My Share
of the Task

My Share

of the Task

| A MEMOIR |

General Stanley McChrystal,
U.S. Army, Retired

Portfolio | Penguin

PORTFOLIO / PENGUIN
Published by the Penguin Group
Penguin Group (USA) Inc., 375 Hudson Street,
New York, New York 10014, U.S.A.
Penguin Group (Canada), 90 Eglinton Avenue East, Suite 700,
Toronto, Ontario, Canada M4P 2Y3
(a division of Pearson Penguin Canada Inc.)
Penguin Books Ltd, 80 Strand, London WC2R 0RL, England
Penguin Ireland, 25 St. Stephen's Green, Dublin 2, Ireland
(a division of Penguin Books Ltd)
Penguin Group (Australia), 707 Collins Street, Melbourne, Victoria 3008
Australia (a division of Pearson Australia Group Pty Ltd)
Penguin Books India Pvt Ltd, 11 Community Centre, Panchsheel Park,
New Delhi—110 017, India
Penguin Group (NZ), 67 Apollo Drive, Rosedale, Auckland 0632,
New Zealand (a division of Pearson New Zealand Ltd)
Penguin Books, Rosebank Office Park, 181 Jan Smuts Avenue, Parktown North 2193, South Africa
Penguin China, B7 Jaiming Center, 27 East Third Ring Road North, Chaoyang District, Beijing
100020, China

Penguin Books Ltd, Registered Offices:
80 Strand, London WC2R 0RL, England

First published in 2013 by Portfolio / Penguin,
a member of Penguin Group (USA) Inc.

10 9 8 7 6 5 4 3 2 1

Copyright © Stanley McChrystal, 2013
All rights reserved
Maps copyright © by Gene Thorp / Cartographic Concepts, Inc.

Photograph credits appear on page 452.

McChrystal, Stanley A.
My share of the task : a memoir / Stanley A. McChrystal.
p. cm.
Includes bibliographical references and index.
ISBN 978-1-59184-475-4
1. McChrystal, Stanley A. 2. Generals—United States—Biography. 3. United States. Army—
Biography. 4. McChrystal, Stanley A.—Military leadership. 5. Afghan War, 2001- I. Title.
E897.4.M38A3 2012   355.0092—dc23
[B]   2012027306

Printed in the United States of America
Set in Sabon LT Std
Designed by Elyse Strongin

With weeping and with laughter
Still is the story told,
How well Horatius kept the bridge
In the brave days of old.

Contents

Leadership ... requires that you inspire, that you build an endurable trust. ... evoking participation larger than the job description, commitment deeper than any job contract's wording. Leaders ... are good because they're willing to learn and to trust. ... inaction has dire consequences. Any war or conflict you enter where you are likely to lose more Americans and expend more treasure is something worthy of very detailed debate. There ought to be a lot of skepticism. There ought to be a lot of discussion. Strength is leading when you just don't want to lead. Throughout my career, I have lived by the principles of personal honor and professional integrity.

Author's Foreword

If every soldier is authorized to make one mistake, then we lose the war. ... Soldiers don't want to follow cautious cynics.

In late 1963, when I was nine, I almost burned our house down.

I had draped my red Mario's Pizza basketball team uniform over a lamp in the room my brother David and I shared because I liked the red glow it produced, and then went off somewhere. Some time later my father detected smoke, raced to my room, and found a melted nylon uniform and a growing fire on a wooden desk he'd built for us.

I was upset and, even more, embarrassed. So a day or so later he sat me down to talk about it. He'd just come home from work at the Pentagon, and I remember his green army major's uniform seemingly covered with ribbons as he sat in my room and talked about how hard it was to take responsibility for mistakes. He used President Kennedy's leadership and courage after the Bay of Pigs fiasco as an example. It had only been a few weeks since Kennedy had been assassinated, so it was a powerful weave of history, leadership, and life, even for a nine-year-old.

If I have accomplished my intent, this book weaves two threads that have always fascinated me—history and leadership—around a third: my memoirs, the story of my life.

The framework is history, the forces, events, and personalities that shaped the extraordinary era in which I've lived. Because things have moved so quickly and changed so radically, it could almost be described as multiple eras. The Army I knew as a child, the one I experienced as a young officer, and the one I left in 2010 were as different as the times they resided in. The history I experienced was the backdrop to my life and largely defined, enabled, or limited all I did or did not do.

Leadership was always the objective. From my earliest memories, leadership was an overt, ever-present theme. The books my mother gave me to read as a boy—stories of Roland, William Tell, and Robert Bruce—were about leaders, courage, and service. In Stonewall Jackson Elementary School's library I found youth-oriented biographies of John Paul Jones and Davy Crockett that I read surreptitiously in Mrs. Lynch's second-grade classroom. In later life it was no less important. I came to judge myself, and others, more on their ability to lead than any other quality.

The core of the story is my life, from my birth in 1954 to Captain and Mrs. Herbert Joseph McChrystal, Jr., at Fort Leavenworth, Kansas, to the present. Like all lives, mine has been a personal journey, enriched by experiences and people that have matured into memories and relationships of unexpected importance to me. If my appreciation for the constellation of family and friendships I've known comes through, I've succeeded.

More than I ever anticipated in the early years of my career, my story intersected with events of historical significance and, in the later years, with policy issues. I attempt to describe what I saw and evaluate its meaning, but I leave current policy prescription to others.

Though this is my memoir, I treated my own recollection of events as only the starting point as I attempted to compile an accurate view of what happened. Doing so required the generous help of comrades and participants. Throughout the course of the writing, more than fifty people were interviewed, most of them more than once. Many more reviewed drafts and episodes, in order to verify the accuracy and fairness of descriptions. I am particularly grateful to the Afghans who participated, giving insights on their lives and their country only they can provide.

To meet my legal and moral commitments to the Department of Defense, my country, and my former comrades, I worked closely with United States Special Operations Command (SOCOM) during the twenty-two-month writing process, and, upon completion, submitted the entire manuscript to the Department of Defense for a lengthy security review. In the end, I accepted many suggested changes and redactions, some reluctantly, particularly where public knowledge of facts and events has outpaced existing security guidelines, while laboring to maintain the coherence of the story. But despite imperfections in the process, I judged compliance with the security review to be essential for me to keep faith with the comrades I had served alongside, and the nation I had served. My goal was to ensure that the following chapters do not endanger our mission or our stalwart personnel in any way. I believe I have accomplished that goal. Those who generously participated with me in the research and writing process were assured the book would undergo a security review, and the professionals who provided their insights and perspectives on this unique time in history would not have done so otherwise. At various points in the book, for their protection, some individuals' names have been shortened to initials, or re-placed with pseudonyms.

Finally, I have no doubt this book reflects the flaws of my memory and biases I've developed, many unconsciously, over a lifetime. I ask the reader's forbearance for these shortcomings.

Part One

God is not on the side of the big battalions, but on the side of those who shoot best.

—Voltaire, *Notebooks*

▼

CHAPTER 1

Ghosts of Christmas Past

December 2009

Christmas . . . is not an external event at all, but a piece of one's home that one carries in one's heart.

—FREYA STARK

The interior of the UH-60 Black Hawk was dark to avoid presenting a glowing target in the night sky. Gunners on either side of the helicopter manned machine guns, maintaining a constant vigil for enemy threats. Below, the rugged Afghan landscape, devoid of any speck of man-made light, was even darker. I could just make out hills, valleys, and an occasional mud-brown compound. Inside the aircraft it was cold, and I pulled my parka tightly around me. The army-issue gear was far better than it had been in the early years of my career, but lately I seemed to feel the cold more than I had back then. It was 2009 and at fifty-five, I wasn't the young lieutenant I'd been thirty-four years earlier. At best, I was a well-worn version of the officer who had spent so many nights like this one alongside warriors.

In a few hours it would be Christmas. Although I didn't know it at the time, it would be my last as a soldier.

I looked around at the other men on the aircraft. Although we all wore headsets connected through the UH-60's intercom system, we rarely spoke. Normally during long night flights, men were lost in thought, and, especially tonight, I respected their solitude. The eight years of war since 9/11 had meant several Christmases away from home for most of these men. For soldiers at war, there's comforting continuity in the traditions and inevitability of Christmas. We savored memories of Christmases past, made the most of, or endured, the one we had at the time, and dreamed incessantly about those we'd have in the future. I felt a bit like Dickens's Scrooge pushing them so hard on a night that should be special. For each of us, Christmas stirred deep memories and strong emotions. But this was the life of our choice.

Sitting directly across from me was my aide, Major Casey Welch, no doubt thinking about his wife and two small children. Casey had spent twenty-seven months in combat in Iraq, including a tough year in Samarra. He had been home for only five months when I had been designated to command in Afghanistan and he had volunteered to deploy again.

Sitting next to Casey was an unimposing figure hunched over a dimly lit laptop. The reading glasses and lines on his face matched mine. I couldn't help but smile slightly as I watched him work. Mike Hall was my old friend and, more important, the finest soldier I'd ever known. After over thirty years of service and then eighteen months at a good civilian job, a phone call had brought the retired command sergeant major back on active duty to become the senior enlisted adviser of all international forces in Afghanistan. Now he would spend yet another Christmas away from his wife, Brenda, and son, Jeff.

Charlie sat to my left, close by, as always. I had known Colonel Charlie Flynn since he was a lieutenant twenty-three years earlier, and I remembered how his first child, Molly, had been born while Charlie was deployed to the first Gulf War. A couple of years later he'd commanded a company for me in the 2nd Ranger Battalion, and his young son Sean was climbing over pews at Christmas Eve Mass in the historic Fort Lewis chapel. Thirteen years later, upon his redeployment in 2008 from his fourth combat tour—fifteen months commanding a brigade combat team in Iraq—I'd asked him to join me in the Pentagon as my executive assistant. When alerted for Afghanistan in May of 2009, the first two officers I sought to form the nucleus of the team were Charlie and his older brother Mike.

Just behind the bird's pilots sat Chief Warrant Officer Shawn Lowery, the man responsible for our security. With a shaved head and a serious countenance, Shawn's all-business gravitas masked a dry, wicked sense of humor. He'd pronounced himself "unenthusiastic" about my decision not to wear body armor some months prior, but took the decision in stride. Shawn had been back from his most recent tour in Afghanistan less than a year when I was notified to deploy. But he had volunteered without hesitation to go forward again.

As the December air rushed in the open windows where the door guns were mounted, I readied myself for the next stop. Continuing a tradition of military commanders, starting that afternoon we'd begun a journey to visit six outposts on Christmas Eve. The next would be the fifth. At each location we spent time with soldiers, gave them a short talk, normally in their mess hall, and took the opportunity to circulate, pose for pictures that they could send home, and, most important, thank them. It was tiring but unfailingly inspiring to me. A few hours later, on Christmas Day, we'd launch

again to six other bases, several manned by soldiers from our coalition partners. Christmases with Polish and Romanian troops, including religious ceremonies in crude bunkers and huts, were deeply spiritual experiences.

Soothed by the rhythmic vibration of the rotors, my mind wandered to
the more than half century of Christmases I'd experienced. I remembered
early-morning excitement as my four brothers, one sister, and I rushed
down to the living room of our small Arlington, Virginia, house, where
presents from Santa Claus were reliably piled for each of us. I most loved
getting toy soldiers I could use with the handcrafted wooden forts my father built and my mother painted. During the years my father was in Vietnam, my mother struggled to make Christmases special. I could only guess
how my father felt until I got a taste as a young captain in Korea during my
first yearlong separation from my wife, Annie. Along the DMZ on Christmas Eve, a well-intentioned morale visit to our unit by a USO tour only
made me miss Annie, and Christmas, all the more.

Becoming a father made Christmas more important to me than ever.
Fatherhood was a great excuse to play with toys again. I remember the fun
Annie and I had staying up late assembling a plastic fort for my son Sam's
Rambo figurines, and I could still hear my father shaming me into finally
buying Annie a color TV. Even memories of punji stake–like pain from
stepping barefoot on a rogue Lego block now brought a smile. I wanted the
young men and women I'd visit that night to know that I understood the
ache inherent in Christmas so far from home.

I had spent four straight Christmases, starting in 2004, in Iraq or Afghanistan, typically traveling to be in one location on Christmas Eve, then
making a night flight to be in the other on Christmas Day. I'd listen to
Christmas music on my iPod, particularly Alabama's "Christmas in Dixie,"
which made me homesick, but I couldn't help it. And I knew that as much
as I missed Annie and Sam, young soldiers bore the heavier burden of missing the all-too-temporary magic of their children's holiday joy.

As we reached the forward operating base, or FOB, we could see from
the air the series of simple buildings constructed of Afghan bricks and mortar. It was a small, fortified outpost manned by a combined U.S. and Afghan force totaling about seventy-five soldiers. Its position on high ground
above Afghanistan's open terrain gave it a deceptively imposing *Beau Geste*–
like appearance. But its only real strength lay in the effectiveness of the
soldiers inside. In a few minutes I'd be able to see that for myself. We landed
a couple hundred meters away and walked with the commanding officer
through the gate and into the outpost.

Because it was dark and cold, we met the soldiers inside. Like most small
outposts, this one was rudimentary but functional. Generators provided
power. There was a small operations and communications center, bay barracks in which groups of soldiers arranged bunks and gear, and a mess hall.
Small trees and other decorations, obviously sent by loved ones, brought

Christmas into the crude surroundings. Except for some of the more modern equipment, soldiers on similar counterinsurgency duty in the American West in 1868, the Philippines in 1900, Malaya in 1950, Indochina in 1952, Algeria in 1956, or Vietnam in 1965 might have found the outpost familiar. It was warfare at its most basic, where success depended more on lieutenants, sergeants, and privates in lonely forts or on small patrols than on grand plans in a generals' headquarters.

As always, the officers and senior noncommissioned officers were polite and forthcoming, but the younger troops were initially distant and uncommunicative, as though they were only there because they'd been directed to show up. Their reticence didn't bother me. It was always that way. Only afterward, when Mike Hall and I spoke to them as a group, presented some hard-earned awards, and then mingled, offering to pose for pictures and answer questions, did they loosen up. Before long, the gathering became animated, and I felt connected to them.

As we prepared to reboard the UH-60 to fly to our final stop for the night, several groups asked to take pictures with Mike and me. While we assembled one group, I introduced myself to a young soldier. As I always tried to do, I began by looking at the rank and name tape on his combat uniform so I could address him as personally as possible. I read his name and paused. Then I asked him quietly if his father had been a soldier. He said that he had. I cautiously asked if his father had been a Ranger. The young man, anticipating what I was trying to determine, confirmed that his father had been a Ranger whom I had known well. After leaving the Rangers, his father had joined an elite Army commando unit and had been killed in 2005 in a nighttime raid on an Al Qaeda safe house. He had been lost under my command, during a summer of bitter fighting in Iraq's Western Euphrates River valley, at a critical juncture in a war that now felt a lifetime past. Now his young son had taken his place in the ranks. For a moment I was silent.

There was no outward drama or emotion. The young man clearly sought no special recognition. It felt strangely natural. I asked about his mother and soon moved on to talk to other young soldiers. But as I did, it struck me that, in an era when military service is a question of choice, he, like his father, had chosen to spend Christmas in rough surroundings. I looked around the room at the young soldiers and their slightly older sergeants. They had all made the same choice.

On the flight north that night, I absorbed the continuity of war. I knew from history that war comes with frightening regularity, often fought over the same ground and similar causes as previous conflicts. Wars often begin with enthusiastic vigor but typically settle into costly, dirty business characterized for soldiers by fear, frustration, and loneliness.

There was also continuity in soldiers. In the young soldiers on outposts, in the sergeants and junior officers who led them, and particularly in the team of professionals I worked alongside each day—the Charlies, Mikes, Caseys, and Shawns—I felt the unbroken tradition of commitment to a mission, and a fierce commitment to one another. Like the generations they followed and those they now led, they came forward when called and sacrificed when needed. They did so quietly, often in shadows, with no expectation of reward. They were no better than their grandfathers, and not a bit worse.

And there was Christmas.

| CHAPTER 2 |

▼

Journey to the Plain

July 1972–June 1976

I was raised to respect soldiers, leaders, and heroes. They were who I wanted to be. They were why I was there.

And in the unblinking sunlight of an August morning at the United States Military Academy in 1972, the colonel in front of me looked like the embodiment of all I admired. Hanging on his spare frame, his pine green uniform was covered with patches, badges, and campaign ribbons. Even the weathered lines of his face seemed to reflect all he'd done and all he was. It was the look I'd seen in my father's face. For a moment I could envision my father in combat in Korea, or as the lean warrior embracing my mother as he came home from Vietnam. He was my lifelong hero. From my earlier memories I'd wanted to be like him. I'd always wanted to be a soldier.

Yet the colonel's words were not what I wanted and expected to hear. As he stood in front of me and my fellow new cadets, he talked about collar stays, the twenty-five-cent pieces of wire cadets used to secure the collars of the blue gray shirts we would wear to class during the academic year.

As he spoke, we tried not to squirm under the sun. Our backs were arched, arms flat to our sides, elbows slightly bent, fingers curled into tight palms, chests out, chins forward, eyes ahead. Mouths shut. I was five weeks into my education at West Point. We were still in Beast Barracks, or simply Beast, the initial eight-week indoctrination and basic-training phase during the summer before the fall term of our freshman year—plebe year, in West

Point's timeworn terminology. There were not many full colonels at West Point, so it was rare for cadets, particularly new cadets like us, to interact with them. It seemed like an extraordinary opportunity to hear from a man who'd done so much. But he wasn't discussing his experiences and the truths they had yielded; he was talking about collar stays.

"Gentlemen," he said, "soon you will begin to wear the class shirt. You'll wear it every day of the academic year and, per uniform regulation, you will secure your collar with the collar stays that have been issued to you.

"It may seem insignificant to you now," he continued, "but you're here learning attention to detail." For the next few minutes the combat-seasoned colonel compared neglecting to wear collar stays with forgetting ammunition for our soldiers in combat. Focusing on even the small things, he reasoned, develops a leader who never neglects the critical ones.

I thought it was stupid. Collar stays were for your collar. Ammunition mattered. And although we were not yet officers, we knew the difference. The soldiers I had grown up admiring were Sam Grant in his dirty private's coat and Matt Ridgway and his hand grenades. They wore mud-covered or sand-dusted fatigues, not collar stays. In that moment, the colorful block of campaign badges on the colonel's left breast seemed less like proof of his having fought in the wars being waged far beyond the academy's granite walls and more like ornaments that flashed as he paced and pivoted.

Following the rules here would make me a good cadet, but that was not my goal. I wanted to be a combat leader. And in the colonel's soliloquy I could not see a connection between the two. What I could not have foreseen then were the lessons of unconventional leadership I would learn during my four years in that most conventional of places.

Weeks earlier, on the night of Sunday, July 2, I didn't sleep much. The next morning I was to report to West Point to begin my training as a cadet. A friend had driven with me from northern Virginia to drop me off. At a motel a few miles from the academy, we sat outside, sharing cans of cold beer from a small cooler, talking late into the summer night. We'd talked often about my desire to be a soldier but rarely about what that really meant. I'd likely be a soldier for the rest of my life.

I was preparing to tread a well-worn path. Cadets had been entering West Point since its founding in 1802, and 140 years later, six months after Pearl Harbor, my father had done the same. Graduating in 1945 as a member of one of the abbreviated three-year wartime classes, he went on to fight in Korea and Vietnam and was a major general as I prepared to enter, thirty years after he first reported as a cadet. But he never pushed me to apply and was supportive but hands-off as I prepared my application. I attributed his stance to the fact that one of my older brothers had attended and then quit West Point a year earlier. I suspected my father worried that he had pressured my brother to go, but he also sensed I was different.

I always assumed I would attend West Point but had never thought much about what it would be like to be a cadet. From my birth to an army captain and his wife, I'd been an "army brat." After that, West Point seemed the natural route. There was not much more to the decision. I never fixated on the school itself, never dreamed of wearing cadet dress gray. I arrived at the academy already looking past it, eager to get to the real soldiering that came only afterward.

The next morning, my friend and I drove through the academy's gates and followed the drive that runs along the edge of the cliffs overlooking the Hudson until it breaks away from the river and veers up a hill to Michie Stadium, where Army's football team plays. It was warm and I was nervous.

At the stadium we found swarms of people. This was Reception Day, better known as R-Day, and 1,378 new cadets had shown up to be officially "received" into the academy. From the stadium we were bused to a series of concrete courtyards walled off by barracks that cadets call "the Area," a desolate stretch that I would come to know intimately. That morning it was controlled chaos.

From the perspective of a new cadet (as we were called until the end of Beast Barracks), upperclassmen ran the show. Postured like sentries in gray trousers and starched white shirts, they clenched their jaws and pulled their hat brims low over stern eyes. They controlled our every movement. Through decades of practice, R-Day processes neared scientific precision. The circuit ensured that all new cadets that day could be sworn in, stripped of outside possessions, supplied with new ones, measured, weighed, outfitted, sheared, scared, and, finally, paraded in front of their families in a matter of hours. For the academy, it was an impressive feat. Families saw the often-shaggy high school graduates they'd deposited earlier that morning reappear as uniformed, disciplined soldiers. For some parents and siblings, it probably felt like a miracle.

For new cadets it felt more like being rats in a maze. Directed through the process by an upperclassman known as the Man in the Red Sash, who tracked our progress on cards safety-pinned to our shorts, we felt like fools. Outfitted in T-shirts, knee-high black socks, and black dress shoes, we looked like fools as well. But it was efficient. Before arriving, I expected the hazing and knew to address the older cadets in formulaic "Yes, sirs" and "No, sirs." But I had always regarded West Point as an inconvenient but necessary hurdle I had to jump to be a soldier. By the middle of my first day, the obstacle appeared gigantic, four years like an eternity.

Of the nearly fourteen hundred who stood on the point of land overlooking the Hudson River that evening, more than a third would not graduate; 180 would leave before the summer was over. Some admitted cadets had quit that first day. But more than thirty of those newly shorn plebes, including Ray Odierno, Dave Rodriguez, Bill Caldwell, David Barno, Frank Kearney, Frank Helmick, Mike Barbero, and Guy Swan, would serve as general officers in turbulent times for our army and nation.

Earlier that day we had eaten our first meal in cavernous Washington

Hall, the cadet dining facility, as we had every other meal before. That evening, we ate our second meal as we would eat every meal thereafter: by their rules. Seated "family style" at a table for ten, two upperclassmen ruled eight new cadets, controlling what and how we ate. Correctly reciting "plebe knowledge" we were all required to memorize might yield a rushed bite, or more, depending on how hard-ass our elders decided to be. Knowing Schofield's definition of discipline—which ironically counsels that the "discipline which makes the soldiers of a free country reliable in battle is not to be gained by harsh or tyrannical treatment"—might allow a cadet a quick forkful of potatoes before a minder ordered the utensil placed back on the table. Routinely, we left plates of untouched food at the ends of meals. Food became a fixation.

After dinner on the first night, we retired to our rooms, where our M14 rifles and other equipment had been placed on bunks before we arrived. I don't remember exactly what I thought as our first day ended. Much of what I had seen that day seemed silly. But the ubiquitous tablets containing names of graduates who had fallen in battle did not. Many of the soldiers I admired for their battlefield leadership had begun where I was now, had navigated the same peculiar process, and had emerged with qualities I sought to emulate. Had this seemingly absurd process molded them? After a long, often disorienting day, it was too much to ponder. When we finally fell into our bunks to sleep, I think I took comfort in the fact that no matter how long I stayed in the Army, I'd never have to have another "first day" as a soldier.

After Beast Barracks, we settled into life as plebes. Like the peas on our plate during Beast, the minutes of the day throughout the academic year were not ours to consume freely. We necessarily became efficient. Reveille was at 0615 hours, and we arrived at formation ten minutes later in complete cadet uniform, clean and shaved. There were no wasted movements in those early minutes, especially in winter. Before entering the mess hall for breakfast, all four thousand cadets stood in formation outside the barracks, and the chain of command inspected our uniforms. The fife-and-drum corps accompanied every movement to, in, and from formation. The rest of the day was spent at class, with forty minutes for lunch. On autumn and spring afternoons, we either paraded for visitors or played sports, before rushing back to barracks to clean up, don our dress gray uniforms, and report to formation. Then the band fifed and drummed us back into the mess hall for dinner. After dinner was time for study before taps ended the day at 2300, when all rooms went dark. Some studious cadets covered their windows with blankets to hide the light or requested official permission to continue studying—known as "late lights." I never much did that.

I had a slow start academically, and for the first two years poor grades were a lurking threat to my cadet career. "The subjects which were dearest to the examiners," Winston Churchill once wrote, "were almost invariably those I fancied least." The same was true for me during plebe and yearling years, when the curriculum was loaded with math and science requirements. The system of daily recitation and grading begun under the early-nineteenth-century superintendence of Sylvanus Thayer, known as the Father of the Academy, was bad news for a poorly prepared student like me. In math class each day, including Saturday, we stood at the blackboard in front of a new problem that tested the previous night's lesson, and "briefed the solution" to the class and instructor. I got crushed in math and over the first two years fared poorly in chalkboard battles with chemistry, physics, thermodynamics, and engineering. When I could, I retreated from my math and science textbooks to histories and biographies. Compared with Grant's account of Shiloh in his memoirs, attempting to prove mathematical theorems in calculus was unbearable.

Normally focused on daily requirements, West Point in 1972 felt estranged from the society it was meant to serve. A decade of fighting in Vietnam and a series of scandals like My Lai had degraded the military's credibility with the country, and as cadets we were periodically reminded that we were out of step with the views, values, and lifestyles of many of our generation. On Saturday, October 21, we traveled to New Brunswick, New Jersey, for the Rutgers football game. We then were bused into Manhattan and allowed our first few hours of freedom since R-Day, but required to remain dressed in our distinctive gray cadet uniforms. Walking near Times Square, a friend and I heard a loud, long honk and looked up to see a forearm and middle finger poking out through a half-opened window of the passing car. As visible symbols, soldiers often receive praise or condemnation, and both reactions feel curiously undeserved. Yet the gap between us and American society was palpable—and disturbing.

Cadets were not alone in feeling alienated. At the end of his tenure as superintendent of West Point in 1974, General William A. Knowlton invoked the academy's historical role as an eighteenth-century fort when explaining to his successor that as superintendent he had spent four years defending "a stockade surrounded by attacking Indians." West Point was training officers for an army that had lost its moral footing in the eyes of its country. And it was commissioning officers into an army that valued the ideals its graduates infused into the force but also thought some of those graduates were "prima donnas and spoiled brats," in the words of Army chief of staff General Creighton Abrams, who had overseen the drawdown in Vietnam.

If West Point felt like a penal colony, the feeling forged close bonds among cadets. My roommate for the second "detail" in the winter (we rotated rooms and roommates three times a year), and one of my best friends for four years, was Arthur Ken Liepold. It was hard to miss Kenny, and I noticed him early during Beast Barracks. He was an offensive tackle with an expansive frame, kind eyes, and dimples that appeared when he smiled and laughed, which he did a lot.

Like most people, I was drawn to Kenny because he did not take anything or anyone at West Point too seriously, and did not suffer kindly those who did. His legendary devotion to friends, easygoing charisma, and disarming humor were antidotes to the rigor and pomp of West Point.

Another friend I made early was Rick Bifulco. Stocky and quick, Bifulco was a star lacrosse player from Long Island but was built like a boxer from Brooklyn. He excelled in math and engineering but had a wickedly quick wit and a mischievous streak. Success in academics and athletics came easily to Rick, but from the beginning it was clear he valued the intangibles of camaraderie more than anything else. Rick, Kenny, and I became an unlikely but close trio for all four years.

All three of us were on hand for the historic mess hall rally-turned-riot of November 3, 1972, the night before the Army football team played Air Force at Michie Stadium. Pep rallies in the mess hall, in spite of the slight damage they caused, were an unofficial tradition and one of the few outlets for the cadets. But thus far that year the academy leadership had ordered the celebrations to be subdued—to the frustration of the corps.

That afternoon, however, the commandant, Brigadier General Philip Feir, had filtered a message down through the companies to all cadets: *The Commandant has determined that damage to the mess hall is of secondary importance to the morale of the corps.* The implication could not have been clearer and the effect was electric. We entered the mess hall and took our places as usual.

The mess hall, with hundred-foot ceilings, stone arches, and light filtering through stained-glass windows, normally felt like a church. Portraits of stern soldiers of yore lined the walls, peering down at cadets, who sat with their respective companies. There were eight companies seated during Beast, then thirty-six companies divided into four regiments when we joined the rest of the corps at the start of plebe year. Laid out like an asterisk, with six wings converging in the center, the mess hall was where General MacArthur, near the end of his life, bade adieu to "the corps, the corps, the corps" in his famous 1962 address to cadets. The wall at the end of the northwest wing was a massive mural from 1936, a Bayeux Tapestry–like panorama of twenty decisive battles.

After a few moments the massive wood doors swung open and an army jeep, laden with members of the pep squad yelling into cone megaphones and pumping their fists, crept slowly down the aisle between the tables. Trailing the jeep, the academy's brass band streamed through the door in double file, playing the Army fight song. The hall echoed with the sounds of horns and drums and the loud gurgling of the engine.

The jeep veered left toward my company, the B Company of 1st Regiment, which sat at the foot of the mural. As it passed us, a cadet from my table took the water pitcher, ran up to the jeep, and dumped it on one of the rabble-rousers, soaking him and igniting mayhem. By the time the jeep completed a U-turn at the end of our wing and came rumbling back down the gauntlet toward the center, a huge layer cake had been smeared across its windshield. At that point, it was all over.

Cadets threw opened milk cartons and heaps of mashed potatoes, dinner rolls, butter, handfuls of salt. I hurled cups of ice cream, pulling off the tabs and lobbing them like grenades. Across the hall, through the clouds of projectiles, cadets stacked dining tables into a multistory tower and climbed to the top. The steely marching band played on, a bit like the quartet on the deck of the *Titanic*, providing a booming soundtrack to the whole scene. When the din settled and cadets had launched their last missiles, the walls and the dark oil paintings had been streaked with food.

In the glorious mess, two things were clear. First, the corps had never felt more like a brotherhood. (The next day, we dramatically upset Air Force.) Second, Feir, normally considered an old-guard martinet, had displayed uncommon leadership. Most would remember that on that day he understood that he led young men, not hollow gray uniforms.

If West Point was hard, I made it harder. During Beast, I recorded my first slug, slang for the academy's punishment following an infraction. In that case it was for "disapprobation towards a cadet superior": After an upperclassman berated a fellow cadet and me, he took a shortcut through a building to cut us off as we walked away, catching us laughing at his reprimand. Depending on severity, slugs earned some combination of demerits, room confinement, or hours marching on the Area. At the end of Beast Barracks I reported to the regular cadet company I would be a part of for the next four years with the uncommon and dubious distinction of a negative disciplinary mark already on my record.

My second slug was more serious. Before spring finals, a girl I had been seeing scored Kenny and me some alcohol, and we drank it in our barracks room, a violation of regulations. What started as surreptitious sips of vodka mixed with White Rock soda evolved into two idiots playing air guitar to increasingly loud music. I'm not sure it was social drinking, but it was fun and I cherish it as a special memory of Kenny.

Of course it ended badly. The next morning, one of our tactical officers, an army captain, found me in the basement showers of our barracks. Friends later told me that I tried, unsuccessfully, to hoist myself up off of the cold tile by grabbing at the stunned officer's pants like a rope. I don't remember. Two weeks later, a commandant's board issued my punishment: forty-one demerits, sixty-six hours walking the Area, and three months of room confinement.

Punishment of cadets had been artfully crafted. In the early nineteenth century, West Point officials deemed manual labor an inappropriate punishment for a cadet: It would have been an ungentlemanly task for a future officer. But they could make him do something that was tiring, embarrassing, and, most excruciating, accomplished nothing. So cadets ever since have been awarded "Area tours," each representing an hour—two hours on Friday afternoon, and then three on Saturday—walking in our dress gray uniforms with rifles across the Area. As my bemused father explained to me, the Area does not make you smarter, braver, or more expert; even trench digging would offer some tangible benefit. At the academy, where we hoarded free minutes, walking the yard meant wasted hours.

While I ran afoul of certain academy rules, I had respect for the tradition of honor embedded in the institution. My slugs were for infractions of West Point regulations, the same rules that governed how much rust was acceptable on a rifle (none) or how our rooms were to be kept (immaculate). The cadet honor code was entirely different, and there was a clear, bright line dividing shenanigans from transgressions against integrity. Failing to clean your barracks sink was a violation of the regulations and earned demerits. Lying to anyone about whether you had cleaned your sink was a violation of your honor and meant expulsion.

When it was chartered in 1802, the academy adopted the unofficial code of honor that covered all levels of officer conduct in the regular Army. Infractions of the code were settled between cadets, usually in a formal fist-fight. Eventually, the scope of the code narrowed, but the underlying aim remained the same: The code existed to ensure that the words of cadets and officers alike could always, in all situations, be taken as truth. Lies, even small ones, threatened that system of trust.

The discussion about military honor was particularly fraught when I was a cadet. In the twilight of the Vietnam War, the Army was broken and sought to heal itself. The scandals of that war—particularly falsified body counts—had sent fissures through the officer corps, and West Point was severely shaken. Although I was probably more aware of these issues because of my father, it was obvious, even to cadets at West Point, that the Army had wounds that would take a long time to heal.

The massacre of South Vietnamese civilians at My Lai in 1968, and the subsequent cover-up, had exemplified the challenge and had reached into the academy a few years before I arrived, when then Major General Samuel Koster was superintendent. A West Point veteran of World War II and Korea, Koster had commanded the 23rd Infantry Division, troops from which had perpetrated My Lai. In March 1970, the Peers Commission recommended he be criminally charged for his part in the cover-up and he was forced to leave the academy. Before he left, he famously warned the assembled corps of cadets, "Don't let the bastards grind you down."

Beyond Koster, other graduates were implicated in the myriad scandals of Vietnam. Although accounting for only one tenth of the officer corps in 1976, West Pointers were meant to catalyze honor and discipline in the rest of the Army. But in the eyes of many, they had fallen short in that mission. During my time there, it struggled to repair the damage. Progress was made there and across the Army, but shortly before I graduated in June 1976, the academy was rocked by the largest cheating scandal in its history. More than a hundred cadets in the cow, or junior, class one year behind mine, including members of the honor committee, faced expulsion for colluding on an electrical engineering exam. The scandal spurred national media attention and congressional hearings. If honor could not be safe at West Point, what chance did it stand in the nation as a whole?

When I arrived, the code had been distilled to a simple directive: "A cadet will not lie, cheat, or steal, nor tolerate those who do." Cadet leadership added the last part, the "toleration clause," only in 1970, but it had existed for many years in the self-policing spirit of the corps. If the code's basic wording became simpler over time, its enforcement did not. In the late nineteenth century, cadets elected a "vigilance committee" to police honor violations and field accusations. When a cadet was found guilty of an honor violation, the committee made sure that he left the academy. Eventually, the committee became an advisory body without explicit punitive powers, although the commandant almost always expelled a cadet whom the committee found to have violated the code.

In the rare case when the committee's recommendation was not followed, the corps' summary justice took over. A year before I arrived, the honor committee had found Cadet James Pelosi guilty of cheating. Pelosi's lawyer got him reinstated on a technicality, so the corps began to treat him as if he did not exist by "silencing" him. No one spoke to him; he had no roommates and ate alone at a separate table; reportedly, plebes in charge of delivering laundry threw his in the dumpster. Being in a different company, I never knew Pelosi, but I recognized how precarious it was to allow vigilantism among eighteen- and nineteen-year-olds. The corps saw that as well, and banned silencing in 1973.

While honor was sacrosanct to me, other academy regulations were not. On the afternoon of Saturday, October 27, 1973, one day after I finished the sentence from my May slug, I screwed up again, this time drinking in my room with classmate and friend Rick Bowman. Rick and I would go on to serve together in the 82nd Airborne as lieutenants and then for many years in special operations, where he flew in, and ultimately commanded, the elite 160th Special Operations Aviation Regiment. But that was later, and for now we were fools in trouble—again.

When I appeared before the commandant's board two weeks later, the colonel in charge, after hearing the details of my infraction, took off his glasses, paused, and shook his head. "Okay, you have *got* to explain this to me. You *just* finished a slug," he said, tapping my files, "and here you are about to eat another one. Explain that to me." I had no explanation, but I was glad to hear him asking for one: It meant that I wasn't going to be thrown out. The colonel could do the math and knew that if he wanted to, he could make the slug big enough to put me over the limit in demerits. I did not offer any excuses and simply explained that I had shown poor judgment. He agreed. Forty-four hours on the Area.

Despite all of my behavioral nonsense, my peers evaluated me well. My tactical officer expressed disappointment in my poor decision making but never wrote me off. Some classmates jokingly compared me to Captain Virgil Hilts, the character played by Steve McQueen in *The Great Escape*, the 1963 film about Allied soldiers in a German prisoner of war camp during World War II. An irreverent, carefree inmate, Hilts is known as the "Cooler King" because he spends his time either trying to escape or being punished for it in the cooler, solitary confinement, where he plans the next attempt. The comparison was a good-natured honor. Sort of.

My fourth and final slug solidified this reputation. After dinner one evening near the end of our yearling year, I joined Kenny Liepold, Rick Bifulco, Rick Bowman, and a few others in barracks horseplay with unloaded vintage weapons from West Point's museum. Being yearlings with more energy than sense, we were soon chasing one another down the hallway, clicking the triggers and yelling "bang," taking cover behind corners, and feigning being hit by rolled-up-sock "grenades." It was literally sophomoric.

We soon spilled out the back door and ran to the entrance of Grant Hall, a few yards behind our barracks. At the time, Grant Hall served as a place where upperclassmen were allowed to congregate and meet dates. Inside is a long, very West Point–like lounge: dimly lit and filled with overstuffed leather furniture. We achieved complete surprise, running through the door, mimicking the *rat-a-tat* of guns, tossing socks at perturbed upperclassmen and their dates, doing combat rolls at their feet, laughing wildly. Then we withdrew to our barracks rooms.

As we caught our breath, flashing lights lit up the walls and ceiling of our room from the street below. We looked out the window to see a military police car. Suddenly our door opened and a tactical officer entered, the hallway behind him full of faces trying to catch a glimpse of the fugitives. "Was it you?" he asked. "Yes, sir," we responded. "You got the weapons?" We handed them over. Disappointed, the crowd in the hallway dispersed. He closed the door behind him and turned to us, only barely concealing his amusement. "What were you knuckleheads *thinking*?"

In the end, he wrote up the event conservatively and we received a light punishment. But I finished the year having walked 127 hours on the Area.

When I entered West Point, some Americans still believed the Vietnam War might end honorably. By the time I graduated, South Vietnam did not exist. As cadets, we watched the war teeter and implode, and the historical sweep was not lost on us.

My interest in Indochina began when my father first deployed to Vietnam in 1965, as part of President Lyndon Johnson's escalation of the war that summer. Then a lieutenant colonel, my father commanded the 2nd Battalion of the 18th Infantry Regiment, part of General William DePuy's 1st Infantry Division, the Big Red One. Their battalion ran search-and-destroy missions in the Bien Hoa area in South Vietnam, near the Cambodian border. Curious about where my dad was going, I read *The Two Viet-Nams* by Bernard Fall, the war correspondent and historian who chronicled the French and later American experiences in Indochina. Only eleven at the time, I struggled through parts of it, but from then on I was captivated by Indochina, and I eventually read all of Fall's books.

The focus of my senior year in high school was a research project on Indochina. Ho Chi Minh, General Giap, Jean de Lattre de Tassigny, Bruno Bigeard, and the other players in the conflict fascinated me. Their outsized personalities and human flaws all converged in the military and political fights of the First Indochina War. The essay ended up well over a hundred pages long. It was not groundbreaking, but I had pursued the topic with an intense curiosity about how the French had failed so spectacularly in their efforts to maintain their colonies and why the Americans and the British had decided against overt intervention in those early years.

While I studied the French war, support for the American one evaporated. Growing up near Washington, D.C., my friends and I went to peace demonstrations in the capital, curious to see the events. I remained supportive of the war but was skeptical of the American war strategy. The echoes of the French defeat, culminating in the disaster at Dien Bien Phu, stuck with me. The war the United States fought in Vietnam was different from that waged by the French paratroopers, for better and worse. As much as the French tried to dress it differently, theirs was a war of empire, and their counterinsurgency was built on untenable colonial foundations. I didn't think America's was.

When I was in junior high school in 1968, my father deployed for a second tour, involving bitter fighting in the central highlands alongside our Montagnard allies. Beginning with the Tet Offensive, the upheaval of 1968—explosive civil rights and antiwar protests, the murders of Martin Luther King, Jr., and Robert Kennedy, Nixon's election, My Lai—was seared into my young mind. At home I watched my mother endure another separation for a war I strongly suspected she opposed. Mary Gardner Bright was a beautiful southern girl with no connection to the military who had met and fallen in love with a young lieutenant. It wasn't an easy life, but she navigated six children through two wars with what, even as a fourteen-year-old boy, I recognized was stoic courage.

From the first day of Beast, it was unlikely that Vietnam would be "our war." In the years before we arrived at the academy, the Nixon administration had steadily drawn down troops, a policy widely supported by the American public. By the time I reported to the Man in the Red Sash, there were fewer than seventy thousand American troops in Vietnam, down from more than half a million only three years earlier. Nixon, like the rest of America, wanted out.

Throughout 1972, the combatants waged bloody campaigns on the peninsula to shore up their negotiating positions that fall in Paris. In October of our plebe year, we watched National Security Adviser Henry Kissinger return from Paris to announce, "Peace is at hand." But negotiations stalled later that autumn and broke apart in mid-December. That winter, Nixon ordered an intense bombing campaign.

On Saturday, January 27, 1973, North Vietnam signed peace accords with South Vietnam and the United States in Paris, formally ending what at the time was our nation's longest war. In April 1975, the corps watched intently from within the walls of West Point as Saigon fell. We followed world events to the degree we had time, but we were first and foremost college students. I never knew who among the cadets were conservatives or liberals; we did not walk down the halls deep in heated discussions about Vietnam or anything else. We were at the academy during the doldrums of the early 1970s, too late to have been ignited by President Kennedy's idealism and too soon to be bolstered by Reagan's confidence. Our president was Nixon, and he resigned in shame over Watergate in August 1974.

Shortly after Nixon resigned, I returned to West Point from summer training and leave. I'd had a good summer experience at Airborne School at Fort Benning, Georgia (where I became qualified as a paratrooper after making five jumps), and then Fort Hood, Texas, with a Ranger unit, and I felt a bit closer to being a real soldier, but at the time I did not know how central being a paratrooper and Ranger would be to my life. I returned to West Point more focused.

But I was carrying baggage. After four slugs and still on the hook to serve the punishment for the last (the Grant Hall raid). With a weak academic record, my future was anything but secure. The implications of my performance in my first two years had been made clear the previous spring when I had tried to take the first step toward what I considered serious soldiering and volunteered to be one of the few cadets allowed to attend Ranger School during the summer break. I was disappointed when I was turned down because of my low academic, disciplinary, and physical training scores. It was a wake-up call.

Soon after returning for the start of cow year, I met my new tactical officer. Then–Major David J. Baratto had graduated from West Point in 1964 and completed two tours in Vietnam, earning a Purple Heart and a Bronze Star and serving with the Army Special Forces. He was aware, competent, and tough—but never petty.

The young tactical officers who arrived at West Point in those years responded to the institution in different ways. Some, even those with combat experience in Vietnam, internalized the spit-and-polish culture of the institution. Others were disgusted that preparing cadets for war meant inspecting the underwear in their bureau drawers. To them, the academy was, to use a West Point phrase, choosing the easy wrong, not the hard right. While I was there, dozens of young officers quit their academy posts.

Major Baratto had scheduled counseling sessions with every cadet under his command in B-1. Until that point, my interactions with tactical officers had generally been positive, but also perfunctory. I was not in handcuffs when I met Baratto, but I had earned a reputation. At that time I was still walking punishment hours for drinking and for raiding Grant Hall the previous spring. I braced for a lukewarm assessment. I expected counseling for my prior infractions and advice that only if I focused more could I succeed at West Point.

"I've got your file here. You have a lot of potential and talent, and you are going to be a great cadet," Baratto said in his soft-spoken manner. "I see you as having a serious leadership position at the academy, and as being a great army officer." I was stunned. He continued, "I see a lot of potential in your peer ratings, and I think you are going to do really, really well."

His words were not empty cheerleading. My personnel file included write-ups of my infractions, but also my peer ratings. At West Point, a cadet's class rank was an amalgam of various scores and evaluations. The quarterly peer rankings on leadership were weighted heavily. In this area, the other members in B-1 ranked me at the top of the company. So while what Baratto said was based on my record, he had chosen to focus on aspects he considered relevant and important—not on my antics.

Baratto knew that I saw West Point as a means to an end and that I was anxious to finish. He held that the academy was a fine place, but more than anything, he addressed me as an officer-to-be, not as a cadet who needed to be lectured on collar stays. At every point in my career I saw people live up, or down, to expectations, and Baratto skillfully lifted mine that afternoon.

I had returned that fall ready to be more serious, and a number of factors, beginning with the confidence of Major Baratto, led my performance as a cadet to surge. I was a bit older, I was tired of being slugged, and I'd learned from my rejection for Ranger School that my poor performance carried costs. Shenanigans ended.

I matched my professional drive with personal focus. Many of my fellow cadets had come to West Point with girlfriends, but often, if a cadet survived plebe year, the relationship did not. I had arrived at the academy with plans to remain a bachelor, to go it alone.

Annie Corcoran changed all that. I first met her at Fort Hood in Texas during winter break in 1973. Our fathers both served there, and we met at a Christmas party organized in the neighborhood. Annie was beautiful, grounded, strong, and quietly but ferociously independent. Like me, she came from a military family. Her father, Colonel Edward Corcoran, had served in Korea as a lieutenant in August 1950. From the Pusan perimeter he had led his tank platoon far into, and back out of, North Korea in the war's bloodiest year. Later he had served a tour in Vietnam. Annie understood what it meant to date or marry a soldier and had decided not to. But we connected, and she accepted my invitation to visit West Point from her college in Pennsylvania twice that spring. When I went to Fort Hood that summer to serve for a month with a Ranger unit, Annie was a lifeguard at the pool near my bachelor officers' quarters, and I courted her aggressively. By the end of the summer we were dating seriously and I, who had planned to be the hard-bitten warrior, was in love.

When Annie wasn't visiting, I often stayed in my room, reading biographies and histories, a passion that I inherited from my mother. A woman of extraordinary energy, when she read, my mother bore into a book and would have to be shaken to look up from the page. Throughout my childhood, she passed me Tennyson, biographies of T. E. Lawrence and John Paul Jones, Greek and Roman mythologies, tales of the Scottish chiefs, and stories of Roland at the pass and Horatius at the bridge. My mother was raised on these stories, and on Scots-Irish stoicism, so that when my father deployed to Vietnam, she not only held down the fort, she made it hum. If she was afraid for her husband, her strength would not allow her to show it. Instead, she changed her world. When Mary started a garden, it became an industrial-size operation; when she engaged in liberal politics in Arlington, she dragged me with her to stand in front of the local supermarket and hand out balloons and flyers calling for better education in the county. My mother was special.

On New Year's morning in 1971, when I was a junior in high school, my mother woke up feeling sick, although they'd not celebrated the night before. My father, a new brigadier general, took her to the army clinic at Fort Myer. She was swiftly moved to the hospital. By midnight she was dreadfully ill, and a few hours later, in the early morning of January 2, she passed away. It was a shock to the family, and to my father especially. We all missed her deeply, but the impact her loss had on the stoic soldier I loved and admired was tragically evident.

Part of my mother's legacy to me, my affinity for history and literature, pulled me through my final two years at West Point. Among those military biographies I consumed, Grant's memoirs seeped into my pores most deeply: "The last two years wore away more rapidly than the first two," Grant wrote of his attitude toward the academy, "but they still seemed about five times as long as Ohio years, to me." So it was for me. Cow and firstie years featured more English and history courses, and these played to my strengths. "History 381: Revolutionary Warfare" was my favorite; it was one of the few classes that focused on small wars and unconventional warfare at an academy otherwise stuck in a World War II–era mentality. We studied the insurgencies and counterinsurgencies in Malaya, Algeria, and Greece, all of which I found fascinating. I studied figures like Lawrence and conflicts like Indochina that seemed to carry lessons relevant to being a soldier in the kind of wars I expected to fight.

Beginning in the fall of firstie year, our general order of merit began to matter: It would determine which branch we joined and our first assignment. By that time, my grades had improved over the prior three semesters, and the academy began to weigh more heavily our military performance, where I scored well. Branch selection was dramatic. With my entire class seated in a Thayer Hall auditorium, starting at the top of the class, each cadet stood and announced his pick: engineering, field or air defense artillery, armor, intelligence, signals, or infantry. Each choice reduced the remaining slots available. As slots in other branches ran out, the lowest one hundred or so cadets that year were "ranked" into infantry by default. I had a choice, however, and went infantry. My grandfather, father, and older brother had all worn the crossed-rifle insignia of infantry officers, and I never considered any other option.

As graduation neared, the gears of my life turned smoothly. Annie agreed to marry me, I excelled academically, and, because of my meteoric leap in class rank, after graduation I would be able to join the storied 82nd Airborne Division. I hadn't expected to be high enough in the class to have a shot at an assignment to the 82nd, so Annie had been studying German in anticipation of going there. But the chance to be a paratrooper and serve in one of the units most likely to be involved in any potential conflict made it an easy decision.

On Wednesday, June 2, 1976, I graduated and my father commissioned me as a second lieutenant. Our graduation ceremony was where we'd begun our cadet experience, at Michie Stadium. As I sat with 834 other members of my class, out of an original 1,378, waiting to receive our diplomas, I realized that I was very different from the seventeen-year-old boy whose friend had dropped him off four years earlier. I wondered if I could, or would, be the kind of military leader I admired, and I was eager to try. When the ceremony ended, in accordance with tradition, we launched our hats into the air and congratulated one another. I rapidly looked for Annie—and the exit. As quickly as possible, I threw everything I owned into the used Chevy Vega I'd bought and set course with Annie down the hill away from campus. As we neared the last bend before the academy gates, I turned to her. "Hey, look back at West Point."

"Why?" she asked, twisting in her seat to look at the tips of the parapets getting smaller behind the hills.

"Because that's the last time we'll ever see it."

| CHAPTER 3 |

▼

The Army in Which I Should Like to Fight

August 1976–March 1982

"**Y**ou're the United States of America. How could you let this happen?" The question was passionate, like the officer who posed it. I had no good answer, either for Lieutenant Thawachi, a Thai Army officer with whom I'd developed a close relationship, or for myself.

It was April 1980, and photographs in the media of wrecked U.S. aircraft and burned bodies in the Iranian desert were stark reflections of a failed attempt to rescue Americans held hostage in Tehran. Despite my respect for President Jimmy Carter's courageous decision to launch the operation, it was clear to me that my nation was struggling with feelings of frustration and impotence.

At the time, I was a first lieutenant in the Army's 7th Special Forces Group conducting a mission on the tidal edge of the Third Indochina War. Five years earlier, after U.S. troops had completed their withdrawal from Vietnam and Saigon had fallen, deep historical and fresh political animosities had ignited a complicated "East-East" contest involving the Soviets and Chinese, as well as the Vietnamese, who then controlled most of Cambodia. I deployed to neighboring Thailand to lead a four-man Special Forces team in teaching the Thai Army how to use the shoulder-fired Dragon missile system against any Vietnamese tanks that might cross the border. Four years after graduating from West Point, I was a seasoned lieutenant and excited to be in the field, leading a small but important mission far from oversight. This was not practice on a barren military range, and my anxious Thai counterparts reminded me of the urgency.

But my discussion with Lieutenant Thawachi that muggy morning on the Thai Army base near Pran Buri carried my thoughts far away from Southeast Asia, to the desert of Iran.

Thawachi was a muscular officer with obvious energy held in check as we sat drinking tea in a small coffee shop. He was one of the first four Thai soldiers selected to train on the notoriously difficult Dragon because of his skills in marksmanship and English. He was pro-American, and his face reflected pain when he excitedly asked me, "Have you heard?" I had. President Carter had told the world that he had aborted the rescue mission, and the news and images moved rapidly, even to Pran Buri. "There was no fighting," Carter had said, "there was no combat." But eight men had died, he explained, when "two of our American aircraft collided on the ground following a refueling operation in a remote desert location in Iran."

I pictured American aircraft smoldering in the desert. And I thought about the men who had perished.

Like most Americans, I had watched Iran closely since Tuesday, January 16, 1979. On that day, after facing more than a year of volatile public opposition, the Shah, Mohammad Reza Pahlavi, fled Iran. Two weeks later, the Shah's longtime opponent, Ayatollah Ruhollah Khomeini, returned to Tehran from his fourteen-year exile. Inspired by the Ayatollah, a mob of more than five hundred Iranian students stormed the U.S. embassy on Sunday, November 4, 1979, and seized sixty-six Americans. Many Iranians believed the embassy had been the headquarters for the 1953 coup that first reinstalled the Shah—a point Khomeini and others hammered in their anti-American diatribes—and many saw the takeover as a necessary step to prevent an impending American intervention. The American public reacted emotionally. Yellow ribbons were hung; nightly newscasts ended with somber declarations of the number of days since the crisis started. Many asked: *Why is this happening to America? What were we going to do?*

Thawachi pressed the same questions. He had high expectations for America's role in the world. So my initial answers, explaining the complexity of hostage rescue operations and the ever-present chance of failure, didn't satisfy him. His question was far broader. He repeated himself, emphasizing, "You're the United States of America," as though I might have forgotten. His reaction reinforced to me that the cost of failure was far higher than just the immediate loss of life. In years ahead I would see more times when the confidence, hopes, and prestige of the nation rested on the shoulders of a small group of committed professionals.

The cost of any failed special operation is high. President Carter bravely accepted responsibility for the failure, but even so, it stung. This felt like a humiliating demonstration of our inability to execute difficult missions like hostage rescues, especially in comparison with recent successes by our allies.

I'd been impressed in July 1976 when Israeli commandos had reached deep into Africa to rescue passengers from a hijacked Air France flight being held at the airport in Entebbe, Uganda. Two years later, as a paratroop lieutenant, I had watched on the news as French Foreign Legionnaires parachuted into southeastern Zaire and saved thousands of French and Zairian hostages from anti-Mobuto rebels. And just ten days after our failed mission in Iran, the British Special Air Service (SAS) had freed nineteen hostages held by Arab separatists at the Iranian embassy in London. Eagle Claw—as the failed operation was known—was more tactically complex and difficult than these raids. But we made it look impossible.

On Wednesday, January 21, 1981, the hostages' release lifted the pall that the ordeal had cast over America. But the failure in the Iranian desert would cast a long shadow over U.S. special operations. A commission under retired navy admiral James L. Holloway would capture in stark terms what had gone wrong and, more important, what needed to be done. It would provide initial direction for a journey that would shape the rest of my career.

That career had started nearly four years earlier, when I reported to Fort Benning, Georgia. There, in early August 1976, two months after graduating, I left behind the largely theoretical world of West Point to begin my real-world education—graduate work in the nuts and bolts of soldiering. I had also volunteered for Ranger School. The nine-week Ranger course was created at the outset of the Korean War as a way to teach leadership by simulating the stress of combat. It had developed its own mythology. Stories of sleep deprivation, hunger, physical exhaustion, and instructors who did their best to make the course hell led many officers to decide against attempting it (fewer than eighty of two hundred lieutenants from my basic course chose to attend) and intimidated those of us who did. Still, wearing the Ranger tab on our left shoulder would be an important step in establishing our bona fides as soldiers.

Rangers have a rich lineage. During World War II Ranger units conducted high-risk missions across North Africa and in the Nazi underbelly in Sicily and Italy. They rescued American POWs from the Japanese prison camp at Cabanatuan in the Philippines. On D-Day at Normandy the 2nd Ranger Battalion, a unit I would later command, climbed the cliffs of an angular bluff called Pointe du Hoc under a downpour of enemy fire to locate and destroy enemy guns. The postwar Army of 1973—struggling to rebuild professionalism and pride badly shattered in a painful, unpopular war—launched a new era of Rangers.

In November 1976, we arrived in the Harmony Church area of Fort Benning. There, in World War II–era wooden buildings, the Rangers had established a Spartan enclave set apart from the more relaxed standards of the 1970s Army at large. Many Ranger instructors (RIs) wore "high and tight" haircuts, made a point of fitness, and prided themselves on their apparent

indifference to physical discomfort. During the military's post-Vietnam na-
dir, Harmony Church was a refuge for the flint of the Army.

Many of the instructors, like Staff Sergeant Swackhamer, were larger-
than-life characters. His Dickensian name haunted the first phase of the
course, and he treated the Fort Benning sawdust pits, where he taught
hand-to-hand combat, like the sands of the Colosseum. When we shivered
under our winter gear during patrols later in the course, another iconic RI,
Sergeant First Class Jutras, erect and seemingly comfortable in a single
layer of summer fatigues, taunted us in a thick Rhode Island accent: "Cold,
Rrrain-jah?" Lore had it that once, in the final phase of the course conducted in the swamps of Florida, Jutras had continued a lecture on poison-
ous snakes despite being bitten, calmly describing for the Ranger students
the feeling as the venom took effect.

After Vietnam, everyone had an opinion on what ailed the military—
and how to fix it. My class's tactical officer waged his personal war for the
soul of the Army. Convinced that West Point lieutenants tended to band
together and "carry" weak classmates through Ranger School, he sought to
make the early weeks of the course so painful and difficult that the weak
would be culled from the ranks and denied Ranger tabs they couldn't earn
on individual merit. His favorite tool was the "worm pit," a long, mud-
filled ditch covered at about eighteen inches with a canopy of barbed wire.
Through the cold of November and December we crawled through the mud
and water, the first of us breaking the ice on top as we crawled. One night
I watched as five lieutenants in my platoon quit. In accordance with Ranger
School policy, they signed Lack of Motivation statements, forfeiting forever
any chance of winning Ranger tabs and accepting a stigma that would follow them for the rest of their military careers.

Leadership lessons often came unexpectedly. One evening, early in the
course, we conducted a six-mile speed march at the end of which our tactical officer took us to the physical training (PT) field. We shivered as the
sweat from the march chilled us, steam rising from our shaved heads in the
cold of the night and glare of the field lights. After a short time we were
ordered to navigate the obstacle course and worm pit, crawling through the
icy slush. Rapidly the cold produced spasmodic breathing and our limbs
and hands became unable to grasp ropes or perform motor functions. It felt
as though we had crossed the line between being hard and being dangerously stupid.

Suddenly the field lights flashed and another Ranger instructor, a master
sergeant, shouted instructions to us to go immediately to our wooden barracks up the hill from the field. Our tactical officer, a major, surprised by
the countermanding order from a subordinate, protested. Yet in our joy to
be released from the cold and pain, we ran from the field as quickly as our
nearly hypothermic bodies would carry us. Even in my haste, I was struck
by the courageous action of the master sergeant in stopping the foolishness.
Tragically, several weeks later when we were in the mountain phase of the

course, cold killed two Ranger students in the class ahead of ours as they patrolled in the swamp phase in Florida.

The essential vehicle for teaching leadership was the small-unit patrol. Instructors graded students on how well they led squads and platoons, frequently rotating the Ranger students assigned leadership positions. Because patrol leaders depended on the support of fellow students, a "cooperate and graduate" attitude permeated the class. Yet cooperation was challenging when fatigue and hunger wore down otherwise good team players. Most of us found the personal discipline required when things were tough was an accurate measure of the man.

Some of our classmates from West Point had been puffed up as cadets but buckled once they were shivering in the woods. One fellow student stood in stark contrast. Lieutenant Dave "Rod" Rodriguez, caught my attention. A six-foot-four-inch, 230-pound defensive end when we were together at West Point, Rod was quiet and modest yet wickedly funny. One night, assigned to lead our exhausted patrol away from an objective to a base on a route calculated to take up to seven hours of walking, Rod studied the map and gave the order to "ruck up," and despite tired legs and heavy rucksacks, we moved purposefully enough to reach the base in less than two hours. A good man, I noted. Doesn't mess around.

At our graduation in February 1977, the Ranger tab did not make us Swackhamers or Jutrases. No one was instantly stronger, braver, or smarter with it on his shoulder. But it changed the way others viewed us and thus changed the way we viewed ourselves.

I followed graduation with the inelegant eating binge most new Rangers undertake. I remember Annie, who had come down to Fort Benning to see me pin on the tab, staring in amazement as I washed down Hershey bars dipped in peanut butter with beer until I vomited, only to repeat the process. But my insanity was temporary, and in early March 1977 I reported for duty to the 82nd Airborne Division at Fort Bragg, North Carolina.

From its inception, the ethos of the 82nd drew from stark realities: Jumping out of an airplane is an egalitarian process, and luck often determines how and where jumpers land. Generals and privates wear the same parachutes and hit the ground with the same bone-jarring force, and on a hot landing zone, there is no "safe" or rear area from which to direct the battle. Great paratroop leaders had leveraged these realities to earn reputations for leadership by personal example. Over Normandy on D-Day, Division Commander Major General Matt Ridgway, and his assistant, Brigadier General Jim Gavin, were famously the first out of their planes' doors. Later, after taking over the 82nd from Ridgway, Gavin broke two discs in his back jumping into Holland for Operation Market Garden, and yet he continued to command. Generals who commanded from the rear often sported ornamental pistols. In contrast, Gavin carried a rifle, which he meant to use.

The division that I joined bore little resemblance to its storied predecessors or my expectations. But like all lieutenants, I watched and hoped to learn. Some of what I saw inspired me. Much did not. The legacy of Ridgway and Gavin had grown threadbare: I remember bitter comments from my paratroopers during a twenty-five-mile foot march when a commander drove by the column in a jeep, only dismounting in order to correct troopers for perceived shortcomings.

I spent the next twenty months in the battalion as a mortar and then a rifle platoon leader, then finally as company executive officer. During that time our battalion commander and I exchanged few words, and I recall nothing resembling encouragement. He would talk about keeping a notebook in which he categorized people as good guys or "peckerwoods." I felt his connection with the battalion was weak.

The Army of the 1970s was particularly hard on commanders. Constrained resources and centralized edicts created an environment that seemed both demanding and limiting. Training was poor, yet units were consumed with mandatory instruction on seemingly irrelevant subjects as well as picayune inspections of garrison-related equipment and functions. Soldiers and units suffered the cost when truly combat-focused activities lost out to things that looked good or briefed well.

Values and integrity were often under pressure. Although the dark days of Vietnam body counts and My Lai were past, small but insidious reflections of corrosive values would surface. Seeking to reduce the visibility associated with having to file investigation reports on lost equipment, many company commanders avoided it by making up shortages through trading or "scrounging." Similarly, there was pressure to meet reenlistment quotas. At the end of one reporting quarter, our battalion commander revoked an action my company commander had taken to prevent one exceptionally substandard trooper from reenlisting. As a result, the soldier was allowed to reenlist, the unit met its quota, and the Army would suffer that soldier for another tour. Because word of such actions spread quickly, speeches on leadership and values from such commanders often fell on deaf ears.

Appearances were deceiving. I was first impressed, then often disappointed, by some of the flashiest or most macho leaders in the division. And I found that even combat badges were unreliable predictors of knowledge or leadership. Similarly, sloppy appearances and nonmilitary demeanor were not necessarily indicators of flagging professionalism.

Such was the lesson when I first joined Charlie Company and met our company supply sergeant, Sergeant First Class Davis, or Old Dave. A tall combat veteran, Davis had reportedly once been a hard platoon sergeant but had badly injured his leg in a training jump and now limped painfully along, unable even to wear combat boots. As a result he was relegated to the supply room and had developed a significant, overhanging belly. In his rumpled uniform, low quarter shoes, and constant sheen of sweat, he was the antithesis of a poster-paratrooper. But he was an important part of my practical education, and I had much to learn.

A few months after I joined the battalion, Sergeant First Class Davis called me down to his stuffy supply room in the basement of our barracks. "Lieutenant Mac, I'm gonna teach you something here," he said when I walked in. He thumbed through my platoon's equipment hand receipt, breathing heavily as he spoke. "Here's the hand receipt you filled out. See these columns here? Well, I could go here, here, and here," he said, his finger bouncing over the page, "and because you signed in the wrong place, you would be responsible for whatever numbers I wrote in." It wasn't a huge mistake, but I had been careless with the form and left myself vulnerable and potentially liable. "Now I could have done that, but I didn't. I was waiting to see if you were a good guy or not. And I have determined you are. I brought you down here to make sure you'll be more careful in the future. Remember, Lieutenant Mac, not everyone in the Army would do that for you."

Years later, when relying on intelligence whizzes or speaking with bearded tribal leaders, I'd remember Old Dave, and that leaders don't always look like they stepped off the plain at West Point.

Pride in craft was an elusive trait in the post-Vietnam Army, but the sergeants and officers known as jumpmasters had it. Because of the inherent complexity and danger associated with military parachute ("airborne") operations, jumpmasters, who led parachute jumps in the 82nd, needed absolute expertise in their craft. They had to lead planeloads of frightened paratroopers to perform the essential, unnatural act of leaping from an airplane. As a result, jumpmaster standards were exacting and the 82nd's jumpmaster school had a famously high failure rate. Many seasoned paratroop leaders passed only on their second or third attempts. During the jump process, jumpmasters not only ensured safety but also instilled critical confidence in the paratroopers about to jump. They began to do so from the beginning, with their meticulous equipment inspection of each paratrooper before he boarded the aircraft: Their hands and eyes followed a rapid yet precise sequence of parachute and equipment checks.

In the air, jumpmasters carefully controlled the final minutes before jumps. As we neared drop time, the two jumpmasters stood in the aft of the aircraft and simultaneously gave hand signals and shouted warnings: *Twenty minutes!* The planeload of soldiers, called a chalk since the World War II practice of using chalk markings to connect planeloads of paratroopers with their correct planes, stirred. Helmets went on and even veteran jumpers subtly checked weapons containers and other equipment. After giving the ten-minute warning, jumpmasters remained standing near the rear of the aircraft, one adjacent to each of the two paratroop doors they would control during the jump.

Exchanging a glance to ensure they were in unison, the jumpmasters next shouted, *Get ready!* Hearts pumped. To raise the men to their feet, jumpmasters pointed first to the paratroopers nearest the outside of the aircraft, then to those in the center, or inboard. Raising their extended arms, they commanded: *Outboard personnel, stand up! Inboard personnel, stand up!* The next commands followed in rapid succession. *Hook up!* Snap hooks clinked as paratroopers connected the static line that would pull their parachutes to open as they left the aircraft.

Check static lines! Check equipment! Beginning at the nose end of the plane, each man checked himself and the trooper in front of him. *Sound off for equipment check!* This indicated they were ready: *Okay! Okay! Okay!* carried down the line until the paratrooper nearest the jumpmaster gave a thumbs-up and shouted, "All okay, jumpmaster!"

With the doors open, the wind and engine roar were deafening, and the final performance began. Each jumpmaster inspected his doorframe for sharp edges that might sever a paratrooper's static line, then moved onto the jump platform, a step that extended about a foot out of the cargo door into thin air. As young paratroopers watched, each jumpmaster bounced on the platform to ensure and demonstrate its serviceability, then firmly grasped the sides of the doorframe and thrust his body as far outside the door as he could without losing his grip. As the wind buffeted his body and contorted his face, he calmly looked around—first for other aircraft or hazards to jumpers, then to the approaching drop zone (DZ). They scanned the ground for the geographic markers that they had memorized as indicators of the distance to the DZ. During the final sequence, they rotated back into the plane and alerted the jumpers: *One minute! . . . Thirty seconds!* With the DZ seconds away, the jumpmasters pulled themselves back inside the aircraft, faced the troopers, and commanded the first jumper, *Stand in the door!* Moments later the light adjacent to the door flashed from red to green and the jumpmaster slapped the first jumper on the rear. "Go!" The first paratrooper disappeared into the darkness. We shuffled forward and tumbled out of the plane until it was empty. The last one out was the jumpmaster.

It was choreographed ritual, and necessarily so. Jumpmasters were the high priests. In an army where too many leaders hid a lack of competence behind crisp uniforms or spit-shined boots, jumpmasters showed something far more real: hard-won expertise. Over the years, I would watch as confidence and willingness to assume responsibility grew in leaders of every rank when we demanded true craftsmanship.

Throughout my lieutenancy, I was never alone. A year behind me in school, Annie finished college while I was in Ranger School, and after a couple of months to allow me to grow back some hair and become "redomesticated," we were married in a military ceremony where her father was stationed at Fort Monroe, Virginia. We had no money for a honeymoon and instead loaded our 1974 Chevy Vega and moved into our one-bedroom,

$180-per-month apartment in a complex near Fort Bragg. Most of our possessions sat on shelves we made of cinder blocks and wood planks. But it felt right.

In many ways, Annie and I learned together. One Friday night, as a platoon leader, I scheduled a parachute jump, which typically finished after midnight, thus stealing part of the men's weekend. As we strapped on our parachutes, I sensed their resentment and decided to raise morale by suggesting that after recovering from the operation they all come to my place for a platoon party. I did not routinely hang out with subordinates, but this was a moment to build the team. The plan was set, but in the age before cell phones, it was not relayed to Annie.

Although it would be late by the time we would finish the jump and begin the gathering, I assumed I could get home before everyone arrived. But the platoon sent Sergeant Emil Holtz, an enormous mortarman, to the liquor store while the rest of them cleaned equipment. In spite of his looming appearance, Sergeant Holtz was a quiet, cerebral teetotaler. Unsure what the boys drank at parties, he bought a lot of everything with the cash they gave him. Soon thereafter, Annie answered the door in her nightgown, still unaware of the party plan, to find what looked like Andre the Giant, holding clinking grocery bags of liquor, wine, and beer. "LT says we're having a party," he said bashfully. Others soon arrived. By the time I got home, Annie had already met most of the platoon and made them snacks. Later, she sat laughing and warmly chatting with a soldier's girlfriend, a nice girl who danced topless locally but who had dressed conservatively for the party. Annie's instinctive ability to make others feel welcomed and, in situations more dire, comforted, shone through.

Although when I first met Annie she had made it clear to me that she did not want to date or marry a soldier, I think she was more comfortable in an army family than she readily admitted. From her "army brat" upbringing Annie deeply admired her parents. Her memories, tinged with bittersweet good-byes and uncomfortable moments as the new kid in school, are invariably dominated by funny stories of her and five siblings being packed into station wagons or small quarters. I soon found that Annie had an indefinable quality—call it pluck—that made duty feel like privilege and made our army life an adventure.

In the fall of 1978 I made the decision to apply for Special Forces training. Lieutenant Colonel Dave Baratto, my tactical officer from West Point, was commanding a battalion of the 7th Special Forces Group at Fort Bragg, and after seeking his counsel, I submitted my request. The reputation of "SF" at that time was mixed at best, but I wanted to become a part of something that long ago had captured my imagination.

Just after I left the 82nd, the chief of staff of the Army, General Bernard W. Rogers, stripped the paratroopers of their maroon berets. To rein in other units that had begun wearing various nonstandard berets and other headgear, General Rogers issued a blanket ban. The loss of the maroon beret, the accepted paratrooper symbol worldwide and a badge of pride, was traumatic for the 82nd. At the time it seemed to me as though Army leadership, despite good intentions, was tone deaf to what mattered to the volunteer soldiers of its own force.

By the time the paratroopers lost their maroon berets, I was wearing a green one. In November 1978, I joined Detachment 714, Company A, 1st Battalion, 7th Special Forces Group (Airborne), part of the U.S. Army's famous—and, in the minds of some, infamous—"Green Berets." Created midway through the Korean War, the Special Forces were modeled on the OSS's World War II Jedburghs, three-man teams dropped deep into Nazi-occupied Europe to recruit and lead partisan militias. In Vietnam, the Green Berets played their largest role to date, and stories of their operations and exploits had fascinated me from an early age.

Assigned to a twelve-man A-Team (Operational Detachment A), I became part of a brilliant concept that remains effective today. Manned with two officers and ten specially qualified sergeants, A-Teams were designed to possess skills, maturity, and cultural acuity. This enabled them to leverage indigenous forces, from militaries to guerrillas, in a wide range of missions in a more discrete alternative to larger, more conventional operations.

Special Forces' history was tinged with politics. During the 1960 presidential campaign, members of then-Senator John F. Kennedy's staff sought to burnish his defense credentials. Other senators had associated themselves with high-profile weapons like the Polaris missile or B-52 strategic bomber. Kennedy would adopt the Special Forces, whose soldiers had worn the green berets illicitly until the fall of 1961, when the new president authorized the headgear as "a mark of distinction."

As he explained on June 6, 1962, to the graduating cadets gathered in the West Point field house, Kennedy envisioned that his infantrymen would likely face small, hot, peripheral wars "new in . . . intensity, ancient in . . . origin," against the "guerrillas, subversives, insurgents" exploiting "economic unrest and ethnic conflicts." The Special Forces were the first troops Kennedy dispatched to Vietnam, where they trained the South Vietnamese. As the war escalated under President Johnson, their mission grew and activities diversified beyond training. They became highly publicized, and despite some extraordinary exploits, by the end of the war, controversies dogged the force. Criticisms ranged from being elitist to being "off the reservation" to *Time* magazine's August 1969 damning description—"enveloped in the sinister"—after the Army investigated the Green Beret commander in Vietnam, along with six intelligence officers, after accusations that they had murdered an alleged South Vietnamese double agent.

By the time I joined the Green Berets in 1978, they only faintly resembled their Kennedy-era forebears. Traditionally, the Army had an aversion to elite units because such units tended to siphon resources, particularly talented soldiers, from the rest of the force. After Vietnam, that resistance reemerged, and Special Forces were allowed to atrophy. Young officers often received terse advice to avoid ruining their careers by joining Special Forces. "So you want to join the Speckled Feces?" an officer in my battalion had put it to me before I left the 82nd.

Early on, some of my worst fears were realized. My Special Forces officers' course included several lieutenants who had been fired in the 82nd—at the time a rare occurrence. Some of the instructors were equally disappointing. A lecture was stopped one day as a senior instructor had to remove an obviously drunk sergeant from the stage. My company commander was relieved for inappropriate conduct during a training deployment. It made for amusing stories, but it really wasn't funny.

It was a difficult time and some talented, combat-experienced Green Beret officers and noncommissioned officers (NCOs) became disillusioned and unmotivated. The routine of peacetime service didn't suit them. For a young leader, these veterans were an intimidating challenge.

I faced that challenge early. As a new detachment commander (A-Team leader), I felt that the respected and experienced team sergeant of our twelve-man A-Team had grown lazy and needed to be moved from the position. For a young lieutenant team leader, a position designed for a more senior captain, making this assessment was difficult, and acting on it was even harder. He had fought a war as a Green Beret; my beret was still new, and I had never been to war.

So I sought and received the support of my chain of command and we made the change, replacing him with a twenty-nine-year-old combat veteran with less experience but vastly greater energy. It was not an action taken lightly, yet I found surprising support for the move across the unit (particularly from veteran NCOs) and realized that the foundation of professionalism in Special Forces was stronger than it had first appeared to be.

The experience I underwent as a team leader helped transform my career. I had about as much latitude as a post-Vietnam lieutenant could have, received great support but no micromanagement from my commanders, and set the standards and direction for my team.

Although theoretically my team were already "elite" soldiers, I found they wanted someone to push and lead them, reflecting the truism that most soldiers respond when challenged. But, as good as my practical education became in the Special Forces, it was incomplete. In 1980, my fourth year of commissioned service, I wanted something more than training, something that mattered, something real. The Soviets had invaded Afghanistan; in Nicaragua the Sandinistas had overthrown Anastasio Somoza, who had been at West Point with my father. And, of course, Iranian revolutionaries had ousted the Shah and then seized the American embassy in Tehran. The global tumult made training at Fort Bragg feel increasingly irrelevant for a young officer who was honing his craft.

In June 1980 I left Special Forces and entered the Infantry Officers Advanced Course at Fort Benning, where I was promoted to captain. While my experience in Special Forces ended well, I hoped to join the Rangers. A one-year tour to Korea, along with a company command, offered the best route, though it meant a yearlong separation from Annie.

Several months before I left, Annie's sister Nora had been widowed suddenly when her husband, Steven Strickland, an army captain who had been a year ahead of me at West Point, was killed in a helicopter crash in Germany. At the time, Nora was pregnant. Annie decided to spend our year apart living with her sister to help with the new baby. On February 20, 1981, Annie, her parents, and I were at the army hospital on Fort Jackson as Nora's baby, Megan, was born. It felt like a special family time. At first light the next morning, amid a few tears, I kissed Annie good-bye and flew away for a year. In September 2008, soon after returning from another long separation, I danced with Annie at Megan's wedding.

Although I'd hoped to command an infantry company in Korea, I was assigned to the Joint Security Area (JSA) at Panmunjom, Korea. The JSA was a small enclave of neutral territory inside the DMZ where discussions between the two warring parties (North Korea and the United Nations) took place in austere one-story buildings that straddled the border. The North Korean soldiers wore hardened faces and glowered at us while we stared back. The area was rarely violent, but it was always tense. In 1975, when the two sides still intermingled within the JSA, a group of North Koreans tried to provoke an American major, knocked him to the ground, and smashed his larynx with their boots. A year later, North Korean soldiers killed two Americans who were in the DMZ trimming a tree that blocked the view from the South.

As I finished my uneventful year in Korea in March 1982, I had also completed my five-year commitment to the Army following West Point. Some of my experience thus far had been disappointing, and what I'd seen caused me to consider leaving. But I decided against it. I'd also seen some amazing leaders and experienced bonds with soldiers that I found fulfilling, and I sensed that changes were afoot in the Army.

My sense was right. While I was experiencing the low point of my career in Korea, the U.S. military had begun its renaissance. A confluence of factors would move the Army forward. Much of the improvement that I would experience firsthand—namely, the revitalization of special operations—was set in motion by the military's reckoning with the failure in the Iranian desert in 1980.

Operation Eagle Claw was designed to rescue fifty-three Americans held hostage at two locations in the heart of Tehran, an urban thicket of more than four million people. Planners decided that to penetrate Tehran and reach those targets undetected, they had to drive into the city. But once the alarm rang, there would be a firefight and they would need helicopters to escape. These helicopters would meet the rescue teams at a nearby soccer stadium within Tehran. The six hundred miles that separated Tehran from the Arabian Sea–based aircraft carriers the helicopters would launch from was beyond the distance that those helicopters could fly without refueling. Thus the need for fixed-wing aircraft. To shuffle teams and fuel between the planes and helicopters, the teams would need to use makeshift airfields during both the approach and escape legs.

To infiltrate the rescue force, two sets of aircraft would fly into Iran across its southern border. First, C-130 aircraft—carrying Army special operators, Army Rangers, and six-thousand-gallon bladders of fuel for the helicopters—would leave from a tiny island off the coast of Oman, one thousand miles from Tehran. Second, navy helicopters, empty except for the Marines piloting them, would be on their heels, taking off from the USS *Nimitz*. All would rendezvous at night on a desert airstrip, code-named Desert One, southeast of Tehran. To avoid detection at the airstrip, the teams would transfer and the helicopters would refuel without illumination. The ground teams would then travel by helicopter to the outskirts of Tehran—Desert Two—where the soldiers would spend the night hiding in advance of an early-morning assault.

When the convoys converged on Tehran early the next morning, Army Rangers would capture, secure, and hold a second air base southwest of the capital city. After the rescue at the embassy, the escape helicopters would fly from the soccer stadium to this air base, where a second fleet of C-141s would be waiting to ferry the force and the rescued hostages to freedom.

In all, the mission called for forty-four aircraft, thousands of gallons of fuel, a fleet of ground vehicles, and a hybrid force culled from the Navy, Army, Marines, Air Force, and intelligence agencies. It required securing a desert landing strip in darkness, seizing and holding a second airfield, striking two urban targets, engaging in a firefight to get out of Tehran, and exfiltrating to friendly airspace. At best, the plan was a series of difficult missions, each a variable in a complex equation. At worst, with an ad hoc team, it called for a string of miracles.

Launched on Thursday, April 24, 1980, 173 days into the hostage crisis, the mission faltered early. As with all operations, the plan had certain built-in criteria that, if not met, would require the mission to be aborted. In this case, if the number of operating helicopters fell below six—out of the eight originally launched—the operation would not continue. Five helicopters could not carry a team large enough to overpower the enemy at the embassy. Shortly after entering Iranian airspace, one was abandoned due to mechanical failure. The remaining seven helicopters, flying low to evade radar detection, flew into a series of *haboob*, vast milk-thick columns of suspended dust that form in the desert. The clouds were the size of mountains: A thousand feet high, they swallowed the speeding helicopters for hours, obscuring anything much farther than the cockpit windows. After one helicopter turned back, only six landed at Desert One.

On the cusp of launching the second leg of the operation, one of the six helicopters was deemed inoperable. With only five helicopters, fewer than the mission minimum, the commanders aborted. Preparing to exfiltrate and blinded by kicked-up sand in the night, one of the helicopters crashed into the nose of a C-130 that was full of soldiers and fuel. The plane caught fire and the fuel bladder in the fuselage ignited, killing eight operators trapped inside.

Eagle Claw was America's first attempt at a new type of special operations warfare characterized by politically sensitive, complex, fast, joint operations. Its failure largely owed to insufficient bandwidth of every type. The force did not have command and decision-making processes in place: While commanders on the ground were in contact with the White House, some of the helicopter pilots later admitted they did not know who was in charge at Desert One until the operation was over. The assembled teams were not a bonded joint force, as they had not operated, or even fully rehearsed, together before crossing into Iranian airspace. The demands of operational security were understandably heavy. But the mission was too corseted. Security concerns prevented weather analysts, who knew the helicopters might encounter a *haboob,* from briefing the pilots; their forecasts were filtered out when the intelligence reports moved through the organization.

The calamity of Desert One was not a failure of political or military courage. The failure occurred long beforehand when the military—faced with limited resources, talent, and focus—failed to build and maintain the force necessary to accomplish these kinds of missions.

In response to this failure, the Holloway Commission recommended creating a "Counterterrorist Joint Task Force" that "would plan, train for, and conduct operations to counter terrorist activities directed against" the United States. Following the Commission's report, there was born a renewed interest in special operations.

Iranian state television looped footage of the charred aircraft and bodies at Desert One, and Iranian officials triumphantly displayed the blackened remains of the Americans at a press conference in Tehran the next day. Within special operations, "Desert One" became a synonym for failure and a powerful, if at times unspoken, rallying cry. Pictures of the wreckage, with the clearly implied message—"Never Again"—hung on office walls and were posted in barracks. Over the next two decades we rehearsed hundreds of operations to ensure we would get it right when we needed to. There were lessons learned and costs dearly paid, but the force that the nation needed would eventually emerge.

CHAPTER 4

Renaissance

February 1982–May 1993

I n February 1982, near the end of my tour of duty in Korea, Annie
flew to Seoul, and we spent ten days touring where I had been
stationed for the previous year. In early March we flew back to the
United States, where I was to report for duty at Fort Stewart, Georgia. Although I did not recognize it at first, the Army I joined when we returned
was already a different one than the one I'd left just a year before.

Cold war tensions in Europe, exacerbated by the Soviet invasion of Afghanistan in 1979, argued for strengthening the U.S. military's capability,
which had been badly weakened by Vietnam and subsequent budget con-
strictions. As a result, beginning in the final year of Jimmy Carter's presidency and continuing through Ronald Reagan's administration, defense
spending rose, peaking in 1986 and in the process transforming the peacetime capacity of the U.S. military.

At first the change was not obvious, but a series of actions taken near the
end of the Vietnam War set a course to revitalize the Army's equipment,
doctrine, training, and, most important, its leadership.

With limited budgets in the 1970s, the Army made the decision to pursue
five primary weapons systems, highlighted by the M1 Abrams tanks and
Apache helicopters, which would serve to transform the force and to out-
class anything fielded by our potential enemies. In 1982, based on lessons
learned from the Arab-Israeli War of 1973, a new doctrine of offensive
maneuver called AirLand Battle was adopted that leveraged this enhanced
weaponry and technology.

To address chronic leadership problems that had been exacerbated by the six-month command tours used in Vietnam, in 1974 the Army initiated boards, composed of senior officers, to select battalion and brigade commanders centrally, which improved quality, while command tours were lengthened, providing greater continuity.

Better pay, better recruiting, and a difficult economy all helped improve the quality of the force. While I'd struggled as a young lieutenant in the 82nd to persuade soldiers to reenlist for a second or third tour of duty, by the early 1980s we held boards to select which soldiers in the battalion would be allowed to reenlist.

The conditions were set for a renaissance.

If the Army was undergoing such a renewal, it wasn't immediately apparent to me as I arrived at Fort Stewart in coastal Georgia. The post appeared to have at least one foot in a previous century.

And I wasn't joining the renaissance intentionally. I'd volunteered for Fort Stewart and its 24th Mechanized Infantry Division with the sole objective of making it easier to reach my goal of an assignment to the 1st Ranger Battalion, stationed only thirty miles away at Hunter Army Airfield in Savannah. To qualify for the Rangers, I still needed to command a conventional company—my reason for going to Korea, only to find myself diverted to be the operations officer in the Joint Security Area. Because Fort Stewart and the 24th Mech were not traditionally coveted assignments, I assumed I could get company command fairly quickly.

After a short visit with her parents in South Carolina, Annie and I drove down Interstate 95 to Georgia, pulled onto Highway 144 near the small community of Richmond Hill, and passed a sign announcing we'd entered Fort Stewart. There was no gate or military police checkpoint, as became ubiquitous after 9/11, but I slowed down assuming we'd soon enter the main post.

We didn't. After driving nineteen miles through dark marshy pine forests, we finally pulled into the small center of the installation and found the welcome center that most army posts have for arriving personnel to complete administrative processing and coordinate details like housing—for military families, always a troubling concern. Fort Stewart's center was in an old wooden World War II–era building, the kind built to be temporary. Now, forty years after FDR's presidency, it remained in use. In 1982, even the nearby post headquarters was the same construction.

At the welcome center, we checked into the availability of military quarters—small but convenient 1950s-era duplexes. A sergeant working the desk assured Annie and me we'd wait at least twenty months. We ended up renting a small apartment for seven months before the housing office called, and a friend and I moved several pickup truck loads of belongings into a set of two-bedroom quarters.

I'd never been to Fort Stewart but had assumed life there would be much like bustling Fort Bragg. It wasn't. Established in 1940 and sprawling across a huge expanse of swampy terrain that once held a patchwork of rice plantations, Stewart was used during the war to train soldiers in antiaircraft skills, first on wooden replicas until the accelerating defense production could produce the real metal ones. In subsequent decades, Fort Stewart had experienced a roller-coaster ride of booms and busts. The limited development of the post's facilities and the neighboring town of Hinesville seemed to anticipate the next bust more than a possible boom.

I reported to the personnel assignment officer, anticipating immediate posting to an infantry battalion. Instead I was told that I had been promised to the Directorate of Plans and Training. The DPT was an installation-level staff responsible for coordinating military schools, ammunition management, and a host of things I wanted no part of. I wanted to lead soldiers, command a company, and then go to the Rangers. I asked the personnel officer to understand. He was sympathetic and said he would try to work something out.

After days of uncertainty while I waited at home, he told me he couldn't work any alternative to DPT. I was deeply disappointed—first in Korea and now in Fort Stewart, I felt deprived of a chance to command. While my peers from West Point were commanding units, I would sit in a wooden building for who knew how long, working with civilians and a few soldiers—whom most people assumed had been rejected by regular units. At home that night, I talked with Annie about resigning from the Army.

I decided not to, but that meant the next morning I had to report to the officer who knew I had sought to avoid his directorate. Lieutenant Colonel Kenneth Lyons was a short, intense officer who'd hoped to command an infantry battalion but had not. Wounded five times in combat in Vietnam and completely dedicated to the Army, he had reason to be disappointed, even bitter—more so than I. As I entered his office, I knew that with my first words and demeanor I would define myself to him.

He was professional but guarded. He said he'd heard I had hoped for a troop assignment, but he needed an officer, and I was it. He looked for my reaction. Part of me wanted to erupt in complaint about the unfairness of the system. But in thinking it through and talking with Annie, I had realized that responsibility for being the soldier I hoped to be lay with me.

"Sir, I very much want to command an infantry company," I started carefully. "But I'm assigned here to you and intend to work as hard and enthusiastically for you as I'm capable." I paused. "If, after I do, you'll help me get command of a company, I'd be grateful."

He broke into a smile. We were both disappointed to be assigned staff jobs, but I realized that if he could serve without whining or complaint, his was an example worth emulating. Not surprisingly, he turned out to be a great boss.

The next seven months were busy. I got to know then-Major General John Galvin, our division commander, and was befriended by his aide-de-camp, Captain Dave Petraeus. Dave's position on the post was unique. Division commanders normally select their aides with great care, and the position bestows special credibility on a young officer. In addition, Dave had been a

Battalion operations officer as a captain, normally a major's job, and was headed off to Princeton before going to teach in West Point's prestigious social sciences department.

Two years behind Dave at West Point, I'd known who he was. Now at Fort Stewart we periodically ran together and he helped introduce me to leaders around the post. For me, a newly arrived officer with no prior mechanized experience hoping for command of an infantry company, Dave's endorsement was invaluable. We began a friendship that intersected intermittently for many years before aligning often after 9/11.

D uring the summer of 1982, units from the 24th Mech conducted the division's first rotation to the Army's new National Training Center (NTC) at Fort Irwin, California. Sprawled across an area the size of Rhode Island in the California desert it was where George Patton's 2nd Armored Division had trained before deploying to North Africa, and where I'd parachuted into with the 82nd as a lieutenant in 1977. Now, two 24th Mech battalions fought a two-week "war" against an army unit called the opposing force (OPFOR) that employed Soviet tactics using U.S. vehicles modified to look like Soviet tanks and personnel carriers.

The NTC represented the inauguration of a new era in army training, and was the brainchild of General William DePuy, who had been my father's division commander in Vietnam. As commander of the Army's Training and Doctrine Command, DePuy stressed the idea that training must include measurements that would add both realism and accountability. The NTC, approved in 1977, was crafted to allow units to train as they would fight.

That summer, the 24th Mech's two battalions were beaten badly by the OPFOR. For the 24th, as for several other posts that were getting similar wake-up calls, success at the NTC became the new objective.

The NTC wasn't actual combat, but in 1982 it was the closest analog the Army had. The new Multiple Integrated Laser Engagement System (MILES) allowed for relatively realistic battles in which there was a winner and a loser. Vehicles and soldiers were "killed" or "wounded" if hit with an enemy laser. An advanced system evaluated the battle, in which each vehicle's location and actions were tracked and recorded and could be played back to provide analysis to the forces being trained.

Like war, the entire experience could be brutally unforgiving. During a December 1983 rotation in which I commanded a mechanized infantry company, our battalion spent forty-eight hours of feverish activity preparing the deliberate defense of a desert pass. I barely slept as we dug fighting positions; erected kilometers of complex obstacles with tank ditches, minefields, and seemingly endless rolls of concertina wire; and positioned key weapons. We left small gaps in our obstacles as we worked to speed our movement, yet cleverly piled the necessary material next to the gaps so we could close them easily before the enemy attacked.

At the critical moment we failed to close the gaps. Under cover of a smoke screen, the opposing force made them freeways through our defense. Clausewitz's 1832 maxim "Everything in war is very simple, but the simplest thing is difficult" proved timelessly correct.

NTC rotations were revealing. For the first time in peacetime, the effectiveness of a unit and its leader was starkly transparent. Lengthy critiques called After Action Reviews, which displayed shortcomings in planning, coordination, and execution, seared the experience into the psyche of the force.

The scar tissue wasn't all bad. "Disasters" on the desert battlefield became shared memories and lessons learned together. Without war, we recounted NTC stories. Funny tales bound soldiers, and even spouses, as they were told and retold around backyard grills. The NTC created a common experience across much of the force and served, as much as anything in peacetime can, to build wartimelike relationships.

On November 20, 1982, I ran the John F. Kennedy fifty-mile race near the Antietam battlefield in Maryland. Despite the pain, I was excited because the previous Thursday, the 24th Mech's chief of staff, then-Colonel Pete Taylor, had informed me that I would take command of a mechanized infantry company the following week. A company commander was going to be relieved of command, and I would replace him.

On Tuesday morning I reported to the headquarters of the 3rd Battalion, 19th Infantry. My first stop was to report to the battalion commander for guidance. I knew him slightly and hoped he had personally requested my assignment to his battalion.

But his office was empty. The plain army-issue furniture remained; everything else was gone. I soon found that in addition to the company commander I would replace, the battalion's commander, sergeant major, and personnel officer had all been removed.

Four leaders had been fired at once. I was stunned. I would never see anything like that happen in all my years thereafter. But their removal was, ironically, a sign of the Army's growing improvement. Four years earlier, my company commander in Special Forces had been fired for mooning someone inside an officers' club bar. Now, as I understood it, the Army had fired the leadership of our battalion because they struggled in the core skills of our profession. That was progress.

I was also told that a new battalion commander, Lieutenant Colonel Pierce T. Graney, would arrive in several weeks. I had no idea of the impact "Tom" Graney would ultimately have on me as a leader, or how his wife LaJuana's example would instruct Annie.

My first few weeks as company commander were dominated by a single concern: property. I signed a document accepting personal responsibility for all the equipment assigned to the company, millions of dollars in value. Complete inventories of everything from barracks furniture to huge tool sets involved identifying and counting everything. Whatever was missing, someone typically paid for. A command inventory was a grueling task, made hellish if the unit's accountability had been shoddy. My company's property was in bad shape, and I spent countless hours counting tools, gas masks, weapons, and typewriters and then preparing documentation to determine responsibility for the losses, which I remember as having been over thirty thousand dollars.

Before Christmas, Graney arrived. He was a slightly paunchy, thirty-six-year-old soldier with sandy-colored hair and a bottomless mine of sarcastic comments. He soon showed he could be disarmingly informal in demeanor but was unwavering in his expectations. Taking command of a unit still in shock from its horrendous NTC performance in the summer, he forwent lofty motivational speeches. He simply told everyone that he knew how a good mechanized infantry battalion should run. In short order, he said, we'd be one.

I wasn't sure how to take Graney. A chain smoker who avoided strenuous exercise as most soldiers do snakes, he held training and staff meetings that would stretch on for hours. He seemed to ignore most of the popularly accepted practies of an infantry commander. "I want you all in physical training at 0630 every day," he once deadpanned, "because when I roll over and go back to sleep, I want to know where you are."

Graney violated most leadership traits except two, and they counted more than the rest. He cared deeply, and he knew his business. He wasted no time pontificating about the merits of being a great unit, he simply began to deconstruct almost every component of the battalion and put it back together again, patiently teaching us how things should be done.

"How do you spell excess class IX?" Graney routinely querried soldiers of every rank in the battalion. "Class IX" was the military term for the spare parts for our vehicles and other equipment.

"C-O-U-R-T-M-A-R-T-I-A-L," we had to dutifully spell out.

It was his tongue-in-cheek but serious way of teaching us how a truly disciplined unit worked. It was a tradition, albeit a bad one, in mechanized units, to steal and hoard spare parts. It was certainly tempting. Possessing extra parts gave a driver or unit the ability to repair a vehicle rapidly, without going through the Army Repair Parts system with its paperwork and time lag for delivery. For a commander, fixing a vehicle rapidly meant better vehicle readiness reporting—a positive metric of performance. For a soldier, fixing a vehicle rapidly meant finishing work earlier and having more time off. In countless movies over the years, Hollywood glamorized the "scrounger" who could come up with scarce parts quickly.

But Graney knew it killed the system we ultimately depended on, and he taught us why. Besides the obvious theft involved, stealing or hoarding parts meant vehicles were fixed without forcing the repair system to work.

The more we went around it, the less responsive it was. It was basic, but getting the basics right was Graney's brilliance.

He also killed lunch. In a weekly command and staff meeting not long after he arrived, Graney announced, "I want to do away with the lunch hour," capturing our full attention. "It will make us more efficient."

When not on field training, it was habit in most units for soldiers of every rank to take a full hour or more over lunch, often using the time for essential personal business beyond eating. Picking up laundry, paying bills, and other activities caused soldiers to get into their personal vehicles and drive, often off base. Graney thought it was stupid and explained why.

It typically took more than two hours to provide soldiers a single hour. Activities in the motor pool or arms room had to be stopped early to allow equipment and tools to be secured, and soldiers had to move to and from wherever they were working. Graney instead offered the idea that if we limited lunch to the nearby mess hall, we could sharply reduce the time used and that we could then finish work and release soldiers by 3:30 P.M. They would then have free time for personal business. There were initial doubts, as it wasn't tradition. But it worked beautifully.

In countless hours of detailed explanations, Graney taught us what to do—and why.

Sometimes in the process, he could seem unreasonably demanding. Riding together in his jeep back to garrison one Friday after a long week of training, we saw up ahead of us on the road a column of M113 armored personnel carriers. They were from one of our companies, heading to the motor pool before the weekend.

"Watch this, Stan," Graney said, grabbing the radio handset. He contacted the company commander up ahead, instructing him to establish secure radio communication with us.

The captain responded to him in an unsecure communications mode, making the familiar excuse that the "Vinson" security equipment—which, when attached to the radios, made their transmissions secure—was inoperable. In earlier days we would have accepted the excuse and told them to fix it when they reached garrison.

"Stay where you are until you can call me secure," Graney said. "I'll wait." The company halted in place and could only proceed in to garrison when they had his permission, which would require them to successfully call him in a secure mode. He brushed off the company commander's immediate entreaty to reconsider—it was Friday afternoon. We settled in to wait.

I figured I might have a long weekend of sitting in Graney's jeep, but as we watched, the company scrambled like ants out of vehicles, moving radios, antennae, cables, and other equipment in an effort to collect enough working parts from the different vehicles to cobble together a working secure radio. In less than thirty minutes they did, calling in and receiving Graney's permission to head in. I learned you get the standards you demand.

It seemed Graney was invariably right, and we soon became disciples operating with extraordinarily high standards under a thin veneer of humorous sarcasm. The battalion's operating premise was that the best way to take care of soldiers was to build standards and processes into a routine until predictable things worked smoothly. That gave leaders the ability to focus on the unpredictable as needed.

It was also a great time for Annie and me. Our son Sam was born in October 1983, and in the evenings, Annie would load him on the back of her bicycle and ride the short distance to my office to bring me home. With Sam perched in the back, we'd walk the bike back across the parade field, talking about the day, satisfied with life.

In May 1984 my younger brother Pete graduated from West Point and after Infantry Basic and Ranger School, he came to Fort Stewart for his first assignment in early 1985. Since we were the only infantry battalion in the 1st Brigade, when he came to the brigade, he came to the 3/19th and "the brothers McChrystal" now served together. It was unusual but great.

I was now Tom Graney's operations officer, responsible for training and operations across the battalion, and although still a captain, I was essentially the third-ranking officer in the six-hundred-man unit. Ignorant, unimpressed, or both, Second Lieutenant Pete McChrystal felt free to come over to our quarters for dinner and critique management of the unit's training. It was valuable to get unadulterated feedback, particularly if it was negative, from a junior lieutenant. As I became more senior, I remembered how much rank could inhibit hearing the unvarnished truth.

In the summer of 1985 I was considered for early promotion to major and not selected. In the years immediately prior, selection rates for early or "below the zone" promotion to major had been extremely low, so I had little expectation of being chosen. But when the list was formally released and I saw the names of a significant number of my peers, many West Point classmates, I was disappointed.

In later years I came to view not being selected as the best thing that could have happened to me. From that time on, I always had a realistic, almost philosophical view of promotions—the same boards that picked me later "below the zone" were those that had passed me by earlier. That disappointment was an important dose of humility.

Also that summer, after three and a half years in the 24th Mechanized Division, I was due for reassignment. From a professional standpoint, although I'd originally intended Stewart as a short stop on my way to the Rangers, I'd witnessed an amazing time, the kind that comes perhaps once in a generation. By 1985, the 24th Mech was a remarkably better unit. Countless leaders had been strengthened in the crucible, and processes had been developed, refined, and refined again.

As an officer I'd grown immensely. Tom Graney's leadership was like graduate school in management, and the different, fast-paced nature of mechanized warfare had given me a new perspective. Making decisions while bouncing across the desert at twenty-five miles per hour demanded a change from the slower, more deliberate mindset I'd formed as a light infantryman. I'd learned to appreciate speed. Leveraged thoughtfully, speed gave you advantages over your opponent. Speed in planning, decision making, executing, and learning became something I pursued for the rest of my career.

But I'd not fulfilled my dream of getting to the Rangers and was sure that because I'd been a captain for over five years, I was too senior in age and my time had passed.

Then the phone rang and in a strong southern accent, the caller identified himself as Major John Vines, the executive officer of the 3rd Ranger Battalion. The 3rd Rangers had, along with a new Ranger regimental headquarters, been formed the previous summer at Fort Benning, Georgia, in the wake of the Ranger participation in Grenada in October 1983, when the Army decided a larger Ranger force was warranted.

"I'm told you might be willing to come to 3rd Ranger Battalion," Vines said to my astonishment.

No call ever came at a better time for me. I joined 3rd Rangers in October 1985 and although it was entirely serendipitous, my timing again allowed me to watch the tectonics of the Army shift. Just as I'd arrived at the 24th Mech at the outset of an extraordinary period of energy and rapid development, I joined the Rangers as they began transforming from elite but simple light infantry into a complex special operations force.

The change did not follow a straight line. Following Vietnam, the Army was so broken that it wanted to make two perfect battalions whose excellence could then seep into the rest of the Army. The first two Ranger battalions, reestablished in 1974 in Georgia and Washington State, served as these incubators of excellence. Unlike other units designed to do specialized missions, the Rangers largely used the weapons and skills of conventional infantry. They just honed them to perfection. When compared to other paratroop units like the 82nd Airborne, the difference lay more in quality of execution than in distinctly different approaches.

Operation Eagle Claw—the mission to rescue the Iranian hostages—had changed the role of the Rangers. Participation in both the failed Iran rescue mission and its never-executed successor, Honey Badger, pulled the Rangers into an association with the new special operations community that eventually matured into a multi-service task force. Strengthened by a number of personal relationships, the Rangers assumed an increasingly accepted role as the "heaviest" component of that force.

The impact on the Ranger regiment was gradual, but over a period of years it transformed the organization. Missions like complex raids and airfield seizures—which came to be the Rangers' hallmark, further distinguishing them from other units—demanded new techniques and skills. Although discipline and attention to detail remained sacred dogma in the Ranger regiment, particularly for the older sergeants, the force evolved into a vastly more precise and nuanced military capability for the nation.

For four years, from 1985 to 1989, I was lucky enough to experience both the "purity" of traditional Ranger operations—long foot marches under heavy packs infiltrating to conduct a raid on a jungle or mountain target—and also to help develop and execute tactics for lightning precision strikes into complex urban areas. Neither was easy, but I found my diverse background as a paratrooper, a Green Beret, and most recently a mechanized soldier gave me a perspective I might have lacked otherwise. I came to see the advantage, when developing leadership skills, of seeking a breadth of experiences, rather than pursuing the tempting path of early specialization.

For infantrymen, walking is a special curse and source of pride. Civil War infantry bore the brunt of combat and joked about having never seen a dead cavalryman. But more than anything else, they walked long miles, often on blazingly hot days while clothed in woolen uniforms. In 1862 Stonewall Jackson led his men up and down the Shenandoah Valley fast enough to earn the moniker "foot cavalry."

In this regard, little has ever changed. Bill Mauldin's World War II cartoon GIs, Willie and Joe, fantasized about dry socks or the occasional ride in a vehicle. Walking, often under crushing burdens of packs, weapons, and sometimes a wounded comrade, has always been an exhausting, necessary aspect of infantry life.

Foot marching became a hallmark of the Ranger battalions and would be a vehicle I used repeatedly during my career to develop discipline, physical endurance, and mental toughness in soldiers I led. It was more than just walking. Because foot marches were executed as tactical movements, we maintained a five-meter interval between Rangers and forbade talking. The pace was fifteen to eighteen minutes per mile—just short of a trot but faster than an amble—stopping for ten minutes each hour to briefly rest or change socks.

That left a man to his thoughts for hour after hour, particularly at night. In long marches, little pains grew as the hours passed and the pack, never less than fifty pounds, began to feel far heavier after the first twenty miles. To avoid blisters I'd paint my feet with tincture of benzoin before rolling my socks on. The effect was to temporarily "glue" my socks to my feet. It prevented blisters but left me for three years with oddly yellow ankles. In summer shorts, I was a sight.

The Rangers were hard men and took pride in it. Things were done to an exacting standard and anything less was derided. Planning was detailed to the point of having fun poked at us by other units, but it created a culture of demanding precision that over time proved infectious across the wider special operations community. To this day senior leaders seeking competent, meticulous planners will specifically ask for a Ranger.

Discipline went to extremes. It was a popular idea that before being captured by the enemy with secret documents, a spy or soldier must destroy them, sometimes by eating them. In 1988 during a training exercise, one of our Rangers was captured while carrying a radio frequency and call sign book. When his captors briefly turned their backs on him, he attempted to eat it, although in this case it was the size of a small paperback book. His captors detected his action but didn't try stopping him. They sat back and laughed until he did too. At least he tried; Rangers always did.

In the spring of 1989 I witnessed an extraordinary demonstration of leadership in which not a single word was spoken. That March, the 3rd Rangers conducted a battalion change of command on Fort Benning's large parade field. The afternoon on which we assembled was cold and rainy. Rather than move the ceremony indoors, someone decided we would continue as planned—leaving the entire battalion, about five hundred Rangers, standing in formation in the drizzle waiting for the ceremony to start. The bleachers and individual chairs arranged for the spectators were empty as people waited inside nearby Building 4, the schoolhouse of the infantry since 1964, where my father and brother had trained for Vietnam.

Then, about twenty minutes before we were meant to start the ceremony, a single uniformed individual emerged from the building, walked across the soggy grass, and sat in one of the wet chairs facing the Rangers. It was a special operations commander, Major General Gary Luck. As the rain fell steadily, he sat there, he looking at us, every Ranger eye on him. He didn't wave or call out. He didn't order us into rigid attention. He simply sat still, under the same rain that fell on us.

At one point, someone sent a young soldier running from the center with an umbrella that he tried to hold over Luck. But with a reassuring pat on the shoulder, the general sent the soldier away. He sat at least a hundred yards from the formation, but I never saw a commander closer to soldiers than he was at that moment.

I spent my final year in the 3rd Rangers as the battalion operations officer, a job I had held before in Korea and at Fort Stewart. Much of the final year was focused on potential operations into Panama against dictator Manuel Noriega. We conducted several detailed rehearsals, and in June 1989, right before I was due to depart, tensions led us to deploy and posture personnel in the United States and Panama in anticipation of imminent operations. Like others in the battalion, I thought I might finally experience combat. I didn't. The decision was made not to act at that time, and my tour with the Rangers ended a week later.

I spent four years in 3rd Rangers, culminating a series of troop assignments in the 82nd Airborne, Special Forces, Korea, the 24th Mech, and now the Rangers. These years had kept me interested and later proved invaluable.

I'd also seen the Army climb out of the hole it had found itself in after Vietnam, restoring its professionalism and pride. And I was lucky enough to have been a part of a dramatic evolution in both the mechanized infantry and special operations force as each grew and adapted to emerging missions and technology.

For the most part, I'd enjoyed serving under a succession of first-rate leaders, several of whom were truly exceptional. And I had been blessed to build lasting relationships of respect and trust with people like John Vines and Dave Rodriguez, who would be lifelong friends. Finally, I served alongside a new generation of army soldiers. At the time, they were young privates or sergeants. Years later, on distant battlefields, I'd serve again with many of them—all seasoned soldiers and many of them fathers. The wars they'd fight in years later had their roots in events occurring then, amid the final act of the Soviet-Afghan War.

M y first contact with Al Qaeda actually took place a year before it existed, in a curious encounter outside Cairo in August 1987. After completing Ranger company command in May, I'd joined the battalion staff. One of my first missions was to lead an advance element to Egypt in preparation for the battalion's participation in Exercise Bright Star 1987. Programmed to conduct operations during the exercise with Egyptian commandos, we set up our small team on the commandos' base and initiated final coordination.

After we arrived, the U.S. 5th Special Forces Group lent us an Egyptian-born U.S. Army sergeant to interpret for us. Normally a supply sergeant, the athletic, outgoing man, named Ali Abdelsoud Mohammad, was quickly invaluable as he accompanied me to some initial meetings. After several days, Ali Mohammad and I went to the headquarters of the Egyptian 45th Commando Brigade. Ali Mohammad was a gifted translator, but the atmosphere with the Egyptians was uncomfortably cool. It was difficult to determine why. Descending the stairs after the meeting, we passed two Egyptian Army majors, and Ali Mohammad greeted them as old friends. They were friendly but reserved, and we left.

On the way back to our tent area, Ali Mohammad explained that before coming to the United States he had been a major in the commandos, and those were old comrades. The next day he was gone. The Egyptians had asked that he leave the country immediately, which he apparently did. The brigade commander later confirmed it but offered no additional explanation.

I never saw him after that. Only years later did I find out about his subsequent membership in Al Qaeda, after he was arrested in conjunction with the August 1998 embassy bombings in Africa, and his public discussions about Al Qaeda as an organization.

The group Ali Mohammad joined was born in 1988 in Peshawar, Pakistan. Peshawar had been a key node from which Afghan mujahideen, split among seven groups of differing ideology, ethnicity, and sophistication, had waged a guerrilla war against the Soviet forces and those of their communist satellite state. Mixed into Peshawar were Arabs who had traveled to central Asia to wage jihad.

The Arab volunteers never had a large role in the anti-Soviet guerrilla war itself. Only fifteen Arabs, by a veteran's account, had joined the jihad by 1984, rising to two hundred in 1986 when they began to fight on their own. But with victory over the Soviets assured in 1988, the Arabs—then estimated by the Islamabad CIA office to be four thousand strong—further asserted themselves.

One of the most influential Arabs was Osama bin Laden, the rich thirty-one-year-old son of a Saudi construction magnate. Born into privilege, as a teenager Osama had become increasingly fundamentalist in his religious views and since his first trip to Pakistan in 1980 had become deeply involved in the Afghan war against the Soviets.

Bin Laden began to develop a mystique through his charitable work. Tales fluttered of the Saudi personally sitting behind the wheels of the bulldozers, supplied by the Bin Laden Group, moving dirt to make defensive positions and roadways for the jihadists in the Afghan ridges. He was known around Peshawar for his visits to the bedsides of the wounded in the hospitals, his uniform—traditional Afghan *salwar kameez* top, English trousers, and Beal Brothers boots—partly that of the respected Saudi scion and partly that of jihadist patron, with the balance between the two quickly shifting.

With impending victory over the Soviets, a central question now divided the "Afghan-Arabs" in Peshawar: Where should the jihad go next? Abdullah Azzam, an itinerant Palestinian cleric, wanted the focus to remain on Afghanistan, ensuring that it became an Islamic state. He had preached that Muslims needed a literal "firm base"—*al-qaeda al-sulbah*—from which to spread the fight. In opposition, Ayman al-Zawahiri, a dour physician and veteran militant in that sphere, wanted to immediately extend the jihad in order to topple Arab regimes, starting with his homeland of Egypt. He and his fellow Egyptians felt a mobile army—a vanguard of jihadists—could undo these regimes through coordinated coups. These issues were not fully resolved but were in some sense transcended from the get-go through the organization's ambitious, if vague, agenda. Al Qaeda's bylaws were as broad as they were soaring: "To establish the truth, get rid of evil, and establish an Islamic nation."

After their planning meetings in August, Al Qaeda officially got to work on September 10, 1988. From the beginning, the group looked for a specific person to join its vanguard army. Testing would cull the "best brothers" from the Arab volunteers; they would need to be obedient and determined. "Trusted sources" would vouch for their integrity and the security of the organization. Al Qaeda soon began to field such candidates and trained them at a new base—separate from the conventional one. Many of the first recruits and advisers to bin Laden were hardened Egyptians, who would remain a powerful faction within the movement.

In late June of 1989, almost exactly thirteen years after we had left West Point, Annie, Sam, and I loaded our car and drove back to school, this time to Rhode Island.

For an army major in 1989, going to the Command and Staff College was important. Only about 50 percent of all officers were ever selected for resident attendance, most to the Army's school at Fort Leavenworth, Kansas. It served as the first significant culling process of the officer corps. Few officers not chosen would later command at the battalion or higher levels.

I was happy to be selected for school but surprised when the Army notified me that instead of attending the Army Command and Staff College at Fort Leavenworth, I'd be going to the Navy's version in Newport, Rhode Island. It proved to be a great year.

Sited in scenic Narragansett Bay, the Naval War College was academically stimulating beyond anything I'd yet experienced. Unlike more structured programs with long class hours, the Navy emphasized extensive reading punctuated by limited but focused seminars. I'd always loved to read, and the instructors pushed me into the works of Clausewitz, Homer, and others that helped build a firmer foundation of knowledge.

It was also a good year to be studying the past and future worlds. The February withdrawal of the Soviets from Afghanistan after nine years of bitter fighting, the Tiananmen Square massacre in China, Solidarity's electoral success in Poland, and the November fall of the Berlin wall created the most fluid international environment of my lifetime. We were forced to think broader than a lockstep Cold War view of the world, and to consider strategy in a more traditional multipolar sense. For a year we had time to do that.

Classes were only four days each week; I played on the class basketball team with Tim McHale and Ray Odierno; I prepared for and ran the Boston Marathon on Patriots' Day; and Annie, Sam, and I enjoyed exploring New England.

There was one personal disappointment. On the morning of December 20, I awoke to run before class and saw news announcements of Operation Just Cause, an American intervention into Panama spearheaded by the Rangers I'd left just six months earlier. I wasn't surprised, but after thirteen years as an officer and over a year of direct participation in the planning and rehearsals, it hurt to miss the operation.

It is difficult to explain a soldier's feeling about missing a combat action. Soldiers don't love war but often feel professional angst when they have to watch one from the sidelines. Reports of the Rangers' performance gave me pride but also guilt and embarrassment that I wasn't there.

Annie let me feel sorry for myself for a few days. Then, standing one evening in our small kitchen, she drew herself up to her full five feet six inches, looked me in the eye, and asked point-blank, "Are you going to get over this? Because you missed it. It wasn't your fault, but you did. And if you can't get past this, then you'd better get out of the Army."

It was the proverbial two-by-four to the forehead, swung as only Annie can. I wanted sympathy, but it was the last thing I really needed. I still loved being a soldier, so I told her I'd buck up.

In June of 1990 we graduated and I headed for another tour at Fort Bragg, this time to a joint special operations task force.

Formed in 1980 following the post–Eagle Claw Holloway Commission, the task force began as a small battle staff designed to command and control the complex special operations, like hostage rescue, that the commission concluded would be needed in the future. It envisioned a lean, secret team capable of avoiding the ad hoc approach that had hampered Eagle Claw from the start.

In the beginning it was not welcomed by the subordinate units it would control. But by 1990 the task force had matured significantly. Its participation in the October 1983 invasion of Grenada had not been flawless, but it had legitimized the command. So too had action against a series of terrorist incidents like the Palestinian Liberation Front's hijacking of the *Achille Lauro* in October 1985. But more than any other event, the task force's central and impressive role in the invasion of Panama—six months earlier— had solidified its reputation and role.

I joined the Operations Directorate, and as the Ranger representative in Current Operations, I shared a small office with Army, Navy, and Air Force special operators. Each day, we handled unit-related issues and helped coordinate forthcoming operational or training deployments. When the task force conducted exercises or real-world operations, we served as operations officers developing plans and then overseeing their execution.

I was on a major exercise at Fort Bliss, Texas, on August 1, 1990, when our intelligence officer informed me that Iraqi forces were massing on Kuwait's borders and an invasion appeared likely. A day later, Iraq bombed Kuwait City, and in less than a day Iraqi units had overrun the country.

With their kingdom threatened, the Saudis received two offers for assistance. The first came during a visit from Secretary of Defense Dick Cheney and Central Command (CENTCOM) commander General Norman Schwarzkopf. On August 6, they met with the king, who approved deployment of a force that eventually totaled 543,000 U.S. and allied troops. They would soon be based in the kingdom, postured to protect Saudi Arabia and eject Iraq from Kuwait if and when necessary. But the arrival of American forces soon provoked ire and an urgent, competing pitch: In early September, Osama bin Laden, recently returned from Afghanistan, proposed to the Saudi king that he could have an army of one hundred thousand Muslims ready in three months to defend the Land of the Two Holy Places. Bin Laden's option was smiled at—and dismissed.

The rejection smarted for bin Laden. So too did the shame he felt at having Christians and Jews defend Muslims. Top Saudi religious authorities fell in line with the regime and sanctioned the American presence, but bin Laden did not. He founded a group in London that produced hundreds of pamphlets condemning the Saudi state, fell out of favor with the Saudi government, and underwent brief house arrest before moving his Al Qaeda group to Sudan the following year. While bin Laden's first enemy had been communism—in Afghanistan, the Central Asian states, and then his father's homeland of Yemen—his ire and the aims of his group now increasingly turned toward America.

The task force did not deploy as part of the initial forces. Instead we planned and rehearsed for a mission to rescue American personnel held up in the U.S. embassy in Kuwait City. The Americans were not hostages in the strictest sense of the word. Iraqi forces had not taken control of the embassy, but their control of the city prevented the Americans' safe extraction, so we were ordered to devise a rescue.

Preparing for the rescue mission gave us something to do while conventional forces staged in Saudi Arabia. But when the embassy was evacuated and the Americans were repatriated on December 13, 1990, it looked as though our role in the crisis would be limited to reacting to possible Iraq-inspired terrorist attacks across the region.

Like others, I speculated on why the task force's part in Desert Shield, soon to be Desert Storm, was so limited. There were clearly challenges to incorporating its specialized skills into a huge conventional effort. Additionally, some leaders were uncomfortable with the force.

The experience helped to shape my belief about what this unique force must be, and how it must operate. We needed better organizational and personal linkages with conventional forces, as well as with other agencies of the U.S. government. We'd have to open up more, educate conventional leaders about what we did, and importantly, we had to avoid even the appearance of elitist attitudes or arrogance.

On January 18, the situation changed when Iraq launched eight Scud missiles against Israel, the first of forty-two eventually fired in an attempt to provoke the Israelis. Although when fired at such extreme range, the Scud missiles were inaccurate and limited in payload, Israeli counterstrikes were expected, and that reaction threatened to fracture the Allied Coalition. Preventing Israeli action became a priority.

In late January, I deployed with the first element of a task force directed to augment ongoing efforts by Coalition aircraft to locate and destroy Iraq's mobile Scud-launch vehicles in the expanse of Iraq's western Anbar Province.

Our concept of operations was to project small ground elements into Anbar, north of where British special forces had already begun to insert small teams. Omnipresent Coalition airpower would support the teams, as would special operations helicopters, which would insert, resupply, and exfiltrate the operators.

To focus our effort, we attempted to view the Iraqi Scud capability as a system. That system included personnel, truck-mounted launchers, missiles, rocket fuel, essential meteorological data, and launch approval, which would clearly require real-time communications. We analyzed the possible launch sites, the hide sites, the best times to operate, and what would trigger a decision to fire.

The approach was correct, but our intelligence simply couldn't generate enough clarity on Iraqi Scud operations to support an effective campaign to cripple the system. As a result, our efforts relied on thoughtful guesswork by intelligence teams and risky operations by forces on the ground. We were largely dependent on luck. It was a position I never wanted to be in again.

I was a staff officer at our base in Saudi Arabia, just south of the Iraq border, so for me the war was less excitement than simple hard work and a chance to learn. At one point in the conduct of an operation, a troop of about twenty Army special operators deep inside Iraq got into a firefight with Iraqi forces. The troop was able to break contact with the Iraqis and move a distance away, but danger remained. With a wounded operator, they requested extraction—a natural decision based on the assumption that the Iraqis now knew their location, and would likely send more forces to pursue them.

The troop's squadron commander, a veteran of high-risk reconnaissance operations in South Vietnam and Cambodia, came to our task force commander, then–Major General Wayne Downing, and recommended extracting the troop. Downing asked some relevant questions and then disapproved the request. The troop would remain on the ground. Downing's decision surprised me, but his calculus was courageous and instructive. He knew that if Iraqi forces cornered and destroyed the troop, he would bear responsibility. And that responsibility would weigh more heavily than if he had been on the ground sharing their risk, which wasn't possible. However, he also knew that if the troop was extracted, CENTCOM's perception would be that we were easily run off the battlefield; that perception would endanger the viability of our mission and our task force's freedom to operate. We'd be marginalized and unable to accomplish our strategic mission of preventing Israeli intervention.

Downing judged that U.S. airpower could protect the troop, but as nothing in war was guaranteed, he had to shoulder the risk. The troop remained on the ground in Iraq and was able to avoid being trapped by Iraqi forces.

As we teamed up with British special forces, I found myself paired for planning with an unconventional Scot, Lieutenant Colonel Graeme Lamb of the British Special Air Service. We quickly became close. I remember little about his appearance except that he was a bit disheveled and wore no socks, so that his white ankles showed between his combat boots and the drawstring of his pant cuffs. Senior to me and with more worldly experience, Graeme was more extroverted and self-confident in that environment than I was. While I often found myself consumed by the details of planning operations, Graeme was constantly thinking and talking about the wider strategy of the war—and he forced me to think.

At one point, when some aspects of operations were frustrating me, I came back to my desk to find a small yellow Post-it note stuck to my notebook with a single, appropriate phrase from Kipling's famous poem: "If you can trust yourself when all men doubt you . . ."

In the years ahead, Graeme and I would go on to two more wars together, and I never forgot the poem, or the Post-it.

I doubt our operations had much direct effect on Iraqi Scud operations. But in the end, Israel never intervened.

The war concluded on February 28, 1991, and I spent two more years in the task force learning the ins and outs of the special operations world. But it was the leadership of three commanders that I remember most. Where Gary Luck had demonstrated empathy by sitting on a rainy parade ground with a battalion of Rangers, and Wayne Downing had shown courage by accepting the frightening burden of responsibility for a small unit being hunted by the enemy, Major General Bill Garrison taught me trust.

In the spring of 1993, in the last months of my initial tour of duty at the task force, I worked for weeks on a long, detailed, real-world contingency plan for relief of a threatened U.S. position in Latin America. Garrison, a laconic Texan famous for once describing a dark evening as being "as black as my ex-wife's heart," was required to brief the U.S. Southern Command four-star. I was to prebrief Garrison and then accompany him.

When I entered Garrison's office, one I would later occupy for almost five years, he invited me to sit in front of a coffee table. Onto it I promptly opened the large three-ring binder containing the plan and prepared to brief him. Instead of nodding for me to begin, Garrison, an unlit cigar in his mouth, leaned back and put his boots on the edge of the table.

"Stan, is it good?" he said, referring to the plan. I said I thought it was, leaning forward again to brief him on it.

"If you think it's good, I don't need a brief; I trust you. Let's talk about something else before we have to go to the airplane," Garrison said, obviously more focused on developing me than on perfecting a plan.

If he'd taken the brief and changed something, or even just scrutinized the details, it would have become his. Instead, it was mine. His willingness to trust was more powerful than anything else he could have said or done. I spent that conversation, the flight, and the time before the meeting hoping I wouldn't let Bill Garrison down.

CHAPTER 5

Preparation

May 1993–June 2000

Soldiers die on sunny days as well as gray and rainy ones: Such was the tragic lesson one pleasant spring morning in 1994. On Wednesday, March 23, after a ten-mile run on the grounds of Fort Bragg with Steve Cuffee, my command sergeant major, I headed to a quarterly training brief. The brief was conducted every ninety days in the 82nd Airborne Division. In it, a brigade commander and his subordinate battalion commanders would review recent and forthcoming training with the assistant division commander for operations (ADC-O). At thirty-nine, I was a paratroop commander, and my unit—2nd battalion, the 504th parachute infantry regiment, known as the White Devils—had just finished a challenging but successful rotation at the Army's Joint Readiness Training Center at Fort Polk, Louisiana. After ten months in command of a battalion I loved, life was good.

I'd been lucky. Hoping to command in the 82nd Airborne, I had ended up in the same brigade I'd started in as a new lieutenant in 1977. I had returned to "the Division" the previous May with some trepidation. I'd been away from it for fifteen years. I knew that much had changed and that the proud unit could be insular. But I joined an organization that was well led and far healthier than the post-Vietnam 82nd I'd experienced fresh from West Point. My brigade commander, Colonel John Abizaid, had forged a close team of commanders yet led with a light touch. While he was my boss, he was also a friend.

When I had taken over ten months earlier, in May 1993, the White

Devils were already a tight unit, and from the start I made teamwork a priority. In the 24th Mech, I'd learned to use technical skills like marksmanship to build confidence, expertise, and a sense of unwavering standards in our noncommissioned officers. We did the same with machine gunnery in 2/504. Likewise, the Rangers had taught me the power of shared physical challenges, so foot marching again became central to forging unit spirit. The paratroopers responded remarkably to my emphasis on cohesion. It would, that March morning, prove essential.

As I left our headquarters for the quarterly training brief, I glanced at paratroopers from my battalion who were loading vehicles for movement to Green Ramp, the marshaling site at Pope Air Force Base, a couple of miles away. There they would complete final refresher training before donning parachutes and taking off to conduct a routine daytime training jump. The jumpers were mostly new paratroopers or cooks, administrators, or other specialists who, although vital to the operation of the battalion, had other duties that kept them out of our larger mass unit jumps. I nodded and smiled at several sergeants I knew well. I envied that they could be outside while I sat in a meeting.

I was a few minutes early, and we gathered in John Abizaid's office talking informally before moving to the basement conference room. After a little while, through John's office window, we noticed a large plume of black smoke rising from the north, the direction of Green Ramp.

"That's got to be a huge fire, and down near Pope," someone said. We assumed it was a controlled burn, and moved downstairs to the brief. A short time later the brigade executive officer, somewhat breathlessly, interrupted the meeting.

"Sir, there's been a big accident at Green Ramp," he told John Abizaid as we all listened.

Brigadier General Mike Canavan, the assistant division commander for operations, said he would drive to assess the situation, and suggested John and I ride with him.

Each minute of the drive made it increasingly obvious that a major accident had occurred, as emergency and other vehicles moved toward the tower of smoke. Having seen my paratroopers next to our headquarters just a short time before, I hadn't considered the possibility they might be involved. But about 250 meters from the gate of Green Ramp we drove past a White Devil paratrooper I knew. Without equipment or a beret, he was walking somewhat aimlessly back in the direction of our battalion. Paratroopers didn't walk around like that.

At Green Ramp, because we were riding with Brigadier General Canavan, we were able to pass quickly through the military police cordon that had been established and into what we now could see was an aircraft crash site. Ambulances, fire trucks, military police, and vehicles from nearby military units that had moved to the site to help were everywhere. Soldiers, both injured and dead, were being moved as quickly as possible to Womack Army Hospital on Fort Bragg, a couple of miles away. I soon found several of my paratroopers and learned that my battalion had been the hardest hit. The accident ultimately killed nineteen White Devils and left over forty injured, many grievously. A sister battalion, the 2/505, lost four of their own paratroopers in the accident.

It was a shock. In combat, losses are painful but rarely surprising. It's the nature of the beast. The scope and severity of this accident was akin to war but arrived with little of the mental preparation that girding for combat allows. The moment called for leadership of the kind I'd long studied and knew would one day be necessary.

We began to piece together what had happened, and over time details of the incident became clear. An in-flight collision of two air force aircraft, an F-16 fighter and a C-130 cargo plane over Pope Air Force Base had resulted in the fighter pilot losing control and ejecting. His aircraft had crashed onto the airfield, striking a parked C-141 aircraft. Pieces of both aircraft, along with a wave of fuel-fed flame, had swept over the adjacent areas of Green Ramp, where paratroopers gathered and prepared to load planes for the jump.

The size of the affected area was limited. Paratroopers fleeing the approaching narrow but hellish fireball who cut one direction escaped unscathed, while those in the direct path of fire and debris suffered terrible burns, or worse. It had ended quickly, but the process of rebuilding the battalion, and the impact on many people, would go on for a long time.

In an accident of this magnitude, as after a significant combat action, there were two immediate priorities. The first was providing medical care to the wounded. Young medics and leaders had to triage on the ground— deciding who would be given a chance to live by determining who would be treated first. At Green Ramp, medical assets arrived after the first few minutes, and relieved that burden.

The second priority was accountability. In combat, soldiers have a sacred responsibility to leave no one behind, yet in the confusion of an evolving situation, accounting for every comrade can be remarkably difficult. At Green Ramp, the mix of units and the rapid evacuation of many wounded soldiers before a firm system could be established to track them left us hustling to ensure we located every paratrooper.

I quickly realized that I needed to communicate a clear message to my battalion about what had happened. Inaccurate accounts or mixed messages would make it harder for us to focus on the tasks ahead. Almost immediately, I also decided that rather than allowing the unit to wallow in grief or self-pity, we would actively focus on honoring our dead, caring for our wounded, and doing everything we could for the families affected. From the airfield I moved to the post hospital.

Not surprisingly, Womack Army Hospital was a confusing whirl of motion. The emergency room entrance area was overwhelmed with arriving vehicles, yet the staff was operating with impressive calm. We set up a small command center to begin to establish accurate accounting for our paratroopers, and I moved to the morgue area to confirm the identity of one of them.

The scope of the event guaranteed immediate news coverage, and we worked to provide rapid notification to families of the paratroopers involved, so they wouldn't hear tragic news from public sources or spend anxious hours in fearful anticipation. Yet we balanced that with a need to ensure that haste did not result in misinformation that might produce anguish in loved ones or friends.

As we assembled and verified the list, familiar names of close colleagues appeared, like that of Staff Sergeant James Howard, only twenty-seven but a veteran leader of our personnel section. Annie and I would later stand by his graveside with his wife and two young children. Paratroopers I'd not yet met, like twenty-two-year-old Private First Class Tommy Caldwell from Senath, Missouri, another husband and father, perished as well. This would have been Caldwell's first parachute jump in the 82nd. I could imagine that he and his young wife would have celebrated it that evening.

As people gathered in a large reception room in the hospital, waiting for information or a chance to visit injured husbands or friends, a young wife from our battalion arrived. Jan Dunaway was married to Captain Chris Dunaway, my battalion personnel officer. Both were from rural Arkansas and had embraced army life, the 82nd, and our battalion with vigor. That day, having heard of the accident, Jan drove from her quarters to the hospital to see if she could help. She had no idea Chris had been involved.

Shortly before Jan walked into the room, I had identified Chris's body in the morgue and seen the distinctive airborne wings tattoo over his heart, a reminder of his passionate commitment. Army procedures dictated that formal notification of spouses include an army chaplain and a careful procedure. But I couldn't risk that she'd hear about Chris from an impersonal list or thoughtless conversation. So I pulled her aside and told her as compassionately as I could.

I'd never personally communicated that kind of news to a spouse, and although I knew Jan well, I wasn't sure what to expect. I think even if I had been a veteran at it, her reaction would have stunned me. Looking directly into my eyes, she drew herself up a bit straighter and thanked me.

"This is a difficult day. I need to see if I can help any of the other families," she said quietly.

From the first, I realized that being organized was the key to real compassion. There was a natural tendency for Annie, me, and other key leaders to flock to the bedsides of injured paratroopers or spend time with grieving, frightened family members. But organizing and focusing the paratroopers and spouses of the battalion allowed us to have a greater impact. We found everyone ready to help, and natural leaders arose, many of them wives, to schedule the delivery of meals to families, provide almost constant child care where needed, and even to deliver 135 Easter baskets to children affected by the crash.

In the first days, Annie, Kathy Abizaid, and other unit leaders spent most of their time at the hospital. The hospital staff was terrific, but White Devil troopers and spouses provided essential support for people facing uncertain futures. Assisting parents and young wives in visiting badly burned, sometimes dying young paratroopers, then making difficult decisions on things like burial locations and insurance money, were searing experiences.

So, enabled by a chain of command above us that would not tolerate bureaucracy preventing us from doing the right thing for our paratroopers and their families, we buried our dead, visited our wounded, and simultaneously prepared ourselves to assume our planned rotation as the division's Ready Force-1 battalion. Immediately after the crash, John Abizaid asked me if, after the losses, I thought we needed another unit to replace us as the first in the division to deploy if needed. I said no. We both agreed that responsibility would help the battalion move beyond the loss.

On March 29, six days after the accident, at an 82nd memorial service for the fallen, I spoke to more than 3,500 people gathered inside the Ritz-Epps Fitness Center at Fort Bragg. The audience included a number of the injured, bandaged soldiers, some moving by crutches, others visible on the white hospital gurneys that had been wheeled in to allow them to watch. I tried to express how I felt.

"The depth of our loss does not mean we are beaten. As long as young men and women volunteer to jump, when no one would question the choice of an easier path, we cannot lose."

While the first days were tough, my reactions were more mechanical than emotional. I grabbed onto the task of leading the battalion through a challenge, and to some degree that focus insulated me from more personal emotion.

Those feelings came later. In the weeks and months after the crash, we visited injured paratroopers at Duke Hospital, and at the Army's burn center in San Antonio. On one visit to Brooke Army Medical Center, in a ward of badly burned paratroopers, most lying flat with little clothing or coverage to avoid infecting sensitive wounds, I spoke with a young paratrooper I knew. I had to lean forward, straining to understand what he said.

"Sir, I'm trying to salute, but my arm doesn't work."

My stomach knotted. I needed to salute him.

I thought often about the risks that the paratroopers I led had accepted. Six months before the tragedy, I'd sat outside my battalion tactical operations center, a waterproofed canvas tent that held maps, radios, and selected members of the staff, with Mike Canavan. We were in a wooded training area on the western part of Fort Bragg but talked about a location some eight thousand miles away: Somalia.

A day or so prior, on the afternoon of October 3, 1993, U.S. forces had launched a raid into the Bakara Market in Mogadishu, Somalia, to capture

clan leaders opposing efforts to bring stability to part of the tragically chaotic Horn of Africa. Although the daylight raid had begun well enough, the
shoot-down of an MH-60 Black Hawk had begun a series of events that
ultimately resulted in the loss of eighteen American soldiers, including
Army special operators, Night Stalker crewmen, and Rangers.

Even from initial, incomplete accounts, it was clear that there had been a
ferocious firefight in which the magnificent courage of the force had been
apparent. But because Mike Canavan and I had both served in and would
eventually command the task force that conducted the raid, the operation
had special resonance for us. We knew that the losses, many of them friends,
would be deeply felt in the small special operations community. In the days
ahead, media coverage that included heart-wrenching photographs of American corpses, our former comrades, being dragged by raucous crowds
through the streets of Mogadishu evoked anger and revulsion.

The fight in Mogadishu was to have lingering effects on America, her
special operations forces, and my experiences in the years ahead. Just as
Grenada, Panama, and the first Gulf War had done much to erase the frustrations of Vietnam, Mogadishu carried a whiff of failure, a reminder that
despite the progress we'd made since Eagle Claw thirteen years earlier, the
possibility of death and defeat was always at hand. That reality focused
and drove us as we labored to develop a force that would win.

S everal months after Mogadishu, and several months before the tragedy
at Green Ramp, the Army Personnel Command had asked if I wanted to
compete for command of a Ranger battalion. Commanding a Ranger battalion was reserved for "second-time" commanders who had already led a
conventional unit. A forthcoming board would consider a slate of candidates from across the Army. I went back and forth in my mind as to whether
I should pursue the opportunity. Ever since my summer experience with a
Ranger company at Fort Hood as a West Point cadet, I'd wanted to lead
Rangers. My four years in the 3rd Ranger Battalion had made that a passion. Yet I loved the White Devils and felt I hadn't yet done all I could in
command. Ranger selection would cause me to leave just halfway through
my command tour.

I was a few days from making the decision, seesawing daily between the
two options, when an old Ranger comrade came to visit. Nick Punimata
had been a senior NCO in the 3rd Ranger Battalion and had since become
a warrant officer in Special Forces. A thoughtful friend in a bearlike body,
Nick sat down in my office and congratulated me on getting a Ranger battalion command.

"Nick, the board isn't until next week," I corrected him. "And I haven't
decided whether to compete for one. It might be better for me to stay here."
Nick gave me a look of surprise and exasperation.

"But, sir, what about the boys?"

I made the decision then and there, and a week or so later I was informed the board had selected me to command a Ranger battalion.

S oon after I was informed I'd return to the Rangers, the Pope crash happened. As a result, my chain of command at the 82nd recommended that my departure be delayed from summer 1994 until November to allow me to help the unit navigate through rebuilding in the wake of the tragedy. It was a good decision, and I was pleased to have seven more months in command of the White Devils.

Those months were exciting. On September 18, 1994, two months before I left the White Devils, I joined most of the 82nd Airborne Division's roughly sixteen thousand paratroopers as we loaded into a fleet of C-130s at Fort Bragg for what was to be the largest American combat parachute drop since World War II.

Contingency planning had been ongoing for many months as turmoil roiled Haiti. The sizable parachute drop and subsequent operations would secure key facilities on the island. My White Devils would jump on the airfield in Port-au-Prince and move on foot through the city to link up with Rangers at the National Assembly building.

Four days before the designated D-Day, we were instructed to move our units into secure holding areas to conduct final preparations while maintaining as much operational secrecy as possible.

With their commanders and key staff having been sequestered for the past week, the paratroopers no doubt sensed something was afoot and were curious as they marched into the personnel holding area where we would be staging. I assembled them in the corner of what once had been a 1950s-era 82nd Airborne Division unit motor pool.

As I looked onto the sea of faces, they were familiar. I'd seen them dripping with sweat on long foot marches, and shivering with cold but grim determination during long training exercises. I remembered their serious but compassionate demeanor carrying coffins or escorting families of their comrades. Most, like me, had never experienced direct combat. They thought they were ready but needed to hear it from me.

"Gentlemen, they've canceled the World Series on us," I said, referring to the ongoing baseball players' strike. I paused to confused looks. "So we've decided to invade Haiti." The paratroopers laughed and cheered.

I wasn't trivializing a combat operation in which people would likely die. But it was important to break the tension. There would be stress enough in the days ahead. As most had already guessed, the operation would be to unseat Lieutenant General Raoul Cédras and his junta, who, having deposed the democratically elected president, ruled over what President Bill Clinton at the time called "the most violent regime in our hemisphere."

After three days of conducting rehearsals and repeated reviews of every part of the plan, we moved to the airfield and, beside a sea of parked aircraft, donned parachutes and loaded up. The energy was palpable—and short lived.

Immediately before takeoff, I was informed that the negotiations former president Jimmy Carter, Colin Powell, and Senator Sam Nunn were conducting with Cédras were still ongoing. I knew no operation would take place while they were still there, and I guessed our imminent launch was being used as a powerful lever to get an agreement from Cédras. So it was no surprise when, a couple of hours into our flight, I was passed a note from the air force loadmaster in the back of the aircraft that said we were returning to Pope. I relayed the word to the paratroopers without much explanation. Most looked surprised; all appeared disappointed.

The aborted invasion was a diplomatic success, and the show of force—sixty-one warplanes thundering toward the island, already ringed by American warships—likely added weight to President Carter's threats that night. It was arguably a textbook use of military power to back up diplomacy. But as we emptied onto the tarmac that night, the force went from being a coiled spring of raw energy to feeling dejected. With time, the aborted invasion was something we laughed about, but often with half-serious teeth gritting.

I departed Bragg in early November 1994 for Fort Lewis, Washington, and the 2nd Ranger Battalion. Annie, our son Sam, then eleven years old, and I packed into our minivan and headed off across the country. We had only six days to make the crossing, which began with a short detour to Fort Benning, Georgia, to meet with my new regimental commander. But we had a great time. I bored both of them with an obligatory stop at the Little Bighorn battlefield in Montana.

We pulled into Fort Lewis on a typically cloudy afternoon, and I prepared to take command the following day. My grandfather had served at Fort Lewis just prior to World War II, and my father and Dwight Eisenhower's son, John, had been friends in the neighborhood of our assigned quarters. With Mount Rainier as a backdrop, Lewis was beautiful, and we quickly felt at home.

Like commanding a second rifle company, commanding a second battalion was still hard work, but even more fun. In my first command I had worried whether I would be up to the job. Now I arrived confident and full of ideas. I suspect Ranger NCOs got a bit tired of self-confident commanders arriving with notebooks full of new directions for the unit to take. But if they did, they hid it well.

Famous for its World War II exploits, the 2nd Ranger Battalion was one of the original two battalion-size Ranger units re-formed in 1974. It always had a slight West Coast attitude. Serving in the 3rd Battalion in the 1980s, we viewed "2nd Batt" as more free-spirited and less disciplined than we were, although they performed well in the field. We also envied their great distance from regimental headquarters, which we could see just one hundred meters away.

I took command in a simple ceremony. From the outset, I determined to set a clear direction for the battalion, identifying agreed-upon priorities and forcing ourselves to perform those to a truly impressive level. We would have trouble maintaining the reputation and confidence of a truly elite organization if we didn't do at least a few tasks better than any other units could.

My senior soldier, Command Sergeant Major Frank Magana, and I identified several areas of emphasis. One was foot marching, walking long distances carrying combat equipment, which typically included rucksacks of fifty pounds or more. We directed weekly marches for every Ranger to build stamina and quarterly marches of thirty miles. Running and marching across Fort Lewis, I'd seen small signs posted by the 9th Infantry Regiment, "The Manchus," guiding their units along a designated twenty-five-mile foot-march route. I knew that Rangers had to do more, so thirty seemed about right.

We also identified the need to increase the physical confidence of young Rangers in hand-to-hand combat. I didn't envision planning operations that would depend upon bayonet charges or fisticuffs, but Ranger operations involving raids or room clearing put Rangers in direct physical contact with enemies. I wanted them to possess the confidence that would come from proficiency in the martial arts.

Training Rangers in combatives, or hand-to-hand combat, was not a straightforward task. First using existing army manuals, then moving to hiring outside experts and nationally renowned college wrestling coaches, we struggled. We could send a few Rangers to specialized training, and they would return proficient and enthusiastic, but their skills wouldn't permeate through the battalion.

Finally, after almost a year of dead ends, we hired two of the Gracie brothers, Royce and Rorion, who were famous competitors and instructors in Brazilian jujitsu, a fighting style their family had pioneered. They would run a two-week course at Fort Lewis. Instead of sending just Rangers who had exhibited interest in or aptitude for it, I sent all of the platoon sergeants.

While we could have chosen any one of several fighting techniques, the breakthrough was sending the right people to training. Platoon sergeants controlled the culture and training schedule of each forty-two-man platoon, which they commanded as senior NCOs. Lieutenants led the platoons, but platoon sergeants shaped the organization and were its heart. As long as the platoon sergeants lacked confidence in their personal mastery of combatives and did not share a strong belief in the importance of the skill, we'd never get real traction. The course proved the point. After finishing the course, the platoon sergeants, now zealots for combatives and eager to demonstrate their skills, demanded their platoons follow their lead. Within months, combatives had infused into the culture of the battalion. In a couple of years, it had spread across the regiment, and soon it infected the Army as a whole. It was a lesson in leadership I never forgot.

I believed that more than anything else, soldiers and units must learn to win, and yet the Army's Joint Readiness Training Center, or JRTC, unintentionally undermined that. Designed to exercise units under demanding conditions against a highly proficient opposing force (OPFOR) who mastered the Multiple Integrated Laser Engagement System (MILES) training device, allowing them to routinely defeat units larger and better armed. Many units blamed their failure on MILES. In my second year in command of the 2nd Rangers, we were programmed for an early spring rotation to the JRTC, and I decided to focus the force on winning.

Winning at JRTC would demand that the 2nd Rangers adjust our tactics away from what would work in actual combat to what would be better suited to the MILES fight. It would require us to spend precious training time mastering MILES, at the expense of more realistic live-fire marksmanship. Many experienced leaders in the battalion felt we were "training to win at training" when we should be training for war. It was a valid point.

But to me, it was training to *win*. Future combat would be unpredictable in nature, and winning at JRTC, with the odds stacked against us, would build the Rangers' confidence that they could win at anything. We trained. Week after week in the field consisted of combat lanes run against MILES-equipped OPFOR that we'd designated and trained from within the battalion. I became a fanatic on MILES marksmanship. Before the start of many lanes I'd pull two or three Rangers from the squad or platoon, place several targets a couple hundred meters away, and demand they demonstrate the ability to "kill" the targets with their MILES on the first shot. In the first weeks, few could do it. I could feel some of the NCOs seething, feeling MILES proficiency a gross waste of time.

Finally, at about 2:00 A.M. one night, after a difficult platoon lane, we were conducting a critique of an operation in a tent we'd erected. We were exhausted and frustrated, and I was tired of haranguing leaders, when a squad leader, Ken Wolfe, who was later a command sergeant major in Afghanistan, stood up. Grabbing his M16 rifle with a MILES transmitter mounted, he erupted.

"This is what we have to do," he said, pointing at the transmitter. "This is the war we'll be fighting and the war we have to win."

I watched him intently, hoping he was saying what he appeared to be.

"It's the MILES fight. We might not like it. But if we're going to win we have to be better at it than the OPFOR." His voice rose. "And goddamn it, we're better than any OPFOR."

He got grudging but genuine concurrence from the Rangers. I could have hugged him. Because at that moment I knew we'd win. And we did. That commitment—to fighting, and winning, the kind of war we were in, not the one we wanted—showed up again in Iraq and Afghanistan.

In June 1996 I relinquished command of the 2nd Rangers and we moved to Cambridge, Massachusetts, for a fellowship at Harvard's Kennedy School of Government instead of attending the Army War College.

Harvard was a tremendous opportunity to explore subjects I'd been too busy to consider while in troop units and to meet a collection of bright faculty and students. I'd expected Harvard to be full of antimilitary sentiment, but instead we received compelling questions and thoughtful looks, as if we were rare animals they'd never seen up close.

And our family life was good. Annie rented an apartment for us close to Harvard Square and got a job at the Kennedy School. There was time to explore Boston, watch the Red Sox, and take occasional trips to elsewhere in New England. Sam's hockey season was in full swing, and we spent evenings and Saturdays watching him play.

On June 23, 1997, I returned to the Rangers. I assumed command of the Ranger regiment in a ceremony on the main parade field at Fort Benning. As it did every two years, the entire regiment had come to Benning for the occasion, with the change of command preceded by several days of athletic and team-building events. Rangers from earlier eras, from those who had landed at Anzio or climbed Pointe du Hoc to those who had fought in Mogadishu, gathered for a reunion. They were bound together by a shared history and values, best reflected in the Ranger Creed.

The Ranger Creed is a six-stanza summary of Ranger values that was adopted in 1974 with the formation of the 1st Ranger Battalion at Fort Stewart. One of the first requirements I was given when I joined the regiment in 1985 was to memorize the creed and to recite it each day at physical training. Memorably, parachute-laden Rangers also shouted it out inside aircraft in the final minutes before the regiment's combat jump into Panama in 1989.

But it was most poignant at ceremonies where it began with a predesignated Ranger somewhere in the formation loudly stating, "The Ranger Creed, repeat after me." The Ranger then recited the first stanza of the creed, breaking it into short phrases that were repeated by every Ranger present.

"Recognizing that I volunteered as a Ranger, fully knowing the hazards of my chosen profession, I will always endeavor to uphold the prestige, honor, and high esprit de corps of my Ranger regiment."

To be heard, the Ranger yelled out each phrase, and Rangers on the field and in the audience repeated them either loudly or quietly to themselves. Some were lost in thought—they all knew the words by heart. The Ranger only kept them in cadence.

For the second stanza another Ranger, normally in another part of the formation, took over, giving a sense of spontaneity.

"Acknowledging the fact that a Ranger is a more elite soldier who arrives at the cutting edge of battle by land, sea, or air, I accept the fact that as a Ranger my country expects me to move further, faster and fight harder than any other soldier."

The third stanza evoked strong emotions.

"Never shall I fail my comrades. I will always keep myself mentally alert, physically strong, and morally straight, and I will shoulder more than my share of the task, whatever it may be, one hundred percent and then some."

Often very young Rangers were selected to lead stanzas, a daunting experience in front of two thousand fellow Rangers and a large audience. On one occasion a young Ranger began the fourth stanza: "Gallantly will I show the world that I am a specially selected and well-trained soldier."

The formation's response was followed by an uncomfortable silence: Naturally nervous, the Ranger couldn't remember the next phrase. Seconds passed, then a nearby sergeant seamlessly stepped in.

"My courtesy to superior officers, neatness of dress and care of equipment shall set the example for others to follow."

Most of the audience never noticed, but to me the sergeant's quick help for a fellow Ranger embodied the very creed he was leading.

By the fifth stanza the crowd's responses were typically stronger. In seemingly practiced harmony, they stated the most important part of the creed.

"Energetically will I meet the enemies of my country. I shall defeat them on the field of battle, for I am better trained and will fight with all my might. 'Surrender' is not a Ranger word. I will never leave a fallen comrade to fall into the hands of the enemy, and under no circumstances will I ever embarrass my country."

Then the final stanza.

"Readily will I display the intestinal fortitude required to fight on to the Ranger objective and complete the mission, though I be the lone survivor."

The creed ended in crescendo: "Rangers lead the way." Although it had a rhythmic quality, the Ranger Creed was neither a poem nor a mindless mantra chanted by masses. It was a promise, a solemn vow made by each Ranger to every other Ranger.

My relationships with senior NCOs had always been important to me, so I saved the final couple of hours that first day for a session with Mike Hall, the regimental command sergeant major. With almost twenty years in the regiment, Mike was an icon to Rangers, and although I knew and respected him, we still had to bond as a team. We talked that afternoon and into the evening, building a relationship that grew first into a partnership, then into a deep friendship. Annie quickly became close to Mike's wife, Brenda, and when Brenda and Mike decided to renew their wedding vows under the Catholic faith, Annie and I attended, along with their son Jeff, as the only witnesses.

Early in our partnership, Mike and I decided to focus the regiment on just four priorities: marksmanship, physical conditioning, first aid, and small-unit battle drills. We'd obviously perform other tasks, but we prioritized and constantly reinforced high standards of mastery on what we called "the Big Four." We'd never have the time to do everything we'd like, but we decided to do what we could do very well.

Marksmanship was an obvious priority. Lightly armed, often outnumbered, Rangers must be able to hit what they shoot at before the enemy can shoot them. Because we operated aggressively at night and new night-vision equipment enabled it, marksmanship was critical in the dark.

In war, especially of the modern era, the vast majority of deaths occur on the field, not in field hospitals, where skilled doctors and technology can offer high survival rates. While we had a dedicated cadre of combat medics, they accounted for a small percentage of the force. To ensure that everyone on the battlefield could provide immediate care, we trained each Ranger in the regiment as a first responder. A tenth of them received advanced training to be emergency medical technicians (EMTs). After the experience of Rangers in Mogadishu in 1993, it wasn't difficult to convince the force that every Ranger must be able to save his buddy.

Mike Hall and I led the Rangers from 1997 to 1999 and never deviated from the Big Four. I'm glad we didn't. Although at the time our nation was at peace, the Big Four would later save lives. During the first eight and a half years of the war on terror, the Rangers conducted more than eight thousand operations. Most were targeted raids, and many of them were under my command. In the course of these missions, thirty-two Rangers were killed, but none of them died in the field from wounds considered survivable; one Ranger with potentially survivable wounds died after being evacuated, because of complications from surgery. This 3 percent rate proved to be lower than some estimates for all American fatalities, wherein 24 percent of those with survivable injuries died.

Commanding the regiment was far different from commanding a battalion. Leading three geographically dispersed units, each led by very experienced second-time commanders, drove a different type of leadership from the more autocratic styles I'd seen, and sometimes practiced, earlier in my career. I learned to demand high standards of performance but to be far more flexible in the approach used to attain them. Increasingly, I also sought for objectives to be jointly developed as people worked harder to meet goals they themselves had a hand in setting.

In my last month of command I was notified I'd been selected for promotion to brigadier general. Mike Hall passed me a note written on a page from one of the small notebooks he carried: "To my friend the new Brigadier General—congratulations." It meant more than all the others.

In the summer of 1999 I found myself in another fellowship, this time at the Council on Foreign Relations in New York City. The year was another opportunity for some unfettered thought. I attended meetings, many with fascinating news makers, and had the opportunity to work on a couple of interesting projects. But perhaps the greatest benefit was another period of time to read, think, and discuss issues that were difficult to spend time on in most army jobs.

As at Harvard, Annie interviewed for and got a job at the Council that allowed us to share experiences and friendships. Sam, exhibiting his too-often-exercised adaptability, attended the local public high school in Bay Ridge, along with more than five thousand other students, and we spent many evenings on then-seedy Coney Island, where his team practiced hockey. To give Sam a glimpse of the memorable experience I was having at the Council, I brought him to the Council's father-son evening. United Nations secretary-general Kofi Annan's face broke into an appreciative grin when I introduced Sam—sporting his most recent look, bright blue hair—as displaying "U.N. blue" in the secretary's honor.

For much of the 1990s, America was the world's sole superpower, buttressed by an ever-expanding economy. Vigorous debates on our foreign policy centered not on what America's role could be but on what America should choose it to be. When should America intervene—as it did in Somalia and the Balkans but declined to do in Rwanda? What was our role in the Israeli-Palestinian conflict? It felt as though America's future was America's to decide.

But not always. On the late morning of August 7, 1998, trucks bulging with explosives tore into the American embassies in Nairobi, Kenya, and Dar es Salaam, Tanzania. The twin attacks killed 224 people and wounded 4,500—mostly Kenyans. Shattering glass blinded one hundred fifty people. Commanding the Ranger Regiment at the time, I remember the horror of the attacks, but even more I remember thinking that it was perpetrated by a faceless, amorphous foe that would be difficult to defeat.

The U.S. government immediately suspected Osama bin Laden. A decade after forming Al Qaeda, the forty-one-year-old Saudi financier, whose anti-American tirades had increased in the previous two years, was still unknown to most Americans. But he had been busy.

After Saudi Arabia forced bin Laden to leave in 1991, he had lived in Sudan. During his years there, he ran military training camps, kept apace as a businessman, and through his money was connected with terrorists across Africa and Asia. A guesthouse he ran in Pakistan sheltered the mastermind of the 1993 attack on the World Trade Center, Ramzi Yousef.

Under American pressure, Sudan evicted bin Laden in 1996 and he flew to Afghanistan, where the Taliban would take Kabul a few months later and begin their five-year reign. That August, purportedly by fax machine from the Hindu Kush, bin Laden sent a letter to Arab newspapers. His long epistle addressed Muslims worldwide, calling on them to wage jihad against the United States in order to expel its troops that still "occupied" Saudi Arabia, the "cradle" of Islam. Bin Laden, still considered primarily a financier, decried the Saudi government but directed to the United States his now-famous taunt, which sounded as giddy then as it does ominous now. "I'm telling you," he said, "these young men love death as much as you love life."

The embassy attacks put teeth on these taunts. And two years after bin Laden's declaration of war by fax, the bombings showed worrisome operational reach and sophistication. For a group hanging its reputation on its violent theater, the simultaneous, deadly attack was a coup—and a name-making moment.

On August 20, 1998, thirteen days after the embassies were bombed, U.S. naval ships in the Arabian Sea unleashed a volley of cruise missiles. Thirteen of them, fired toward Khartoum, hit what American intelligence believed was a factory connected to bin Laden and producing chemical weapons—including nerve gas. The intelligence was later judged to be wrong; the building had in fact produced pharmaceuticals. A Sudanese worker was killed, and to the ire of many, the destruction of the factory deprived thousands of Sudanese of medicine. The true owner of the factory—who was not connected to bin Laden's murky business holdings, as was once believed— later filed suit against the United States.

The same day, sixty-six Tomahawk cruise missiles sailed toward Al Qaeda training camps in eastern Afghanistan, where the United States thought bin Laden would be; he was instead on the road to Kabul, ninety miles to the north. In the aftermath of the explosions, Al Qaeda observers counted five or six dead Arabs, while the Taliban accused Americans of killing twenty-two Afghans and wounding twice that number. The Clinton administration estimated up to thirty militants were killed.

There were other casualties of the strike, largely unaccounted for at the time. Prior to the strike, U.S. officials feared the Pakistanis would think the U.S. missiles crossing over their country were from India. But they worried more that members of Pakistan's military and intelligence establishment would tip off the Taliban or bin Laden about the impending strike. So they gave the Pakistanis notice, but just barely: Over a late-night chicken tikka dinner in Islamabad on the night of August 20, Vice Chairman of the Joint Chiefs of Staff General Joseph Ralston told the head of the Pakistani army, General Jehangir Karamat, that in ten minutes, missiles would be entering Pakistani airspace.

Not only were the Pakistanis kept in the dark, but they also lost men. Some of the buildings blown apart by the missiles were in fact used by Pakistan's Inter-Services Intelligence (ISI), killing, by some accounts, five of its intelligence officers and twenty of its trainees. The event left the Pakistani leadership irate and the Americans ever more skeptical, asking why Pakistani officers were near bin Laden's camps in the first place.

The relationship continued to degrade. After bin Laden disappeared into the snow-tracked Afghan mountains, the United States increasingly pressured the government of Pakistan to intervene with bin Laden's hosts—the Taliban, who received significant patronage from Pakistan—to turn him over. These demands were met with indignant replies.

"Quite honestly," one Pakistani official complained in a *New Yorker* article printed during the winter I spent at CFR, "what would Pakistan gain by going into Afghanistan and snatching bin Laden for you? We are the most heavily sanctioned United States ally. We helped you capture

Ramzi Yousef . . . and all we got were thank-you notes. You lobbed missiles across our territory with no advance warning! You humiliated our government! You killed Pakistani intelligence officers!"

So started, long before we knew how much it would matter, an unhealthy tradition of American administrations, skeptical of Pakistan's allegiance, demanding that the Pakistanis bring them bin Laden, all the while leaving the Pakistanis feeling less and less like an ally—and feeling less inclined to act that way.

Sometime that winter, my old friend and mentor John Vines from 3rd Rangers called me and asked whether, if he were fortunate enough to be selected to command the 82nd Airborne Division the following year, I'd be interested in being his assistant division commander for operations. I said yes immediately.

In June 2000, two months before my forty-sixth birthday, I began my third tour as a paratrooper in the 82nd Airborne. I replaced Dave Petraeus as the assistant division command for operations. Vines commanded some sixteen thousand 82nd paratroopers through seven capable brigade commanders and his experienced chief of staff. That left the two ADCs, one each for operations and support, with tremendous freedom and authority but little bureaucratic responsibility. The position gave us time to focus on training, mentoring subordinate leaders, and serving, along with the division's command sergeant major, as additional eyes and ears for the commander. Being an understudy to Vines was also a great opportunity to learn how to be a general officer.

Some of that education came by watching. John Vines was a charismatic leader, known in the Army for taking care of subordinates and putting tremendous thought into the leadership climate of his commands. Looking to overcome the common problem of getting candor from subordinates in a hierarchical organization like the military, Vines came to my office near the end of a long day with a plan. We were known to be close, and he calculated that if I strongly and openly disagreed with him in a large meeting, it would encourage others to do so. The appropriate venue came several days later in a meeting of about twenty-five commanders and staff. I waited for the right moment in the meeting and executed John's guidance by speaking out strongly against his plan of action.

"Sir, doing it that way will be a serious mistake," I said, looking at Vines, forthrightly proud of my candor.

Nicknamed "the Viper" earlier in his career and feared as well as loved, Vines appeared to be furious. Had he been wearing his combat equipment, his hand would have been slowly pulling his 9-mm pistol from its holster, his long bladed knife from its sheath, or both. He seemed to have forgotten our plan.

In an instant, albeit a very long instant, John smiled. He thanked me for my honesty and signaled to everyone that that was the kind of feedback most helpful to a commander. He reinforced the fact that good leaders defined the environment and created opportunity for candid discussion at the right moments.

I spent June 2001 in Camp Doha, Kuwait, in an army program that rotated brigadier generals there for monthlong tours as forward commanders for CENTCOM. At the time, this seemed absurd, guaranteed to cause turmoil through constant turnover of leadership. But the month I spent in the region—which included exploring Kuwait up to the Iraq border, touring the critical port facilities, and traveling to Qatar to visit prepositioned equipment sites—was a lesser version of Eisenhower's mapping of World War I battlefields in 1929 or Patton's tours of France. The month allowed me to look at ground that I would later tread.

A key theme of the month there was Osama bin Laden–related intelligence reporting that included threats of attacks against U.S. facilities in Kuwait. At the time, Al Qaeda's 1998 embassy attacks in East Africa had once again been on the front page. On May 29, a jury in Manhattan had convicted four men for their role in the 1998 attacks, following a four-month trial that included ninety-two witnesses, 1,300 exhibits, and 302 counts against the accused. Two of those witnesses were former members of Al Qaeda, and the trial provided a window into the largely opaque organization. The next day, the Taliban, who were hosting bin Laden in Afghanistan, announced they would not send him to the American courts.

Prior to my trip, terror had seemed more an amorphous danger with countless sources, like air pollution, than a threat from a specific group with a charismatic leader. Being in the region and reviewing intelligence every day made me more aware of Osama bin Laden and Al Qaeda and gave the threat new meaning and urgency.

| CHAPTER 6 |

▼

The Fight Begins

July 2001–October 2003

M y world changed suddenly on a warm Tuesday morning in September. I'd again replaced Dave Petraeus, this time as chief of staff of XVIII Airborne Corps, and, along with my boss, Lieutenant General Dan McNeill, I went to conduct a daylight parachute jump from a C-130J aircraft, a new variant of the old workhorse with which we'd all grown up. After an orientation at Pope Air Force Base, we donned parachutes. As on every jump, the jumpmaster inspected us. His commands and steady movements followed a pattern I'd experienced hundreds of times before. He checked our helmets and the edges of our packs, then tugged and cinched our straps tightly across our shoulders and thighs.

That same morning, a group of men had instructions to do the same before they boarded an airplane in Boston. "Tighten your clothes well," the man in charge, named Mohammad Atta, had instructed them in a set of guidelines. "And tighten your shoes well, and wear socks that hold in the shoes and do not come out of them." The commands were meant to help make what they were about to do that morning—something they'd never done before and never would again—feel routine. They were liable to be nervous about getting into the air.

At Bragg, we took off for the short flight that would carry us over Sicily Drop Zone. In my career I'd probably jumped seventy-five or more times on Sicily's large, sandy expanse, but none would be like this. Inside the airplane, we listened as the jumpmasters barked out their well-worn recitations. "Stand up!" We stood and faced the back of the plane.

Atta's men had their own recitations to say to themselves, silently, as they too prepared to get up from their seats in their plane. "When you board the airplane," he had advised them, "proceed with the invocations, and consider this is a raid on a path." If all was going to plan, they too were standing now and repeating the commands to themselves.

After the jumpers had stood up, we "hooked up," snapping our static lines onto the anchor line cable. Starting at the back of the plane, each paratrooper gave a firm tap on the shoulder of the man in front of him, cascading down the plane until the man at the front felt his shoulder tapped.

"All okay, jumpmaster," first jumper Dan McNeill yelled, indicating that the "stick" of jumpers was ready. The loadmaster turned a steel handle and slid the aircraft door up until it was fully open.

"Each of you is to hold the shoulder of his brother." Atta and his men had since moved into the cabin of their plane, which now crossed the sky at more than four hundred miles per hour, pointed toward Manhattan's southern tip. Hold your brother's shoulders, he said, in "the plane, and the cabin, reminding him that this action is for the sake of God."

As the warm wind blew into the open door of our aircraft, the air force loadmaster leaned close to my boss. I overheard him say that an airplane had struck one of the World Trade Center towers. I had a few seconds to ponder the obviously terrible accident. Then the green light came on. We jumped.

We'd left Pope that morning with America enjoying an imperfect but relatively stable era of peace; our feet landed on a nation at war. Soon after retrieving my parachute, my driver informed me that a second aircraft had hit the other tower and, mistakenly, that a bomb had gone off at the Pentagon.

"I think this changes everything," he said presciently.

I didn't immediately respond. I was lost in thought, trying to process the information, as we drove back to headquarters. We went directly to the office, where my secretary had the unfolding events on television. We watched together, helplessly, as one, then the other, tower collapsed. Only a year earlier I'd seen those towers every morning as I ran across the Brooklyn Bridge. Now the iconic structures were piles of smoke and wreckage, shrouding almost three thousand perished souls. Much later, as accounts captured the horror of the morning and the courage of common people and the fallen and their families, I felt the sadness of loss. But that Tuesday, like most Americans, I felt the urgent need to do something. My first reaction, as it had been after the Pope accident, was to get organized.

Dan McNeill was an unflappable leader, which was good, because barely controlled bedlam ruled Bragg the first days and weeks after 9/11. We instituted security procedures that had been planned but insufficiently tested. The morning of September 12, lines of cars attempting to enter the base found checkpoints quickly overwhelmed with the volume. On some roads, the wait extended to hours; many people simply turned around and went home. Nurses and doctors were considered essential personnel during high-threat periods, but child-care specialists were not. Many with kids couldn't come to work. At higher levels, Army Forces Command, headquartered in Atlanta, hosted hourslong video teleconferences that simulated effective coordination more than they actually achieved such synergy. Everyone meant well, but like all of America, we were navigating uncharted waters.

Reactions that now seem ridiculous felt prudent at the time. Someone called in a potentially serious threat of an anthrax attack on the area of Bragg where we processed the flood of reservists called to duty to meet a variety of requirements—some of the fifty thousand reserve troops President Bush activated three days after 9/11. Military police did indeed find suspicious white powder on the floor of one of the World War II–era buildings we still used but quickly determined its origin: a nearby box of doughnuts.

As such silly issues arose, Dan McNeill used rural North Carolina wisdom to remind us to maintain perspective. "Sometimes the dogs are going to run us up into a tree," he'd counsel. "But let's not get treed by Chihuahuas." Over time, Bragg settled into a more sustainable pattern.

Six days later, in the House of Representatives, President Bush announced the start of what he called the global war on terror. To the Taliban he issued a set of demands, including delivering Al Qaeda's leaders and dismantling all terrorist camps in the country. To other nations on the periphery of this new war, he delivered an ultimatum whose simplicity earned applause that evening but controversy later: "Every nation, in every region, now has a decision to make: Either you are with us, or you are with the terrorists."

Far away, in Kandahar, the reaction to these demands was less than urgent. In the days that followed, Mullah Omar, the head of the Taliban, met with his ambassador to Pakistan. For the past seven years, Omar, an elusive, one-eyed former mujahideen commander, had led the Taliban in Afghanistan's grinding civil war, and controlled all but a small enclave in the north. His group's relationship with Al Qaeda was more complicated than we understood, but after Omar wrapped himself in the Cloak of the Prophet in front of a large crowd in 1996, bin Laden had sworn allegiance to him. Now Omar's ambassador, just back from Pakistan, explained nervously what he knew of the impending American assault—including air strikes and coordination with opposition groups to unseat the Taliban. To the ambassador's dismay, Omar was unmoved. He thought America was full of bluster and "there was less than a 10 per cent chance that America would resort to anything beyond threats."

He was wrong. On October 7, military operations against the Taliban began with a torrent of strikes against training camps and Taliban leadership. The ground invasion started twelve days later with the insertion of Green Berets into northern Afghanistan. The same night, Rangers executed a dramatic parachute drop onto an airstrip in southern Afghanistan, while Army commandos raided Mullah Omar's compound outside Kandahar.

Back at Bragg, in the XVIII Airborne Corps, noted for its ability to deploy rapidly, we mostly waited for something to do.

Most of us still knew relatively little about bin Laden or the threat he represented. At first we tended to simplify Al Qaeda, assuming it was a tightly bound terrorist band like many we'd faced in the previous three decades. But over time we began to understand that the enemy was really three things in one: an organization, an idea, and most recently a brand. September 11, 2001, represented the confluence of all three—and the culmination of the last.

After sporadic attacks that Al Qaeda claimed to support throughout the early 1990s and bin Laden's forced departure from Sudan to Afghanistan in 1996, the East Africa embassy bombings in August 1998 made Al Qaeda's name. While Al Qaeda had until then been an organization—the *base*—and an idea, its attacks in Africa in 1998 and two years later against the USS *Cole* began to make it recognizable as *the* Islamic group landing blows against the United States.

The emergence of this brand coincided with, and was inseparable from, a significant change in the group's organization and outlook. Three years before 9/11 and a few months before the embassy attacks, bin Laden had issued a joint statement with Ayman al-Zawahiri and four other terrorist leaders. Since he was fourteen, Zawahiri had been obsessively focused on the Egyptian regime, which later tortured him in prison until he informed on his comrades. But now he accepted a turn in strategy. The jihadists could not defeat the apostate Arab regimes—the "near enemy" that stood in the way of a restored caliphate—directly. Instead, they had to attack Israel and the United States, the "far enemy," whose indispensible backing of the Arab regimes made them impossible to take down head on. The "crimes and sins committed by the Americans are a clear declaration of war on God, his messenger, and Muslims," bin Laden wrote. In the face of this aggression, bin Laden issued a fatwa, or "finding," endorsed by his cosigners. It was the duty, he declared, of all Muslims to kill Americans "wherever they find them." Al Qaeda would wage a global struggle in order to achieve regional results.

But focusing on the "far enemy" made it harder to build a movement. At the time, nearly all other terrorist organizations had regional or irredentist aims—fighting for Palestine or Kashmir or overthrowing the government of Libya or of Egypt. Concrete grievances and feasible projects were more appealing to recruits. Al Qaeda had no single front where it could make its name, so bin Laden attempted to fold the specific political fights into an age-old religious war. He talked not of American policy in the Middle East but of the "Jewish-Crusader" crimes against Muslims. He unified these conflicts, from the Sahara to Asian jungles, by reminding his listeners of the common humiliation of Muslims, everywhere abetted by the United States.

In this way, the feasibility of bin Laden's project became secondary to the piety affirmed by fighting with Al Qaeda. They were the true Muslims, defiant amid apostasy, defending the faith from its enemies.

But even if it were nearly impossible for them to win—to destroy the United States—they would be hard to defeat.

Through the fall of 2001, XVIII Airborne Corps responded to orders to deploy forces in support of what was then called Operation Enduring Freedom. First we sent limited forces to secure an air base and logistics hub at Karshi-Khanabad in southeast Uzbekistan. Then we deployed a culled-down brigade combat team to secure Kandahar Airport. Finally, part of a division headquarters went to control operations from Bagram, a newly captured air base built by the Soviets in the 1950s and later used during the 1980s fighting.

Each deployment order we received required reshaping the units and reducing their normal combat power. Although I recognized the necessity of tailoring forces and limiting the U.S. footprint, our operations felt dangerously ad hoc. The failure to trap bin Laden in Tora Bora in December and the messy Operation Anaconda fight in the Shah-i-Kot Valley in early March 2002 seemed to validate this concern.

I was also frustrated. Watching war from afar is torturous for most soldiers, especially when comrades are fighting in difficult terrain. In Afghanistan they were engaged in fights I could watch remotely but to which I could not contribute. So it was a relief in the spring of 2002 when XVIII Airborne Corps was ordered to deploy our headquarters to establish Combined Joint Task Force 180 (CJTF 180) at Bagram and take control of all conventional military operations in the country. In May we deployed.

Deploying is always an emotional event. By nature soldiers focus on the task ahead and are usually a bit excited by the adventure. But leaving loved ones was always heart-wrenching. In some ways it got easier with practice; in others, particularly as soldiers aged, it became harder. For veterans there were fewer unknowns, but life seemed more finite and the costs more clear.

My son Sam, then seventeen, tended to put things into perspective. As we prepared to deploy on a series of flights from Pope Air Force Base, I put on the distinctive sand-colored desert uniform we'd wear and said good-bye to Sam as he headed off to high school. I'd miss his graduation in two weeks. I told him I was proud of him and loved him. He asked when I'd be back.

"I'm not sure, Sam, probably when we've finished the job in Afghanistan," I said, wanting to steel him for an extended tour.

Sam nodded, wished me luck, and headed off to school.

I went to the headquarters, and within a couple of hours our aircraft broke and my flight's departure was postponed for twenty-four hours. So that evening when Sam came home, I was there.

"That job didn't take long," he said impishly.

Any war is serious business, but when we arrived in Afghanistan in May 2002, it wasn't clear whether there was any war left. The hunt for Al Qaeda continued, but the Taliban seemed to have been decisively defeated; most had essentially melted away, and we weren't sure where they'd gone. Later it became clear that some had moved to regroup in Pakistan but that most of the rank-and-file, and some senior leaders, had gone to their homes to wait and gauge the new developments.

Afghanistan in the spring of 2002 had a slightly wild-west feel to it. Bearded Afghans and similarly groomed American and Coalition special operators mixed with conventional military made for an atmosphere of adventure and confusion. And Afghanistan was maddeningly difficult to understand. As CJTF 180 got oriented to our mission, it was rapidly apparent that a major task would be to develop an understanding of what was happening and what people and which forces were driving events.

For most Americans, Afghanistan was a colorful, distant place. Once a destination for free-spirited wanderers, we later knew it as a brutal, mountainous battlefield between the Soviets and heroic tribal resistance fighters—mujahideen, or "holy warriors." We knew that the Soviets had been beaten, but most of us didn't know much else. Later the Taliban achieved dubious fame with their public executions and the demolition, in Bamyan Province, of ancient Buddhist statues. But until 9/11 few Americans ever contemplated fighting them.

Even for the Afghans the place was confusing. The 1978 coup that replaced President Daoud with a socialist regime and the subsequent twelve-year civil war between the Soviet-backed Democratic Republic of Afghanistan and the mujahideen opposition had begun a series of events, culminating in the post-9/11 defeat of the Taliban, that turned much of Afghan society upside down. For Western diplomats and military forces, Afghanistan was a maze of mirrors, and we too easily framed issues or interpreted actions through our own lenses. And for many Afghans, appearing to be what Westerners wanted them to be was at least polite and often expedient. Like many others, I had a nagging feeling that a whole world of Afghan power politics—with ethnic groups jostling and old and new characters posturing—was churning outside our view. I felt like we were high-school students who had wandered into a mafia-owned bar, dangerously unaware of the tensions that filled the room and the authorities who controlled it.

We launched an effort to understand and, where appropriate, influence. But we were poorly prepared to do so, tending to see the problem in military terms. We had Lieutenant General McNeill travel the country and engage various leaders. As he did, we leveraged the most effective tool at our disposal: Afghans imagined American power to be infinite. But our ability to develop the relationships that would produce long-term influence was limited. The strategy to help build Afghan institutions was well conceived, but the West's effort was poorly informed, organized, and executed.

Later in the summer of 2002, I was recalled from Afghanistan to the Joint Staff. I wasn't happy to be pulled from CJTF 180, particularly for the first assignment of my career in Washington, D.C.—and at the Pentagon. I'd avoided both for the twenty-six years I'd served, and I was disappointed to leave Afghanistan. But I knew John Abizaid, now a lieutenant general and director of the Joint Staff, had been behind the move. I trusted he knew what he was doing.

Although my initial posting indicated I would serve as the J34, the joint staff director responsible for force-protection issues across the military, when announcement came of my selection for promotion to major general, Abizaid redirected me to be the vice director J3 (VDJ3). In that role, first under Marine lieutenant general Greg Newbold and later for an old friend, air force lieutenant general Norty Schwartz, I assisted the J3 with management of the large operations staff directorate.

Before I returned from Afghanistan, Annie began to prepare for our move to D.C. We knew my job would involve long, often unpredictable hours, so to avoid a commute she decided we'd rent an apartment that was only about eight hundred meters from the Pentagon. Once settled, we quickly established a routine. I'd run very early each morning, shower, then walk the short distance to my office, arriving about 5:15 A.M.

In the evening, I'd call Annie and she'd walk toward the Pentagon, meeting me halfway. As soon as we saw each other, we'd extend our arms out in distant greeting, a silly habit we'd taken from something Sam used to do when very young. We'd then walk back toward our apartment, normally stopping at the grocery store to buy premade salads for dinner. Once home, we'd talk while eating and soon go to bed. It was a life with distractions pared to a minimum.

Initially designed by two army engineer officers in July 1941 in response to rising office-space requirements for military staffs, the Pentagon was envisioned to provide four million square feet of air-conditioned office space in a four-story building with almost no elevators. The final result was a five-sided, five-story behemoth with 17.5 miles of corridors that held thirty-three thousand workers at the height of World War II. It opened to its first occupants in April 1942 and was completed by January 1943—less than eighteen months from concept.

Although I claimed it as such, this wasn't my first "work experience" in the Pentagon. My father had served multiple tours there in the 1950s and 1960s and would periodically take my brothers and me along. I'd marvel at the huge hallways and the tradespeople who would pedal the hallways on large white tricycles. Usually our visits were short, but if my father had weekend work to do, he'd sit us at a desk with pencil and paper so that we could amuse ourselves.

One Saturday we became fascinated with a metal "tree" on the desk that held about fifteen rubber stamps. To keep us quiet, my father found an ink pad and paper—and we were in business. After a while we left, my father driving our sand-colored 1955 Chevrolet station wagon back to our Arlington, Virginia, home. My mother was waiting at the door.

"Mac, you need to go back to the Pentagon right away," she told him. "Security called."

He deposited us, climbed back in the car, and took off, no doubt a bit worried. He told us later that he'd forgotten the scrap papers we'd tried all the rubber stamps on, and a security guard doing routine checks had found papers marked "Top Secret" and other classifications strewn on the desk, unsecured. Years later the memory made me smile when reading articles about over-classification of government documents.

About forty years later, my next Pentagon experience began with some of the same wonder I'd felt as a boy. From outside, the enormous structure conveyed an imposing message of might, purpose, and a bit of intimidation. The Pentagon had an amazingly functional design and was in the midst of a long renovation when, at 9:37 A.M. on September 11, 2001, Flight 77 slammed into the western face of the building, killing fifty-three passengers, six crew members, 125 Pentagon employees, and five hijackers. Aggressive repairs were under way when I arrived in August 2002, and a large American flag hung at the work site. Inside, the increased post–9/11 security reinforced the serious aura.

Unlike many officers, including Annie's father and mine, my first Pentagon tour was as a general officer, which came with advantages and disadvantages. It spared me some of the pain of working endless actions in rabbit-warren-like office space, but the hours and frustrations with bureaucracy seemed equally distributed. Reassuringly, the quality of the people was good, and many of the actions we worked on were clearly important.

Without question, my biggest surprise was Iraq. At XVIII Airborne Corps, we'd focused our attention on Afghanistan and to a lesser degree on Pakistan. But when I arrived to the Joint Staff in August 2002, the primary focus was on planning for potential operations against Saddam Hussein's regime. Couched as contingency planning against the possibility of hostilities, we conducted a war game soon after I arrived that served to identify and frame solutions for many of the challenges analysts predicted would arise in the event of war in Iraq.

At that point I judged the likelihood of war there to be remote. Although Saddam Hussein was an almost perfect caricature of an evil dictator, I didn't take Iraq's military prowess seriously after the first Gulf War. Further, it seemed to me in 2002 that the international response to 9/11 would further constrain Saddam's ability to act. Although the example of North Korea countered the theory that such regimes inevitably collapse, I suspected that would be Saddam's eventual fate.

As fall passed into winter, the probability of war rose steadily. The bill authorizing President Bush to use force against Iraq passed the House of Representatives on the afternoon of October 10 and cleared the Senate—by a vote of seventy-seven to twenty-three—just after midnight on October 11. Saddam's seemingly illogical reactions to international pressure seemed to confirm assessments of WMD programs that ultimately proved incorrect. Our inexorable buildup of facilities and then combat power, which initially could be interpreted as necessary levers to pressure Saddam into compliance, increasingly looked like concrete steps toward war. Sometime shortly before Christmas of 2002, I remember assessing that our deployments and other preparations had passed the point of being designed to pressure Saddam. It seemed that a decision had been made to go to war.

The VDJ3 position offered me a good vantage point to see how the Pentagon worked. Senior enough to be included in many key meetings but junior enough not to be consumed or constrained by them, I developed a feel for the general mood and trends in the place. I watched how guidance or questions from key leaders in the building were digested and acted on in the "engine rooms" where action officers worked.

Overall, morale at the Pentagon was not great, but I did not see nonstop internecine warfare. When I arrived in August, Secretary Rumsfeld and his team of appointees had been in place for about eighteen months. But many of his anticipated reforms had been postponed due to the tumultuous post-9/11 environment. Still, among the officers, some of the proposals produced angst, exacerbated by the secretary's famously abrasive style. I'd best describe the atmosphere as often tentative and sometimes anxious.

Early on, my duties involved working actions through the bureaucratic process. Many of those decisions could have been made in short conversations or video teleconferences. But many Pentagon decision makers liked the safety of process. There was little recognition that slavish adherence to rigid processes could create inflexible mind-sets across the organization.

Working with Donald Rumsfeld was an adventure, but also instructive. Law required the secretary of defense to authorize the overseas deployment of any forces, and his written approval was called a deployment order (DEPORD). Weekly, we would consolidate all the proposed DEPORDs and conduct a session with the secretary to seek his approval and signature. But the process began much earlier, when staff officers fielded requests from combatant commands—during this period they were mostly from Central Command—for forces. In the days, weeks, and occasionally months that followed, action officers would work long hours with the military services to identify potential sources for the forces, time lines for deployment, and other details. The proposed DEPORDs and supporting documentation were then compiled into a set of about twelve identical three-ring notebooks used to coordinate the actions with key Pentagon leaders in the days before the brief to the secretary of defense.

"DEPORD brief day" was often painful, although occasionally humorous. Secretary Rumsfeld would sit at one end of a conference table in his office, flanked by a briefing officer who was armed with encyclopedic knowledge of every DEPORD. Typically at the table were also the Chairman of the Joint Chiefs of Staff, a couple members of Rumsfeld's staff, and the J3 or VDJ3, the position I then held.

The notebooks were exquisitely organized, with a summary of each proposed deployment, a map showing where it would go, its purpose, and size. Page by page the secretary scrutinized each DEPORD, often asking pointed questions on its importance to the mission and the timing of deployment. In several cases I watched him dig into more detail on a two- or three-person detachment than he did on a fifteen-thousand-soldier combat division. I can't say it was fun, but the rigor of the process forced diligence and scrutiny on the critical decision to deploy service members.

As we postured for war in Iraq, the military's deployment process became an issue. Major military deployments were traditionally designed in support of existing war plans and involved force packages—combinations of forces with all the necessary capabilities for the mission. They were easiest to deploy when a single decision was made for the entire package and military logisticians and transportation planners could flow the force as efficiently as possible.

But Rumsfeld wasn't buying the traditional mindset. He believed military planning was unnecessarily inflexible in what forces would deploy and when they would flow. He felt that a scrub of both would produce a more tailored force and would avoid having to posture it before it was needed. His approach provided him and the president valuable flexibility and ambiguity in their intentions toward Iraq. But operational commanders were left concerned they might not have what they needed if and when fighting began. Logisticians became terrified they'd not be able to make such an ad hoc approach work.

It was an almost classic struggle of cultures and will. Both the secretary and the military were making their best efforts to accomplish the mission. Both were right on a number of points. All were good people. Without question, the secretary's intractability forced the military to be more flexible. But in the process we also experienced a painful period of uncertainty and doubt, which better communication among all the players could have ameliorated.

One of the actions I was involved with should have given us pause. In the fall of 2002, John Abizaid called me to his office and issued guidance to begin working with selected Rumsfeld staffers to build, train, and ultimately deploy a force of Iraqi expatriates. That force was to assume a role a bit like that of the Free French Army units that led the liberation of Paris.

The concept was straightforward. Iraqi expatriates would be recruited by a network of Iraqis, supported by American money, and transported to a location where they would be organized, equipped, and trained to participate in the liberation of their homeland.

But the expatriate community could not, or would not, produce. In what should not have been a surprise, both the Supreme Council for the Islamic

Revolution in Iraq, a main Shiite opposition group exiled in Iran, and the anti-Saddam Kurds refused to contribute to the Free Iraqi Forces. Ultimately, instead of thousands of stalwart freedom fighters, only seventy-four Iraqis volunteered. In Hungary my classmate then–Major General Dave Barno and a team of U.S. Army advisers worked to mold them into a force. Despite great effort and ninety million dollars, little meaningful came from it, and their employment in Iraq proved inconsequential. Over time, I came to believe the inaccuracy of Iraqi expatriates' claims about their ability to marshal opposition to Saddam should have made us question their overall credibility.

When hostilities were clearly imminent, I received two unexpected assignments. The first was to conduct briefings to Congress six days each week. The Armed Services Committees of the House and Senate hosted the briefings, about ninety minutes each, but any member of Congress who had sworn a confidentiality oath was invited to attend. Along with Ambassador Ryan Crocker, an experienced diplomat I'd come to admire deeply in the years ahead, and Colonel William Caniano, an army intelligence officer, we'd brief members in a secure room on the latest developments in Iraq.

The briefings were part of an effort to maintain better relations with Congress, keeping it informed and providing a venue to ask questions on request information. I came to admire the way Senator John Warner of Virginia and Senator Carl Levin of Michigan maintained a seemingly bipartisan friendship and a supremely professional environment, despite the fact that Warner had voted for war in Iraq, while Levin had not. I found this relationship helpful later when commanding both in special operations and the war in Afghanistan.

The second task was to periodically perform the role of Pentagon military spokesman for briefings to the Pentagon press corps. I wanted that role about as much as I wanted a root canal. As VDJ3, I was normally up to speed on operational details, but there was every opportunity to misspeak or to appear a buffoon on national television.

I lucked out. The Joint Staff's public-affairs office assembled a team of young officers with extensive experience who labored to keep me prepared, since I still had my normal duties as VDJ3. I was fortunate enough to be paired with the assistant secretary of defense for public affairs, Torie Clarke. Torie's easygoing manner and mastery of media issues helped me avoid serious damage, and her propensity for colorful clothing sometimes distracted the press from my obvious nervousness.

From my vantage point in the Joint Staff, I also observed a small sideshow in the march to war. Although we did not know it at the time, at least one actor in that sideshow would soon take center stage in Iraq.

I arrived in the Pentagon to find the military mulling plans to attack a small mountain-bound training camp in Kurdistan, in northern Iraq. Fifty-five miles south of the lower limit of the no-fly zone policed by American and British jets, the camp was in a place called Khurmal and run by a little-known Kurdish jihadist group called Ansar al-Islam. The group, with ties to bin Laden, had enacted a mini Talibanized society in its ungoverned enclave in Kurdistan. It forced the men to wear beards and pray at the mosque five times a day; it outlawed music, television, movies, and alcohol. Recently, a small, bedraggled group of Al Qaeda members, who had fled American bombs in Afghanistan and made their way across Iran, sought refuge with Ansar. Most troubling, however, was solid intelligence that at Khurmal, Ansar was manufacturing potent chemical and biological weapons—including ricin—and intended to use them in Europe and per-haps beyond.

CENTCOM and Joint Staff planners had developed several options to destroy the camp. One set of plans, which did not include a ground force, involved sending a volley of missiles or dispatching American bombers. An-other option—which the Joint Chiefs advocated to the White House—involved inserting a ground force after degrading the camp with air strikes. Putting "boots on the ground," as it was called, would allow us to confirm that we had destroyed the target and follow up on the intelligence reports on the chemical and biological weaponry.

A concept was developed, but ultimately, as the march to war acceler-ated, President Bush and his National Security Council waved off the raid. Some have surmised they did so because eliminating the camp and Al Qaeda–linked terrorists—whom some in the administration believed were aided by Saddam Hussein—would have removed a pillar of their rationale for attacking the Hussein regime.

I drew a separate lesson from the experience. Special Operations Com-mand (SOCOM) had been tasked to develop a plan for the ground option and had passed the mission to a subordinate task force. The concept that came back to the Pentagon received little enthusiasm and drew informal criticism. It called for weeks of planning and a considerably larger force package than envisioned.

"Stan, this isn't a special operations mission," one senior officer complained to me. "It's big enough to be an invasion. You were in special operations—can't they do anything small anymore?"

Despite being relatively popular within the Pentagon and in D.C. overall, special operations forces (SOF) had generated a growing frustration among officials. People who viewed SOF as a low-cost, simple solution to all prob-lems were inevitably disappointed. I recognized it was critical for SOF to engage, educate, and communicate effectively with the people—including, at times, the president—who would ultimately make decisions on the most sensitive missions.

It wasn't until after the full American invasion in March 2003 that U.S. Special Forces attacked the Khurmal camp. After a significant firefight, they found traces of ricin and cyanide and the hazard suits, manuals, and equipment Ansar al-Islam had used. Unfortunately, one of the top Al Qaeda operatives who would have been a target of a preinvasion attack had long since fled. It would be some months before the man, an itinerant terrorist named Abu Musab al-Zarqawi, would reappear.

In the months following the invasion of Iraq, I watched as initial satisfaction at the success of operations gave way to concerns over looting, as well as frustration over our inability to capture Saddam or to locate his suspected weapons of mass destruction. At the same time, we were challenged to repair infrastructure and suppress a growing, ill-defined resistance. We worked to establish metrics that would clearly reflect conditions and, we hoped, progress. But in the relatively chaotic conditions of Iraq, it was hard to collect accurate data that could effectively communicate the situation or drive necessary actions.

Additionally, we found it difficult to field the necessary forces to stabilize the country. We'd tried but failed to secure at least three divisions from other nations to help with the occupation. So the U.S. burden would remain high. I worked with action officers on countless iterations of force rotation plans to determine how best to distribute the requirement between the Army and Marines. But even in the summer of 2003, we could see that the endeavor was clearly going to stretch the force.

I was particularly concerned about our ability to fill positions on the Coalition Provisional Authority (CPA) staff and similar political and reconstruction positions on the ground. These roles were being filled slowly and often by inexperienced people. Rotations were too short to allow even good professionals to be effective. I'd see the damaging effect of this later when I was in Iraq.

During the summer of 2003, I could sense growing disquiet in D.C. over the situation. In mid-July, the 3rd Infantry Division, which had participated in the initial invasion, was extended, to the deep dissatisfaction of the Fort Stewart soldiers and their families. A large parade to celebrate their return, planned for New York City's Canyon of Heroes, was quietly canceled. Meanwhile, Saddam's two sons had been killed by U.S. forces, but terrorist attacks in Baghdad and Saddam's continued freedom made policy makers palpably uneasy. By late August, more Americans had died in the postinvasion occupation than in the initial combat operations to unseat Saddam's regime. No one was panicking yet, but the way ahead was unclear to me.

That September, after fourteen months on the Joint Staff, I headed back to Fort Bragg. I hadn't volunteered for Pentagon duty and was happy to leave. But understanding the politics, processes, and personalities in the Pentagon, and in the wider U.S. government, proved indispensible for my later service in Iraq and Afghanistan. What would have seemed unreasonable and ludicrous viewed only from downrange had logic and meaning because I knew the environment in Washington or the individuals involved. Similarly, knowing the secretary of defense, the chairman and vice-chairman of the the Joint Chiefs of Staff, and other key players and—as important—having them know me would be essential when I was faced with sensitive operations easily misunderstood from afar.

All that said, when the time came, Annie and I loaded the car quickly and headed south. We were eager to come "home" to Fort Bragg, and I didn't want to give anyone in D.C. a chance to change his or her mind.

Part Two

The eagerness of our search for firewood turned us all into botanists.

—George Orwell, *Homage to Catalonia*

▼

CHAPTER 7

Through the Hourglass

October–November 2003

On a dry night in February 2004, I was likely standing less than a block from Abu Musab al-Zarqawi. I did not know he and I were that close, nor did the Army special operators who, in a darkened house half a block away, were nearer to him than I was. We were all in the northeastern Askari neighborhood of Fallujah, just south of where the city ended and emptied into sun-caked yellow dirt fields. This was the nicer area of town. The row houses, rectangular with flat rooftops, each stood back from the walled street, with small courtyards in front and dented, rusting metal gates. Constructed with low-grade concrete, the homes and walls were streaked and stained with ocher dust. Half a block away, I stood watch at the corner with Gabe, a major in the special operations task force I was commanding.* Through night-vision goggles, we watched the one courtyard gate that hung half open. Inside, Green operators quickly, deliberately cleared the house's unlit rooms.

If Zarqawi was in fact there, he got away, we think by jumping out of a second-floor window. He would have dropped down into the alleyway around the corner from us, hidden by townhouses. It would have been hard to hear him land on the ground. There wasn't debris for him to disturb, as the houses were still intact then. And, this being Iraq, unseen stray dogs yelped from all corners of the neighborhood. That would all change in a

---

*Gabe is a pseudonym. Throughout this section, for purposes of anonymity, some individuals are identified by their initials, partial names, or pseudonyms.

month, when a crowd at the opposite end of the city murdered four American private security contractors, stringing two of their charred bodies from the beams of the green trestle bridge that spanned the Euphrates. That display spurred the Bush administration to order two massive Marine operations, the second of which, in November of that year, would leave over twelve hundred dead insurgents and the city they had hunkered down in a hollowed shell.

Had Zarqawi's stop at the townhouse that night been a visit for him to motivate his troops, he might have dressed in all black, his signature look. More likely he wore bland Iraqi garb, the type he donned before passing undetected through countless American checkpoints over the next two years. Regardless, he would have been unlikely to bump into anyone else on the street; everyone had retired behind their walls hours earlier and remained there even if our flashbang grenades and shouting woke them. Not once during the scores of raids I went on over the next four years in Iraq did I see anyone stir behind the darkened windows above a street, nor did curious onlookers ever appear on the streets. After decades of Saddam's brutal control, Iraqis seemed to instinctively avoid anything that could bring attention to themselves during night operations by security forces. The process was one they knew well and feared.

Zarqawi was fitter that night than he was in the final months of his life, when he grew heavy and pale from staying indoors to avoid our surveillance. Between the uninterrupted barking, the darkness, and the empty streets, he could have slipped north over the railroad tracks into the open fields to wait us out. Or he could have turned the other way and disappeared into the denser city that sprawled beneath Fallujah's motley minarets. Or he may not have been there at all.

Earlier that evening I had joined the operators at our compound at Baghdad International Airport (BIAP). They came from an Army special mission unit known as "Green," one of the units that formed the core of the globally deployed special operations task force I now led, Task Force 714 (TF 714). After the team briefed the operation, we drove out of the heavily guarded northwest gate of the airport's perimeter. We weaved through a serpentine maze of obstacles, laid out like bumpers on a pinball board in order to slow approaching vehicles that might contain car bombs or shooters. Above our vehicle's windows, dark barrels of machine guns protruded over the security light-bathed HESCOs, refrigerator-size wire baskets filled with earth and rock that served as protective walls.

As we left the relative security of the airport, our small collection of specially outfitted armored vehicles and Humvees got onto Highway 10, which ran west from Baghdad along the Euphrates and out all the way to Jordan. The drive took an hour on the unlit and eerily quiet freeway. At the eastern edge of Fallujah, our single-file convoy slowly exited the highway using the cloverleaf off-ramps. We passed under the same green highway signs with white text and arrows you'd find in any city in the United States. It felt like we were commuting to war.

These operators were unlike other soldiers. They were painstakingly selected, exquisitely trained warriors. Calm but intensely focused, they did not display any nervousness in the vehicle, nor did they engage in the idle chatter shown in war movies. I heard only the low groan of the engine and the periodic electronic beep of the radio set on the dash.

I had worked with operators from their unit on training events and during the first Gulf War, and many of the commissioned and noncommissioned officers were former Rangers with whom I had served. I respected them and wanted their respect. But only four months into my command of TF 714, I was still unsure of where I stood with them. Their demeanor around me was correct but cautiously stiff. I did not lead the operations I went on—and did not try to insert myself into the action. As on this night, I went to observe. Accompanying operators on these missions was essential if I wanted to understand what was happening on the ground in our war against an ever-shifting and increasingly wise network. Critically, in this fight, which only got harder from that night forward, these were opportunities to build relationships and mutual trust with the men and women I led.

We searched and cleared a number of houses that evening. As I climbed the stairs to the second floor of one of those homes, my head came into view of the Iraqis above the landing. Grouped together in the corner and partially illuminated, they turned from watching the operators comb through their belongings to look at me. I'll never forget their stare. It was controlled, but I sensed pure anger, radiating like heat. Perhaps they understood from watching how the operators reacted when I entered that I was the one who had sent these men with lights and guns to their house that night. Maybe theirs was a more instinctive response of indignation and fright to someone invading their homes. That we were foreigners made the process worse. Theirs was a look I would see repeatedly in the years to come.

The Green operators were being as sensitive as anyone could be when searching someone else's house. Poise came naturally to them: They were older, in their thirties and forties, and they were seasoned. They did not need to smash things to prove their manhood or to feel powerful. Most were fathers, and that night, as on the hundreds of raids each went on during the war, they couldn't help but see their own children in the young Iraqis who hid behind their parents' legs.

But the operators' care mattered little to the Iraqis, who never ceased glowering. We were big men, made bigger with body armor, it was one o'clock in the morning, and our searching their home was as humiliating to them as if we had stripped their bodies. They had no way of knowing that we too were fathers; without language, there was no chance even to attempt human connection. I knew we needed to do these raids, but I also knew these searches—on top of the lack of electricity and the backed-up sewage and the lack of jobs in a chaotic, post-Saddam Iraq—were producing fury, understandably directed at us. With calculated barbarism, Zarqawi was already at work exploiting our failures, making us look powerless or sinister or both. His disappearance into the dark that night was troubling, but I was consumed with this Iraqi family. Watching them watch us, I realized this fight was going to be long and tough.

Less than a year after the initial U.S.-led invasion, the beginning of 2004 had brought new sobriety to our mission in Iraq. A month earlier, the number of Americans killed in the war had risen from 497 to the grim figure of 500 when explosives stuffed inside two artillery shells and hidden beneath the ground killed three soldiers as they drove through a field in Taji. At this point few could foresee that the war would grind on until that figure of 500 Americans killed would be reached another eight times over. This was before Iraq became truly hellish as it turned into a civil war, before driving through Baghdad at night in 2006 and 2007 and 2008 meant viewing scenes from a postapocalyptic movie, with masked men illuminated by the fires they lit at the checkpoints they manned. And this was before each new morning brought more bodies floating in the city's brown, soupy irrigation canals. Those images were the grisly markers of Iraq's civil war, a war Zarqawi helped ignite through a ruthlessly efficient campaign of murder. Sometimes his bombs killed Iraqis a crowd at a time. Sometimes his victims died in lonely torture cells in obscure corners of the country.

So on that dusty night in February 2004, while we were disappointed to have missed him, the bloody consequences of our failure were not immediately apparent. On that night, Zarqawi was not yet Iraq's bane.

Had we picked up Zarqawi that evening, the recent history of special operations might have been very different. The raid launched into Fallujah was part of a nascent campaign waged by TF 714. Although TF 714's fight was much wider than Iraq, our role and reputation grew more than anything as a result of our close-quarters fight against Zarqawi and his branch of Al Qaeda. This is a story about how an organization of units and people that began in the wake of Desert One in 1980 radically transformed to fight a new threat. Our transformation also pushed me to grow from an operational commander, where I was most comfortable, to a strategic-level leader. This was not preordained, nor did those with whom I worked always welcome it. But by the time of that raid, I had come to see that for us to succeed, I could not simply command TF 714. I would have to be a part of a new vision of how America had to fight modern wars.

From their creation in the 1970s and 1980s, special operations units were an impressive collection of talent. A chain of visionary leaders forged them into the most effective force of its kind, one that had proven its value repeatedly in its first twenty years. But the escalating war on terror in the aftermath of September 11 compelled the relatively small hostage-rescue and counterterrorist force to adapt to new, more ominous threats. TF 714 needed to become a more complex organization with unprecedented capability, and we needed to employ that on a daily—and nightly—basis, year after year.

The change was historic. The organization I rejoined in 2003 was fresh off impressive operations in the invasions of Afghanistan and, more recently, Iraq. But it was only the kernel of the force I was to depart in 2008. To transform ourselves from a traditional military unit into a network, we changed how we were organized and how we made decisions; we grew a new culture within proud and idiosyncratic communities; we continually added partners. In 2003 our "product" was our "shooters"—our ensemble of tactically unmatched strike forces. By the end, in the months when Iraq's fate would be decided, TF 714's formidable offering was its network—its ability to gel diverse talents into an organic unit that gathered information swiftly and acted accordingly.

TF 714's reinvention and success were neither straightforward nor inevitable. There were numerous failures. I made countless mistakes. And we evolved in response to the distinct historical moment in which we found ourselves. Ultimately, this chapter in military history is a story about the professionalism, creativity, and unwavering courage of those with whom I served. The TF 714 operators' rare stamina and commitment to hunt and fight night after night, month after month, year after year was essential to our effort. But such effort would take an immense toll on these men and women.

I did not arrive with a vision for changing TF 714 when I took over the special operations command whose members formed the core of the task force on Monday, October 6, 2003, at the command's nondescript compound at Fort Bragg, North Carolina. Though this Fort Bragg-based command and the forward-deployed TF 714 were not the same entity, the command provided the predominance of the task force's members and leadership. Starting that day, I would be commander of both. The ceremony was held in the parachute-packing facility. For security reasons, the number of outside guests was limited, and Annie was my only family member to attend. The room was quiet and empty but for the small gathering of us on a dais and an audience in metal folding chairs. Silky, pine-colored parachutes, waiting to be folded, draped the walls like deflated balloons. It lacked the pageantry of a normal army change-of-command ceremony conducted on a sunny parade ground. But the small, muted event reflected the low-key nature and quiet professionalism that were TF 714's hallmarks.

I was excited, but I harbored doubts. Although I had served in special operations for much of the previous eighteen years, I was from the Rangers and had never served in either of the other units—"Green" (the Army's elite commando unit) and "Blue" (the Navy SEAL special mission unit)—considered the crown jewels of the command and of TF 714. The week before, my thick in-box of paperwork had included the unit's most recent Command Climate Survey, which tabulated a consistent complaint about the command: "Too many Rangers." But it was not surprising, as Rangers, long viewed as the junior varsity of TF 714, continued to struggle in this small world to be recognized as equals of the more specialized forces they were increasingly serving alongside. This did little to bolster my confidence.

I was more worried, though, about rejoining the force at this particular time. I had deployed to Afghanistan after 9/11, but to my chagrin I had been stuck in the halls of the Pentagon for the invasion of Iraq the previous spring. I had missed the operations that helped topple the Taliban and later Saddam, which most people within the military probably judged TF 714's greatest accomplishments to that point. Like any soldier who joined a unit after a major engagement, I felt I carried the stigma of not having been on hand for the trial by fire. But I tried not to worry about something I could not control.

Instead, as I sat on the stage, I looked at Annie. After I had left the Pentagon three weeks earlier, she and I had flown to Denver, rented a car, and spent twelve days in late September driving around Wyoming, hiking and sightseeing. In the years ahead, at dawn each day when I would retire to my room in Afghanistan or Iraq for a few hours of sleep, I would spend a few moments staring at pictures from this trip—Annie in hiking shorts and baseball cap, suntanned and smiling. The photographs, taped to walls between my combat gear hanging on hooks, promised sunny days after dark nights of war. From the front row of folding chairs at the ceremony, Annie caught my gaze. As she often did at public events when she could sense my thoughts, she mouthed the words "I love you." So began what turned out to be the longest, most difficult, and most rewarding job I ever had.

When I returned with Annie to Fort Bragg, we came "home." It was the fourth time we had lived there. But the feeling on base had changed. I had been at Bragg for the first year after 9/11, watched the increased security, and I had been among the first from the base to deploy. Now, as America finished its second year in Afghanistan and its sixth month in Iraq, the base was resigned to increased deployments. Thus far, casualties had been limited, and few anticipated they would rise significantly. But disturbingly, our effort, named the Global War on Terror, had no clear end in sight.

A few days after assuming command, I made a trip to Tampa, Florida, to see Generals Doug Brown, who led SOCOM, and John Abizaid, who had left the Joint Staff and was now commander of CENTCOM. I'd known Doug since the late 1980s when, as a Ranger company commander and then operations officer, I worked with him in his role as a special-operations aviator in the Night Stalkers, the aviation unit created from the Iranian rescue-mission effort. Our relationship was entering its second decade when several months earlier Doug called me, not long after he was selected to command SOCOM. He asked if I would take TF 714 that October. The phone call was an uncomfortable moment. Part of me had been hoping to command the 82nd Airborne Division, and I thought I might have been out of the special operations world for too long to be welcomed back by its purist circles.

"Sir, isn't there a more logical choice than me?"

"There might be, Stan," Doug responded. "But I want you to command the task force."

I told my old friend I would be honored.

Now, in Tampa, I sat down with John Abizaid for his guidance, but also to get his approval of a technical but important tweak in our command relationship. Overseeing operations from North Africa to Asia, including wars in Iraq and Afghanistan, John had what was then the most challenging job in the U.S. military. When I took over, TF 714 was commanded by a two-star, but one of its two one-star deputies was constantly in Iraq, running the day-to-day special operations there. Naturally, CENTCOM would be tempted to work directly with that deputy, rather than through me. But I wanted John to agree that I would be the commander of all my forces in his theater. No matter my location, I would be his single point of contact and of responsibility. It may seem an arcane point of military hierarchy, but intuitively I believed the unprecedented campaign TF 714 was faced, across a wide geographic area would demand as much unity and consistency in leadership as possible. I also sensed that my relationships with senior leaders and my physical presence downrange would enhance TF 714's freedom of action, which would otherwise be difficult to obtain. On paper we had a wide legal berth; but the degree to which we could maneuver when the risks were high and costly would actually depend on the trust and confidence of those whose approval we sought.

Like almost all my meetings with John, this one was friendly, informal, and often irreverently funny. We would laugh at the absurdities of military life, and his trademark relentless, dry sarcasm moved like an undertow through the conversation. After our years together in the 82nd and on the Joint Staff, we had formed a bond. As we got to serious business, he expressed his concern with the situation in eastern Afghanistan, where some of Al Qaeda's senior leadership had recently been reported. I agreed to conduct a major operation in the area. Significantly, he agreed to change the way he viewed my role. As my boss in the 82nd ten years earlier, John had liked to communicate with me personally, not through our staffs. So my proposal for direct interaction suited his style.

"Okay, Stan," he said. "But if I call, I've gotta be able to reach you. If I call and can't get you, the deal's off."

It was vintage Abizaid: friendly and unwaveringly demanding. As I looked at him, now with four stars on the lapel of his sand and brown desert fatigues, I pictured the ragged, sun-bleached Oakland Athletics baseball hat he used to wear on the weekends at Fort Bragg a few years earlier. He had the demeanor and temper of an experienced, wry baseball manager. He was supportive but unsentimental and wouldn't hesitate to go to the bullpen if I stopped throwing strikes.

While I had enjoyed other jobs, I loved command. I had been in a command position for ten of the previous twenty-six years. But each new position was initially daunting. As I suspect many leaders feel, I was never sure if I could command at that next level until I actually assumed the job. I remembered how Douglas Southall Freeman, in *Lee's Lieutenants,* had described Lee's challenges in determining which brigade commanders could actually handle the wider responsibilities of a division or corps. The most aggressive brigade commanders often lacked the intangible qualities required for more senior leadership. Of course I wondered about myself.

As the demands of the positions differed, and as I grew in age and experience, I found that I had changed as a leader. I learned to ask myself two questions: First, what must the organization I command do and be? And second, how can I best command to achieve that? Experience taught me that many factors would shape my "command style," and it would be some time before I settled into it.

D uring the first weeks of command, I visited Green. Like our headquarters, Green's compound was based at Fort Bragg, in a separate corner of the base. And yet the true distance between TF 714 and this subordinate unit was much greater than the ten-minute drive. At that time, someone on the TF 714 staff would not feel welcome just dropping by the Green compound, or that of the SEALs or those of other units, if he wasn't himself a member. Many within these organizations viewed any higher headquarters as an unnecessary appendage.

The same qualities that made the units I now commanded so valuable also made them aloof. Although envisioned as a "team of teams," in many ways TF 714 was more a "tribe of tribes." The volunteerism at the heart of each unit, the unwavering standards, the rigorous selection processes, all gave them unmatched competence and cohesion. But in many instances that same tribalism made them insular.

Early on I saw each of TF 714's subordinate units pushing their capabilities with competitive energy that needed only periodic direction from me. But I would need a much more nuanced understanding of these idiosyncratic bands to be an effective commander. While I had grown up in the Rangers and worked with the other units off and on in the 1990s, I knew they had changed in subtle ways. In time, I came to know more intimately each unit's amazing talents, internal politics, and weaknesses.

Green was the most influential of the units. Created from the vision of General Edward "Shy" Meyer, then the Army chief of staff, in the late 1970s, it was an unprecedented organization, one modeled on the British Special Air Service. The force was a collection of experienced commissioned and noncommissioned officers forged into teams that specialized in surgical, direct-action missions, like hostage rescue and pinpoint assaults.

The magic of "the unit," as they referred to it, was its people. Most new members came from the Rangers and Green Berets, but some came directly from the Army's conventional units. An extraordinarily rigorous selection process tested each applicant's fitness, intelligence, courage, and mental balance. The process was so good at selecting for certain characteristics that the operators shared many traits. They tended to be hyperfit, opinionated, iconoclastic, fearless, intelligent, type A problem solvers who thrived without guidance. They affected nonchalance around garrison and between missions. But beneath the beards and civilian T-shirts were to-the-core military professionals. I often joked that if I had inspected their bureaus, I'd have found their underwear neatly folded. As one veteran operator told me, "a place for everything, and everything in its place." They couldn't help themselves.

Enlisted men weren't eligible to attempt admission until they were sergeants, but once in, most stayed until retirement. This embedded the unit with an unprecedented level of expertise and talent. In a conventional army brigade, there were about five sergeants major—the highest enlisted rank—and over two thousand young privates. In Green, a brigade-size organization, there were sixty-three sergeants major and no privates. Given the seniority of the force, rank was less important, and operators earned credibility through performance. Because few ever left the unit, joining Green, meant taking on a separate career altogether. Its members forsook traditional career advancement upon entering, as the small unit had only so many command spots. While few ever left the unit voluntarily, membership was always provisional—and could be revoked if an operator were to go slack.

During its early years, Green gained a reputation as an old boys' club and a refuge for the cowboys of the Army. Even later, some saw them as prima donnas, too long pickled in the privileges and esteem that came to the finest military unit in the world. When I worked in special operations in the early 1990s, I considered Green an effective—but also arrogant—organization.

Entering the Green compound was always a bit intimidating, seemingly by design. But the commander, then-Colonel Bennet Sacolick, and the command sergeant major, Jody Nacy, welcomed me warmly. We moved to one of the larger conference rooms, where I found myself standing in front of a collection of operators. Many were fresh from combat in both Iraq and Afghanistan. I was the new commanding general, just out of the safe halls of the Pentagon. I scanned the faces of the fifty or sixty operators there that day as they sat in rows of chairs in front of me. I quickly realized that I knew many of them from their earlier service in the Rangers. Familiar faces were reassuring. But though many were old comrades, they had graduated to a higher level. We no longer shared the same haircut, and they were not as young as they had been when I first served with them. I needed to recalibrate our relationship.

These men were older—the average age on any operation was often at least thirty-five—but they were immaculately fit. A paunch triggered scorn. Their maturity and experience when molded together in small teams made them extraordinarily effective. During the previous decades, when most of America had enjoyed peaceful lives, they had repeatedly deployed. Many in the folding chairs had fought as Green operators or as Rangers in Mogadishu, some in Panama. More recently they had done quiet work in the

Balkans before being thrust into the war on terror. Their hard-wrought intuition would deepen in the years to come.

Unlike many young, untested soldiers, the men in the seats did not think they were bulletproof. They had built up lives beyond mere soldiering. Nearly all were married and had children. Often their children were not infants but teenagers growing into adults while their fathers fought overseas. In the years ahead, more than one would have a child fighting in the same war, elsewhere in the country. I would have the wrenching duty to write a letter of sympathy to a veteran operator and his wife, a couple I'd known for years, when their only son was killed serving in the fight as a young paratrooper.

That day, I wondered what the members of the unit saw in me. As always, their demeanor betrayed nothing. They appeared patient and attentive but not obsequious. I saw none of the slouching that signaled disinterest or disdain. As usual, I hadn't prepared a speech; I wanted to get their attention and dispel any feeling that the wars we faced were nearly over or that TF 714 could limit its role. Instead, we needed to display unconventional adaptability.

"I need you to do *whatever* the customer wants," I said.

There were some stunned looks in the seats at this. Indeed, the veterans' reaction was similar to my own when I had initially bristled at the term "customer" twenty years earlier. It had been in 1985, through the headsets of a helicopter being flown by a veteran Night Stalker named Steel. Being called a customer put me off. It felt too much like business, too transactional—not how warriors should think of their comrades. I soon came to see that the Night Stalkers' constant use of the term was a skillful way of reminding themselves that they existed to support and enable the forces—the customers—whom they flew. The culture that formed around this word was one of the Night Stalkers' great strengths.

In the end, I think they got my point. I sensed a serious curiosity about how I would command and where I would take TF 714. T. E. Lawrence, who himself wrangled and led tribes during World War I, wrote that they "could be swung on an idea as on a cord: for the unpledged allegiance of their minds made them obedient servants. None of them would escape the bond till success had come, and with it responsibility and duty and engagements." These strong-willed, opinionated operators were far from servants, but they shared a fundamental quality with Lawrence's tribes: If there were a worthy mission—an idea they could come to believe in—they committed to it unlike anything I had yet seen in my military career.

Indeed, in time I came to see that the older faces of these Green operators and the SEALs were leathery but not grizzled. They were not hardened, cynical soldiers for pay who floated from one battlefield to the next, without regard for the cause for which they employed their skills. In fact, they were often more outwardly patriotic than many other soldiers I'd served with, quick to hang American flags on the walls of their barracks and headquarters. Believing in our cause, and in their leaders, was critically important to them.

After I answered questions, our meeting ended, and I left the conference room and walked down the long, sunlit hallway to the front of the compound. Spaced along one wall were glass-encased displays a couple feet deep and a few feet wide. Each documented one of the unit's significant operations or missions. Dusty guns, equipment, maps, and photos rested behind blurbs about each accomplishment.

In the years ahead, they would have reason to install more displays.

Before arriving at my new command, I'd communicated to the TF 714 staff that as soon as practical I wanted to take a trip to the region where our forces were operating, a theater that included Iraq and Afghanistan and stretched from the Mediterranean to the end of the porous Durand Line. We programmed about ten days for the trip. Several key leaders accompanied me, including my J2, or intelligence officer, Colonel Brian Keller, a former Ranger whom I'd known and trusted for years. Brian was soon to move on from TF 714 to another command in a few months, and would eventually be promoted to brigadier general, so I wanted to leverage his experience and expertise before I lost him.

The other half of the key J2-J3 dynamic was my operations officer, Colonel T.T. He and I had worked together as Ranger captains in the 3rd Ranger Battalion in 1987–89. I had recognized his talent, but we were both intensely focused young officers, maybe a bit too much alike, and our relationship was initially strained. As we both advanced in rank and experience, so too did my appreciation for T.T.'s qualities—his amazing vision, unwavering loyalty, and personal courage—and we developed a deep friendship. T.T. subsequently joined Green, but in 1995 he agreed to return to the Rangers as my deputy at the 2nd Ranger Battalion. Now, eight years later, I was again benefiting from his experience and unshakable values.

The TF 714 senior enlisted adviser was Command Sergeant Major C. W. Thompson, a laconic former rodeo rider turned soldier, and a trusted friend. My aide-de-camp was air force major Dave Tabor, a young, humorously sarcastic, but veteran MH-53 helicopter pilot who'd flown initial operations in Afghanistan in 2001. Also on the trip was the deputy commander of Green, then–Lieutenant Colonel Austin "Scott" Miller. Bennet, Scott's boss, had wisely dispatched him with me on this first trip both to keep an eye on me and to begin shaping my perceptions of his unit. Scott did the latter superbly and would become a key figure in the years ahead.

Those four, along with my communicator, navy petty officer Vic Kouw, formed the core of the command team. Starting that fall, for 60 percent of any given day, I would be close enough to literally reach out and touch any of these men (or their successors). The command team would grow in size and evolve with personalities in the years ahead. We would share countless hours on every type of aircraft and would struggle together to shape the command. The bonds would grow deep.

The purpose of this first trip was to begin to establish my relationship with those TF 714 forces that were currently deployed and, also important, to see the situation in each location and to assess our requirements for the future. Although I had served in Afghanistan in 2002, I had not been to Iraq, and I knew my view from the Joint Staff had been distant and incomplete. As always, I wanted to see the battlefield for myself.

L ike most things in Iraq that looked stable and orderly from a distance, the Republican Guard palace in Baghdad was, upon closer inspection, a mess. The American-led coalition had turned the palace into its headquarters following the March invasion, and on Friday, October 24, 2003, it was the first stop on my first trip as TF 714 commander to the theater in which my forces were most heavily deployed. The palace lay deep within the Green Zone, the four square miles staked out as a sanctuary for coalition civilians and military forces on the western bank of the Tigris River, which bisects Baghdad. With Dave Tabor, we drove from BIAP west of the city along a road that the Coalition then called Route Irish. The drive was uneventful, the roadway not yet the notorious shooting gallery it would become a few months later. As we approached the Green Zone, over the tops of the palms that lined the driveway to the palace we could see the outlines of the huge busts of Saddam that perched on the facade. In each, the deposed dictator—whom we had yet to capture—was refigured as a vintage Arab warrior. His cold, jowly face peered down from within a pith helmet and kaffiyeh, apparently worn by the Iraqis who rose against the Ottomans. Iraqi cranes hired by the Coalition had not yet ripped the busts from their perches, and the palace had largely survived the initial bombardment of Baghdad in the opening hours of the war. On the outside, its beige outer walls conveyed an air of order and calm. Inside was a different story.

Over the summer, the initial postinvasion elation of April and confidence of May had quickly muddied, turning to growing unease in June. By August, nervousness tempered the halls and offices of the Pentagon. Data foretold more unrest and more violence that autumn. But there remained a hope, if only a halfhearted one, that if we could just find Saddam and get the lights on in Baghdad, the country would straighten itself out.

Following the March invasion, the Bush administration had eventually assigned Ambassador L. Paul Bremer to reconstruct Iraq after its rapid defeat and the collapse of Saddam's regime. As the head of the newly created Coalition Provisional Authority (CPA), Bremer was responsible for governing the country with the objective of rapid transition to Iraqi sovereignty. The CPA had been using the palace as its headquarters for five months, but inside it felt like confused entropy.

The whole coterie of professionals, soldiers, contractors, and wide-eyed "augmentees"—some of them twentysomething political operatives—seemed as if they had either arrived just hours earlier or they were about to be overrun by the proverbial barbarians beyond the gate. Boxes of documents lined some hallways. Those working in the palace had partitioned the cavernous Italian-marble rooms into offices using plywood. Some sat at imitation Louis XIV chairs and desks—with gilded, curved legs and turquoise cushions—left behind by the Iraqis. Many on the staff looked aimless. I was amused by those who wore what I called their "adventure clothing"—hiking boots, earth-tone cargo pants, and Orvis shirts with multiple Velcro pockets purchased with the allowance many had been given to stock up for their tour.

That day I was there to meet Lieutenant General Ricardo Sanchez, one of the newest three-star generals in the Army and the top military commander in Iraq. I had met Sanchez a few years earlier, and this time, in his Baghdad office, we shared a courteous rapport. In desert fatigues, he looked out from big rectangular eyeglasses.

"Your guys are doing what we need them to do," he said.

But he left it at that. He did not slap a map down on the coffee table and explain what he was trying to accomplish and how our forces could help. His reticence was natural. TF 714's relevance to Sanchez was probably unclear. At that moment, we were tasked with capturing or killing the high-value former Baathist leaders—a set known colloquially as "the deck of cards" after the Pentagon had printed packs of playing cards with the grainy photographs and names of the top Baathists and distributed them to soldiers before they rolled across the Kuwaiti border.

The previous summer, our units had been key in the fight that killed Saddam's sons, Uday and Qusay, but we had not yet captured Saddam himself, the ace of spades. Sanchez had a lot to worry about in the fall of 2003, and I sensed that he did not know whether I would just be another of the countless visitors who appeared on his calendar every few months, or whether I was committed to becoming a real partner. We never got much beyond pleasantries, and I had no sense of the big direction of the war. Elsewhere in the palace, I met with the chief of staff of the CPA and second-highest ranking civilian in Iraq, Ambassador Patrick F. Kennedy. I explained to him what TF 714 was.

I arrived with some prejudice about the uneven and often unserious national resolve to make hard decisions in the months after the invasion. Many agencies were at fault for that, but the atmosphere in the palace added to my doubts about the CPA. Certainly many smart people worked hard to overcome great odds that summer and fall. But seven months of spotty progress had left many cynical. Policies kept them cloistered behind the palace walls, where they often worked alongside unqualified volunteers whose tour lengths were far too short to gain adequate, let alone advanced, understanding of the complexities of Iraq. The CPA ordered fundamental challenges—that would affect the lives of Iraqis and the Americans fighting among them—to be tackled by spectacularly unqualified people, like a twenty-five-year-old with no financial credentials responsible for rebuilding the stock market. I left the palace that day thinking, *Holy shit.*

The next morning, October 25, I helicoptered with Dave Tabor and Scott Miller to Mosul, 250 miles upstream of Baghdad on the Tigris. The second-largest city in Iraq, with some 1.8 million people, Mosul was the responsibility of then–Major General David Petraeus. His 101st Airborne Division had fought up from Kuwait through southern Iraq and into Baghdad, at which point they had been moved north. The city sat where the Arab and Kurdish regions met uneasily, with the Sunni Arabs predominantly in the traditional city center south and west of the Tigris and the Kurds in suburbs to the northeast.

In a former palace overlooking the city, Dave Petraeus was full of energy, as always. His office was a huge, marble-floored room turned into a warrior's den by the combat gear hanging on hooks and the cot he slept on, covered with the camouflage poncho liner issued to every soldier. Dave and I had shared an early fascination with irregular wars and the counterinsurgents who had fought them in Indochina and Algeria. As effectively as any commander at the time, Dave had read the situation in his area of Iraq, recognized the tremendous threat of instability, and moved rapidly to seize the fleeting opportunity to forestall it. He made early progress by spending energy and money on economic and political development. His force established governing councils, opened schools, and corralled, equipped, and dispatched a local Iraqi security force. But when the twenty thousand soldiers of the 101st turned over Mosul to an American unit only a fraction of their size the following January, the insurgents soon destroyed what calm Dave's force had been able to win.

TF 714 had a small detachment working in Mosul in conjunction with Dave's division, and we enjoyed his strong support. Still, when I reviewed with our team how they ran targeting missions periodically, based on the trickle of tips and intercepts they were able to scrape up in the early days, I was convinced they were having limited effect. In October 2003, Saddam and his network of former regime members remained our primary focus, but at this point the picture we could draw was very rudimentary. Rare bits of intelligence came from the task force headquarters in Baghdad or from the other outposts throughout the province. They were working hard to understand the people who lived in the big city down the hill from their compound and were accomplishing as much as a team of sixteen could. But they were largely cut off from the rest of our force. I thanked them for their work and went to the helicopter pad feeling that despite their talent and dedication, the team's isolation limited their ability to contribute effectively. The price of that isolation was made clear on the airlift down to Tikrit.

As we flew single file in two Black Hawks, our helicopter suddenly took a sharp, aggressive turn, banking hard off course. We tilted sideways,

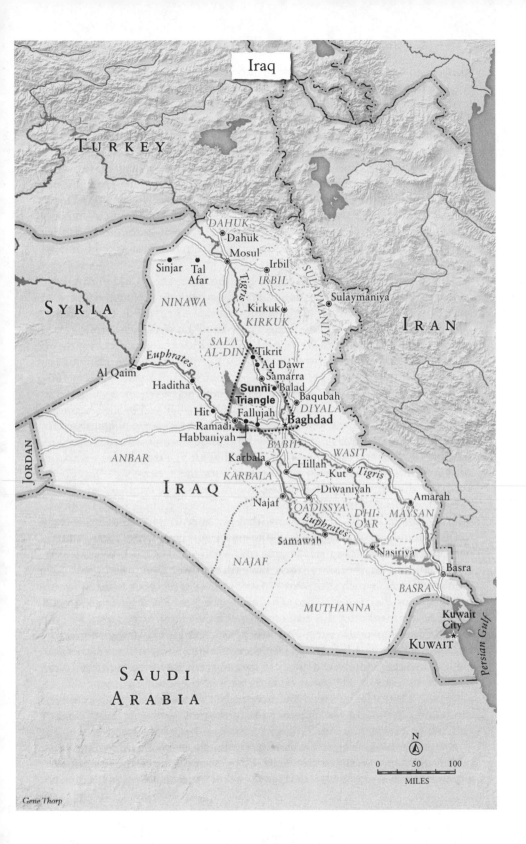

bringing the desert rushing below us into view through the open side doors. As we circled up and back, the pilots said over the headsets that the helicopter behind us had been shot down, clipped by a rocket-propelled grenade. Thankfully, before leaving for Mosul, I had left my key TF 714 staff behind in Baghdad to draw up a campaign plan for the upcoming operation in Afghanistan that John Abizaid had requested. Therefore, the second of our two UH-60s, originally meant to be full of the planning staff, was empty except for the crew. It was further fortunate that the craft did not instantly explode when hit. We landed near where it had made a hard landing, unloaded all of the crew, and took off as the downed helo burned, hissing and popping as each piece exploded off. One of the pilots, with a leg wound already bandaged, joined our helicopter. In the air, I asked him how he was.

"I'm pissed off, sir," he said through the headset. "Goddamn it." He leaned over, looking back at the smoke. "They shot down my helicopter." I smiled, and after a few moments he continued. "Sir, you don't remember me, but I was a Ranger in 2nd Rangers for you." I hadn't recognized him in his flight suit and helmet. We reminisced, and I was reminded how small our special-operations world was. And I was reminded of the resilience of its ranks.

As we continued to Tikrit, I turned my thoughts to our enemy. I tried to picture the man who had bravely shot at us and what had brought him out to the desert to do so. He would have needed a certain level of commitment to stand in open ground, in broad daylight, and take a potshot at two heavily armed Coalition helicopters. Surely, in that area of Iraq and at that time, he was Sunni. But what motivated him? With the accuracy of his rocket, was he a disenfranchised Baathist soldier? Or was he younger and more devout than his Baathist counterparts, taking orders from Ansar al-Sunnah, an Al Qaeda–allied jihadist group with a presence in that region? Contrary to the administration's official line, the attack did not, to me, smack of desperation. It seemed to signal, "Game on."

On landing on the hard-caked helipad, we moved to another of Saddam's mansions, which then–Major General Ray Odierno was using for his headquarters. Ray and I had grown close at the Naval War College. His son Tony, now an infantry lieutenant, had babysat Sam often, and we had shared more than a few beers after weekly Hash House Harrier runs. Now he commanded the 4th Infantry Division, a brigade of which my father had led in Vietnam before serving as its chief of staff. Ray met us in the colorful, cavernous foyer. He knew we had lost a helo but not any men.

"Stan." He reached his big hand out, his baritone filling the high-ceilinged room and echoing off the chamber's hard marble walls and floor. "Heard you had an exciting trip in."

Ray was responsible for Tikrit, the northernmost of the three cities that, with Ramadi out west and Baghdad in the center, formed the Sunni triangle, where the insurgency would rage. He described the situation as serious.

Tikrit was Saddam's hometown, and he was thought to be hiding within its limits. High-level Iraqi officers had returned to the surrounding province, a Sunni stronghold, after the invasion. Some journalists concluded that Ray had failed where Dave succeeded. Cerebral Dave fought with money and good governance, the story went, while Ray, the bald, towering lineman, was blunt and brute and alienated the population with huge sweeps and arrests. Reality was less clear cut. Ray's physical presence belied a nuanced approach to the complexity he was encountering. Tikrit was different terrain from Mosul, and both cities would host bitter fighting in the years ahead. Like Dave, Ray appreciated the work of our small team that was linked up with him. But I quickly saw our main obstacle. Without real-time links to an effective TF 714 network, the team's good relations with their 4th Infantry Division hosts wouldn't mean much.

Like the team in Mosul, the force in Tikrit largely toiled away on its own, with inadequate support or guidance. Like the wider Coalition effort, TF 714 suffered without a common strategy or a network to prosecute one. This was most glaring in the way we handled raw intelligence, a significant amount of which came out of the raids that the TF 714 operators conducted throughout Iraq and Afghanistan. On each mission they found documents and electronics, as well as people who knew names and plans that we wanted to know. But human error, insufficient technology, and organizational strictures limited our ability to use this intelligence to mount the next raid. The sole intelligence analyst in Mosul or Tikrit was unable to digest the information brought back in dumps by the operators to the outstations in the early hours of the morning. The teams were ill equipped to question suspected insurgents they found on the targets or detained briefly at their forward bases. And they could not easily seek assistance from Baghdad. We considered our communications robust for a small element, but we quickly found them inadequate for sending and receiving the vast amounts of classified information to and from Baghdad fast enough to make it relevant to targeting. Single e-mail messages went rapidly, but modern intelligence depended upon large volumes of data—scanned images of maps or documents, videos found on computers and camcorders—which required significant bandwidth. Without the ability to share these quickly, we were hamstrung.

These strictures led the force to adopt a standard practice that summer and fall that looks farcical in hindsight. After the teams in Mosul or Tikrit or Ramadi digested what little they could from the captured material, they filled emptied sandbags, burlap sacks, or clear plastic trash bags with these scooped-up piles of documents, CDs, computers, and cell phones and then sent them down to our base in Baghdad. Some bags started the trip with a yellow Post-it note on the outside explaining their origin; others didn't. Detainees thought to be important made the trips with the bags.

Fundamentally, the senders and receivers, in this case the forward team and its higher headquarters, had neither a shared picture of the enemy nor an ability to prosecute a common fight against it. This inspired territoriality and distrust. Outstations rarely saw the benefits of the raw intelligence they collected, which often disappeared into a black hole once they sent it up. Equally frustrated, the analysts on the receiving end often had little context for the bags' contents or the detainee's identity—even when the sticky notes didn't fall off in transit. They had little indication of whether the hard drives or documents came from a mansion owned by an old Baathist or had been found underneath prayer rugs at a jihadi safe house.

When I inspected our intelligence-processing facility at BIAP later that month, I opened a door to a spare room to find it filled with piles of these plastic and burlap bags stuffed with captured material. They appeared unopened.

I returned to Baghdad that evening itching to put my thoughts down on a whiteboard and to hear what everyone else had observed. This is how I do my best thinking, and it was the first of many such collaborative sessions.

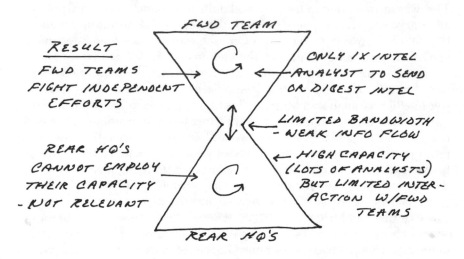

FWD TEAM

RESULT
FWD TEAMS
FIGHT INDEPENDENT
EFFORTS

ONLY 1X INTEL
ANALYST TO SEND
OR DIGEST INTEL

LIMITED BANDWIDTH
- WEAK INFO FLOW

REAR HQ'S
CANNOT EMPLOY
THEIR CAPACITY
- NOT RELEVANT

HIGH CAPACITY
(LOTS OF ANALYSTS)
BUT LIMITED INTER-
ACTION W/FWD
TEAMS

REAR HQ'S

① NEED TO RAPIDLY INCREASE BANDWIDTH TO/FROM FWD TEAMS — CONNECT THEM TO REAR HQ'S

② NEED TO REDISTRIBUTE INTEL PERSONNEL TO BALANCE WORKLOAD

③ NEED TO TIE FWD TEAMS + REAR HQ'S INTO A SINGLE FIGHT

Talking with Scott Miller, I drew an hourglass. The top triangular half represented a forward team, the bottom was the rear headquarters. They met at a narrow choke point, allowing for only a trickle of interaction between the two.

"Would removing this half affect the forward team?" I asked, putting my hand over the bottom triangle.

From what Scott had seen, he said it wouldn't. The rear headquarters were not relevant to the forward teams, as each was fighting an independent campaign. At the very least, targeting a terrorist network was both tedious and violent; starving the teams of information, as we were in the fall of 2003, made the fight sluggish and excruciating. The hourglass diagram portrayed a simple defect in our force's structure. I copied the sketch to a legal pad and left Iraq for Afghanistan with the rudiments of the vision that would drive TF 714's change for the rest of my command.

On October 27, two days after we left Baghdad, Zarqawi's group ushered in Ramadan with the latest in a line of its strategic bombings. That morning, an explosion outside the International Committee of the Red Cross (ICRC) building killed two of its staff and ten Iraqi bystanders. This was the latest in a pattern, although its significance was not then apparent. It began on August 7, when a bomb in a car parked outside the Jordanian embassy in Baghdad exploded, killing seventeen and wounding forty. Two weeks later, at 4:30 P.M. on August 19, a suicide bomber driving a KAMAZ flatbed truck laden with military-grade munitions breached the front gate at the United Nations headquarters in Iraq, detonated the cargo in front of the facade, and collapsed part of the three-story building. Among the twenty-two victims who died was Sergio Vieira de Mello, the head of the U.N. mission in Iraq and a famed expert in postwar reconstruction. The blast also killed Arthur Helton. I had known and liked Arthur from my year at the Council on Foreign Relations in 1999, when I was a colonel and he was the new director of its peace and conflict program. After a second bombing targeted the remnants of the mission on September 22, the U.N. withdrew all but a handful of its staff to Qatar. They wouldn't return in force until late 2007.

Although it was unclear at the time, these attacks against humanitarian organizations proved to be part of Zarqawi's incipient strategy to isolate the Americans and shape the battlefield. Zarqawi clearly hated the Jordanian government, so unalloyed vengeance may have been at play. He blamed the U.N. for giving Palestine "as a gift to the Jews so they can rape the land" and, according to one of the operatives responsible for the attacks, he sought revenge against Vieira de Mello for having helped dismantle an Islamic nation through his work during East Timor's independence. But the real logic to the violence was less histrionic. With the U.N. and ICRC gone, Zarqawi eliminated two organizations that had the experience and niche capacity to help reconstruct Iraq. Perhaps more important, as the war became one of perceptions, by scaring away the U.N., the Red Cross, and other international organizations, Zarqawi ensured that Iraqis increasingly saw only American troops in the streets.

The American efforts to cobble together a wider coalition were largely undone in a handful of explosions. As the months progressed, it looked much more like an American occupation than an international effort.

Meanwhile, in Afghanistan, our forces were planning what we jokingly referred to as General Abizaid's "big-ass operation." The final plan would send a large number of TF 714 forces into eastern Afghanistan, where intelligence reports had placed senior Al Qaeda leadership in the remote crannies of Kunar and Nuristan provinces. Abizaid knew that American presence there—and in fact across all of Afghanistan—was stunningly thin. He could not raise the overall troop numbers because of a cap attributed to Secretary Rumsfeld, so he ordered a temporary surge of TF 714 forces because of our unique agility.

The American military's normal process for moving troops in and around theater was bureaucratic in design and cumbersome in practice—almost the polar opposite of what we now needed. We realized that for TF 714 to execute with the speed and precision this campaign demanded, only a new construct would do. Fortunately, my predecessor, Dell Dailey, had taken a critical step to secure authority for TF 714 to reposition forces without the traditional staffing. It was a farsighted move that proved invaluable.

In November, I was back in Afghanistan for the final days of planning and then implementing what by then was named Operation Winter Strike. Although like most soldiers I was most comfortable when immersed knee deep in the tactical details of an operation, as much as possible I left the planners alone. As Bill Garrison's leadership had taught me, displaying trust and instilling a sense of ownership—and the confidence that comes from it—among the soldiers on the ground was almost always more important than any slight tactical tweaks I might make.

As Winter Strike approached, I moved into an office at the back wall of the tent. The operation would demand long days, so initially I put my rickety aluminum cot next to my desk and encouraged others to do the same. I had watched commanders who remained aloof from their units' actual operations, and I had long ago decided that wasn't right for me. But that was only the first in a long chain of small decisions and tweaks. I had to take into account not only our mission but also the team around me and the tools, like communications and aircraft, at our disposal.

Within weeks of assuming command, I appreciated the complexity of TF 714's task, its geographic dispersion, and the array of relationships we needed to maintain in order to succeed. All of this convinced me that I needed to leverage technology to be able to exercise full command, whether forward in Iraq or Afghanistan, or back in the United States.

Our dispersion also drove us to try different distributions of key leaders across our network. After some trial and error, we spread our three flag officers among our main centers, with one each in Afghanistan, Iraq, and our headquarters at Fort Bragg. Although over the next two and a half years I grew close to my two assistant commanding generals, Dave Scott and Bill McRaven, and I grew close, we weren't able to be physically together in the same room until April 2006, a month before they were promoted to new positions outside TF 714.

The technology and team around a commander were keys to the unit's success, but the command style still depended heavily upon the leader's personality. By nature I tended to trust people and was typically open and transparent with colleagues and subordinates. By providing them tremendous latitude, I believed I accessed greater intellect and judgment. Inclusiveness also instilled a shared sense of ownership, which reduced the danger of my becoming a single point of failure. But such transparency could go astray when others saw us out of context or when I gave trust to those few who were unworthy of it.

While tactically smooth, Winter Strike failed to yield any top Al Qaeda affiliates. Although we already knew slow, ponderous sweeps were no way to target terrorists, the operation confirmed my hunch that the the authorities that provided TF 714 with increased flexibility, was brilliant— but slightly flawed. We needed its proposed web of teams and the preapproved authority to reposition them to respond to emerging threats. But the forces that would respond couldn't be back in the United States waiting for the call. The distance and the necessary bureaucratic deployment approvals would make them too slow and would cause them to lose focus. We needed small nodes, tightly linked together and with an unprecedented ability to act locally. Those local teams would need to be able to make decisions far from the center and would require a network that rapidly marshaled resources, information, and support. To get there TF 714 would need to develop better intelligence.

Winter Strike showed this might be a long road, but we were moving.

▼

CHAPTER 8

The Enemy Emerges

December 2003–April 2004

A bout midday on December 13, 2003, I received a phone call
while back at Fort Bragg. "Sir, we have intelligence. We think
we know where Saddam Hussein is and we're moving on
him now."

The voice on the other end of the secure phone was Rear Admiral Bill
McRaven, one of TF 714's two assistant commanding generals. Bill, then
TF 714's senior officer in Iraq, was a Navy SEAL I'd known off and on for
many years. I had enjoyed the book he wrote, *Spec Ops*, and earlier that
year I had attended his promotion ceremony at the White House, as he
moved from working for Condoleezza Rice at the National Security Council to TF 714. Energetic and iconoclastic, he would be a passionate force in
shaping the command.

Bill's call was welcome news. When I took over TF 714 in October 2003,
Saddam Hussein was still the biggest target in Iraq. We were not the only
unit responsible for his capture—everyone was on the hunt—but the administration and the military looked to us as the premier element. While
his role in the growing violence in Iraq was unclear, we knew we had to
remove him from the equation.

After Bill's call, I went immediately to TF 714's Joint Operations Center at
Bragg. The room, with rows of workstations manned by staff and unit operators facing a wall of video screens, was a buzz of controlled excitement. One
screen displayed an operational log of ongoing activities, and another showed

a live Predator feed of the operation moving on Saddam's assessed location. As we watched, operators from Task Force 16 and soldiers from Ray Odierno's 4th Infantry Division moved down a road that cut through farmland in Ad Dawr, south of Tikrit.* We could see operators moving purposefully through empty courtyards. Bill, calling from the TF 16 operations center at the Baghdad airport, reported intermittently. Although I did not know it at the time, our force had brought along a detainee who had been flipped through the smart manipulation of the task force's interrogation team. After a period of silence, Bill spoke again.

"Okay, they went in there and . . ." He paused. "We've . . . got a guy."

"Do you think it's Saddam Hussein?" I asked. For a few tense moments, the line was quiet.

Then we heard Bill get back on. "He claims he is, sir."

"Well, that's *one* indicator," I said, laughing.

Although less refined than many that would follow, the operations that led to the capture of Saddam gave a glimpse into how TF 714 operations would evolve in the coming years. Using a complex combination of intelligence collected from a variety of sources, including detainees, we slowly laid bare the network around Saddam. While the process was slower and less precise than it would ultimately become, our efforts with conventional-force partners, painstaking exploitation of information, and rapid reaction to emerging leads proved an effective combination.

But I cringed when, on December 14, Ambassador Bremer declared, "Ladies and gentlemen, we got him!" This was the kind of triumphalism that I knew would not play well with the Iraqi people. To me, the presentation evoked memories of the previous April. Soon after the capture of Baghdad, newspaper photographs showed U.S. generals sitting on couches and smoking cigars in one of Saddam's palaces. Annie observed that if she were an Iraqi, even an ardent opponent of Saddam, she would have resented what looked like foreign invaders humiliating Iraq. After Saddam's capture, my gut told me, the Iraqis should have made the announcement and celebrated it as a victory for the new Iraq. The country's government, although it did not technically exist, would need as much credibility as possible when it gained sovereignty the following summer, according to the American timetable.

The scene that followed increased my unease. After Bremer finished, Lieutenant General Sanchez moved to the podium and cued up a video. The monitors on stage first showed shaky nighttime footage of the hole in which

---

*The subordinate task forces that composed Task Force 714 also went by numerical designations. Those numbers changed continually over the years, but for the sake of simplicity I will use one number for each component task force throughout these chapters, even where it is anachronistic. For example, Task Force 16 operated in Iraq, Task Force 328 in Afghanistan, and separate task forces in other locations. Additional task forces were organized over time as our TF 714 mission expanded.

our men had found the toppled dictator. The video then displayed an American medic sifting through his mangy hair with white latex gloves. Sanchez began to narrate, but when he said "Saddam"—clarifying that the raggedy man being prodded was indeed the tyrant—loud whistles and cheers from the audience interrupted him. "Death to Saddam! Death to Saddam!" the Iraqis in the audience, ostensibly reporters, shouted. Men in the front stood up from their seats to cheer. The video rolled on, showing Saddam with a cowlike expression, mouth open and tongue out. Sanchez tried to continue but was interrupted again by shouts and clapping.

The death shouts, likely most loudly voiced by Shia Iraqis, reflected an anger that was largely unimaginable to most Americans. Meanwhile, these images of Saddam and cheers likely amplified fearful questions that had been growing among Sunnis that fall. With Saddam gone, what revenge would these Shia seek? On that day, thermal emotions erupted in outbursts at the monitors. But the anger and fear they both represented and provoked would be cynically tapped and manipulated by both Zarqawi and his Shia opponents, and would lead to mind-numbing internecine cruelty.

Because I had always shared the fairly common army ethos that self-promotion was something quiet professionals eschewed, I was disappointed soon after Saddam's capture when I found out that members of my force had given President Bush the pistol found with Saddam in his spider hole. While I understood the desire of the team to thank a president they had followed in combat since 9/11, I felt such an act smacked too much of currying favor. My opinion changed somewhat in 2008 when I went with then–Brigadier General Scott Miller to the Oval Office to brief President Bush. He showed us the pistol, which he had kept in a framed exhibition case. I realized the gesture had, in fact, meant much to a person in the loneliest of jobs, wartime commander-in-chief.

Any optimism Saddam's capture brought was short lived, and a growing Sunni insurgency was emerging as the principal threat in Iraq. The de-Baathification decision from the previous summer, which reduced Sunni presence in key positions, reinforced Sunnis' fears that the fall of Saddam would leave them disenfranchised in the face of Shia dominance. The dissolution of the Iraqi army stoked those fears and pushed thousands of trained potential fighters into an economy wracked by unemployment. Severe electricity shortages—which deprived Iraqis of fans or air-conditioning in the searing summer and convinced many that the high-tech American military withheld basic services out of spite—brought frustrations to a boil.

Particularly troubling was the assessment that one of Green's top intel analysts, then-Major Wayne Barefoot, brought when he came to my office in Iraq two weeks after Saddam's arrest, during the first week of January.

"Sir," Wayne said, "we have good reason to believe Zarqawi is in Iraq." Although we knew he had been in northern Iraq on the cusp of the American invasion, and attacks over the summer and fall had borne his hallmark, this was the first time we had felt certain he was setting up shop in the country. "And, sir," Wayne continued, "we believe he's building up a network." Most troubling, the Jordanian operative seemed to be angling to control the growing Iraqi uprising.

At the time, my focus was still primarily on the venues where we believed Al Qaeda's command structure lay, Afghanistan and Pakistan. I sensed but didn't fully appreciate at the time what Zarqawi's presence in Iraq augured. He was preparing to shift the group's center of gravity from the Hindu Kush to Anbar. But his growing impact also represented a broader post-9/11 change in the nature and networking of Al Qaeda, as our pressure had forced the group to move beyond its core-guided organizational model in the 1990s. We were seeing more, but Al Qaeda's command structure remained opaque.

On 9/11, Al Qaeda still largely organized its movement as it had at its inception thirteen years earlier. On an international scale, it mirrored the model of native insurgent movements I had studied throughout my career. This model included three concentric circles: a core group, enclosed by support elements, with auxiliary components on the periphery.

The core was a bureaucracy. Bin Laden led from the top as emir, consulted with an advisery council, and directed the group. Beneath him were committees in charge of religious authorization, military affairs, finance, the group's security, and propaganda. From here, bin Laden exerted command and control and distributed resources. Still building its brand, Al Qaeda needed its attacks to be spectacular and successful. Through what an Al Qaeda defector called "centralization of decision and decentralization of execution," the leadership selected targets and approved proposals that came from below. The bulk of the planning, equipping, and execution was delegated to the local parts of the network, which received guidance and funds as necessary from the professionals in the top-level Military Affairs Committee.

As they planned and executed the attacks, local cells adopted a more traditional terrorist "blind" cell model, whereby the links among its members were limited. Single intermediaries—cutouts—connected different clusters, so arresting one or a number of members only made a limited dent in the organization. If a detainee could resist questioning long enough, the people he knew could scramble and reposition, maintaining the integrity of the cell. The night before the attack on the embassy in Nairobi in 1998, all members of Al Qaeda left East Africa except those preparing to kill themselves in the trucks and those staying to clean their tracks.

The auxiliary support for the group included the networks that funneled donations from sympathetic patrons in the Gulf, in Europe, and elsewhere. Al Qaeda had unofficial partnerships with at least twenty other groups, some of which bin Laden attempted to bring under his control.

Attraction to the brand during the late 1990s was most noticeable in the robust training camps Al Qaeda established, primarily in Afghanistan.

These camps trained and indoctrinated between ten thousand and twenty thousand (estimates ranged as high as seventy thousand) young Muslim men in the way of modern jihad. Some of those trainees came from hard, poor lives. Many were well-to-do men who had science and engineering degrees but had never fired a gun. Al Qaeda adopted the pedagogy of bin Laden's influential high-school gym teacher, who had mixed Koranic study with soccer—running violent, macho physical training alongside indoctrination classes that fed a narrow but potent ideology.

To spur innovation, the leadership invited attendees to brainstorm and share their own macabre ideas about how to kill a lot of Americans and Jews. At the same time, the organization enforced some strict tenets of its own. For example, it ensured that suicide bombing became an Al Qaeda trademark by belaboring the prestige of such "martyrdom operations."

Like a spinneret, these camps spit out the threads that would compose the web of the growing network. While a small portion of these trainees remained in the core—staying to fight the Northern Alliance or graduating to advanced training—the camps ensured that the organization had supporters and agents of varying commitment worldwide. As the men returned to their corners of the world, including western Europe, they did so with strong links to fellow jihadists. At times, those global relationships crossed social strata or cultural divides they wouldn't have crossed before the camps. Even as these men dispersed, they did so bonded by a shared consciousness. They saw the same "problem" and endorsed the same strategy for redress: to restore Muslim pride and dignity by demonstrating moral and political strength, largely through violence. By 1999, their increasingly thick network stretched across sixty countries.

Those durable relationships made the movement difficult to target, as its dynamics were often known only to the people who shared those bonds. We tried to think of it less as an organization easily defined by a hierarchical chart and talked instead of associations and a network of relationships: Who communicated with whom? Who was married to whose sister or daughter? Who, ultimately, influenced whom?

September 11 represented the high-water mark of Al Qaeda's triumph. Even a dedicated enemy of Osama bin Laden could acknowledge the impressive operational feat of simultaneously hijacking four airliners and crashing three into different buildings. The attacks also established Al Qaeda as a brand. Thenceforth, no group was more recognizable as the credible, effective Islamic resistance to America. Its appeal swelled beyond the confines of the jihadist community. But the swift response by the United States quickly forced the organization to adapt.

By 2004, a number of trends were making the group more effective but also more vulnerable. Bin Laden and his core group were increasingly isolated and on the run, and he was less able to maintain meaningful control over the disparate network. For the survival of the brand, the group needed to remain active. As a result, power and authority devolved from the center to the outer parts of the network, which would thenceforth make decisions that central committees had previously made.

Beginning in 2003, this decentralization forced Al Qaeda to rely on what became known as its "franchises"—in Algeria, Libya, Saudi Arabia, Yemen, Somalia, and Iraq. The first of these had appeared the previous spring in Saudi Arabia, when in May 2003 a new group operating under the name Al Qaeda in the Land of Two Holy Places set off car bombs in three Western housing compounds in Riyadh. Their cells comprised core Al Qaeda members operating under orders from bin Laden, though most of the country-based franchises would not be created through large transplants from central Al Qaeda. Veteran Al Qaeda cadres would offer guidance, but the franchises were increasingly jihadist groups that had existed or started somewhat independently. As they grew in prominence and ambition, they joined Al Qaeda by taking its name and benefited from its image as *the* global resistance to the United States. What had been a weakness of the Al Qaeda brand—its narrowly extreme but global ambitions—now reinforced it. We would soon learn much more about how these groups functioned through our close-quarters battle with what became the most violent and most powerful of the franchises—that which was led by Zarqawi in Iraq.

As Al Qaeda increasingly decentralized, the core's practical role changed. It did not act as a central hub of funding or logistical support. If anything, funds flowed from local groups back to Al Qaeda central, though the network was not designed to distribute resources. Rather, each of the local elements became self-resourcing and self-reinforcing, drawing recruits and money on its own. Cut off from central support, these elements rapidly adapted to local conditions.

But Al Qaeda's core still mattered as more than a symbol of the organization's survival. Foreign volunteers increasingly went directly to a battlefield, not through training camps, though directing this flow by endorsing certain fronts remained one lever Al Qaeda's senior leadership retained over the outer network. Moreover, it was still a resource pool, only now it offered men who had a decade or two of experience and specialized training. As jihadists, they had risen to the top of the organization and survived hot conflicts and Western intelligence efforts. They were vulnerable when they circulated battlefields, but less so when they mentored and guided through communiqués. So while decentralization made the core less relevant in day-to-day operations, it made the top leadership in some ways even more valuable, as it sought to preserve the brand and maintain disciplined messaging while often relying on less experienced, less loyal affiliates. But interactions with the center were slow, as CDs or letters literally had to be carried across countries, and leaders could only make some decisions in rare meetings. The jihadists knew communicating by cell phone or e-mail was dangerous.

I concluded there was no single person or place we could strike that would cause Al Qaeda to collapse; there was no coup de main option. But TF 714 could target two of the enemy's surfaces. We had to attack the organization head on as it sprouted up locally while also targeting its upper echelons of leadership. Doing so would deplete the organization of its entrenched expertise and institutional wisdom, although such skills and know-how existed in the increasingly powerful local elements. If onlookers saw that the organization was losing—fleeing territory, hemorrhaging people—its brand would suffer.

While we had some tactical advantages, we were, in some ways, years behind the enemy. Defeating Al Qaeda would be a protracted campaign.

Early on, counterproductive infighting among the CIA, State Department, Department of Defense, and others back in Washington threatened that campaign. No one had less patience for this than did John Abizaid, so he chose his Tampa headquarters to hold the January 2004 conference in which he convened and focused key organizations for the war on terror. The United States was fighting most of the war in General Abizaid's theater, and he was not satisfied with the way it was going. At this meeting, which we later called Tampa I, Abizaid brought together the key intelligence officials and military commanders assigned to hunt Al Qaeda's senior leadership in Afghanistan and Pakistan. I was TF 714's senior representative; General Doug Brown and then–Vice Admiral Eric Olson came from SOCOM; the National Security Agency sent representatives; and my friend for two decades, Dave Rodriguez, then a brigadier, represented the Joint Staff. But the attendee who mattered most for Abizaid's purposes—to free the war on terror from the pettiness of D.C. so we could redouble our focus and cooperation—was CIA director George Tenet.

At the circular table, Abizaid explained his conviction that, two years after 9/11, the United States had lost focus against Al Qaeda. The fight would be longer and more difficult than the initial decimation of Al Qaeda in the opening salvo of the Afghan war might suggest. Our focus, durable commitment, and ingenuity needed to be extraordinary.

"We need a new Manhattan Project," he said, referring to the American effort during the Second World War to beat the Axis powers in the race for an atom bomb.

It was important, then, when Tenet struck the same chord of renewed commitment and teamwork. "Okay, everybody, let's dedicate ourselves to getting UBL *this year*," he said, tapping the table with his two forefingers as he said these last two words. His appeal seemed feasible, and the room nodded. I was impressed with Tenet's obvious desire to increase partnership. With that, Tampa I set the precedent for organizing our effort. Abizaid convened the group and ran the meeting, and the CIA sent its top man. It was an important first step toward moving cooperation from gestures to action.

At the end of the meeting, I proposed translating this enthusiasm into military gains by bringing to bear all of the potential intelligence resources of the U.S. government. "In no class of warfare," C. E. Callwell had written a hundred years earlier, about the "small wars" of the nineteenth century, "is a well organized and well served intelligence department more essential than in that against guerrillas." The same qualities that made intelligence so important when countering guerrillas then—the difficulty of finding the enemy, of striking him, and of predicting his next move and defending against it—were increased a hundredfold when trying to counter terrorists in the age of electronic communication and car bombs. I began to see that in addition to rewiring our own force, we had to make our relationship with the intelligence agencies, particularly the CIA, deeper and broader. Based on an assumption that we could not be a SOF-only task force, or even a military-only task force, I had earlier accepted Bill McRaven's recommendation that we seek to form a true joint interagency task force (JIATF). While the concept of a JIATF was not new, it would prove a transformative step for TF 714.

I explained to the group that this JIATF would be a way to fuse the various intelligence agencies' specialties in order to better understand the enemy. It would leverage the CIA's "human intelligence" from spies and sources; the National Security Agency's intercepted signals; the FBI's forensic and investigative expertise; the Defense Intelligence Agency's military reach; and the National Geospatial-Intelligence Agency's (NGA) dazzling mapping ability.

Previous attempts at this fusion had existed before and after 9/11 with varying success. But for counterterrorism efforts, while the intelligence was collected in theater, it was typically consolidated in the United States. This allowed for centralized analysis by the limited community of experienced counterterrorism (CT) professionals and senior-level decision making for the sensitive, high-risk operations periodically required. But proximity to Washington also had costs. The Beltway culture compelled, or allowed, the agencies to be less collaborative. Valuable information that might slide across a table downrange had to cross miles and clear bureaucratic hurdles back in the States. In Washington, the myriad essential but competing priorities, from bureaucracy to family life, always slowed action.

For this reason, the JIATF would bring analysts from each agency into the same literal tent—and that tent would be on a base in Afghanistan or Iraq. Obviously, this would enable intelligence to be analyzed downrange, close to the fight, making the process faster and the information potentially more relevant. Less obvious but more important, having the analysts live and operate forward, teamed with counterparts from other agencies, decreased the gravitational pull of their headquarters back in D.C. and dramatically increased the sense of shared mission and purpose. It was extraordinarily powerful for analysts to share information, to brief operators on their assessments, to hear the rotors of an assault force launching on their information, and then to debrief together after the operation.

Very quickly after the conference, the JIATF took its place at Bagram in a tent next to others originally erected for Operation Winter Strike but now permanent fixtures at the old Soviet air base. The goodwill and camaraderie that brimmed in the room in Tampa undersold just how big a challenge it would be to get the agencies—through their representatives in that tent—to work together. And while the day-to-day leadership inside the JIATF tent fell to our most deft TF 714 members, much of my next four and a half years was consumed with shoring up support at the top levels by keeping participation in the JIATF and our wider task force a top priority.

No alliance could be as infuriating or as productive as my relationship with the CIA. We worked more closely with it than with any other agency, and the effort tried the patience of both sides. Some of my closest friendships at the end of the fight were with CIA partners. In a frame on my wall at home I have a note, written on a page torn from a small notebook while in the back of a helicopter flying over Kunar in 2005. The man who scratched the note was a CIA officer who became a close comrade and friend. The note reads: "I don't know the Ranger Creed. But you can bet your sweet ass I won't leave you!"

And yet more than once, my most trusted subordinates had to stop me, in moments of utter frustration, from severing all ties with our "Agency brothers," repeating back to me my own guidance to preserve our relationships through specific conflicts. I knew my Agency partners had equally mixed sentiments about me, and I admired them for their tolerance. On my initial October tour, I had visited the CIA headquarters at Langley, as well as the posts downrange where we had liaisons. Depending on the locale and the personalities, special operations and the CIA worked together only marginally better than they had during Operation Eagle Claw in 1980. At best, we were fighting parallel, fractured campaigns against Al Qaeda; ours had to be a unified fight.

Not everyone in the CIA agreed. For those people, the relationship with us was good because it was limited. Their hesitance was understandable. Many of them were skittish as the military—led by TF 714—began to take a more active role in the counterterror effort. The entire CIA had about as many people as a single military division, and some feared that when the Department of Defense directed its immense resources toward counterterrorism, it would overwhelm the CIA, reducing their role. Some maintained a legitimate concern that our proposal ran contrary to how the Agency operated, as Langley had been the furnace of their intelligence work, while security concerns meant that they maintained a light footprint forward. Others had a more instinctive cultural aversion that fueled their intense professional territoriality. As the junior varsity, thundering in loud and large, TF 714 was liable to muck up their careful spy work, and we would have leaks. I had to clench my teeth at one meeting when a not particularly impressive ex-military CIA officer smugly said, "Welcome to the war on terror." Building a durable relationship was an exercise of persistence and patience more than brilliance.

Government agencies signaled their feeling toward TF 714's expanding presence in their community through the caliber of representatives they sent to the JIATF and the orders they gave them. Some sent their best talent; others deployed people they wouldn't miss. They deployed some talented people with instructions to be polite, but narrowly limited their cooperation; a few others came fully committed to the team.

With this mixed influx of people, the JIATF was an early step in expanding TF 714 beyond its traditional core elements, and the diversity brought its ups and its downs. Participants came with fascinating stories or created them by their actions. A young navy lieutenant told me of her Afghan birth and how she'd fled the Soviet invasion with her family as a young child, riding on the back of a donkey through the Khyber Pass. Now an American citizen, she was back, and her determination carried a buzz felt by those she worked alongside. Another officer, gifted in intelligence analysis but less so in weapons, accidentally discharged his M16 rifle inside the JIATF tent. No one was hurt, but the bullet pierced a fire extinguisher, and out of the gaping "wound" white foam spewed into the NGA's computer servers, which stored all of the map data for the task force, ruining one of our key databases of information. Although it became a much-loved anecdote within the command, it wasn't funny at the time.

For many, the JIATF was an entirely new experience, in some ways an adventure. Whether fresh out of school and only weeks out of their host agency's training, or nearing retirement, few were accustomed to the demanding rhythm and spare living of deployments. Away from the ties, traffic, and fluorescent-lit cubicle pens of D.C., they found themselves living crudely and briefing broad-shouldered operators who, often in a matter of hours, and sometimes in minutes, would launch on missions using the intelligence the JIATF provided. For most of the twenty-five to thirty-five people working there, this was the most exhausting, frustrating, but deeply rewarding work of their career.

The JIATF at Bagram was not a tipping point for our effectiveness, but it was an essential step forward. It wasn't until 2005 that the JIATF and its counterpart created at Balad that year really began to hit their stride as nodes for focused analysis and hubs to connect the contributing organizations. The stand-up of the JIATF that spring began the process of turning TF 714 from a collection of niche strike forces into a network able to integrate diverse elements of the U.S. government into a unified effort.

As we built our new network, Zarqawi used his to spark the recrudescence of a bloody, centuries-old hatred. After a spring attack on the Shia in southern Iraq, a French diplomat in Baghdad summed up the terror in his report: "We have recently seen a horrible example of the Wahhabis'

Valuable background

cruel fanaticism in the terrible fate of Imam Hussein," meaning the holy Shiite mosque in the city of Karbala. His reaction would be a familiar lament to any observer of the Iraq war.

Yet the attack the Frenchman described had occurred in the spring of 1802, when Wahhabis were a new puritanical Sunni movement, led by Muhammad ibn Abd al-Wahhab, an Arabian desert preacher who believed that Islam had been diverted, deceived, and made weak. Only strict Koranic literalism would restore Islamic society to its pure, strong form. Wahhabis had come north to Iraq from the Nejd and Hejaz as part of Ibn Saud's army, which he was using to conquer the peninsula. That day in Karbala was a chance to enforce one of the Wahhabis' precepts: The Shia were infidels, corroding the nation of Islam. Their mosques were monuments of idolatry, their rituals blasphemy. And this demanded action.

Witnesses later reported to the French consul in Baghdad that "12,000 Wahhabis suddenly attacked Imam Husain," killing men, women, and children. "It is said," he reported, "that whenever they saw a pregnant woman, they disemboweled her and left the fetus on the mother's bleeding corpse." The Wahhabi attack was religiously motivated but caused political disruptions. It weakened the central authority in Baghdad, showing it unable or unwilling to protect Shiites and their holy sites. This provoked the Persians, who would need to come guard their fellow Shiites and their sacred mosques.

In the two centuries between the rise of al-Wahhab and the emergence of Zarqawi, a number of strains competed and overlapped within the radical wing of Sunni Islam. Zarqawi's Salafist jihadism owed much to the Wahhabi creed, though in its violent political manifestation that Zarqawi pushed, it sought to outdo the Wahhabis where they were too passive or too compromising. While anti-Shiism was ingrained in these ideologies, even the most violent Salafist groups that emerged in the late twentieth century had largely avoided the sectarian targeting on display in Karbala in the spring of 1802. Strategically, Zarqawi resuscitated that hatred, and in the spring of 2004 he prepared an attack on that same Iraqi city with largely the same religious motivations, aiming to achieve strikingly similar political aftereffects.

The strike augured a campaign strategy that had become clearer to us at the end of January. In spite of the attacks Zarqawi orchestrated in the fall of 2003 against the U.N. and the ICRC, we were not certain he was in Iraq until the end of the year. But with Saddam now captured and the remnant Baathists increasingly rolled up, Zarqawi became our primary focus. As he did, our understanding of him took an ominous leap forward.

During the third week of January, Kurdish Peshmerga forces arrested a Pakistani Al Qaeda operative named Hassan Ghul near Iraq's northeastern border. Acting as a courier, Ghul was carrying two CDs and a thumb drive, which yielded a letter written from Zarqawi to bin Laden and Zawahiri. A dispatch from Iraq, the letter described the scene for the senior Al Qaeda leaders holed up in Pakistan, and laid out the strategy Zarqawi would pursue with brutish consistency for the next two and a half years. The Americans were a threat, he acknowledged. But like bin Laden before him, Zarqawi dismissed us as a paper tiger. "They are an easy quarry, praise be to God." Rather, the Shia were the "insurmountable obstacle, the lurking snake, the crafty and malicious scorpion, the spying enemy, and the penetrating venom."

The Iraqi Sunnis had yet to realize this threat—or to coalesce behind Zarqawi's ranks. So he cast his foreign jihadists as the true keepers of the faith, the hard edge of the insurgency, and the only defense against the Shia. To jolt the Sunnis from their torpor, in which, he contended, the Shia would slaughter them, Zarqawi had a simple strategy. He planned regular and merciless attacks against Shiite civilians, which would provoke Shia reprisals until the back-and-forth escalated to full sectarian war, stoking the rage and sympathy of Sunnis worldwide and bringing the "Islamic nation" to the fight as volunteers and supporters. The new Iraqi government, which the Shia were clearly going to dominate, was the main obstacle to making Baghdad the seat of the reestablished caliphate. Only in the high pitch of an ethnic war would the Sunnis win. In that hell, Al Qaeda would reign.

The Coalition released the letter to the public. Three weeks later, Zarqawi made good on his promises. On Tuesday, March 2, Shia believers from around Iraq and from abroad entered Karbala, the site of the Wahhabi massacre 202 years earlier. For the first time in almost thirty years, these Shia were free to celebrate Ashura in that holy city. For decades, a political desire to suppress Shia identity had driven Saddam to ban the festival.

That Tuesday morning, Zarqawi's operatives, outfitted with suicide bombs assembled in Fallujah garages, were positioned inside Karbala. Others waited to fire mortars into the crowd, as a prominent Kuwaiti cleric damned the Ashura rituals that would take place that day as "the world's biggest display of heathens and idolatry." At 10:00 A.M., with the streets lined, multiple suicide bombs exploded where people were most densely packed in the streets, near choke points, outside a hotel and a shrine. Desperate pilgrims beseeched the panicked crowds not to step in the pools of blood or on the bits of flesh and limbs scattered on the pavement, to avoid profaning them. At roughly the same time, multiple bombs popped in a Shia neighborhood in Baghdad. All told, the day ended with at least 169 dead and hundreds wounded.

Zarqawi's campaign against the Shia was more than political. It was fueled by a visceral hatred and repugnance and a dogmatic theological commitment. But as the 1802 massacre had done for a spell, Zarqawi's Ashura bombings, the loudest of an increasing drumbeat of anti-Shia attacks, succeeded in nudging the political realignment his strategy required. Zarqawi wanted Iraq to be contested by extremists, not forged by moderates. Shortly after the twin attacks in Baghdad and Karbala, militias patrolled these cities, portraying themselves as the protectors of their fellow Shia. If Shia lost faith in the ability of the new Iraq project to secure them, they might turn to the volatile militias, the Iranian-backed Badr Brigades, and the growing if more ragtag ranks of Muqtada al-Sadr. These more radical, demagogic groups were liable to conduct anti-Sunni reprisals.

And yet civil war did not erupt that spring. Zarqawi's persistent and fatal campaign of anti-Shia attacks did not set off the sectarian schism he sought as early as we thought it would. At that time, at least, sectarian war was not in the long-term interest of the Shia, who, as the majority, would be empowered under a democracy. Even while patrols of Shia militias took to the streets, Shia clerics worked to discount Zarqawi's narrative and dampen sectarian feeling, blaming the Americans instead of the Sunnis. This reflected considerable restraint and, less charitably, a fractured and disorganized Shia political community.

Armchair analysts too often caricatured Iraq as a place of sectarian tinder that was easily lit after we removed Saddam. It was easy to forget, having watched the country fall into civil war, that Iraq in the fall of 2003 and spring of 2004 was not riven along sectarian lines. Iraqis rarely thought of themselves primarily in religious or ethnic terms. Although the Sunni-Shia split had been exploited and frozen under Saddam, there did exist a national Iraqi identity—in part attained through common aspirations toward unity, in part forged in the trenches and minefields along the border war with Iran in the 1980s. While a contest over resources and political power was inevitable, there remained genuine interest—among Shiites and Sunnis—to work with the Americans following Saddam's fall. The ease with which we forget this fact—and the stubborn refusal of Iraqi leadership to overcome the sectarian paranoia once it became entrenched—is a legacy of Zarqawi.

Zarqawi aimed to get Iraqis to see one another as he saw them. And to him they were not countrymen or colleagues or neighbors or in-laws or classmates. They were either fellow believers or an enemy to be feared and, in that fear, extinguished. Zarqawi's rabid anti-Shiism increasingly drove his organization to be less focused on driving the Americans out of Iraq and more bent on attacking Iraqis. In the years ahead, Zarqawi—obstinate and powerful enough to fend off critics—almost succeeded.

That spring, the logic of Zarqawi's violence was hazier than it would become later. But the sheer ferocity of these attacks, and the terroristic tendency they lent to the insurgency, convinced me this fight would be long and difficult. From history, I knew of the moral and political traps awaiting forces conducting counterinsurgency or counterterrorism operations, and I wanted us to confront them directly before we found ourselves acting in ways counter to our values or our cause. TF 714 would need to acquire roles and expertise that would demand clear mental, moral, and operational focus. For this reason, I called my commanders together for a conference at Bagram the first week of April 2004.

Periodic commanders' conferences were especially valuable for TF 714.

Given our geographic dispersion and the insularity and elitism ingrained in some of our units, they helped us build a sense of teamwork across the force and aligned our strategy. The Bagram conference convened key TF 714 staff; the flag officers heading the country task forces; and commanders, deputy commanders, and senior enlisted advisers of the component units. Everyone flew into our base on the Bagram airfield. There we still operated out of big canvas tents and rudimentary plywood huts filled with metal folding chairs and folding tables.

As early as our October trip, Scott Miller, the Green deputy at the time, had said we would be deluding ourselves to think we weren't facing a full, and growing, insurgency in Iraq. He had been reading about the French experience in the insurgencies of the midcentury. We had both read *Modern Warfare*, a compact 1961 treatise by the French military theorist Roger Trinquier, but I read it again that spring after Scott passed me a photocopy of the book. While we disagreed with many of the hard-edged solutions Trinquier endorsed, his analysis of the challenge was instructive.

At the conference I decided to show *The Battle of Algiers*. The film is a fictional but historically accurate portrayal of the French 10th Parachute Division, which deployed in 1957 to secure the city after the National Liberation Front (FLN) insurgency overwhelmed the ability of the Algiers police to suppress it. Additionally, I had the commanders read *Modern Warfare*, but I did not attach any message or opinion when I sent it to them. I wanted them to come with fresh opinions. We also brought Professor Douglas Porch, one of the foremost scholars of French military counterinsurgency campaigns, to Bagram from California.

On the morning of the second day, we watched the film and then had a lively two-hour discussion. Intentionally, I allowed the conversation to flow. As is so often the case, the senior enlisted advisers, in particular, were sharp students of these issues. I felt it was critical that these leaders drew and articulated their own conclusions. But they also needed to understand my personal view, so there could be no ambiguity about what I expected. In order to show the thinking that led to my conclusions, I reminded the group of two powerful scenes from the film. The first showed the fundamental ignorance of the French about the deeply ingrained nature of the FLN insurgency in Algerian daily life. Pointing to one of the walls, I told the group assembled, "We fundamentally do not understand what is going on outside the wire."

The second scene addressed torture head on. I believed that—even with the heated post-9/11 outrage felt by Americans—such a tactic would be self-defeating, and the film opened a window for me to address concerns I had about our nation's detainee operations since I had taken command. I had been deeply unimpressed with the interrogation facilities at Bagram when I first deployed to Afghanistan in 2002. Our nation's lack of institutional wisdom gnawed at me. In preparing for the conference, I distilled two thoughts. First, how we conducted ourselves was critical, and the force needed to uniformly believe that. Doing less would dishonor the service of those I led. Second, I was convinced that detainees presented an operational risk: If we got it wrong, TF 714 would be taken out of the fight and might even be disbanded. Three weeks after our conference, we saw the pictures CBS broadcast of Americans abusing prisoners at Abu Ghraib prison. The rest of the world, of course, saw them as well.

As we were meeting, events in Iraq were altering the course of the war and TF 714's relationship to it. On the day the conference began, then-Colonel Bennet Sacolick, the commander of Green, called from Baghdad. He needed to stay in Iraq, he explained, because four American contractors had been ambushed and killed in Fallujah, which was then beginning to tremor with widespread violence.

When I had made the decision the previous fall to hold the April commanders' conference at Bagram, our main focus had been in Afghanistan and neighboring Pakistan, where the primary Al Qaeda threat was amassed. The events in the weeks that followed the contractors' killing would change all that. The grisly images from the Fallujah attack—and the convulsive violence they augured—soon made the purse bombs and chicly dressed Algerian terrorists from *The Battle of Algiers* seem quaint.

▼

CHAPTER 9

Big Ben

April–June 2004

I n early April 2004, the meltdown in Fallujah cut short my stay in Afghanistan. Until that time, my command group and I had largely flown around theater on scheduled conventional military flights. Now we summoned one of our MC-130 special operations aircraft in the middle of the night. Listening to the throaty rumble of the planes' engines across the darkened tarmac, I was anxious to get to Iraq. I sensed that the tenor of the war had changed and that a critical point in the fight against Al Qaeda was waiting for us there.

A week earlier, a very public horror show in Iraq had prevented Bennet Sacolick from attending our commanders' conference in Afghanistan. The previous Wednesday, three trucks with empty flatbeds had driven down Highway 10 into Fallujah, en route to the American base west of the city to pick up kitchen equipment. This was more dangerous than it sounds. Four American contractors, working for the private security firm Blackwater, split between two unarmored Mitsubishi Pajeros, escorted the trucks. At the entrance to the city, a group of Iraqi national guardsmen joined the convoy. The vehicles were stopped at a checkpoint on the east side of the city and apprised of the Marines' assessment of the dangerous situation. But they continued on. Already, insurgents had planned an ambush. That morning, shop owners along the route had reportedly shuttered their storefronts and terrified residents hid indoors, while the insurgents had prepared the emptied street for the assault.

The American convoy drove along the main road through Fallujah. It continued past the corner where, weeks earlier, our TF 714 vehicles had taken a right into the residential neighborhood where we had searched houses, looking for Zarqawi, and found glaring faces. Once into the denser commercial center of town, the contractors entered the kill zone. The cars in front of the second American SUV halted, boxing it in. Insurgents rushed toward the car from the sidewalks, firing AK-47s, perforating the Pajero's red doors and windows. With the pop of gunfire behind them, the lead SUV tried to maneuver, accelerating, then leaping the raised median. But insurgents were quickly only feet away from the vehicle's windows, raking the car with bullets. They fired until the Pajero slammed into another car and juddered to a stop, its driver slumped over. The four Americans died in their seats.

With camcorders rolling, a crowd rushed to the cars and set them ablaze. When the flames subsided they dragged the bodies onto the pavement. They beat the corpses with sticks until they fell apart and trailed the bodies, or parts of them, behind cars. A maroon sedan honked playfully as the crowd—which reportedly included Iraqi police, children, and women— circled around the back bumper and shouted, "Fallujah is the cemetery of the Americans!" Paper fliers saying the same had been printed and distributed to the crowd to hold up in front of news cameramen. The crowd and cars moved to the southwest edge of town, where they tied the charred remains of two Americans to the beams of the green trestle Old Bridge. Men and young boys climbed the supports in order to reach out with sticks and shoes to hit the blackened, deformed corpses swaying over a crowd assembled and chanting below. One Baghdadi told the Los Angeles Times "with disbelief" that in Fallujah he saw "adolescent boys . . . carrying pieces of charred human flesh on sticks 'as if they were lollipops.' "

This was the most grievous display of overt resistance to American control since the war began. It hit close to home: One of the contractors was a former Navy SEAL, and the other three were former Rangers. Wes Batalona, who had been our operations sergeant at the 3rd Ranger Battalion in 1988 and 1989, was in the driver seat of the lead vehicle. The images recalled the decade-old videos showing the bodies of men from our command being dragged through the streets of Mogadishu.

Even before this event—and the two subsequent loud, dusty, bitter urban battles fought in the city—gave the name "Fallujah" a sinister if vague ring to Americans, the place had been tinder under the American occupation. I had visited a few times that spring and knew the city of 285,000 was a religious place. Once an ancient nexus of trade routes, it was now a tough trucker town and a smuggling hub. But it was also deeply conservative and proud of its moniker "city of mosques," boasting 133 of them. Industrial compounds just north of the city had produced chemical weapons for Saddam, drawing the suspicion of the U.N. inspectors.

By the time I arrived in Baghdad on Monday, April 5, Marine battalions had breached Fallujah's outer rim, entering all four quadrants of the city in the opening stage of what became known as the First Battle of Fallujah.

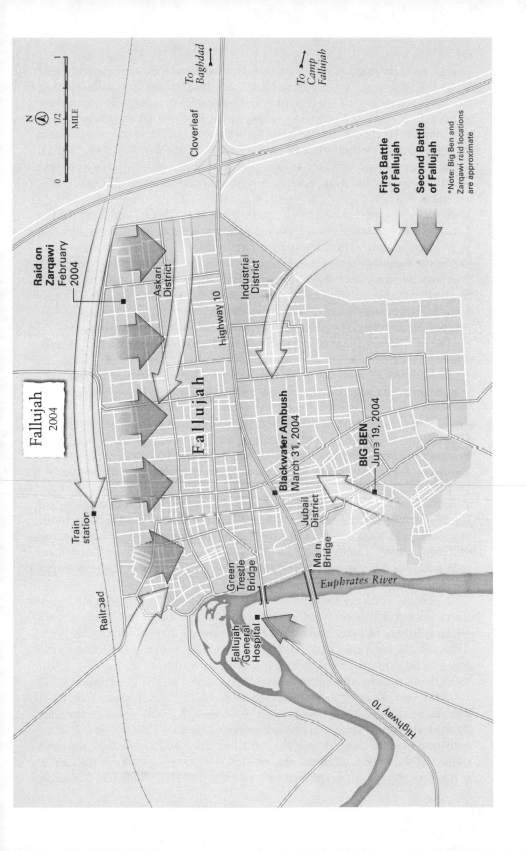

Fallujah
2004

N

0   1/2   1
MILE

To Baghdad

To Camp Fallujah

First Battle of Fallujah

Second Battle of Fallujah

*Note: Big Ben and Zarqawi raid locations are approximate

Cloverleaf

Raid on Zarqawi February 2004

Askari District

Industrial District

Highway 10

F a l l u j a h

Train station

Railroad

Blackwater Ambush March 31, 2004

BIG BEN June 19, 2004

Jubail District

Main Bridge

Green Trestle Bridge

Euphrates River

Fallujah General Hospital

Highway 10

They began their assault at 1:00 A.M., having cordoned the city the night before. Others have well documented the grinding, costly battles for Fallujah, waged largely by the Marines. But unknown to most, the events there shaped TF 714 and changed our story, as we accepted an expanded role in the fight. Even then I didn't know the city would take center stage—and that events there would alter the course of the war. Nor did I fully understand the conditions in the city that would vault Zarqawi and his network, in turn spurring our force's evolution to contain the jihadists' violent expansion.

The city that would host this first clash between TF 714 and Al Qaeda in Iraq had a long, combustible history. To limit resistance to his control in Fallujah, Saddam established a system of patronage with the Sunni tribesmen of the town, frequently recruiting his government officials from the city, which was home to many military officers. Many of these Baathists returned to Fallujah after their army was disbanded in May 2003, seeding the city with disgruntled, trained military men. The city's complex social mixture, relatively inert under Saddam, grew more combustible due to American actions.

The 82nd Airborne was responsible for the city following the fall of Saddam in April 2003, but the population quickly turned against them. In truth, the people may never have been theirs to win. Rumors—like that suggesting that the paratroopers' night-vision goggles allowed them to see through the garments of Fallujah's women—increased distrust and hostility. On April 28, 2003, soon after the U.S. invasion, a crowd of about 150 Fallujans marched on a school the 82nd had occupied, demanding the paratroopers vacate. Reports differ as to what provoked the violent clash that followed. According to the 82nd, they returned fire after being shot at by youths in the crowd. Fallujans claimed the crowd had no guns and called it an atrocity. In the end, seventeen Iraqis were dead and another seventy-five injured. They remembered that the Americans offered no apology, no monetary compensation even as a gesture. Fallujans would refer to the shooting as "the massacre" for years afterward, and although the Marines who took over from the 82nd sought to dispense money for the damages, many of the proud Fallujans rejected it.

A year later, during the final week of March 2004, the 1st Marine Expeditionary Force was set to take over all of Anbar. In the weeks leading up to the transfer, Fallujah had become increasingly hostile. In addition to the unsuccessful night raid described in the previous chapter, I had gone to the city several other times to meet with 82nd Airborne leadership. Stretched thin, the 82nd ran only limited patrols through the city. On February 12, General Abizaid had gone with the division commander to visit a new Iraqi army unit organized in Fallujah. As John and the Iraqi boss of the unit chatted in Arabic, rocket-propelled grenades hit their compound, fired by insurgents from nearby rooftops. John left calm and unscathed, but two days later the same compound was hit again. In a sophisticated assault, fifty insurgents spread across the city and attacked that Iraqi army compound to prevent its soldiers from coming to the rescue of the much less fortified mayor's office and police station, which another group of insurgents was striking. They freed eighty-seven prisoners and killed at least twenty Iraqi policemen. As insurgents gained a foothold in Fallujah, they used it as a base of operations. From there, earlier that March, Sunni insurgents had dispatched the suicide bombers to Karbala and Baghdad for the attacks on the Ashura procession. Later that spring, a jihadist tape surfaced. "If John Abizaid escaped our swords this time," said the speaker, believed to be Zarqawi, "we will be lying in wait for him."

Before the attack on the contractors, I spoke with then–Major General James Mattis, commander of the 1st Marine Division, about his plans for handling Fallujah and the other hot spot down the road, Ramadi. Our conversation was the first time we had spoken. For the bitter fight he was heading into in Anbar, he would need both of his personalities—Mad Dog Mattis, commander of the lethal Devil Dogs, and the cerebral student of people and ideas who had an anthropologist's curiosity and appreciation of nuance. Backed by the specter of the former, he would lead with the latter.

"We're planning to do this differently," he said. "I want us to take off the Kevlar helmets." He talked about engaging the population. "We're going to go in on foot and fan out in small patrols across the city."

His intent was to establish a more continuous, more visible presence among the residents, and in the short time before they deployed, Jim tried to give one platoon in each battalion additional language and cultural training. He even arranged for help from the Los Angeles Police Department. The Marines grew mustaches as a small but resonant gesture of cultural assimilation and amity toward the Iraqis. At the time, I knew there was a plan for his Marines to wear dark green forest camouflage print and shiny black boots for the first part of their rotation. The uniform choice was meant to differentiate them in the eyes of the Fallujans from the 82nd, who had worn beige and brown desert fatigues. Neither of us thought simply being in soft caps would win Fallujah. But Mattis, early on, understood that perceptions were at least as important as any tactical gains.

As they assumed control of the city that March, the Marines began to carry out Mattis's approach, starting with foot patrols. Against determined insurgents, this was dangerous. On Thursday, March 25, in the same Askari neighborhood with row houses that I had walked through a few weeks earlier, insurgents killed one Marine and wounded two more with homemade bombs. The Marines returned to the neighborhood the next day, eventually taking control of the cloverleaf to its east. Our TF 16 forces worked closely with the Marines, gathering intelligence and running pinpoint raids while the Marines provided a steady presence. On the night of March 24, one of our Green convoys was ambushed outside of town. In the massive ensuing firefight, with operators using vehicles as cover, one of the detainees got away. A week later, the American contractors drove into this rising simmer.

It was the beginning of a difficult chapter in the Iraq war. For the first few days after the March 31 ambush on the Blackwater convoy, the attack did not appear to derail the Marines' plan for clearing the city of insurgents. Mattis's troops focused on retrieving the remains of the contractors, which they did with the help of the local police chief in Fallujah. The Coalition collected intelligence on the crowd and ringleaders and would have enlisted our help in plucking them from the city. From Afghanistan, I waited and watched. But Washington wanted to answer the murder and mutilation of the security contractors, and rapidly secure the city. The Marines bitterly disagreed, wanting to manage Fallujah on their terms, not as a rushed reaction to the insurgents' baiting. They were overruled. General Mattis was ordered to attack the city within seventy-two hours. Helmets would go on and stay on.

The commander of our Fallujah-based team decided to seed Marine platoons with Green operators, in ones and twos. These dispersed teams were not only valuable for their experience but also better connected to one another and to the command center in Fallujah than many of the Marine platoons with which they found themselves. Our technology, combined with the agility and experience of the operators, allowed us to gain a quick, robust picture of what they found inside Fallujah. I became addicted to this ground-level reporting for the rest of the war.

Shuttling between my headquarters in Baghdad and outposts in Fallujah and nearby Ramadi, I did not find the teams' reports encouraging. The Marines faced significant but yet unspecified resistance shortly after entering the city limits. We knew Fallujah hosted nationalistic Sunni insurgents seeking to expel the Americans and win political and economic privileges in the Shia-dominated new Iraq. More modestly, these Iraqis were fighting to preserve their pride. We also knew that Fallujah was a nexus for tribal criminal networks, making for a glut of arms and money. Most troubling were the Salafist jihadists in the mix. The same trading routes that now made Fallujah a smuggling nexus for refrigerators and cars had imprinted the city with the ideology of the fundamentalists who had sacked Karbala in 1802. Fallujah sat along the corridors that connected the wellspring of Wahhabism in Saudi Arabia with the region's other great cities—Mosul, Aleppo, and Amman. Much of Anbar was insular, but Fallujah's sympathetic mosques and history as a place of transit lured a trickle of foreign jihadist volunteers.

The Green teams reported throughout that week, with some amazement, that fighters had seemingly come out of the woodwork. What disgust Iraqis may have had after seeing their countrymen string up corpses was quickly replaced, a few days later, by a smarting sense of solidarity with the embattled Fallujans. For some Iraqis, the invasion of Fallujah was the American occupation in its ugliest form: they viewed the Marines as acting out of revenge, carrying out collective punishment against many innocents for the crimes of a guilty few.

The perception that Americans were committing widespread atrocities quickly spread, largely through the Arab TV networks that reported significantly inflated civilian casualty figures. There were TV reports of injured civilians in Fallujah even before the attack began, and the networks played stock footage from other battles. Al Jazeera reported that U.S. artillery shells had hit mosques or wiped out whole families of twenty-five, and American newspapers repeated these claims. In reality, the Marines did not shoot any artillery during the entire first battle of Fallujah, using only precision weapons from aircraft. But the rumor resonated.

This feeling was so profound that it brought Sunni and Shia Iraqis together in a momentary period of sympathy and cooperation. Shiites in Baghdad reportedly sent money to the city and took food from their pantries and medicine from their own cabinets to donate. They urged their own brothers and sons to fight while taking in Sunni refugees. Shiite leaders solicited blood donations for Fallujah. Of course, the short spasm of cross-sectarian unity didn't endure.

Political pressure mounted on the Coalition, which had done little to compete with enemy propaganda, to stop the offensive in Fallujah. The U.N.'s representative to Iraq, Lakhdar Brahimi, threatened to quit. British prime minister Tony Blair implored President Bush to cease the assault. Most vitally, the Iraqi Governing Council, the interim body of Iraqis working with the CPA until Iraq regained sovereignty at the end of June 2004, threatened to disband if the assault did not desist. Its dissolution would have been potentially fatal to a new Iraq. So Bush ordered the assault stopped.

At the time, I was aware of only part of this political maneuvering, so I was surprised to receive a call from Mattis informing me that Washington had halted the assault. I was largely to blame for my own confusion. I had established too few links with the Marine command—a mistake I worked hard not to repeat. Beginning with the Marines, I began sending liaisons to as many units and commands as I could. Those liaisons fed back information, and we quickly set up fusion cells to combine and compare intelligence. Before Fallujah, coordination had been an important but tangential component of TF 714's effort. Now I learned it was central to our effectiveness.

On Friday, April 9, 2004, John Abizaid flew to Iraq and then out to the Marines' Camp Fallujah. John had come to tell the Marines in person to cancel the entire offensive, knowing they would be irate. I would join him out in Fallujah later that day, the one-year anniversary of the fall of Baghdad. Things were meant to be going well. Instead, it was arguably the worst day for the Coalition since the invasion had begun, with Sunni and Shia extremists making gains. The Sunni insurgency had won a tactical draw in Fallujah: for them, a triumph of legendary proportions.

The war was not going well elsewhere. Much of the rest of Iraq was erupting. Even with Fallujah teetering, the CPA had, the previous week, chosen to confront Muqtada al-Sadr, the thuggish thirty-year-old son and nephew of a prestigious Shia cleric assassinated by Saddam. Bremer shut down *al-Hawza*, Sadr's mouthpiece newspaper, and arrested one of his top aides. In response, Sadr's Jaish al-Mahdi (JAM) militia rose up in the streets of its Shia strongholds—Najaf, Karbala, Kufa. In Sadr City—the Shia "neighborhood" of Baghdad, home to 2.5 million people and recently renamed from "Saddam City" in honor of Muqtada's martyred father— JAM attacked soldiers from the 1st Armored Division, commanded by then–Major General Marty Dempsey. By the time I met with Abizaid on Friday, Sadr City was in full revolt. That day, Dempsey's soldiers in Baghdad read his letter to them, explaining that their yearlong tours would be extended another three months to continue fighting Sadr's militia. His men had fought too hard, Marty wrote to them, to allow "one thug to replace another."

The remaining weeks of April and the beginning of May saw Iraq further unravel. Route Tampa—the main artery running supplies from Kuwait into Baghdad—was effectively shut down as insurgents lit up roadside bombs and blew out bridges and trucks stopped moving. I continued to jog beside the taxiway on the runway at our airport base, but it had a surreal feel as I watched insurgents' 107-mm and 240-mm rockets land in the airport infield, blowing craters in the grass. Running was neither bravado nor lunacy. The rockets were inaccurate, and our nearby headquarters was an unfortified building, so running in the open air was no more dangerous than sitting at the computer terminal. But sucking in the sour, metallic smell of the explosives that lingered in the dry midday air was an irritating reminder that things were not going well.

On April 23, as we focused on the deterioration in Iraq, I flew from Baghdad down to Qatar, where I met with John Abizaid at his forward headquarters. We discussed the situation and TF 714's potential contribution. While there, Craig Nixon—the Ranger regimental commander, at the time in charge of all TF 714 forces in Afghanistan—called me from Bagram with news that a Ranger had been killed in a firefight near the village of Sperah in the southeast part of the country. I passed the sad news to John as we talked. Later that day Craig called again with an update: the Ranger lost was Pat Tillman, the professional football player whose enlistment in the Army after 9/11 had been widely reported. I hadn't met Ranger Tillman, but the loss of any soldier was significant. Craig informed me that standard notification and other administrative processes were under way. He also informed me that the chain of command would be recommending Tillman for a Silver Star award for valor, based on his actions while maneuvering against enemy forces. At that time, most soldiers killed in action were recommended for an award, typically the Bronze Star. We followed what was then standard practice to process the award as quickly as possible so that it could be presented to the family at the memorial service.

As I'd previously planned, the next day I flew with the Command Team to Bagram. In addition to ongoing operational activities, Craig briefed me on the circumstances of Corporal Tillman's death. He described a late after-noon/early evening firefight in broken terrain in which Tillman had been fa-tally hit by small arms fire. He continued that although further investigation was required, he had concluded that Tillman was likely killed by friendly fire from fellow Rangers. He drew out the engagement on an easel and we dis-cussed how it likely occurred. After the discussion, as I would have for any suspected incident of fratricide, I called SOCOM headquarters at Tampa to relay a tentative conclusion of friendly fire. General Brown was out, so I passed the information to his deputy, then–Vice Admiral Eric Olson.

In the discussion with Craig about the incident, I asked about the Silver Star. Lieutenant Colonel Jeff Bailey, commander of the 2nd Ranger Bat-talion, said he felt that although friendly fire was suspected, Tillman's actions—maneuvering against what the Rangers at the moment believed were enemy forces ambushing the column of Tillman's fellow Rangers—warranted the recognition. I agreed, and a short time later approved a cita-tion that had originated within the Ranger Regiment.

A few days later I was told that a high-profile memorial service in San Jose was planned for Corporal Tillman. I had already passed the assess-ment of the potential that he had been killed by friendly fire to SOCOM, and advised them that an investigation of that possibility was under way. But because I became aware of the memorial service, I decided to send a direct message to emphasize to Generals Abizaid and Brown that friendly fire was the likely cause of death. The message was classified secret, as all my official communications were required to be. I also sent the message to Lieutenant General Phil Kensinger at U.S. Army Special Operations Com-mand, the administrative headquarters responsible for handling actions surrounding the death of members of Army Special Operations Forces like the Rangers.

In the years that followed, controversy arose and continued over the cir-cumstances of Pat Tillman's death by friendly fire and his family's notifica-tion. Five investigations were conducted and accusations of intentional deception, cover-up, and exploitation of Corporal Tillman's death for politi-cal purposes were propagated. Sadly, truth and trust were lost in the process. Genuine concerns over slow and incomplete communication with the family increasingly became mixed with suspicions of intentional misconduct.

As the TF 714 commander in operational control of the Rangers, but not tasked with administrative communication with the family, I had an in-complete view of all that transpired. But in Afghanistan I watched the Rangers deal with the loss of a comrade, and I saw nothing but genuine efforts to take care of a fallen Ranger and his family in ways that reflected the deep values of the force.

I learned later that the family was not immediately notified of the pos-sibility of friendly fire. From the beginning, I assumed they would be noti-fied of the ongoing investigation into the possibility of fratricide, but I believed final determination would not be publicly announced beyond the family until the investigation's conclusions were final. From experience with how long investigations typically took, I knew that the investigation's findings were likely to be complete after the planned memorial service.

The initial phone call I made, and the message I transmitted, only days after Pat Tillman's loss, reflected my intent to fully inform the multiple commands and commanders who would be involved in administrative matters associated with Corporal Tillman's death.

Concerns were raised over wording in the Silver Star narrative, which some found misleading as to the reason for Tillman's death. Before this, I had seen Silver Star citations carefully framed and proudly hung on walls of homes I'd visited. In the citation, we thus sought to document what I believe was his heroism, without drawing official conclusions about friendly fire that were still premature. Any errors, which I should have caught, were not the result of any intention to misrepresent or mislead. I believed that the fact that Pat Tillman was killed by friendly fire, a sad reality in every war, did not diminish either his service or his sacrifice.

To this day, I am saddened by Ranger Tillman's death, as I am for the loss of every service member I served with, and for the pain such losses cause each family.

I was back in Baghdad in late May when Scott Miller knocked on the plywood doorframe to my office. "Sir, I've got the Berg video," he said, and handed me a DVD. Prior to this, there had been a spate of kidnappings. But Nicholas Berg had recently become the most infamous victim because of what was on the DVD Scott brought me. Berg was a twenty-six-year-old from Philadelphia who had come to Iraq to repair telephone towers, moving alone throughout the country that spring. He was kidnapped on April 10, as kidnappings started to occur more frequently that summer. By the time Scott came to my office, I had received reports that Berg had been executed on camera. Soldiers had found his body under an overpass in Baghdad, and the video of his execution had been uploaded to a jihadist website. As I loaded the DVD, Scott sat down across from me. He shook his head.

"Sir, I don't think he knew it was coming. As he was sitting in front of those guys, I don't think he had a clue that he was going to be beheaded."

After weeks of intelligence updates and briefs from our hostage cell, I had come to know quite a bit about Nick Berg. So there was a flash of familiarity as his image came up on the screen. In the video, he appeared in an orange jumpsuit in front of five men clad in black, their heads covered. Intelligence sources told us the bulky man in the center was Zarqawi. After delivering a diatribe to the camera, he removed a long knife from the black folds of his shirt and tipped the shackled Berg over onto his side. His henchmen held Berg down until it was finished. Even though I knew the outcome, at the end of the video I had to consciously relax my clenched hands.

By virtue of our close-quarters fight with Al Qaeda, our force began to see a lot of these videos. War drives strong emotions. American outrage over the Alamo produced the Texan victory at San Jacinto but also the brutal pursuit and killing of hundreds of Mexicans attempting to flee the defeat. During the Second World War, Fleet Admiral Halsey, one of only nine officers to ever wear five stars, placed a billboard in the entrance to one of his harbors in the Pacific that said, "Kill Japs, Kill Japs, KILL MORE JAPS!" Frustrated by the suicidal tactics of the insurgents in the Philippines, John Pershing, another man the United States eventually awarded five stars, buried the corpses of his Muslim enemies with pig carcasses. These and similar moments from our military's past were on my mind as the enemy in Iraq appeared ever more sinister.

I sought to emphasize in my force, and in myself, the necessary discipline to fight enemies whose very tactic was to instill terror and incite indignation. Maintaining our force's moral compass was not a difficult concept to understand. Armies without discipline are mobs; killing without legal and moral grounds is murder. But after the first shot, the first bloody corpse, war is no longer theory. As we moved further from the theoretical, like every commander before me, I found it critical to maintain as much discipline over my emotions toward what we encountered, and the losses we suffered, as I could. I remembered Grant's admission that he rarely visited his wounded in field hospitals because he felt seeing the cost of his decisions so starkly would prevent him from making the difficult decisions he believed were necessary. I found strength in Grant's candor.

In the end, Nick Berg's murder and the experience in Fallujah that spring made us more resolute, more serious. Until late 2006 or 2007, Coalition leaders shied away from using the word "war" in our briefings and conversations. It was always "the problem" or "the situation" or "the conflict." But after the events that spring, I began to tell my command group, and to repeat until I gave up command: "This is a war. And this war will have a winner, and it will have a loser. We are not here to fight the war on terror. *We are here to win it.*"

We were not winning when I met with John Abizaid on Friday, April 9, 2004. Historically, insurgencies had taken time to incubate, as anger evolved into coordinated resistance. The initial stages of their organization typically went unseen by governing powers. So it was on that Friday that, for the first time since the war began, the Sunni insurgency openly controlled terrain—parts or all of Fallujah—within the country.

Restarting the Marines' offensive on Fallujah was politically untenable. They would be forced to withdraw from the city limits. As they prepared to vacate the city, which they would do three weeks later, they searched for a stopgap measure. In the week before their formal exit, the Marines began to assemble a local security force, called the Fallujah Brigade. They chose a former Baathist general to command it, provided limited equipment, and filled the ranks with Iraqis, some from Fallujah. It was clear from its inception that the Brigade was a big risk. Few had any doubts the militia might switch sides en masse or be quickly overrun by the very insurgents and foreign fighters they were meant to police. But having some representation inside the city was better than nothing.

Violent skirmishes filled the days leading up to the Marines' withdrawal. On April 26, a platoon entered the northwest district and linked up with a handful of Green members from our task force. They were there to teach the Marines how to use a new weapon. But soon insurgents found their position. As insurgents began arriving by the truckload outside the buildings, the Americans were in danger of being overrun. In the course of the assault, as insurgents unleashed on the buildings, a Green medic, Staff Sergeant Dan Briggs, ran six times across the bullet-swept street in order to administer care to wounded Marines in two separate buildings. Meanwhile, on the roof of one of these building, two Green operators and a small force of Marines fought off the encircling insurgents who fired from alleys and the windows and rooftops. As he covered the evacuation of the remaining force, one of the operators, Master Sergeant Don Hollenbaugh, found himself alone on the rooftop, shuffling from one spot, firing a few times, and moving to the next, in order to hold at bay what were estimated to be three hundred insurgents. For their exceptional courage, Briggs and Hollenbaugh were awarded the Distinguished Service Cross, the award for valor second only to the Medal of Honor, and Larry Boivin—wounded twice in the firefight, only to return to it each time—was awarded a Silver Star. They earned them. A few days later, the Marines withdrew from the city.

At the end of May, less than a month after the Marines left the city to the Fallujah Brigade, Abizaid summoned me to meet with him, Lieutenant General Ric Sanchez, Ambassador Bremer, and the Marine commanders on the outskirts of Fallujah. Our task force already believed the city was, in all but a few pockets, a free zone for the insurgency. For some of the Sunni recruits, joining the Brigade was a way to make it past our checkpoints into the city in order to join the insurgent ranks. The remaining contingents of the Fallujah Brigade were no match when they contested the insurgency. Some guerrillas were battle hardened. All were high on the recent "defeat" of the Marines and heavily armed. Moreover, during this spring and summer of 2004, much of the Sunni insurgency took on a religious tone and logic that had previously been absent from the Baathist resistance. Iraqis increasingly joined the ranks of Zarqawi and began acting like his Salafists, who sold themselves as the vanguard of the resistance. The dye helping color the reservoir were foreign fighters, non-Iraqis sneaking into Iraq to volunteer as jihadists. They arrived emboldened by inflated tales of the brilliant resistance to the invaders in Fallujah. But for many, burning anger over the recent stories and images of degradation at Abu Ghraib had provoked them to come to Iraq and would fuel the fire for years to come. Fallujah became both symbol of, and command base for, the jihadist wing of the resistance, separate from and at times in conflict with the nationalistic insurgency. While the outcome of the jockeying among the insurgent factions was still murky, we had little doubt the Fallujah Brigade had withered within weeks of its inception.

"The Fallujah Brigade is completely ineffective," Jim Mattis said at the meeting. "They're broken, probably beyond repair."

The meeting felt surreal, as we held it in a room inside Camp Fallujah, a base bristling with American military power. Just a short distance away sat an entire city, increasingly opaque and inaccessible and under the sway of insurgents. The agreements that established the Fallujah Brigade and the political sensitivities in the background prevented the Marines from setting foot inside the city. Abizaid made it clear we could not allow the situation stand.

"We need to hit some targets," he said, hitting the table with the edge of his hand. He was looking to us.

To hit with precision within Fallujah, a city we had no ability to enter that summer, would draw on TF 714's existing capabilities, and some not yet developed. Two incidents in particular reflected the changes. First, the actions of Briggs, Hollenbaugh, and Boivin alongside Marines reflected our growing relationship with conventional forces. Second, our employment of every piece of technology, combined with painstaking analysis, meant we could develop and strike targets with increasing speed and precision. By the fall of that year, when the Marines had forcefully recaptured Fallujah, TF 714 was a different force.

The process began slowly and out of necessity. By early summer, our intelligence on Fallujah had been reduced to a trickle. The violent reprisals of the insurgents snuffed the few sources who lived there and made recruiting new ones almost impossible. But in the near term, we were at a loss for credible on-the-ground insights into how the city's power vacuum was filling, and the enemy amassing there.

Of most value was our increasingly sophisticated employment of unmanned aerial vehicles (UAVs), with the Predator being the most common version. These remotely piloted aircraft, equipped with video cameras on their underbellies to transmit live feeds back to the monitors in our Joint Operations Center (JOC), allowed us to watch locations or vehicles for extended periods. We had used UAVs before, but with uneven results. When I took command in 2003, for all of Iraq we normally had access to just one Predator, which we augmented with a helicopter we had outfitted with a camera on its fuselage.

The control of the few UAVs that did exist that June was still an awkward process. The Air Force viewed UAVs as a strategic collection platform and was inclined to centrally manage them, which it could do given the limited number of systems. The technology allowed for Predators to be physically based, launched, and recovered in theater but piloted from distant bases, even from the United States. Downlinked video could be viewed and analyzed anywhere the correct equipment existed.

Unlike surveillance of larger or more static targets, TF 714 missions normally required constant surveillance of people or moving vehicles, often looking to identify subtle movements or specific mannerisms. TF 714 teams would direct the Predator to look at a building or follow a car—usually a white sedan in a country where white sedans were ubiquitous.

It was a fascinating situation in which new, emerging technologies made dispersed operations possible, but our processes had not yet figured out how to effectively leverage them. We quickly recognized the need to fully integrate every available intelligence source, both operationally and psychologically, into our force and spent the next few years perfecting approaches that would do that. Ultimately, we used a combination of liaisons, constant communication, and eventually the formation of SOF Predator units, to create the close partnership needed.

As wartime often does, the challenge had moved two of Green's key leaders in the country to act. Lieutenant Colonel Steve was the commander of the Green squadron in Iraq, based in Baghdad.* Also in Baghdad, then-Major Wayne Barefoot was acting as the intelligence chief for the Iraq country task force, TF 16. Steve had come to Green directly from the conventional Army—not through the Rangers or Green Berets. He retained more of a regular-army style in his appearance and command than some of his peers but he earned respect in Green through consistent performance and later commanded the unit. Wayne came to the command from tracking Islamic extremist groups in the Philippines. He was one of a very small group of analysts who, in January, had told me with confidence not only that Zarqawi was in Iraq, but that they saw signs of an incipient, violent jihadist network taking root there. At the time, many of their peers disputed that analysis.

During May and June 2004, the final two months of their three-month rotation, Steve and Wayne sought to meld the sometimes-divided spheres of intelligence and operations. With Fallujah inaccessible, Steve required his operators to take turns sitting alongside Wayne's analysts, watching the Predator feeds on uninterrupted twenty-four-hour shifts. He required the operators to keep a logbook, tracking vehicles, houses, and routes in order to accrue a picture of life within the city. We began to develop what became known as "pattern-of-life" analyses that followed the targets' habits as they undertook their daily routines.

In addition to producing detailed maps of enemy movement in the city, these shifts introduced a number of important intangibles into our force. Operators, the Brahmins within TF 714, developed deep respect for the

---

*Steve is a pseudonym.

intelligence professionals. They became better operators by learning to think like analysts and by acquiring vast knowledge about the enemy. Both analysts and operators increasingly owned the mission, which in turn increased activity on the ground by moving targeting decisions down the ranks.

Some operators relished immersing themselves in the intelligence grist. Others resented the added work, as handling the tactical aspects of raids was difficult enough. But by tweaking behavior we were trying to transform attitude: Instead of waiting passively to receive a targeting assignment, we wanted them actively helping the analysts to find targets. To win, all of us would need to be knee deep in the fight, all of the time.

Unexpectedly, that process accelerated in mid-June, thanks to the work of one of the operators' most dedicated partners. Jimmy D., a Green imagery analyst who later retired as a sergeant major, had become a fixture in the tactical operations center. "Jimmy D., what you got?" was the jaunty refrain when entering the operations room—which he rarely left. Near the end of his squadron's tour, Jimmy D. in fact had something very promising.

After reviewing recorded video from the previous few days, Jimmy noted that a tractor had blocked off the entrance to one stretch of street in Fallujah, keeping all foot and vehicle traffic away. When he checked the imagery from a few days earlier, there was no tractor. So through the pilots thousands of miles away, he directed the Predator back to that area for a live shot. He started looking up and down that road and at one end saw a group of men in the process of loading and unloading two trucks, with scrunched cabs and long flatbeds, parked outside one of the houses. After a few minutes of unloading carpets, the men began carrying suspicious crates from the house to the flatbeds, covered in canvas. Then came armloads of AK-47 rifles and munitions. At some point, a second truck at the site, still loaded, lurched to life. We followed it through the streets, out of Fallujah, east on Highway 10, and once it was southwest of Baghdad, we intercepted it on the ground. As suspected, it was packed full of all kinds of munitions—rockets, machine guns, grenade launchers, and raw explosives for car bombs. We flew the UAV back to the city and the blocked-off section of the street, where we watched men continue to hurriedly load material into trucks and then get into cars, both of which subsequently moved down through Fallujah in a convoy, passing through the commercial strip where the insurgents had laid their March 31 ambush. Eventually they entered a suburb on the southwest edge of the city and stopped in front a concrete-and-block house. The location became a potential target for us—Objective Big Ben.

The intercepted truck had been driven by two men, with a thirteen-year-old along for the ride, likely to help them avoid suspicion at checkpoints. The men professed to be hired help and under questioning confirmed the others they had just left were moving the arms cache to a new house. They described the neighborhood, which matched the area around the new house. With this, we had a viable target—and an urgent one. The insurgents in Fallujah had commandeered many of the city's garages and warehouses to set up "factories" for the car bombs that they would dispatch to Baghdad's bazaars and Sadr City.

It was only through intense persistence, and some luck, that Jimmy D. had found this load of unexploded weapons. The insurgents might disperse the cache over the next day or two, and with only two sets of eyes periodically on the city—our Predator and the outfitted helicopter—we could easily lose them in the urban maze. We had to move quickly.

But striking inside Fallujah was complicated by the strong political forces swirling around the city. On June 18, I flew to the Marines' nearby base to meet with Abizaid, Mattis, and his immediate boss, Lieutenant General Jim Conway, commanding the 1st Marine Expeditionary Force. Steve, Wayne, and a TF 16 officer named John Christian joined me. Abizaid was frustrated with the situation in Fallujah. Intuition told him to prevent it from becoming an internal safe haven for the insurgency.

"We need to turn up the heat on the enemy," Abizaid said.

Steve briefed Abizaid on their plan to take out Big Ben. They would drop a bomb and move a ground assault force to be at the scene just after the initial explosion in order collect intelligence from the rubble, survey the aftermath, and arrest insurgents. The assault force would fly in on MH-6 helicopters, fast-roping from the highly agile Little Birds piloted by the Night Stalkers. A second group would drive in with the vehicles needed to leave the city, as there was no place to land the helicopters. Fighting in April had taught them to expect enemy fighters to mass rapidly around the objective, and surveillance now reflected fighters nearby. Remembering the bitter lessons of Mogadishu, where Green operators and Rangers had fought their way down congested streets without armored protection, Steve's team determined armored vehicles were essential.

"Good," Abizaid said. "Hit them, watch them, then hit them again." Turning to Conway and Mattis, he reiterated the point. "I want you to find some targets for Stan's guys to hit. We need to get more aggressive here."

Later that evening, as we planned the final tactical aspects of the raid, I got a phone call from Conway. Understandably reluctant to give the insurgents any propaganda ammunition, he didn't want to drop a bomb on the target because of the potential for civilian casualties. I called Steve just as his team was about to walk out to the darkened helipad to begin the assault. The armored vehicles, motors running, were lined up in battle order, vibrating in place and ready to roll. I explained that we couldn't bomb the site. It bothered me, as I was asking them to take on greater risk. Steve understood this, as did his men.

"Yep, okay, sir," he said. "Let's do it."

Instead of a precision-guided bomb, the rockets and machine guns on

the helicopters carrying the Green teams could pummel the safe house before the teams dismounted and breached it. I communicated back to the
Marines but received another caveat. There could be no tanks or other armored vehicles on the operation. The Marines had promised the leadership
of the Fallujah Brigade that U.S. forces would not enter the city. American
armor would be too visible and would undermine what little standing the
Fallujah Brigade held within the city. The armor would also undercut the
bargaining position of the Marines, whose credibility among the various
factions continued to tremble.

I didn't like it, and neither would Steve and his force, but I understood. I
felt the value of denying the cache to Zarqawi and demonstrating Coalition
strength warranted the political risks. But I appreciated that the Marines had
to deal with the complex politics of Anbar and would absorb the reverbera-
tions of any operation. Such tensions would arise with varying degrees of
urgency, and would be negotiated with varying degrees of effectiveness, on
each of the thousands of operations TF 714 conducted over the next few
years.

That night the calculus of whether to strike was a particularly thorny
issue. From it I distilled an important lesson of leading TF 714 as our role
expanded. I could have asked Abizaid to overrule the Marines in order to
allow us to use armored vehicles for the operations, and he might have. He
had clarified earlier that day to everyone in the room that he wanted TF 714
to hit the cache and that the Marines were to assist. But I also appreciated
the Marines' position and felt that building our relationship was the more
crucial objective. So I didn't go to Abizaid. It became standing guidance
throughout the command, for teams coordinating with either conventional
commanders or other intelligence partners: In most cases, the long-term
relationship was more important than the immediate operation.

But by both following this rule and not canceling the raid, I was ratchet-
ing up the potential risk to Steve's force, a move I wouldn't make without
Steve's input. He and his operators had studied the situation in minute detail and had an instinctive feel for how things might play out. They knew
the Jubail district, where the house was located, was a particularly dense
harbor of extremists within the wider Fallujah stronghold. And they had
spent days watching throngs of insurgents do calisthenics or man checkpoints throughout the city. They knew these fighters would quickly swarm
Big Ben, making the roads dangerous gauntlets. When I told him of the
restrictions on armored vehicles, Steve voted no. He couldn't send men in
without armor to protect them on the way out. I agreed. The raid was off.

My exchange with Steve went as I felt it should have—and gave me a
sense that my command style and my relationship with the force were taking shape. I knew that our units, and leaders like Steve, would not request
assets like armor without good reason. It wasn't a question of courage, as
members from the Green detachment outside the city had, around the time
the Blackwater SUVs were ambushed, ventured into Fallujah alone in

beat-up old Iraqi sedans that we bought and outfitted, surveying parts of the city simply inaccessible to American Humvees or even unmarked SUVs.

 But Steve made a sophisticated call as a leader by calling off the assault. Missions—especially special-operations raids—can be whittled down through a back-and-forth of caveats and tweaks until a leader can find himself agreeing to a raid with manpower and protection levels that would have been unacceptable in the planning stages. Instead, Steve had a line in his head, and when it was crossed, he concluded the operation no longer made sense. For my part, I wanted subordinates to feel comfortable telling me no.

Still, Big Ben remained a potential fountain of weapons for a growing insurgency. So we persisted, negotiating to get approval for an air strike. Later that night, June 18, we were cleared to hit Big Ben with a precision weapon.

At 8:00 A.M. local time on June 19, our bombing window opened. Hours before it did, screens at both the Fallujah and Baghdad operations centers had been focused on Big Ben. On the screen, the safe house revolved slowly as the Predator filming the scene circled in a tall gyre above the city. The strike aircraft flew its own circular pattern in the sky, over the empty desert, out of earshot of Big Ben's Jubail neighborhood. Eventually, the airpower coordinator in our Fallujah base relayed the order to the pilot, freeing him to engage. In minutes he would drop a precision-guided bomb through the roof of the house in the center of our screens. Now after 9:00 A.M., it was already approaching ninety degrees Fahrenheit on that street in Jubail, and the heat made the sky bright, cloudless. The safe house was quiet and unaware. The streets in front of it were empty.

As the plane sped toward Big Ben, I knew that our credibility as a force would be hugely shaped by the success or failure of this air strike. Beginning that summer, I constantly reiterated an equation to the force:

Credibility = Proven Competence + Integrity + Relationships

We were about to validate our competence.

In planning every air strike, we performed painstaking analysis to estimate the risk of possible noncombatant injuries or deaths. Computer-based algorithms calculated estimates for potential unintended civilian casualties. To provide the most informed analysis of the risk, these took into account the sizes and blast ranges of the explosives, the probability of their accuracy, a count of the number of civilians likely to be there at that exact time of the day, the structure and strength of the building, and the shrapnel it might produce. What this scientific rigor underscored was a deeply human desire within my force to avoid hurting innocents.

I was tense watching the safe house as the aircraft approached. I was confident about Big Ben, or we wouldn't be bombing it. We had watched it from the time the insurgents moved the weapons until that morning and had confirmation from the men detained as well a source inside the city. But perhaps they had moved the arms cache without our knowing, or civilians had slipped into the home unnoticed.

At 9:30 A.M., an hour and a half into the bombing window, the pilot reported his approach. We watched the screen. A few seconds later, we saw a white flash, which expanded and darkened to shades of gray and black as it became a thick cloud of dust and smoke. The house beneath it was leveled. But for one, two, three seconds nothing happened. We waited for the secondary explosions from the munitions. The smoke and dust blossom expanded and thinned. My stomach tightened. Faces around the JOC were clenched, watching the screen. The image seemed frozen.

And then munitions stored in the house started to cook off. Rockets flew through the air with sparkling tails, while smaller explosions bubbled up from the house. It was awkward to feel relief at seeing the secondary explosions, which might harm bystanders, but they meant we had hit the cache, not an innocent home. Backyard propane tanks or gas kitchen stoves could occasionally cause a single secondary explosion, but this was different. For the next twenty minutes, the arms cache, likely piled densely in the safe house, continued to burn off. Small arms shimmered and the bigger bomb-making materials, intended for car bombs or suicide vests, made larger thuds. There was no cheering, no joy, in the operations centers. But we had validated our techniques. And we were confident that we could replicate the process.

Because we were unable to put an assault force on the ground, we could not verify other results of the strike, beyond the obvious munitions cache. Sources inside Fallujah and signal intercepts indicated that roughly twenty people had died in the blast, almost all of them Tunisian foreign fighters killed when the house exploded and collapsed. Fallujans told newspapers that a noncombatant family had been killed. This was possible but hard to verify. Those same witnesses claimed we had dropped a second bomb, which we had not. They had likely mistaken the initial explosions of the munitions cache. Reports of civilian casualties from inside Fallujah at the time often came from individuals hostile to the Coalition, and in later air strikes in Fallujah, we received reports of insurgents placing teddy bears and dolls among the rubble before news photographers arrived.

With the rubble still smoking, we saw a crowd congregate in the street outside Big Ben. Hundreds of Fallujans, reported the *Los Angeles Times*, rushed to the site, "chanting anti-American slogans and vowing revenge." Despite the clear importance of the strike, it was a reminder that the term "surgical strike" is often poorly used. Even with a sharp scalpel, a surgeon has to break the skin and cut through live tissue. There is chance of infection. And sutures close a wound only imperfectly until the skin fuses. Strikes like Big Ben had to be seriously considered for their costs as well as their benefits.

Still, given the carnage Zarqawi's forces had been inflicting on innocent Iraqis and his group's growing toll on Coalition forces, I was satisfied.

A couple of weeks later, at the end of June, Steve's squadron rotated out of Iraq. They copied all of the imagery and video onto a hard drive for the next squadron, so that their replacements would not be starting from scratch. Later we institutionalized and expanded these principles: Squadrons that rotated home continued to monitor operations, watch feeds, and listen to video teleconferences (VTCs) at their stateside bases. Operators trained and studied with analysts on top of honing their tactical and operational edge against an ever more hardened enemy. Our men and women might not have been in Iraq or Afghanistan, but we expected their focus to be, and we relied on their skill set expanding and diversifying.

Over the course of the next four months, we worked to refine our ability to find, monitor, and map targets. As our intelligence stores accrued and our coordination improved, we started, as Abizaid had implored us to do, hitting them, watching them, and hitting them again. Where the city dispersed into empty fields on its southern edge, we watched insurgents hold physical training formations, and we bombed those. We watched the circles where the insurgents sat when they would gather for ceremonial meals of lamb in the compound courtyards just prior to suicide bombing missions. And we bombed those. We saw this patchwork of movement from our eyes in the clouds and rounded out the picture with increasing human and signals intelligence. It was a tense education, because we knew the cost of a mistake. Each strike was a test of our force, and we treated each like one.

The mosaic we constructed was revealing. Through June, internal wrangling among insurgent groups and personalities yielded no single dominant force; instead, powerful families maintained control throughout parts of the nicer northwest section of Fallujah, while foreign fighters rooted themselves in the southern parts of the city. Civilians largely fled the commercial parts of the southeast, where jihadi-Salafi volunteers took up in guesthouses and restaurants. At the time we struck Big Ben on June 19, the already moribund Fallujah Brigade was no real challenge to Zarqawi's rising influence. By the end of July, while some of the city's blocks remained parceled, Zarqawi's foreign-backed jihadists had largely wrested control of the resistance away from the Sunni nationalist insurgency.

Although we could never fix him in Fallujah definitively enough to support a strike, sources described the kabuki Zarqawi performed. A chauffeur would drive him through the city's bazaars and commercial districts, and he would hold meetings in the backseat of his car between stop and start points. We believed that for most of the summer Zarqawi operated north of Fallujah, pulling strings within the city while staying outside the area under our scope. He deftly managed alliances and eventually co-opted local insurgent celebrity leaders to be his deputies. On some level, I admired Zarqawi's cunning.

The Jordanian and his supporters professed a desire to make Iraq the seat of a resuscitated caliphate, governed by the puritan formulation of Islamic law. The parts of the city they controlled offered a chance to try out this draconian rule. They shut down hair salons and movie theaters. They forbade Western clothing. Weeks before our air strike, the jihadists had flogged liquor sellers, displaying them half naked in the back of a truck that roved through town. We watched them line up "spies" on their knees and shoot them in the back of their skulls. One video surfaced that showed members of Zarqawi's network burning Iraqi policemen alive. After the coalition wrested the city back the following November, forces found crude torture chambers, where these jihadists had brought frightened Shia or Iraqi policemen kidnapped in Baghdad or the south. Zarqawi's troops—through their cruelty, fanaticism, and glut of resources—emerged as the strongest group. And he was still ascendant.

Although coalescing within Fallujah allowed Zarqawi's influence to gestate, his choice to control much of the city was a strategic mistake. He burnished his legitimacy with insurgents, but as our targeting matured over the summer, we stripped his network of a cadre of mid- and senior-level leaders who operated within Fallujah's limits. More important than any losses to his force, however, were the gains to our own. Our UAV-centric approach to targeting in Fallujah was dangerously limited, but the experience forced us to hone our aerial surveillance skills. Those soon proved even more effective when combined with maturing signals, human, and other intelligence disciplines.

Of course, the enemy was more agile than Fallujah reflected and would soon be far more dispersed. Pressuring him across his network would require that our methods of intelligence development become far more efficient, so that we could replicate the process in many locations simultaneously. Small teams of men, in a time span of days or hours, would have to do intelligence collection, planning, and coordination that in June 2004 spanned weeks and consumed the focus of an entire squadron and task force. In April of that year, we ran a total of ten operations in Iraq. Later that summer, in August, we conducted eighteen. In two years, we would average more than three hundred per month, against a faster, smarter enemy and with greater precision and intelligence yield. Getting there would require further revamping our force by pursuing many of the principles that enabled us to destroy the arms hidden inside Big Ben.

As we grew stronger and more agile, however, our enemies grew more ruthless. And Fallujah was just the opening salvo.

▼

CHAPTER 10

Entrepreneurs of Battle

June–December 2004

I t was the machine guns and munitions we found in the flatbed of the truck driven by two Iraqi men out of Fallujah that convinced us we needed to strike Big Ben. But in the days before we hit the arms cache on June 19, 2004, a thirteen-year-old boy, whom the drivers had placed in the front seat as a decoy, gave a hint of an even bigger target.

At the outstation in Baghdad, while the two men were detained, task force operators sat with the kid in one of the rooms of the old Saddam-era mansion used by Green for living quarters and an operations center. They gave the thirteen-year-old a cold Coke from their refrigerator and, through a translator, started chatting. When they asked him about the two drivers, the kid explained that he had seen them meet a few days earlier with a very important man. Between sips of soda, the youngster described the meeting as a thirteen-year-old would. The important man arrived and greeted the group of assembled men, including the two drivers. When the important man arrived, everyone was excited to meet him. Making room for the important man, they sat on the floor and shared hot tea. The men in the circle sat quietly and listened to this important visitor, who spoke for a long time.

The thirteen-year-old recounted the important man's speech. He was very enthusiastic, the kid explained, and told the truck drivers and other men to continue what they were doing. Things, the important visitor had said, were going well.

The Green troops looked sideways at one another, and one asked the boy whether he could recognize the important man in a photograph. Oh sure, he said. The operators brought in a big flip book, with rows of pictures but no names, and set it in front of him. After scanning it a few moments, the kid pointed to one of the mug shots. It was an old picture of Abu Musab al-Zarqawi.

"That's him," he said in Arabic. "I'm sure of it."

Although told in youthful tones, the young boy's story conveyed a troubling truth that summer: Things were, indeed, going well for the network Wayne Barefoot had warned us about six months before. Even as Zarqawi sowed enmity among many of the Iraqis stuck in Fallujah, his international notoriety continued to grow and, in a phenomenon peculiar to our media age, it brought him recruits from around the world, in turn widening his influence within the local insurgency beyond his minority group of jihadist followers. Meanwhile, through his Jordanian tribal connections in Baghdad and Anbar and his history with Ansar al-Sunnah in the north, he was forging crucial alliances between traditionally antagonistic groups: deeply xenophobic Iraqi Sunnis, insular Kurds, and his foreign Arab fighters. As he became both transnational terrorist and insurgent leader, he positioned himself at the center of that insurgency's constituencies.

While Al Qaeda's leaders, with whom Zarqawi still had no official partnership, eyed his rise coolly from afar, our side experienced a turnover of leadership.

The veteran diplomat John Negroponte, who had arrived in Iraq in June to be the new U.S. ambassador, became the top civilian when Bremer turned sovereignty over to Iraq and its new prime minister, Ayad Allawi, on June 28, 2004. On the military side, General George Casey, Jr., arrived to replace Ric Sanchez on July 1. George was the first four-star general to command the military coalition, now called Multi-National Force—Iraq. I was glad that I had known him for several years. Our fathers had been classmates at West Point, graduating in 1945, and I vividly remember my mother's reaction when George's father, then–Major General Casey, was killed in Vietnam. For my mom, who had stoically endured my father's multiple combat tours, the death of a peer was a jolting reminder that not only young soldiers die.

George, whom I'd worked with on the Joint Staff, was easy to underestimate. Like John Abizaid, he wasn't physically imposing, and he shared John's disarmingly casual demeanor. But while John bounced with a certain swagger and was endearingly sarcastic, George was quieter, more outwardly professional. Although stocky and square-jawed, he had a subdued manner closer to that of a high-school teacher. I wondered how that would play with the Iraqis, to whom he needed to be a symbol of American strength and competence. But I knew that as a captain, George had passed the grueling Green selection process, only to choose instead to remain in the conventional Army. In thirty years I had never heard of another person passing selection and opting not to join the unit. His self-confident decision impressed me.

As these new leaders entered the scene, they came to find TF 714 assuming a larger role in the war. Beginning with the destruction of Big Ben, we were on the offensive against the Sunni insurgency across Iraq, periodically striking targets in Fallujah and tracking Zarqawi's network around the yellow, dusty cinderblock cities of Anbar. This was the early part of what was to become a significant campaign.

That summer, I tried to envision how that campaign would take shape. Strangely, the fight in arid Anbar Province made me think about a desperate sea battle between Admiral Horatio Nelson's British navy and the allied French and Spanish fleet at Trafalgar on October 21, 1805. Early in the famous battle, Nelson was incapacitated. One of the thousands of musket balls fired point-blank between the ships during the battle caught him in the shoulder, detoured through his lungs and ribs into his spine, and dropped him to the deck. Three hours and fifteen minutes later he was dead. But his force, outnumbered by thirty-three enemy ships of the line to his twenty-seven, fought on to a decisive victory.

Nelson's force was able to win without him in command because of what had happened long before the first shot was fired. In the years leading up of Trafalgar, Nelson cultivated traditional strengths inherent in the British navy by making technical mastery and a capacity for independence prerequisites for command. His command style then maximized these qualities: His famous instruction to his ship captains before the Battle of Trafalgar— which concluded, "No Captain can do very wrong if he places his ship alongside that of an Enemy"—embodied the value he placed on his subordinate leaders' taking initiative. He sent this guidance confident in their professional competence and in the entrepreneurial hunger he had stoked in them. Napoleon had done just the opposite, prohibiting his commanding admiral from sharing the larger strategy with the French captains.

Nelson knew that while the plan mattered, ultimately the actions of the captains would determine the outcome. His genius was to organize the force into a lethal machine, bring the enemy to battle on his terms, and then unleash the apparatus on that enemy. Even as Nelson lay dying, his machine ground on to victory.

Although Nelson had been dead for almost two hundred years, I found that we in TF 714 faced a similar challenge. And we began with similar fundamental advantages.

To confront Zarqawi's spreading network, TF 714 had to replicate its dispersion, flexibility, and speed. Over time, "It takes a network to defeat a network" became a mantra across the command and an eight-word summary of our core operational concept. But the network didn't yet exist. Building it would prove to be one the largest challenges I faced in my career. It required turning a hierarchical force with stubborn habits of insularity into one whose success relied on reflexive sharing of information and a pace of operations that could feel more frenetic than deliberate.

I knew I was no Lord Nelson, but thinking about what was demanded of him clarified how I could help build, shape, and lead this revamped TF 714.

In command of a dispersed force facing a dispersed enemy, Nelson endowed his low-level leaders—talented, ardent men—with the freedom to maneuver, and the fleet was in turn propelled to success by their zeal. Likewise, our units' strict meritocracy demanded professional expertise, and our highly competent members had the confidence and training to operate without detailed instructions or constant supervision. So I came to see my role as setting the conditions where these qualities were stoked and where initiative, creativity, and dedication to the mission were demanded and supported. Our strategy had to be sound, but success would hinge on how well every level in TF 714 executed it.

I would demand commitment, and offer it myself, to a campaign that would at best be long and arduous. I felt that success against Zarqawi would require nightly raids into gritty neighborhoods to systematically dismantle his network and capture insurgents who hardly appeared to be high-value targets. To many in the elite units, and to some critics outside the command, these less glorious tasks were better left to police or conventional military forces. Inevitably, our campaign would lead to more graveside gatherings in Arlington. Preparing the force and seeking their devotion was ultimately my responsibility but would only be possible through the efforts of leaders across the command. Like Nelson's officers, they would have to stand tall on the deck under fire, leading with competence but also with courage.

And, although we rarely talked of it, we knew we could fail.

Early on, TF 714 lacked a clear mandate to either build a network or get other organizations to join it. Already critics in different parts of the U.S. government felt we were straying outside our traditional role—which we were. But I saw no other organization weaving the kind of web that was needed, and I received strong encouragement from leaders like John Abizaid.

The network I sought to build needed not just physical breadth but also functional diversity. This required the participation of the U.S. government departments and agencies that were involved in counterterrorism, like State, Treasury, the CIA, and the FBI. But we faced a circular dilemma: Because their participation was essentially voluntary, TF 714 needed to be more effective at targeting Al Qaeda for other agencies to want to join our project. But we often needed their support or compliance to be noticeably more effective. The solution, I realized, was to do what we could to improve TF 714 internally to make us more appealing to partners. We began by rewiring TF 714's units into a network better connected to itself and more accommodating to those agencies we were courting.

To do so, and to posture TF 714 for a more decisive role to defeat Zar-qawi's network, we needed a central hub with a clean deck. In July 2004, amid plans to give control of Baghdad International Airport (BIAP) back to the newly sovereign Iraq, we found that new hub at a former Iraqi air base in Balad, a rural area west of the Tigris, almost fifty miles north of Baghdad.

American forces had occupied the base since the invasion, but the tem-porary infrastructure reflected the initial Coalition mindset: Get in quickly; get out just as fast. When I visited our section—a dusty area in the north-west corner, crisscrossed by cement roads and runways—nothing usable remained. For security and secrecy, we walled off our plot with concrete blocks and rock-filled HESCO barriers. Across the airfield, on the other side of its two large runways, Coalition forces occupied tents and Saddam-era buildings. Over time, that area sprouted retail shops and several fast-food restaurants housed in small trailers. But our plot remained spartan—which I considered essential to our focus. Lieutenant Colonel Richard Williams, who commanded the British Special Air Service task force later in the war, captured the atmosphere inside our compound viv-idly: "We were there to fight, to do PT, to eat, to sleep, then to fight again. There was no big-screen TV or other diversion in the barracks. It was a world of concrete, plywood, and gun oil, and it was absolutely intoxicating in its intensity."

To build that world, we set about clearing and rebuilding, deliberately laying out our facilities and equipment to channel the sustained fight ahead. We put our hooches as close as possible to work areas, including the task force screening facility (which would hold new captures for initial interro-gations before we transferred them to internment at Camp Bucca), so that TF 714's leaders could frequently visit and observe, in the process reinforc-ing our mission and our values.

We placed our headquarters and that of the Iraq-focused TF 16 inside one of the three hardened air shelters that sat within the TF 714 footprint. A big concrete dome the size of a circus tent, with beige reinforced walls several feet thick and bowed openings at each end, it resembled a giant caramel-colored turtle shell. Its vaulted interior was ideal: By this time, we were convinced the secretive and compartmentalized traditions of special opera-tions forces, particularly TF 714, would doom us. The hard lessons from the previous months—of Big Ben and the unnerving speed of the enemy network—had chipped away at this dogma. But we knew to deliberately craft our work spaces to channel interaction, force collaboration, and ease the flow of people and information.

Rather than divide the interior into a honeycomb of offices, we congre-gated all of TF 16 in the middle of the hangar and, in an unprecedented move, made the whole cavernous interior a top secret–secure facility: Ev-erything could be discussed on the open floor, so secrecy was no excuse for not cooperating with the rest of the team. Facing a wall of screens

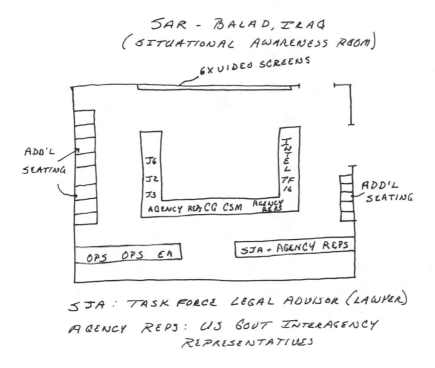

SAR - BALAD, IRAQ
(SITUATIONAL AWARENESS ROOM)

6X VIDEO SCREENS

ADD'L SEATING

J6
J2
J3
AGENCY REP CG CSM AGENCY REPS

INTEL
TF 16

ADD'L SEATING

OPS OPS EA

SJA + AGENCY REPS

SJA : TASK FORCE LEGAL ADVISOR (LAWYER)

AGENCY REPS : US GOVT INTERAGENCY
REPRESENTATIVES

displaying a ticker of updates and streaming real-time video of operations, the TF 16 commander and his key staff sat at a rectangular horseshoe table. Behind them were four rows of tables, divided like a theater. Although a few offices lined the perimeter, the sixty or so people who coordinated TF 16's work—intelligence analysts, operations officers, military liaisons, intelligence, surveillance, and reconnaissance (ISR) operators, airpower controllers, FBI agents, and medical planners—sat in these rows.

My command-and-control headquarters, a few feet away through a plywood door, followed the same logic. Most of our quarter of the hangar comprised what we called the situational awareness room (SAR): I worked primarily at the head of a rectangular horseshoe table that faced a wall of screens. My intelligence director, operations director, and command sergeant major flanked me. Liaisons from more than half a dozen agencies eventually sat at the same *U*-shaped table, though in the summer of 2004 only the CIA seat was filled.

The SAR reflected how my command style and command team were evolving. As I stressed transparency and inclusion, I shared everything with the team sitting around the horseshoe and beyond. E-mails that came in were sent back out with more people added to the "cc" line. We listened to phone calls on speakerphone. (Rare exceptions to this policy of transparency were sensitive personnel issues and cases when sharing would betray some-one's trust.) As a result, I increasingly found T.T. and other senior officers could frequently anticipate my position on an issue and make the decision themselves.

While effective, this immersive command approach was also a bit like playing the run-and-gun style of basketball I'd preferred in my youth. It required almost nonstop focus. My command staff and I often discussed urgent decisions, all while keeping an eye on the screens depicting ongoing operations in Iraq, Afghanistan, and elsewhere. It could also lead my full attention to snap to near-term issues—what we called "pop-up targets" after the silhouette figures on army marksmanship ranges. Aware of this pitfall, I tried to create venues for strategic thinking—frequently gathering members of my command group, subordinate task forces, and an intelligence analyst with in-depth knowledge so we could stew in a topic.

I lived in a plywood hooch about twenty meters from the entrance to the bunker. I shared it with my command sergeant major, Jody Nacy, and operations sergeant major John Van Cleave—both extraordinary soldiers and close friends. I slept on a cot-size, metal-framed bed that spanned the width of the room. On nails and screws I put into the plywood walls I hung back-packs and equipment and tacked up pictures of Annie. The room was spare but convenient. I believed it reinforced the message I preached about focused, unadorned commitment.

Until we won, this was home.

As we were establishing our base in Iraq, so too were Al Qaeda's top leaders. Sometime in the late summer of 2004, Abdul Hadi al-Iraqi, a Mosul-born Al Qaeda lieutenant working in Pakistan, reportedly made his fourth and final trip to Iraq as an emissary between bin Laden and Zar-qawi. He arrived to mediate an agreement at what was a tense time between the two camps. Al Qaeda was increasingly hampered, while news-making Zarqawi was still not fighting under its formal banner.

Since Zarqawi had sent his letter to bin Laden and Zawahiri the previous January, tentatively requesting their formal support, they likely were hung up on whether to endorse the most controversial pillar of Zarqawi's Iraq strategy—the unrestrained targeting of Shia Muslims. The rogue Jordanian likely forced Al Qaeda's hand, as the strategy was already going full bore. In their discussions, Al-Iraqi probably told Zarqawi he needed to cur-tail his "messaging"—the carnage and beheadings his group broadcast abroad—to avoid tarnishing the Al Qaeda brand. They likely haggled over whether Zarqawi needed permission to launch attacks outside Iraq. A red line was surely that Zarqawi could not publicly challenge Al Qaeda's lead-ership. When al-Iraqi left Iraq and returned to Pakistan, he likely did so with an agreement from Zarqawi in hand, for soon Al Qaeda's network would officially have a new franchise.

Around this time, Bennet Sacolick, commanding Green, came into my office to brief the command. Tall, with long limbs, a thin face, and closely cut graying hair, Bennet looked more like a high-school basketball coach than a veteran commando. And he was different. Thoughtful, talented, and pleasingly iconoclastic, he could also be headstrong and slow to carry out changes with which he didn't fully agree. I could live with that. This was a force of strong-willed professionals, and I had learned it worked best to harness, not constrain, their energy and ideas. He had the tricky responsibility of commanding Green as it moved from what it was—an insular, powerful fiefdom—to what it would be—one of the most important nodes in an integrated network.

Bennet put a single PowerPoint slide on the monitor, with five words in a line. Its simplicity belied how profoundly it would drive our mission to be a network:

FIND—FIX—FINISH—EXPLOIT—ANALYZE

The words represented our targeting cycle: A target was first identified and located (Find), then kept under continuous surveillance to ensure it hadn't moved (Fix), while a raid force moved to capture or kill the targets (Finish). Material of intelligence value was deliberately secured and mined, while detainees were interrogated to find follow-on targets (Exploit); the information this exploitation yielded was then studied to better know our enemy and identify opportunities to further attack its network (Analyze).

The military had used targeting cycles like this for a generation. But the task in Iraq—finding and stopping insurgents, not Soviet tank columns—demanded radically faster and often very precise execution. Innovative Green operators and commanders, including Scott Miller and Steve, the squadron commander from Big Ben, had outlined F3EA, as we called it, the previous January as they turned their attention from rounding up former Baathists to attacking Zarqawi's emergent organization.

Bennet's brief captured an important and sometimes misunderstood layer of complexity—what he described as the "blink" problem. A blink was anything that slowed or degraded the process, which often involved a half dozen or more units or agencies working in as many locations. Between each step, information crossed organizational lines, cultural barriers, physical distance, and often time zones.

"By the time we're ready to go after another target," he said, impassioned but focused, "it's often days later, the situation has changed, and we're essentially starting from square one." The process felt slow at the time. In retrospect, it was glacial.

Only part of this was due to our not-yet-robust technology infrastructure. Most of it owed to a lack of trust among the participants. In the world of intelligence, information was power, leading people at each stage to ask themselves a set of questions: *Should we pass this intelligence, and if so, how much? If we share it, will we lose control over it? Will we get in trouble for sharing this information? Will those we pass it to use it in the way we agreed they would?* These doubts cost us speed and often diluted the intelligence, making it less likely to lead to targets.

An initial and soon fixed example involved the National Security Agency, one of our closest partners, which specialized in signals intelligence. By practice, the NSA provided us with condensed summaries and analyses of the signals it intercepted. TF 714 wanted to see raw intercepts right away, before receiving the NSA's summaries a few days after the fact. Initially, the agency refused. The NSA was understandably concerned that we lacked the in-house expertise to avoid misinterpreting and misusing unfiltered information. But it also saw the analysis of signals intelligence as its proprietary domain and was reluctant to relinquish that unique role. Discussing this in terms of "blinks" helped us to identify and parse these choke points and to empathize with the viewpoints and incentives of our partners, like the NSA.

We knew eliminating "blinks" would have a dramatic payoff but would require changes equally significant: They had to be physical, organizational, procedural, and—most important—cultural.

Indeed, the greatest chance for improvement lay in how people felt about their involvement. Everyone needed to trust counterparts (especially those whom they'd never see in person) and believe in the network premise itself. To spark this, we in TF 714 leaned hard on our operators to use video teleconferencing to improve the frequency and quality of their interactions. We instructed our people to share more than they were comfortable with and to do so with anyone who wanted to be part of our network. We allowed other agencies to follow our operations (previously unheard of), and we widely distributed, without preconditions, intelligence we captured or analysis we'd conducted. The actual information shared was important, but more valuable was the trust built up through voluntarily sharing it with others.

M uch of my and my command team's time was spent solidifying the partnerships with the half dozen agencies involved in a single cycle of F3EA. I knew the creative solutions to eliminate blinks would originate from those closest to the fight—and closest to the hiccups.

So while most members of the force were self-starters by nature, I needed them to operate without waiting for detailed instructions or approvals. TF 714's leaders and I tried to set a climate in which we prized entrepreneurship and free thinking, leaned hard on complacency, and did not punish ideas that failed. "As long as it is not immoral or illegal," went my frequent refrain, "we'll do it. Don't wait for me. Do it." On nearly every visit across the force, I asked, "What more do you need?" then fought tooth and claw to get team members any resources they legitimately needed. I wanted to leave them with the sense that nothing was impossible, that there were few valid excuses for not accomplishing the mission, and that even those processes not broken needed fixing. I was rarely disappointed and frequently awed by their solutions.

Although some decisions had to be approved by TF 714's leadership, we pushed authority down until it made us uneasy. More than once I encountered equipment we'd purchased or tactics we'd adopted that made me worry I was negligent in oversight. But I thought of the alternative— corseted centralization—and that squelched my inclination to grab control. At the end of 2005, I listened to the audiobook of Adam Nicolson's *Seize the Fire*; it did a lot to clarify why Nelson came to mind as TF 714 redefined itself. "He would create the market," Nicolson wrote about Nelson, "but once it was created he would depend on their enterprise. His captains were to see themselves as entrepreneurs of battle."

Rarely did any one thing transform our capacity, and few ideas could be traced back to one person. Rather, after weeks and months of incremental changes, what we had once considered swift was slow, rudimentary, or inefficient by comparison. In order to better triage and translate captured documents, for example, we first hired more Arabic linguists. But we only saw exponential improvement after the Defense Intelligence Agency's (DIA) National Media Exploitation Center contributed a powerhouse of capability we could never have created ourselves. To pump terabytes of images and video to them, we augmented the thicket of antennae on our hangar roof with a grove of huge satellite dishes. We learned to feed their linguists intelligence about raided targets, so they had valuable context to help them parse the material. The operators, seeing greater value arise from captured documents, became more focused and effective at retrieving them—no more trash bags labeled with a sticky note.

As one part of our process improved, a new choke point would appear, and the innovation would continue. TF 714 instituted "exploitation VTCs" by installing cameras in the garagelike rooms where our exploitation teams worked in Balad, so that by video link specialists in D.C. or in other parts of Iraq could weigh in on the material only minutes after it was captured. We developed a "portal," essentially a Bloomberg-like terminal that stored a library of intelligence on Al Qaeda. We also uploaded instructional videos— "How to Be a Liaison Officer" was one of the best—and posted important memoranda everyone needed to read. The number of people accessing the information soon bloomed to thousands.

The catalyst to turn so many of these concepts into reality was then-Colonel Mike Flynn, TF 714's J2 or intelligence chief. After I sought his appointment, he joined our force in July 2004 and for the next three years would direct every aspect of the intelligence that is the lifeblood of counter-terrorist and counterinsurgency operations. Mike was pure energy, and it infused his aquiline face and posture. With neatly parted dark hair, a sharp jaw and nose, and a lean athletic build, he looked spring-loaded. In conversation, his eyes locked your gaze and his passionate, raspy Rhode Island clip quickened when he hovered over a notepad. He had an uncanny ability to take a two-hour discussion or a thicket of diagrams on a whiteboard and then marshal his people, resources, and energy to make it happen. The green notebooks he kept—filled with elaborate notes and printouts of slides and images—were bulging compendiums of TF 714's conceptual growth.

Mike's impact was distinct. He arrived as it became clearer than ever that our fight against Zarqawi was, at its heart, a battle for intelligence. And yet when he and I surveyed TF 714's outstations and liaisons during the first few weeks of his tenure, we found ourselves largely focused on the fix and the finish—the tactical strikes—even though the exploit-analyze portion of the cycle would determine our success or failure. Some time would pass before the whole force—which saw itself as the best tactical and operational wing of the military—bought into this. Our physical expansion that summer sped the process: We weren't building more shooting ranges at Balad. We were accruing facilities and resources devoted to collecting intelligence and to understanding the enemy. By the time he left, we had a brigade-size force of intelligence people throughout Iraq, Afghanistan, and elsewhere. This did not happen easily. We often had to scrounge for analysts and interrogators, and Mike built much of this force a pair or a handful at a time.

This market we sought to create yielded a product that came online that August and allowed us to curb the growth of Zarqawi's metastasizing network.

The product in question was, that August, being installed to a group of aircraft whose motley appearance belied their importance. On the cement runways north of our Iraqi hangar, past the sleek black helicopters of the Night Stalkers lined neatly nose to tail, lay our fleet dedicated to intelligence, surveillance, and reconnaissance, or ISR.* For months I'd been fighting to get more ISR aircraft, and we soon resorted to buying, borrowing, leasing, and modifying an odd array of substitutes to create what we dubbed the Confederate Air Force for the amusing diversity of aircraft types. After a visit to Israel in February, I'd wanted SOCOM to bypass the creaky acquisitions process and buy ready-made Israeli models. The air force had objected and promised to field remotely piloted Predators quickly. Frustrated when the air force didn't follow through, my boss at SOCOM, Doug Brown, suggested that as a near-term fix we buy manned aircraft and retrofit them with the ISR packages.

We purchased six commercial single-engine, turboprop planes. We gutted the insides of amenities, stripping them down to the metal frames to reduce needless weight—every ounce consumed fuel and shortened the time they could spend over targets—and filled them back up with the necessary communications and surveillance equipment.

The piece of equipment added that August was the product of the two operators trying not to merely fight the war but to win it. The previous spring, they had come to my office at BIAP and briefed our command that a technology they'd encountered, if slightly tweaked, could prove game changing by allowing us to capitalize on our enemy's own increasing use of technology—particularly communications devices. Indeed, Zarqawi and his group were the first insurgents in history whose rise and success was inextricable from the emergence of broadband Internet and cell towers. When Zarqawi first arrived in Iraq in 2002, there were hardly any cell phones in use (they were technically illegal under Saddam) but they had quickly spread after the American invasion. They relied on high-speed bandwidth to upload propaganda films to the Internet, as did the recruits and funders who watched these videos. In Iraq, they used cell phones to communicate internally and to terrorize Iraqis by sending gruesome clips of executions and torture phone to phone.

The potential the two operators described was obvious, and I directed that we develop the capability. After a few short months coordinating with interagency partners and technology experts, our operators had the product in the field. It lacked the elegance of the all-knowing systems depicted in movies, but in the hands of talented operators, it could lead to Zarqawi's leaders and key lieutenants, who relied on communications to remain networked. To my amazement, the operators invented software that revealed relationships among the owners of captured equipment, giving us a vivid understanding of the enemy's organization. In short order, it was an accelerant to F3EA and had a distinct impact on those in Zarqawi's

---

*"ISR" was the family of assets—including remotely controlled unmanned vehicles, as well as piloted, manned planes—that collected intelligence. Technically, spies were also an ISR tool, but in this war ISR typically referred to manned and unmanned aerial surveillance platforms.

network, forcing them to modify how they communicated and making it much harder to hide in the expanses of Anbar.

These operators' mentality and sense of ownership of the outcome in Iraq had also taken root on an organizational level. Shortly after my first visit to the Green compound during the fall of 2003, I had "given" Iraq to them. My guidance was simple: Green would be in charge of TF 16 until we won. They could rotate squadrons and alter deployment schedules, but no outside unit would replace them. *We're not here to fight; we're here to win.* This put whoever was the Green commander in operational control of all TF 16 forces in Iraq—at the time, primarily Green, Rangers, and Special Operations Aviation units. (At the same time, I put TF 328 in Afghanistan, under the rotating command of the Rangers and the SEALs.) Giving the Iraq fight to Green led them to tap their best talent in a way a higher head-quarters could not: They brought top officers and NCOs, even when they were technically on their three months of rest, to Iraq to serve in odd but important jobs before returning a few months later to their normal posi-tions within their squadron.

Our command had come to accept our central role in the fight against Al Qaeda. The next round of that fight was heating up again in Fallujah. Ever since the United States had lost control of the city, Coalition leaders had known we would have to wrest it back. After a long summer, that operation was imminent.

On September 12, 2004, Lieutenant General John Sattler assumed com-mand of the 1st Marine Expeditionary Force, and I felt like I had an-other close friend in a key role. John had been General Abizaid's operations chief at CENTCOM the previous year, and I was fortunate that he was now overseeing Anbar at such a critical moment.

Beginning with John's arrival, each Friday I would helicopter down from Balad to Camp Fallujah, southeast of that city, to meet with him and his Marines for informal dinner meetings. I was normally accompanied by T.T., Mike Flynn, and the Green planners and commanders who operated in that area. After landing in a dry field inside their base walls, I met John outside the mess hall. With him was usually a mix of his chief of staff, his director of operations, the regimental commander responsible for Fallujah, and his battalion commanders.

Inside the mess hall, our group snaked past flimsy white plastic chairs and folding tables covered in Marine Corps–red tablecloths where British and American service members ate dinner. These men and women, bent over their food in conversation on those nights, would in a few weeks take Fallujah block by block. I knew they and their comrades would bear the burden and costs. But I also sensed the cloth from which they were cut, and in their faces I saw the same fortitude and heroism of those who had gone before, at Okinawa, Inchon, and Khe Sanh.

At the time, the relationship between the Marines and our TF 16 forces remained cool, which was understandable. The Marines had the difficult job of containing and eventually clearing Fallujah, and the value of our operations and air strikes—which had continued steadily since Big Ben—was not always clear to them. Much of the Marine leadership we dealt with that summer had not been convinced that Al Qaeda or Zarqawi was active in Anbar. But the offensive to recapture Fallujah was to be bigger, faster, and nastier than the April operation, and we needed to build relationships in the lead-up. John and I hoped our warm friendship would cascade down the ranks. He made this easy and was an ideal partner. Although a tough Naval Academy wrestler who would soon oversee the bloodiest battle of the Iraq war, John was deeply humble and quick with self-effacing humor. With his friendly, coarse voice, he set a warm atmosphere and had a knack for disarming any stink eyes.

Designed to build trust, these dinner meetings were low-tech affairs without computers or slides. We talked about the previous week and coordinated upcoming operations. Members of TF 16 distributed targeting folders, which were becoming increasingly advanced. These could consistently show where targets were in the city as well as when and how they moved. As we discussed how to shape the battlefield prior to the inevitable ground assault, the tabletop became Fallujah's neighborhoods—we turned saltshakers and napkin dispensers into buildings, while knives, laid end to end, became roads that needed to be blocked or taken.

While our meetings were upbeat, they were not cavalier. TF 16 had accrued a reservoir of credibility from over two months of strikes—so far, a perfect record except for the one bomb diverted into an open field. John knew this. Before he arrived in Iraq, John's previous post at CENTCOM had made him our point of contact when we sought approval for strikes. But like me, he also understood the stakes: A bungled strike with significant civilian casualties could cause us to lose the independent authority to conduct air strikes—which remained the sole means of interfering with insurgents in what was otherwise an internal safe haven.

The growing rattle of insurgent bombs—like the one that exploded the afternoon before one Friday meeting with the Marines—was an urgent reminder that a sovereign Iraq could not allow Fallujah to be a staging area from which insurgents were able to prepare increasingly sophisticated and sinister attacks. On Thursday, September 30, a suicide car bomb exploded half a block down the road from a new sewage facility in Baghdad. The families who had just attended the facility's opening ceremony wandered over to the cordoned-off area. As they often did, children crowded near the site to pick up debris and greet American soldiers. While they loitered, a second car, black, sped down the street. Thirty-five of the curious children were killed when the driver detonated his payload. Ten Americans and more than 140 Iraqis were wounded. In addition to Shia civilians and

Americans, reconstruction projects and the contractors building them were targets of Zarqawi's suicide bombings.

Between our Friday-evening dinners throughout September and October, TF 16 commanders went to Camp Fallujah to coordinate their targeting with the Marines, who lent key support—providing cordons, putting doctors and triage hospitals on standby, and offering spare barracks for our operators. This level of coordination and cooperation eventually became routine, but in the fall of that year it was not.

Even as our task force attacked the insurgent nodes in Fallujah, John Sattler wisely enlisted Prime Minister Allawi to exhaust all opportunities to negotiate with the insurgency to turn over the city without an assault. But the negotiations broke down, the insurgents ignored Allawi's ultimatums, and the Coalition scheduled the invasion for the first week of November.

With the date set, the task force went into high gear at the end of October. TF 16's full focus turned to Fallujah, and we transitioned from hitting targets every couple of nights to striking multiple targets throughout the day. We targeted leaders, trainers, and mortarmen in order to eliminate their skilled labor. We knocked out key command-and-control centers and barriers the insurgents set up to channel American vehicles and foot patrols into ambushes and traps. At the same time, then–Major General Rich Natonski, commanding the 1st Marine Division, ran feints at the south of the city, while the Marines planned to bring the real attack from the north. As the British had done there in 1941, the Marines dropped leaflets urging civilians to leave Fallujah. Most did, while the jihadists entrenched and fortified the terrain.

John later recounted one of the strikes on these insurgent traps that reflected why our continued efforts at partnership were so important. One night just before the offensive, a group of Marine leaders, including John and the ground division commander, gathered in their combat operations center, where they watched videotape from one of the targets hit that day. After the air strike destroyed the initial target, smaller explosions cascaded down each of the roads leading away from it: pop, pop, pop, like chains of fireworks or lines of electrical charges. These were daisy-chain IEDs the insurgents had buried under the road, stringing together bombs for meters on end that would explode together. As the charges continued exploding on the soundless video, the room was silent. The hushed commanders watched, imagining what would have happened had a file of Marines attacked that position with the IEDs still unexploded, waiting in the packed dirt beneath their feet.

In an effort to ensure that no targets went unserviced, strikes continued up until the Marines' ground assault. That invasion began when Iraqi commandos and Marines seized the main hospital just before midnight on November 7. Air strikes continued throughout the following afternoon, the Marines cut the power at 6:00 P.M., and later that night they crossed the berms and railroad tracks at the city's northern edge. Accompanying them were TF 16 operators.

Zarqawi's jihadists who fought in the streets during the battle were doing so under a different name. On October 17, three weeks before the Fallujah offensive began, Zarqawi's group posted a message to its website declaring that Zarqawi pledged *bay'ah*—swore allegiance—to Osama bin Laden. The message hinted at Al Qaeda's senior leaders' unease with Zarqawi's campaign design. After eight months of back-and-forth messages, Zarqawi's group explained, "our most generous brothers in al Qaeda"— the upper echelon of leadership, mostly in Pakistan—"came to understand the strategy of the Tawhid wal-Jihad organization in Iraq, the land of the two rivers and of the Caliphs, and their hearts warmed to its methods and overall mission." While tensions would remain, Al Qaeda blessed the decision on one of its websites a few days later. Zarqawi's group now went by "Al Qaeda in the Land of the Two Rivers" or "Al Qaeda in Iraq" (AQI), the latter being the name we had already called the group since Zarqawi first emerged into the fray the previous January.

Less than a year after writing to bin Laden and Zawahiri for support, Zarqawi was quickly eclipsing Al Qaeda's patriarchs as the most active, violent, energetic commander of jihad—especially for a younger generation of aspirants who were less theologically minded and more violent. The United States was partly at fault, as the constant chorus of blame assigned to Zarqawi in the press—much of it warranted, some of it misappropriated—had inadvertently inflated his stature. But the ruthlessness and ambition he would continue to display in the years ahead convinced me he would have grabbed the spotlight anyway.

That fall, as bin Laden accepted, however reluctantly, Zarqawi's strategy, I was thinking hard about our own. Unless we developed a more effective Coalition program, working with credible Iraqi security forces, we would have limited options. I had already concluded that a strict decapitation strategy was unlikely to work. Top Al Qaeda leaders were well hidden, and their capture or death was rarely decisive. Moreover, a string of effective operations could give us a false sense that we could slowly grind Zarqawi's network out of existence.

I believed, however, that if we controlled the tempo, rather than merely eliminated personalities, we could halt Zarqawi's momentum. Then, partnering with a more robust Coalition and Iraqi effort, we could ensure his defeat. Such a campaign design, however, confronted the reality that in irregular warfare, successful guerrillas won by controlling the speed of the war. They forced the incumbent to fight at their pace—slowing it when they were vulnerable by reducing their profile, quickening it when they sensed fatigue or weakness in their foe.

Our campaign would flip this and seek to deny the insurgents this inherent advantage: If we could apply relentless body blows against AQI—a network that preferred spasms of violence followed by periods of calm in which it could marshal resources—then we could stunt its growth and maturation. Under enough pressure, AQI's members would be consumed with staying alive and thus have no ability to recruit, raise funds, or strategize.

Meanwhile, instead of trying solely to decapitate the top echelon of leaders, we would disembowel the organization by targeting its midlevel commanders. They ran AQI day to day and retained the institutional wisdom for operations. By hollowing out its midsection, we believed we could get the organization to collapse in on itself.

To pursue this strategy, our force needed to operate at a rate that would exhaust our enemy but that we could maintain. Key to this was a regular TF 714-wide regimen, what the Army terms a battle rhythm. Disciplined routines get a bum rap in today's world, where we celebrate spontaneity and often look for the game-changing sprint to the end zone. But this war was a marathon, and distance running had taught me the importance of pace. Moreover, it was my message to the force that we could not be rattled: In times of both quiet and chaos, we would maintain a calm, disciplined, even rhythm.

This began on a personal level. I needed to have a regular, worthwhile presence as I commanded from the theater and moved locations every few days. When in Iraq, I retired at dawn, slept for several hours, then replied to the day's first tranche of e-mails. During these quiet midmorning hours, I'd spend a few minutes in the Joint Operations Center, talking to the skeleton staff who planned for the evening's actions or performed maintenance. Then, come noon, I ran for an hour parallel to the runways at Balad. During summer the pavement baked at 120 degrees Fahrenheit, but I tempered my pace and found every run a good diversion.

During my run or while lifting weights, I listened to audiobooks. I've always loved to read a wide variety of books, and I found audiobooks offered the best way for me to digest them. After loading them onto my iPod, I listened through headphones while working out, then used small speakers to continue listening while I dressed. Annie checked out every good audiobook she could find in local libraries and bought me countless others she thought would interest me. My tastes remained eclectic—from *Freakonomics* to *Don Quixote*, *Moscow 1941* to *Intelligence in War*—and they made me think more broadly than the constant staccato of e-mail or daily briefs.

After my midday run, meetings began—the first of which became a hallmark of TF 714: Our operations and intelligence video teleconference or O&I. On the surface, the update—we aimed for ninety minutes, but it could run to two hours—looked like the kind of standard review of operations and intelligence that I'd attended in green canvas army tents and that other units held internally. But we created the O&I to tie together a geographically dispersed command, and it differed from other updates in three key respects: its regularity; the size, diversity, and dispersion of the forum; and (made possible by the first two) the richness of information discussed.

As the core heartbeat of our battle rhythm and the nucleus of each day, the O&I ran six days a week and was never canceled. Our force, spread across time zones, operated uniformly on Zulu time (Greenwich Mean Time), so the O&I began at noon Zulu time (4:00 P.M. inside our Balad hanger, 9:00 A.M. on the East Coast of the United States—by design at the start of the workday for the agencies in D.C. that we wanted to participate.

The O&I audience began relatively small that winter of 2004, when we could connect a constellation of D.C. conference rooms, our bigger bases in Iraq and Afghanistan, and teams in embassies across the region. But by the following summer, the video link was seamless and reached all the way to our austere forward operating bases in the Iraqi desert or Afghan hills. We developed prepackaged communications bundles that could connect from anywhere in the world. We installed secure communications in embassies to entice our partners to participate. Eventually, every member of TF 714 and partners in D.C. could view the meetings on their personal computers, listening through their headphones. Especially as TF 714's battlefield success gained notice, by 2007 the O&I was a worldwide forum of thousands of people associated with our mission.

The size of the forum invited an array of perspectives that built a collectively richer understanding of the topic at hand. So too did the depth of information we discussed and the regularity of our conversations. Few topics were off limits: Granular tactics were discussed alongside strategy, intelligence alongside operations, resourcing alongside values. The best moments came when a briefing sparked a conversation among multiple people at different agencies that disclosed information that was known but had not been shared across the community.

I quickly saw, however, that beyond its value for the information shared, the O&I was the single most powerful tool I had at my disposal in leading a dispersed force. A video teleconference couldn't replace a hand on a shoulder. But the O&I provided me nine hours a week during which I could seek to influence, inspire, and learn from those I led. I asked probing questions, but also ones I knew the answers to, in order to give them a moment to demonstrate their mastery in front of an audience of thousands of their peers. I would restate something I feared was unclear or provide my personal assessment of something I wanted to ensure was accurate, only to have the experts correct me. These exchanges were helpful in calibrating my thinking, but they also hopefully demonstrated to everyone that we were less a team led by me than we were a team leading one another. The regular briefings also reinforced the briefers: As Admiral Nelson knew, decentralizing did not mean disengaging, and those farthest out could not have any doubt that their work fit into a wider mission.

Unless someone in my room was talking, one camera was on me the whole time. By nature an introvert, I found the requirement to be on camera for so long exhausting, but it forced me to be a better leader. My interactions with one person were amplified to the thousands—subordinates, peers, superiors—who were watching. If I probed until people were uncomfortable, I tried to resist chastising them in the open forum. I tried hard to address all the briefers by their first names, something that got easier the longer I was in command. I was glad one day to get a cheeky but well-meaning e-mail from a subordinate who had tried to calculate the number of times I said "thank you," or some form of it, in the morning stand-up. He had lost count before it was over.

Critically, the O&I fostered decentralized initiative and free thinking while maintaining control of the organization and keeping the energy at the lowest levels directed toward a common strategy. This was meant to liberate subordinates and remove unnecessary hesitation. When I told a major, for example, that he did not have to ask permission to do something, I simultaneously broadcast that directive to all of the other majors. They now didn't have to waste time dialing up headquarters. Everyone left the O&I confident they knew the latest update of our organization's intent, strategy, rules, and approvals. Our discipline of schedules, processes, and standards did not reduce adaptability or creativity. It was the foundation that allowed for it.

In subtle and overt ways, the O&I helped us to animate Beltway conference rooms and cubicles with the "This is a war" ethos that filled our austere, dusty outstations downrange. By spanning time zones, we were gluing together groups of people with different levels of devotion. We relied on people in the States for whom this was a nine-to-five job, who picked up their kids from soccer practice after work. Even when their commitment was outsize for D.C., it often didn't match the grueling pace maintained in three- and four-month spurts by people downrange. The O&I helped stoke further commitment. In most stateside locations, the military wore the dark green uniform or the blue blouse to the office. So after months and eventually years of appearing in the tan uniforms worn by those deployed, we built up moral suasion. The impact was more immediate when people outside the war zone watched the operators brief. They saw their days-old beards and the guns, helmets, and body armor hanging on the wall. They knew those men would in a few hours be out in dark, tight spaces. The stand-up reminded analysts that their work was not just paper traffic; it affected lives. Those who were frustrated by sending intelligence reports into the ether had the simultaneously sobering and exciting experience of hearing that their work did, or could, lead to a senior leader being captured or to a car-bomb factory being shut down.

These moments were motivation enough for much of our force, so in concluding remarks, I would summarize some of what I had heard and try to connect it to our bigger goals. We didn't have time to drive this with emotions, to huff and puff. We needed constant, demanding, driven vigilance and professionalism. I tried to build that up a few sentences at a time through forceful but even tones. *Do your job. People's lives are on the line. Thanks, as always, for all you are doing.*

The O&I ended in the early evening, and preparations for battle filled the rest of the day. Although we conducted a few operations before sunset, as night fell, the operations centers hummed with serious, focused activity. Soon the rumble of helicopters and aircraft, some throaty, some a high whine, bounced across the darkened gravel and off the cement walls and barriers of our compound. The sound grew in layers, building like a chorus singing a round, as one set of rotors, propellers, or jet engines came alive, joined the cacophony, and then departed the airfield. Gradually, the chorus dissipated until silence returned to the darkened base. Elsewhere across Iraq and on bases in Afghanistan, smaller outbreaks of mechanical sound cut into the night.

On some nights I walked to the dark tarmac, took a seat in a helicopter, and joined the raids. On other nights, I sat on the back bench of the operations center, watching the screens and listening to radio traffic and updates read aloud to the room from the operations log. After the initial assaults were called in, I often went to the gym for a second workout—exactly thirty-two minutes on the treadmill—and then returned to headquarters until light broke and the teams headed back from the targets.

When the dry heat of a new day began to creep in, supplanting the relative cool of the desert night, I retired to my hooch. Propped in my bunk, I'd read for bit, often waking to find myself nodding over pages I couldn't remember. Above my side table, Annie smiled at me from the photographs tacked to the wall. It had now been a year since I had taken command, deployed forward for most of it. As a captain in Korea, during our first long separation, I had ended each night by writing her a letter. Now I went to bed each night knowing that in the morning I would have an e-mail from Annie and a few minutes to reply before the day's activities gained momentum.

These developments, during the second half of 2004, laid the essential framework for a machine that would become larger, better synchronized, and smarter in the years ahead.

As we grew our network, solidified the relationships that bound it, and committed ourselves even more to the fight in Iraq, our enemy did the same. On December 16, Osama bin Laden issued a long audiotape, much of it a detailed screed against his homeland's leaders. But in imploring action, he turned to the more vulnerable front next door, in Iraq. A year earlier, he had "urged" young Muslims to wage jihad there. He now took a direct, almost scolding tone: "Mujahideen . . . you scare the enemy but they do not scare you, and you are well aware that the burning issues of the *umma* today are the jihads in Palestine and in Iraq. So be very sure to help them, be sure to know that there is a rare and golden opportunity today to make Americans bleed in Iraq, in economic, human, and psychological terms. So don't waste this opportunity and regret it afterwards."

Eleven days later, amid the Christmas news lull in America, Al Jazeera broadcast an abridgment of another audiotape. In addition to warning Iraqis not to participate in their forthcoming January parliamentary elections, bin Laden named Zarqawi the emir of Al Qaeda in Iraq. Zarqawi's men, he added, needed as much as two hundred thousand euros a week to maintain their good work.

The year ended with the highest-profile terrorist leader doing more than channeling recruits and donations to that year's most violent. By knighting Zarqawi and elevating his fight, bin Laden had tied his own fate, and his organization's, to the success of Al Qaeda in Iraq, now the most crucial front in the global jihadist movement. Al Qaeda staked its vision—of American humiliation, jihadist victory, and a resuscitated caliphate—on that new front.

Contesting that vision, and the men who flocked to Iraq to achieve it, would soon lead us to an arid stretch of western Iraq.

| CHAPTER 11 |

▼

Out West

November 2004–October 2005

A t lunchtime on December 21, 2004, five days after bin Laden urged young Muslims not to miss the "golden opportunity" in Iraq, a man dressed in an Iraqi security forces uniform walked to the middle of the football-field-size mess tent at Forward Operating Base Marez in Mosul, northern Iraq. He wound his way through the long rows of white folding tables, covered with Tabasco bottles and napkin dispensers, where Iraqis and Americans sat eating. Some reports had him loitering by the sandwich bar. Others who survived saw him sitting and, at the last moment, bowing forward in silence. In either case, a few minutes past noon, he ignited. The BB pellets packed in a thick layer over the explosives of his vest cut through the packed mess hall in a metallic cloud. Unseen shock waves pulsed out, scattering tables and bodies. The glowing heat scalded the room and ripped open the tent ceiling. Beneath its charred tarp and in the bright, smoky column of sunlight coming through the gash, twenty-two people lay dead, including an operative from my task force.

After the mess-hall attack, Ansar al-Sunnah, the group that had sheltered Zarqawi before we toppled Saddam and that maintained a close but rocky alliance with Al Qaeda, was quick to take credit. In its Internet boasts, Ansar claimed the attacker was an Iraqi, a hometown recruit from nearby Mosul. But intelligence instead indicated Ansar had dispatched a twenty-year-old Saudi medical student, one of the many foreigners imported for these martyrdom attacks.

Contrary to Ansar and Al Qaeda propaganda efforts, Iraqis rarely volunteered for martyrdom operations at that stage of the war. These attacks were instead the hallmark of foreign volunteers, whose increasing infiltration into Iraq had been one of TF 714's main concerns in the months leading up to this bombing. The operative we lost that day was part of a team we had dispatched to Mosul to help combat that flow.

Foreign fighters had fought in more than a dozen conflicts since bin Laden and his fellow volunteers had first become "Afghan-Arabs" in the 1980s. Iraq was the latest and, we believed, quickly becoming the largest battlefield destination for what the jihadists called the "Caravan of Martyrs." Most were young men who considered themselves jihadists. Few came to Iraq with dreams of restoring the caliphate there. Rather, most left their homes in North Africa, Saudi Arabia, the Levant, Central Asia, and Europe roused by a more visceral sense of Muslim duty. Like the generation before them who flocked to Afghanistan, Chechnya, and Bosnia, many came fired by righteous indignation of real or perceived injustices committed by the West against their Muslim brothers and sisters.

I was in Afghanistan with Mike Flynn when I learned about the attack, and our loss, later that evening. Mike had been doing a superb job making our network smart about the growing threat. But as the event that day reinforced, we needed to get smarter, faster. We needed to scale our network to combat the tide of young Muslim men funneling into Iraq.

A lthough the war in Iraq was becoming international, TF 16 was not. Our operative was killed in Mosul, but the explosion was a product of a network that extended far beyond Iraq's borders. Increasingly, its supply lines of material, money, recruiters, handlers, and, most important, volunteers, stretched to Riyadh and Aleppo, Tunis and Hamburg. But this periphery of AQI remained vague to us. To uncover and then dismantle these outer rings would require that our network overlay theirs. This meant finding creative ways to employ the international reach of other agencies and units, usually existing local security forces, like the police. To coordinate our effort to tie this together, we decided to replicate the proven model of JIATF-East in Bagram by creating a parallel structure in Balad. While JIATF-East focused on locating senior Al Qaeda leaders in Central Asia, the mission of the Balad-based JIATF-West was to reverse engineer the problem we were seeing in Iraq.

I knew the success of JIATF-West, like so many of the new teams and units we created, would hinge on effective leadership. So I called two men whom I had known since they were young soldiers, Tom D. and Tres H., into the Operations Center in our Bagram compound. T.T. and I had carefully selected each man for the task. Tres was an intelligence professional, but his real gift was getting people to do things and then feel particularly good about having done them. He could, as necessary, alternate between being animated, stern, demanding, and consoling. He had been a private in my Ranger company from 1986 to 1987; now, almost twenty years later, I was sending him as an experienced major to work a difficult assignment. He would be deputy to Tom D., who had been a Ranger captain when I commanded the regiment, which he had left to join Green. Tom D.'s wry, irreverent humor formed a veneer over his dogged leadership skills, which he later used to great effect in command of a Green squadron in Iraq. T.T. and I judged that together, Tom D. and Tres could corral, convince, coerce, and inspire a motley group of military and civilian analysts to gel into a team. Within a couple of hours of receiving their new mission, they had computers and gear quickly packed and had joined Mike and me on the plane for Iraq.

A biting, wintry desert wind swept Balad when we arrived in the early morning the day after the mess-hall bombing. December turned the ubiquitous dust, powderlike during the scorching summer, into a soupy, adhesive mud, and we walked carefully to avoid it as we returned to our hangar. At daybreak, Tom D. and Tres moved into two empty white corrugated metal trailers and began to set up shop. That day the trailers had no chairs, tables, or computers. JIATF-West had only Tom D. and Tres. But within weeks, analysts from the CIA, FBI, NSA, NGA, and DIA were working inside. The trailers quickly became a critical piston of our war machine, now moving in wider concentric movements.

TF 714's demonstrated battlefield effectiveness made us increasingly legitimate in the counterterrorism community. By affiliation, the JIATF grew in prestige. Its own weekly VTC began with a modest audience but soon included chiefs of station from across the Middle East, deputy directors, and three dozen agencies. Because we did not hesitate to share operational details with them, D.C.-based analysts knew that a weekend in their office doing work for "the task force" might lead to an arrest in the back alleys of a casbah. Deploying forward to serve in a JIATF became sought-after duty.

The JIATF's essential products were information-rich, five-page targeting folders on key enemy operatives. Each included exhaustive background on the target, his activities, and often enough specific location and pattern-of-life information for a host nation to capture him.

A key to doing so was the web of liaisons whom we had seeded across the region and who worked with U.S. country teams to ensure that local authorities saw the JIATF's communiqué so they could make an arrest. I learned early on that our influence in the embassies and agencies we were wooing often depended on the simple charisma, integrity, and competence of our liaisons. So I carefully selected the professionals we placed there, routinely diverting world-class commandos or peerless intelligence professionals to serve as liaisons, despite the impact on our operations. The trust they had earned toiling away by themselves in isolated embassies—far from their tight-knit units and the comparative glory of the fight—was vital.

Our concern about the strategic threat that the refreshment of foreign fighters posed had been building in the months prior to the December mess-hall bombing and the inception of JIATF-West. Beginning that fall, I met with the leaders of TF 714 and TF 16 in a series of two- and three-hour-long sessions. In front of maps and whiteboards, we discussed the evidence and potential ways to combat the problem. Bennet Sacolick, the Green commander, had returned to the States to oversee the unit there, leaving Colonel John Christian in charge of TF 16. "Big John," as Graeme Lamb later warmly called him, was indeed that. With cropped whitish hair and a big, sculptural face, he looked like a bust of a Hellenistic soldier. He was articulate and persuasive, speaking in a distinctive baritone and cleanly enunciating the last syllables of his sentences. He had been commander of TF 16 during Big Ben and throughout the previous summer had gone back and forth with the Marines' intelligence shops, who disagreed that there was a significant "Al Qaeda problem" in Anbar.

John was a perceptive leader who often saw and understood trends before hindsight put them in relief for the rest of us. He had been deploying to Iraq since the summer of 2003 and before then had been a military adviser in the Philippines with Wayne Barefoot. There, the two had followed Islamic extremist groups like Abu Sayyaf and Jemaah Islamiyah, elements with regional and national agendas but aspirations toward Al Qaeda's sophistication. Their experience watching these groups as they networked, cohered, and grew helped Wayne and John divine some of Al Qaeda in Iraq's more opaque patterns.

During these sessions, we tried to do more than parse calculations of foreign fighters. We questioned our underlying assumptions about the insurgency—its strategy, depth, and leaders—that led us to see what we thought we were seeing. These debates inevitably turned to discussions about Zarqawi and what the influx of foreign volunteers revealed about his proficiency as a manager: AQI's swift fielding of these volunteers required mature processes. The increased number of volunteers implied they believed Zarqawi's was a winning team, while the strict deployment of suicide bombers against select targets revealed an ability to design and execute a strategy with discipline. That Zarqawi could keep this regional network glued spoke to his pull as a leader.

Zarqawi's charisma was the topic of one of the more memorable of these sessions that fall, when we sat down with raw transcripts eavesdropped from a broadcast he had made. He began with a lengthy preamble. For minutes, Zarqawi enthusiastically praised each of his cells in Iraq.

"To the brave lions of Samarra," he said, "you strike fear in the hearts of the invaders. . . . And to sons of the sword in Diyala Province . . . To the vanguard in Tikrit . . ."

After a while, John Christian cut in. "He does it by township," he said, reluctantly impressed. What could be more powerful to a struggling group of jihadists in some dusty basement than to have Zarqawi himself praise their outfit on a broadcast that would soon rocket around the world on the Internet?

"This guy is the real deal," John said. "He understands what he's doing." I agreed. The speech confirmed the image we had stitched together of Zarqawi as a leader. Recovered videos showed him circulating the battlefield, motivating his disparate frontline cells. Firsthand reports of his visits described him as exceedingly quiet and gracious yet visibly confident enough to be inspiring. To the awe of his followers, Zarqawi personally went on missions, donning disguises to get past American checkpoints.

Zarqawi's reputation as a battlefield commander was the foundation for his mystique. That jihadist mystique—a potent mix of violence and real charisma, perfumed by thick propaganda efforts—was wafting outside of Iraq's borders. As it did, he became the face of the insurgency. Without that personification and his celebrity, the otherwise anonymous Iraqi resistance groups would have had a harder time pulling in foreign volunteers.

At the time, we believed between 100 and 150 jihadists were entering Iraq every month, but that calculation, based on a combination of assessments, was less than scientific. Against the Coalition's estimate that the Sunni insurgency comprised between 12,000 and 20,000 men of varying levels of enthusiasm and expertise, this might have appeared small. But I believed their impact on the violence was disproportionately large. The leadership of Al Qaeda in Iraq remained heavily foreign, replenished by outsiders who were sometimes experienced operatives with personal and ideological connections to Al Qaeda's regional network. At the lower end of the spectrum, the younger, harsher, and more enthusiastic jihadists infused energy into the insurgency. Without competing commitments like jobs or families, these foreign volunteers had nothing to do but fight full time. Unlike aggrieved Iraqis, they had no indigenous stake in the future of Iraq. So a functioning electric grid or more jobs or even greater political concessions for Iraq's Sunnis would not convince them to lay down arms. They came to hurt and kill Americans.

Most critical was the steady resupply of suicide bombers. If even a fraction of the hundred men crossing the borders were willing to blow themselves up on suicide missions—and documents TF 714 later captured and released showed the majority crossed the border with that stated intention—they could do great harm. Through increasingly seismic car bombs that left whole city blocks charred and relentlessly decimated Iraqi police and army recruits, a single suicide bomber could exact a disproportionate toll.

As we studied the problem, we found the enemy network had a frighteningly efficient system to recruit, intake, move, and employ foreign fighters. We were most amazed by cases where, in a year or less, they could reach a young man with no prior history of violence, pluck him from his daily life, get him into Iraq, and convince him to strap a suicide vest across his torso or torch off a car bomb in a crowded, daylight market. Although each person volunteered for individual reasons, we began to see a template emerge.

For many, the journey began in the glow of a computer screen, watching slick propaganda videos posted to the Internet. Carefully constructed montages, overlaid with hymnal chanting or righteous sermons, played on the man's guilt and anger, while propagandists challenged his sense of manhood with stories of Iraqi women raped by Americans. But often, slick videos were superfluous: In my experience, we found that nearly every first-time jihadist claimed Abu Ghraib had first jolted him to action. Ginned up, he started to hang around a local mosque. There, a spotter picked him out, detecting in him the same fidgety, adolescent yearning he'd seen in dozens of other young men. The spotter befriended him and soon introduced him to a wider group of men. These guys, the recruit found, also liked to discuss the American war in Iraq and the jihad. They met regularly at the mosque to listen to the smooth, airtight lessons of their mentor or cleric.

Soon the young man began to grow a beard and wear different clothes. He started praying five times a day. It felt good to have the rigid discipline, the direction, and to think of himself as a hard man. In many ways he appeared no different from hundreds of millions of devout, peaceful Muslims. But the ideas he imbibed were narrow and potent. For some in the group with guilt over a wayward youth, jihad offered redemption, as it had for Zarqawi, who had ruined his adolescence with drugs and gangs. Soon the young man had no friends outside this circle. If the recruiter introduced the young recruits to a jihadist just back from Iraq, they would envy the older, prouder bearing of this veteran. One day, the young man came to the mosque and found that a handful of regulars were absent. It had been their turn. Violent jihad became not just a pillar of the particular faith preached to the young man's group. It was now compulsory as a source of esteem in his enclosed world. With a companion, or a maybe a few friends from the mosque, the young man decided to set out for Iraq.

We found that most jihadists entered Iraq through Syria. Using their own savings or money from a wealthy sponsor, they typically flew into Damascus with little more than a gym bag of clothing. From the airport they were split up and rapidly put into what we called ratlines that moved them through safe houses in Syria. Usually passed between single recruiters, not teams, the jihadists moved up to Aleppo, then gradually down the Euphrates through Dayr az-Zawr to the Syrian side of the border, just across from the industrial town of Al Qaim, Iraq. After nightfall, a taxi deposited them at crossing points thirty miles up and down around Al Qaim, and they crossed the final few hundred yards on foot.

Once in Iraq, handlers whisked them to safe houses and confiscated nearly everything. They took volunteers' donations to Zarqawi's organization— sometimes only a handful of bills, but usually hundreds, if not thousands, of dollars. AQI kept meticulous records during this intake. The questionnaire we later recovered revealed the enemy had a serious, sophisticated managerial concern with the integrity and breadth of its network. Because its ratlines in Syria tended to rely on paid criminal smugglers, not true believers, AQI asked jihadists what fees the handlers had extracted and how well they had been treated. To plumb potential partners, AQI had recruits list which other "mujahideen supporters" they knew and how strong their relationships were.

At these early way stations, the handlers sorted the jihadists. Nationalities appeared in spurts and cycles, though Saudis were the largest, most consistent contingent. Men with visible smarts or a science background might go to Mosul to help make bombs. But handlers would be most anxious to gather those who volunteered to be suicide bombers or peel away those who appeared vulnerable enough to be turned into them.

Inside Iraq, potential suicide bombers were normally handled like rounds of ammunition, moved from safe house basement to safe house basement. Expedited down the pipeline, they were sequestered from outside contact and constantly indoctrinated—all to prevent them from changing their mind. By design, often the first time a suicide bomber saw Iraqis in the flesh was in the moments just before he killed them.

Attacks were carefully orchestrated. The operative who was to film the 2000 attack on the USS *Cole* overslept. Zarqawi brooked no such risks. On nearly every suicide bombing, a car with a videographer trailed behind. To safeguard against last-minute hesitation, the follow-on car or a lookout on the street often controlled detonation. In some cases the driver—like the Saudi behind the wheel of a fuel truck that exploded in Baghdad on Christmas Eve that year—did not know his was a suicide mission. But, at least early in the war, most went willingly. In many of the videos filmed on the day of an attack, the men appeared almost ecstatic.

Periodically, we had information that young men were planning to martyr themselves. The messages they left behind were chilling harbingers of attacks we often could not prevent. There was no humanity or humor in anything surrounding a young person willing to blow himself up to kill innocents. But I had to smile when I saw one message to a mother and read her stern response: "Stop this foolishness now and get your rear end home and back to work." I hoped the young man complied. There was no way to know.

During the last week of November 2004, as the second battle of Fallujah waned, I invited General Casey and key members of his Multi-National Force–Iraq (MNF-I) staff to our compound at Balad to discuss our concerns over the foreign-fighter flow.

Although I had a good relationship with George Casey, I was glad that he brought his operations officer, Major General Eldon Bargewell. I'd known Eldon since we were captains at Fort Benning. A highly decorated Vietnam veteran, Eldon and I had worked together many times in later years during his service both in Green and on the TF 714 staff. Eldon was unfailingly helpful in smoothing tensions between MNF-I and TF 714. The setup of our two headquarters invited friction: Although we fought in Iraq, TF 714

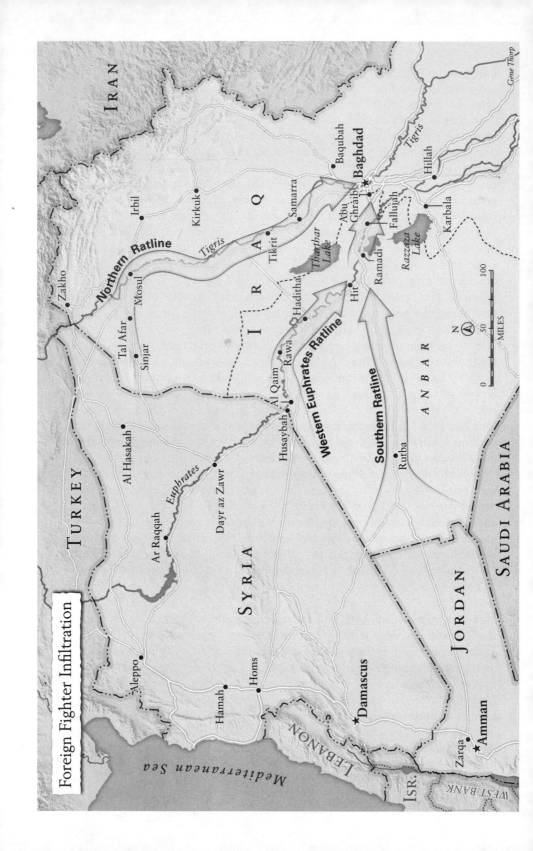

Foreign Fighter Infiltration

Mediterranean Sea

TURKEY

IRAN

SYRIA

IRAQ

JORDAN

SAUDI ARABIA

LEBANON

ISR.

WEST BANK

ANBAR

Northern Ratline

Western Euphrates Ratline

Southern Ratline

Zakho
Irbil
Kirkuk
Mosul
Tal Afar
Sinjar
Al Hasakah
Ar Raqqah
Dayr az Zawr
Husaybah
Al Qaim
Rawa
Haditha
Hit
Ramadi
Rutba
Samarra
Tikrit
Baqubah
Baghdad
Abu Ghraib
Fallujah
Karbala
Hillah
Razzaza Lake
Tharthar Lake
Aleppo
Hamah
Homs
Damascus
Amman
Zarqa

Euphrates
Tigris
Tigris

N

0   50   100
MILES

Gene Thorp

answered to CENTCOM, not to MNF-I. Meanwhile, the ground-holding commanders' occasional annoyance with TF 714—over disruptive targeting missions in their domain or our greater share of resources—all percolated up to MNF-I headquarters. By being there, Eldon could translate our mission and culture to those he served with on the conventional side.

In the long meeting, Mike Flynn and some of our best minds, like Wayne Barefoot, laid out the case for the threat this foreign flow presented. I was disappointed at how much our read on the enemy differed from that of some of Casey's key staff. One senior officer on the MNF-I team openly doubted our assessment of AQI's central role in the insurgency.

I sympathized with the concern that emphasizing the role of foreign fighters could be a way to unintentionally sidestep the reality that Iraqis were, in large numbers, joining the insurgency motivated by earthly grievances, not religious jihad. Especially early in the war, we in TF 714 and much of the rest of the Coalition problematically used "AQI" as a catchall designation for any Sunni group that attacked Americans or the Iraqi government. In truth, more than fifty named insurgent groups fought at one time or another. These distinctions were important but also could be misleading. By numbers, AQI never constituted the majority of the insurgency. But AQI usurped the insurgency's leadership and gave it direction and shape—often through sheer intimidation. So while in 2004 and 2005 an Iraqi fighting for a nominally nationalist group did not consider himself a card-carrying member of AQI, his group was fighting within Zarqawi's strategic framework. The insurgent groups were like local gangs, while AQI—richer, crueler, and better linked across the country—was the mafia.

No major MNF-I orders or initiatives flowed from that November meeting at Balad, but our discussions continued. Unfortunately, the thinking at our respective headquarters continued to diverge. Around the time we met with George Casey and his staff, a month before Tom D. and Tres stood up our JIATF to combat foreign influence in Iraq, MNF-I assigned its own Baghdad-based JIATF to target "former regime elements"—essentially old Saddam apparatchiks.

"The fat, old, jowly Baathist generals holding meetings in hotel lobbies in Amman and Damascus are not controlling the insurgency," John Christian lamented after the meeting, voicing our collective frustration. "They are not the instigators of violence." Nor were they the levers to success, despite some of their aggrandizing claims to control the spigot of insurgent attacks.

Although disappointed, I appreciated it was an antidote to groupthink for two major headquarters in the same theater to come up with such different assessments. And we could not fault Casey's staff for eyeing us as a kind of special-interest group. TF 714 global mission was almost entirely directed toward Al Qaeda and its close affiliates. So in Iraq we focused on AQI and its terrorist allies like Ansar al-Sunnah. That narrow lens could produce assessments that inflated Al Qaeda's role. And because threat measurements guided resource allocation, TF 714 had an interest in portraying

Al Qaeda as the central enemy. As TF 714's growing credibility gave us greater sway in the war's decisions, I knew we needed to maintain a culture of self-scrutiny and humility, lest we have it wrong. Our divergent outlooks also told me our integration and communication with MNF-I was too weak. This we could, and would, labor to fix. At the conclusion of the meeting, while I felt his staff had it wrong, I sensed General Casey remained unconvinced but open-minded.

E very Friday that I was in Iraq, I flew from Balad to Baghdad to meet with General Casey. Periodically, in addition to my operations officer, T.T. (or his replacement, Kurt Fuller), and Mike Flynn, I brought two members of TF 16. I wanted Casey to see the knowledge and commitment that defined the task force.

Most of my travels around Iraq were at night. But flying over Baghdad every week for more than four years gave me a time-lapse-photography-like view of a city as it convulsed from the relative calm of 2004 to the dark days of 2006 and 2007 and settled back into a seething equilibrium in 2008. In January 2005, the streets we flew over were tagged with reminders of that pivotal juncture in Iraq. Colorful election posters and banners with flashy Arabic text hung alongside wanted posters for Zarqawi, with tip-line phone numbers running below his cold face staring out under a black kufi.

Since taking over, George Casey's two strategic priorities had been to build up Iraq's security forces and to support the emergence of a legitimate government. According to this plan, midwifing a new Iraqi government required that Casey secure the three Iraqi votes scheduled that year: in January to elect an assembly to draft the permanent constitution, in October to ratify that constitution, and again in December to vote for the government that would serve under that constitution.

We were increasingly focused on integrating our efforts with the larger MNF-I objectives. So in the lead-up to the January 30, 2005, election, we were doing everything we could to contain Al Qaeda's plans to undermine them—which Zarqawi announced a week before the election. On January 23, Zarqawi released an audiotape calling democracy heresy. Eight years earlier, while the two were locked away together in Jordan's Suwaqah Prison, Abu Mohammad al-Maqdisi, a leading ideologue of the jihadist movement, had mentored a younger Zarqawi. Maqdisi made his name in the 1990s, in part through an innovative treatise that argued democracy constituted not just a separate political process but a religion unto itself. For true believers, then, voting was a veritable act of heresy.

Zarqawi now invoked this logic as religious top cover for what were surely more clear-eyed strategic concerns. His sectarian scheme relied on keeping Sunnis paranoid and fighting. This wasn't hard: Whether or not Sunnis voted, the elections were going to entrench the majority Shia in power in Baghdad. But Zarqawi needed Sunnis fully disenfranchised—to make the specter of Shia domination more fearsome and to prevent insurgents from getting the idea that integrating into the political process might have its benefits. So, joined by other hard-line insurgent groups, Al Qaeda in Iraq prepared to unleash hell on the polling sites and the vulnerable queues of Iraqi voters. Its online warning that week was ominous— and essentially an admission that Zarqawi would target Sunnis. "Take care not to go near the centers of heresy and abomination . . . the election booths," it threatened. "The martyrs' wedding is at hand."

Violence on election day was far more muted than Zarqawi's histrionics portended. Insurgents overran no election sites. But their threats were enough to keep many Sunnis home; others boycotted in genuine protest of the new government, which would freeze them into a minority role. Only 3,775 people voted in all of Anbar Province—2 percent of the population. Sunnis secured a mere 17 of the new National Assembly's 275 seats.

W ithin the military, the elections had crystallized the increasing competition over resources, which had grown more acute that winter. The conventional forces understandably sought to employ intelligence, surveillance, and reconnaissance (ISR) aircraft, like UAVs, to monitor polling sites in the days preceding the vote. We had asked for control of these assets in order to ramp up an offensive effort to preempt AQI's attacks. We sought a balanced approach of using the ISR to pressure AQI's network up until the day before the elections, then shifting them to monitor the voting areas.

Although not the first occasion for passionate competition between special and conventional operations over select resources like ISR, the January elections foreshadowed an extended debate over the best use of what were always scarce, highly useful tools. For relatively new assets, like the Predator UAV, demand continued to soar as more units identified valid, innovative ways to employ them.

The same applied to us. We first tended to use the vantage offered by ISR to observe ongoing operations, which was valuable but not game changing. But by 2004, we had integrated ISR into F3EA, learning to weave together information from detainees and human sources with expanding communications intelligence and then use aerial assets to build an understanding of a target's behavior and potential links to the insurgency. This "target development" lay at the heart of the F3EA process and enabled vastly faster and more successful raids. So that our strike forces could be used each night, we employed part of our ISR each day to develop future targets and used another chunk to support ongoing raids. After asking our staff to analyze the likely impact of increasing our ISR assets, I briefed General Casey that if our ISR capacity were doubled, our output, or the number of enemy targets we could hit, would more than double: Since Big Ben we had organized and trained ourselves to get more out of every hour of ISR flight time. With consistent support from Generals Casey, Abizaid, and Brown, the ISR available to TF 714 increased and my claim proved true.

I knew, however, that much of the military resented our disproportionate piece of the ISR pie. While not apologetic for our share, I reminded
our teams that we needed, day in and day out, to prove why we deserved these
tools. I used the O&I one afternoon that winter to make the point.

"Okay, so we've got twenty-four hours in the day," I said, addressing a
member of the operations staff. "What is the maximum amount of time the
plane, as a piece of machinery, can be in the air? Forget the human component—
let's find out many hours it needs for maintenance and refueling."

"Yes, sir," he answered, and told me how long it took to refuel and rekit
one of the drones.

"So out of the remaining hours, how many can we push the live video
feed to our operations center?"

The officer knew immediately and answered.

"All right," I said. "So my directive is simple. If it's not flying and pushing the feed that many hours, every day, I need to know why."

This tone was becoming familiar to those in the force: As 2004 ground
into 2005, I was leaning hard on TF 16 to ratchet up the number of raids
we conducted. In the O&I and personal interactions with our force, I'd
articulate the need to pressure AQI as much and as rapidly as possible, before it could expand its hold on the Iraqi people. Operators understood how
sacred their lives were to us, but they also understood the importance of
their role in a fight that would be won by slim margins.

Our increasing operational tempo prompted me to send a more sober
message to General Casey. Termed a Personal For, or P4, it was designed
for point-to-point communications between senior officers, avoiding the
normal route through staffs. I used these communiqués sparingly but did so
when I felt it was important my message not be lost or delayed. As we increased the pace and precision of our targeting, we correspondingly captured more and higher-ranking members of Al Qaeda in Iraq. Yet our
capacity to interrogate them lagged. In my message, I reemphasized my
concern that we suffered from a shortage of trained interrogators. I told
him flatly that I could not ethically send my force on dangerous raids to
capture enemy leaders if we could not adequately question them. Without
more interrogators, I wrote, TF 714's ability to strike targets was limited.

The interrogator shortage wasn't George Casey's fault or a problem he
could solve, and I knew that. He was one step up the pipeline from me. The
problem lay in the slowness of the government bureaucracy to adapt to
the requirements of the war on terror, particularly in Iraq. Half a dozen
corners of the military—from the Pentagon to the services to training
centers—had a part in producing and fielding a professional interrogator,
so following up on urgent manpower requests often felt like punching a
cloud. On 9/11, our shortage was understandable. By 2005, it was indefen-
sible. At wit's end and desperate for a way to help Casey get us the needed
personnel, I wanted my stark message to be ammunition he could use to

press for more interrogators. In the years ahead our shortages decreased, but the situation was never close to good enough.

By spring, it appeared elections would do little to bring unity to Iraq— and were in fact energizing the causes of violence. It took until May for the new government to be seated, under Ibrahim al-Jafari, a Shiite. The Ministry of Defense went to a Sunni, but the Ministry of the Interior went to a Shiite believed to be a leader of the Badr Brigade, a revenge-minded militia linked to Iraq's largest Islamist Shia party. Before long, the Ministry of the Interior—whose police and commando units, unlike the Iraqi army, functioned independently of the Coalition's control—began expunging Sunnis from its roster and putting uniforms on Badr militiamen, who used their badges and guns against Sunnis and ex-Baathists. Surely to Zarqawi's delight, the government's sectarian direction confirmed Sunnis' worst fears. He and his insurgents appeared an ever more necessary buffer.

Throughout it all, General Casey was a disciplined, methodical thinker. His was not a mind that turned like a weather vane based on the last briefing he had received, only to turn back the other way. TF 714's intelligence conclusions and reasoning suited his temperament, as our industrial grind gathered information from ground actions, detainees, documents, cyber operations, liaisons, our JIATFs, and other nations' police and intelligence. Although never perfect, there was a special value to the volume of intelligence, as it fostered a more well-rounded view that a single source or a biased samples were less likely to corrupt.

By May 2005, which alone saw more than sixty suicide bombings, Casey was increasingly convinced that the foreign-fighter flow was a strategic vulnerability. He had decided the Coalition needed to conduct major operations along Iraq's western border, in an attempt to shut down the ratlines of foreign fighters. The biggest of those ran down the western Euphrates River valley, connecting Syria to Baghdad. Al Qaeda had rooted itself throughout the valley, setting up way stations and safe houses in rural desert compounds and riverside cities, from Al Qaim down through Rawa, Haditha, Hit, Ramadi, and Fallujah. I believed that as part of a larger MNF-I effort, our task force could play an effective role. The smaller size and greater agility of TF 16 enabled us to swiftly shift our focus to this contested waterway, pressuring parts of the enemy network conventional forces could not. I offered to Casey that our strike teams and the focus of our targeting apparatus shift to be part of the effort out west.

But I worried our efforts would only be decisive if the Coalition went full tilt. "Conventional forces have got to do their part," I told Casey. "We can only be part of the solution."

He agreed and said we would contribute to a significant effort to reinforce the conventional forces that, through no fault of their own, were hopelessly overstretched along Iraq's western border. The Marines who owned much of the terrain were forced to rely on the Iraqi Department of Border Enforcement to manage the "forts" that dotted the border in Anbar and Najaf provinces. That spring, the Coalition was building new forts in these provinces, planning to have thirty-two installations facing Saudi Arabia, Syria, and Jordan. But many of the posts were deserted. A handful of chronically underequipped Iraqis—with little ability to check the flow of men, trucks, and cars—manned others. Many of the abandoned posts that pocked the desert border got most use from nomadic shepherds, who commandeered the buildings as temporary mangers for their sheep.

Soon after meeting with Casey, I sent General Abizaid a message, explaining my decision to support this push out west. *These operations will be riskier,* I explained, *because our teams will be a greater distance from our bases.* Although I worded my message in terser military-speak, I knew my old friend would understand the stakes. *Fewer conventional forces exist to act as quick reaction forces if operations go sour. I'm going to send us out there in greater numbers, and I think it is going to be very dangerous. I think it is going to be bloody. And so I am steeling everybody for greater casualties.* Abizaid called me when he got the message. We skipped the usual joking back and forth that started most of our conversations. John thanked me for the forewarning and said he concurred with the decision.

As we considered how to unseat Al Qaeda from the western Euphrates and dampen its ratlines, I became convinced that we would need more TF 714 forces in Iraq. To supplement what we then had—a Green squadron and smaller detachments of Rangers and SEALs—I decided to deploy a second squadron of Green to Iraq and bring some of our SEALs and aviation from Afghanistan. I did not make the decision lightly. In the year and a half since I'd taken command, I had already increased our forces, as well as expanded our liaisons across the region. We were nearing the highest deployment pace we could sustain. In a year, an individual TF 714 operator spent four months in combat, doing near-nightly operations; four months on the short tether of alert, on call the entire time; and four months recovering from or preparing for deployment, sometimes overseas if he was pulled out to serve as a liaison. By 2005, the men had been at this for four straight years. That cadence was sustainable but couldn't be taken for granted; now, for a number of months as we surged, our pace would become an unsustainable sprint. I knew that sprint was the only way we could help arrest the deteriorating situation in Iraq.

In truth, our need to increase forces required no special insight. It was almost mathematical. The much more difficult—and far more crucial— challenge came after I made that calculation. Alongside the other leaders of TF 714, I needed to get the force to believe, as I did, that this push would be decisive—and thus worth the costs.

I convened the top commanders of TF 714 and TF 16 in Iraq to explain why the surge was necessary. Kurt Fuller, a bulky, fox-sharp Oklahoman and the newly arrived TF 714 operations officer, was there, as were Mike

Flynn, Jody Nacy, and the top leaders of TF 16, at that time led by Colonel John Christian. The meeting wasn't easy. As I explained the campaign plan I proposed, the Green leaders sat with still faces. Only their eyes moved, alternating between me and the whiteboard where I wrote and drew a map of Iraq. Until this point, TF 714 had drawn up targeting decks, not maps: We executed missions; we did not wage campaigns.

"Listen," I said, turning from the whiteboard to the still faces. "The western Euphrates is damn near occupied. Look around. I don't see anyone else who can do what we can do out there." I told them about my conversations with General Casey, and I explained why I thought it would work.

I sat down at the table and asked for their thoughts. They expressed sentiments held within the unit that were apparent over the next few months. Many felt other Coalition forces were not pulling their weight in Anbar and that the campaign would be increasingly conventional and therefore not our kind of fight. They had concerns this emergency setup—two squadrons forward and one back—would become permanent once the surge dislodged those squadrons from their traditional cycle, ultimately depleting the force. As I had to John Abizaid, they expressed concerns that in the further reaches of the desert, they were dangerously far from medevacs and quick reaction forces. They were professional but candid—as I needed them to be.

As I often did, I watched Green's command sergeant major, Chris Faris, to gauge his reaction. By position and personal credibility, he was the unit's elder, both bellwether and opinion maker. At the time, I perceived he was worried about my decision, but felt he was less opposed to the concept of a surge than seriously concerned this one just wouldn't work. But despite misgivings, the Green leaders seemed to recognize that we could not win in Baghdad without clamping down on these ratlines that funneled violence into the capital city. And without Baghdad, we could not win the war.

In truth, during the months leading up to this discussion with the leaders of Green, I believed that failure in Iraq was tangibly close. My force's ability to target kept improving through the fall of 2004 and into early 2005, but no matter how good we got tactically—and we were energetically tearing away at the network—the situation was getting worse. We had been alarmed a year earlier, when Al Qaeda held large parts of Fallujah. Now, by the early months of the summer of 2005, Al Qaeda essentially controlled stretches of the western Euphrates River valley. It needed to be stopped.

The biggest leadership challenge fell to Chris Faris and to Scott Miller, who was then replacing Bennet in command of Green. Just as he was taking over, I asked Scott to order Green to do something unprecedented in its nearly thirty-year history. He believed in the operation, but he would be weakened if his unit perceived that he supported the surge just to curry favor with me. He handled it masterfully. Through calm, firm, but not unsympathetic pressure, Scott and Chris broke through some initial intransigence and continued to develop momentum and support for what remained a highly controversial decision. It increased the already high regard in which both their unit and I held them.

Ultimately, it fell to John Christian, as the head of TF 16, to name the operation. Typically, these code names had little rhyme or reason. But this time John chose one that reflected the gnawing fear in Green that sending two squadrons was a roll of the dice: Snake Eyes.

As I had confided to John Abizaid, I knew my decision could result in losing men. Even before our surge forces began to arrive en masse in July 2005, three heavy losses reminded everyone how dangerous the summer would be.

On May 31, Sergeant First Class Steven Langmack was killed by small-arms fire while entering a fortified enemy position in Al Qaim, near the Syrian border. As a Ranger NCO, Steve had been the patrol leader for my command group, and we had enjoyed the comfortable relationship of long-time comrades. Steve's wife was a strong lady who had operated an independent coffee stand on Fort Benning during our tour there. Annie attended Steve's funeral at Arlington and that night sent me a note describing the stoic courage of his wife. Less than three weeks later, on June 17, Master Sergeants Mike McNulty and Bob Horrigan were killed, also in close-quarters combat with tenacious enemy fighters.

These deaths hit the unit like a shudder. Losing a McNulty, a Horrigan, or a Langmack meant losing a man who had been in the unit for a decade or more, where he had grown from a young soldier to a veteran one. Senior members had children who played on the same soccer teams; their wives were close friends. Bob Horrigan, for example, was a fixture in Green and in TF 714. He and his brother had been privates in my Ranger company back in 1986 and 1987, and I remembered the young, happy-go-lucky Horrigan twins with fondness. Bob had been in Green for years and had grown into one of its patriarchs. As an instructor of new operators, he had earned a special respect across the force and had a following of younger operators who looked up to him. He made beautiful custom hunting knives in his garage between deployments and had decided this tour would be his last. He was to retire the following spring.

These losses on the cusp of the major offensive made the upcoming danger very raw. *If a man and an operator like Bob Horrigan can get killed*, the unavoidable reasoning went, *so can I.*

As the second Green squadron flowed in that July, we put them outside Al Qaim. A contingent of Rangers and SEALs joined them. Our push into that area of the upper Euphrates would not be the first time this stretch of desert had hosted bitter fighting. The landscape appeared largely unchanged from the summer of 1941, when then–Major General William Slim, the British general later famous for his operations in Burma, having worked up the valley, prepared to attack Vichy French forces ninety miles upriver. "Toward us flowed the winding Euphrates, broad, placid," Slim wrote, while "on either side stretched, mile after mile, the desert, flat and featureless, a muddy brown." In the summer of 2005, the area looked like a Nevada mining town, full of little brown buildings and a dusty, desolate horizon. Ten miles southeast of the city itself lay a big, defunct phosphate plant that abutted an industrial rail depot. We constructed a base around there, and the squadron set up shop inside the old, run-down factory. At this critical, tough post we installed one of our most talented commanders.

By the time we arrived that summer, Al Qaim and Husaybah, closer to the Syrian border, were nasty. Our Green teams, Rangers, and SEALs worked alongside the Marines from the 2nd Regimental Combat Team, ably commanded by then-Colonel Steve Davis, whose South Carolina–size bailiwick ran to the border area. Davis, one of the few Marines who had served previously on the TF 714 staff, shared our conviction that the foreign infiltration through the Al Qaim area was a major threat. The Marines had encountered wily, well-trained foreigners, and their Camp Gannon, in Husaybah, had suffered a deluge of bold attacks. That spring, while insurgents engaged in a diversionary gunfight, a dump truck bomb exploded at the camp entrance while a fire engine—driven by suicide bombers wearing Kevlar vests and protected by thick plated glass—sped in behind it and attempted to breach the gate. They were repulsed, thanks largely to the heroics of a Marine lance corporal.

As the Marines and TF 16 contested the area near the border, a seperate force of Marines worked their way east to west, fighting a hopscotch series of battles against insurgents up the Euphrates River valley. Our forces joined them.

If the black Al Qaeda flags that insurgents draped over the sides of compound walls or flew from rooftops weren't evidence enough of how deeply entrenched Zarqawi sympathizers were in the upper corridor, the violence that ensued when we contested these areas proved it. The engagements were some of the largest since the initial invasion of 2003. And yet in the vast desert expanse far from Baghdad, they went mostly unnoticed by the American public. At a time when Iraq was supposed to be emerging as a secure and sovereign nation, western Anbar was exploding. Largely away from civilian populations, our forces waged bitter fights against confident AQI militants, periodically requiring thunderous bombing runs on isolated mud and cinderblock safe houses. The United States was meant to be rebuilding Iraq, but my old mentor Lieutenant General John Vines had to destroy five bridges along the Euphrates River to constrict the enemy's lateral maneuvers.

Early in the push, the close-quarters engagements quickly gave us a deeper understanding of the enemy. We began to see the structures and relationships that allowed AQI to nest so thoroughly into this stretch through Anbar. AQI had purchased some of the safe houses it used, but it really relied on an archipelago of guesthouses run by sympathetic or permissive villages and tribes. When insurgents fled, they scaled fences using carefully placed but otherwise innocuous-looking piles of junk against the back walls. As they scattered into villages, they relied on what John Christian aptly termed a biblical system, using Old Testament–era techniques—sympathizers left small markings on the lintels of their compounds, for example—invisible at first to our technology and untrained foreign eyes.

When we did encounter insurgents willing to make a stand, the fight was different from most of what we had experienced in Iraq to date. As a hostage-rescue and strategic-raid force, our inclination was to do deliberate, intelligence-driven planning, then conduct fast point assaults—landing helicopters on roofs and fast-roping into compounds. These were high-risk tactics based on knowing more than the enemy, achieving absolute surprise, and having forces that, pound for pound, were always superior to the enemy ranks.

That approach had largely worked, but by the summer of 2005 our adversaries had wisened up and hardened into a different foe. AQI leaders, even midlevel ones, began wearing suicide vests constantly, usually sleeping in them so that if our men breached their doors and headed toward their cots, they could light themselves off in the darkness. They lay traps, setting up makeshift pillboxes in the slits between staircases and rigging the walls of compounds with explosives. Whole units of foreign fighters barricaded themselves in basements, firing up through the floorboards or at the ankles of operators. We adapted, landing helicopters kilometers away, walking to the targets, cordoning the areas and methodically working our way through them. Although the fighting was bitter, some of our operators felt a certain relief that, for once, the insurgents were out in the open, not melting into cities or hiding among civilians.

Not since Fallujah had we seen AQI fighters defend houses or hold and retain terrain. Their actions out west seemed to signal that they possessed new resolve and increasing confidence. We needed to break both.

By August, the costs of the surge I had feared were realized. On Thursday, August 25, 2005, a pressure-plate triple-stacked antitank mine hit a convoy of our men in Husaybah, between the Syrian border and Al Qaim. Green operators Master Sergeant Ivica Jerak and Sergeant First Class Trevor John Diesing, and Ranger Corporal Timothy M. Shea were killed. A fourth operator, Sergeant First Class Obediah Kolath, was critically wounded in the blast and flown to Germany. Others in the troop were badly wounded. All were professional soldiers, volunteers for their elite units, and fully cognizant of the risks. But it left us all with the ominous feeling that our losses would mount.

Before dawn on Sunday, August 28, as I prepared to fly out to visit this team at their outpost, I wrote an e-mail to Annie that captured the challenge I faced as their commander: "A lot of emotion attached, naturally, but we need to maintain absolute focus right now."

On the helicopter ride, I thought about something T. E. Lawrence had written in *Seven Pillars of Wisdom*, a book I've revisited countless times. Writing about his own fight in the desert, not far from where these Rangers and operators had fallen in Iraq, he reflected on the fragility of the tribes in the face of heavy fighting: "Governments saw men only in mass; but our men, being irregulars, were not formations, but individuals. An individual death, like a pebble dropped in water, might make but a brief hole; yet rings of sorrow widened out therefrom. We could not afford casualties."

Writing about World War I, Lawrence had experienced a very different theater from that in Europe, where men died en masse—hamlets lost an entire brood of boys and men to a few minutes of shelling in wet, gas-filled trenches. There, commanders risked seeing their men not as men but as mere numbers in the columns of a War Office ledger. But the tribes Lawrence corralled and led were constituted so thickly, with such interwoven histories and personal ties, that the loss of one member sent fissures through them. Our forces, more tribes than modern military units, were the same way to me.

We landed in the evening near the phosphate plant outside Al Qaim and met with the squadron inside the run-down factory they used as a base. The commander at Al Qaim, Lieutenant Colonel Trevor, had a small work space, not much bigger than a storage closet, in the shabby, trailerlike building that adjoined one end of the factory.* I sat down with him there before meeting with the rest of his men. I had known Trevor a long time. He had served as a Ranger captain for me. He had lost his wife to sickness a few years earlier. Then, as on this night, I had been proud of—and steeled by—his determined strength. I let the door close and looked him in the eye.

"How are you, Trevor?"

"Sir, I'm good," he said. We were speaking quietly.

"Well, how are the guys?"

"I think they're all right, sir," he said. "But they're beat up."

That same day, Sergeant First Class Kolath, who had been flown to Germany after the mine attack there in Husaybah, had died from his wounds. Loss was compounded by the stress of combat. Getting hit by an IED is unnerving. There is no enemy to fight back against. It strikes and brings a few moments of chaos and noise, but in the silence afterward there is no enemy to engage, no contest where each side has a chance.

We met with the operators in a small room in the compound. I'd known many of them for years. For a few it was the first time we had met. I began by offering my sincere condolences for their losses. They knew how I felt, but I wanted them to hear it directly. Losing comrades is hard, and I didn't patronize fellow professionals by telling them that. I rarely prepared remarks beforehand and for small groups never did. On the ride out I had thought through key points I want to make, but now I mostly tried to understand the tenor inside the room.

"Listen," I said, "this really hurts. But let me tell you what would make these hurt even more: if it is all in vain. Now I am not fucking around. I am here with you, not just physically here, but I am completely committed to

---

* Trevor is a pseudonym.

this thing. We can beat these bastards, and we're going to." Victory could not offset the terrible price already paid—a price that would increase as the fight expanded. But losing would make the pain unbearable.

I explained how the nighttime raids they were running in that corner of the war were vital to TF 714's mission and to the larger strategy. "Let me tell you what your brothers up in Mosul are doing," I said, building out a wider view of the fighting that summer. I told them what we were seeing in Baghdad and east of them in the rest of Anbar. I shared what I thought George Casey was thinking, based on my most recent conversations with him.

Within a couple of months, by October, we were able to see real evidence of the strategic impact I hoped would materialize when I explained it to the operators in Al Qaim that day. We had no way of scientifically proving the effect of the push out west, but the trends were promising. By August, the Coalition believed suicide attacks accounted for a decreasing proportion of the car bombings. According to the National Combating Terrorism Center, in July 2005, before the campaign, 51 suicide attacks killed 277 people and wounded 751 in Iraq. In September, nearly 40 such attacks killed 431, and wounded a similar number. November saw 11 attacks that killed 270. In December, 10 incidents killed 97 people.

In October, Chris Faris, the command sergeant major of Green whom I regarded as the unit's elder, weighed in with his assessment. In one of our routine strategy sessions, he said, "The western Euphrates push was the right thing to do. I was worried it wouldn't work, but it did." Our successes out west solidified a significant shift in how we, as a force, regarded ourselves. Previously content to conduct periodic point assaults, the western Euphrates campaign gave us a larger sense of possibility—and responsibility.

Although we did not fully appreciate it that summer or fall, the hot contest over Al Qaim became about more than tamping the foreign-fighter pipeline. There in the dusty border juncture, the first sparks for a much larger, more definitive strategic shift flashed. In addition to fighting the Marines and our TF 16 operators, Al Qaeda found itself facing a third enemy: the Albu Mahal tribe, many of whom not long before had fought with the insurgency against the Coalition. The tribe turned, joined the Americans, and rose against Al Qaeda for a number of reasons. In part, they found themselves on the losing end of an alliance between AQI and another tribe.

But also, by all accounts, the Albu Mahal's was a reaction to the tyranny and barbarism that ran amok when AQI governed anything bigger than a city block. Al Qaeda degraded the tribal structures and overtook smuggling and other criminal sources of wealth. It forced intermarriages between its foreign men and Iraqi girls. Reports from the mini emirates AQI established, like the one in Baqubah north of Baghdad, reported that they punished grocers who kept tomatoes alongside cucumbers in the same stall—as the vegetables' shape suggested male and female body parts commingling. Sunnis throughout Anbar were having similar reactions to Al Qaeda's mix of the infantile and the sadistic. Al Qaeda shifted in the eyes of many Sunnis from protectors to parasites. As it did, many Sunnis real-ized that they had made a nasty Faustian bargain by accepting the jihadists. If they resisted, Al Qaeda brutally forced them into submission.

So it was in Al Qaim: The defiant Albu Mahal uprising was quickly snuffed out. A week after I left Al Qaim, Al Qaeda pushed into the town center up the road from the phosphate plant. Its men openly patrolled the streets, where they promptly executed nine members of the Albu Mahal-led resistance. They hung Zarqawi's black flags from buildings and, at the city's edge, brazenly announced their coup: "Welcome to the Islamic Re-public of Al Qaim."

Although the Mahal failed, other tribal leaders took note as they and their people squirmed in the grip of AQI. These onlookers saw that resis-tance to Al Qaeda was possible, but highly dangerous. Such resistance needed the full, coordinated backing of the Americans—something the Albu Mahal complained they lacked. Moreover, throughout Anbar that summer and fall, tribal leaders saw that when Americans showed up to a place in full force, when they surged, they defeated Al Qaeda. John Chris-tian spent much of the summer out west. He would later play a critical role in helping the Coalition capitalize on the promising dynamics that flashed in Al Qaim and would soon spread wider.

Any payoff from our push was, however, many hard weeks of fighting away when I left Al Qaim that evening of August 28. On the long night-time helicopter ride back to Balad, with the gray desert rolling beneath, I thought about the team I had just seen and the previous two years. I thought about where I stood with my force. I wasn't a full member of their small subtribe out in Al Qaim, which had grown even tighter through its toil and losses along the border. But I was more than a mere visitor to their camp.

Back in Balad, I walked from the tarmac across the gravel buffer, silver under the glow of the spotlights, to my office to write another e-mail to Annie. "Just got back from a long helicopter flight to see the guys farthest out, who lost so many recently. Great trip and I am very happy I did it," I wrote to her. "Some very genuine comments afterwards about how much they appreciate me doing that regularly like I've been able to do." Upon reflection, the note was more upbeat than I felt. But it showed my resolve—and that of my men.

By now the force knew I had been forward for almost two years and had extended for a third. I was fiercely proud to be associated with the people in TF 714, and leading them had become inseparable from how I thought of myself.

I had told the men that day what I believed and what had come to be my life: *It's the fight. It's the fight. It's the fight.*

CHAPTER 12

The Hunt

June 2005–May 2006

"Good morning," the president said in a brisk but friendly manner as he took his seat at the head of the conference table. On June 29, 2005, the White House Situation Room felt miniature. The principals' black leather chairs, with high backs and deep seats, felt outsize, and it was difficult to move around due to the tight quarters. The walls' lacquered wood paneling shined plastic-like under the fluorescent glow. They were undecorated except for a Frisbee-size presidential seal, hung at eye level directly behind the president's chair, and a digital clock with red LED numbers that clicked away near the ceiling.

I'd been in a number of Situation Room meetings during my earlier tour on the Joint Staff, but never with all the principals or the president. Big personalities filled the tight space. To the immediate right of the president sat Vice President Cheney, on his other side was Condoleezza Rice, five months into her tenure as secretary of state. Next to her was Secretary Rumsfeld and, to his left, General Richard Myers. As Rumsfeld's plus-one, my seat was along the wall, behind his. Across from Rumsfeld sat John Snow, secretary of the treasury. National Security Adviser Steve Hadley and Homeland Security Adviser Fran Townsend were also present. Notably absent were any members of the National Security Council staff with the Iraq portfolio. This meeting, like those leading up to it, excluded these Iraq officials, drawing a line between the counterterrorist fight and the war in Iraq. This was a division of labor at odds with my thinking about Al Qaeda's ascendant role in Iraq.

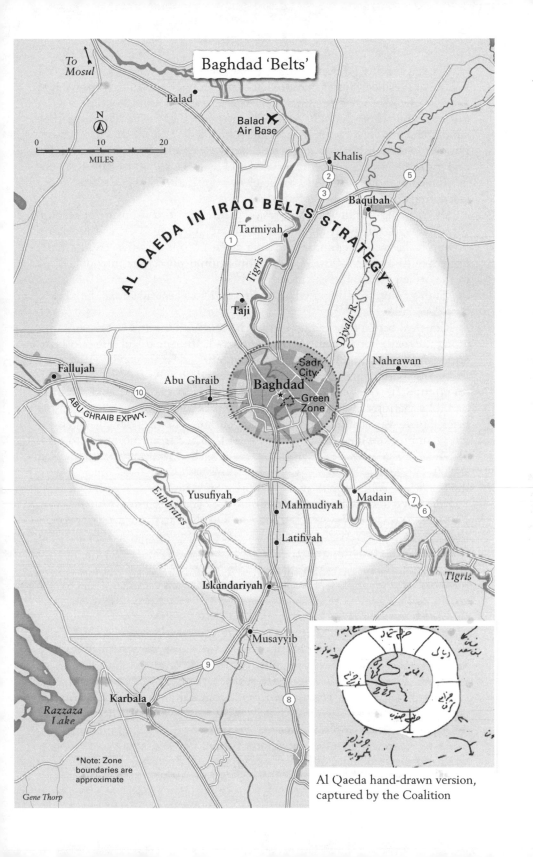

Al Qaeda hand-drawn version,
captured by the Coalition

Two days earlier I'd been asked to come down to the White House for this session of President Bush's National Security Council meeting. I was back in the States for a TF 714 commanders' conference we were holding at Gettysburg, and when the NSC staff caught wind that I was Stateside, they summoned me. Field commanders rarely attended these meetings in person, but the topic, by the president's request, was Abu Musab al-Zarqawi. He and his national security team wanted to know, as Secretary Rumsfeld put in his memorandum, "what [was] being done to get him." As the commander overseeing that hunt, I was to tell them.

The meeting began and the president directed it at a businesslike clip. John Snow began with an update on his department's efforts to clamp down on the terrorist funding flowing from Europe and the Middle East. Secretary Rumsfeld followed. After some initial points, he introduced me to the principals around the table.

"Stan's going to tell you what we are doing to get Zarqawi," he said to President Bush.

Rumsfeld began to stand up to switch seats with me and to take my spot along the wall, but General Myers demurred. Rumsfeld slid left into General Myers's chair, and I sat down between him and Secretary Rice. It was an awkward shuffle, moving the big chairs around on their wheels. The monitor to my left, in front of the president, turned to the briefing slides, prepared by the Joint Staff and not TF 714. It was the first time I had seen the brief, but it was straightforward and accurate. The president listened intently and looked me in the eye each time I turned from the screen to him. His interjected questions were not cross-examinations, but he was focused and obviously interested in the mechanics of our hunt. After I finished with the brief, he gave me a half nod. "Thanks, Stan."

He paused and looked intently at me. "Are you going to get him?"

I had assumed he'd ask this question. On the early-morning helicopter flight down from Gettysburg, over the green fields of southern Pennsylvania, I had thought about how I would answer. I knew I wasn't just there to read a brief, or even to draw on my ground knowledge of the operations, fresh from the front. In truth, my being there allowed President Bush to size me up, to look me in the eyes, get a straight answer, and assess whether he thought I could deliver.

"We will, Mr. President," I said. "There is no doubt in my mind."

There wasn't. This wasn't bluster. I saw our force growing, learning, and becoming ever more effective against Zarqawi's network. And I knew as long as Zarqawi was in Iraq, we would find the leads to him. But in the summer of 2005, after almost two years commanding TF 714, I also appreciated that the mission was larger than one man—he needed to be stopped, but his network had to be destroyed.

As we neared the end of the allotted time, I talked about some operations and the challenges of capturing targets like Zarqawi.

"Do you want to kill him, or capture him?" the president asked.

"I'd like to capture him, Mr. President," I responded.

"Why don't we just kill 'im?" the president said quickly, flatly. Nervous laughter in the room gave way to a few beats of silence. I assumed his comment referred to Zarqawi.

It was a fair question, neither theatrical nor simplistic. He had been watching American men and women die to stop Zarqawi's effort to incite civil war and tear down the new Iraqi government. On one level, to risk losing more of our people trying to capture a man who led a psychopathic campaign of violence seemed illogical and almost immoral.

"Well, Mr. President," I said, "to be honest, I really want to talk to him. He knows things we want to know."

No raid force ever went on a mission under my command with orders not to capture a target if he tried to surrender. We were not death squads. But my calculus was not about Zarqawi's well-being. I told the president that our nightly operations to gather the intelligence allowed us to understand, and ultimately to dismantle, his network. I felt a living Zarqawi might be a decisive source of intelligence, and that was worth the risks.

"Yeah, I've got it," he said, nodding. He smiled. "Good point."

The meeting concluded. Our mission hadn't changed, and Zarqawi remained a major part of it. The hunt would require us to be increasingly sophisticated in how we operated. We had to negotiate a difficult, at times contentious, balance between maintaining as much pressure and preventing as many immediate threats as possible by continuing to hammer Zarqawi's network and conducting deliberate, painstaking target development. I was confident we could do it, but this would be long and bloody.

I spoke briefly with Secretary Rumsfeld, then headed north to rejoin my commanders at Gettysburg.

When I was a boy, my father, recently returned from combat in Vietnam, brought my brother and me to Gettysburg. At the time, I thought of the confusion and violence that had violated Gettysburg's serenity a century earlier. July 1, 1863, had been a difficult day of fighting for Union forces, as they resisted Lee's army, then converging from the north and west. By the early evening, the Union had fallen back through the town to defensive positions on nearby Cemetery Ridge.

For more than two years the Army of the Potomac had fought hard, and it was maturing into a seasoned force, but success eluded it. Earlier that day, Brigadier General John Buford had led his cavalry division in a brilliant delaying action, buying time for hard-marching infantry units to concentrate. But by nightfall, Confederates pressed aggressively through the town for what appeared to be another Lee victory. The next night the Union commanders met in a small farmhouse behind Cemetery Ridge with George Meade, the army's new commander. They decided to stand and fight a battle that many in the crowded, smoke-filled room thought might decide the war.

By the summer of 2005, TF 714, like the Army of the Potomac, was a seasoned force, but the situation in Iraq looked grim. And I'd gathered my leaders at Gettysburg to ensure we were united in our strategy for the way ahead.

On June 25, 2005, I had traveled from Fort Bragg to Austin, Texas, for Bob Horrigan's funeral. I flew in a military plane with Bennet Sacolick and about forty of Bob's Green brethren. As we sat in the pews of St. Mary's Cathedral in downtown Austin that morning, the sound of bagpipes swelling through the stone arches and ceilings, men from Green were arriving in Iraq as part of our surge into the upper reaches of the Euphrates, where Bob had been killed.

In the early months of 2005, as jihadists heeded bin Laden's call to seize the opportunity to fight with Zarqawi, in one aspect I began to think of Iraq as the Gettysburg of the war on terror. When John Buford decided to dismount his men and fight the Confederate forces he encountered outside of town, he committed the Union Army to fighting the decisive battle of that war in tiny Gettysburg.

I saw the evolution of our fight in Iraq against Al Qaeda the same way. Al Qaeda had never planned or desired for Iraq to be the place in which it clashed with and bled the United States. Afghanistan had always been the more appealing country to which to lure the Americans. For our part, America did not invade Iraq in order to fight Al Qaeda. Despite some re-ports and claims of Saddam's purported late-in-life connections with bin Laden's network, any ties were insignificant. No one on either side, except perhaps Zarqawi, wanted or expected Iraq to be the main battleground for the war on terror. But by mid-2005, it was precisely that.

To win in Iraq, Al Qaeda did not need to destroy our army. It needed only to demonstrate that our success in Iraq was impossible. It needed to show that the thesis of a politically moderate Muslim world, engaged with the West, was invalid, that American power was illusory. We needed to defeat it in what became its self-stated main effort. We also needed to suc-ceed in ours. For us, the war against Al Qaeda could not be won in Iraq. But it could be lost.

Now in late June, as commanders were gathering in Gettysburg and I pre-pared to brief the president, we had gotten news from Afghanistan of another loss. Eight men from our 160th Special Operations Aviation Regiment had been killed. After a small team of SEALs under a separate command was ambushed in a remote valley, the 160th pilots had taken off from a nearby base, flying the urgent rescue mission. Insurgents shot down one of the Chi-nook helicopters, carrying eight SEALs. All sixteen men on board died.

In Gettysburg, several commanders and I gathered in one of the small hotel rooms outfitted by our team as a temporary communications center, drew the curtains, and conducted a video teleconference with the leader of our Afghanistan task force, then-Captain Ed Winters. Ed, also the com-mander of TF 714's SEALs, had an impressive ability to drive elite forces in tough situations.

As we talked on the VTC, Ed was preparing to send members from his task force, which included SEALs, Rangers, Air Force Special Tactics operators, and others, into the valley in an attempt to find survivors or, more likely, recover bodies. He was forward and solidly in control of the situation, and we were thousands of miles away. But in the new way in which we had constructed and operated our network, my command team and I were always in the fight, even at Gettysburg. That night, weather prevented Ed from launching the mission. When they could get to the site two days later, the operators who searched for their comrades had to search intensively through the charred crash site before they were able to account for each of the fallen.

From notes I'd received before the Situation Room meeting, I'd known that President Bush wanted to know about Zarqawi the man and the leader. After a year and a half of hunting Zarqawi, we had studied him closely.

He was born in 1966 as Ahmad Fadil al-Khalayleh into the dun, industrial city of Zarqa, northeast of Jordan's glitzier capital of Amman. Ahmad grew up—along with two older brothers and seven sisters—in one of Zarqa's drab, boxy concrete apartments. With no parks in the dusty, hardscrabble neighborhood, Zarqawi spent his time playing among the headstones of the cemetery near his apartment.

He was unremarkable in his youth, but not the dunce some made him out to be. He captained his soccer team and earned Bs in school but suddenly dropped out at age seventeen. He married and got a job sweeping Zarqa's brown streets but before long was drinking heavily. He used and sold drugs. He earned a reputation for his temper and became known as the Green Man for the tint the ink of his many tattoos gave his skin. During this time he was, by various accounts, either arrested for a case of attempted rape or questioned in relation to it and briefly detained for wounding a man with a knife in a fight.

Reportedly at the insistence of his mother, Ahmad attended a mosque in Amman recognized for its strict Salafist bent. As with others schooled there, it soon led him to Afghanistan. Only by the time he arrived, in the spring of 1989, he had missed the war: The Soviets had already withdrawn back across the Amu Darya. He instead worked as a correspondent for a Peshawar-based jihadist mouthpiece, traveling around Afghanistan interviewing mujahideen, chronicling their heroic exploits. Drawing up these burnished portraits would surely be useful to him later in fashioning his own persona.

As the Afghan factions began fighting one another, Ahmad returned to Jordan in 1992. He quickly joined up with a militant group led by Abu Mohammad al-Maqdisi, a rising jihadist ideologue. But after guns and bombs were found hidden in the walls of his house, purportedly for use against Israel, Ahmad was, along with Maqdisi, shipped off to Suwaqah prison in 1994.

It seems the next five years, which he spent in Jordanian prisons, molded him into the Zarqawi we would later face on the battlefield. Behind bars, he became right-hand man to Maqdisi, who led the fundamentalist faction of prisoners. Under Maqdisi's wing but in his shadow, Zarqawi became more pious. He memorized the Koran and tried to scrub his skin of tattoos using hydrochloric acid. He also began to lead. He organized prisoners in his cellblock for protests and first practiced violent bullying as a way to keep people in line. He took to lifting homemade weights, building the physical bulk visible later on the grainy videos from Iraq. His brash resistance to the authorities won him the right to wear what he wanted—Afghan robes—and the respect of his followers. As Ahmad became harder, Maqdisi relinquished leadership of the organization to him. By the end of his prison time, Ahmad could, according to a prison doctor, "order his followers to do things just by moving his eyes."

Released in March 1999 after the new king of Jordan, Abdullah II, granted a blanket amnesty, Ahmad soon traveled back to Peshawar with his Jordanian wife in tow, then to Afghanistan, where he established his own training camp in Herat in 2000. There he married a second wife and adopted the name Abu Musab, a *kunya* meaning the father of Musab, from Zarqa. Zarqawi's Jordanian credentials and connections brought recruits from the Levant, an underrepresented group in Al Qaeda. He maintained a working but informal relationship with bin Laden's organization, largely mediated by Saif al-Adl, Al Qaeda's deputy military chief.

During the invasion to oust the Taliban the following year, Zarqawi escaped the bombing with only a set of broken ribs. With a small band of jihadists, he fled to Iran, and he was then dispatched to lead a contingent of fighters to Iraq. Just before leaving, he visited and said good-bye to Saif al-Adl. Revenge, al-Adl recalled, was on Zarqawi's mind.

Shortly after the June 29 meeting in the White House, we started following a promising lead to Zarqawi: Mohammad Rabih, also known as Abu Zar. Abu Zar was believed to be a top leader in Al Qaeda in Iraq and was a connection between the network's component pieces. Al Qaeda in Iraq comprised localized networks—in Baghdad, in the Fallujah-to-Ramadi corridor, in the western Euphrates, and in Mosul—that used and contested specific areas of terrain through traditional terrorist-insurgent attacks. Overlaying the geographic infrastructure, Zarqawi developed capacity-based networks that specialized in particular functions—foreign fighters, car bombing, and propaganda, among others. Networks rose and fell based on the acuity and energy of their leaders. As a native Iraqi and a key facilitator of the car-bombing operations, Abu Zar was connected to each of the geographic networks—making him a possible line to Zarqawi himself.

After trying to track Abu Zar down for more than a month, we received surprising news. He was about to be buried in Abu Ghraib city although we had not heard of his death. Skeptical, we decided to "attend" his funeral. It wouldn't be the first time a target tried to fake his own funeral or spread rumors of his death. With sources watching from the ground, we circled aerial surveillance above, recording the funeral, which I later watched. While we often watched funerals, we never bombed or raided one. In most cases it was a moot point—there were too many civilians present. But even when the attendees were likely only militants, we didn't. It was important as a force to set limits. So on that hot afternoon, we watched.

On the recording, men shuffled into neat rows in front of an inelegant plywood coffin, unadorned except for Arabic script painted along the sides. An imam, with a longer beard and headdress, led the men, most in Western-style clothes, through prayers. The rows raised and lowered and then folded their hands in unison, then repeated the gestures. Although we could not distinguish the details on the ground, these funerals typically had a group of women who rocked in ritual mourning. On this day we heard that one was Abu Zar's mother, her body contorted in pain. The words of the imam and wails of the women weren't captured on the aerial surveillance recording, but our sources on the ground believed they were genuine.

Eventually the men carried the coffin through narrow, rutted streets to a nearby cemetery. They set the coffin in the dirt, next to a deep slit in the ground. Men carefully passed the limp body, wrapped head to toe in white linen, down to men standing in the hole, who laid it on its right side, holding it in place as the first shovelfuls of dirt fell over their shoes and covered the white shroud. They climbed out, and the hole was filled in. With the back of the shovel and then their hands, they smoothed the dark mound of dirt, and one of our main lines to Zarqawi ran cold.

Days later, the month ended with a gross demonstration of our failure to stop Al Qaeda in Iraq. On August 31, in northern Baghdad, hundreds of thousands of Shiite pilgrims made their way toward Imam Musa Kadhim shrine. The streets along their route had been blocked off for protection, and the roads swelled with the crowds moving under colorful banners and chants. Eventually, the crowd bottlenecked on Aimma Bridge, leading across the Tigris toward the shrine on the other side. At 10:00 A.M., with the bridge choked with people, shouts emerged from within the crowd of a suicide bomber. Earlier that morning, the crowd had heard explosions from the mortars Sunni insurgents fired at the shrine. The rumors transformed the shuffling procession into a stampede. In the rush, the Iraqis—especially the weakest of foot, the women and children—were crushed to death under the feet of others. As the crowd surged, others suffocated when squeezed against the cement blast barriers lining the route to protect from suicide bombings. Some leaped or were pushed off the bridge, only to hit the sloping concrete banks fifty feet below. Some drowned. Without a fuse even lit, 953 Iraqis died, and nearly that many were injured.

To many people, the noise of violence across Iraq was growing to such a pitch that one day's atrocities and explosions didn't stand out from the next. But I remember this day well. So much of a devolving Iraq was wrapped up in the tragedy of that afternoon. Reports that evening were of a surreal death toll, of hospital hallways choked with bodies, of sectarian paranoia tragically entrenched. Back in the States, news of the stampede on the Baghdad bridge ran at the bottoms of newspaper front pages, underneath stark images from Hurricane Katrina's deadly toll and news that President Bush was dispatching thirty thousand national guard troops to the South.

The deadly stampede that hot August day fell into the middle of a roiling internal argument among the jihadist community over Zarqawi's campaign in Iraq, particularly his emphasis on killing Shia civilians. The same energetic, ruthless, stubborn program that had catapulted Zarqawi to his position of leadership now brought him into conflict with serious jihadist thinkers and leaders.

On June 28, as I was in Gettysburg preparing for the meeting with President Bush's national security team, Abu Mohammad al-Maqdisi, Zarqawi's former mentor, was released from prison in Jordan. The Jordanian government likely hoped Maqdisi, out in public, might injure the magnetism of Zarqawi. Since their time together in prison, their trajectories had risen in relative parity: While the murderous Zarqawi was the most notorious practitioner of jihad, Maqdisi was its most influential ideologue.

Maqdisi's writing had soured on Zarqawi in Iraq recently. He complained that the default use of suicide bombing, even when other means were available, had made Iraq a "crematory" for young pious Muslims. He explicitly condemned the widespread attacks on Shia civilians, writing that Zarqawi misunderstood the concept of *takfir*—or excommunication. Unlike their heretical imams, he said, ordinary Shia civilians, who "only know how to pray and fast and do not know the details of [the Shia] sect," were not so different from Sunnis that they could be wiped out like another race. Now out of prison, when he appeared on Al Jazeera on July 5, Maqdisi protested that "Six months ago, every day we read in the newspapers and saw on television dozens of killed Iraqi civilians, women and children, while barely one or two of the American occupiers were killed."

Compelled to respond, Zarqawi flung aside his old mentor, casting him as a queasy theologian with an academic view of jihad, while Zarqawi was on the front lines of a messy war against a Shia who wanted to "liquidate" the Sunnis.

Ayman al-Zawahiri, the second-in-command of Al Qaeda, may well have watched this back-and-forth—in which Zarqawi invoked Zawahiri's earlier calls of support—as he composed his own letter to Zarqawi, dated a few days later on July 9.

The fifteen-page letter, which the U.S. government obtained that summer and released publicly in October, began with fulsome if perfunctory praise. But after stoking Zarqawi's ego, Zawahiri cautiously prodded his "political angle" in Iraq, reminding Abu Musab that "the strongest weapon which the mujahideen enjoy—after the help and granting of success by

God—is popular support from the Muslim masses in Iraq, and the surrounding Muslim countries." At issue was the targeting of Shia. In hushed tones, Zawahiri assured Zarqawi the Shia would one day get their comeuppance. But at that critical moment, "many of your Muslim admirers among the common folk are wondering about your attacks on the Shia." He urged Zarqawi to tone it down, to stop inciting so much wanton carnage, and to turn his attention to the more urgent target: "Expel the Americans from Iraq."

Zarqawi never answered Zawahiri directly, but later that summer he weighed in on the Shia question. Al Qaeda in Iraq, he announced in a speech posted to Al Qaeda's "Jihad Media Battalion" website on September 14, "has decided to declare a total war against the . . . Shi'ites throughout Iraq, wherever they may be." "Beware," he warned. "By Allah, we will not treat you with compassion, and you will have no mercy from us." That same day, Baghdad shuddered with twelve separate bombings, including a van bomb in the Shiite neighborhood of Khadamiya that exploded near a crowd of poor Shiites waiting in line for day labor, killing 114 of them. Six hundred Iraqis were wounded in that day's blasts.

Zarqawi's ability to deflect these attempts to rein him in reflected his growth as both a commander and an ideologue. Zarqawi's campaign, as Maqdisi portrayed it, looked less like one designed to restore the caliphate and more like nihilistic revenge on a wide scale. But to many entering Iraq, that mattered little: Unlike the generation before, these less ideological, more violent volunteers were less concerned with the creation of an Islamic society than with drawing blood in the name of Islam.

While Zarqawi largely deflected this outside criticism, he soon made a critical mistake. On the evening of Wednesday, November 9, 2005, coordinated explosions rocked three hotels in Amman, Jordan. The deadliest attack came inside the Radisson, which Zarqawi had tried to blow up six years earlier during millennium celebrations. That night an Iraqi from Anbar, who had driven across the border four days earlier with three other members of AQI, made his way into a wedding reception in the Philadelphia Ballroom, mingling quietly with the partygoers. Shortly after 8:50 P.M., he detonated a belt he wore under his clothes, the RDX explosives sending a hail of ball bearings through unsuspecting guests. More would have died, but the attacker's wife, also wearing a suicide vest, was unable to set hers off and ran out of the room moments earlier. Two other suicide bombers exploded themselves elsewhere in Amman nearly simultaneously, one inside the lobby of the Grand Hyatt and another just outside the Days Inn. In total, more than 60 people died from the blasts, and 115 were wounded. At the Radisson, bodies were wheeled frantically out of the fume-filled lobby on hotel luggage carts.

The Jordanians quickly suspected Zarqawi, and indeed Al Qaeda in Iraq claimed responsibility for the attack the next day. It was worrying proof of his ability, gestating over years, to strike outside Iraq and to establish his part of Al Qaeda as a regional power. In April 2004, Zarqawi had aspired to use chemical agents against Jordan's General Intelligence Directorate headquarters, the office of the prime minister, and the U.S. embassy in Amman. The Jordanians estimated that such attacks could have resulted in horrific civilian casualties in and around those buildings. A mix of talent, ruthlessness, growing mystique, and unprincipled ambition enabled him to lead both a national insurgency inside Iraq and a transnational terrorist network, leveraging his connections throughout Jordan, Iraq, and Syria. His long-harbored ambitions to compete with the top echelons of Al Qaeda were not delusional.

I was disgusted when I heard the news of the November 9 attacks. But they had perverse value for our mission. They unequivocally demonstrated Zarqawi's growing ability to prosecute targets outside Iraq, but it was obvious to me that he had overreached. A few Jordanians blamed the United States and Israel, but most reacted defiantly against Zarqawi. On Friday, thousands of Jordanians protested in the street, and Zarqawi's hometown mosque forbade Salafists from praying there. He had miscalculated.

Al Qaeda in Iraq responded with a flurry of statements, until finally Zarqawi himself released an audiotape on November 18 explaining the attack. The man who had in the months before defiantly defended his targeting of Muslims in public spats with top Al Qaeda leaders and thinkers now struck a very different tone, defensive and almost apologetic. "The report [which claimed] that the brother who carried out the martyrdom operation exploded himself among the celebrants at a wedding feast is nothing but a lie," he claimed, saying they died when explosions aimed at other targets brought the ceiling down in the banquet room. "[I]t was an unintended accident."

On December 15, 2005, Iraq held a third round of elections—to vote in the first permanent parliament—but they neither stabilized nor unified Iraq. Against the rising din of Sunni-Shia violence, the votes perpetuated the sectarian slide of the country. But amid so many deaths, we soon got word of a curious resurrection.

On January 6, 2006, one of our liaison officers reported that Iraqi forces had captured a man they believed was Abu Zar. If true, he was not dead after all, and given his importance, we were anxious to interrogate him ourselves. Working through Department of Defense procedures, we arranged for him to be transferred from Iraqi custody to our control. Soon, Abu Zar was flown to Balad and escorted the short distance from the flight line to the task force screening facility, which was now a truly professional operation. It had taken eighteen months of relentless focus, leadership, and attention at all levels of our task force to make it so.

Sixteen years earlier, while I was studying at the Naval War College in Rhode Island, one of my instructors had related a conversation he'd had with an Israeli officer. When asked what to do first when faced with an insurgent or terrorist threat, the Israeli officer said firmly, "Build a big jail. You're going to need it." The Israeli's wry answer came from experience.

As the Israeli had implied and Abu Zar would soon reconfirm, detainee intelligence was vital. HUMINT, or human intelligence, along with several other collection disciplines like SIGINT (signals intelligence) and IMINT (imagery intelligence), formed the spectrum of ways we could gather information and understanding of a situation, a population, or most often the enemy. HUMINT involves on-the-ground human sources, from patrols that speak to local villagers to spies. One of the most important of these has always been prisoners, or detainees. Detainees can explain the meaning of what we see from other intelligence sources and can let us step into the mechanics, mindset, and weaknesses of the enemy organization. Detainees, whether they talk out of fear, because they think it's pointless not to, or because their egos can be manipulated and played, can reveal not just what the enemy thinks but *how* he thinks and *why* he fights.

Detainee operations were as difficult and sensitive as they were vital. The resources required and the complexities and risks associated with them caused most organizations to avoid such duty. Some who called loudest for better intelligence on Al Qaeda were happy to have someone else to "bell the cat."

So it was a thankless but necessary task that selected agencies and military units took on in the aftermath of 9/11. And they were unprepared for it. Beyond the legal and diplomatic complexities, the United States had not institutionalized the policies or devoted the resources required to professionalize detention operations. Trained interrogators were woefully few. Essential language skills in Arabic, Dari, and Pashto were almost nonexistent, and other relevant expertise and experience were largely unavailable to the forces that needed them. Well-intentioned but unqualified people struggled to perform a dauntingly complex task, with predictable results. When I took TF 714 in the fall of 2003, more than two years into the fight, little had changed.

I was one of the leaders who lacked experience in detainee custody and exploitation. I had studied history and understood the theory but had never done anything remotely like running a prison. My peers and subordinates were similarly positioned. I was clear on the legal and moral imperatives, but they were just a foundation on which to build enough expertise to command TF 714's detainee operations. We dealt with the limited but complex population of Al Qaeda–related detainees that had the highest likelihood of providing critical intelligence. From the beginning, the importance and sensitivity of the mission was clear.

It began the day I assumed command of TF 714. Lyle Koenig, the air force brigadier general then commanding our task force in Iraq, called me from Baghdad to welcome me to the command. After pleasantries, he stated flatly, "Sir, we need to close the screening facility we're operating at our base at BIAP. We don't have the expertise or experience to do this correctly."

I asked him for options, but we agreed that in the near term, none were evident. We concluded that I would visit the facility on my forthcoming trip to the theater and determine a way ahead.

When I visited the building we used at the Baghdad Airport to screen new captures about a week later, I was unimpressed with both the facility and our ability to staff it. It was housed in a one-story building that the task force had modified internally to contain holding cells, several interrogation booths, and a common work area for analysts and interrogators. The holding cells were constructed of wood and were clean and functional. But the overall facility was cramped and had old linoleum floors and white ceramic tiles crumbling off the walls. On the positive side, it was a short distance from the Joint Operations Center, making it easy for key staff and the commander to provide frequent personal oversight, which I knew was crucial.

Most dangerous, the facility was not manned with the right expertise. That day I met two or three interrogators and a couple of interpreters. They seemed dedicated to getting it right but lacked the requisite experience or manpower. As important as detainee handling and interrogation were to any effort like ours, we were not yet up to the task. We were not obtaining the necessary intelligence, and we had not yet implemented the right facilities and controls to handle detainees properly.

"This is our Achilles' heel," I told the task force staff. "If we don't do this right, we'll be taken off the battlefield." I knew that mistreating detainees would discredit us.

Changes began almost immediately, competing for attention and resources with daily operations and a range of other initiatives vital to our effort. In December we held Saddam Hussein in our small screening facility at BIAP in the first weeks after his capture, but at that time we were still only partway through the necessary process of developing a truly professional capability.

The importance was reinforced when, on April 28, 2004, three weeks after we'd focused our commanders' conference in Bagram on the complexities and sensitivity of counterinsurgency operations, particularly detainees, *CBS News* broadcast images taken by Americans working at Abu Ghraib prison, in the city of the same name west of Baghdad. Pictures from the guards' digital cameras clearly showed American soldiers abusing Iraqis. On a personal level I was sickened by the images of arrogant superiority. In a nation we sought to liberate from an oppressive dictator, we seemed to mirror all we opposed.

The pictures sent shock waves through units deployed in both Iraq and Afghanistan. My force was disgusted by the soldiers' stunning and immature depravity, and we immediately felt effects of the misconduct, even though we had no connection with Abu Ghraib. The more important effect was Abu Ghraib's impact on America's perception in the world.

Abu Ghraib represented a devastating setback for America's effort in Iraq. Simultaneously undermining U.S. domestic confidence in the way in which

America was operating, and creating or reinforcing negative perceptions worldwide of American values, it fueled violence that would soon worsen dramatically.

I knew that our task force was vulnerable to misperceptions. Some reported that our screening operations constituted "black" prisons in which commanders ordered the mistreatment of detainees. That wasn't the case before I assumed command and wasn't true under my command nor under my successors. But creating the right facilities and building our expertise took time and meant addressing buildings, standards, leadership, and most important, the mindset of the force. Abu Ghraib demonstrated what can happen when even a well-intentioned army attempts to conduct sensitive operations, like the handling of detainees, without the preparation and resources required to do it correctly.

By the summer of 2004, the new screening facility was clearly the most important building constructed during our critical move to Balad. It was clean and sterile, with cells, offices, and interrogation booths inside a building with aluminum paneling, glossed cement floors, and high ceilings. Only a few months after its initial construction, we doubled it in size while maintaining the same capacity. At its highest levels, the facility contained only a small number of captures.

We made the facility as internally transparent as possible. Interrogations were monitored, and inspections conducted regularly. We hosted partner representatives from the FBI, conventional military units, and other agencies, and distributed interrogation reports to their headquarters. We established ways for partners from the United States or other countries to watch selected interrogations. This allowed experts on particular topics, or even on certain personalities, to judge detainee responses. This transparency meant that screening a capture, like Abu Zar, in our facility leveraged expertise and intelligence from across the spectrum of groups doing counter terrorism.

Recognizing that people typically assume the worst of whatever they can't see, we would take most visitors to our task force, especially those from the States, on a full tour of the facility. I wanted to dispel incorrect perceptions these congressmen, national security officials, or partner agency representatives might have. It was also a subtle, frequent reminder to my force that we were accountable for how we handled detainees. Most visitors said they were impressed, but continuous refinement and improvement were needed.

On one such occasion not long after we had begun using the Balad screening facility, Senator Carl Levin visited and toured it. He saw the facility in its first weeks of use, when the cells had been built smaller than some others in Iraq and were painted black. They weren't dirty, and the paint choice had been made with no particular intent. But it sent a negative message. Senator Levin said nothing during the visit, and I judged him satisfied with what he saw. But soon afterward I received a letter he'd sent to the secretary of defense, expressing concern with the black cells. His letter was a surprise, and

I wished I'd known his concerns on the spot, but it served as a good outside check on us. We immediately painted the cells a brighter color and simultaneously began a construction program to expand the screening facility, including cells that matched exactly with the standards that had begun to be carried out across all of the MNF-I force. We continued to learn as we fought.

I emphasized through written guidelines and face-to-face conversations throughout the task force that not only were screening operations critical but the conduct of those operations was elemental to success. Mine was a direct message: *If you screw up, you will be punished. Simple as that. I won't wait for someone else to act; we won't "protect our own." I will personally make sure you are kicked out of the task force and court-martialed if necessary.* I was clear and unequivocal. Anything less than emphatic prohibitions on mistreatment might be taken as implicit consent.

I learned quickly as we went along. But I also made mistakes. As late as the spring of 2004, six months into my command, I believed our force needed the option of employing select, carefully controlled "enhanced" interrogation techniques, including sleep management. I was wrong. Although these techniques were rarely requested or used, by the summer of that year we got rid of them completely, and all handling inside our centers followed the field manual used by the Army.

Intuitively I knew leadership was key, but in the first months after I assumed command, we tended to place outside "augmentees," not organic members of TF 714, in leadership roles in the screening facilities in Iraq and Afghanistan. By the spring of 2004 I realized that was a serious mistake. The thought had been that we lacked the in-house expertise, so we'd leverage outside experience. But we quickly found out that augmentees lacked it as well. Our screening operations demanded mature, seasoned leaders whom I could trust completely, so from that point on we assigned only leaders from inside TF 714, professionals I knew and trusted, to the responsibility. To reinforce oversight I sent a cadre of TF 714 leaders on routine circulations to every one of our locations that conducted screenings. On these unannounced trips, they reviewed facilities and procedures and came back with best practices that could be applied across the force. Higher commands like CENTCOM also routinely inspected us.

There were lapses of discipline, but they were never tolerated. Never a wink and a nod. During the difficult summer of 2004, when we tracked and interdicted the truck leaving Fallujah carrying the two men and the thirteen-year-old, whose actions indicated to us that they likely knew Zarqawi's location in real time, we knew that information like this was extraordinarily time sensitive: Zarqawi would quickly learn of the capture and move, rendering the intelligence valueless. Within minutes the detainees were taken to a forward operating base in Baghdad for questioning, while other parts of the force were alerted in preparation of acting on any useful intelligence.

Although trained interrogators appropriately conducted initial questioning of one of the men, two members of the capture force monitoring the interrogation, anxious to get Zarqawi's location, mistreated the detainee by electrically shocking him several times with a Taser. The incident was clearly serious, and our reaction to it reflected the mindset I sought in the force. Human Rights Watch recovered and reported on a June 25 e-mail from an FBI official to FBI headquarters stating that several days earlier a detainee with burn marks had been brought in from one of Task Force 6-26's outstations (TF 6-26 was then the numerical designation for TF 16) and noting that "immediately this information was reported to the TF 6-26 Chain of Command, and there is currently a military 15-6 investigation initiated. This information was shared with all members working at the [screening facility] (military, FBI, . . . DHS) and all were reminded to report any indication of detainee abuse."

At the conclusion of the investigation, we acted swiftly. Included in the punishment of those responsible was expulsion from the unit, a uniquely difficult blow for soldiers whose very identity relied upon being part of the finest unit of its kind in the world. They weren't the first to fall short of our standards and values, nor were they the last. But each time we acted.

Over time, as our experience and expertise grew, detention operations became a noted strength for the TF 714. They had to be. For operators, risking their lives night after night, capturing insurgents was not a theoretical undertaking. A calculus that felt self-evident in a classroom in Connecticut was more difficult in blood-drenched Baghdad, when Zarqawi's bombers were wreaking havoc on innocent civilians. Finding themselves face-to-face with a person they believed was an insurgent who might have killed comrades and who might possess the information needed to help end the fighting, our operators had to have confidence that capture and exploitation would help us stop the violence. I could never have sent our forces out every night, pushing hard for more and more raids, without a screening facility that produced results in a manner that stood up to rigorous scrutiny and, even more important, to the values we sought to embody.

True to form, in January 2006 the men and women at the task force screening facility got valuable information from Abu Zar. Shortly after being picked up, he identified a grouping of buildings in Yusufiyah that he told interrogators Al Qaeda in Iraq periodically used for meetings. Specifically, Abu Zar said, Abu Ayyub al-Masri used the houses for shelter. Al-Masri was an Egyptian who had previously been part of Zawahiri's al-Jihad organization before its union with Al Qaeda. His relationship with Zarqawi reportedly stretched back to 1999, when they met in Afghanistan. Now he was the second-in-command of Al Qaeda in Iraq, running its daily operations. He did so as the emir of the foreign-fighter network, which, together with car-bomb operations, was the bread and butter of Al Qaeda in Iraq. They filmed the suicide and car attacks for propaganda, which created revenue and more recruits for the wider network.

Lying on the southwest outskirts of Baghdad, Yusufiyah was a largely rural area that Al Qaeda used as a staging ground for attacks in the capital.

It sat in what the enemy called the Baghdad "belts"—the suburbs and cities ringing Baghdad. Beginning the year earlier, as we had seen the ratlines from Syria pouring violence into Baghdad, captured documents, detainee interrogations, and other sources had allowed us to refine our understanding of Al Qaeda's strategy in operation. While a network, its campaign increasingly reflected a geographic overlay. It used the ratlines from Syria, west along the Euphrates and southwest through Ar Rutba, to move foreign fighters. A third ratline ran north into Mosul, which AQI used as a rear support area, raising money and building cells but committing relatively fewer operations there. While Al Qaeda never tried to hold terrain in Baghdad itself, it increasingly sought to control the belts around the city—more sparsely populated, with less Coalition troop density. It aimed to funnel violence into Baghdad, the country's seat and most visible city, in order to demonstrate the futility of MNF-I's efforts, paralyze the government, and help spur civil war.

When our intel team in Baghdad first surveyed the buildings Abu Zar had identified, they saw nothing—no abnormal security measures, no enemy movement to and from or around the sites. But the squadron's top intel analyst, a sergeant major named Allan,* was convinced the site was important. When unused ISR orbits were available, he directed the aircraft toward what became known as Named Area of Interest 152 (NAI 152), monitoring for activity until the ISR was needed for more urgent tracking. At first, NAI 152 was just another plot point among a country's worth of locations we kept tabs on, some of them for years.

During Allan's eighth week of directing spare ISR toward Yusufiyah, two explosions one hundred miles to the north, in Samarra, rerouted the war. Before dawn on Wednesday, February 22, 2006, attackers had placed bombs inside the huge gilded dome of the Askariya shrine. Although in a city with a roughly 90 percent Sunni population, the shrine, known as the Golden Mosque for its glistening teardrop-shaped dome, was one of Shiism's holiest sites. Shiites believed that two of the main sect's twelve revered imams were buried beneath the dome and that the Mahdi—now namesake to Muqtada al Sadr's extremist militia—had visited the site before his disappearance. At around seven o'clock that morning, the bombs inside the dome exploded it like an eggshell, leaving behind a stump of crumbled cement and twisted rebar.

Within hours, spontaneous sectarian killing broke out through most of Iraq. Thousands of men gathered outside of Muqtada's headquarters in Sadr City, loading onto the backs of flatbed trucks and slinging weapons. Sunni mosques were torched or strafed with bullets. Hundreds of Iraqis died in ethnic violence in the days following the attack, and perhaps a thousand Iraqis were killed in the five days after the bombing.

Although shocking, the full implications of the destruction of the Golden Mosque were not immediately obvious to me. The first spasm of Shiite

---

* Allan is a pseudonym.

reaction was predictable, but it took a number of weeks before the full scope of the Shia counterattack was clear. We'd watched Zarqawi's cruelty for more than two years, but now the violence went both ways, as Shiite militias acted with brazen impunity. The ethno-sectarian targeting campaign waged in the following weeks and months was methodical, appearing to reflect the cold-blooded release of frustration and hatred. But some deaths reflected emotional, intimate methods of murder. Bodies arrived at morgues melted by acid or were found with their heads still covered in the plastic bag used to suffocate them, one by one. Sunni bodies were found with their kneecaps drilled hollow, while severed heads of Shia were carefully spotted for public view and horrific videos were circulated.

Throughout March the violence emanating from Samarra rippled through Baghdad and into the belts like Yusufiyah as Al Qaeda sought to expel Shia from these suburbs. And yet amid this simmer, NAI 152 remained unperturbed.

The Green squadrons were set to rotate out in early April. The new squadron's intel team arrived in Iraq before the assault forces to reimmerse themselves in the effort. The team was led by the squadron's J2, Sergeant First Class J.C. I knew J.C. and much of his team well from regular visits with them. Throughout my command, I scheduled chunks of time—usually two or so hours at a shot—to sit down with intel teams. Like hounds on a scent, by 2006 they didn't need much encouragement. In a community of impressive intelligence talent, J.C. was one of the best. He was tall, but not bulked out like the operators he worked with. His slightly shaggy hair and slow, calm cadence begged you to dismiss or underestimate him. But his muted appearance and delivery betrayed intensity and strong opinions formed over years of hunting Zarqawi. When you got him going, he could rattle off connections ("and his sister is married to . . . ") and names, the Arabic *kunyas* twisted a bit by his slight southern accent. J.C. and the other intel men and women working for the unit had spent more than two years doing nothing but studying and hunting the Al Qaeda in Iraq network. Zarqawi was an obsession.

J.C. and his team had seen the Samarra bombing and its aftermath from the States and sensed the stakes were now higher. After digesting the current intelligence traffic and digging up some past leads, they identified a number of intelligence lines to pursue. Before they deployed, J.C. had given his team a challenge: This would be the rotation on which TF 714 got not only Zarqawi but also the man we thought would replace him, Abu Ayyub al-Masri, the second-in-command. The TF 714 machine, he felt, was simply too proficient to allow Zarqawi to survive their three-month rotation. The information being pumped through it was richer than it ever had been. The capacity to exploit intelligence had taken another huge leap in the six months since his last rotation. The hard bargaining of the previous two years had won us more surveillance assets. And Zarqawi was getting sloppy.

When J.C.'s team arrived, they developed a set of targets for the squadron to hit at the beginning of their rotation. By the spring of 2006 this was a standard, if unstated, practice in our task forces. Striking a series of targets in the first days after arrival would shake any cobwebs off the operators, but more important, the strikes could yield a wealth of intelligence leads that could then guide follow-on operations. This fight was about gaining and maintaining momentum, and our forces sought to grab it immediately.

On that target list the task force added NAI 152. Allan remained convinced that it was an important site, and his assessments were respected. Even though it was squarely in the middle of AQI territory, it had been quiet. This made it a good target for the new squadron, coming in cold, to warm up on.

They wouldn't get the chance. In the late morning of Saturday, April 8, before the squadron assault teams rotated, Allan saw a convoy of vehicles approach NAI 152. After three months of monitoring the target, he knew the activity merited a strike. The operators trusted him, boarded helicopters in Baghdad, and launched a daytime assault.

A short time later, just before 1:56 P.M., the Green teams landed at NAI 152. In the firefight, five insurgents were killed. The Green team suffered no fatalities. Inside the house, the teams found suicide vests and an explosives-laden van with a huge tank inside—likely bound for Baghdad's streets. The operators who entered the house, like TF 714's SEALs and many of the Rangers, had been trained in forensic techniques at our Sensitive Site Exploitation (SSE) course, one of a number of schools we set up to develop in-house expertise. There in Yusufiyah that afternoon, they meticulously searched the house, tagging each item of intelligence value and recording exactly where in the house it had been found. They transmitted any key data back to the headquarters in Baghdad and the Iraq task force's headquarters in Balad. As had become the norm, analysts there immediately began exploitation, while pumping both the raw information and their initial assessments to the wider intelligence community.

As the assault teams were airborne toward NAI 152, the Baghdad outstation monitoring the operation had seen a car drive to a second location up the road. Soon the task force picked up more vehicles approaching the follow-on target. Helicopters went airborne, and the second target was hit at 4:11 P.M. Two hours and fifteen minutes had elapsed since the assault teams first landed in Yusufiyah earlier that afternoon.

The second target, now named Objective Mayers, went down more quietly than the first. The operators arrested all twelve of the men they found at the mud-and-brick farmhouse. In the backs of the helicopters that lifted off from Yusufiyah a short time later, the assault teams squeezed in next to the flexi-cuffed men and returned to Baghdad.

"We picked up twelve guys at Mayers last night," Wayne Barefoot said, bringing up a slide on-screen in an intel brief the next day, April 9. Wayne was in Iraq coincidentally. He was in transition to a new job, but

Scott Miller had asked him to come back to Iraq and make any final adjustments, now that Wayne was free of the time constraints that came with
being the TF 16 intel chief. That role was newly filled by Major M.S., Wayne's
deputy at the time and a seasoned intelligence officer. An avid athlete, M.S.
had the combination of intellect, common sense, and people skills necessary to succeed in the traditionally all-male community of special operations. She was serious, unflappable, and demanding.

Immediately sensing the importance of these new captures and concerned something might fall through the cracks, Wayne had flown down to
Baghdad to ensure everything was properly sorted out, and that a plan was
in place to prioritize the detainees and work through the extensive material
found on the target. Now, he briefed Scott, M.S., J.C., C.M., who was the
officer in charge of the screening facility, and me on his initial conclusions.

The one-page slide he showed had a map and a few bullet points summarizing the target. Also on the slide were pictures of each of the captures.
Their faces were those of older men, not twenty-year-old thugs.

"This is *very* interesting," Wayne continued. "Only one phone." To find
twelve Iraqi men in 2006 with only one phone among them was nearly
impossible. One of the many irrigation canals that crisscrossed Yusufiyah's
lush farmland passed along the edge of the objective where they were captured. We later surmised that they must have thrown all the phones into
the water when they heard our team approach. Or all but one of them
was smart enough not to show up with a phone. In either case, it indicated
savvy.

"This is not just a bunch of fighters," Wayne said. "These guys are
different."

It wasn't just the age of the detainees that piqued the interest of interrogators and analysts. By 2006, most of our intelligence people had been
working Al Qaeda in Iraq for two years. Many had prior experience in
Afghanistan, some in the Balkans. The best had made an art form out of
reading detainees. While at the time still hindered by an almost complete
lack of Arabic skills within our force, many had learned to quickly parse
demeanor and came armed with enough understanding of the environment
to recognize inconsistencies or holes that detainees deliberately left in their
accounts. Almost immediately that night, those skills paid off. During the
detainees' initial questioning, the intel teams knew something was awry.
The team could see them thinking at a higher level. In some the team sensed
a stubborn but concealed professional pride, as if they wanted the Americans to recognize they were not mere thugs but had tradecraft.

Within a couple of days, all the Yusufiyah captures had been brought from
Baghdad up to Balad. That week, the second of April, I walked over to
the screening facility for one of the multiple meetings they held each day to
review the current evaluation of each detainee. The pace of the meeting was
rhythmic. With the detainee's name, biographical information, and picture
displayed on a large screen, the lead interrogator would make the case for why

a detainee should be retained for another day in the task force screening facility, turned over to the larger Coalition-run facilities, given to the Iraqi court system, or released. The Department of Defense and CENTCOM had set firm policy limits on how long we could keep captives for screening. Outstations, like those in Fallujah or Mosul, could hold detainees only briefly before either releasing them or sending them up to our Balad screening facility, where we could keep detainees for only days before having to submit a written request to CENTCOM. When detainees were thought to be especially important, we could request authorization from the secretary of defense to hold them longer. The approval process was bureaucratic but necessary to ensure that detainees were not held for inappropriate times in temporary facilities and that every detainee was properly accounted for throughout the process.

The substance of these discussions and briefing slides was the product of an intense exploitation effort conducted in a honeycomb of adjacent rooms. Inside rooms for captured phones, documents, and computers, like surgeons over a patient, analysts huddled around the electronics and documents laid out on big stainless-steel tables. By design, they worked in the same building as the interrogators who questioned the men whose handwriting or names were on the documents and who were the onetime owners of the phones and computers.

As we evolved, the amount of talent and manpower we were able to put against detainees became a key strength. At this time, we had interrogators working both night and day shifts, so that important detainees were questioned during each cycle. Even at full capacity, our screening facility's staff of analysts and interrogators was six times as large as the number of captives they oversaw. In stark contrast, at its fullest, Camp Bucca—the Coalition's central-theater detention facility—held more than eighteen thousand detainees. As was common practice in historical counterinsurgencies, the United States used incarceration to reduce near-term violence. Although detention took fighters off the battlefield, these holding facilities unfortunately became incubation chambers in which the insurgency grew in intensity and commitment—where more hardened insurgents radicalized young Iraqis.

We focused our interrogation efforts on detainees whose information might lead to follow-on targets. This compelled us to be precise in whom we captured in the first place and discriminating when choosing to hold a detainee. The average detainee stayed in the screening facility for a matter of days. We quickly moved detainees deemed not to have information or unlikely to cooperate to Camp Bucca or Abu Ghraib. Once there, they joined and were subject to the influences and coercion of a large population of other detainees.

Using material retrieved from the site and triangulating their answers, the Yusufiyah detainees' identities grew clearer. They were mostly subcommanders. We decided to focus the interrogators' efforts on four of the twelve:* Abu Omar, a senior lieutenant cutout who helped run the religious wing; Abu Sayyif, a leader of the Combined Extremist Media Forum who ran all the media operations in Baghdad; a man at first believed to be working for him on the day of their capture, Abu Mubassir; and finally, most promising, Abu Felek, who had been in the car that went from NAI 152 to Mayers. Called "Taha" by the other detainees, Felek was Ansar al-Sunnah's emir of the north, where he was in charge of all Iraqis. We soon discovered that Felek, older than the others picked up that day, who were in their thirties, was one of Zarqawi's emissaries to bin Laden.

For a variety of reasons, most detainees chose to cooperate. Some had egos and could not resist taking credit for what they had done—eager to show their importance. Others found themselves uncomfortable with AQI's tactics—especially the targeting of Shia civilians. Some arrived to the interrogation booths with regret and shame. Still others burned with raw anger that Iraqi lives were expendable to Al Qaeda in Iraq's leadership. Confronting them in moral language was often powerfully persuasive. They were quick to offer up information on impending attacks if we could convince them it was the right thing to do. Early on we learned that our worst mistake with a detainee was to confirm the negative stereotypes of Americans that animated the enemy's mosques and safe houses.

The Yusufiyah detainees were a special challenge because only two had been on the task force's radar before the raid. We put three of our best interrogators against them. During the day, Amy partnered with Jack. A young, petite woman, Amy was pulled out of one of the outstations and given the priority of the detainees. She devoted four years of her life, starting at age twenty-six, to working for the task force. Her partner, Jack, was another longtime interrogator with the command. Paul conducted the interrogations in the evenings. Paul had served in the navy in the late 1980s, but after watching the Twin Towers collapse from New Jersey, where he was working an IT job, he returned to service.[†]

Amy, Jack, and Paul slowly began to triangulate the detainees' answers and play them against one another. The interrogators were immediately suspicious of Abu Sayyif. A pediatrician from Baghdad, he was also known as Dr. Mahjub. Soft-spoken and well educated, he was quite smug and appeared to hold himself above the others. When questioned, he was resistant and angry—at times, it seemed, with himself. At first he spoke only in Arabic, answering through the translator. But the interrogators intuited he knew more than he was letting on. They could see a glint in his eyes when they said something in English, before it was translated. And while most detainees needed a few moments to process the question after the interpreter finished speaking, Dr. Mahjub launched into his answers right away.

---

*All detainee names are pseudonyms.
†Paul, Amy, and Jack are pseudonyms.

At one point the interrogators brought all the detainees—commanders and their drivers—into one booth and had them write on a piece of paper the name of the most important man among them. Everyone, including Dr. Mahjub, wrote down Dr. Mahjub.

Dr. Mahjub remained prickly and maintained that he had hired the fourth detainee, Mubassir, as a one-off to help with media operations that day. Mubassir repeated this account and was less of a priority than the others. As many hard-core members did, Taha continued to be obstinate, while Abu Omar continued simply responding to questions with a laugh or a wide, menacing smile.

Toward the end of April, however, a couple weeks into the interrogations, the task force grew more suspicious of Mubassir. He was tall and heavyset, in contrast with many of the scrawnier, shorter Iraqis. In his youth he had been a soccer player and a wrestler, which accounted for his bulk. Now in his thirties, he cast a playful look at his interrogators. Shortly after the initial capture, Paul had sat down with Mubassir for the first time in the Baghdad outstation. When his blindfold was removed, Mubassir's face had twisted into a wide, toothy smile.

"Oh, hello," Mubassir said cheerily, in crisp English.

"You're an English speaker," Paul, the night interrogator said, taken aback.

"Yes," Mubassir said dismissively, as if it weren't news. "How long do you think this will be?" he continued in a bouncy, fluid tone, his posh Tory accent emerging as he spoke. "Because I do need to get back to my family."

As on that night, in his subsequent sessions Mubassir appeared to enjoy the back-and-forth and peppered his answers with English colloquialisms. He was confident, charismatic, and clearly very intelligent.

Initial questioning at the outstations was often direct, aimed to use the detainees' relative disorientation following capture to pry details that could unearth follow-on targets. By the time they arrived at the the screening facility, one or two days into their detention, detainees were more comfortable. They now knew they were fed three times a day and given a shower and weren't going to be abused. As with all interrogations, the interrogators' strategy was to manufacture, as fast as possible, a durable rapport that they could manipulate over time to our advantage. Interrogators offered as much information about themselves—making it up as necessary—as the detainees divulged, in order to establish a history of back-and-forth sharing and, ultimately, trust.

From Mubassir's demeanor to his clownish smile to his showy displays of English proficiency, the interrogators detected an undercurrent of pride that might be tapped. They soon got him to talk more at length about himself. They learned that he fancied himself a religious scholar. He claimed a connection, through clerics, back to Mohammad, and claimed to be associated with the mufti of Iraq. They allowed Mubassir to lecture them on religious doctrine. Just as the interrogators built up semifictional personas inside the booth, their questions allowed Mubassir to project himself as a budding religious authority. It was an identity they wanted to tease out.

One of the early sources of suspicion with Mubassir was a picture of a man that had been taken on his street. J.C. had sent it up to the screening facility because the task force knew the man in the photo was one of a handful of runners for the Dardiri courier network, coordinated by Abu Ayyub al-Masri. (One of al-Masri's aliases was Yusif al-Dardiri.) When Paul showed the picture to him, Mubassir waved it away, claiming not to know the man. The interrogators remained unconvinced, and Paul took to hanging it on the wall behind him at the start of each session, so that the picture faced Mubassir. For weeks, Mubassir refused to recognize the face in the picture.

Near the end of April, that changed during a marathon nighttime session with Paul. Toward the end, Mubassir was wearing thin. He had not seen his family in weeks. His mother was sick and needed surgery. And after five or six hours of conversation, he was tired. Again, Paul asked him about the photo. This time Mubassir sighed. He looked at the photo with a quiet resolve, as if he had made peace with the response he was about to give. "I love that man very much," he said warmly. "That's my brother." He told Paul his brother's name was Karim.

Interrogator and detainee exhausted, Paul left the booth so that he could get the information to his analyst. When he returned, Paul brought breakfast for the both of them. It was now early morning, and they sat together and ate. The warm eggs, fresh fruit, and cold juice they shared at the small plastic table marked a new stage in the relationship between the two men.

Mubassir divulged more about Karim and agreed when told the task force would bring him in. "Good, good," he said. "I can talk to him. I know he'll start talking."

In Mubassir's eyes, bringing in his brother was a way to keep him protected and a way to make his own part of the ordeal end by giving us what we needed in order for us to be done with him—even if it meant giving up a bigger fish. For us, it was a promising lead.

As the task force began monitoring Karim, Paul traveled from Balad down to the Baghdad outstation with Mubassir in tow. While there, Paul lived in the same small hooch with Mubassir, leaving him unshackled the whole time. He sat together in the small room with Mubassir, listening to Iraqi radio, or allowed Mubassir to lecture him on religion and Iraqi culture. Paul brought him the same food the operators ate, including ice cream. It was all about trust.

Unfortunately for both Paul and Mubassir, Karim spooked. Around May 3, roughly twenty-five days into Mubassir's detention, Paul and the Baghdad team watched Karim, as they had for a few days. But his demeanor was ominously different that day. They watched as he walked briskly up his street, talking on his cell phone, then went up to his home's rooftop, where he burned a pile of documents and material. At midmorning the next day,

Karim drove to his sister's house and entered the front door, and that was the last we saw of him. Unbeknownst to us at the time, he fled out the back door of the house, out of view of our cameras. He confided in a sheikh, who told him to confer with Abu Ayyub al-Masri himself. When Karim met al-Masri outside Baghdad, al-Masri gave him one thousand dollars and told him to flee to Syria, which he did.

The task force was steamed. They were not alone. When Paul returned from the operations center to their shared hooch and told Mubassir his brother had fled, Mubassir was crushed. This left Mubassir with no more leverage, as everything else he had offered us was worthless. Karim was his lifeline.

Meanwhile, more new captures came in, taxing the capacity of the screening facility. Mubassir increasingly appeared to have nothing more to offer, and it was nearing the time when we would need to submit a request to extend his stay in our facility. During the first few days of May, the screening facility team proposed sending him off to Camp Bucca. But when C.M. brought the recommendation to M.S. that night, she vetoed it. She knew Mubassir was the only detainee with a connection to al-Masri's courier network and wanted the interrogators to keep mining.

On the same night M.S. vetoed the suggestion to move Mubassir, one of the other interrogators not normally assigned to Mubassir got him to admit a piece he had been holding out on: Karim was not the only connection to al-Masri. Mubassir had met with al-Masri a few times over the past two years, after first hosting the Egyptian at his house in Ahmadiya in the spring of 2004, as the insurgency was materializing.

As M.S. sensed Mubassir could give more on al-Masri, she and the intel teams working for her came to me for approval to continue holding him. I had already written to CENTCOM for permission to keep him this long, but I wrote again seeking Secretary Rumsfeld's approval. As always, an extensive intelligence package was required to justify the request. By this time our credibility had been built on a strong record of getting it right, and the extension was approved.

"This has been, and will be, a long and serious war," I wrote to all of our task forces that spring, posting the message on our portal. "Although initial structures and TTPs* have evolved tremendously from where they were even two years ago, we are still operating with manning and operating processes that need to be improved to be more effective and professional.

"We must increasingly be a force of totally focused counter-terrorists— that is what we do. . . . This is as complex as developing a Long Term Strategic Debriefing Facility that feeds out in-depth understanding of the enemy, and as simple as losing the casual, 'I'm off at my war adventure,' manner of dress and grooming.

---

*"TTPs" stands for tactics, techniques, and procedures.

My father, then–Colonel Herbert J. McChrystal, Jr., pictured in 1968. A 1945 graduate of West Point, he went on to serve tours in Korea and Vietnam, earning four Silver Stars. He embodied for me what a leader should be. He retired as a major general in 1974, while I was a cadet at West Point.

Annie entering the Chapel of the Centurion inside moated Fort Monroe, Virginia, on our wedding day, April 16, 1977. Her career-soldier father, Colonel Edward Corcoran, escorted her down the aisle.

My battalion commander, then–Lieutenant Colonel Tom Graney, hosting foreign military officers as they observe our unit training on Fort Stewart in 1984. Over his right shoulder, our division commander, then–Major General Norman Schwarzkopf, watches. I learned an immense amount from Colonel Graney and his sometimes unconventional leadership.

The burned-out wreckage of a C-141 at Pope Air Force Base on March 23, 1994. An F-16 Fighting Falcon collided with the C-141, which was parked at Green Ramp, a section of runway on the base. The resulting explosion killed twenty-four paratroopers and wounded more than one hundred others. Many of the dead and wounded were from my battalion, the "White Devils" of the 82nd Airborne.

ABOVE LEFT: On the National Mall with my son, Sam, then seven years old, and Annie in 1991, shortly after I returned from the first Gulf War.

ABOVE RIGHT: In the late summer of 1999, speaking to the men of the 75th Ranger Regiment and wearing the signature "high-and-tight" haircut after my final physical training session as the regimental commander. Following each daily physical training session, all those assembled repeated the six-stanza Ranger Creed—a daily promise to those around them to uphold Ranger standards, and never leave another Ranger behind.

BELOW: Planning in the village of Mangretay, Paktika Province, Afghanistan, in January 2004. Rangers were conducting operations a short distance from the Pakistan border. Second from right is then–Colonel Craig Nixon, the Ranger regimental commander. At the time, our fight against Al Qaeda led us to focus primarily on Afghanistan and Pakistan, but our attention soon shifted to Iraq.

RIGHT: Chaos on the streets of Karbala, Iraq, on March 2, 2004, moments after bombs exploded among the thick crowds of Shiite pilgrims who had gathered for the first time in decades for the Ashura festival. Abu Musab al-Zarqawi and his group targeted the crowds in Karbala and Baghdad, leaving at least 169 dead and hundreds wounded. It was the loudest opening salvo of a vicious, persistent effort to instigate civil war between Iraqi Sunnis and Shia. That spring, our central focus quickly turned from Afghanistan to Iraq.

ABOVE: My friend and mentor Lieutenant General John Vines (left) in December 2005, when he commanded Multi-National Corps–Iraq.

OPPOSITE TOP: Then–Major General Graeme Lamb welcoming Jack Straw, the British foreign secretary, into Basra, southern Iraq, in November 2003. Graeme and I served together in the first Gulf War, and again in Iraq. During 2006–2007, we worked together when he oversaw the Coalition's sometimes controversial reconciliation efforts during a critical juncture in the war. One of my best friends, Graeme would later come out of retirement to serve with me in Afghanistan.

OPPOSITE BOTTOM: My Task Force 714 command team in front of the flight line at our headquarters in Balad, Iraq. From left are Donny Purdy, Kurt Fuller, Jody Nacy, Bud Cato, me, Mike Flynn, and Vic Kouw.

Here wearing his trademark all-black outfit, Abu Musab al-Zarqawi built a mystique as a battlefield commander. His group, Al Qaeda in Iraq (AQI), deftly employed video and audio messages to recruit and inspire followers. This screen capture was taken from a rare public video appearance during the spring of 2006, at a time when we were trying to provoke his ego in an effort to cause him to make a misstep, and come into our sights.

ABOVE: The ruins of the safe house where Zarqawi was killed, in Hibhib, north of Baghdad. On June 7, 2006, Task Force 16 dropped two five-hundred-pound bombs on the house, which was nestled among a thick grove of palm trees.

LEFT: The night after Zarqawi was killed, I thanked members of the Task Force in the backyard of our Baghdad compound abutting the Tigris River. It was not a time of celebration: They knew, as did I, the fight was far from over.

A badly disabled Stryker armored fighting vehicle, rendered inoperable by an enemy improvised explosive device, on the streets of Ramadi during the summer of 2006. The Stryker had carried a group of Rangers, assigned by Task Force 16 to run raids into the city. At the time, Ramadi was the most dangerous place in Iraq, and tested our special operators and conventional forces who, under the creative leadership of then–Colonel Sean MacFarland, partnered to subdue it and midwife the first durable movement of Sunni reconciliation.

In what we termed the Situational Awareness Room at our Balad headquarters in July 2006. Though I had an office, I rarely used it. We had designed our office spaces to be open to make our communications quick and robust. This meant I spent nearly all my time an arm's length from my command team—at the time, Kurt Fuller to my left, Mike Flynn to my right, and Jody Nacy to his right. The briefing on the screen is called "Defeat AQI Brief," and according to its date was delivered six weeks after Task Force 16 killed Abu Musab al-Zarqawi. That fall, we thought we felt Al Qaeda in Iraq breaking, though larger problems still loomed.

LEFT: With the hardened aircraft hanger that held our Iraq headquarters in the background, I addressed members of Task Force 16 in 2007. On sadder occasions than the one pictured, the motley members of our task force—young, old, male, female, military, civilian—gathered at the foot of this flag for memorial ceremonies.

RIGHT: On June 2, 2009, I testified before the Senate Armed Services Committee as a nominee for the post of commander of NATO and U.S. forces in Afghanistan. The position meant more years away from Annie, seated behind me. She understood.

Command Sergeant Major Mike Hall (front right) my senior enlisted adviser in Afghanistan, visiting soldiers at one of our remote combat outposts in Nuristan. This small base was home to some forty or fifty troops, half of them Afghan, and took direct and indirect fires daily. From the time I first met Mike and served with him in the Ranger Regiment a decade before his visit to this outpost, he was the finest soldier I knew.

The Flynn brothers: Charlie (right) here at his promotion to brigadier general, and Mike. A trusted friend, Charlie was my indispensible executive officer both at the Pentagon and then Afghanistan, where he shared with me the highs and lows of command. At the same time, his older brother, Mike, was my chief intelligence officer in Afghanistan, and fulfilled the same role during my command of Task Force 714 before that. He has since been promoted to lieutenant general.

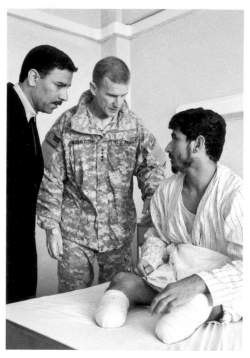

LEFT: At the Afghan National Army Hospital with a wounded Afghan soldier in December 2009. On this day, I was accompanying President Hamid Karzai. During our visits to hospitals, the president's deep emotions for his people were evident beneath his dignified exterior. He would quietly pass envelopes of money to the wounded.

OPPOSITE TOP: On April 4, 2010, while in Kandahar for the first of the two *shura*s, or traditional consultations, held by President Karzai in advance of our efforts to secure that city. Surrounded by tribal elders from in and around Kandahar, Ambassador Mark Sedwill, the senior NATO civilian authority, and I are seated cross-legged to the president's left. During the main meeting that week, this basement floor of the governor's palace was filled to the brim with some 1,500 tribal leaders.

BELOW LEFT: Afghan Minister of the Interior Hanif Atmar, during a large spring 2010 review of the joint civilian-military efforts. Hardworking and soft-spoken, Minister Atmar was a close partner during my time in Afghanistan.

BELOW RIGHT: Another close ally: Amrullah Saleh, head of the National Directorate of Security, Afghanistan's intelligence service. At one time a trusted deputy to the celebrated mujahideen commander Ahmad Shah Massoud, Director Saleh brought an unmistakable fervor and powerful intellect to bear in the fight against the insurgency.

LEFT: During his May 2010 visit to the United States, I accompanied President Karzai to Arlington National Cemetery. My trusted friend, Afghan Minister of Defense Abdul Rahim Wardak, and my boss, Secretary of Defense Robert Gates, are second and third from left. Here in Section 60 of Arlington, where many of the fallen from the wars in Iraq and Afghanistan are buried, we came across headstones of men I knew. This was one.

In Berlin on April 21, 2010, Dr. Theodor Freiherr zu Guttenberg, the German minister of defense, and I visited the Bundeswehr memorial, where we conducted a memorial service for fallen German soldiers. During the visit, the minister presented me with fourteen Gold Crosses of Honour to give to fourteen U.S. Army aviators, still in Afghanistan, who had earlier that month flown courageous medical evacuation missions in support of German soldiers during a fierce firefight.

Giving a speech, April 16, 2010, to the Institut des Hautes Études de Défense Nationale in Paris. As commander of ISAF, I was not only the top American officer but also the commander of all NATO nations' forces. This and other such speeches, primarily in Europe, were part of my responsibility to build a team out of a diverse coalition of allies and respond to their concerns over the war and its prosecution.

BELOW LEFT: With General Ashfaq Parvez Kayani, the chief of Pakistan's army, visiting ISAF headquarters in Kabul, December 2009. Our relationship with Pakistan was crucial to the overall strategic situation in Afghanistan but was complicated by decades of mistrust.

BELOW RIGHT: Meeting with a local on the street in Maimanah, Afghanistan, March 15, 2010. My tours around the country were as much about connecting with troops and allies dispersed to combat outposts as listening to and trying to understand men like the one I am greeting in this photo.

ABOVE: Then–Lieutenant General Dave Rodriguez—better known as General Rod—meeting with Afghan National Army officers. With more experience in and knowledge of Afghanistan than any other senior military leader, Rod commanded the daily battle during my tenure as commander of ISAF forces. He was, throughout, my best friend and a close partner with a difficult task.

BELOW: Two of the finest special operators I've known. Then–Brigadier General Scott Miller (left) led Task Force 16 in Iraq and was the architect of many of our successes there. Here in Afghanistan, while leading the ISAF coalition's special operations, Miller is with then–Major Khoshal "Kosh" Sadat, an exemplary officer and my trusted aide de camp.

ABOVE: On the receiving end of a bear hug from my classmate, comrade, and friend General Ray Odierno at my retirement ceremony, held at Fort McNair on July 23, 2010. At the time, Ray was commanding general of U.S. forces in Iraq. He has gone on to become chief of staff of the army.

LEFT: We met these two young boys during a visit to Jalez, Afghanistan, a hotly contested area not far from Kabul. I thought their faces captured what was ultimately at stake in the war. I had this picture hung in the small room at our Kabul headquarters where we ate meals.

"In every case it will not be about what's easy, or even what we normally associate with conventional military standards. It will not even be about what is effective. It will be about what is the MOST effective way to operate—and we will do everything to increase the effectiveness even in small ways.

"If anyone finds this inconvenient or onerous, there's no place in the force for you. This is about winning—and making as few trips to Arlington Cemetery as possible en route to that objective."

I probably wrote five such messages during my years commanding TF 714, but I made many of the same points in the O&I VTC almost daily. A leader must constantly restate any message he feels is important, and do so in the clearest possible terms. It serves to inform new members and remind veterans.

TF 16 increasingly pushed to be ever more effective, and that spring, even as Al Qaeda in Iraq wreaked havoc, we had been pummeling the organization. I stressed the importance of pace, or "OPTEMPO" as we called it, as key to maintaining pressure. Where we'd executed eighteen raids per month in August of 2004, by that month in 2006 we were up to three hundred. I also felt that we were closing in on Zarqawi himself. Many in the task force shared the feeling. We looked for every way possible to provoke him or someone near him to make a mistake and appear on the grid.

That May, one way we thought we could flush him out was to manufacture discord between him and Abu Ayyub al-Masri. Egyptians like al-Masri were to a degree the dominant aristocracy within Al Qaeda, and Zarqawi had displayed a fixation with his status in the movement. So we aimed to diminish Zarqawi's stature while raising al-Masri's profile. We petitioned to reduce the reward offered for information on Zarqawi—which had been at twenty-five million dollars since 2004—down to five million, while simultaneously raising the money attached to al-Masri to the same amount. From my assessment of Zarqawi, any diminution of his status would sorely upset him.

At about the same time, we obtained a video taken by Zarqawi's propaganda team of him shooting a U.S. M-249 squad automatic weapon, or SAW, in a bermed desert area somewhere inside Iraq. The footage was meant to be grist for a propaganda film showing a macho-looking insurgent leader demonstrating his warrior skills. We intercepted that footage, as well as the full, unedited version, which revealed the supposedly pious Zarqawi ignoring a call to prayer from a muezzin off camera and lacking even rudimentary proficiency on the weapon. As Zarqawi and his team swaggered back to their trucks after firing, one of his aides achieved buffoon status when he took the SAW from Zarqawi by grabbing the barrel, still hot from being fired. The hot metal seared his hand, and he dropped the weapon. It was amusing to watch and also an opportunity to undercut the terrorist leader's mystique. So we arranged for it to be released by MNF-I on May 4, nine days after AQI's edited version hit the Internet. We felt we were closing in—and it was worth making every effort to provoke his vanity, threaten his standing, and hopefully cause him to make a fatal slip.

By Wednesday, May 17, after two more weeks of interrogations, Mubassir's flippant attitude had increasingly given way to weariness. His family was now completely on its own, without his brother to watch over them. The screening facility team sensed they could make his desperation more acute. Again working together, the analysts and interrogators had put together a time line of Mubassir's travels to Jordan. Amy and Jack saw that Mubassir had been there prior to bombings in Amman the previous November. He had admitted a connection with al-Masri, who, along with Zarqawi, was closely linked with the Atrous family, which had yielded the female suicide bomber for the attack. Knowing this, they saw a chance to play on his self-preservation instinct and goad him into revealing something they thought he was holding back.

Now, several weeks after Mubassir's capture in Yusufiyah, Amy, the young female interrogator, and her partner, Jack, sat down again across the table from Mubassir. They told him they knew of his trips to Jordan and his connections to al-Masri and top status in AQI. They presented these as dangerous secrets they had uncovered.

"We're trying to hold on to you, but if the word gets out that you are tied to this, it could be really bad," the interrogators said. Mubassir sensed how significant the hotel bombings were.

"I can't give you anything," Mubassir said. "I don't have anything."

Jack, pretending to get mad, got up and walked toward the door. He passed a knowing glance to Amy over his shoulder. She understood. He stopped in the doorway. "I'm going to get a guard, we're done with you," he said to the detainee, and slammed the door.

Amy turned back around in her seat and looked at Mubassir squarely. Across the small molded-plastic table from her small five-foot-four frame, Mubassir's bulk hid much of the white plastic chair. "You need to talk to us," she said. "You need to tell us what's going on. We're going to be able to tie you to those bombings, and at that point, it's going to be out of our hands."

"I don't have anything," he said.

Behind her the guards knocked on the wood door. The weeks of rapport now tugged at him. His only meaningful interactions since capture had been with Jack and Paul and Amy, sitting in front of him. They were now his best and only advocates in this bizarre world he increasingly wanted to escape, and the surest way to make it be over for him. The knocks on the door threatened to upend all of that. The knocks meant a new prison, new interrogators, new uncertainty.

"Wait," Mubassir said, "I have something to tell you."

CHAPTER 13

Hibhib

May–June 2006

A t around 10:00 A.M. on May 18, 2006, an interrogation report was on the desk of J.C. when he entered the operations center. T.S. and T.C. had convinced Mubassir to talk the day before, and the result was stunning. Midmorning was normally dead time at the Baghdad compound, the squadron's central headquarters. J.C. had gone to bed only a few hours earlier, when the raids had finished and the assaulters called in "objective secure." Those operators were now asleep in the bunk beds berthed throughout the house, one of a row of identical villas Saddam had built for favored supporters. The villa sat inside the Green Zone and backed to the Tigris River. It had at one time been nice, with stucco patios and verandas. After five years of heavy use by the seventy-man squadrons that rotated through for ninety days of breakneck operations, the amenities were neglected and in disrepair. Most of the pools out back were covered in a film of algae. The interior was austere and practical. Plywood shelving had been built into the walls. A TV went rarely watched, and a gym was heavily used. Former living and dining rooms had been converted to operations centers with monitors and workstations. The rooms and hallways were crowded and had a hodgepodge look, but it was anything but casual. In these slow hours of the morning, and into early afternoon, a few operators scrutinized intelligence and quietly coordinated necessary support. But by late afternoon it would become tense with focused activity in anticipation of the night's raids.

J.C. had sat there many mornings before, studying Mubassir's interesting but still inconclusive interrogation. Up until then, each had normally been a couple of pages in length. Today's report, from Mubassir's fifty-first inter- rogation, was eight pages of commentary from a man who seemed to be unburdening himself. The day before, after Mubassir had told Amy to wait as she rose to answer the guards knocking on the door, she and Jack had deftly pulled out of him all the details they knew J.C. and his team would need. It was all now in the report, which J.C. quickly skimmed: Zarqawi's spiritual adviser, Mubassir said, was Sheikh Abd al-Rahman. He lived in Baghdad with his family. He had a wife and three kids. Two daughters and a boy. The boy was the youngest. Abd al-Rahman never drove himself. He had a chauffeur.

And, Mubassir claimed, Abd al-Rahman met with Zarqawi regularly, every seven to ten days.

Reading Mubassir's full portrait of Abd al-Rahman, it was almost too good—perhaps bluffs from a desperate detainee. But the address Mubassir had provided for Abd al-Rahman in Baghdad was a way to start to verify. At this point the squadrons and troops—two and three levels below the TF 714 headquarters—had control over the task force's ISR flight paths. Not needing to go through the higher headquarters, J.C. turned to a team member.

"Hey, fly over to that address. Tell me when you're there."

As the aircraft flew toward the house in Khadra, Baghdad, J.C. contin- ued reading the report. When the UAV arrived overhead, the house was quiet. By Baghdad standards, the neighborhood was upper-middle class, and oddly, given Abd al-Rahman's supposed connections, the house was in a Shia area. This might be a waste of time, J.C. thought. But after a few minutes, the image on his screen stirred. A silver sedan pulled up in front of the house. The driver got out, disappeared under the roof of the house, and came back out with another man. Both got in the car and drove off.

"Stay with that car," J.C. said.

As the cameras followed the car weaving through the residential streets, J.C. read the report over again. As he turned to the section about Abd al-Rahman's family, the sedan returned to the house. The passenger went back into the house, while the driver stayed in the car idling out front. Five figures reemerged from the house a few minutes later—two adults and three smaller figures. To lay eyes, it would have been hard to tell that the second figure was a woman. But her distinctive movements and size were visible to the Green intel team with years of watching aerial surveillance. Three young children trailed them, one small enough to be picked up by the man. The man, woman, and children got into the car.

The sedan drove to a nearby market, busy now as midday approached. The man on the passenger side stepped out of the car. The driver popped out as well. While the scene was mute on the screen, J.C. and his team could read their exchange as the passenger told the driver to get back in the car. The passenger turned toward the bazaar, stopped at a few stalls, and eventually returned to the sedan, which wound its way to another house. What now appeared to be a family got out of the car and walked into the house, the driver shutting their doors behind them. J.C. watched and knew he had to cancel the planned surveillance for that day. As if on script, these six people on the screen matched the description and movements described in the detainee report in his hands. Suspicious, J.C. pulled up the database that plotted all the known areas of interest. The second house the sedan ended at was tagged as one of the five known locations used by the Abu Ayyub al-Masri's courier network. It made sense—al-Masri functioned as a sort of real estate agent for the network.

J.C. called his boss, M.S., who was at Balad, and described what he was seeing and how it matched the detainee report. J.C. was skeptical as to whether Mubassir's report was trustworthy—and had good reason to be. M.S.'s experience had told her to put great stock in the intuition of colleagues, so she arranged for her, J.C., and the interrogators to discuss this at more length in a series of VTCs. The interrogators—Amy, Jack, and Paul—laid out why they thought this report from Mubassir was worth betting on. As they did, J.C. was convinced. It was now up to him and M.S. to convince the task force leadership.

"All right," said M.S., "let me get the boss, and let's do a VTC." They would propose to the task force leadership that J.C. and his team watch Abd al-Rahman—or the person they thought was Abd al-Rahman—constantly. Approval would not be automatic. Diverting limited ISR assets to concentrate on any target was a decision with significant operational implications for our ability to maintain pressure on Zarqawi's entire network.

M.S. and Scott Miller, the commander of Green in charge of TF 16, videoconferenced in J.C. and Joe, the commander of the squadron about to rotate out, both of whom were in Baghdad.

"Here're the facts," J.C. began, being sure not to mix what he thought with what he knew: Although the man, woman, children, and driver matched what Mubassir was saying, it wasn't a sure thing that the guy being driven around was Abd al Rahman or that, if he was, he met weekly with Zarqawi. But, he said, if this panned out, it would be the closest we had been to Zarqawi yet. The two colonels and the major listened patiently to this sergeant first class, who had been eating, living, sleeping, breathing Zarqawi and the Al Qaeda in Iraq network for the past two years. He was credible for his reservoirs of knowledge and for his straightforward reputation.

To monitor Abd al-Rahman, they would need to watch him constantly, twenty-four hours a day, in a busy city. J.C. asked to control at least three ISR assets at all times. He wanted two to stay with Abd al-Rahman and a third to follow anyone with whom he met. This would require using up the bulk of the task force's valuable ISR, pulling orbits away from the other TF 16 teams spread throughout Iraq to be solely under J.C.'s control.

"All right, we'll do it, J.," said Scott.

From that moment on, J.C. almost never stopped monitoring the screen. He slept minimally. Guys brought him food. He occasionally stole away for a VTC to keep the rest of the teams and us up at Balad informed, knowing that updates bought him time.

On Saturday, May 20, as J.C. and his team spent a second day watching Abd al-Rahman in Baghdad, the Iraqi parliament gathered for a vote in an auditorium inside the Green Zone. With typical drama, including a group of Sunnis storming out, the parliamentarians approved the first permanent government since Saddam. After three years in which the Iraqis had a governing council, a transitional government, and then an interim one, they now had a constitutional administration. At its head was a Shiite member of parliament, Nouri al-Maliki, a balding man with glasses and a gourd-shaped head. He was influential within his Dawah Party but lesser known by most spectators. Fifty-five years old on that day, he had lived much of his life outside Iraq—he had fled to Iran via Syria and then, once able, moved back to Syria where he spent his adult life until 2003. It was hard to know what to make of al-Maliki. Would he be a Shiite hard-liner? Or would he prove the much-hoped-for conciliator? Would Iran and Syria have undue sway now? Would he be a democrat or an authoritarian in utero?

In addition to selecting al-Maliki as the prime minister, Parliament also approved thirty-six of his cabinet posts, all except for three: the national security adviser and the ministers of both interior and defense. These most contentious positions were all connected to the security forces, which over the past year had been infiltrated by Shiite extremists. Wearing their light gray and deep blue uniforms and carrying the badge of the ministry of the interior, they had targeted Sunnis—young men, mostly—abducting and killing them. Sunnis worried Maliki's temporary appointments would stay long enough that he could make them permanent.

The urgent question, further delayed by these empty posts, was this: Would, or could, al-Maliki create a unified Iraqi government not defined by sectarian infiltration and divisions? If he did, would it slow the apparent slide to open civil war? That looked doubtful. Many of the politicians meeting in the auditorium that day supported—and were supported by—the Sunni and Shia groups who were meanwhile producing a thousand corpses each month in the streets outside the Green Zone.

In April and May, I visited the task force screening facility more frequently, walking across the gravel path to sit in on the evening session of their twice-daily update. More informally, Scott Miller would stop in to my office for quick updates, or I would sit down next to him on the small bench in the back of his TF 16 JOC. One night, as we sat before the moving mosaic of current operations screens, Scott turned to me.

"Sir, we're really starting to get something out of Mubassir," he said.

"He's starting to cooperate. We've never had someone who we can ask about what we're seeing."

As J.C. and his team monitored Abd al-Rahman's movements, they showed pictures—of buildings or people Abd al-Rahman visited—to Mubassir, who explained whom or what we were looking at. Most recently, Mubassir had identified a second house, belonging to Abd al-Rahman's brother-in-law, where Abd al-Rahman had recently moved his family. The task force gradually built up fourteen sites throughout Baghdad that were part of Abd al-Rahman's routine movement.

I had heard people get excited about detainees before, but I listened to what he was saying. Across the gravel, where Mubassir was detained, the interrogators continued to build rapport. One day they set him up in one of the interrogation booths so he could watch a movie. At his request, his interrogators brought in their own chairs and took turns watching it with him. They had managed to find a copy of the film he had asked for, which he said was his favorite: *The Exorcist*.

J. C.'s focus remained controversial within the command. The squadron was doing its best with limited ISR, and during the weeks we watched Abd al-Rahman, it hit one or two targets a night throughout the country. But this was way below the operational tempo I had been pushing—and that I felt was necessary to keep Al Qaeda in Iraq disjointed and wheezing. The assault troop based out of that compound in Baghdad was essentially sitting on hold, as the squadron's intelligence staff and 70 percent of its ISR assets were focused full time on Abd al-Rahman.

The wait was grating. Every day that we watched Abd al-Rahman, other targets went undisturbed. I was worried that if he was a wash—and we had seen other seductive leads go cold—we would have allowed Al Qaeda in Iraq weeks to heal and strengthen. The days that Abd al-Rahman relaxed at home and out of sight were excruciating.

Meanwhile, outside the field of view of the ISR feed, Baghdad was on fire. In the weeks after the Samarra bombing at the end of February, the violence was carried out in impulsive spasms. Now, by the end of May, three months after the bombing, the sectarian killing programs were accelerating. Armed militias of Sunni and Shia led systematic campaigns of ethnic cleansing neighborhood by neighborhood in Baghdad. By the end of May 2006, more than eighty thousand Iraqis had been uprooted, seeking shelter elsewhere in the country. Meanwhile, Baghdad's central morgue had taken in 1,398 bodies during the prior four weeks, the most since the invasion. And yet this was only a portion of the real death toll in the capital city, as the morgue didn't perform autopsies on victims of the city's bombs.

During these tense weeks, I went down to Baghdad to meet with J.C. and his team as I had on each of his previous rotations. I wanted to show them my support and interest. Given the stakes, I also wanted to know more about their thinking. I met J.C. at the squadron's Green Zone villa during daylight, when most of the assault teams were still asleep from the previous night's operations. J.C. left the monitors under the watch of his team and joined Mike Flynn, Joe, the commander of J.C.'s squadron (headquartered at Baghdad), and me on the couch in the next room. We cradled Styrofoam cups of coffee as J.C. ran through what he had been watching.

Every morning, normally at around 9:00 A.M., the silver sedan showed up outside Abd al-Rahman's house. Abd al-Rahman came outside to the street, said good-bye to his wife and family, and got in. The driver always opened and closed the front passenger door for him. They drove around the city, stopping for meetings, until dinnertime, when Abd al-Rahman returned home. He repeated the routine each day, varying only the locations throughout the city. They mapped and logged each location in a database—from the gas station at which they filled the tank to where Abd al-Rahman bought bread to his regular, sketchy meeting places.

But it was J.C.'s eye that made the difference. When Abd al-Rahman emerged from Friday prayers, which are very busy, J.C. picked him out of the crowd almost instantly. Abd al-Rahman made it slightly easier by wearing similar outfits, but J.C. could spot him based on his distinctive demeanor. He walked, J.C. explained, as a Westerner would walk in the Middle East. He seemed to float with arrogance. When he got out of his car, he did so deliberately, snapping his lapels down to straighten his jacket. Of greater consequence, J.C., steeped in Iraq for years, could decode Abd al-Rahman's intimate relationships. He knew, for instance, how important the brother-in-law's house would be if Abd al-Rahman ever left town and needed his wife and family to be with a trusted male relative.

As on most visits, I wanted to hear about the granular details of his work, but I also liked to push and prod the premises underlying their targeting philosophy. *How can we think more outside the box? Are we too far afield? Are we overthinking or underthinking?* J.C. and his boys enjoyed debating targeting philosophy, and although his eyes were ringed from lack of sleep, he was animated when I pushed him on his contention that we should watch Abd al-Rahman rather than capture him now.

"Why not police up Rahman now and use what we have to get him to tell us where he meets AMZ?"

"Sir, Rahman's a true believer. Even if we got him in the booth," J.C. said, referring to the interrogation rooms, "I don't think we could get him to talk. If we move on Rahman, and what Mubassir's saying is right, it could spook AMZ."

"Rahman obviously knows we've had Mubassir for a while now. What if he has stopped seeing Zarqawi? Or what if he disappears?" I asked.

"Why would Zarqawi give Rahman regular access? He hasn't survived this long being careless. I don't think that you can draw a direct line between Zarqawi and any one person."

"See, I disagree with you, sir. Everybody is connected to somebody, but you've got to find the right guy and draw a line. I think Rahman's it."

"I'm not sure," I said, "but I'll let you go with it."

So far, we had seen what Mubassir said we would, and he had told us that every seven to ten days, Abd al-Rahman met with Zarqawi. J.C. and his team had been monitoring, mapping, and patterning Abd al-Rahman's movements for almost that long. One day, as they watched Abd al-Rahman, swells of dust obscured the ground and Abd al-Rahman with it. They switched the cameras to infrared, but in doing so the picture went from color to black and white. Abd al-Rahman became a small, dark figure inside a crowd of small dark figures, and they lost him.

They still had eyes on Abd al-Rahman's family, and after a couple hundred hours of watching his movements, the team was convinced he wouldn't leave them. They also had eyes on the man who had driven with him that day, later thought to be Abu Ghadiya, a young Anbari who helped run the foreign-fighter pipeline. They watched Abu Ghadiya go north of Baghdad and stop. After a few uneasy moments when they wondered what Ghadiya was doing, a car bomb went off nearby. Now we had a strong reason to move on Ghadiya—who had likely been there to film the bombing. But picking up Ghadiya meant moving on Abd al-Rahman's house, where Ghadiya was staying. J.C. made the case that picking up Ghadiya would spook Abd al-Rahman—and we potentially could lose our trail to Zarqawi. We gritted our teeth and waited for Abd al-Rahman to reappear.

Two days passed without any sign of him. On June 1, Tom D. arrived in the country as the new commander of J.C.'s squadron, replacing Joe. It had been seventeen months since I had flown with Tom D. and Tres from Afghanistan to Balad after the suicide bomber destroyed the mess hall in Mosul and I asked them to stand up JIATF-West. Tom D., like all commanders, held strong opinions about how best to hunt. He preferred to develop targets and err on the side of running less frequent missions if it meant fewer "dry holes." This made him inclined to support J.C.'s program. But, Tom D. told J.C., realistically, if Abd al-Rahman didn't come back in another two days, they would have to give up monitoring his family and house. They couldn't burn assets if Abd al-Rahman had fled the city.

J.C. nodded. "He'll be back."

Two days after they spoke, and after four days gone, Abd al-Rahman returned—fresh, many assumed, from having seen Zarqawi.

Around this time, the leadership above J.C. again shifted. As all commanders did periodically, Scott Miller returned to the States, and Steve, his deputy at Green, came to lead TF 16. (As commander of TF 16, Steve was my subordinate and Tom D.'s commander.) Steve's inclination, like mine, was to act on targets rather than cultivate them. He knew the task force expected him to arrive and make them move on Abd al-Rahman and the rest of the targets. But Steve let the process play out, and his arrival bought J.C. a few more days of watching Abd al-Rahman.

The tension over whether to watch or strike a target was a recurring one and increased at the beginning of June. Watching a target often held the potential for a bigger payoff, mostly by revealing valuable connections to other targets. This slow work was popular with law-enforcement people who served as augmentees in the task forces and with intelligence analysts who looked to unravel the enemy network. But prolonged target development was less popular with the action-oriented operators. Striking targets rapidly had put tremendous pressure on AQI in the two years since TF 16 had accelerated its tempo, and these operations had yielded countless troves of intelligence. We would never have been where we were in June 2006 if we had taken an overly deliberate approach. Moreover, leaving targetable AQI operatives undisturbed as they continued their reign of violence on Iraq was a difficult moral judgment.

Well before Steve's arrival, every day in their forcewide VTCs, TF 16 debated whether to arrest Abd al-Rahman or leave him under surveillance. Tempers began to flare during the early days of June. Green drew opinionated and often vocal men and women, and the unit's ethos held that if you shied from speaking your mind, you shouldn't be in the unit. On top of this, everyone in the room had spent long years chasing Zarqawi. During that time, I had sought to breed a sense of ownership that demanded everyone be interested not only in their small part but in the big decisions. Everyone was expected to be a strategist. So by June 2006, the men and women under me wanted to win—and thought they knew how. J.C. and M.S. were both highly respected and were absolutely convinced we should not move on Abd al-Rahman. Tom D., who was a strong, vocal presence within the unit, supported them. Steve's more conventional army background made him disposed toward a more direct approach, and he shouldered an immense burden: No colonel had ever run anything as large and complex as TF 16, which was what Steve was doing at its most critical juncture. Meanwhile, he spent his days only paces away from me, a demanding three-star general (I had been promoted three months earlier, in mid-February) who, by personality and explicit guidance, was inclined to strike more than to sit and watch. But I respected the intelligence assessment of people like J.C. and M.S., and so, ultimately, did Steve, who allowed the process to continue to play out.

Aware of the mounting pressure to move on Abd al-Rahman and anxious to buy even more time, the squadron decided to try to positively identify Abd al-Rahman. Until then, J.C. and his team hadn't been able to say for certain "their" Abd al-Rahman was the right guy. Many remained unconvinced he was: He was much younger than we expected AQI's religious scholars to be, given the credentials needed.

Two dedicated analysts working for the task force recovered a good-quality picture of the real Sheikh Abd al-Rahman that they could use. The squadron decided to see if he was the man being followed by J.C. when he went to the mosque that Sunday, June 4. A two-man team, part of the squadron's specialized reconnaissance troop, dressed up in Iraqi clothing and planned to drive through Baghdad in a nondescript sedan and see Abd al-Rahman in the flesh as he emerged from the Sunday-morning services. This was highly dangerous. Now, three months after the Samarra mosque bombing, the ethnic contest for Baghdad had turned the city into a maze of checkpoints manned by militias who stopped cars and checked ID cards. If the ever-more-brazen and paranoid militias decided the occupants' names indicated they came from the opposite sect, they often simply pulled the riders from their car and shot them in the street.

Nonetheless, the reconnaissance made it to the mosque, parked half a block away, and waited. They planned to drive by just as Abd al-Rahman walked to his car door, so they could see and photograph his face. As the crowd emptied out of the mosque, Abd al-Rahman made it to his car, parked right out front, faster than the reconnaissance team had anticipated. He got in and started moving as our team was still down the street. From the air, J.C. and the squadron watched as the two cars—al-Rahman's and ours—drove toward each other. On the ground, for only a moment as the noses of the two cars were almost abreast of each other, our reconnaissance team and their camera lens got the right angle: From the diagonal, Abd al-Rahman's windshield lost its glare and his face was visible through the glass.

They sent the photograph up to Balad and placed it, along with five or six pictures of other men, in front of Mubassir. They asked him which one was Abd al-Rahman. He put his fingers on the photograph taken that day: "That's him."

Upon returning to the Baghdad compound, one of the reconnaissance operatives came to see J.C. He had studied the picture of Abd al-Rahman before venturing into Baghdad that day and told J.C. the man he saw on the road was him. Having seen the cars whip past each other on the screen, J.C. pushed him. How could he be sure?

"Hey, look," the operative said, standing there in the Iraqi garb. "It's him. I'm one hundred percent on this." There was no one better at the craft than the reconnaissance team that had gone out that day, and J.C. trusted his judgment. It was the same trust the task force had placed in J.C. Without it, our complex machine would have seized up.

Two days later, just before sundown on Tuesday, June 6, J.C. and his team were in place in the JOC when they saw a moving van pull into the frame and park in front of Abd al-Rahman's house. Almost nightly during the weeks before, the intel and operators had been refining the plan for a move on Abd al-Rahman when or if the time came. Based upon what Mubassir had explained of his routine and Abd al-Rahman's pattern and regimen observed over the past nineteen days, the operators and J.C.'s intel team had determined certain movements that would trigger a raid. One was moving his family.

They watched as the van, similar to a big, thirty-foot U-Haul, was loaded with packing boxes. It was dusk just as the last boxes were put in the back and the hatch closed. That night we had in the sky a brand-new, hard-won set of manned surveillance planes. The van was now theirs to track. But in the difficult lighting as dusk grew quickly darker, they lost the van as it made its way through Baghdad. Tracking targets from the sky was not automatic, not done with simple flicks of the joystick. The men in the manned surveillance aircraft overhead sat in their seats for hours on end, following targets through their cameras but also relaying what they saw over the radio. It was a finicky process in which even a van could get lost.

J.C. was frustrated but still had Abd al-Rahman and his family in his sights. They returned to the brother-in-law's house, a couple blocks away from the house Mubassir had first directed us to, where J.C. had first seen Abd al-Rahman nineteen days earlier.

The next morning, June 7, J.C. again found himself watching the screens. The JOC was empty except for one member of J.C.'s team. Midmorning, as usual, Abd al-Rahman went in the silver sedan from his brother-in-law's home back to his own house. He and his driver started out the same as usual, only this time the car stayed in the immediate district. They wound around its streets and then, curiously, circled back to the house. At around noon, Tom D. entered the JOC, just as Abd al-Rahman returned to his house after circling about. He and J.C. agreed: It seemed like a maneuver of someone worried about being followed to wherever he was going next.

Under continuous surveillance, the silver sedan drove to the northeastern part of Baghdad, where it caught the on-ramp for the route Iraqis called Sabbah Nissan, which ran north through the sparser neighborhoods east of Sadr City and out, eventually to Diyala Province. It was now midafternoon, and the highway's six lanes were flush with traffic. As J.C. and Tom D. watched, the silver sedan slowed and veered to the side of the road, where Abd al-Rahman got out. It was not uncommon for Iraqis to get out on the side of even busy highways, hop the side walls, and go to the stores along the road. But the silver sedan took off and Abd al-Rahman started walking backward, against traffic. They saw him with his cell phone to his ear. Within the time it took him to walk twenty or thirty or feet, a blue Bongo truck—the kind with a small, snub-nosed cab, short flatbed, and car-sized wheels—appeared in the field of view and quickly slowed to a stop in its lane. Abd al-Rahman swung himself into the passenger side, and the truck driver punched the accelerator. It was over in a few seconds. J.C. and Tom D. looked at each other.

"That was slick," Tom D. said. It was classic countersurveillance behavior, called tradecraft in the "business" of clandestine operatives.

One of the three ISR planes followed the silver sedan, while J.C. and

Tom D. focused on the second feed, showing the Bongo truck. They figured he was going to the neighborhoods in the northeast quadrant of Baghdad, where they had watched Abd al-Rahman circle around in the preceding weeks, likely talking on his cell phone. But then the Bongo truck missed one turnoff, then the next. Soon, it had left the city limits.

"Well, he's out of Baghdad," J.C. said, turning to Tom D. Leaving the city was one of the preestablished triggers to move on Abd al-Rahman. "We thought he was going to go to the west, not north. But he's out." He sucked air in between his teeth. "It looks like we're waking everybody up."

The roused operators, who had returned to the villa and shed their equipment only a few hours earlier, soon joined J.C., Tom D., and the rest of the intel team in the JOC. They also called up to TF 16 headquarters at Balad. Steve, the task force commander, and M.S., its intelligence chief, were in the O&I VTC when someone came in and told them Abd al-Rahman was moving. They came out into the JOC and watched a replay of the feed showing the vehicle swap. The feeds went onto the JOC screens, and Steve started pulling in more ISR assets from across Iraq.

A few minutes later, Steve came into my office on the other side of the plywood wall. He was businesslike, but this wasn't business as usual. As I listened, I knew the frustration he had experienced as a squadron commander over a year earlier, when lost surveillance had let Zarqawi slip through his fingers.

"Rahman's moved, sir. He swapped vehicles and left Baghdad," he said.

"Okay. Where's he going?" I asked. I assumed he would head to Yusufiyah.

"He's going north. We're pulling in assets to cover this guy."

"Really?" I said, surprised at the direction. "Okay. Don't spare anything."

"Roger out," Steve said. He returned to the JOC, and I stayed in my office.

On the screens in both the JOC in Balad, and down with Tom D. and J.C. in Baghdad, they watched the Bongo continue up Sabbah Nissan. I came out a couple times to look at the feed. The JOC was buzzing. Normal operational coordination continued, but most kept an eye on the Bongo truck on the screen.

A little less than an hour later, Abd al-Rahman pulled into the capital city of Diyala Province, Baqubah. It was now late in the afternoon. The city the Bongo truck had entered had a mixed Sunni-Shia population of about five hundred thousand. The Sunni insurgency was deeply entrenched in the province around it, where Al Qaeda enjoyed alarming support. In the previous days, four Shiite mechanics had been gunned down, six Iraqi policemen had been attacked, and the heads of eight Sunnis had been found together in banana crates. Four days earlier, at a fake checkpoint on the road into the city, insurgents had killed twenty Shiite bus passengers, including seven students preparing to take their final exams at a university in Baqubah.

The Bongo pulled off the street into a parking area in front of a building, apparently a restaurant, in a commercial part of town. Abd al-Rahman got out and went in, past a figure who appeared to stand watch on the curb. A minute, maybe two, later, a pickup truck pulled into the lot. It parked nose to nose with the blue Bongo truck. This struck everyone as odd. After the kicked-up dust settled, the pickup's coloring came into view—white with a red stripe. The JOC froze. They had seen that truck before or, rather, dozens like it. Zarqawi used a fleet of white pickups with red stripes, part of an unnerving countersurveillance shell game. Five or six white pickups would pull up, he would hop in one and climb through the cab to the next, and they would peel off in separate directions.

An odd figure emerged, dressed in full Gulf-like attire, with flowing white robes and kaffiyeh. He entered the building, walking past the guard without any visible exchange, as if they knew each other.

The Baghdad JOC was on edge. *Here he is, dropped off outside of Baghdad. This is it; this is what we've been waiting for.*

"What do you think?" Tom D. asked J.C.

"No, no, hold on," J.C. said. "This isn't it." Not everyone there agreed. *He's in there, right now, meeting with Zarqawi.* But the meeting spot didn't feel right to J.C. Too congested. Too insecure.

Luck had slipped Zarqawi through countless checkpoints in the past two years. It had hidden him from our helicopters in Yusufiyah a few weeks earlier and had been there when our camera gyroscope locked up and spun out and lost him on the road between Ramadi and Rawah a year earlier. Luck helped every bomb that went undetected beneath a roadway or hidden behind clothing. But luck now swung to our side: Before we had to decide whether to move on the building, two figures walked out its front door.

No more than three or four seconds passed between when the two emerged into the sunlight from under the building veranda and when they got into the white pickup a few feet in front of it. In that time, both J.C. and one of his team members picked up his movements.

That's Rahman, they said. *Follow him.*

The white pickup with a red stripe, which had deposited the sheikh-looking man with the flowing robes, peeled away from the building. The car began to look like a shuttle, ferrying between this building and, inevitably, somewhere else.

Steve came in again and told me Abd al-Rahman had left Baqubah. It was now late afternoon, and the JOC beyond the plywood wall was loud. People were on phones, coordinating the ISR that Steve had pulled in and that was flying high overhead toward Baqubah. Soon we had six, and then nine, orbits stacked in the sky, watching four targets—the silver sedan still in Baghdad, the way station in Baqubah, the blue Bongo still parked there, and now the white pickup hauling out of town. We needed that many eyes, but we risked spooking the targets as the airspace became congested. Inside the JOC, Steve's team began to work out how it was going to go down. *What are we hitting? What is Baghdad saying?*

The white pickup drove northwest out of Baqubah five kilometers to a small town identified as Hibhib, where it got off the main road. It passed through the sparse streets and continued onto a single-lane dirt frontage road, running alongside a narrow concrete irrigation canal half full of turquoise water. Dense groves of palm trees, with thick shrubs and undergrowth, extended back a few hundred meters from the track on the passenger's side. In the early-evening light, the groves were dark and shadowy. The truck approached a boxy two-story house tucked among the trees, sitting half a dozen car lengths back from the road at the end of a driveway. It had a carport under the front edge of the second floor. Only the beige facade of the house was fully visible, as the rear part of the building disappeared into the shadows and palm trunks that surrounded it.

At 4:55 P.M., the truck turned right off the frontage road and stopped halfway up the driveway, in front of a closed gate. While Abd al-Rahman stayed in the passenger seat, the driver got out and went to the driveway gate. A figure emerged from under the carport roof and walked down the driveway to meet him. After a short exchange, the second man went back to the house and then came back and opened the gate. Back in his white pickup, the driver pulled through the open gate and parked in the carport. Our team saw Abd al-Rahman get out and enter the house. The white truck reversed out of the driveway and went back the way it had come. As they watched this down in Baghdad, Tom D. turned to J.C. "What do you think, J.?"

"I have no reason to tell you not to hit it," J.C. answered.

"I'm not going to promise you that's Zarqawi," J.C. said, pointing to the screen. "But whoever we kill is going to be much higher than anybody we've ever killed before. So I'm saying, absolutely—whack it." Inside, he felt, would be al-Masri, Zarqawi—or both.

Tom D. told his operators at Baghdad to go. Steve came into our SAR up in Balad. "We're launching Tom D.'s boys." Down at Baghdad, the troop of Green operators suited up and waited for the helicopters to land in the front yard of their villa safe house.

Steve came in a few minutes later. "Sir, you've got to see this."

We brought up the video feed on the screens in front of our U-shaped desk. Mike Flynn and Kurt Fuller were next to me. The video replayed Abd al-Rahman's arrival and the white truck's departure. Then he played a scene that had just occurred. On the video, a figure emerged from the shadow of the veranda and walked down the driveway. As he got into the sunlight, we could see more clearly. He looked heavy and was dressed head to toe in black. He walked past the gate and continued to the end of the driveway, where it met the frontage road going back to Hibhib. He stood, looked left up the road, looked right, and walked back to the house.

"That's AMZ," I said, turning to Steve standing by the doorway.

"Yes, sir. We're going to bomb it," he said.

Steve remembers my reaction being one of irritation—I'd hoped to get Zarqawi alive. I remember calmly telling him to do what he had to do.

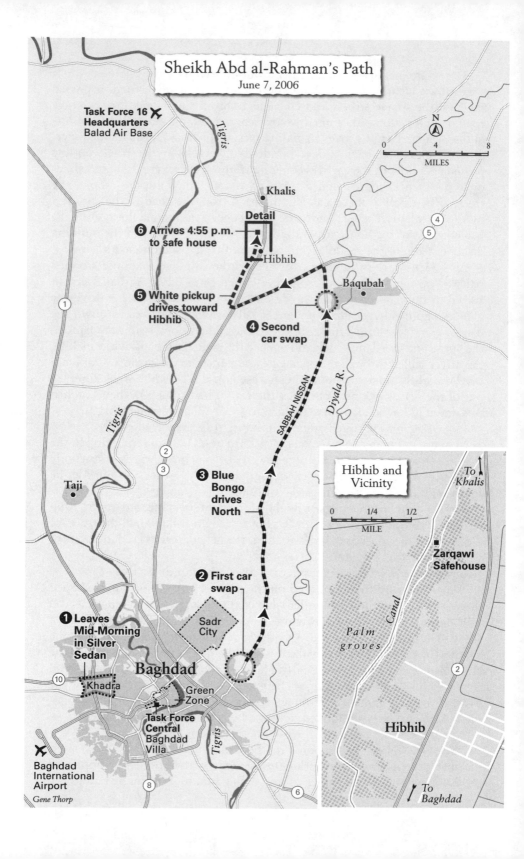

Sheikh Abd al-Rahman's Path

June 7, 2006

Task Force 16 Headquarters
Balad Air Base

Tigris

Khalis

Detail

6 Arrives 4:55 p.m. to safe house

Hibhib

5 White pickup drives toward Hibhib

4 Second car swap

Baqubah

Diyala R.

SABBAH NISSAN

3 Blue Bongo drives North

Tigris

Taji

2 First car swap

Sadr City

1 Leaves Mid-Morning in Silver Sedan

Baghdad

Khadra

Green Zone

Task Force Central
Baghdad Villa

Baghdad International Airport

Gene Thorp

0 4 8
MILES

N

Hibhib and Vicinity

To Khalis

0 1/4 1/2
MILE

Zarqawi Safehouse

Canal

Palm groves

Hibhib

To Baghdad

Having worked so closely with Steve, I'm confident his recollection is more accurate. We'd always planned to capture Zarqawi for his obvious intelligence value, but not at the risk of his escape. To give up that possibility was a difficult decision that had to be made quickly in response to the situation as it was developing, and Steve had the experience and authority to make the call. I'd made a point of, and we'd been very successful, trusting subordinates to use their best judgment. This time should be no different. I did not interfere.

There was good reason to strike. As Tom D. and his operators recognized, a ground raid would be difficult, with a high probability of failure. The house did not appear to be a formidable defensive position, but as we'd learned in the Western Euphrates River valley fight, appearances could be deceiving. More important, palm trees surrounded the house, and the closest bald patch of ground to land our assault helicopters was a quarter mile away. To do a direct assault, because the trees were so tall, the assault force would have had to fast-rope ninety or a hundred feet down, a towering, dangerous distance—and one that would require the helos to float, in daylight, over the house. Doing a fast-rope would be asking to get a helicopter shot down. Most troubling, anyone inside the house could easily slip out the back, disappearing into the thick vegetation and groves. We likely wouldn't even see it happening.

Mike Flynn, Kurt Fuller, and I came out from our office into the TF 16 JOC. We took our spots on the bench at the back of the JOC room. As I had on hundreds of nights in the past two and a half years, I sat quietly and watched.

The JOC in front of us was in pained, tense anticipation. In order to secure the site and arrest anyone who escaped the blast, we wanted Tom D.'s operators to land just after the explosion. So Steve was waiting on them to be airborne and nearby before having the F-16 engage. Unbeknownst to many of us in Balad, as the troop down in Baghdad was first kitted up and loaded into the two helos taking off from in front of their villa, one of the engines wouldn't start. Tom D. and his team were stunned. This was unheard of for 160th helicopters. They sent for another helicopter, but it would be thirty tense minutes before it arrived from Balad.

As they watched the house on the screens, many in the JOC played over in their minds the worst-case scenario: They imagined seeing Abd al-Rahman and the Man in Black, spooked by the sounds in the busy sky overhead, dart from the house, disappearing into the foliage. They scoured the edges of the house, looking for movement under the carport or around the house's stucco walls. For now, it was quiet. The only movements on the screen were made by the tall palm trees, their top fronds rustling slightly, casting dark shadows across the house.

As we imagined what was happening inside the boxy, two-story house, we knew that if Zarqawi was there, he was not alone. His family—including perhaps both of his wives and their children—often stayed with him and would be killed in the strike.

Steve decided they couldn't wait for the Baghdad troop to be nearby. He called down to Tom D. at Baghdad. Through the receiver pressed to Tom D.'s ear, J.C. could hear Steve's go-ahead.

"Blow that motherfucker up."

Tom D. set it in motion. "Get the first helo airborne; the other one will catch up," he ordered. He turned to his joint tactical air controller (JTAC). "Go ahead and execute. Drop the bomb." The JTAC relayed the order to two already airborne F-16s on a normal combat patrol flown to provide near-immediate response to emerging requirements, like bombing a target. But the answer came back that only one of the two F-16s was available. The second was on the tanker, refueling midflight, and would be delayed fifteen minutes.

It was now after 6:00 P.M., and Tom D. shook his head. Weeks of patient, persistent focus had gotten them here, and the final operation now seemed to be running off the rails. "We don't have fifteen minutes." He told them to send the one that was free. The lone F-16 canted and roared through the clouds toward Baqubah.

"You are cleared to engage," the JTAC relayed, and the JOC waited. The jets were in a three-minute hold.

A minute passed. Two minutes out.

One minute.

The jet was within miles, and the residents of Hibhib would soon hear its engines crackle through the sky overhead.

At 6:11 P.M., it came in on a dive, rushed over the house, and peeled up. Tom D. and the JOC watched the screen. There was no explosion. The house was still there. The F-16 had screamed low over the house's roof but left it unscathed. They called the F-16. The JTAC's earlier bomb command had been improperly worded, they were told, so the F-16 hadn't released its munitions. Tom D. couldn't believe it. They looked to the screen, waiting to see Abd al-Rahman and the Man in Black flee into the palms.

They prepped the F-16 with the right command, and it circled back around.

At 6:12 P.M., a laser-guided, five-hundred-pound GBU-12 bomb traveling nine hundred feet per second hit the house. The explosion flashed, turning our screens in the JOC white for a split second, as smoke and dust burst up and out laterally in three columns, like the prongs of a toy jack. The F-16 circled again, and a minute and thirty-six seconds later, using GPS coordinates, a GBU-38 hit the same spot.

Thick billows of smoke streamed diagonally up from the house and frontage road, thinning over the tops of the palm grove.

"Tom D.'s boys are eighteen minutes out," said someone.

At 6:40 P.M., the skis of the Little Birds skidded into the dirt of a clearing four hundred meters from the house's driveway. Before the helicopters rocked forward and settled, the teams had bounded off. Leading them was Major Jason,* a physics-Ph.D.-turned-soldier who had been a Ranger first lieutenant for me years earlier. As the operators burst through the brown curtain of dust kicked up by the rotors, they moved quickly up the frontage road. Up ahead, parked in the driveway leading from the road to the crater, the operators saw an Iraqi ambulance. As they neared, they saw a group of Iraqis in police uniforms. A few of them were at the back of the ambulance, struggling to lift a stretcher into the trunk.

The Iraqi policemen turned to see our teams approaching in fast, coordinated movements, as if on rails. Very quickly the Americans had fanned out and claimed the geometry of the scene. With rifles poised, they yelled at the Iraqis. *Step away from the vehicle!* An Iraqi police lieutenant, standing separate from his men, eyed our operators. He put his palm on the pistol at his hip. *Put your arms up!* Our Green team moved closer with steady shuffle steps. The Iraqi lieutenant paused, then slowly lifted his hands to match the men around him, already holding their arms up around their ears. The operators swarmed in and took their weapons.

They quickly went around to the back of the ambulance and saw a gurney halfway out of the ambulance's swing doors. On top was a heavyset man in black clothes. They pulled the stretcher out and set it down into the dirt.

"Do you know who this is?" an operator asked one of the policemen.

"We do not know the Jordanian," the Iraqi said. That was unlikely. He was the only person at the scene they were evacuating.

Our medic leaned over the Man in Black, who was alive, but barely. Under the medic's forefingers, Zarqawi's carotid artery was deflated. His breathing was shallow, and blood seeped out of his nose and ears. The pressure caused by the blast waves had cascaded through the concrete walls of the house and pulsed through his chest cavity, bursting vessels and air sacs in his lungs. Behind the kneeling medic, members from the rest of the troop methodically searched the crater for evidence. Five other bodies were in the rubble, including Abd al-Rahman, another man, two women, and a young girl.

The medic continued to work on Zarqawi. When he cleared his airway, Zarqawi gurgled blood. The damage was fatal. Twenty-four minutes after the Green team had descended, under an orange evening sun and the long shadows of palm trees extending across the crater, beneath the clenched faces of the operators standing over him, Zarqawi's lungs failed. At 7:04 P.M., our medic called it. Zarqawi was dead.

Not long after, the ground team arrived at Balad, along with the bodies of Abd al-Rahman and Zarqawi, so we could definitely confirm their identities. I did not meet the operators on the tarmac when they touched down outside our hangar. I told Steve to let me know when he had a free moment, and we would go over together to the screening facility, where they would place the bodies. He nodded. Around us, the JOC was still electric.

---

*Jason is a pseudonym.

On-screen, we were still tracking the three vehicles that had shuttled Abd al-Rahman to the house. Ground teams were launching shortly, in Little Birds and Black Hawks, to interdict the vehicles. They would soon appear on-screen, swooping in behind the cars and cutting them off.

"We need to pull the trigger on the other targets," Steve said. By plan, making a movement on Abd al-Rahman was the trigger to take down the fourteen other sites in Baghdad, Arcadia 1 through 14, that had become targets based on Abd al-Rahman's suspicious activity. In addition, teams would interdict the vehicles that had ferried Abd al-Rahman to the safe-house. TF 16 was activating its strike teams from around the country so we could hit the targets within twenty-four hours, before Zarqawi's network heard about the strike and scattered. The machine was about to hit a fever pitch, and the JOC buckled down.

I returned to the SAR and continued to work until Steve came by and we walked over together with Mike Flynn. The low sun darkened the compound's dun walls and pathways and turned the dust-choked horizon and stray clouds orange.

At the screening facility, they had placed the bodies of Abd al-Rahman and Zarqawi in one of the exploitation rooms. Two guards outside the door let Steve and me in. Inside, Zarqawi and Abd al-Rahman had been laid on separate tarps spread on the cement floor. The room was empty except for two other operators. I walked over to the edge of the tarp and looked down. Killed by overpressure, Zarqawi's skin was unbroken. Even in death he looked stunningly like the figure we had seen weeks earlier in a propaganda video—soft and ashen.

It had been two and a half years since that first night in Fallujah, when we thought he leaped out the window. It seemed a long time ago. Since then, the war had twice ripped through that city. Zarqawi had gone from an important but stock jihadist operative slipping through our fingers to the most feared, active, deadly, and controversial Al Qaeda leader. We were only a few meters from my command center, and even closer to the small wooden hut where my command sergeant major and I had lived for most of the past two years—working toward this moment.

I looked at one of the operators, Luke,* kneeling on the other side of the body. I watched him as he quietly examined equipment captured in the operation. His chiseled face was drawn tight in focus as he sifted the material, his fingers smudging the film of dust on the phones and computers. His curly hair was still damp and matted with sweat—he had been a member of the assault force that had gone out to Hibhib and brought back the body. I had first served with him a decade earlier, when he was a staff sergeant squad leader in the Rangers. He was now about thirty-eight and a sergeant major in Green with almost five years of combat experience since 9/11. In a few hours, he would go back out into the night for another raid.

As our eyes met and we exchanged nods of recognition, respect, and

---

*Luke is a pseudonym.

friendship, I thought about what he saw when he looked at me. I'd been a forty-year-old Ranger battalion commander when we'd first met at Fort Lewis. I had technically still been a one-star general when I had joined him and his comrades in this fight in October 2003. Now, two months short of my fifty-second birthday, I wore the three stars of a lieutenant general and commanded a deployed force that had grown from a few hundred to many thousands on multiple continents, backed up by an even bigger structure in the United States. What had been impressive but rudimentary was now a relentless counterterrorist machine. In a honeycomb of rooms adjacent to the room in which I stood, teams of analysts pored through material recovered from the house in which Zarqawi was killed. In the hangar next door, screens were showing the first of the raids going out against the Arcadia targets. Similar processes were under way in ten different nodes worldwide.

I looked back at the body. Seeing him as a man, I couldn't exult in his death. Nor did I wring my hands. I took satisfaction, standing there, knowing that this work, our work, was necessary. Tonight, it had moved us closer to being finished.

"What do you think, Luke?" I asked the operator.

"Oh, that's him, sir," he said.

I nodded.

With Steve, I returned to my office to phone George Casey. I had called him prior to the strike, and he now knew we were waiting on the FBI to run the fingerprints back in the States. Until it did, we could not definitively say it was Zarqawi. But we'd shared this fight together for two years and I told him what I thought.

"Sir, I've seen the body, and I think it's him."

"How sure are you?" he asked.

"I'm sure, sir," I said, my voice cracking from fatigue or emotion.

Elsewhere in the screening facility, Amy, Paul, and Jack gathered outside Mubassir's room. They had agreed they would do this part together. They entered, closed the door, and told Mubassir about the strike. The information he had provided, they said, was correct. Zarqawi had been killed. What about Abd al-Rahman, his friend? Mubassir asked. They told Mubassir and stayed with him in the room as he sobbed.

In the early morning, as we waited for the FBI to call, I sat down with Mike and Kurt and Jody at our horseshoe desk in the SAR. The farewell ceremony for Bill McRaven had been planned for that evening at Fort Bragg. After three years as one of its assistant commanding generals, Bill was preparing to move on to become the commander of all special operations forces in Europe. But tonight he was at Fort Bragg, where they were holding a dinner for him. As we often did for ceremonies we couldn't attend, we cued up our VTC cameras so we could participate from afar. A projector screen at the front of the auditorium at Bragg showed us from the front, sitting at our horseshoe desk. From our side, we could see a wide angle of the room, with rows of tables and people. After scanning the figures, I saw Annie, sitting toward the front. In the public venue, I didn't try to speak to her, but I caught myself staring.

No one in the audience knew about the strike. Annie watched on the screen as every few minutes someone walked behind our chairs, leaned down, and whispered in my ear. Each time they said, still nothing back from the FBI. We grinned as teams at various outposts, connected by VTC, performed skits, and friends and colleagues in the auditorium at Bragg gave toasts as part of Bill's farewell. A few minutes after 3:30 A.M., a member of the task force staff walked briskly over and leaned in.

"FBI's come back, sir," he told me, "It's a match. PID." This was the abbreviation for positive identification.

As the audience watched one of the skits, Annie saw me get up and walk out of the frame. I went a few paces to my office and called George Casey again. The FBI had confirmed it, I told him. The man lying in our screening facility was Zarqawi.

Down at Baghdad, J.C. was still up. He would be for a little while longer, until all the teams called in "objective secure" near 4:00 A.M. Only then did he retire for his first real night of sleep in weeks.

Just before noon the next day, June 8, George Casey, Ambassador Zalmay Khalilzad, and Prime Minister Maliki held a press conference in Baghdad announcing Zarqawi's death. Prime Minister Maliki began, speaking in Arabic in front of a glossy wood-paneled wall. In a scene that evoked the Saddam announcement two and half years earlier, members of the audience broke out in cheers and clapping, eventually together in unison, *clap, clap, clap*. But the triumphalism on the podium was far more muted this time around. "Although the designated leader of Al Qaeda in Iraq is now dead, the terrorist organization still poses a threat," said General Casey. "Iraqi forces, supported by the Coalition, will continue to hunt terrorists that threaten the Iraqi people until terrorism is eradicated in Iraq." Shortly after the press conference ended, dueling factions in the Iraqi parliament dropped their vetoes and approved Maliki's outstanding cabinet nominations, putting the ministries of national security and interior under Shiites and the ministry of defense under a Sunni.

Later that day, Steve gathered everyone inside the JOC in our Balad hangar and gave much-deserved awards to five members of the task force screening facility—the three interrogators, Jack, Amy, and Paul, as well as two analysts who had worked side by side with them. The three interrogators continued to deploy back to Iraq for the rest of my time in command.

That night, I went from Balad down to meet with Tom D.'s squadron at their villa. A small group of us gathered in their conference room, a few paces from where J.C.'s team had spent the past few weeks watching Abd al-Rahman. Inside, I gave J.C. a bronze star medal. Everyone in the squadron liked and respected J.C. They knew how much he had contributed and how much he had staked his considerable reputation in the process. In many ways, his work and all the operations leading up to the strike was the culmination of what Steve and Wayne Barefoot had begun two years earlier in the lead-up to Big Ben, when they sat analysts and operators together to patrol the skies over Fallujah. He accepted the award in his typically humble, subdued way, speaking immediately of his team—who were at that moment riffling through the unprecedented trove of intelligence we had collected from the safe house in Hibhib and the seventeen other targets.

We then moved to the backyard, where the rest of the Green operators, pilots, intelligence officers, and other members of the task force who lived and worked at the villa gathered in a half circle. The grounds backed to the Tigris, the river's slick black surface reflecting the orange-ish glow of nighttime. The backyard was otherwise unlit. I could make out only darkened features or pairs of eyes when they caught the ambient light from the house or the city across the river.

"Listen, a lot of people are talking about all of this, what a big deal it all is," I said. "Let me tell you, I know what it took to get here. I know the price you have paid to do this. We have been at this a long time. We all know how important this was, and I just want to thank you." I spoke about Tom D.'s leadership and that of Major Jason. I talked about the work of J.C. and his team.

In typically laconic fashion, no one cheered or clapped. Age and rank still separated me from them. But in that moment, in the dark, I sensed I was as close as I would come to being a brother and friend with the men half visible around me.

"Feel good about what you've done, but you know, and I know, we *cannot* let up," I said. "This is far from finished."

They knew this. Indeed, no one in our task force believed killing Zarqawi would be the end of Al Qaeda in Iraq or the insurgency it leavened. But his ability, for more than two years, to evade us had given Zarqawi a dangerous aura and handicapped the Coalition's credibility.

His death was more than symbolically important. It was a trite reaction among some to point out that there were thousands of men ready to replace Zarqawi—or any leader we removed. It was of course true that the organization regained a leader: Within days of Zarqawi's death, Al Qaeda in Iraq announced that Abu Ayyub al-Masri would head the group. And yet there were not, in fact, thousands of "Zarqawis." He was a peculiar leader. His mix of charisma, brutality, and clear-eyed persistence was never matched by al-Masri or al-Masri's successor. While Zarqawi's leadership style had opened rifts within the insurgent movement in Iraq, he also had the ability to keep the insurgency largely congealed. Al-Masri lacked the magnetism or deep connections to marshal the factions as coherently.

Given how badly Zarqawi's campaign of ethnic murder had eroded global support for Al Qaeda, it's likely that the Al Qaeda leaders in Pakistan just hearing of Zarqawi's death that night were partially relieved to see him go. Indeed, Zarqawi's final message—a four-hour-long anti-Shia screed recorded that spring but released four days before his death—again defied bin Laden and Zawahiri's desire that he attack Americans, and not so many Shia. "We will not have victory over the original infidels," Zarqawi preached, unless "we fight the apostate infidels simultaneously." Some within our force made a convincing case that if we had not killed Zarqawi, he would have been retired from Iraq by bin Laden and given a top post in Al Qaeda's central leadership from which to project violence in the Levant. Indeed, before Zarqawi's death, Al Qaeda's senior leadership sought to salvage their project in Iraq by dispatching Abdul Hadi al-Iraqi, the Mosul-born operative who had helped broker the agreement between bin Laden and Zarqawi two years earlier. Our Afghanistan-based Task Force 328, however, monitored al-Iraqi as he grew restless in Waziristan, and when he set off for Iraq, Turkish authorities intercepted him on their soil and sent him back to Afghanistan, where he was detained.

And yet the more important, ironic point we understood even at the time of Zarqawi's death was that the success of his campaign in Iraq had made him, or any leader of Al Qaeda in Iraq, less relevant. While he did not do so single-handedly, Zarqawi's focused sectarian killings helped inaugurate a system of violence that was, by the time he died, a self-propelling cycle. The antigovernment Sunni insurgency was no longer the sole furnace of violence—the ethnic killing was—and Iraqis' fear of unbridled civil war was increasingly self-fulfilling. Across the Tigris from us, extremist Sunni and Shia factions contested Baghdad, while previously mixed neighborhoods drained of one ethnic group or the other, with Shia often fleeing to the south and Sunnis to Anbar. We were halfway through June, during which 3,149 Iraqis died from the war's violence. That number would rise to more than 3,400 for July, when the coroner in Baghdad alone took in more than 1,855 Iraqi corpses, 90 percent of them executed. We had killed Zarqawi too late. He bequeathed Iraq a sectarian paranoia and an incipient civil war.

After I finished speaking in the backyard, I met individually with some of the men I knew well. I said good-bye and flew back to Balad, while the operators gathered inside the villa. There they lifted on their equipment— the thick canvas of the shoulder straps softened from years of use, the helmet padding carrying permanent indents—and went back out into the dark.

CHAPTER 14

Networked

June 2006–June 2008

On June 5, 2006, two days before Zarqawi was killed, I went to Ramadi to go on a raid with the Rangers stationed there. I'd been there many times before, but Ramadi was now the worst city in Iraq. The Coalition and Iraqi government had largely ceded the city to the insurgency. Only one hundred policemen showed up for daily work in a city of four hundred thousand—and most holed up in their stations. A stoic company of Marines held the only ground there—a patch of buildings at the city center surrounded on all sides by neighborhoods where insurgents operated undisturbed. Absent a significant population of Shia they could target, the insurgents focused on the Americans, and our conventional-force casualty rates there were extraordinarily high.

The next twelve months would be the most difficult we faced in our long war in Iraq, yet TF 714 was more capable than ever to contribute to the fight. Because I was so focused on the task, I was happy I'd been extended for a fourth year in command. But I knew that meant Annie had been extended for a fourth year alone.

While Iraq was our main effort and highest priority, TF 714's role in what was then called the war on terror continued to mature and expand. I had the additional influence that came with my third star, and we had resources, from ISR aircraft to interrogators, that I'd only dreamed of in 2004. Across the embattled region, we continued to build a network that spanned more than two dozen countries at one point, with nodes ranging from full task forces capable of combat operations to single operators or intelligence analysts embedded in embassies.

While only two years earlier, in the summer of 2004, hitting the single Big Ben safe house in Fallujah had consumed most of our bandwidth, any given day during these final two years of command consisted of managing counterterrorist operations in Iraq, Afghanistan, and elsewhere; engaging with VIP visitors to the task forces; strategically coordinating in theater, including visits to Baghdad to meet with General Casey and his replacement, General Petraeus; and holding VTCs with D.C. to continue stoking our interagency partnerships. In spite of our breadth, if we still had real problems to confront, it wasn't due to a lack of communication.

As I moved more frequently and more widely, I was naturally drawn to areas where we faced particularly tough fights or challenges. I aimed to assess invariably complex situations and to simply demonstrate my commitment. That summer, this led me to Ramadi. Although I went to Ramadi to show my support to a captain who, true to our decentralized culture, had made an on-the-spot decision suited to his situation, I encountered there a vision for part of TF 714's role in the next stage of the Iraq war.

Our operations in Ramadi fell to a company of Rangers led by then-Captain Doug P., operating under a commander of a TF 714 SEAL squadron who had charge of Anbar. Unlike a few years earlier, having Green operators, SEALs, and Rangers integrated so seamlessly was becoming commonplace.

On the day I'd accompany his force on an operation in Ramadi, I met Doug and some of the Rangers at their base, called "Shark Base," before we went out. At their outpost, on the southern edge of the Euphrates, fumes from garbage and sewage, stewing in the 120-degree sunlight, drifted across the compound, which existed under a permanent haze of suspended dust. It was hard to find a clean mouthful of air. From their location north of the city, they had been running raids into areas the conventional commander had told Doug were off limits as enemy territory.

But the enemy quickly learned and left the city at night. The Rangers were breaching the correct houses, only to wade through the dark rooms and find empty cots. So Doug decided to start running daytime operations into the city. Rolling in broad daylight into the city across the main bridge leading in from the northwest, the Rangers quickly learned contact was inevitable. The only question being how nasty the firefight would be as they fought their way into insurgent strongholds. AQI seeded the few roads the Ranger convoys could use with IEDs, and time and again as they left the wire, a Stryker in the line would disappear in a fount of dust and black smoke. As the Rangers aggressively prosecuted operations, casualties mounted.

As they did, other parts of the task force openly questioned Doug's decision to assume the risk of daylight operations. Moving in the stark light of the Iraqi summer deprived his ground force of the speed, element of surprise, and cover of night that were hallowed tenets of our raids. It made close air support a less reliable option. But even with this added risk, I supported Doug's decision. As we'd done in the early stages of our campaign in the western Euphrates River valley a year earlier, it was essential that we do what we could until a stronger conventional force could retake Ramadi.

After a few weeks of watching the progress of Doug's operations and seeing the casualties, I decided to go out with them. When my aide called TF 16's Anbar headquarters and told them I wanted to go on a daytime operation with the Rangers in Ramadi, they initially thought he was joking. No, my aide said, he's serious. The Rangers could do the job without me, but I wanted them to know that I understood theirs was a perilous task and that I appreciated their courage.

At their base, as Rangers donned body armor and weapons for the operation, I spoke with Doug. He had an unlikely appearance for a Ranger commander. His lanky frame, thinning hair, and understated manner, however, overlaid a boiling energy that became apparent only after some time. When I asked him the purpose of the operation we were about to conduct, he paused as a slight smirk came across his face.

"I'm going to take a bite out of crime, sir," Doug said drily. He was riffing on the tagline of McGruff, the cartoon hound featured in 1980s public service announcements aimed at kids. In the context of Ramadi, it was necessary gallows humor.

"Do it, Doug," I said, chuckling.

Doug and his Ranger company weren't trying to solve the problem of Ramadi by themselves. But even though they were getting hurt on nearly every raid, the Rangers felt good about their impact on the otherwise unpressured insurgents. Just before I arrived, they had waged a four-hour gun battle and taken down a huge IED factory whose bomb makers were stunned to see Rangers burst through the door in what they thought was a safe haven deep in Ramadi.

We left the building and emerged into the courtyard, hot under the sun and filled with the loud, low gurgling of Stryker engines. After the last of the forty or so Rangers loaded their vehicles, we departed. We received a few shots on the way to the target, but nothing dramatic, before stopping outside a rural Iraqi version of a strip mall—three or four low, one-story buildings, with a patch of concrete in front where vehicles parked.

As the Rangers bounded out of the Strykers, I took my usual position toward the back, watching them set a perimeter and begin a search of the buildings. As always, I didn't insert myself into tactical decisions on the ground. It was their responsibility and, I felt, their right.

Instead, over the past three years, I had learned to carefully watch the operators at work: After years' worth of daily raids, their instinctive movements and mood often told me more about the situation than they could describe back at base.

The Rangers moved quickly and gathered a group of local men from inside and around the buildings on the concrete parking areas in the front.

To ensure security, as they moved to identify each man, they had him lie on the pavement with his hands behind his head. One Iraqi was notably older than the others, and a young Ranger, without instruction, retrieved a white plastic chair for him from an automobile maintenance shop. As was normally the case, even in daytime, there were no women in the immediate area. But I saw a boy, probably about four years old, standing near one of the men, no doubt his father.

As the Rangers motioned for the men to lie down on the ground, I watched the boy. He stood quietly, as if confused, then, mimicking his father, the child lay down on the ground. He pressed one cheek flat against the pavement so that his face was turned toward his father and folded his small hands behind his head.

As I watched, I felt sick.

I could feel in my own limbs and chest the shame and fury that must have been coursing through the father, still lying motionless. Every ounce of him must have wanted to pop up, pull his son from the ground, stand him upright, and dust off the boy's clothes and cheek. To be laid on the ground in full view of his son was humiliating. For a proud man, to seemingly fail to protect that son from similar treatment was worse.

As I watched, I thought, not for the first time: *It would be easy for us to lose.*

The professionalism of the Rangers in the sweltering heat, paradoxically, suggested just how arduous our task was. As much as Doug and his Rangers were doing to keep the insurgents off balance, they couldn't change the dynamics in Ramadi simply through raids—which, even when done as professionally as they were on that day, could produce enmity in the population. Absent a campaign to protect the people, we could only hope the residents understood these raids were necessary. But even then, the targeting operations could not address the deeper structural sources of the violence that only a fuller-spectrum counterinsurgency effort could. Doug and his Rangers could help, but it was going to take much more.

Within days of my Ramadi trip, Scott Miller brought an army colonel named Sean MacFarland to see me in the bunker at Balad. Sean was commanding the 1st Brigade Combat Team of the 1st Armored Division. Armed with ideas they had seen pacify Tal Afar under then-Colonel H. R. McMaster, MacFarland and his force—comprising five Marine and army battalions—were to take charge of Ramadi. I'd heard good things about Sean but was anxious to judge for myself.

Sean's visit to our command was part of a concerted effort, on both sides of the fence, to lash our efforts tighter with conventional forces. It was working. Brigade commanders increasingly stopped through to see Scott, Mike Flynn, Kurt Fuller, and me. Conversely, I encouraged conventional flag officers and their commanders to embed for a day or two with our strike teams and to go on raids. Scott, meanwhile, established a weekly video teleconference with all the brigade commanders in Iraq. Far from its stereotype as an overly secretive unit running its own war, our task force, which was then hardwired to succeed through internal collaboration, worked hard to drive an all-of-military effort.

As Sean sat down, I took stock of the tall, soft-spoken cavalry officer. "I'm going to retake Ramadi," he said quietly. "We're going to reoccupy the city itself."

I was skeptical, not because of Sean, whom I liked immediately, but because a number of brigade commanders had tried and been unable to root out insurgents in places less violent than Ramadi. Yet his firmness struck me.

Sean explained he would not have his forces live concentrated in a large forward operating base, but he would nest them among the people in smaller combat outposts (COPs) spaced throughout the city. He spoke of the importance of standing up a police force drawn from local men. Keen to resuscitate a tribal uprising—undone six months earlier by dissension and a meticulous AQI assassination program—Sean knew he needed to provide American backing and protection to tribal leaders willing to band together against Al Qaeda.

"So this is going to take some time," he said. He estimated around nine months.

"Sean, if it takes you that long, we've got a real problem," I said. "You've got to get on that horse and ride."

He did just that.

The full story of how Sean and his Iraqi partners turned Ramadi is theirs to tell. But on every idea Sean shared with me before arriving, he drove hard, and his team made them work. Like all counterinsurgency, it was slow, difficult, and deadly work.

Perhaps most important, Sean understood the indispensability of fielding a local police force that could target Al Qaeda, and the need for a strong Iraqi partner to lead the aggressive recruitment effort. The man Sean quickly identified as that partner—Sheikh Abdul Sattar Abu Risha—seemingly came out of central casting for a desert chieftain, with a thin face and falconlike eyes. Although he belonged to the powerful Albu Risha tribe of the Dulaim confederation, in the normal pecking order he was a third-tier sheikh. But Ramadi was not normal—most of the local government and higher-ranking tribal leaders had fled the violence.

As was the case so often, Sattar was motivated by a number of frustrations. As he realized AQI was his real enemy, not the Americans, whom he reimagined as his guests, pride motivated him to fight Al Qaeda. But so too did baser motives: He sat atop a number of lucrative criminal enterprises in Ramadi that were threatened by AQI incursions.

In any case, he was the partner Sean needed, and on September 9, Sheikh Abdul Sattar formally announced that the "Awakening" was officially under way. Eight days later, on behalf of twenty-five of Anbar's thirty-one tribes, Sattar wrote to Nouri al-Maliki requesting money to fund and arm his tribal coalition to fight Al Qaeda. Maliki had agreed (perhaps because Ramadi was uniformly Sunni and so he was confident armed locals could target only AQI and not Shiites) and the Ramadi police recruits soon went on the Iraqi government payroll.

As the sheikh's movement was gaining momentum, our task force commander for Anbar, Commander Ethan,* came to see Sean.

In command of a TF 714 SEAL squadron after gutsy, distinguished tours in Afghanistan, Ethan was on the vanguard of a growing trend within our force to be better linked to the battlespace owners, and worked to incorporate—and sometimes subordinate—his targeting teams to the conventional commanders. Bald, with a thick beard that gave him a slightly messianic look well suited to his passionate approach to leadership, Ethan came to Ramadi keen to see the city holistically, beyond his aperture of direction-action raids.

"Sir, what's your center of gravity?" Ethan asked Sean MacFarland in his polite but direct manner.

"Well, it's actually Sheikh Sattar," Sean replied.

"Right. We've *got* to keep that guy alive."

At Ethan's suggestion, the brigade took an American M1 Abrams tank and parked it in front of Sheikh Sattar's house. In addition to the protection offered by its menacing barrel, the tank itself came to be a set piece in the larger drama of Ramadi—and a bellwether for changing Sunni sentiment. At first, Sheikh Sattar did not like having an American tank in front of his house, and at his request, the Americans replaced it with an Iraqi one. When the Iraqi tank unit eventually left Ramadi, however, an American tank again sat in front of his house. By this time, however, Sattar and his American partners had become more credible, and the people around Ramadi now saw the American tank as evidence of the sheikh's clout over the Americans. As the tribes turned, a liability was now a token of power.

The task force's experience across Iraq increasingly resembled what was occurring in Ramadi—which was the first all-of-military counterinsurgency fight in the war. There, conventional and special operations coordinated, and it was a case study in the application of surgical strikes in support of the first two stages of what became known as the "clear-hold-build" process of counterinsurgency. Evolving from our first role of targeting Former Regime Elements, then AQI senior leaders, TF 714 was now heavily partnered with conventional forces and other government agencies. Our network enabled us to see and understand the broader situation rapidly, and our intentionally decentralized culture allowed us to act rapidly.

What Ethan and Sean had done with the tank in Ramadi, General Casey looked to do from his strategic perch: nurture and marshal the promising but fragile reconciliation movements. Casey understood that the

---

*Ethan is a pseudonym.

dynamics needed to change. Simply grinding harder against the dual Sunni and Shia threats would not suffice. To this end, he found a deft weapon in my old friend Graeme Lamb, who arrived to Iraq the same week Sheikh Sattar announced the Awakening was under way in Ramadi.

Almost immediately upon Graeme's arrival to be his deputy commanding general, Casey asked him to pursue strategic reconciliation—the process to bring opposition groups, even those currently fighting, toward a durable political solution. Graeme would help marshal "the Awakening," which was not in its early stages nearly as monolithic nor as Damascene as the name conveyed. In the beginning, the Sunnis did not gather in a caucus and declare a national position.

General Casey's direction to Graeme was not surprising to me. Although not much noticed in writings about this period, George Casey had been beating the drum to do counterinsurgency, often called COIN, and do it well. At the end of 2005, he had created the "COIN Academy" in Taji, to root out the conventional mindset and jittery tactics that sowed enmity in the people and inflamed insurgencies. Sean MacFarland's soldiers cited its teachers' precepts during the early stages of their immersive approach to Ramadi.

Shortly after meeting with Casey in September, Graeme came to visit me at Balad. I met him on the tarmac, and although he entered Iraq at its bleakest moment yet and had been handed a hard assignment, he appeared fresh and upbeat as he decamped the helo. After a two-year hiatus from Iraq, he was freed of the peculiar guilt that gnaws at a soldier like Lamb who, when stuck in garrison, can come to feel like a charlatan as wars are fought without him. After a bear hug, we walked across the pavement toward TF 714's big brown hangar.

Lamb, a Scot, was a rare soldier and comrade. His default pose, with forearms folded across his chest, erect stance, dark eyes, and latent tenacity gave him the air of a nineteenth-century bare-knuckle boxer. Despite his protestations otherwise, Graeme read deeply, but with a sort of utilitarian drive, finding and then rereading a few books—Hart's biography of William Tecumseh Sherman, Junger's *Storm of Steel*, and Rousseau's *The Social Contract*—turning their heavily dog-eared pages into handbooks for fighting and leading and living. He plumbed the past for guidance, and it gave him a stoic appreciation for history's hard truths. Where the American military could produce soldiers who lapsed into earnest, jargon-filled bullet points, Lamb could offer profanity-laced parables. His explanations had academic nuance but were tinged by his Scottish brogue and often infused with a Churchillian vocabulary—*we'll give it the ol'* . . . His delivery contributed to his mystique, as did a certain darkness. In a way few others did, especially Americans newer to these nasty small wars, Graeme, a veteran not only of Basra but also of Afghanistan and the Troubles in Northern Ireland, conveyed an intimate appreciation for Hobbes's view of man.

As we entered our hangar and walked past tables and screens, Graeme said hello to the many familiar faces. Since he had finished commanding in Basra in December 2003, the British special forces had become full-fledged and highly valued members of Task Force 16. In addition to their work down south, they had been invaluable in suppressing the Baghdad car-bomb networks since mid-2005, when we emptied much of our forces out of central Iraq to fight up in Al Qaim. Without the Brits keeping the insurgent cells in Baghdad under pressure, we feared the insurgents would simply relocate away from our push on the Euphrates, and the effort would do nothing more than move mercury on a table. As a former troop and squadron commander in the SAS and, later, commander of all British special forces, "Lambo" was a beloved member of their tribe. From his emeritus perch, he had remained a close observer of our task force.

Inside the SAR, we chatted for a bit and got down to business. Graeme explained the concept for establishing a cell that would pursue strategic reconciliation. Put simply, Graeme proposed talking to the most violent of our enemies to see if we could nudge their thinking.

In parsing the different "types" of enemy we faced, Graeme spoke of these groups existing along a spectrum from "reconcilables" to "irreconcilables." While the extremist edges of both the Sunni and Shia combatants might fall into the latter category, most of both branches fell into the former. In between sat the government of Iraq—or those actors and groups either assisting the new Iraqi project or at least not actively resisting it. Certain groups—namely, the jihadist wing of the Sunni insurgency and the Iranian proxies on the Shia end—could not be reconciled to the Coalition project. But the rest might be persuaded, through threats or enticements, to move toward the political center. While others might have spoken with this nuance before, Graeme's language of reconcilables and irreconcilables soon permeated the rest of the Coalition. His terms helped us conceptualize—and visualize, in what we called the Squeeze Chart—how these groups might be split or how they might be redirected. He was fond of reminding skeptics that Clausewitz hadn't finished the sentence when he argued war was "not an independent phenomenon, but the continuation of politics by different means." "And to politics it must *return*," Graeme added.

Even so, Graeme remained an advocate for relentless targeting. As the Coalition targeted insurgents ever more effectively, they would either back into a corner and fight to the death, or they would come toward daylight. Graeme's reconciliation program would be the latter choice, a choice made more appealing if they feared the alternative. Graeme proposed finding the groups just shy of the most extreme poles on the spectrum and convincing them that even if they didn't want to align with the American or Iraqi government, it was in their interest not to be allied with the irreconcilables. The key would be to feel for the fissures between the groups, and rip.

Linking our targeting efforts with Graeme's strategic engagement—which operated under a few names but eventually took the name Force Strategic Engagement Cell, or FSEC—would further redefine the "precision" we aspired to achieve with our targeting. In this context, precision did not just mean killing or capturing targeted individuals and leaving the

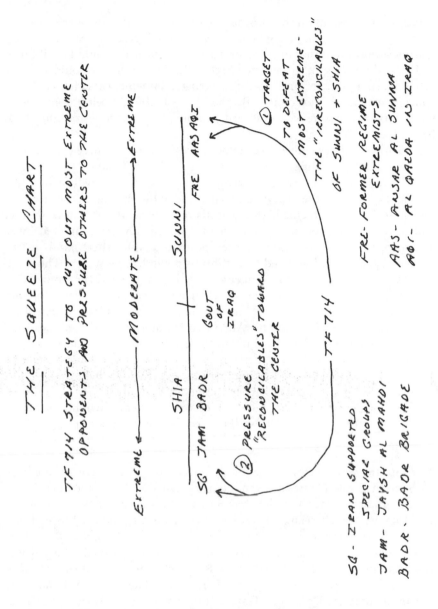

THE SQUEEZE CHART

TF 714 STRATEGY TO CUT OUT MOST EXTREME
OPPONENTS AND PRESSURE OTHERS TO THE CENTER

EXTREME ← MODERATE → EXTREME

SHIA | SUNNI

SG JAM BADR | GOVT OF IRAQ | FRE AAS AQI

② PRESSURE "RECONCILABLES" TOWARD THE CENTER

TF 714

① TARGET TO DEFEAT MOST EXTREME - THE "IRRECONCILABLES" OF SUNNI + SHIA

FRE- FORMER REGIME EXTREMISTS

AAS- ANSAR AL SUNNA
AQI- AL QAEDA IN IRAQ

SG - IRANI SUPPORTED SPECIAL GROUPS
JAM - JAYSH AL MAHDI
BADR - BADR BRIGADE

houses or civilians around them unharmed. Rather, these precise actions would need to bring about desirable second- and third-order effects by moving certain groups' thinking or behavior in the right direction.

While it sounded logical, what Lamb proposed would be extremely controversial, especially within TF 714. Many of the hard-line leaders Graeme would propose releasing were those whom my men had spent years of their lives trying to capture, losing limbs and friends in the process. Graeme's program meant setting them free in the hope that, once convinced, they could be more useful on the outside by altering the calculus of their former comrades in a way that benefited us. It was a tough case to make, and without my support and that of those under me, his project would be stillborn.

I agreed on the spot to lend members of TF 714 so that he could staff the cell. I did so in part because I knew and trusted Graeme. I also felt Graeme's concept was a necessary tack. By that fall of 2006, I felt the dynamics needed to change were we to succeed. Simply getting enemies talking could be a start.

Graeme's military career, from experiences as a soldier three decades earlier, had uniquely equipped him for the task at hand. Graeme's first assignment as a young officer was to patrol the streets of West Belfast in 1973, during the height of the Troubles. During one of his later numerous tours in Northern Ireland, Graeme had to grit his teeth beneath his tam-o'-shanter and watch as men convicted in court of killing his mates sauntered by as free men, with sinister smiles as they pointed at him, their hands in the shapes of pistols, and snapped their thumbs down like hammers. The experiences armed Graeme with a longer view of how these wars are fought and how they end. Martin McGuinness, a convicted leader of the Irish Republican Army, had been notorious on the Belfast streets Graeme patrolled. Now, Graeme would remind his American counterparts, McGuinness had just finished a stint as Northern Ireland's deputy minister of education.

Graeme talked with a soldierly respect and even a certain sympathy when he described the need to understand our enemies' beliefs and logic. And yet his tone could easily pivot from generous to menacing.

"We can offer them a way out, we can show them daylight, yeah," he said, "but if they don't take it, we'll put 'em in the fucking grave."

W ith the war's tectonics seemingly seized up, the domestic debate back in the United States grew in intensity. On Tuesday, November 7, during the midterm elections, the Democrats retook a majority in Congress. The vote was widely seen as a verdict on the Iraq war and the Bush administration's handling of it.

The day after the election, President Bush appeared in the East Room and announced that he and Secretary Rumsfeld had "agreed that the timing is right for new leadership at the Pentagon." The president announced he would nominate Dr. Robert Gates for the vacant post. At the time, Gates was serving as president of Texas A&M, but he had been a career CIA man. By that month, many Americans judged the war to be dangerously close to failure. More Iraqi civilians died in October than in any other month of the war. One hundred seven Americans died, and nearly eight hundred were wounded. Upwards of one hundred thousand Iraqis were fleeing every month, mostly from the secular, educated, and moderate classes that had the means to get out. Confidence in Nouri al-Maliki's ability to lift the country out of sectarian killing was perhaps at its all-time low. And yet the nascent Sunni Awakening was growing.

The Pentagon and White House discussed competing courses of action. A continuation of the current strategy was an option, and reportedly some called for a rapid withdrawal of U.S. forces. Others argued for scaling up troop levels. But would additional forces, along with the Awakening, be enough to make a difference?

As the administration debated and American support slid, Sunni insurgents did their best to keep the sectarian violence roiling. On Thanksgiving, Sunni insurgents exploded five car bombs into a dense crowd in Sadr City, while dropping shells into the Shiite slum and assaulting the Ministry of Health. All told, the day saw 202 Iraqis killed and another 250 wounded. It was the deadliest single attack of the war. Tragically, it would not hold that record for long.

"Sir," I told Casey that fall, "we're going to beat Al Qaeda. The leadership is cracking right now. We can feel it. I can't prove it, but I can feel it." Some of our assessment may have been wishful thinking—code for *How many of these guys do we need to kill before they break?* But there were also metrics behind my optimism—persistent targeting of AQI's leadership, for example, had pushed younger, less experienced leaders into key positions. Adding to my confidence were a series of swift raids by TF 16 that had delivered a prime opportunity to divide—and potentially cripple—the Sunni insurgency.

Toward the end of November, I sat and listened to M.S.—whose relentlessness and poise had been fundamental to the final stages of the Zarqawi hunt six months earlier—as she spoke in front of the whiteboard in a small room Task Force 16 used in the back of the bunker at Balad. In a series of raids that month, Task Force 16 had captured most of Ansar al-Sunnah's leadership, including at least ten of the organization's topmost leaders—three national-level administrators, a founder of the group, and seven geographic emirs from Al Qaim to Baqubah to Tikrit. Pointing to a diagram of the enemy's network, M.S. described each capture and the cumulatively crippling impact to the organization.

To be convinced to reconcile, an enemy organization normally has to think it's losing—or at least be convinced it cannot win. Decapitating the leadership of the organization, as we had just done, went a long way toward doing that. Graeme soon made these leaders, now in our custody, a focus of his efforts. Among other things, Graeme sought to slip a wedge into the fissure between Ansar al-Sunnah (AAS) and AQI.

After offering sanctuary to Zarqawi and other Al Qaeda operatives who fled the American bombing runs in Afghanistan, AAS had adopted many of AQI's tactics during the insurgency, including beheadings and wanton killing of civilians. Closest to home, two years earlier AAS had dispatched the Saudi suicide bomber into the mess-hall tent in Mosul. For years, Al Qaeda in Iraq had sought to formally bring Ansar al-Sunnah under its control. But, leery of Zarqawi, the group's Kurdish leaders had reported through back channels to Al Qaeda's leaders that Zarqawi—impious and power hungry—was not the man in propaganda reels, and that they had made a terrible choice staking their fortunes on him. Despite these persistent tensions, rumors had surfaced again that fall of a potential merger between the two groups.

Graeme initially focused his time on a detainee, the religious emir of Ansar al-Sunnah, a man named Abu Wail. Every ten to fourteen days, Graeme had Abu Wail brought out of detention to talk with him. Graeme made sure the emir was allowed to change out of his orange jumpsuit, cleanse himself, and put on Iraqi robes. The guards would bring the emir into the room, unshackle him, and leave him alone with Graeme, who would be preparing tea to serve to the emir. As the door closed, a primal electricity would fill the small room, or even the larger Maude House salon where they met. In any other moment or place, the two men sitting there, separated by a table and two small glass cups of hot golden tea, would have attempted to kill each other. It was this mutual recognition—that Graeme had spent most of his life hunting men like Abu Wail and that, given half a chance, the emir would saw Graeme's Scottish head off—that allowed them to have a conversation. Hard recognized hard. These were conversations that no United Nations technocrats or State Department diplomats, no matter how skillfully schooled, could have had.

At the end of their conversations, the emir would be taken back to detention until their next meeting. Slowly, somewhat impossibly, a respect built that would later pay off. Toward the end of their meeting early that December, the emir addressed Graeme.

"You know," he said matter-of-factly, "you're a force of occupation, and don't try to tell me differently. That's how we see it—and you're not welcome." He explained to Graeme in his deliberate way that his guidance from the Koran was that he must resist the force of occupation for years—for generations even—if it threatened the faith and his way of life. He paused, as Graeme continued to listen. "We've watched you for three and a half years. We've discussed this in Syria, in Saudi, in Jordan, and in Iraq. And we have come to the conclusion that you do not threaten our way of life. Al Qaeda does."

It was a remarkable breakthrough—and opened up possibilities for what effect the emir might have if freed. So during the final days of December 2006, when news from Iraq was dominated by the bungled hanging of Saddam Hussein, the Coalition released Abu Wail from prison—FSEC's first strategic release. They released him without conditions. We needed him to be a credible member of Ansar in order to stir their thinking and divert their direction. Requiring him to meet with a westerner or to spy for us would put that in jeopardy. Regardless, we worried suspicious comrades might well kill him.

" Annie, another Christmas apart," I wrote to her by e-mail. I was to spend the day in Afghanistan with our force and then after dark fly in one of our aircraft to Balad, arriving after midnight. Christmas Day was spent seeing parts of my force in Iraq, while Annie, with Sam home from college, followed their tradition of Christmas Eve dinner in a local Chinese restaurant. This was the third Christmas in a row that I was gone, and while she wasn't alone, it had to be lonely.

"We never really expected this kind of thing at this stage in our lives," my e-mail continued, "but I still believe we are doing what is our duty—as a team—to the nation and to the people we serve with. You know the frustration I feel when I see the packed malls and overfed greed of so many Americans. But when I meet in small posts in harm's way with young Americans who believe in their cause and their duty—and who desperately need to see leaders who reflect the values and dedication they want in the people they follow—it is pretty easy to stand the separations with the quiet confidence we are living up to all the values we were raised to uphold."

My thoughts were as much for me as they were for her, but Annie always seemed to understand what I was trying to say. For me, it meant staying forward deployed. And as hard as it was for her, Annie wouldn't have had it otherwise. It was fundamental to the kind of leader I believed I should be. Being apart so long was painful, and she worried. But she was proud of me, and that meant everything.

By the time I wrote to Annie and thousands of other soldiers sent e-mails home or called families who missed them, President Bush had decided on a new strategy in Iraq, following months of review stretching back to the spring. During Christmas and the final days of 2006, he weighed the heavy decision of how many troops he would "surge" to Iraq as part of this new way forward. He eventually decided to send five army brigades that would primarily focus on Baghdad, and two Marine battalions to reinforce Anbar. The war in Iraq was about to hit an even higher register.

On the cusp of this expansion in Iraq, pressing developments on a different continent demanded my attention—and drew me to Addis Ababa.

On Christmas Eve 2006, Ethiopian troops had invaded neighboring Somalia, then riven by a civil war. Six months earlier, in June, the Islamic Courts Union, an umbrella group of Sharia courts and Islamic militant groups, claimed control of Mogadishu and most of southern Somalia. One of the main militant groups of the ICU, Al Shabab, or "the youth," had developed increasing ties with Al Qaeda, largely through its charismatic founder, Aden Hashi Ayrow. We believed Al Shabab was sheltering some of Al Qaeda's senior operatives, including Abu Taha al-Sudani, leader of Al Qaeda in East Africa, as well as a number of those behind the 1998 embassy bombings.

Although the Ethiopian operation was not a huge surprise—they invaded to suppress an insurgency they thought threatened eastern Ethiopia—

American policy was poorly postured for what looked like a potential opportunity. As the Islamist rebels were forced to flee the Ethiopian forces, Al Qaeda operatives, on the run, would be more vulnerable and perhaps come into view long enough for us to target them.

With a small number of intelligence-collection assets, and the periodic assistance of American aircraft and ships, U.S. forces targeted the Al Qaeda leaders we could pinpoint, and pressured the others. It was sensitive, difficult business due to our limited access into Somalia. Over the coming months, the United States expanded its capacity to both find and target Al Qaeda leaders in Somalia who had previously eluded us. As the United States relied on a good rapport with the Ethiopians, my team and I visited Addis Ababa repeatedly to do the slow, deliberate work of building a relationship with them. Most instructive for me, as my position increasingly required forging partnerships with other countries, was the Ethiopians' frank skepticism toward U.S. intentions and reliability, echoed on my trips to Islamabad and Sanaa.

These trips, sometimes to Addis Ababa and back in a day, were typical of the final two years of my command. The constant movement around the region was often choreographed down to the minute. My command team—which evolved as original members were promoted to new jobs and replaced by men of equal talent—spent flights hunched over e-mails on their Toughbook laptops, talked through secure in-flight voice links and VTCs to headquarters on the ground, wore civilian clothing, and kept Ambien close at hand. From the look of our group as we'd gather preflight in the dark outside the SAR or stumble back in, exhausted, a few days later, our travels came to be known as the Pain Train.

J ust after 9:00 P.M. eastern time on January 10, 2007, President Bush stood at a podium in the White House library and spoke frankly about the course of the war in Iraq. He admitted the many challenges the mission faced and announced a "new way forward." Bush described the way in which troops would change how they operated, embracing counterinsurgency tenets. Most controversially, he announced that he would surge nearly thirty thousand troops, most of them to secure Baghdad. It was a courageous decision taken at a time when currents of opinion were flowing strongly in the other direction.

The physical impact of these troops on Baghdad, and all of Iraq, would become clear only in the months ahead. But by the time these troops began to arrive early that spring, Iraqis had experienced nearly four years of violence and uncertainty and were, by and large, exhausted.

For Sunnis, the future was fraught with danger. Fearing the disenfranchisement that came with Saddam's fall, de-Baathification, and the emergence of an Iranian-influenced Shia-majority national government, many had joined an insurgency increasingly dominated by Zarqawi's extremism. At first, they thought they could succeed—expel the Americans and

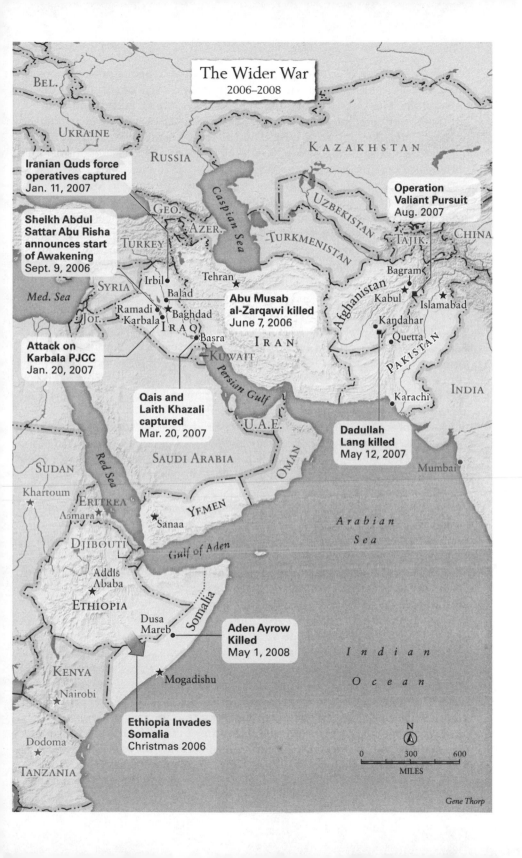

The Wider War
2006–2008

Iranian Quds force
operatives captured
Jan. 11, 2007

Operation
Valiant Pursuit
Aug. 2007

Sheikh Abdul
Sattar Abu Risha
announces start
of Awakening
Sept. 9, 2006

Abu Musab
al-Zarqawi killed
June 7, 2006

Attack on
Karbala PJCC
Jan. 20, 2007

Qais and
Laith Khazali
captured
Mar. 20, 2007

Dadullah
Lang killed
May 12, 2007

Aden Ayrow
Killed
May 1, 2008

Ethiopia Invades
Somalia
Christmas 2006

Gene Thorp

reclaim rule of Iraq from the Shia. But after years of struggle, prospects for doing so looked bleak—and with the increasingly vicious onslaught by the Shia militias, the U.S.-led Coalition appeared less like an enemy and more like a necessary protection against the Shia death squads and a vital arbiter in the struggle for power in Iraq. The emerging Sunni awakening movements reflected this calculation, and America signaling its commitment with the surge reinforced it.

The size of the surge force was no more important than its quality. By late 2006, the U.S. forces were the best we had yet put on the field. The troops in, or returning to, theater were increasingly experienced and wise. They included commanders like Sean MacFarland and Mike Kershaw, whose brigade ultimately tamed the Baghdad suburb of Yusufiyah, the southern belt that had been an AQI sanctuary.

Against all of these positive intangibles, however, we as a nation and a force were undeniably tired as well.

During his televised address to the nation in which he announced the "new way forward" in Iraq, Bush spoke provocatively about the threat posed to the Iraqi project by Iranian proxies. "Succeeding in Iraq also requires defending its territorial integrity and stabilizing the region in the face of extremist challenges," he said. The Syrian and Iranian "regimes are allowing terrorists and insurgents to use their territory to move in and out of Iraq. Iran is providing material support for attacks on American troops. We will disrupt the attacks on our forces. We'll interrupt the flow of support from Iran and Syria. And we will seek out and destroy the networks providing advanced weaponry and training to our enemies in Iraq."

For nearly three months, TF 714 had been targeting the Iranian proxies President Bush spoke of. The previous fall, General Casey had asked us to start targeting specific Shia extremists, particularly Iranian-backed "Special Groups." At the time, as Robert Gates explained that winter, there were four vectors of violence in the country: attacks from the Sunni insurgency directed at the Coalition and Iraqi government; terroristic attacks by Al Qaeda against Shia and western targets; sectarian conflict between the Sunni and Shia; and Shia-on-Shia violence, largely nonideological power struggles in southern Iraq.

Shia organizations like Jaish al-Mahdi, or JAM, tiptoed along a line of opposition to MNF-I and made an uneasy truce with the status quo. Beneath the surface, however, were more sinister elements supported by Iran's secretive Quds Force. These elements operated an aggressive, seemingly unconstrained network that funneled material, including the explosively formed projectile IEDs, known as EFPs, that were devastating Coalition forces. They also provided training and advice to Iraqi Special Groups.

After seeing how Green had responded after I made them own TF 16, I thought it would be a mistake to graft the Shia target set onto an existing task force, diluting its focus. So I decided to create a new task force: Task Force 17 (TF 17) would focus entirely on the Shia target set. As with many things, it was easier said than done. We now had double the mission but not twice the ISR, helicopters, or detention facilities. We'd beg or borrow what we could, but the new mission would inevitably put Task Forces 16 and 17 in competition over the same resources.

The sympathy and active support that hard-line, Iranian-backed Shia militias enjoyed from Iraqi officials at the highest levels meant our raids sent us wading into a murky world of politics. On January 11, 2007, the day after President Bush's speech, TF 714 forces, acting on short notice, raided an Iranian facility in Irbil in northern Iraq, aiming to capture Mohammad Jafari, who we believed was guiding Quds Force activities in Iraq. Instead, our force detained five Iranians, later called "the Irbil Five," judged to be members of the Iranian Revolutionary Guards Corps (IRGC). The men were interrogated and ultimately held for the next two and a half years, pawns in a determined diplomatic struggle with Iran. Nine days later, perhaps as revenge, one of the most notorious Shia Special Groups staged a perfidious, goading attack.

In the early evening of January 20 a line of eight SUVs with thickly tinted windows stopped at the outermost gate of the Provincial Joint Coordination Center in Karbala, Iraq. Iraqis and Americans manned the small outpost and lived alongside one another. At the outpost's front gate, witnesses later said, some of the men inside the SUVs wore U.S. Army uniforms and flashed fake identification. They were allowed in, and the vehicles rumbled past a further series of gates. Once inside the inner courtyard of the camp, roughly a dozen militants bounded out. Some beelined it to the American soldiers' quarters and began firing their weapons through the doors. Others set fire to the American Humvees. They killed one American in his room and gravely wounded three others. Within minutes, the attack was over and the assailants had sped away into the evening. No Iraqis on the base were harmed or, according to the Americans, showed any alarm, raising suspicions about their involvement. As the Humvees billowed jet smoke into the sky above the courtyard, the Americans came to the sickening realization: The attackers had captured four Americans.

Later that night, Iraqi policemen who had given chase after the convoy passed one of their checkpoints came upon five of the SUVs. They were parked, doors ajar, about 20 miles from Karbala, in the neighboring province of Babil. Inside, the four Americans were found handcuffed and shot, some point-blank in the chest, others in the limbs or head. Three were already dead, and the fourth, with a gunshot wound to the head, died as one of the Iraqi policeman attempted CPR. The attackers had stripped the men of identification. But in the dark, flashlights illuminated the name of one of the perished Americans: a young lieutenant, less than two years out of West Point, had in his final moments scrawled his name into the film of Iraqi dust covering the SUV he had been left to die in.

We couldn't immediately identify who had directed or conducted the operation. I was determined we would find out.

| CHAPTER 15 |

▼

The Long War

February 2007–June 2008

On February 10, 2007, General George Casey turned over command of MNF-I to General Dave Petraeus. Because I avoided public events in Iraq and Afghanistan while commanding TF 714, I didn't attend the morning ceremony. But I flew down in time to say good-bye to General Casey before he left the country. We met after the ceremony in a guesthouse he was using before departing for the States. After two and a half years together in Iraq, a bond had been forged between us through countless difficult moments. Ever balanced and upbeat, Casey expressed his appreciation for all our force had done. I presented him with a small memento from TF 714.

It was important for me to communicate my appreciation for his stoicism and support of my team. We both knew that in the years ahead he'd receive less credit and more blame than he deserved, but that often went with the territory. He had been rock solid—the epitome of a professional throughout his time in command.

A month later, John Abizaid ended his tenure as commander of CENT-COM, having served for nearly four years at the post. A narrative arose of a fresh start after failed leadership. Some press and pundits picked up on the theme as grist for the media mill.

That was a simplistic binary to which I couldn't subscribe. I tended not to personalize mistakes, as there were plenty to go around. I certainly had made my share. In hindsight, the strategy we'd all been executing was insufficient. John had long argued that the very presence of Americans in the country had instigated the violence, providing a nationalistic insurgency with a raison d'être. Based on my experience, this was hard to dispute. He felt that by limiting our footprint and accelerating our withdrawal, we could avoid producing antibodies. Similarly, George Casey's strategy was to quickly raise the capacity of Iraqis to secure and govern their country. What few accurately anticipated was the devastating sectarianism that quickly contorted the conflict from a largely one-directional Sunni antigovernment fight to what became a brutal civil war. In the end, the surreal levels of violence that sectarianism produced were too much for the Iraqi government, which needed American force to subdue it.

Could things have been different? Of course. We learned and improved, but in February 2007, we had to navigate from where we were, not from where we wished we were.

Both John Abizaid and George Casey had guided the effort through difficult times, and both had given unfailing, critical support to TF 714. The incredibly lethal targeting machine that Dave Petraeus would soon have at his disposal would not have existed without their guidance. As I saw the often-simplistic criticism directed at them, I remembered what retired General Fred Franks, the one-legged general who led a corps in the first Gulf War, had once told me.

"Remember, no matter what you do during your service, or what you accomplish, your last interaction with the Army," he said quietly, "will be one of rejection."

For years I mistook Franks's comment as one of bitterness. Over time I realized he was admonishing me against looking for esteem in the wrong places. And he was reminding me whose respect was truly important.

That month also marked the end of Sean MacFarland's tour commanding in Ramadi. I had returned regularly to the embattled city over the previous nine months, but during one visit I was struck by the feedback I received.

"Ethan," I asked the SEAL squadron commander I knew so well, "how is it going now?"

"Sir," he said passionately, "the change is eye-watering."

I cocked my head. "In what way? Good or bad?"

"Eye-watering *good*, sir," he said. Ethan outlined the changes he and his SEALs were seeing up close. "Colonel MacFarland and his guys are taking Ramadi back."

The eye-watering changes there had come at a steep price. Five hundred of Sean's troops were wounded and eighty-five of their comrades died in the fight to retake Ramadi.

As Sean and his troops left, having pried back the fingers of AQI's grip on the population, TF 17 was about to execute a mission whose intelligence harvest would, in the right hands, drive a growing wedge between the Maliki government and the Shia extremists who influenced it.

On the night of March 19, 2007, then-Commander John B. brought me pressing information. Since the previous September, he had commanded a squadron from SEAL Team 4 as part of TF 17, which had relied on TF 714's airpower and intelligence architecture throughout the fall. But to streamline TF 17's operations, by the beginning of January we formally placed it under TF 714's full tactical control.

Built like a logger, John B. had been one of the first TF 714 people I'd met in Afghanistan when I deployed to Bagram in May 2002 with Combined Joint Task Force 180. Wearing civilian clothes and an enormous beard, John B. initially struck me as one of a number of dilettantes I'd met. But he was different.

John B. lacked the crusty arrogance I'd always despised in some special operators and sought to eliminate in TF 714. We'd worked together when I joined the command in 2003, and it was reassuring to have a trusted partner in the new TF 17. He had been part of most of their operations into strongholds like Sadr City, Karbala, and Najaf, and he understood the political aftershocks that could ripple out from even the most precise of raids. That night, he was asking to conduct one that would, inevitably, upset a number of powerful Iraqis.

At the time, political sensitivity had created an unofficial list of Shiites whom we could not knowingly target. One such no-go target was Qais Khazali, a thirty-three-year-old who had served as an aide to Muqtada al-Sadr's father, Grand Ayatollah Mohammad Sadeq al-Sadr, before he was killed in 1999. Khazali then assisted Muqtada in the first years after the U.S.-led invasion in 2003, before splitting off to lead one of the designated Special Groups. His network was considered particularly dangerous, yet he also had powerful political connections and was periodically discussed as a potential alternative to Sadr.

But while Qais was off-limits, his younger brother Laith was not. That March night, John B. explained, Laith had popped onto the grid. The weather was particularly bad that evening and had grounded aircraft. But from intercepts, John B.'s team was confident they had found the younger Khazali brother. Then, and for the next few nights, they believed Laith was in a house in the heavily Shia port city of Basra. John B. proposed capturing him before we lost the scent.

The operation carried all kinds of risks. Launching a raid from Balad to Basra involved a lengthy flight down. More significant, we had a light presence that far south, and although we had good partnerships with the Brits, the operational infrastructure in and around Basra was unfamiliar. I knew we risked political backlash from inside Maliki's regime, but I gave John B. the go-ahead.

On the night of March 20, John B. climbed into the aircraft alongside his TF 17 operators for the almost three hour flight to Basra. There they would link up with British special operators who, augmented by conventional troops and intelligence partners, were moving. The Brits in Basra had played a vital role in the lead-up, helping with intelligence and planning and now in the coming assault. The British troops positioned themselves around the area in Basra as blocking forces, as the TF 17 teams approached by vehicle, quietly established a cordon in the dark, and took the house without fire. Elsewhere in Basra, British troops got into a series of gunfights, diverting the Shia insurgent groups, including Laith's own Asaib Ahl al-Haq, which might have turned the objective into a much more costly affair.

As expected, they found Laith Khazali inside the house, along with seven other men. After a few minutes, they realized that one of the men they'd captured on the target was about to complicate things.

"Hey, sir," John B. called into our JOC. As usual, I had him on speakerphone. "We've got Qais."

It was an interesting moment. Although we hadn't been targeting him, Qais' presence wasn't all that surprising, and his role as a Special Groups leader was something we already suspected. TF 17 was still relatively young, and some of the fallout from the January capture of the Irbil Five was still fresh in our minds. But given the other men on the target, we knew we had to hold him and quickly passed word to Dave Petraeus.

Soon after returning to the airfield in Basra, the teams gathered all the detainees—Laith and Qais, as well as an Arab who appeared to be both deaf and mute—and the sizable intelligence haul and flew north to Balad. Upon landing in the early morning, our teams spent hours feverishly triaging the material. As they pored through the seized computers, a young Marine captain who spoke fluent Arabic came across a twenty-two-page document. The document appeared to link Qais persuasively to the attack on our outpost in Karbala, with details of the planning as well as postoperation assessments. Included in the material were the military IDs taken from the Americans left to die anonymously in the desert.

While the contours of the relationship would become clearer from subsequent interrogations of the Khazalis, the document showed clear support of their network from the Iranian Quds Force. Specifically, the Iranians had supported the Karbala assault by providing Khazali's men with details of life inside the camp. We had long suspected Iranian involvement, but never had it been laid in such bare, unmistakable terms.

On previous raids, we had been forced to let well-linked detainees go, and I expected strong and immediate pressure to release Qais. But I saw the twenty-two-page document as a smoking gun that made releasing Qais impossible. To argue our case, we sent one of our best analysts, a young army captain named Sara,* down to Baghdad in a helicopter to give the book of material and her analysis of its importance to Petraeus. In the rush to relay the material, the intelligence team had time to translate only parts of the document. Sara arrived in Baghdad, gave the material to Dave, and then, at

---

*Sara is a pseudonym.

his request, went with him to the palace to see the prime minister. Immediately upon sitting down, Petraeus decided to roll the dice. He handed Maliki a copy of the original document, seized only hours earlier. When he stuck the paper in front of the prime minister, Dave did not know everything it contained.

Dave steadily raised his voice as he explained to Maliki just what he should make of the document. We are here, he seethed, to help you, and these people are killing Americans. They are not on your side, Dave said, and you need to cut ties to them.

Maliki began to absorb the document and blanched. It showed clear disdain for him and his government. Its contents made painfully clear to the prime minister that the Khazali network, as a proxy for Iran, was undercutting him.

"Where did you get this?" he demanded.

Dave explained it had just been pulled off of the Khazali brothers, who were being held.

"We have to keep them; we have to hold them," Maliki said emphatically.

The meeting ended, and Sara and Dave got into the SUV outside. Sara was shaken from the confrontation. The doors of the Suburban closed, and Dave turned to her.

"Well, I thought that went pretty well," he said jauntily, and smiled. "Don't worry. That's the way it works."

It was a gutsy move on Dave's part, and one that I respected. Barely a month into his tenure, he had seized an opportunity to begin changing the paradigm of the man—Maliki—who stood at the center of Iraq's future. A Shia prime minister after generations of Sunni dominance, Maliki walked a tightrope of ethnic, religious, and political complexity. The last thing he wanted was more pressure from Shia groups or their Iranian supporters. But we had Qais, and the evidence was damning.

Dave's effort received a further dose of energy with the arrival, eight days later, of one of America's finest diplomats, Ambassador Ryan Crocker. I had known Ryan from Pakistan, where he was ambassador from 2004 until coming to Iraq.

Fluent in Arabic, Crocker managed an unusual personal connection with Maliki. After larger meetings, he would request to meet with the prime minister one-on-one, without a translator. Contrary to the hard-charging American inclination to slap down a list of requests when speaking with our counterparts, Crocker sat down without an agenda.

He talked to Maliki about the prime minister's past—about his life under Saddam and the danger of being a member of the Dawah Party, which he now led. Crocker had been in Iraq in 1980, when Saddam's thugs had murdered Baqir al-Sadr, the head of the Dawah Party. He had seen Dawah Party members hanging memorial posters of Sadr faster than the secret police could tear them down. It must have stirred deep emotions and opened new trust when the ambassador told Maliki that he recognized what a monumental act of courage it was for Dawah Party members to go out on the streets and hang those posters—one of which Crocker had kept and hung on his wall. At a time when America was desperate to know whether Nouri al-Maliki would have the will and desire to rebuff Iranian influence, these deeply personal discussions yielded clues. In a window to his feeling about Iran, Maliki once confided to Crocker, "You can't know what arrogance is until you are an Iraqi Arab forced to take refuge with the Iranians."

On May 3 and 4, six weeks after we captured the Khazalis, Ambassador Crocker and Secretary of State Condoleezza Rice traveled to Sharm el-Sheikh, Egypt, to attend a regional conference, which included representatives of Iran, on the future of Iraq. In the building at the time was Mohammad Jafari, the Quds leader we'd sought to capture in Erbil. Later that summer, an Iranian delegation met with Ryan to discuss the U.S.-Iranian relationship, especially as it regarded the future of Iraq. It was quickly apparent the Iranians were uninterested in substantive talk. The Iranian ambassador excused himself repeatedly. He appeared to have a weak bladder. In fact, he was calling back to his handler, Quds Force leader Qassem Suleimani, and, in later talks, meeting in a separate room with Jafari. While the talks yielded no ground with the Iranians directly, they were, like the Khazali documents, helpful with Maliki. The unseriousness of the Iranians in these talks did a lot to convince him that he could not dissuade them from their nefarious meddling in his country.

That spring, two new TF 714 people had joined Graeme's reconciliation cell. In February, John Christian—the Green colonel who had earlier commanded TF 16, including during its push into the western Euphrates River valley—returned to Iraq. With considerable time in Iraq since the summer of 2003, and trained as a foreign area officer, he was well suited for the task. He now came to work on a movement he'd seen the early glimmers of firsthand on the upper Euphrates, where the Albu Mahal had turned, unsuccessfully, on Al Qaeda in Iraq in the summer of 2005.

Having John Christian on the cell was crucial to me. He had commanded in the same squadron that had picked up many of the guys now being considered for release, and he could pose the problem to colleagues in stark terms. "I've done the math," John would say, "and it's going to take us two hundred and forty-seven years to kill them all." Reconciliation was the alternative. While most in the task force quickly grasped the logic, stomachs turned when it came to actually freeing terrorists. John's history of shared sacrifice gave the project essential credibility.

John came to me that spring as he started work with Graeme.

"You know, sir," he said, "this involves meeting with a lot of generals. I don't like talking to generals or dealing with their offices."

"Neither do I, John," I joked.

So John proposed bringing on an experienced Department of Defense civilian, Anne Meree, who had impressed me when I had met her two years earlier and—to Graeme's marvel—was able to get just about anyone in D.C. on the phone. With the addition of John and Anne Meree, the team—which also included an SAS officer, picked by Graeme, and an American intelligence representative—became, in Graeme's words, four blokes and a bird. The cell was small and, during the crescendo of the war, demanded improvisation. Their office was a small plywood cube accessed by a flimsy molded-wood door, which sat like an island in the middle of the ballroom on the east side of the embassy. Every morning, the team gathered in Graeme's office and combined the intelligence reports from their respective organizations—TF 714, the Coalition, and the British and American intelligence agencies.

Between these meetings, whenever he could manage a moment free, Graeme stole away from his office and went to the area across from the MNF-I headquarters in the Green Zone, where, behind tall blast walls, lay the combat support hospital. Called "the cash" from its acronym, it was the Coalition's main emergency room. Helicopters descended and departed throughout the day and night as nurses and medics waited on the edges of the helipad poised with stretchers. Inside, its hallways were filled with the injured, beneath blankets and clear plastic tubing that snaked around them like vines. Graeme spent time with the young medics and staff, men and women with thousand-yard stares. Their long days and nights were spent taking in the ruined frames of young people who had come to Iraq in the peak of their physical fitness. Graeme met men and women with everything to live for who arrived at the hospital, quite literally, in bits.

Graeme carried that emotional weight into the room each time he sat down across from men whose groups were fighting our own. These meetings were not negotiations—no rewards were offered. Graeme tried instead to slowly forge a mutual respect—even a contemptuous one—based upon an understanding of the other's character and motivations and a recognition that both men were trying to do right by their clans. This meant getting beyond the bluster of who could outlast the other, whose force had more men and limbs to sacrifice in the contest.

In the case of Ansar, FSEC sought to convince its leadership of the truth from the Coalition's perspective. First, the Coalition was not there to convert them to Christianity, as they had feared. Second, Ansar would be better off the further they were from Al Qaeda, which had shown a disregard for Iraqi aspirations and a contempt for Iraqi life. Third, AQI was one of the main reasons that the Coalition remained in Iraq. Finally, in the sectarian war AQI continued to provoke, the Iranian-backed militias—or "Safavids," as the Sunni insurgents sneeringly called them—were going to win, and the Sunnis faced potential slaughter. The sooner AQI was neutralized, the better it would be for Iraqi Sunnis and the quicker Ansar would see the Coalition leave.

Ansar would not turn and fight with the Coalition. But leaders who had seen the light might lead the group to downgrade from an AQI-allied jihadist force to another insurgent organization with political demands. Short of that, these leaders could sow doubt and discord.

Graeme's discussions had already showed promise, and given greater latitude by Petraeus, the reconciliation cell pressed hard on other fronts. Graeme expanded his efforts wider than the Ansar leadership. Among others, Graeme contacted and vetted Abu Azzam, a former Sunni insurgent leader who wanted to partner with the Iraqi government; by July, Azzam had twenty-three hundred men patrolling the streets of Abu Ghraib city. Graeme met that winter and spring with the mayor of Sadr City, Rahim al-Daraji, working to check the sectarian killing emanating from the slum and seeking to win safe passage for Coalition forces to enter in advance of the surge campaign to control Baghdad that summer. Their talks were cut short when Daraji was ambushed on March 15, 2007, near Habibiyah Square in Baghdad, leaving the Sadr City police chief dead and the mayor riddled with shrapnel.

The Ansar efforts, meanwhile, continued to show promise. So it fell to John Christian to meet with a particularly unsavory leader of Ansar captured the previous November. An avowed enemy of our task force, Abu Mustafa was a founding member of Ansar and the leader of its operations in Iraq. Most notorious, he masterminded the suicide attack two years earlier on the mess tent in FOB Marez that had killed an operative from our task force. John flew regularly to Camp Cropper, where he met with Mustafa—a big, smelly man with a large head, thick mustache, and bulbous nose. And yet in spite of everything unseemly about this man, FSEC became convinced that Abu Mustafa, like Abu Wail, believed and could in turn convince a core mass of AAS that AQI's program would ultimately spell disaster for Iraqi Sunnis. Thus, FSEC worked to prevent a potential merger of the two groups.

Because Petraeus, as MNF-I commander, had the sole authority to release prisoners, FSEC would need to present its case to him at our weekly meetings. It would be a difficult decision.

A s I had done with Casey, I flew down to Baghdad every Friday that I was in Iraq to meet with General Petraeus and the other senior commanders. Part of the battle for Baghdad had already been fought, without the Coalition. By the spring of 2007, Shia militias methodically pushing westward had ethnically cleansed many of the neighborhoods. Flags of different colors flapped on rooftops of different neighborhoods. In an attempt to stem the violence, long lines of tall blast barriers segmented neighborhoods as the Coalition walled off the city into a honeycomb of cement-encircled enclaves to immobilize the roving militias and cars packed to the brim with bombs. The city felt like it was slowly dying.

Upon arrival at Camp Victory, we drove to the Water Palace, headquarters of both MNF-I and its subordinate command Multi-National Corps–Iraq, or MNC-I. Al Faw was an imposing marble structure perched in the middle of a turquoise man-made lake. As we passed armed guards and entered the cool, cavernous foyer of polished marble floors, I often had images of General Allenby in Cairo, a soldier on the edge of the empire.

As George Casey had done, Dave met with key subordinates for an informal lunch discussion. Around a rectangular table with Dave at the head sat his deputy, Graeme Lamb; his senior enlisted adviser, Command Sergeant Major Marvin Hill; three-star operational commanders Ray Odierno leading MNC-I, Jim Dubik at the Multi-National Security Transition Comamand–Iraq, and me at TF 714; and the key one- and two-star generals responsible for contracting, public affairs, engineering, detainee operations, and other functions. The talk was all business, but unscripted. It was an important time to bring busy leaders together.

As was evident in our weekly meetings, one facet of Dave Petraeus's genius was to scan an often-cluttered field, recognize a good thing or an able commander, and throw his personal energy and hunger and the brunt of his organization behind it. He scrambled to capitalize on the emerging Awakening movement, creating the Sons of Iraq program and giving Graeme greater latitude. In a campaign where demonstrable progress was essential, Dave's ability to create or harness energy was indispensable.

After lunch, a group of us moved the short distance across the massive inner hall to Dave's office. There we'd provide a detailed update on TF 714's operations and current read of the fight. I'd typically bring my operations officer, Kurt Fuller, my intel chief, Mike Flynn or his replacement Gregg Potter, as well as one or two key leaders from TF 16. I wanted Petraeus to interact directly with my team often to build as much confidence as possible in our effort.

Beginning in the spring of 2007, at the conclusion of our TF 714 update we would conduct a second meeting to discuss the work of FSEC. Graeme and his team would provide an update and then propose potential prisoner releases—including, in late March, Abu Mustafa, the Iraqi emir of Ansar. These were difficult decisions, and each of us came into the room from a different vantage of the fight, and with different baggage.

Although he had undisputed bona fides, being a Brit handicapped Graeme. As America was surging, it became clear that Gordon Brown's new administration in London was anxious to withdraw. To some, the Brits appeared to have lost Basra by the start of 2007. By the time Graeme left his post in July, Whitehall had ordered the bases in Basra to be packed up, and the last British convoy from the south departed to the airport in September. In this light, the reconciliation Graeme was pushing could have appeared more like a British-concocted scheme to save face, rather than what it was—a vital component of an aggressive surge.

But not being an American also bore advantages. Although officially the deputy commander, as a Brit, Graeme could maneuver with less concern over American sensitivities or internal politics. His nationality allowed him to say and do things that few Americans could have, and that was invaluable for the effort.

In the discussions, although committed to the process, Ray Odierno harbored serious concerns about the strategic releases. He had been leading the day-to-day battle since December and was the one writing stacks of condolence letters to families of the fallen that spring, when fighting claimed 81 Americans in March. The number of envelopes waiting on his desk would increase that summer, as 104 Americans died in April and 126 in May. More than 600 were wounded each of these months. In one discussion, Ray objected to the release of men like Abu Mustafa, who had American and British blood on their hands.

"Yeah," Graeme responded, "tell me one man in this room that doesn't have blood on his hands. We're drenched in the damn stuff."

In between these meetings, Graeme, Anne Meree, John Christian, and the other members of their team met weekly with Ray's trusted staff. Graeme had a powerful ally in Emma Sky, Ray's political adviser. A brilliant Brit who had started as a bitter critic of the war, Emma became nearly inseparable from her boss, Ray, during his time commanding in Iraq. It was a testament to Ray that he kept close and relied on such an outsider whose unvarnished critiques of the Coalition's campaign could be uncomfortable but necessary antidotes to the too-often insular world of military high command.

But even as FSEC made its case, Graeme instructed the team never to sugarcoat or obscure the crimes of the men they proposed releasing. So when it came time to propose releasing Abu Mustafa, John laid out all the details of his crimes in their presentation at the Friday meeting at the Water Palace: among others, masterminding the deaths of twenty-two Americans and twelve Nepalese construction workers, one of whom was beheaded.

Dave's style took into account the emotions these releases could rile. When it came time for a decision, he turned to his right. "Ray, what do you think?" Ray would give his piece. "Stan?" I would give mine. And so it happened for Abu Mustafa. With our accession, Dave approved his release.

Five months after the release of Abu Wail, the religious emir, we saw him resurface on the outside. On May 2, 2007, three insurgent groups announced that they had come together under a new breakaway coalition, the Jihad and Reform Front (JRF). Although intensely anti-American, the group's announcement set it in opposition to AQI, explicitly declaring its goal to avoid killing innocents. In addition to the Islamic Army in Iraq and the Mujahedeen Army, the faction included a new group called the Sharia Committee of Ansar al-Sunnah—led by Abu Wail. Reports indicated that Abu Wail had sought to lead Ansar into this new coalition, but only a faction came with him. Abu Wail's actions earned him the ire of Ansar's members, who accused him of collaborating with the United States. Soon thereafter, AQI began to target the leaders of the new Jihad and Reform Front. Some reports indicated that JRF, as it clashed with AQI, petered out. Others saw it survive, continuing to cause dissension within Ansar's ranks.

All of these measures had a half-life, and creating a durable competitor to AQI was not the goal. Instead, when the U.S.-led Coalition had everything on the table, Graeme looked for a way to nudge the dynamics in our direction, to create a spurt of momentum in our favor. Doing so would add to the momentum gathering elsewhere, through the quiet work of the CIA, enterprising Marine commanders in Anbar, and then–Brigadier General John Allen, who deftly negotiated deals with Iraqi sheikhs who were residing in Jordan.

At the end of July, two months after Abu Wail's faction appeared on the Internet, Graeme's tour ended and he returned to Scotland. It's unclear whether either Abu Wail or Abu Mustafa survived the war.

I had moved my flag to Iraq during the uprising in Fallujah in April 2004, but during these years I still devoted roughly a quarter of my energy and focus to Afghanistan and Pakistan. Now, as Iraq showed fragile indications of improvement during the summer of 2007, the bigger and more worrying war in Afghanistan increasingly drew my attention.

Until 2006, TF 714 had limited its role in the Afghanistan-Pakistan region to pursuing Al Qaeda leaders. Given the reconstitution and growing strength of the Taliban, I directed our task force in Afghanistan, in careful coordination with the NATO military coalition—the International Security Assistance Force (ISAF)—to begin targeting Taliban leaders.

The initial routing of the Taliban in the fall of 2001 had not so much destroyed it as fragmented it. The less ideologically extreme members of the movement returned home to wait and see how the new government of Afghanistan would perform, while the hard-line factions melted into Pakistan. There, under the direction of Mullah Omar and others, they began to turn themselves from a dislocated government into a full-fledged insurgent movement.

That summer, one of our top targets was one such hard-line Taliban leader: a cruel, one-legged mullah named Dadullah Lang, or Dadullah the Lame, who drove the movement's regeneration and lent it a particular bent. His life trajectory tracked the Taliban's own rebirth post–2001. Born in Uruzgan in 1966, as a teenager he joined the first generation of jihadists in the anti-Soviet resistance of the 1980s. When the communists were expelled, Dadullah returned to his studies in Pakistan but quit school to join the gunslinging students across the border as they formed the Taliban movement in 1994.

During the Taliban's fight to retake the country in the 1990s, he stepped on a mine near Herat and, as one of his Al Qaeda eulogizers put it, "his leg preceded him to Paradise." After Dadullah's men massacred hundreds of Shiite Afghan civilians in the Hazarajat, Mullah Omar retired him. Indignant after being fired, Dadullah presented Omar with his AK-47 and prosthetic and declared, "If you no longer need me, I no longer need them." Omar would indeed need Dadullah again and dispatched him to the bitter fight against the United Front in the north, where his name was cursed for the atrocities he carried out.

As the Taliban regrouped after 2001, Dadullah helped make them into a twenty-first-century insurgency. Unlike their forebears who fought against the Soviets, the post-2001 incarnation of the Taliban relied increasingly on suicide bombs. Arabs provided inspiration and some technical instruction on IEDs, based upon the success of the bombs on the roads of Iraq. Men like Dadullah, who claimed tighter ties with Al Qaeda Arabs and other non-Taliban terrorist groups in Waziristan, often facilitated these exchanges. Dadullah, meanwhile, had a more direct role in the introduction of suicide bombing to the Afghan battlefield. Although some in the Quetta *shura*— the Taliban's leadership council—were queasy with the tactic, Dadullah pushed it enthusiastically.

To field the first tranche of "martyrs," he skimmed from Pakistan's mental asylums and orphanages, strapped the parentless and infirm with suicide vests, and sent them across the border. The propaganda and mythology surrounding those attacks lured further recruits—madrassa students and refugees. In 2004, only six suicide bomb attacks occurred in Afghanistan. In 2006 there were 141. Dadullah developed a cultlike following through his regular media appearances, and his boasts of global aims and tight ties with Al Qaeda were often to the chagrin of Taliban leaders, who sought to maintain distance from Al Qaeda. He granted regular interviews to Al Jazeera, while the Taliban media arm produced a steady stream of DVDs— hawked in Quetta and in Peshawar for four dollars a disc—that showed Dadullah trekking ridgelines and beheading "spies."

By 2007, we were aware of Dadullah's periodic trips into Afghanistan, during which he dispensed funds and guidance and motivated Taliban forces. Like Zarqawi's, Dadullah's personal visits were a powerful leadership tool. But they also made the self-styled top Taliban field commander vulnerable to our forces.

Typically we would detect Dadullah's movements only after he was in Afghanistan, and then it was difficult to obtain pinpoint locations and react with forces fast enough to target him. However, partly by tracking his recently released brother, Mullah Shah Mansoor, we were able to learn about a forthcoming trip into Afghanistan before he traveled. We positioned collection and raid forces in advance.

On Saturday, May 12, 2007, Dadullah crossed the border, and we were able to track his movement to a compound in southern Helmand Province. There, in a raid that included air strikes and both ground- and helicopter-delivered forces, British commandos engaged in a four-hour fight in which we had indications Dadullah was killed. We tracked the enemy's movement, and in an operation the next evening, Dadullah's body was found, absent his prosthetic leg.

As when Zarqawi died, Dadullah's bosses possibly felt some relief when he was disposed of. But his death nonetheless brought eulogies from Al Qaeda bigwigs like Abu Yahya al-Libi and Ayman al-Zawahiri. The hunt for those top leaders had never ceased, even as Zarqawi and Iraq became a higher priority. Later that summer of 2007, our task force in

Afghanistan began to collect intelligence that indicated bin Laden might be in or returning to the notorious mountain area of Tora Bora. Known to locals as Spin Ghar, it was famous as bin Laden's "mountain lair" and the location of the December 2001 battle in which the United States sought, and failed, to corner and capture him and his closest compatriots.

For the past six years, the hunt for bin Laden had included doggedly persistent efforts by a variety of individuals and agencies around the globe. I watched extraordinarily complex and clever technical initiatives employed to track devices, multidisciplinary analysis leveraged to predict and locate potential hiding spots, and daring human intelligence operations conducted to identify potential sources who might lead us, as Sheikh Rahman had with Zarqawi, to the elusive Al Qaeda leader. But his apparent discipline in avoiding phones and Internet and limiting personal interaction had left behind only theories to his whereabouts, and a mostly cold trail.

We were unable to verify the limited but tantalizing hints that bin Laden might appear at Tora Bora but also unwilling to ignore that there was to be a confirmed gathering of insurgents there. So I moved my headquarters temporarily to Afghanistan, and over a period of more than a month we refined our intelligence about the area, then conducted an operation—Valiant Pursuit—to search and clear known or likely insurgent pockets. The initial phases were intense as we focused an unprecedented array of ISR surveillance aircraft, manned and unmanned, over the area, with a particular focus on mapping every communication signal being transmitted. It provided a fascinating, if still inconclusive, picture of insurgent activity, and we subsequently conducted helicopter insertion of Rangers and SEALs on initial targets, some at extraordinarily high altitudes.

Bin Laden wasn't there, as I'd doubted he would be. But the operation worked to shut down insurgent sanctuaries inside Afghanistan, a critical goal in counterinsurgency. As was so often the case in this long war, however, the relationships we in TF 714 forged with Dave Rodriguez's paratroopers of the 82nd Airborne Division—then in charge of eastern Afghanistan— were invaluable. Rod was quickly accumulating more time in Afghanistan than any other general officer, and the importance of my friendship with him would be fully apparent to me only a year later.

Back in Iraq, Dave Petraeus and Ryan Crocker worked hard to manage our relationship with Prime Minister Maliki. Although supportive of aggressive targeting of Sunni extremists, the Iraqi prime minister remained skittish about going after Shia. On several occasions Dave sent me to Baghdad to brief Maliki on TF 714's operations and to make our case for confronting the Shia groups.

Each occasion was almost exactly the same. Armed with a briefing book of PowerPoint slides summarizing recent operations, their effects, and the intelligence that underpinned our targeting, I'd pass through Iraqi security and sit in a large meeting room with chairs arranged in a rectangle along the walls. There was no main table, and when the prime minister arrived we sat side-by-side with a small table in front of us on which I laid the book.

Maliki was always cordial but not effusive and seemed to know little about my force. Sometimes Dave's trusted cultural adviser Sadi, and on occasion Ryan, sat in and interpreted. Each time I reminded Maliki who my force was and what we did, and then started with a summary of our operations against Sunni extremists. Maliki asked few questions but nodded energetically in agreement as he listened to my accounts of raids and the effects they had against AQI, Ansar al-Sunnah, and other insurgent groups. For that part of the brief I felt the glow of approval.

Then I'd flip to the section on Shia groups and he'd perceptibly stiffen, almost recoil. I'd review the operations, emphasizing the accuracy of our intelligence, and, seeking to convince him of the necessity of the effort, I'd review information we'd gotten from captured documents and interrogations. He remained civil, but it was a hard sell. He clearly understood and accepted the overall premise, but in many cases, we were targeting his constituents.

On Sunday, October 21, 2007, my aide Chris Fussell stopped by my office during the first part of the morning, while I was still in the gym, to get a jump on any pressing issues. The operations center was in its quiet lull, a few hours after dawn. As usual, Chris checked in with the daytime operations officer, who gave a rundown of the previous night's raids.

"And seventeen is just wrapping up an op," he added, referring to TF 17.

"Long one, huh?" Chris asked, concerned. Something didn't seem right. We tried to avoid operating in daylight, when more civilians and traffic were out.

"Yeah, in Sadr City. No friendlies lost, but they think more than fifty fighters were killed," the ops officer said.

Chris stared at him, stunned. "Wait. You're saying we just killed fifty people in Sadr City? In *daylight*?"

The operations officer nodded. Chris asked whether I had been notified. No, the operations officer said, looking quizzically back at Chris, "no friendly casualties."

Chris took off for the gym and caught me as I was walking along the hot gravel back to my hooch. He told me quickly about the operation: a big gunfight in Sadr City, went into daytime, maybe fifty killed. I went straight to the SAR to get a better understanding of the situation.

As I sat in my gym shorts and shirt, the staff gathered as many details of the firefight as possible. For nearly three months, there had been a cease-fire in effect between Muqtada al-Sadr's Mahdi Army and the Iraqi government and Coalition. As in this case, our only raids into Sadr City were against the Special Groups that shunned Sadr's agreement with the Maliki government and continued to attack both Iraqi and Coalition forces with devastating rockets. The operation in question had begun as a night raid to target a Special Groups leader in charge of kidnapping and death squads. But quickly, it had gone bad in the thicketlike backstreets of Sadr City.

While clearing the target building, the team came under fire from surrounding buildings, as fighters fired machine guns and rocket grenades at them. Helicopters came to their support, firing from the air. The team fought street to street in order to escape the slum, departing under gunfire and hitting an IED as they withdrew. As I watched the recorded aerial surveillance of the fight, the violence and the rapidly gathering swarms of enemy fighters moving to the site reminded me of the Battle of Mogadishu, where in October 1993, special operations forces fought a desperate battle against Somali fighters who gathered like antibodies against an infection.

By the time this battle in Sadr City was over, our force reported that forty-nine fighters had been killed, but there were no known civilian casualties. Despite the immense violence, TF 17's assault force was able to withdraw.

Dave Petraeus called, and I closed the door to my office.

"Stan, this is bad. This could be really ugly," Dave said. He was a masterfully cool commander, but as he spoke, his words carried an edge of worry.

"Sir, I understand," I said.

"Stan," he said, "Maliki called; he's really upset." He paused. "He said the whole government may fall."

"Sir, I understand," I said. "It's over; there's nothing I can do about it now."

After a couple of hours, our force made it back to its outstation. In the meantime, the insurgents had cranked into gear their propaganda machine, filming at the local hospital, igniting outrage and barraging the Iraqi government with complaints. Iraqis in the neighborhood reported that bullets from the helicopter had killed teenagers and children, and the Iraqi government spokesman said that fifteen people, not fifty, had died, but that all fifteen were civilians. Dave was taking the heat from Maliki and would later meet with him to discuss the raid.

I understood how fragile a moment this was for the Coalition—and for Dave Petraeus in particular. A month earlier, he and Ryan Crocker had returned to Washington, D.C., for a highly scrutinized public update on the surge in front of Congress. He faced strong skepticism and outright hostility from many of the legislators. And yet he presented—most memorably, in a thirteen-slide PowerPoint presentation—evidence of a truly dramatic reduction in violence. He showed improvements on a number of key metrics. Civilian deaths, ethno-sectarian killing, and weekly attacks were down. American fatalities had spiked as more troops entered the war during the early summer, but now fewer Americans were dying. In May, 126 Americans were killed; in October, that number was 38. It was far from clear that these trends were real and would continue, and the political reconciliation that the added security was meant to midwife was not yet moving. But it appeared for the first time that a spectacular turnaround of the war, under Dave's leadership, seemed within grasp.

From the very beginning, Dave had been supportive of TF 714's targeting missions in Iraq. And while there was one level between the political heat and me, I felt the burn. My teams needed immense freedom to operate in order to achieve the required operational tempo. But I was always personally responsible for what they did. In practice, the only way I could manage the balance between assuming the risk for their actions and allowing them enough autonomy was through trust, and lots of it. It had taken four years to build the machine that produced the intelligence that located the Special Groups leader deep in Sadr City. But, more important, those four years also had built up the trust that allowed TF 714's leaders to act on it.

So in the days following, we did a significant review with the operators of what had occurred and how to move forward. But it was important the men understood I did not question the decisions they made once bullets started flying. I did not want them to feel that they could go from heroes one night to villains the next depending on the whims and friction of war.

As much as the networked organization of our force was novel, sustaining the bonds among warriors, particularly during these difficult months, demanded age-old leadership. On the night of November 20, 2007, a month after the Sadr City raid, a British Puma helicopter was flying near Baghdad, carrying operators from the SAS on an operation. As it descended to land, the helo was caught in a brownout, engulfed in the plumes of desert earth kicked up by its rotors. The helicopter crashed and rolled, and one of the SAS operators was pinned inside, conscious as the helicopter burned and his teammates tried in vain to pull him from the wreckage. The crash killed two of the SAS operators, while others on board were left injured.

After the crash, the British pilots stopped flying for a few days to review the incident—a standard thing to do following a crash like that. I knew they might be self-conscious about getting back into the air after a rattling crash and might worry that the rest of the task force—namely the operators who depended on them—would doubt their ability. During the stand-down, I told my aide Chris Fussell that the first time they got back in the air, I wanted to fly with them. Days later, I rode with the Brits in the Pumas on a run from Balad down to Baghdad.

Graeme captured it in his typically profound and gnomic way: "Soldiering equals trust."

Our war demanded relentless focus and a hardening of natural emotions. I knew that required me to regularly reflect on what we were doing and how to keep myself moored to what I believed. Chris Fussell later reminded me of such a moment that spring of 2008. It was Sunday morning, and we'd left TF 714's small enclave inside Balad Airfield to get a haircut.

I was irritable as we left the barbershop. Seeing the fast-food restaurants and electronics sales displays around the PX did that to me. From the earliest days of our presence in Afghanistan and Iraq, I'd been frustrated by the seemingly unstoppable growth of facilities that I considered a serious distraction from the business at hand. I wanted soldiers well fed and housed, but attempts to replicate the comforts of home could deceive us into thinking we weren't in a deadly fight.

Pulling out of the lot and back onto the roads that led to our compound, the car was quiet. Chris tried to make conversation.

"You see that one of the dogs died on the target last night?" he asked, referring to the dogs the assault teams outfitted with cameras and sent bounding into dark, often booby-trapped houses before the team entered. Chris shook his head. "Really sad."

"Fuss," I snapped, turning toward him and squinting. "Seven enemy were killed on that target last night. Seven humans. Are you telling me you're more concerned about the dog than the *people* that died?"

The car fell silent again.

"Hey, listen," I said. "Don't lose your humanity in this thing."

He looked me in the eye for a few beats, nodded, and turned to face the road again. We drove back to base. My reaction was unfair. I hadn't raised the dog that died. I hadn't enjoyed his companionship during lonely nights at some dusty outpost. I hadn't had my life saved by the dog.

But, nearing the end of my command, four and a half years in, I had an acute awareness of the incredibly lethal machine we had built in order to defeat the enemy, and the amount of killing that machine had required men like Chris—young, moral, fearless—to bear. I reacted to Chris like this not because I saw in him any bloodlust or brutishness or imbalance but because I feared these qualities might gnarl the upright men I led.

We found ourselves in a situation wherein an enemy ideology had spread and corrupted thousands of young men. By the time they came into contact with our machine, by the time they had a vest strapped to their chest and were planning to cut down a score of Americans on their way out, the only way to deal with them was to fight them and, often, kill them. Operations reports put the toll into tidy acronyms—EKIA, enemy killed in action—while the aerial feeds of operations showed men fleeing our helicopters as antlike specks, too small to show their blanched faces. But they obviously believed in what they were fighting for. And while some men showed an innate, unalloyed cruelty, many who ended up fanatical and dangerous had begun as misguided, gullible kids. That they had to die was something to lament.

On May 1, 2008, I waited in the SAR at Balad for a missile impact some two thousand miles away in a rural compound in Somalia. We'd done the same thing eight weeks earlier, however, and had failed. In that case, our intelligence was accurate, but to be conservative, we'd fired only two missiles when four would have covered the entire compound. Al Qaeda leader Saleh Ali Saleh Nabhan was in a separate part of the compound, escaped the edge of the blasts, and survived. The miss was a bitter lesson for me.

Another opportunity arose quickly. In late April 2008, we located Al Shabab leader Aden Hashi Ayrow near Dusa Mareb, Somalia. Like Dadullah in Pakistan, Ayrow seemed an eerie mirror of Zarqawi. A stubborn but charismatic extremist known to be personally volatile and ruthless, he was responsible for the deaths of foreign aid workers, Somalis, international peacekeepers, and BBC journalist Kate Peyton, who was shot in the back near her Mogadishu hotel in February 2005. Since the Ethiopian invasion sixteen months earlier, Al Shabab had split from the Islamic Courts Union. No longer a "youth wing," Al Shabab was growing into an autonomous terroristic organization with aims to disrupt political reconciliation inside Somalia. It also had aspirations, albeit boastful ones, of striking beyond its borders. Aden Ayrow's continued personal ascendance had helped spur Al Shabab's dangerous rise. Now we felt we had him in the crosshairs.

Waiting for the operation brought me back to the tense moments surrounding Big Ben, the arms cache on the southern edge of Fallujah we had struck in the summer of 2004, when insurgents controlled the city and TF 714's credibility was far more fragile. And yet, in spite of everything we'd done in the past four years, I again worried about the potential impact of a second failed strike on TF 714's standing and its hard-won freedom of action.

As the missiles impacted, we waited anxiously for indications that Ayrow was dead. Sometimes the target's voice came up on a phone call after the strike. Ayrow's never did. The operation represented an important step in TF 714's ability to contribute in even difficult, denied areas. A September 2009 U.S. raid that killed Nabhan reflected the continued maturation of this capability.

A month later, in June of 2008, immediately before I left Iraq for the last time, I walked the three hundred meters from a new headquarters and billet area we had occupied since March of that year for a last look at the original area we had built and occupied since the summer of 2004.

In the fading light of early evening, with the frequent roar of departing jets or helicopters in the background, Jody Nacy and I walked into the bunker, through the SAR, TF 16's operations center, and then across the gravel patch I'd crossed thousands of times to our small wooden hooch when retiring at dawn. All the areas were deserted but still largely furnished, as they had been when we had lived there. The plywood tables, worn chairs, and shelves, often built quickly, all remained. It was as though everyone had suddenly disappeared. It was as though we were exploring a sunken ship.

Memories poured back. I recalled good times, like modest ceremonies to pin medals on deserving young people. And I remembered moments of frustration and loss.

At what had been the entrance to the bunker area—a small wooden guard shack flanked by cement blast walls—we paused. As much as there was sacred ground for members of the task force, this was such a place. Here, on more occasions than Jody or I liked to recall, the small patch of concrete would fill with weathered and bearded Green operators, young and focused Rangers, our SAS brothers-in-arms, the tireless men of the Night Stalkers, a broad assortment of SEALs, intelligence analysts, interrogators, communicators, and countless others.

As had become our tradition, it was here that our task force would assemble at dusk whenever we lost a comrade on the battlefield. In an admittedly ragtag military formation, beneath half-masted American and British Union Jack flags folding and unfolding easily in the warm breezes of the Iraqi desert, we would listen to a brief and solemn remembrance of our fallen comrade. We would then remain at silent attention as bagpipes played and the flags were returned to their positions at the top of the flagpole. With our Balad bunker in the background, the team would disperse, returning to a fight that did not pause for losses.

I doubt there's anything there now to mark the spot or record what took place. It remains only in the memories and hearts of the incredible men and women who gathered there. Jody and I said nothing and walked away from our Balad war bunker for the last time.

A few days later, on June 3, 2008, I flew back to the States a different person from the one who'd first flown to Iraq in October 2003. In my pocket I carried a letter from my aide Chris Fussell, who had written to me about his year.

> Sir: You asked me once what I would consider the "perfect day," and I've thought of that often this year—especially during a few of the not-so-perfect days. I know that day would include Holly, a good running trail, crisp morning air, a meal with good friends. I also know it would not involve a war, a helicopter, or an assault rifle; there would be no air support, medical plan, or five-paragraph order. But it would most certainly involve stories and debates from a time when those were the daily norm. And it would involve friends who shared these days and lived to see a more peaceful world. It would also involve stories of great men and leadership and what our mentors taught us, and I will speak with pride of this year.

Well said.

Part Three

The power of the mighty hath no foundation but in the opinion and belief of the people.

—Thomas Hobbes, *Behemoth*

CHAPTER 16

The Ticking Clock

June 2008–June 2009

The black civilian vehicle drove onto the palace grounds and pulled up in front of a small residence where we would stay. On the entire early morning drive through Kabul, Annie had been perched in her seat in wide-eyed wonder trying to take in every sight, asking questions about all that was new and curious. It was vintage Annie, on her first trip to the country that had so impacted our lives.

The box-shaped, two-story residence sat next door to a similar structure where President Hamid Karzai lived. Both were in the shadow of the historic palace accommodations of kings, but were a far cry from palatial. As the vehicle slowed to a stop, Annie and I saw a collection of members of President Karzai's protective force and staff who were waiting to greet us. I knew most from before, and their genuine smiles and traditional hand-on-their-heart gestures brought back a flood of memories.

It was November 19, 2011, and I was once again in Afghanistan. It had been nine and a half years since I'd first arrived with Combined Joint Task Force 180 early in the war and seventeen months since I'd left on a June evening amid controversy over a magazine article. I'd never expected to return but now found myself excited to see old friends.

We'd traveled at President Karzai's invitation. I'd delayed accepting for many months, but in October, after consulting Ryan Crocker, our new ambassador in Kabul; General Jim Mattis, now the commander of Central Command; and Chief of Staff Bill Daley at the White House, I decided to go, and as we exited the airplane I was glad I had.

Annie and I spent only two days in Afghanistan—I knew how distracting visitors could be for busy leaders, but it was enough time for Annie to visit an American-sponsored center for the vulnerable street children of Kabul she supports as a board member. And it was long enough for me to meet with ministers, generals, ambassadors, and President Karzai. I was able to renew friendships and express in person the respect and thanks I'd only been able to write in letters. After all we'd done together, I owed them that.

As we entered the building to a waiting breakfast of Afghan fruit, tea, and the flatbread I'd always enjoyed, I pointed out to Annie the room where, twenty-one months before, President Karzai had come from being sick in bed to approve, as commander-in-chief, the combined Afghan-ISAF operation into the Helmand district of Marjah. There was history in that room, another chapter in Afghanistan's long, often twisted tale. It was history I had been a part of.

Over lunch Karzai talked to Annie about Afghanistan, and later escorted her on a short tour of the palace. He took special care to explain the restoration that had been required to repair, as much as possible, the needless damage inflicted by the Taliban to the artwork. It was a subtle message of what he was trying to do for his country.

On our last night in Kabul we had dinner at the home of Abdul Rahim Wardak, Afghanistan's minister of defense since 2004. Wardak was a career soldier who'd trained in the United States, but had defected to be a mujahideen leader for a moderate Sufi faction during the Soviet war. An ardent royalist, he had experienced Afghanistan when it had proud institutions, like the army he joined. Since 2001, Wardak had been a consistent advocate of rebuilding a credible Afghan military, and we had become close during my tour.

In the fading light of early evening we passed through checkpoints manned by poorly uniformed security guards and bumped along potholed streets flanked by grayish brown cement walls until we came to a battered metal gate. On a call from our security detail the gate swung open and we pulled into a small courtyard.

The chilled fall air was immediately warmed by the glow of light from an open door and the familiar face of Wardak and his wife, who came quickly to the car to greet us. Clasping my hand firmly, Wardak thanked Annie and me for coming and escorted us into their house.

The inside felt like an oasis of color and culture in the somber landscape of Kabul. The home had been in his wife's family for many years and was decorated with tasteful furniture and beautiful red Afghan carpets. As Annie and his wife chatted, Wardak escorted me to a small studylike room toward the back of the house. On the walls and shelves were mementos of his military career. Some, like diplomas from military schools, were self-explanatory; others were seemingly innocuous objects that needed backstories to explain their significance. And there were photographs. A younger Wardak, often against a backdrop of harsh terrain, peered at me from alongside other soldiers. It was a soldier's room and testified to all he was, and that which was important to him. He didn't bring me into it to brag or impress, but to connect.

I was home, or at least I could have been. In my father's house the room is the same, except the hills are Korea and Vietnam instead of Jalalabad and Khost. In mine they are Iraq and Afghanistan. And there are always photographs showing comrades who have shaped and defined us. Earlier that day, I'd given Wardak a gift of a small statue of Washington crossing the Delaware, and it was already on a shelf in a place of honor. My office holds a nineteenth-century rifle Wardak had sent to me after I'd left Afghanistan.

For dinner Wardak had gathered a small group of Afghan officials with whom I'd worked closely. Over lamb and plates of steaming rice topped with raisins, we shared an evening of friendship and candor. We knew that the following morning Annie and I would fly home; they would stay in troubled Afghanistan. It would likely be the last time I saw many of them. Unexpectedly, Afghanistan, and most important, Afghans, had become a major part of my career, and my life.

The story I will tell of my command there is from my perspective. I will describe the evolution of my understanding of the challenges we faced in Afghanistan, the mission I believed I'd been given, and the strategy I felt could succeed. I'm not unbiased. Afghanistan can do that to you. In Iraq, though we fought to destroy Abu Musab al-Zarqawi and Al Qaeda with all the ferocity we could muster, I never connected with the population. In Afghanistan, as my time in command progressed, I would develop strong feelings for the Afghans and their nation.

At the heart of the story is Afghanistan itself, a complex swirl of ethnic and political rivalries, cultural intransigence, strains of religious fervor, and bitter memories overlaid on a beautiful, but harshly poor, landscape. Without internal struggles or outside interference, Afghanistan would be a difficult place to govern, and a challenge to develop. And there have always been struggles and interference.

But it's not just that. In her beauty and coarseness, in her complexity and tragedy Afghanistan possesses a mystical quality, a magnetism. Few places have such accumulated layers of culture, religion, history, and lore that instill both fear and awe. Yet those who seek to even budge her trajectory are reminded that dreams often end up buried in the barren slopes of the Hindu Kush or in muddy fields alongside the Helmand River.

When I arrived to take command of the war in June 2009, in addition to the rising violence and sense of insecurity, I found a creeping, fatalistic pessimism, as though the fight were over, the effort failed. Some pointed to history and declared the country intractable. Few countries or NGOs were leaving, but many wanted to. There was growing unease with the viability of the mission.

Indeed, in those early days, as I assessed the war, I wasn't sure the mission could be done. Although I'd known it would be difficult, the situation was even worse than I'd anticipated. I was further cautioned by the fact that I would be the twelfth commander to lead the NATO effort in Afghanistan, the latest in a succession of experienced professionals. Any solution would not be only a military one; it had to encompass much more. But as we looked closer and considered a range of strategies, I concluded that it was possible. The intimidating specter of Afghanistan as an impossible challenge belied the reality. The obstacles were numerous, but the accrued problems were not insoluble, just incredibly difficult.

Against the fatalism that the cause was doomed, I believed a unique confluence of factors, personalities, and events in Kabul, Washington, D.C., and other locations offered a real opportunity to succeed. But radical change was needed, quickly. We needed to leverage the movement those factors had created in order to convince Afghans, ISAF, and other players that the status quo had changed, that the trajectory had been altered for the better. It couldn't be false—cynicism would overtake any progress that was too slow or wasn't real. But I thought that if we did smart analysis, got the strategy right, worked to exhaustion, and came into a bit of luck, the mission could be accomplished. I would never have sought additional forces to fight an effort I felt was doomed.

As the story unfolds many things appear: extraordinary sacrifice and teamwork, often alongside an atmosphere of mistrust, uncertainty, media scrutiny, and politics. There is a temptation to seek a single hero or culprit— a person, group, or policy—that emerges as the decisive factor. This makes for better intrigue, but it's a false drama. To do so is to oversimplify the war, the players, and Afghanistan itself. Because despite their relevance as contributing factors, I found no single personality, decision, relationship, or event that determined the outcome or even dominated the direction of events.

Afghanistan did that. Only Afghanistan, with her deep scars and opaque complexity, emerged as the essential reality and dominant character. On her brutal terrain, and in the minds of her people, the struggle was to be waged and decided. No outcome was preordained, but nothing would come easily. Few things of value do.

This story begins one year to the day before I arrived to command in Afghanistan. On Friday, June 13, 2008, in the same parachute-packing facility at Fort Bragg where Annie had mouthed the words "I love you" seventeen hundred days before, I passed command of TF 714 to my friend and former deputy, then–Vice Admiral Bill McRaven. My boss at SOCOM, Admiral Eric Olson, officiated. Friends and colleagues from throughout our career, like then–Lieutenant General Marty Dempsey and his wife, Deanie, and Dave and Ginny Rodriguez, were there. But mostly the rows were filled with familiar faces I'd shared the turbulent years with since 2003.

"There will be few markers from this war," I said to those present, and those still far away, "and much of the history will be inaccurate or incomplete. Cannons won't reflect where you stood and bled, or markers to record the cost. But in the minds and hearts of those who have known you, and in the soul of the nation, the fact that you were there is indelibly written. You have done your duty—and it was the honor of my life to have been here to witness it. Thank you."

With those words, I gave up command of TF 714.

A few weeks earlier, I had been confirmed by the Senate to become director of the Joint Staff, essentially chief of staff to the chairman and the joint chiefs. DJS, as it was called, was a prestigious post, one John Abizaid and then George Casey had held during my previous tour at the Pentagon. I'd been told that the chairman, Admiral Mike Mullen, had sought me for the position. Having appreciated his keen interest in how TF 714 operated when he was the chief of naval operations, I suspected he'd be a kindred spirit.

The Senate confirmation process had been unexpectedly jarring. Although every military officer's promotion to field grade or higher must be confirmed by Senate vote, my experience to that point in my career had been as a name on long promotion lists that the White House recommended and the Senate confirmed. My promotion to lieutenant general in February 2006, when I was deployed in Iraq, had not involved individual testimony or significant issues.

This time the experience was much different. I was informed in December 2007 that I'd be nominated for the DJS job and to anticipate an early 2008 confirmation and departure from TF 714. In the end the process took until the first week of June. Although questions surrounding the death of Pat Tillman were raised and I addressed them, the major issue regarded TF 714's detention operations. Legitimate questions and concerns were intertwined with an ongoing inquiry into the Bush administration's overall detention policies led by Senator Levin. I was happy for the opportunity to address any questions about TF 714 head-on, but it felt as though the delay was the product of a larger political issue.

I reported for duty to the Joint Staff on August 13, 2008. Because I'd disliked the ponderous Pentagon bureaucracy during my previous tour I was pleased with the guidance I received in my first meeting with Chairman Mullen.

"I want you to do what you do," he said. "I want you to attack and destroy the network."

I was confused. We were sitting in his quiet office in the Pentagon, not Baghdad. "Chairman, what network are you talking about?"

"Ours," he said. He was referring to the Joint Staff, and by extension to the parts of the Pentagon and military we in the Staff interacted with. "Tear it down and rebuild it to be faster, more transparent, and more effective."

That was clear enough, even for an infantryman. A navy admiral with extensive experience in the Pentagon had identified an enemy who must be defeated, and it was us. Much of my next ten months were spent implementing changes to shape the Joint Staff into the more agile, focused team that Admiral Mullen desired. My close partner in this, and in Afghanistan afterward, was my executive officer, Charlie Flynn. Since he had commanded a company under me in the 2nd Ranger Battalion in the mid-1990s, Charlie and I had stayed close. He was, on the surface, charismatic and easygoing, with a quick smile and kind face. But as the youngest of a rough-and-tumble Rhode Island brood of nine, Charlie had a scrappy, hard-charging energy. He came to the Pentagon that year directly from commanding in Iraq—his third combat tour since 9/11. He and his wife decided the family would stay in North Carolina to let their kids stay in the same schools, so Annie insisted he bunk in a small third-floor room in our quarters on Fort McNair.

During our year at the Pentagon, we shared most moments of what became a mechanical schedule: Each night, he and I ate a quick dinner together before I got up the next day at 3:30 A.M. to run to the Pentagon, in time to shower, change, meet Dave Rodriguez at six and then host the 6:30 A.M. standup—a knock-off of the TF 714 O&I—that I soon instituted to tie together the Joint Staff and other offices in the Pentagon. When the day ended around 8 P.M., Charlie and I walked across the Pentagon's big plateau-size parking lot to his car, drove home, ate, and did it again the next day. But as busy as we were, I was home with Annie.

When I arrived at the Pentagon, I found, as I had six years earlier, the nation's energy and resources shifting from the theater I'd left to a war I'd soon rejoin. When I joined the Joint Staff from Afghanistan in 2002, I was surprised to find the Pentagon's focus on Iraq. Now, returning from Iraq in August 2008, I was less surprised to find a growing focus on Afghanistan. From the day I became the DJS I sensed that Afghanistan and neighboring Pakistan would dominate our energy. In 2003, there had been a troubling velocity to the decision making. Now, with rising war fatigue and an impending change in administrations, I sensed the opposite.

As we knew better in 2008 than immediately following the 9/11 attacks, our war in Afghanistan did not begin in 2001. The fighting reflected forces brewing in Afghanistan for centuries, and the conflict's modern roots dated back to 1973. That year, after a forty-year reign, King Zahir Shah was unseated in a bloodless coup (he was vacationing in Europe) by his former prime minister and brother-in-law Daoud. Daoud's soft entrance belied his authoritarian reign, which soon prompted a group of eager Afghan communists to overthrow him in 1978. As these communists' early attempts to rule faltered and provoked a violent backlash that showed signs of an impending insurgency, the Soviet Union intervened on Christmas 1979.

For the next ten years, the Afghan government and ever more Soviet troops fought against a collection of diverse opposition movements. They were eventually subsidized by Saudi Arabia and the United States, but largely manipulated by Pakistan, which dispensed the funds as it saw fit. The long struggle polarized Afghanistan's many ethnic groups, and turned the mujahideen resistance more extreme. The perennial warring catapulted into positions of power a group of nontraditional leaders like Abdul Rashid Dostum, Gulbuddin Hekmatyar, and Ahmad Shah Massoud, whose talents ranged from military acumen to cold-blooded murder. Ultimately, the Soviets withdrew their military forces in 1989, but the government they left behind, under President Mohammed Najibullah, survived for three years. When the Soviet Union fell in 1991, however, Najibullah's regime lost funding, credibility, and was weakened by infighting. The amassing opposition movements soon took control of the nation, advanced toward Kabul, and began fighting one another in civil war.

The year the civil war had begun, 1992, wasn't that long ago, and adults in Afghanistan remembered well the behavior of the groups that had struggled for wealth and power. Alliances arose and shifted quickly. Fortunes were amassed and used to construct garish homes or private fiefdoms. The traditional relationships that balanced local and national interests, and formal and informal power brokers, struggled to reemerge from the wreckage of war. In the chaos, Afghans retreated to relationships most familiar and trustworthy to them: family, tribe, and ethnic group. A cadre of well-educated elites labored to stitch together structures on which to build the future, but most were upended with each new spasm of violence and turmoil.

In 1994, the Taliban rose to power. They emanated from the Pashtun south and were populated by young Afghans often schooled in madrassas, or religious schools—*talib* means "student"—across the border in Pakistan. These idealistic, religiously inflexible young men seemed at first like a summer rain that would wash away the excesses of "warlords" who had robbed, raped, and terrified Afghans living under them. The Taliban's personal piety and quick punishment of pederasts and thieves appeared, at first, a welcome respite for a people weary of conflict. They skillfully advertised it as such. Of course it was too good to be true. Quickly, the Taliban exhibited administrative incompetence and displayed a stunning propensity for draconian violence and intolerance. Their cruel and tone-deaf actions, like public executions for adultery, and the destruction of ancient Buddhist statues, eventually earned them the contempt of the international community. So too did the sanctuary they gave to Osama bin Laden and Al Qaeda, who helped the Taliban lay siege to the few remaining holdouts of resistance in northern Afghanistan.

For many Afghans, the tragedy of 9/11 and the American response represented an opportunity. With Afghanistan again the attention of the world, they had a chance to remove the Taliban and reshape their country. For a short period it would be possible to leverage the presence of international peacekeepers and donations to establish a government dominated by neither extremist ideologues nor the predatory warlords who'd haunted the country. Nearly seven years later, their vision remained unfulfilled.

For the first few years following the Taliban's overthrow, Afghanistan appeared under control. But after a period of waiting to see how the Karzai government would perform, and treat former Taliban, an insurgency soon gestated. To the degree that the insurgency had a central command, the Taliban regime's former leaders dominated it. Most decamped to Quetta, Pakistan, eighty miles from southern Afghanistan, and the city became the rallying point for turning the now-exiled Taliban government into an insurgent movement to contest the Karzai government. Theirs was a natural reinvention. Although they had largely fought costly conventional campaigns in the civil war of the 1990s, many of the movement's elders had cut their teeth in the guerrilla war against the Soviets. The structures they'd used to govern Afghanistan—*shuras*, or councils—were reconstituted, populated by leaders who'd survived the initial salvo of war as well as new up-and-comers.

They led heavy recruitment efforts throughout Pakistan's madrassas, and began to root themselves into the country by dispatching small bands of fighters. Primarily in the south and east, these mobile units pestered NATO forces but, more important, waged blanket assassination campaigns against any Afghans—government officials, civilians, NGO workers—who collaborated with NATO or the Afghan government. The memory of these fatal visits by roving bands ensured that Afghans did not regard future Taliban threats as empty. Larger bands of fighters, and more distinct military commands, followed.

The Taliban benefited heavily from the weakness and predatory behavior of the Afghan government. Frustration, then rage, at the inability or unwillingness of the government, despite its clear progress in certain sectors like education, to provide basic justice and economic opportunities yielded fertile ground into which the Taliban planted the seeds of resistance. Worse still than the disappointing nondelivery of goods were the predations of the warlords, who gained political sway, entrenched themselves economically, and built up military clout in their corners of Afghanistan, which they often ruled as corrupt autocrats.

It was a dynamic we'd exacerbated. For years, seeking to maintain a light footprint in the country, the NATO approach had largely been to remain in Kabul and use local power brokers—too often the corrupt and despised warlords—whom we paid handsomely. An effort to extend a greater NATO presence into the provinces had begun in 2004, creating regional commands in the north, west, south, east, and in Kabul, but a lack of both Afghan and ISAF forces limited their ability to influence events on the ground. As the Taliban made inroads, sometimes without firing a shot, they sought to compete with the Afghan state. Particularly appealing to many Afghans were the Taliban's rudimentary but swift courts. In 2005, they had "shadow governors" who sought to institute a parallel government to compete with the Afghan government in eleven of the country's thirty-four provinces. Now, three years later, they were established in thirty-one provinces.

In May 2008, shortly before leaving TF 714, I'd spent an afternoon with ISAF commander Dan McNeill, my old boss and mentor. In a series of briefings and discussions, Dave Rodriguez, then commanding the 82nd Airborne Division in eastern Afghanistan, Dan, other key leaders, and I had reviewed the war. As always, indicators were mixed and often contradictory, but both empirical data and the anecdotal observations of my strike forces convinced Rod and me that trends were negative. More Americans—and more Afghan civilians—were dying each year. The insurgency was laying bigger IEDs, and more of them—four times as many as they had implanted in 2005.

Now, in September 2008, it looked even worse. So I was not surprised when General Dave McKiernan, who had led ground forces in the 2003 invasion of Iraq and replaced Dan McNeill at ISAF in June, requested additional forces in order to reverse Taliban gains in southern Afghanistan and improve security in advance of the Afghanistan's upcoming 2009 presidential elections. Improving security would be essential to achieving durable improvements in governance and development.

Also in September, after several years largely fixated on the crisis in Iraq, President Bush launched what would become the first in a new round of assessments on Afghanistan and Pakistan, conducted by Central Command, the Joint Staff, and the National Security Council in order to align current policy with on-the-ground reality. The reviews were each fairly comprehensive but ultimately identified no silver-bullet solutions to seemingly intractable problems. The obvious options—do more, do less, or do the same—were unappealing.

General McKiernan's request for forces arrived at an inconvenient time. The ongoing White House assessment, and the resource limitations of the military services stretched thin by expanding requirements in Iraq and Afghanistan, made a quick decision difficult and unlikely. So too did a natural reluctance to make major adjustments in advance of the U.S. elections in November. Thus, a decision on whether to send more forces into what was soon to be America's longest war would be awaiting the new president.

All of these factors intersected with the emergence of a serious financial crisis that would compete with issues like Afghanistan, and even Al Qaeda, for America's attention and resources.

The election of Barack Obama on Tuesday, November 4, 2008, promised new energy. Like many Americans, I welcomed his freshness and call for bipartisan action that came amid all the challenges buffeting our nation.

Within the Joint Staff, we had already done preliminary work to prepare for a transition that would take place in January 2009 regardless of the election outcome. Chairman Mullen created a cell within the staff whose sole purpose was to bring about the most seamless transition possible. We were at war, and the chairman stressed the importance of no hiccups. That task was greatly simplified when, in December 2008, President-elect Obama asked Secretary Gates, a Bush appointee I found exceptionally effective, to remain in his position. From a practical standpoint, that decision significantly reduced near-term personnel turnover in the Pentagon, easing transition. I also read it as the signal of his intent to operate in a bipartisan fashion.

On January 20, 2009, inauguration day, I went to work to be in place in case some kind of incident arose requiring our response. To reduce traffic in D.C., we'd directed most of the Pentagon staff to take a day off, so the halls were uncharacteristically deserted. Earlier that day I'd bundled Annie into one of my large quilted army jackets so she could walk from Fort McNair to join the huge crowd on the Mall for the inauguration without freezing. Meanwhile I watched the proceedings from my office. That evening, she animatedly described to me the sense of excitement she felt radiating through the crowd.

Having read about previous presidential transitions, I anticipated an initial period in which decisions on complex issues would naturally be delayed. Staffs need time to conduct due diligence on issues before recommending long-term projects or commitments. But in 2009, with the development of events and the approaching Afghan elections, President Obama's new administration quickly found itself faced with important decisions.

The immediate driver was General McKiernan's request for new forces, roughly thirty thousand troops, which had been on hold since he'd submitted the request in late summer. A key part of the rationale for additional forces was the desire to halt, and then reverse, Taliban momentum in the south, hopefully in advance of the August elections. That conclusion was logical, but it also created an unwelcome dynamic. In the eighth year of the war in Afghanistan, a new president found himself facing a time-sensitive decision. It reminded me of President Kennedy's experience with the Bay of Pigs.

The next ten months saw the emergence of an unfortunate deficit of trust between the White House and the Department of Defense, largely arising from the decision-making process on Afghanistan. To me it appeared unintentional on both sides. But over time, the effects were costly.

The first sign of mistrust arose around the initial decision on General McKiernan's troop request. Instead of approving the entire request of thirty thousand troops, in February, the president announced that seventeen thousand forces would be deployed, and any decisions on further deployments would depend on further analysis. This partial decision was logical. Put in perspective, after less than a month in office, and in a single decision, President Obama had increased U.S. forces in Afghanistan by 50 percent.

But the situation in Afghanistan pressed relentlessly, and the Department of Defense quickly asked for additional parts of Dave McKiernan's original request. The military felt a sense of urgency, seeing little remaining time if any forces approved were to reach Afghanistan in time to improve security in advance of the elections. More important, confusion arose almost immediately between the White House and Department of Defense over the exact numbers involved, and the specific makeup of the forces. Not long after President Obama approved sending the seventeen thousand troops, the military reported back that an additional four thousand troops were needed. From a White House perspective it surely appeared as though the Department of Defense hadn't done enough detailed staff work or, worse, that the military was playing games with the numbers.

In truth, suddenly cutting a chunk out of a larger force package was complex business. Ensuring that the reduced force has all the necessary capabilities, yet stays within a specified number, is more difficult than it would appear. Brigades are not self-sustaining units: They require "enablers," additional units that provide aviation, logistics, intelligence, and medical support. These enablers are like overhead in a business—they are not needed in direct proportion to the number of brigades whom they deploy to support. Yet to those unfamiliar with the arcane system and often complicated math, it would seem like a basic, fair request to ask the military to tell exactly how many soldiers it was deploying, and what each of them would do. As I confided in Charlie Flynn that spring, "This is, after all, our *profession*—they have a right to be upset."

On the morning of Friday, March 27, 2009, President Obama, flanked by his national security team, took to a podium inside the Eisenhower Executive Office Building. His morning address followed another intensive White House assessment of Afghanistan, this time led by Bruce Riedel. Its conclusions formed the basis of a "comprehensive, new strategy for Afghanistan and Pakistan," which the president outlined that morning: The United States' goal in fighting the war in Afghanistan was to "disrupt, dismantle, and defeat Al Qaeda and its safe havens in Pakistan, and to prevent their return to Pakistan and Afghanistan." To do so, the United States would pursue the terrorists directly, but it would further require "executing and resourcing an integrated civilian-military counterinsurgency strategy in Afghanistan." The counterinsurgency's focus would be to secure the most contested terrain in Afghanistan—in the east and south—while mentoring the Afghan army and police so they could "take the lead" and, in time, fight the insurgency without Americans by their side.

Noting the "situation is increasingly perilous," President Obama announced the deployment of four thousand American troops to train Afghan soldiers and policemen—the troops the military had most recently re-quested.

Although President Obama did not say so in the speech, in the Pentagon we understood we had strong guidance from the White House to deploy and employ the forces on operations as rapidly as possible. We also under-stood that a decision on the final part of McKiernan's request would be delayed until after the August elections.

Watching from my office in the Pentagon, I thought the speech was pow-erful as the president evoked a strong sense of mission to help Afghanistan craft its future.

> For the Afghan people, a return to Taliban rule would condemn their country to brutal governance, international isolation, a paralyzed economy, and the denial of basic human rights to the Afghan people—especially women and girls. The return in force of Al Qaeda terrorists who would accompany the core Taliban leadership would cast Afghanistan under the shadow of perpetual violence.

I used the words from this speech and the National Security Council's Strategic Implementation Plan for Afghanistan to craft my understanding of the mission President Obama was defining for America in Afghanistan. We would prevent the resurgence of Al Qaeda in Afghanistan and, through a counterinsurgency strategy, defeat the Taliban's effort to topple the gov-ernment of Afghanistan and retake the country. Simultaneously, we were to help develop Afghanistan's capabilities so that it could eventually resist the Taliban and protect its own sovereignty. This was the lens through which I testified during my confirmation hearings that June, and then later used to guide my own strategic assessment.

From a White House perspective, with this decision, President Obama had given the military almost all that it had recommended, and had pub-licly announced troop increases twice after the military had to come back with an additional request. Indeed, ultimately President Obama would make difficult decisions that tripled U.S. forces in Afghanistan. And I un-derstood that for an administration that needed to factor domestic support into its strategic calculus, it could seem like taking unnecessary political pain to announce, in the spring of 2009, the deployment of troops who could not physically deploy to Afghanistan before the election that August. I also understood the appeal of not deploying additional forces until the first tranche of troops arrived and their impact could be assessed.

The view from the Pentagon, which I shared, was different. Forces are shaped and deployed in packages to ensure they have every capability re-quired. Also, military leaders, many of whom were students of counter-insurgency, recognized the dangers of incremental escalation, and the historical lesson that "trailing" an insurgency typically condemned coun-terinsurgents to failure. From a military planner's perspective, incremental decisions to provide forces over time are not the same as a clear decision up front that facilitates effective force employment.

From ISAF headquarters in Kabul, there was likely another perspective. A commander analyzes the mission his team has been given; assesses the situation; crafts a strategy to accomplish the mission; and then identifies the resources, including time, needed to achieve the mission. Receiving only part of the forces, or even getting them in a series of decisions, requires a commander to modify his campaign strategy. If that threatens his ability to accomplish the assigned mission, the commander must request that mission be changed.

In the end, the rising mistrust was disappointing. As an experienced soldier, I knew that any perceptions of military incompetence or manipulation were unfounded, and I believed that the intentions of leaders in the White House and across the government were equally focused on what was best for the nation. I saw good people all trying to reach a positive outcome, but approaching the problem from different cultures and perspectives, often speaking with different vocabularies. I hoped time working together would create more trust and a common picture.

During the second week of May 2009, Chairman Mullen asked me to his office, an unconventional space I'd spent many hours in. Instead of the dark polished wood of Pentagon tradition, his office included a half-moon desk of white wood, a set of canted bookshelves evoking a sensation of being in a ship tossed at sea, and a small conference table. As usual, he came from behind his desk, and we sat at the table.

"Stan, the secretary has decided to make a change in Afghanistan," he began. "General McKiernan will be replaced. You will assume command of ISAF. Rod will go, initially as your deputy at ISAF, and then he will take command of a new three star-level headquarters as soon as we can stand it up."

I had conflicting feelings. I was still interested in Afghanistan, and had hoped to replace Dave McKiernan in the summer of 2010 at the end of his standard two-year term. I was also happy to be paired with Rod. At the Joint Staff, I had kept a note in my desk that he had sent a young sergeant to give to me late one evening when we were both in Afghanistan in 2007. It quoted a line from a letter Sherman, in command near Memphis, wrote to Grant on March 10, 1864: "I knew wherever I was that you thought of me, and if I got in a tight place you would come—if alive." Returning to Afghanistan, Rod would command the day-to-day battle, while I focused on strategic-level issues. I would also be a commander again, which I preferred.

But I was uncomfortable with replacing Dave McKiernan—an officer whom I liked and admired, and whose command I felt had suffered from years of relative neglect due to requirements in Iraq. I'd developed a relationship with him over the previous year, trying to shepherd through the Pentagon's bureaucratic maze actions he needed.

I also knew I was taking command of an increasingly difficult and unpopular war. Given all the factors involved, I wasn't sure a successful outcome was achievable, no matter what we did. Nations had dispatched more talented generals than I—Jean de Lattre de Tassigny, Creighton Abrams—to command faltering wars that many thought were past saving. I knew many felt the same about Afghanistan. I'd watched the decision-making process that had transpired in D.C. over the past ten months, and knew it had been awkward at best. At worst, it reflected deep conflicts in U.S. policy toward Afghanistan and Pakistan. After eight years of combat, and a much improved, but still tenuous, situation in Iraq, I saw little enthusiasm among policy makers for what I sensed was going to be needed in Afghanistan. In the weeks before deploying, Rod and I talked nightly about the challenges ahead, often gauging our chances at fifty-fifty, and only then if we made serious changes.

Finally, there was Annie. I'd left her in 2003 for what had turned out to be most of five years. Now, for the past year, she'd been paralleling my job as director of the Joint Staff by helping to bring together the Joint Staff team. She held regular Friday-night dinners at our quarters for small groups of younger staff officers and their wives, functions that competed for any time we had away from work. But being together again was magic. On weekend mornings we'd both run separately and then meet somewhere for coffee. There, for a precious hour or sometimes two we'd talk. As I thought of those moments, I knew they were finite. We were no longer young and I had told myself that to do this job right, I needed, and planned, to commit to commanding ISAF for at least three years.

It was a lot to ask of Annie, but I never had to. There was no cautious conversation in which I broke the news to her, or asked her permission—I didn't need to. I knew that for as long as I wore the uniform, whatever I had to do, Annie would support me.

On May 19, 2009, I was taken to the White House to meet President Obama. We'd met once before when he'd visited the Pentagon during his first week in office, but as DJS I'd been in a collection of other civilian and military leaders, so it was unlikely he remembered the man who would soon command his military effort in Afghanistan.

I'd been in the Oval Office before with President George W. Bush, but the atmosphere in the West Wing in the final and opening months of administrations differed perceptibly. Although it was four months into Obama's term, there was still a feeling of newness to the people, who moved with an air of excited purpose through the hallways. When the president was available, the door opened and Obama walked to the entrance to greet me into the room. The meeting was short, but cordial. The president offered no specific guidance but locked his eyes with mine and thanked me for accepting the responsibility.

Senate confirmation was required and it was easier than it had been coming out of TF 714 the year before, although I again addressed questions surrounding Corporal Tillman's death. I appreciated concerns raised by the Tillman family and others, but after multiple investigations and testimony the year prior, I knew I had already provided full and forthright insights on my role and all I had observed.

On June 2, 2009, I testified in front of the Senate Armed Services Committee. I knew the hearing, while focused on the nominees, was also a venue for the senators to voice their own opinions on the war and the administration's handling of it. In the background was General McKiernan's still outstanding request for ten thousand additional troops. But it also offered a chance for me to offer my own statement of the war as I saw it.

"In Afghanistan, despite impressive progress in many areas since 2001, the situation is serious," I began. "Afghans face a combination of challenges: a resilient Taliban insurgency, increasing levels of violence, lack of governance capacity, persistent corruption, lack of development in key areas, illicit narcotics, and malign influences from other countries. Together, these challenges threaten the future of Afghanistan and regional stability."

To prevent Al Qaeda's reemergence, to maintain stability in a region where Pakistan's fate was linked to Afghanistan's, and to provide Afghans, "battered by thirty years of almost unbroken violence, an opportunity to shape their future," I told the committee, "we must succeed."

I also stressed the importance of NATO protecting the Afghan population. Despite NATO's efforts, the previous year, 2008, had been the deadliest yet for Afghan civilians. The Taliban killed the vast majority of Afghans—largely through their IEDs—but the NATO Coalition was also responsible for a troubling number of those civilian deaths.

Fresh in my mind was an air strike that had occurred a few days before it was announced I'd take over in Afghanistan. On May 4, in Farah, western Afghanistan, insurgents had attacked Afghan troops and the American trainers embedded with them. After air support from F 16s, the gunfight subsided. While Afghan and American ground troops held their ground, waiting for helicopters to evacuate two wounded, a B-1 bomber pursued Taliban who were maneuvering from the fight and dropped 8,500 pounds of bombs on compounds in a small rural village.

The situation was confusing, and the Afghan government claimed nearly 140 Afghan civilians were killed. A later independent investigation estimated roughly 90 civilians died in the incident. In the days afterward, Afghans rioted in the provincial capital after men from the village drove into the city and parked a truck, loaded with fifteen bodies of dead Afghans, in front of the governor's house. Their shouts—"Death to America . . . Death to the government . . ."—caused anguish in Kabul, and serious reflection in the Pentagon.

"Our willingness to operate in ways that minimize casualties or damage, even when doing so makes our task more difficult, is essential to our credibility," I testified. "I cannot overstate my commitment to the importance of this concept."

I would soon find in the villages and office parlors of Afghanistan voices confirming just how critical this point was. What I only partially understood that day in the Senate, and would soon come to grips with, was how monumentally difficult it would be to change how we operated.

From experience, I knew I had to build a team of talented, experienced, and deeply committed professionals. I started at the core. My executive assistant, Charlie Flynn, would go, and he would be the primary architect of the team. As it was on the Joint Staff, his role in Afghanistan would be to understand my intent on a host of issues—everything from tactics to diplomacy—and ensure what I wanted done was translated into action. Never far away, Charlie would be a trusted, forthright adviser. But more than that, he would share with me the emotional highs and lows of command that provided witness to awesome heroism and humanity, as well as spells of frustration in the face of an obstinate, complex war.

It was asking a lot of my enlisted aide Sergeant Major Rudy Valentine, back less than a year from an eighteen-month tour in Afghanistan, to return there with me. But he looked at me quizzically and stated with quiet finality, "I'm going."

When the chairman had first told me I'd be heading to Afghanistan, I'd had the presence of mind to ask him to let me take selected talent from his staff, and immediately identified Charlie Flynn's older brother, Mike, as the first and most important. Mike had helped transform TF 714, and I had a hunch the Afghan war effort's gathering and use of intelligence needed similar retooling. The chairman smiled, having fully expected the request, and agreed on the spot. In the weeks that followed, he let me strip his staff of further talented members. Lesser leaders might have balked. But the chairman's strong, quiet conviction to do what's right, and his instinctive admiral's sense of control for everything around him led him to act swiftly when pressing priorities required it.

The rest of the team came together in the following days and weeks as we reached out to talent we needed. On a phone call, Mike Hall, who'd helped me lead the Ranger regiment a decade before, came out of retirement to be the senior enlisted adviser of ISAF. Charlie meanwhile caught Colonel Kevin Owens, a former Ranger who'd spent a year at the Council on Foreign Relations as I had, while Kevin was having a beer in Germany.

"Count me in," Kevin said. "Where do I go, what job will I do?"

"I have no idea," Charlie said. "Get here, get in-processed, we'll get you a flight to Afghanistan. From there we'll figure it out."

Others simply appeared, most of whom had served in Iraq or Afghanistan before, ready to drop everything and rejoin the fight. A joke circulated that "the band's getting back together," and calls came in offering to put lives on hold, to take on any position we needed filled. There was a sense of purpose that drew steadfast, dedicated women and men.

On June 11, 2009, we boarded a military aircraft that would fly to Brussels and then to Kabul. I had no illusions about the difficulties ahead of us. But as we settled into our seats on board the flight, and I looked around, Lincoln's words—"The better part of one's life consists of his friendships"—came to mind.

Less settling were words that I had heard repeated in the quiet offices of the senators and representatives whom I had visited in the previous weeks. In my confirmation hearing, I had spoken of the need to see progress in eighteen to twenty-four months. Those in Congress had a sharper view of things. In office calls on the Hill before departing for Afghanistan, congressmen had told me repeatedly that I had, at most, a year to show convincing progress. Representative Ike Skelton had set the bar clearly. "All you have to do is win," he said.

Easier said than done. It would require that we restructure, reorient, and reenergize the war coalition, and set it in pursuit of a sound strategy. To do so, the scale of change that we had made over the course of years in TF 714 would have to be done in months. That change would include building, staffing, and mobilizing a three-star command to run the campaign; running a thorough, countrywide strategic assessment to design that campaign; expanding the existing training command to a three-star operation that would be able to recruit, equip, train, and partner with the inchoate Afghan security forces that would continue fighting the insurgency after we left; renovating our detainee operations; shifting how our troops thought about and engaged with the enemy and population; and creating a cell to engage in reconciliation.

I had six months to accomplish these tasks and more. So, one week before we boarded our flight, I'd gathered the initial members of my team in the basement of the Pentagon where we were getting organized, and explained what that meant for us.

"By the end of this calendar year, our organization must demonstrate it is competent and credible," I said, looking at the small group of men and women who would be critical to doing that in six months.

"And in one year," I continued, "we'd better demonstrate progress—something that we said was going to happen, happened—or political support, left and right, will evaporate."

Jeff Eggers, a brilliant SEAL whom the chairman had allowed me to pluck from his strategic advisory group, put the matter of time to me starkly in a dead-on assessment that I read that week: "This campaign may not end for a decade, but it will be decided within a year."

As we flew east toward the war, clocks were ticking.

CHAPTER 17

Understand

June–August 2009

Ⅰn the final minutes of an early-morning flight on June 13, 2009,
rugged, nearly bare mountain peaks gave way to the fertile Sha-
mali Plain, lush green with summer vegetation, stretching north
from Kabul toward the famous Salang Pass. As the aircraft maneuvered to
land, Kabul's lights, flickering yellow in the creeping dawn and hovering
smog, blanketed the sheer slopes of the foothills encircling the capital. The
lights were evidence of the city's dramatic growth since 2001, the population having tripled to over four million inhabitants. And yet I knew the
picturesque sight was deceptive: Many of those lights, as well as the unlit
homes on the higher ridges around the city, belonged to displaced Afghans,
refugees from the war raging in their home provinces.

The Gulfstream's wheels touched the runway of Kabul International
Airport a few moments later. It was my first time back in Afghanistan since
May 2008, when I had made my last visit there as TF 714 commander. As
the aircraft taxied, I reminded myself this experience would be very different, and very difficult.

I pondered our mission. America's aims and expectations had evolved in
the preceding eight years. From President Obama's decisions and speeches
I understood his priority was to defeat Al Qaeda, which was primarily in
Pakistan. In Afghanistan, our mission was to prevent the reemergence of
terrorist safe havens by conducting an integrated civilian-military counterinsurgency strategy focused on the most threatened areas of the country. By

any measure, it was a tall order that implied Afghan sovereignty, protected by Afghans. I would take some time to assess the situation and decide whether, and how, we could accomplish the mission.

Intuitively I knew that the key to success lay in getting people to believe. Afghans of every ethnicity, Pakistani leaders, donor nations, U.N. agencies, the media, and ISAF soldiers, had to believe that we could win, and that we would. So too did our insurgent enemies.

Believing would require changing our strategy, our structure, and our relationship with Afghans. The undertaking would ask much of Coalition nations frustrated by limited progress after eight years of contributions and sacrifice. It would ask the most of Afghans, our most important audience. Afghans, after three decades of war, were smart, discriminating, and wary survivors. They had to be. And after years of unmet expectations, even the most hopeful had become cynics. They were safer that way. Their government would have to show them progress, show them a future that they wanted and believed was possible and worth fighting for. But in the minds of many, both Afghans and others, the onus was on us.

As the aircraft slowed on the tarmac, I reached into my backpack and pulled out the Velcro-backed cloth insignia that my enlisted aide, Sergeant Major Rudy Valentine, had passed to me earlier in the flight. I looked for a few moments at the three-star rank on my chest, which I'd worn since February 2006, four months before we killed Zarqawi. I thought of all the memories of those years, then pulled it off and replaced it with the other strip of cloth bearing four stars.

Charlie and Mike Flynn were both sitting across from me in the aircraft and chuckled at the lack of formality. I'd promoted Charlie three different times during his career, the last time to colonel. I'd promoted Mike twice, most recently to major general. Each occasion had featured their big Irish family, a ceremony, and then a party. This promotion was different. Although I wished Annie and my father could have been there, the four stars simply felt like a new task looming before me. But it was a task I shared with a team of people I trusted, and it was time to get on with it.

After touching down in Kabul, we drove through quiet streets to ISAF headquarters, which lay about a half mile north of the presidential palace and across the street from the American embassy. The walled compound had been the site of a pre-Soviet-era Afghan military club, and the yellow building that now housed ISAF's headquarters offices had been the main facility. The compound also fell within the footprint of the British army's 1842 cantonment site. It was from there that General William Elphinstone's force, encumbered with baggage and thousands of families and other noncombatants, began a tragic winter retreat that left a single British army surgeon alive after a gauntlet of ambushes and freezing temperatures to reach the gates of Jalalabad. Later, I had a replica of a period map of

Kabul, complete with the route tracing Elphinstone's ghastly march, placed under the Plexiglas top of our dining table as a backdrop to warn against hubris.

As I entered the headquarters, briefly greeting the young guard at the entrance, I reminded myself that the command was still dealing with the trauma of the unexpected departure of a respected commander. There would be some resentment and much uncertainty. But I was aided by the fact that Dave McKiernan, to his great credit and my benefit, had epitomized professionalism throughout.

After a quick visit to headquarters, we moved to the prefab modules used for housing. In the small, convenient quarters I unpacked and arranged my gear as I had so many times before in other places, and then returned to the headquarters. As rapidly as possible, I needed to pursue two objectives. First, I had to understand as fully as possible how the war was going, and how prepared our Coalition was to win it. Second, I had to make the changes necessary to make ISAF ready for the challenge ahead.

In one of our conversations before I left D.C., Secretary Gates had given me four specific tasks. He asked me to conduct a strategic assessment of the war and to determine any necessary changes to the mission, strategy, or how our forces were organized. He told me to take sixty days, and specifically asked me to make no resource requests before its completion. Before flying into Kabul, I had visited the NATO headquarters in Brussels en route to Afghanistan. While there, at my recommendation, NATO secretary general Anders Fogh Rasmussen also asked me for an assessment. By combining the two assessments, I hoped to reduce any perceived gaps between my dual-hatted role as a NATO commander and that as commander of all U.S. forces in Afghanistan.

In addition to the strategic assessment, Secretary Gates had directed me to establish the ISAF Joint Command (IJC). As a three-star-level command, the IJC would run the day-to-day operations of the war and directly supervise the five regional commands that divided the country among the capital, north, west, south, and east. Although we'd operated with both three-star-level and four-star-level commands in Iraq beginning in 2004, in Afghanistan, ISAF had been required to operate both at the strategic level in Kabul, and also direct operations of the regional commands. The secretary was convinced we needed an intermediate level of command, and I agreed.

Additionally, he'd instructed me to review how our forces were currently employed to look for ways to reduce requirements or gain efficiencies. The U.S. military was stretched thin between Afghanistan and Iraq. We needed to look for ways to remove unnecessary positions and make every person count.

Finally, the secretary was deeply troubled by Afghan civilian casualties. He asked that I take all possible steps both to reduce them and to improve how we handled those we did cause. Like me, the secretary sensed an urgent need to mitigate Afghan resentment. This would be an ongoing effort.

M y first imperative, then, was to develop the best possible understanding of the war. This was always tricky, particularly for senior leaders in a complex, politically charged environment. My own ignorance, combined with agenda-laden opinions and flawed, incomplete information, challenged me to gather, evaluate, contest, and finally synthesize a mountain of information into a clear sense of reality. I had to be humble about my ability to truly comprehend all that was happening, and why.

Not only did I need a grasp of the war raging beyond Kabul, I also needed to understand the situation within our own walls. The ISAF compound was a crowded hodgepodge of buildings and trailers connected by twisting, casbah-like alleyways. In its way, the headquarters' plot reflected the amalgam of forty-two nations—from Turkey to Sweden, Australia to Bulgaria—that comprised our war-fighting coalition.

Across from the yellow headquarters building, I found a landscaped garden area with picnic tables and gazebos, where ISAF staff relaxed with coffee. It seemed blatantly inappropriate given the austere and dangerous conditions our troops faced only a few miles away. So too did the fourteen bars inside the compound that served alcohol to non-Americans (U.S. forces were forbidden by policy to drink anywhere in Afghanistan or Iraq). The garden gave me a chill of frustration and worry that I'd experienced vicariously before—over the pages of Bernard Fall's *Street Without Joy*, a searing chronicle of the French war in Indochina that I'd read in high school and many times since. While in Siem Reap, Cambodia, in 1953, Fall found himself watching two French officers play tennis and sip drinks at an officers' club mess. When the sun fell and a nearby bugle played "lower the flag," they ignored it. Only a nearby master sergeant—a Cambodian member of the French Marines—snapped to attention and saluted the French flag. "And in one single blinding flash," Fall wrote, "I *knew* that we were going to lose the war." I didn't draw as abrupt a conclusion from the symbolism in the quiet garden. But given my intent to reenergize and refocus our war coalition, the garden and bars were relevant pieces of terrain. It took some time, but in early September I banned alcohol in the ISAF compound. When I visited in November 2011, the coffee garden remained.

As I continued walking along packed gravel paths, the myriad uniforms reminded me anew that this would be a Coalition war. Most common were the familiar grayish green digitized camouflage of the Americans, varying only slightly in hue among the branches. Elsewhere, the sand-colored desert print of the Dutch stood apart from the Norwegians' lime-green highlights. I saw the familiar caramel-streaked fatigues of the Brits and brown-spotted shirts of the Australians, as well as the unfamiliar, dark, lizardlike print of the South Koreans. Ubiquitous were the beige boonie hats and wood-stocked weapons of the Macedonian guards who protected the headquarters. Rarer were the neo-British uniforms of Pakistani liaisons. Conspicuously absent, to my eyes, were any uniforms of our Afghan National Army partners. There were stars on some, epaulets on others, NATO patches on most. But beside some common markings, each uniform represented a different culture, set of marching orders, tour length, work ethic, language, experience level, and historical perspective. At the time, forty-two different nations contributed troops to make up a 61,000-strong ISAF force, of which 28,850 were American. The rest of the United States' 57,600 troops in country that month served under U.S. forces–Afghanistan, as part of Operation Enduring Freedom, which I also commanded.

Forging an ad hoc multinational force into a cohesive team was always challenging, as Dwight Eisenhower had found. In ISAF we not only needed to construct a countrywide battle rhythm of daily processes to synchronize the fight, we also needed to reframe an effort originally intended more for peacekeeping than a coordinated war against an insurgency. For many nations whose domestic constituents had never envisioned a combat role, the deteriorating security situation was a difficult reality. I probably increased concerns by bringing a high-energy team of experienced war fighters into what had been a more deliberate headquarters atmosphere. But I didn't see another option to move as quickly as I felt necessary.

We would have to make these changes while conducting ongoing and planned operations. In this case that included not only ever-more-violent daily combat around Afghanistan but also the campaign just then beginning in southern Afghanistan's Helmand Province. Additionally, we had to prepare for the upcoming presidential elections in late August. These were significant endeavors, larger than anything in Afghanistan since 9/11.

To lessen the gap between what we knew and what we needed to know about the world beyond our walls and windows, Mike Flynn and I determined to establish regular "feeds" that would combine hard, often classified reporting with the perspectives of units, media, and other excellent sources of data. Experience had taught me that commanders too often relied on traditional intelligence reports and focused on metrics such as insurgents killed and levels of violence. But understanding the broader picture required accurately gauging the attitude of the people, levels of economic activity, and, most challenging, indicators of deviations from "normalcy." For many Afghans, normal was a faint memory, long tattered by violence that had come to define the image of a country that had enjoyed nearly fifty years of peace prior to the 1978 coup. A normal life, protected from government predations and insurgent threats, was still the goal for those who remembered, or heard stories of, that time. Understanding how Afghans defined normal, and gauging whether they believed we were moving toward it, could help us engage them effectively and win their support.

Almost immediately, Mike began building a network capable of providing this kind of holistic ground truth. One tactic was to empower talented observers, like a brilliant Marine lieutenant named Matt Pottinger, to circulate through the country and provide unvarnished reports. Matt's background as a journalist, including seven years in China, combined with experience in both Iraq and Afghanistan, made him prototypical of the informal side of Mike's network.

But, as I always had, I wanted to see for myself. I remembered first reading about Afghanistan many years before in a paperback version of James Michener's 1963 novel *Caravans*. The advice offered to a young American girl seemed more prescient every day I spent in Afghanistan: "Ask a lot of questions. Learn the country. Don't be afraid of looking stupid, because one of these days we could be driven into war across this terrain, and you'd be the only American who'd ever seen parts of it. Keep your eyes open." Those words, as well as all my experience in Iraq, told me that to understand, you must first be quiet and listen. In that spirit, I determined to conduct an immediate listening tour around Afghanistan, to hear directly from Afghans and ISAF personnel.

The first few days in Kabul, before I began the listening tour, were a whirlwind. I met with other Western leaders in Kabul, including U.S. ambassador Karl Eikenberry, as well as officials from NATO, the U.N., and ISAF nations. But my most important visit was to President Hamid Karzai on June 14, the day after I arrived in his country.

I'd never met Karzai, but I had watched from afar his evolution as his nation's chief executive. I sensed he had grown frustrated working with foreign governments and organizations that both provided necessary assistance and applied constant pressure. But a strong relationship with him was essential. On the recommendation of one of my aides, I put on my green army service dress uniform, one I typically wore only when forced to do so. I wanted to show respect for Afghanistan's head of state.

This visit, like the countless others that followed, had a similar rhythm and feel. We drove out of ISAF's compound and south on Bibi Mahru Road, a wide old boulevard now truncated by checkpoints and blast wall barriers. We passed the Spanish ambassador's residence, housed in a graceful old mansion, and after another checkpoint entered a traffic circle with an old building, now used by U.S. intelligence and overlooked by a machine-gun position mounted on a guard tower, on our left. It was near this circle in 1996 that the Taliban had coaxed former president Mohammed Najibullah from his refuge in the U.N. headquarters, then tortured and reportedly castrated him before hanging him for public display. The drive was a grim reminder of the perils of Afghan politics.

We drove straight and entered the palace grounds. The palace had the look of an old fort, but its location on low ground meant serious defense was never intended. The stone walls enclosed a compound of inner buildings, a courtyard, and modest but pleasant gardens. As we arrived, workers were repairing outer walls and some of the inner buildings, but the heaviest damage had been fixed a few years before. Even in its heyday, I suspect the complex possessed dignity, but no Versailles–like grandeur.

President Karzai's office sat in one wing of a two-story building within the compound, not far from what had once been the quarters of the king. Security was tight and each visit took me through the President's Protective Service, or PPS. By 2009 the U.S.-trained PPS, similar to the U.S. Secret Service, had become highly professional. Many spoke English and over a year of visits and multiple trips around Afghanistan, I developed a deep respect and fondness for them as they looked out for me with almost obsessive care, often pulling me through crowds or into vehicles.

After a friendly greeting to the PPS detail on duty, and a head nod to the uniformed military guards at the door, I'd walk up a flight of stairs to a large second-floor waiting room where an array of chairs and couches held waiting visitors. Some stood nervously alone as though rehearsing in their minds what they would say to their president; others huddled in small groups in animated conversations as if plotting. Three-piece suits mixed with traditional Afghan outfits from every region of the country. On some days, I ran into noted personalities who were there seeking favors, or chatting quietly with ministers or diplomats I knew. On other days, I'd smile at bearded men in turbans, often in from distant provinces, as we sat in silence, uncomfortably separated by our languages. And I was always amused by the practiced nonchalance some officials and visitors displayed, as though entering the president of Afghanistan's office was nothing remarkable. I tried to remember that it was.

In that room I was reminded of the intricate challenge of ruling Afghanistan. Tajiks and Uzbeks from the north; Hazaras from central Afghanistan; and Pashtuns from almost every corner of the country were represented by tribal or business leaders, many of them powerful khans or landowners, carrying demands, entreaties, and sometimes threats. In addition, government officials, foreign ambassadors, and even an occasional general like me would come to convince, cajole, and pressure. The flow of people placed a nonstop succession of issues and opportunities on the desk of a president with precious few resources to provide and little direct political power. His was a perpetual balancing act to retain support, influence, and legitimacy across a diverse range of constituencies. It was a high-wire act in the stiff wind of Afghan politics.

The president was invariably punctual. An aide would open a door to the waiting room and would ask me to enter. Even if the president's previous meeting had involved heated discussion, Karzai walked to the door and warmly greeted each visitor. I learned to appreciate the physical stamina, the compartmentalization of other frustrations, and the personal self-control required of the man. Karzai was now into his eighth year of a job that was not only exhausting but dangerous. Nearly all his predecessors—the kings and leaders of Afghanistan—had been assassinated or deposed.

The Taliban energetically sought to maintain this track record, and their attempts on President Karzai's life since 2001 were sure reminders of this history.

On that day, after greeting me at the entrance to his office, he led me to a chair and sat in its twin on the other side of a small table. Two sofas accommodated other attendees, normally his chief of staff and security ministers. An aide quickly served tea.

"General McChrystal, you are most welcome to Afghanistan," the president said in fluent English with a slight British accent. I nodded my thanks.

"I know you have been to Afghanistan many times before, and all you did commanding special forces in Iraq is most impressive," he said. "But welcome in your new position." He'd done his homework.

President Karzai was familiar with my background, and was clearly trying to determine what it meant for his country now that I would command. After five American ambassadors, eleven other ISAF commanders, and a number of other interlocutors since 9/11, Karzai found himself unsure how to deal with the United States. Back in 2001 and 2002, following the Taliban's demise, both Afghans and the West viewed Afghanistan as a place of promise. The liberation of Afghanistan was proof positive of both our military might and the justness of our cause against terror—and Karzai was lauded for his part in this project. He was honored with state dinners at the White House, and given ready audience with all the top American officials. But as the military shifted to Iraq, and Afghanistan quickly proved more obdurate than fixable, the spotlight dimmed. Late in his term, President Bush had maintained weekly video teleconferences with Karzai, something President Obama's administration opted not to continue. Now, in the summer of 2009, as Karzai ran for reelection, I sensed he was almost desperate to figure out how to balance maintaining a firm relationship with the United States while reinforcing Afghanistan's sovereignty. I also guessed he was still gauging how influential I was, and how relevant I would be to his job as the nation's leader.

While President Karzai was curious, I was, more than anything, anxious to begin defining our relationship, which I wanted to be based on candor and trust. I don't know if wearing my dress uniform that day made any difference—though Afghan confidants told me it did—but as time passed I learned to place great importance on gestures of respect, large and small, for the Afghan people and their leaders.

The need for effective, productive relationships went far beyond President Karzai. Before deploying, I had sat down with Dave Rodriguez, who began as my deputy before moving over to lead the daily battle as the commander of IJC. We'd mapped out the important Afghans and Pakistanis, and divided responsibilities for establishing relationships with them. We needed functional ties, but we aimed for durable, genuine friendships. In these early weeks, we bonded with them over small dinners in my office, battlefield circulation trips, and regular meetings. Over time those relationships proved invaluable in addressing sensitive or fast-moving situations without being slowed by formality and bureaucracy.

The effort was not without setbacks, some self-inflicted. One day that summer, we'd invited Afghan partners to a meeting at ISAF headquarters. Then–Lieutenant General Sher Mohammad Karimi, the army operations chief, was asked to come. As a young lieutenant, Karimi had won a coveted spot at Britain's Sandhurst military academy, and later had gone to Fort Benning to earn American parachute wings and slither through the chilled mud pit at Ranger School. Following the 1978 coup, that Western training made him suspect, and the communists jailed him. In prison—dead for all his family knew—Karimi lived in the same pair of clothes for eight months, and endured relentless interrogations. Just as prison was about to leave his back crippled, he was released.

Under Dr. Najibullah's rule, Karimi found work in construction, and rejoined the military amid the communist regime's decline. But he refused to join any of the ethnic factions jostling for power in the civil war, and eventually he left the army and his country and lived out Taliban rule in Peshawar, Pakistan. There, while at home translating a newsletter for the U.S. consulate, his wife called him to the television where he watched, again and again, planes colliding with the World Trade Center. Not long after, he returned to Afghanistan. He'd spent the intermittent years working to rebuild an Afghan army few in the international community seemed truly interested in.

Karimi was a critical partner, but when the soft-spoken, sixty-four-year-old general arrived at our compound that summer day, just weeks after I'd directed a closer ISAF partnership with Afghans, our guards turned him away. Though an invariably gracious man and the ultimate team player, he was humiliated, and naturally livid. After years of hearing that we were partners with Afghans, and my recent renewal of that promise, the senior Afghan planner couldn't enter a base in his own country—one that had been an Afghan military club at the beginning of his career. We had habits to break.

My command team and I began our listening tour on June 18, with a visit to Regional Command–Capital, the French-led organization responsible for the security of Kabul and some adjoining areas. Brigadier General Michel Stollsteiner, a fifty-three-year-old veteran of operations in both Africa and the Balkans, commanded the French forces. He'd been in command only twelve days when, on August 18, 2008, an estimated 140 insurgents ambushed a French patrol in the Uzbin Valley, killing ten French soldiers and wounding twenty-one. In that ambush, France suffered its heaviest loss since the 1983 barracks bombing in Beirut. Shock waves had rippled in Paris, but France had maintained her commitment to the Coalition.

While French forces were highly professional, a combination of relatively short six-month tours and limited helicopter mobility constrained their potential effectiveness. In later visits to other ISAF forces, I found that the structure, training, and operational limitations—often called "caveats," like some nations' prohibition from conducting offensive combat operations—prevented them from being as effective as they might have been. Invariably, I sensed the limitations frustrated these forces more than they did me.

Beginning with the listening tour, I made the decision that whenever I left the headquarters to visit forces, or meet with Afghans in Kabul and beyond, I would not wear body armor. I also did not carry a weapon, or wear sunglasses. (I stuck to this for all but a few trips where I accompanied actual combat operations.) As with my decision to go on raids with TF 714, it wasn't bravado. Rather, I quickly concluded it was necessary for me to be successful in my role. For Afghans, as the commander of international troops, I was a symbol. How I appeared in their offices or in their newspapers and newscasts would significantly impact their view of the international presence writ large.

The unadorned way I presented myself was specific to Afghanistan. During the occupation of Japan, General MacArthur drove in a large, black sedan car and conducted himself aloofly. To the Japanese, accustomed to their emperor as demigod, MacArthur's model was comfortably familiar. My situation required the opposite. We needed to appear humble and aware of our status not as occupiers, but as guests. Moreover, we needed to project calm. For that reason, when I met with Afghans, were I to be half-hidden by body armor, a helmet, and a retinue of guards, it would make the whole Coalition look scared, even as we were trying to convince the Afghans that the Taliban were not to be feared.

Showing up as we did in just our cloth uniforms often elicited useful feedback from the forces I led. On one visit to Surobi, east of Kabul in the fall of 2009, Mike Hall, ISAF's senior enlisted adviser, my team, and I visited a French unit. The French officer in charge—who had a great reputation for competence and bravery—looked at me, concerned, as we were preparing to get in the armored personnel carriers to leave his base.

"General, aren't you going to wear your body armor?" he asked.

"I think things will be all right," I said.

"You know, General, it's funny," he responded. "I can come back from this mission and get completely run out of this province—but I'd get back to France and probably be promoted and get a medal. But if I have one soldier killed that didn't have his body armor on, I'd be relieved of command."

The concern wasn't limited to a single nation's forces. German, Italian, British, and American commanders echoed the French officer's lament.

Also beginning with the listening tour, and for the duration of my command, I tried to travel as lightly as I could, typically with an aide or two; Charlie Flynn, my executive officer; and Shawn Lowery, my security detail. I knew it would be difficult for me to get an unadorned, fully authentic experience at the ground level. But as much as possible, I wanted to avoid

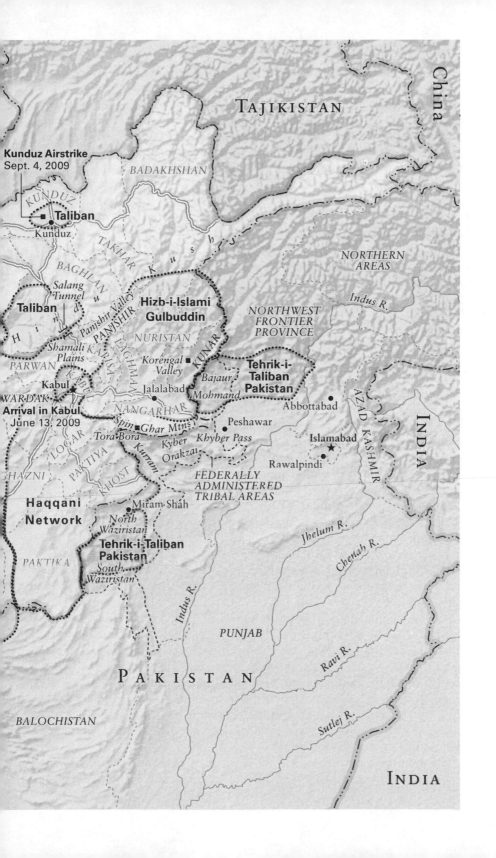

anything Potemkinesque. We sought to simply slide into units' normal routines. Even so, I knew they could easily tell me what they thought the commander wanted to hear, so Rod and Mike Hall often followed in my wake. So too did the civilian and military members of a new group I set up—the Counterinsurgency and Advisory and Assistance Team—who dispersed throughout the country. These experienced veterans spread best practices and provided me direct feedback on whether my guidance was being followed, and whether it was working.

On the second day of the listening tour, June 19, we visited eastern Afghanistan. We stopped off first at Bagram Airfield, north of Kabul, where I'd spent so much time between 2002 and 2008. What had been a mine-strewn former Russian base in May 2002 was now a bustling array of aircraft, buildings, and seemingly continuous construction. It served as the headquarters for Regional Command–East. Rare in this Coalition war, the RC-East headquarters was not a hybrid staff of many nations. Rather, it had the advantage of being formed around the headquarters of the 82nd Airborne Division, a cohesive team. My longtime comrade and friend Major General Mike Scaparrotti was commanding.

RC-East's area of operations was enormous and difficult. It encompassed the mountainous provinces of Nuristan, Kunar, (where TF 714 had conducted Winter Strike in 2003), Nangarhar and the Khyber Pass, and the Khost "bowl" that looked across the border into Pakistan's northern Waziristan region. Remote outposts sat perched on hilltops while patrols traversed steep, winding valleys.

In addition to its unique terrain, RC-East had the Haqqanis. Formed around their patriarch, former mujahideen commander Jalaluddin Haqqani, yet supervised by sons Siraj and Badruddin, the Haqqani network boasted between four and twelve thousand fighters. They operated out of the Pakistan frontier town of Miram Shah, where T. E. Lawrence had done Royal Air Force service in the late 1920s. Aligned with both the Taliban and Al Qaeda, the Haqqanis waged a semi-independent, vicious campaign against the Afghan government and ISAF to control a large chunk of southeastern Afghanistan.

After staying the night in Bagram, on June 20, we visited Khost and the 4th Brigade Combat Team of the 25th Infantry Division, commanded by Colonel Mike Howard. Mike, now in his forties, retained the wiry frame, red hair, freckles, and penchant for startling frankness that he had when commanding B Company under me in 2nd Ranger Battalion, thirteen years earlier. Mike had commanded two different battalions in combat in Afghanistan. That day, both he and his command sergeant major, Dennis Zavodsky, expressed frustration with the difficulty of delivering development aid to a skeptical population.

"The number one complaint from Afghans is that the Afghan government doesn't deliver on promises," Mike stressed, as Zavodsky nodded.

It was a predictably sobering message. The countless challenges posed by the Taliban insurgency and Pakistan's apparent complicity had to be addressed. But many of Afghanistan's problems and solutions lay on her own doorstep.

My visit to RC-East confirmed the difficult environment in which they operated, and the threats, like the Haqqani network, they faced. The east's proximity to Kabul and the Haqqani's penchant for jarringly spectacular attacks made the decision to focus arriving forces in southern Afghanistan a difficult one. But in addition to the need to increase security in the Helmand River valley and around the strategic city of Kanadahar, I judged RC-East, and in particular Mike Scaparrotti, to be capable of operating effectively until additional forces were available.

On Sunday, June 21, my ninth day in country, Karl Eikenberry and I chaired a civilian-military coordination meeting, one of the regular engagements designed to maintain the teamwork essential to any counterinsurgency campaign. In a private discussion we also reviewed the forthcoming strategic assessment I'd been asked to conduct. In retrospect, it would have been valuable if the U.S. embassy had also been directed to conduct a parallel analysis. Although we coordinated our review with the embassy staff, the failure to clearly identify and bring to the fore any differing assessments proved to be a problem during the White House's subsequent decision-making process on our ISAF strategy and troop request. We also discussed the civilian-military plan, designed to provide an outline for coordinated execution of operations, that our staffs were jointly developing.

That afternoon, we headed to RC-North, based in Mazar-e-Sharif, and commanded by German Brigadier General Joerg Vollmer. At the time, his area was the most stable part of Afghanistan, but its nine provinces and population of almost seven million was not the quiet domain of the former Northern Alliance that it once had been. Named the United Front by its founders, it was pejoratively labeled the Northern Alliance by its opponents to create a divide between the Pashtuns in the south and the ethnic Tajiks and Uzbeks in the north. In truth, RC-North included a broad ethnic mix, including numerous Pashtun enclaves established in the nineteenth century by Pashtun Afghan kings.

Coalition forces in RC-North were not routinely attacked, but they were stretched thin and unable to adequately secure threatened areas from Taliban infiltration. Such infiltration had by then begun in earnest, particularly in the province of Kunduz. Sitting astride Afghanistan's critical line of communication to the north, which included the vulnerable Salang Tunnel near Kabul, an unsafe Kunduz felt like someone choking the nation's windpipe. I quickly sensed the need to expand and strengthen our ability to secure key areas in the north.

Our trip to the north included a meeting, on June 22, with Balkh Province's governor, the Tajik former high school teacher turned mujahideen commander, Atta Mohammad Nur. This was the first of the contentious meetings I encountered, as Governor Atta, in his "welcome" speech to a room of about forty local leaders and my command team, pointedly complained about Western leaders classifying him as a warlord.

"We and the people of Balkh Province have removed narcotics from our province but no one praised us, supported us or lent us a hand," he complained. "Meanwhile, we are stepping up efforts to prevent the trafficking of narcotics throughout Balkh Province every year."

As Atta continued his speech, my translator whispered in my ear. "He's not happy . . . He's saying Western officials unfairly criticize him, even though he's doing the right things for his province and Afghanistan." I clenched my teeth to avoid smiling, amused by Atta's posturing to a new commander.

Atta's on-again, off-again support for President Karzai became a constant source of intelligence reporting and I viewed it as one barometer of Northern Alliance thinking. It also highlighted the domestic political maneuvering President Karzai needed to execute in order to build and maintain often fragile coalitions of support.

We'd traveled to and from Atta's provincial center in a ground convoy. Experiencing how an ISAF unit drove in populated areas of Afghanistan disappointed me. Even in a peaceful city like Mazar-e-Sharif, our units drove in an aggressive way they believed was essential to protect against car bomb attacks. But in reality, by forcing Afghan drivers off the road and pointing weapons at an Afghan family, we endangered and insulted the population whose support we needed. It was another practice we needed to fix.

That week, on Tuesday, June 23, I suspended our listening tour for a day for a visit by retired general Jim Jones, President Obama's national security adviser, accompanied by reporter Bob Woodward of the *Washington Post*. In a morning meeting in an ISAF conference room, with Woodward present, I was surprised when the national security adviser said that the administration would not consider further American forces until the full effects of the currently arriving units could be evaluated. Because the last units approved thus far were due to arrive in September, I judged it would be the end of 2009 before we could realistically assess their effect. I was working on what I thought was different guidance from Secretary Gates, to conduct a detailed assessment and an analysis of required resources, which I would submit in the middle of August.

In retrospect, I should not have been surprised. President Obama had voiced strong support for the effort in Afghanistan during his campaign, pledging to add two brigades, which he did. But since the inauguration, despite the partial approval of existing troop requests, and a thorough strategy review of the war culminating in the White House's spring announcement prescribing a better resourced, better coordinated counterinsurgency campaign, the administration had signaled that the U.S.

commitment needed careful assessment. They felt we needed to recalibrate the strategy and objectives. I didn't disagree with that. In fact as I deployed to Afghanistan my gut feeling had been that we needed a new approach, not additional forces. But this early in assessing the situation, before I could draw fully informed conclusions, the delayed time line National Security Adviser Jones articulated worried me.

The final leg of our listening tour took us to RC-West, commanded by an Italian paratrooper, Brigadier General Rosario Castellano. RC-West had traditionally been more secure than either the south or east, but had also been the site of the two most significant civilian casualty incidents within the past year. I was concerned about the relatively weak force levels there, the limited interaction they had with Afghan security forces, and the rise of some seemingly intractable resistance in several areas.

In stops across Afghanistan, over countless cups of steaming golden tea, I met with Afghan political leaders, tribal elders, soldiers, and shopkeepers. All were polite, but I sensed a wearied frustration from people whose inflated expectations in the fall of 2001 for political stability and economic progress had been largely unmet. In 2003, "How can we help?" or "What do you need?" still elicited detailed, hopeful answers. By 2009, the questions evoked polite nods but little excitement. They'd been asked too many times with little to show for it. Governance was weak, security was deteriorating, and our apparent ineffectiveness had disappointed once optimistic Afghans.

To be sure, Afghans were the architects and engineers of many of their problems, which they would reluctantly admit. But too often, ISAF and our civilian counterparts seemed disconnected from their lives, unwilling or unable to bridge the gap. To convince the population that we could, and would, win, we needed to engage dramatically more Afghans at every level.

I had hopes for a program first hatched by Scott Miller, Mike Flynn, and me in my office at the Pentagon earlier that spring. Watching from afar, I'd grown frustrated by what I thought was an unserious national approach to the war. As one solution to that, we decided to field a cadre of several hundred American military officers and NCOs—"Afghan Hands," after the "China Hands" of the 1930s and 1940s—who would be trained in the languages, history, and cultures of Afghanistan and Pakistan, and then employed there over a five-year period. On rotations in country and back in the United States, their focus would be the same region or topic. We would send them back to the same districts each time, so that they would maintain relationships with the Afghans with whom they worked. Despite enthusiastic support from Chairman Mullen, the military services' reluctance to contribute personnel slowed the program. It would be early 2010 before the first Afghan Hands arrived and quickly dispersed throughout the country.

The listening tour ended on June 26. That night, the final leg home was in a Chinook helicopter. Earlier that day I'd asked Charlie Flynn to write down his impressions from the last eight days of moving around Afghanistan. As we sat next to each other, leaning close to talk over the rumble of the aircraft engines, Charlie said he'd already recorded his initial impressions. I told him I'd look at them tomorrow, but then told him what was weighing most heavily on my mind.

"It seems like we're fighting five very different wars, not one coherent plan."

He smiled. Pointing with the small headlamp he wore so he could take notes on night flights, Charlie opened his notebook to show me the first point on the page. It matched my concern exactly: "5 Regional Wars—Not One Fight."

As we flew on in darkness I thought how it was even more complex than that. While ISAF was fighting five distinct, uncoordinated campaigns we were actually facing something more like twenty-five wars, and scores of insurgencies. The monolithic image of the Taliban personified by the ominous image of one-eyed Mullah Omar was in fact a loosely connected collection of local insurgencies that were energized by local grievances and power struggles. The largely local nature of the insurgency gave it certain advantages, but also revealed its inherent weaknesses and, I thought, fundamental limitations.

During the Taliban's first big coordinated offensives in 2006 and 2007, the Taliban's senior leadership had dispatched trusted commanders—like the one-legged Dadullah—and delegated the campaign to them. These commanders had managed dispersed but responsive units. But when many of these commanders died or defected, the tethers between the Quetta-based headquarters and the field units grew weaker. Since 2007, the movement had become less hierarchical, less centrally controlled.

As that trend had continued, by the summer of 2009 the Taliban was a heavily local phenomenon. While the senior leadership desired to overthrow the Karzai regime and institute a Pashtun-dominated Sunni theocracy, few Afghans who called themselves Taliban did so explicitly to bring this about. Affinity for the movement's ideology and vision for the country were not the primary motivations, though a sense of Islamic duty was inextricable. Rather, the Quetta-based leadership attempted to swell its ranks by leveraging Afghans' fear of recent experience—with bad government, warlords, foreigners, and, to some degree, modernity itself. In other cases, young men went to fight, and hopefully command, because doing so offered a chance at prestige in the world they knew, a world that offered little else. Others sought a place in the movement to carve out local political power, so that what on the surface appeared like antigovernment insurgent violence was in fact score settling, or clashes over criminal enterprises.

The Afghans' vocabulary grew to account for the diverse taxonomy of groups we lumped together as "the Taliban": "fighting Taliban" differentiated active insurgents from simply the pious but quiescent madrassa students; "clean Taliban" were good mannered, while "thief Taliban" used the insurgency as a guise to engorge themselves; "local Taliban" typically had a more sympathetic reception than those from even a province away, who were eyed warily because of their capacity to run roughshod; of least concern were the "Taliban sitting at home," older members of the former regime, all but retired.

In Iraq, Zarqawi did not care whether fighters underneath him identified themselves as "Al Qaeda" so long as their sabotage and bombing fell within his strategic framework. Not so for the Taliban leadership. They needed fighters and supporters alike to think of themselves as Taliban, and be recognized as such. It was crucial to the Taliban's desired—but phony—image as a cohesive, national liberation movement on the march. Meanwhile, the perception of a unified Taliban movement benefited local fighters, who looked more legitimate and fearsome to foes and recruits. The connection between the local units and top-level leadership was the *mahaz*, or "front," which ranged in size from as few as twenty fighters to as many as a thousand. To have the prestige of commanding a smaller *mahaz*, a young man had to win approval from the Quetta-based leadership, who in turn provided him arms and mentorship. By co-opting these *mahaz*, the leadership made its disparate movements look cohesive, and helped them, through a chorus of spokesmen they fielded throughout the theater, claim quick credit for any and all violence that suited their interest. Even so, the links between the two levels often remained tenuous—in some areas, senior leadership was unable to fire the local commanders.

The local nature of the insurgency meant that "the Taliban" was not a fungible group that the leadership could reposition at whim. While there were some particularly vicious roving bands of more fanatical militants who gained notoriety acting as shock troops, most locally recruited insurgents would not stray far from the property and family and tribe whose safety and dignity were often a reason for taking up arms. Outbreaks of insurgency we were seeing in the north and west that summer were not the result of big tranches of southern Pashtun fighters infiltrating the north, but rather concerted efforts to turn local resentment into violence. While some argued that pursuing the Taliban in one area of the country would simply displace them to another—like squeezing a balloon at one end only to see the other side expand—our view of the insurgency argued against this happening to any significant degree. Insurgent field leaders were relatively mobile, and they could focus on inflaming a new area, but, as a sign of their weakness, they could not relocate whole armies of fighters.

This prevented the Taliban's senior leadership from orchestrating a national strategy with any of the sophistication we saw in Iraq. The Taliban were seeking to build a national political infrastructure, with varying degrees of success. But their strategy was, more than anything, opportunistic, even when seeking to choke off Kandahar or control swaths of Helmand. The insurgency grew where it could grow, where the government was weakest or worst. Their reliance on local grievances, not nationalism or ideology, was a glaring liability. The introduction of minimally decent and competent governance could cause the local resistance to wilt.

But their composition also, I knew, made for a daunting tactical, intelligence, and development challenge. To our frustration and bewilderment, security and popular sentiment could often be night-and-day on an opposite ridgeline, between towns, or across far more subtle geographic features: In one of the most violent areas in the corridor connecting Helmand and Kandahar, one of my civilian advisers reported that the few lanes of a highway formed the dividing line between relative stability in the arid stretch to its north and a vicious fight among pomegranate orchards and grape vineyards to the south. To prevail, we needed to create a counterinsurgency effort that was synchronized across Afghanistan but agile enough to adapt to the war we faced in each village and valley.

Not long into the summer, during a morning update—at ISAF, I had instituted a forum similar to the O&I meeting we'd run in TF 714—a briefer from one of the regional commands noted that there had been a civilian casualty recently in his area of operations. This death came on the heels of other incidents in the days prior, in which one and two civilians had died. I asked the circumstances of this latest event, which was forty-eight hours earlier, and the briefer admitted he had no details. Neither did my staff there in ISAF headquarters. The steady trickle of dead Afghans appeared to be an afterthought.

I slammed the table.

"What is it that we don't understand? We're going to lose this fucking war if we don't stop killing civilians," I said, looking at the staff and at the commanders on the screen. It was uncharacteristic for me to swear during the morning update. I took a second, and began again. "I apologize for losing my temper, but we *cannot* continue to do this."

This was a conclusion that the listening tour had strongly reinforced. I'd watched as a focus on the enemy in Afghanistan had made little dent in the insurgency's strength over the past eight years and, conversely, had served to antagonize Afghans. Not only was Afghans' allegiance critical, but I did not think we would defeat the Taliban solely by depleting their ranks. We would win by making them irrelevant by limiting their ability to influence the lives of Afghans, positively or negatively. We needed to choke off their access—physical, psychological, economic—to the population.

In the year before my arrival General McKiernan had pursued a counterinsurgency approach. But he had faced a shortage of Afghan and ISAF manpower, as well as limited infrastructure, like roads, that would have enabled effective operations. Additionally, NATO had no doctrine for counterinsurgency, and ISAF forces on the ground had offered a fair amount of institutional resistance to adopting the tactics and interaction with Afghans essential to an effective counterinsurgency campaign.

As Secretary Gates had stressed, protecting the Afghan population was paramount to the counterinsurgency we had to wage. This included reducing Coalition-caused civilian casualties. The year before I had arrived at ISAF, I'd watched from afar as two high-profile incidents had raised tensions between Afghans and the international mission. On August 22, 2008, a Coalition air strike near the village of Azizabad in Herat Province killed scores of noncombatants. More recently, following the May 4, 2009, air strike in Farah Province that set off riots, I'd sat with Chairman Mullen to listen to my old comrade Brigadier General T.T., who had been assigned to investigate. His chillingly detailed analysis of a series of mistakes and Byzantine command structure that had led to tragedy had stayed with me. One of my early moves after arriving to ISAF was to clean up the lines of command.

The listening tour confirmed my conclusion that Afghans' perception of our airpower had largely formed during the opening salvo of the war, in the fall of 2001, when the precision of American bombs had awed them. Lore grew that our bombers, tens of thousands of feet up in the sky, could read the label of a cigarette pack on a car dashboard. This perception of our exacting omnipotence made it difficult for Afghans to believe that when we killed civilians accidentally, we did so truly unintentionally. "We didn't mean to" often elicited squinted, skeptical looks from Afghans. So, over time, as Coalition air strikes continued to hit misidentified targets like wedding celebrations, Afghan tolerance grew brittle. These stray bombs reminded some Afghans of the Soviets' periodic, murderous carpet bombing against the mujahideen and innocent civilians. President Karzai had been complaining for years about civilian casualties, but over time many in the international community viewed his protests as political rhetoric for domestic consumption. Though doubtlessly motivated in part by politics, Karzai apparently believed that his responsibility to represent his citizens required that he provide a loud voice in their protection. While never completely ignored, his protests to Coalition forces appeared largely discounted. I decided it was important to reverse that impression.

The instinctive way we reacted to alleged incidents made it worse. Americans frequently responded defensively to charges of misguided strikes. Afghans viewed our skepticism about the validity of their claims as obfuscation, even if we followed our comments with thorough investigations. They thought our hesitation to quickly, publicly apologize for Afghan deaths was an indicator of callousness. Americans cared, of course, but perceptions mattered. Even when an apology was forthcoming, Afghans would rarely, if ever, see any change in our behavior. "Afghans hear with their eyes, not just with their ears," a group of elders had reminded members of my staff on the listening tour.

I prioritized ensuring ISAF made careful use of its awesome firepower. But from the start I knew doing so would be sensitive. Resistance would come from both the take-the-gloves-off proponents of more aggressive counter-guerrilla operations, but also from thoughtful commanders and units whose experiences in Iraq were seared into their psyche.

I would ask soldiers and Marines to demonstrate what we soon termed "courageous restraint"—forgoing fires, particularly artillery and air strikes, when civilian casualties were likely—even if it meant a firefight dragged on longer, or a group of insurgents was allowed to flee only to ambush ISAF forces another day. I was emphatic that fires could and should be used if the survival of our forces was directly threatened, but in cases where the only purpose was to kill insurgents, the protection of civilian lives and property took precedence. To communicate as clearly as I could, I personally wrote the key parts of a tactical directive that was designed to explain my intent in straightforward, nonlawyerly language. I wrote it not to prescribe tactical decisions for sergeants and junior officers closest to the fight, but to help them understand the underlying logic of the approach I was asking them to employ.

"I expect leaders at all levels to scrutinize and limit the use of force like close air support (CAS) against residential compounds," I wrote. "I cannot prescribe the appropriate use of force for every condition that a complex battlefield will produce, so I expect our force to internalize and operate in accordance with my intent." They were points I reinforced almost daily in commandwide VTCs.

More important, the directive did not change any part of the soldiers' rules of engagement—the military's legal code that governs how and when soldiers can use force when confronted by the enemy. I left untouched the rules by which soldiers could defend themselves. "This directive does not prevent commanders," I wrote, "from protecting the lives of their men and women as a matter of self-defense where it is determined no other options . . . are available to effectively counter the threat." I wanted them to think creatively about how they could avoid getting stuck in a situation where, to defend themselves, they needed airpower. But I never took that right away from them.

Many of the lower-level battalion and brigade commanders had reached these conclusions long before I issued my tactical directive. They had been prudently restricting their use of firepower. Some made it a de facto policy to drop munitions on compounds in only the most dire situations.

But I also knew that the military coalition was an immense organization, and that there was a constant risk of misunderstanding the directive at the lowest levels, where the fight and these decisions were the most difficult. This was especially true since many lieutenants and sergeants never directly read the directives that top-level commanders, like me, put out; they often received the guidance secondhand. One young Marine, for example, told me that as a lieutenant in Iraq, he learned of new tactical guidance or directives through TV news reports about them. Thus, I used every opportunity, and leveraged the leadership and credibility of combat leaders like Dave Rodriguez and Mike Hall, to articulate the policy. Charlie Flynn, my exec, who quickly grasped the importance, also spread the gospel by answering e-mails from battalion and brigade commanders, many whom he knew, or by talking with them frankly, commander-to-commander, when we visited outposts and regional headquarters.

My decision to limit fires wasn't primarily a moral one, although a single visit with a child, staring blankly at where her legs had been, or a widowed spouse, mouth twisted in grief, was enough to convince many people that it was the right thing to do. Rather, mine was a calculation that we could not succeed in the mission I thought President Obama had outlined for Afghanistan without the support of the people. That support was based upon the premise that we were there to protect them—and to support the Afghan government. For many Afghans, we were in their country because their government had asked us to be. Thus, every time we killed or maimed civilians, it not only made us more unwelcome but it corroded the government's reputation. We needed to curate and grow that reputation in order to make it a bulwark against the insurgency.

Additionally, as I sought to make our force more mindful of civilian casualties, I also wanted to dissuade a myopic focus on insurgent deaths. Thus, shortly after taking over, I directed that all of the units cease reporting, in their public affairs releases, tolls of insurgents killed. While these units were not using insurgent deaths as an official metric, I knew that forces performed according to what was measured and scrutinized. So I wanted to take away any incentives that might drive commanders and their men to see killing insurgents as the primary goal.

We were, of course, not alone in trying to fight smarter and learn from the mistakes of the past eight years. So too were our enemies. That summer, the Taliban's senior leadership—the *rahbari*, or Quetta, *shura*—released an updated version of the *layha*, the rule book that ostensibly governed how its insurgent ranks could conduct themselves. The Taliban had distributed the *layha* internally since 2006. But that summer they revised it, and then leaked it to the media as part of their campaign to counteract our counterinsurgency. The new *layha* aimed to rein in the conduct of insurgents—or at least appear to do so—so as to make the insurgency more acceptable to the Pashtun population.

"Mujahedin," Mullah Omar instructed that summer, "are obliged to adopt Islamic behavior and good conduct with the people and try to win over the hearts of the common Muslims," by which he meant ordinary Afghans. The sixty-seven sections of that summer's *layha* regulated a range of behavior—from smoking cigarettes to cutting off Afghans' noses or lips, both "fiercely" forbidden. They reiterated rules for taking prisoners and managing funds—likely worried that their "brand" would be tarnished if their fighters ran kidnapping rings or other criminal enterprises under the guise of holy resistance. The Taliban in Helmand, however, were allowed to continue financing operations through drug trade.

We took most notice of the provisions that mirrored our own directives: The *layha* advised all fighters to take all precautions not to unnecessarily kill Afghan civilians. Significantly, to this end, the directive appeared like an effort to limit the use of suicide bombing. "A brave son of Islam should not be used for lower and useless targets," it said, "The utmost effort should be made to avoid civilian casualties." The Taliban leadership was reckoning with the mixed legacy of Mullah Dadullah Lang, the one-legged commander whom British special forces killed in 2007. Through his personal sadism and his success integrating suicide bombings into the Taliban's repertoire of tactics, Dadullah had made the insurgency appear more radical and less pious to many Afghans. Suicide bombings were not just scandalous among Afghans, but remained highly controversial among Islamic extremists, clerics, and fighters. (Throughout the entire 1980s, the Afghan mujahideen never used a suicide attack against the Soviets.) The Taliban leadership knew this. And they had taken notice of the blunders made farther afield in Iraq: They knew of the damning criticism of Zarqawi—his sympathizers complained that his default use of suicide bombing, particularly against fellow Sunnis, had turned Iraq into a "crematorium" of young Muslim men—that had undercut his movement.

But the fact remained that in many cases the Taliban's leaders now had only tenuous supervision over their dispersed units and local commanders, who were often obsessed with making short-term gains to the detriment of the strategic contest. Omar's efforts with the *layha* were, thus, mixed—and mostly for show. The Taliban continued to forsake the rules of war on nearly every battlefield in the country. And while the insurgency killed fewer Afghans through suicide blasts the year following the book's release, they started killing more civilians through targeted assassinations.

But they also continued to selectively mitigate their fanaticism in order to win the support of the people, and to avoid looking ridiculous or draconian. The Taliban, for example, soon began working with Karzai's government and the United Nations—whom they branded as slaves and infidels, respectively—to run polio vaccination programs. Mullah Omar's signature appeared at the bottom of a letter that vaccinators carried in order to gain safe passage into Taliban-controlled areas (local commanders had sworn an oath to Omar), and showed to Afghan villagers to persuade them to participate. This ensured that the villagers knew the Taliban had allowed these vaccinators in.

I took satisfaction seeing these developments, not least because it might mean fewer Afghans would suffer and die. The effort to moderate the movement divided the Taliban's pragmatists and hard-liners, presaging a larger schism within the insurgency over whether it could, and should, alter its principles and become a political movement. Moreover, that the enemy leadership felt compelled to respond in kind to our efforts (many of them started by my predecessor) to protect and engage the population affirmed our strategy. They knew what we did: Afghans did not automatically detest the Afghan government and back the Taliban, who enjoyed active support from only a sliver of the population, even in areas like Helmand where they'd made alarming gains. The crucial support of Afghans was not to be taken for granted, by either side.

In our fight with the insurgency, we were making an argument to the people—that we would win, that the future we promised was better, and that we could deliver it. The insurgents made counterproposals. Ours was a kinetic debate, growing more heated that summer.

▼

CHAPTER 18

Design

June–August 2009

On the afternoon of June 26, 2009, I walked to the small theater across from our primary headquarters. By this time, most of the civilian experts we'd gathered to help advise on our strategic assessment had arrived into Afghanistan. They joined members of ISAF whom we had specifically chosen for their intellect and candor. It would be the first of many sessions with the full team.

By that afternoon, I had already begun to rethink the importance of the strategic assessment. When Secretary Gates had first assigned me the task before I deployed, I had viewed it as merely another in a series of assessments, from the previous fall and spring, that would plow the same ground. I expected ours would produce no discernibly different conclusions and merit no greater notice than the others. But as each day passed since my arrival in Kabul, I realized the stakes were rising. The deteriorating situation and my arrival had focused attention on Afghanistan to the point that despite all the previous work done, what we reported would be more prominent and important than I had anticipated.

I thought again about a question National Security Adviser Jim Jones had asked during his visit three days earlier: "Where do we want to be a year from now?" He indicated that was President Obama's question as well. The assessment would help us determine where we could be. It was easy to criticize Afghanistan and our effort, but we had been asked to distill the situation and to prescribe a solution.

The assessment had to be unbiased. Not only were circumstances in

Afghanistan quickly making it more urgent. But after long fights against insurgents in Iraq and Afghanistan, the renewed interest in counterinsurgency seemed to peak that summer. Two years after the surge introduced the concept to many lay Americans, our assessment fell amid an ever more robust and heated intellectual debate among policy makers and the military over counterinsurgency's value and limitations. So as I reviewed the composition of the team, I was happy we'd included a wide range of thinkers. Energetic former Ranger and think-tank fellow Andrew Exum, Iraq assessment veterans Fred and Kim Kagan, and the helpful, ever-skeptical Tony Cordesman were joined by Steve Biddle, a clear-eyed authority, Catherine Dale, Jeremy Shapiro, Terry Kelly, and others. Kevin Owens, who'd come to Afghanistan on a call from Charlie Flynn, not knowing what role he'd take, would orchestrate the effort. It would benefit from the knowledge and passion of Colonel Chris Kolenda, one of the Army's most experienced Afghanistan experts, and the insights of Lieutenant Commander Jeff Eggers.

With the full team assembled, I gave them the same initial guidance. Keen not to pollute the process, I gave no indication what I thought the problem was. Instead, I asked three questions.

"First, tell me: Can we do this mission?"

"Second, if so, how would we do it?"

"Finally, what will it take to do it?"

In this and subsequent discussions, I used a car-mechanic analogy to describe the mindset I wanted us to maintain. We were to avoid becoming emotionally tied to any particular course of action or outcome. As "car mechanics," we would diagnose what was wrong with the car and recommend what actions and resources we would need to fix it. It was up to the car owner to decide whether they wanted the car fixed, whether they wanted only limited repairs, or, indeed, whether the car was worth fixing at all. Our role was to conduct an accurate diagnosis and offer effective fixes.

"Remember," I reminded them, "we don't own the car."

The team then traveled across the country to speak with every regional command, several brigades and battalions, most Afghan ministries, and a variety of government officials and local Afghan elders. What they saw in many places astonished them and matched what I saw on my own circulations. They noted a persistent focus on force protection. In many places, our forces had actually sealed themselves off from the Afghan population, whether on base, while driving, or even on dismounted patrols. Few units appeared to take interaction with the population seriously. Most units had little idea what ordinary Afghans were thinking. Those Afghans' decisions to side with either the government or the Taliban would determine our success, but many distrusted our efforts and those of the government.

"The government robs us, the Taliban beat us, and ISAF bombs us," said one group of elders. "We do not support any side." Partnering with the

Afghan Security Forces was episodic at best. In most places, ISAF and the Afghan National Security Forces operated separately. ISAF units would sometimes ask for a few Afghan National Army soldiers to "put an Afghan face" on a mission.

The assessment team's inputs and my own observations, which had been building since my listening tour, convinced me that more than anything else, Afghanistan was gripped by fear. Lack of faith in their government, concern, bordering on paranoia, over Pakistani-supported Taliban expansion, and an almost primal fear of abandonment by the West: These factors left Afghans angst-ridden about the future. Whatever actions ISAF took would have to be as much about building Afghan confidence as killing Taliban insurgents.

When I'd arrived on June 13, one of the largest operations ISAF had yet conducted was to begin in less than a week. In the pitch of night on June 19, twelve Chinooks, their elongated hulls loaded with 350 troops from the 3rd Battalion, Royal Regiment of Scotland, known as the Black Watch, descended into Babaji—a heavily contested area northwest of Lashkar Gah, the provincial capital of Helmand. The Scots' first steps out of the blacked-out helos and into the caked sandy ground marked the opening stage of a systematic campaign that summer to retake control of Helmand Province.

Their operation to clear Babaji initiated Operation Panchai Palang, or Panther's Claw. It would soon introduce more than three thousand British, Afghan, Estonian, and Danish troops into a series of towns along the Helmand River valley. They aimed to secure and connect key population centers and agricultural areas, many long controlled by the Taliban, with the provincial capital of Lashkar Gah and then Kandahar. In the near term, we hoped expanded security in the Helmand River valley would enable greater participation in the August elections, but we knew at the outset that real progress would be measured in months, if not years. Indeed, the problems we faced had been gestating that long.

The intersection of tribes, corruption, insurgency, poppy, tyranny, and family feuds and loyalties that would make waging counterinsurgency in Helmand so complicated had its most visible roots in the anti-Soviet jihad of the 1980s. Although 92 percent Pashtun, Helmand's tribal structure was a rich tapestry of tribes and subtribes. Competition for power and resources among the Barakzai, Alizai, Noorzai, and Ishaqzai was old and remained, and in some districts twenty or more tribes were represented and sought sway. Since the 1980s, the power of *maliks*, khans, and elders to represent constituents to the government and control land had been largely superseded by the rise of nontraditional strongmen.

One of the strongmen to emerge from that time was Nasim Akhundzada, a mullah from Musa Qalah. A devout, effective man, Nasim rose quickly in one of Helmand's most prominent anti-Soviet insurgent groups. The fighting in Helmand, however, quickly got messy and the factions began fighting one another, not just the Soviets. They pursued criminal, tribal, and family feuds under the guise of jihad. In this grapple, Mullah Nasim showed himself tenacious. He reportedly executed his prisoners—Russians and Afghans alike—buried them, and then sat and ate his meals on the platform he built overtop the soil of their graves.

The anti-Soviet war was good for Nasim's family; his personal ascendance gave the Akhundzadas a prestige they previously lacked. Looking to transform his martial clout into a political and economic franchise, Nasim brought the province an innovation: The expansion of poppy. Though farmers had long grown the bulb-headed crop in the arid, northern tip of Helmand, he succeeded in integrating it down through the agricultural band of the snowmelt-fed Helmand River, where the vast majority of Helmandis live, and into the province's south. He expanded his work under a fatwa he issued in 1981, justifying the seemingly unholy trade of opium by citing the poverty of the river valley farmers. As Soviet troops withdrew in 1989, Nasim contacted the U.S. embassy in Pakistan and offered to shut down the opium trade exchange for two million dollars. He was on his way to doing so when assassinated by a rival faction that stood to lose from the eradication. Nasim left behind the structures of a durable drug cartel, which became the Akhundzada family business.

The withdrawal of the Soviets from Afghanistan in 1989 only exacerbated the fray among insurgents-turned-barons and pettier gangs of criminals. Amid these clashes over land, money, and ideology, the population of Helmand suffered. Most of Helmand's roadways became a checkerboard of roadblocks where militia commanders and local gangs shook down passersby.

When the Taliban arrived in 1994, and dispensed with these warlords and their client gangs, the Akhundzadas put up only brief resistance. Instead, they retreated to Pakistan. It was there the family became close with another exiled Pashtun family—the Karzais.

Across the border in Helmand, the Taliban program took hold with relative ease. Especially in the province's sparser areas where a rural, conservative Islam was the norm, the simple religious dogmatism of the Taliban found a sympathetic audience. But the sharia was strict, and Helmandis lost their right to music, flying kites, and dogfighting. Worse, the Taliban showed themselves unqualified to bring about any substantive economic or infrastructural improvements. Thus began the dilemma of the Helmandis, which persisted in 2009, to be caught between the usurious militarism of warlords and the harsh, incompetent rule of the Taliban.

With the American invasion of Afghanistan in 2001, it was the Taliban's turn to flee across the border to Pakistan. When President Karzai returned to Afghanistan and sought a strong anti-Taliban force to install in Helmand, he turned to the clan with the roots and connections to subdue the province:

the Akhundzadas. At the ready was Nasim's nephew, Sher Mohammad, whom Karzai made the provincial governor in 2001. Worst among the old comrades, the Akhundzadas brought back into power was a man named Abdul Rahman Jan, who became the tyrannical provincial police chief. He ruled a small district called Marjah as his own drug-financed fiefdom, where he and his men stole boys from local families for their sexual pleasure.

From a distance, their rule gave an appearance of stability; up close, the population chafed. While violence in Helmand only simmered after 2001, small groups of Taliban trickled back into the province and mustered networks of aggrieved locals. Abdul Rahman Jan became the frequent posterboy of insurgents' propaganda, and a steady refrain in their stirring sermons.

The situation in Helmand began changing rapidly toward the end of 2005. The British were preparing to deploy a brigade-size task force to the province as part of wider NATO effort to reclaim momentum from the Taliban across the country. Understandably seeking a better governmental partner than Akhundzada after authorities found him with nine metric tons of opium inside the governor's office, the British pressured Karzai to replace him as governor. Such a move would be a family matter: Perhaps to prevent feuding, or to gain a foothold in the other's sphere of influence, Sher Mohammad and President's Karzai's half brother Ahmed Wali Karzai had married two sisters. Karzai relented under British demands, however, and removed Akhundzada in December 2005 by promoting him to parliament, away in Kabul.

Akhundzada's ouster came just months before the Taliban's deliberate 2006 offensive into Helmand, led in full force by Mullah Dadullah Lang in February. In spite of a greater Coalition presence—forces grew with the deployment of British troops in April 2006, and by late 2007 they numbered seven thousand soldiers—the Taliban made serious inroads. The insurgency was soon strong enough that British forces were challenged to move outside of the network of small bases they had established. Many were essentially besieged inside sandbagged outposts the Taliban had surrounded with a "reef" of mines and improvised booby traps that made simply leaving base time-consuming and treacherous. Intentions to establish an "Afghan development zone" around Lashkar Gah and Gereshk were frustrated. Among the last places taken by the insurgency, in August 2008, was Marjah. It was rumored that Abdul Rahman Jan, seeking to discredit the new governor and give cause to bring back his patron Sher Mohammad Akhundzada, had let his district fall to the Taliban.

While the Taliban had grown stronger, their strength throughout the province derived more from the poor character of existing governance than the appeal of their narrative. In the areas they took over, the Taliban eased the population back into their rule, allowing music and dogfighting again, and looking the other way when men went without turbans and a beard.

Dadullah's ranks swelled as he gained local recruits in the districts that fell under his sway. He and the insurgency were able to leverage a natural xenophobia and some religious extremism. But for many the motivation for supporting the insurgency was to resist the Kabul government, whose face in Helmand had been that of the Akhundzada clan. We believed that if we could address the underlying problems of predatory governance and corruption, we could help establish secure zones along the Helmand River valley.

That summer, as we introduced new forces in a widened effort, we did so fully cognizant that ISAF's track record in Helmand was unimpressive. Both conventional and special operations forces had successfully targeted the insurgents. But many operations had inflicted damage on homes and caused civilian casualties, unintentionally undermining our effort. We intended that future operations would be different by including a robust Afghan component, having enough manpower to maintain areas once they were secured, and offering a more effective program of creating governance free of warlords.

The strategy was neither new nor guaranteed to work. It was a version of the "ink spot" approach French General Lyautey made famous in Madagascar and Morocco and one often adopted in counterinsurgency campaigns of the nineteenth and twentieth centuries. The concept called for providing secure zones inside which the population could be protected, governed, and allowed to conduct economic activity free from insurgent pressure. The theory held that as people were free to live their lives, this would enhance the government's legitimacy and strength. And as these domains of government control expanded—like inkblots seeping on a page—they would conjoin. The United States' counterinsurgency doctrine, which outlined the steps of "clear, hold, and build," was a manifestation of this approach. That summer, we added "sustain" as a fourth tenet. Success in counterinsurgency was less dependent upon the brilliance of the strategy—the concept is not that hard to understand—than it was on the execution. Counterinsurgency is easy to prescribe, difficult to perform.

In order to gain a sense of the early stages of the fight in Helmand Province, on June 25 I visited the British soldiers of the Black Watch who had been the first into Babaji. Standing in a damaged compound they'd cleared and were now using as a temporary base, I met with these soldiers and their leaders. With wisps of smoke, the aftereffects of combat, floating through the air, they told how, in the scorching heat of the Afghan summer, they and their comrades had methodically cleared compounds of insurgents and countless IEDs buried beneath the dirt or built into the mud walls of homes and alleyways. Their dead and wounded, more than one hundred men, had been evacuated. But after only several days of fighting, even the unwounded gathered around me looked gaunt and weary, their matted hair blanched and skin yellowed from the film of sand clinging to it. And this was early in their current six-month tour in Afghanistan.

After talking with the soldiers and being struck by the details of the fighting, we moved by helicopter a few kilometers to the south to meet with a group of Afghan elders in a quiet, shaded spot alongside an irrigation ditch. The war seemed distant as we sat under a small tree. Tea was served, conversation was careful and nonconfrontational. The elders had only a vague appreciation for the position I held, and weren't awed by four stars. After some thirty to forty minutes, one of the elders responded to our offer to build roads, schools, and bridges. He hesitated for a moment, as if pondering his answer.

"It is security that must come first," he said, looking me in the eyes as the interpreter translated. "Security is the mother of all development."

In the end, the villagers were hospitable but cautious. They would not commit themselves to any side until convinced it was safe to do so. Theirs was "brutally rational behavior," I reminded my team. "Exactly what we'd do in their position." Like most people caught in this kind of warfare, they were simple people who couldn't afford the luxury of backing the side they hoped would win over the side they believed would. In Helmand, we had cleared parts of the province during each of the last four summers, only in many cases to leave without holding the terrain won. ISAF's history of doing so left the people increasingly skeptical of our promises—and fearful of the violence they knew a fresh Western assault augured. The villagers knew from experience how easily the Taliban seeped back into the pockets we vacated. That summer, insurgents had been punishing "spies" and "collaborators" thought to be working with NATO or the Karzai government. A single Taliban night letter could undo weeks of grueling ISAF fighting.

As the Brits continued disrupting Taliban routes and havens north of Helmand's capital, the Marines focused their efforts south of it. On July 2, four thousand Marines launched Operation Khanjar, or Strike of the Sword, into the Nawa and Garmsir districts. In the weeks and months that followed, in multiple locations along the river valley, operations continued with the Marines, Brits, Estonians, and other Coalition forces. Along with their Afghan partners, they did the slow, gritty work of rooting out insurgents, establishing security, then laboring to institute the first small shoots of Afghan government control. The face of counterinsurgency was typically the grimy mug of a young sergeant and his small squad or platoon walking patrols and leading beardless young warriors in protecting markets and clearing roads.

To some observers, a counterinsurgency "ink spot" strategy seemed ill-fitted for Helmand. It was a largely rural province with only 4 percent of Afghanistan's population, and its capital city, Lashkar Gah, was home to just over one hundred thousand. But the Helmand River valley was a key geographic center for the south—a narrow lane where 85 percent of the province lived, and, importantly, where its agriculture was based and where commerce flowed. The Taliban used their significant, often contiguous strongholds along the Helmand River valley to string interior lines, moving supplies, men, and communication to and from Pakistan. Denying these lines would seriously hinder the insurgents' operations.

The more relevant questions were: Why Helmand now? Why not focus initial efforts on the much larger, and strategically essential cities like Kabul and Kandahar? Or why not work to seal the border near Khost in order to contain the Haqqanis' aggressive attacks?

Like most things in war, the answers are both simple and complex. On the simple side, it is because Helmand was where our forces already were. When I took command, ISAF was in the final stages of positioning troops and preparing for operations in the Helmand River valley. Construction of Marine bases, movement of mountains of necessary supplies, coordination of unit boundaries and operational plans, reconnaissance, and engagement with the population: all were far along. And unlike maneuver warfare where mobile forces dash across battlefields toward decisive objectives, counterinsurgency is methodical and chesslike, requiring deliberate spadework for each successive step. Redirecting to a different location and repeating these efforts there would have required months I judged we didn't have.

The complex side of the equation had multiple components. Time was significant. With two months until the August elections, operations that demonstrated even the first glimmers of progress in a contested area could be important. Confidence was a big consideration. President Karzai's government naturally wanted to allow more Pashtuns to vote by securing Helmand. But I judged that wide voting in the upcoming election would enhance Afghan confidence, or at least increase their involvement, in the governance of their nation. This was a vital long-term objective. More broadly, Afghans had grown cynical of short-term fixes that quickly eroded, and I hoped to show that we could concentrate our forces and capabilities to secure an area, and make it stick. It wasn't proof of principle; I knew the principle worked. It was an opportunity to demonstrate it to people and governments who were too tired for theory.

Politics were a reality. The Marines had sought a contiguous area, Helmand, where they could operate with relative independence, and the Brits welcomed the opportunity to reduce the territory their overstretched forces needed to secure. I knew that both would be more vested in the success of the effort if it also supported their internal objectives. Going forward with the Helmand operations took advantage of these dynamics.

I did have concerns that an initial main effort in Helmand delayed our ability to place more focus on securing the south's key city, Kandahar. But while Kandahar's security was a serious concern as the districts around the city were inflamed, it wasn't besieged or in imminent danger of falling. Rather, we would be able to wage a deliberate campaign in a year's time to better secure Kandahar.

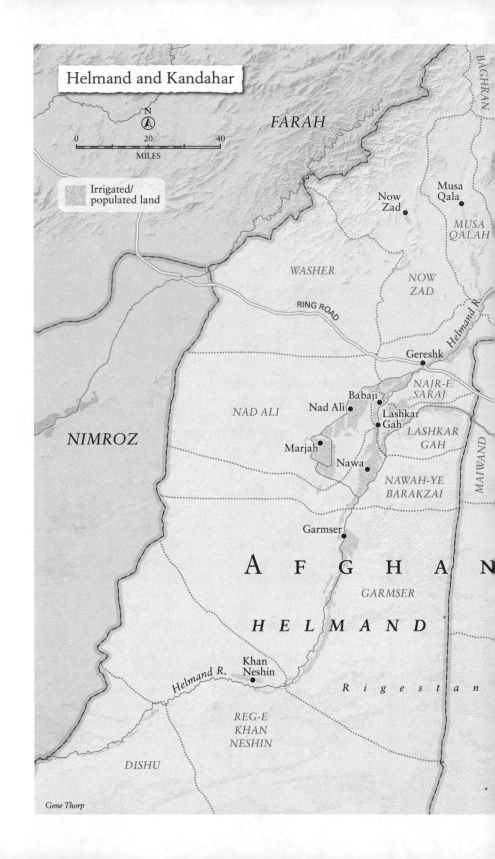

Helmand and Kandahar

N

0   20   40
MILES

Irrigated/
populated land

FARAH

Now
Zad

Musa
Qala

MUSA
QALAH

WASHER

NOW
ZAD

BAGHRAN

Helmand R.

RING ROAD

Gereshk

NAJR-E
SARAJ

Babaji

Nad Ali

Lashkar
Gah

LASHKAR
GAH

NAD ALI

Marjah

Nawa

NAWAH-YE
BARAKZAI

MAIWAND

NIMROZ

Garmser

A F G H A N

GARMSER

H E L M A N D

Khan
Neshin

R i g e s t a n

Helmand R.

REG-E
KHAN
NESHIN

DISHU

Gene Thorp

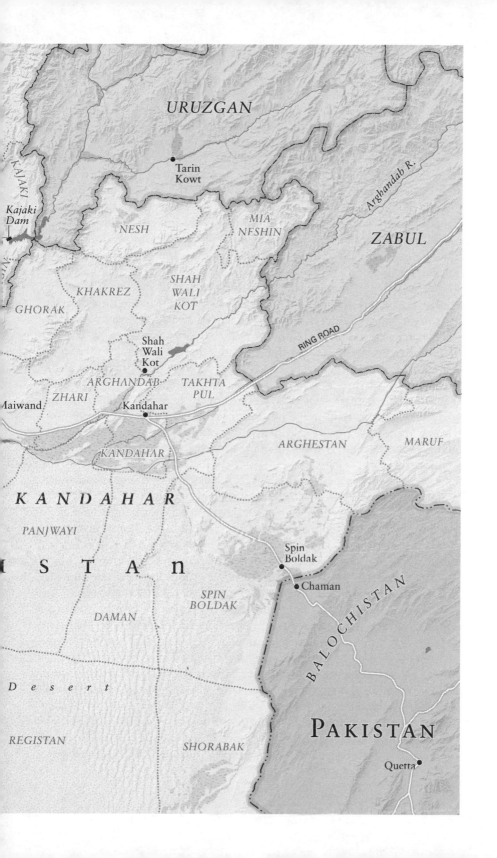

Some critics argued that our resources were misspent on Helmand. But such views typically underplayed Helmand's importance, and just how bad the situation was there. With limited effort and facing little resistance, the Taliban had captured districts closely encircling Lashkar Gah, giving them a perch from which to seriously threaten the provincial capital, and make it untenable. I reasoned that clear success in a Taliban stronghold like Helmand could be a convincing first step in puncturing the perception of the Taliban's strength. And more than anything else, this was a war of perception and confidence.

Outside views of the Helmand operations were mixed. Media coverage ranged from descriptions of positive signs to proclamations of total failure. Reality was confusingly somewhere in the middle, and it would be months before we could judge either way. For me, the war's inherent ambiguity created a delicate balancing act. A convincing portrait of success would have helped give Afghans greater confidence and built Coalition-nation support. But I sought to avoid advertising any perceived gains, as I was more concerned that I maintain my credibility and that of the command. This required that I understand the on-the-ground situation and the slow pace of successful counterinsurgency. I had to be honest enough to provide realistic appraisals.

I instructed my team that they were allowed to speak freely with the media, but if they were to make a case for progress, they were to use numbers, not anecdotes. For every positive vignette they might come across, Afghanistan would surely offer up depressing scenes in equal measure.

The insurgencies waged in southern and eastern Afghanistan were primarily fought and led by Afghans, who had Afghan aspirations. But to a troubling extent, they relied on sanctuaries in Pakistan to protect their leadership, recruits, staging areas, and supply lines. They kept their headquarters in Quetta and used infiltration routes in Pakistan's Federally Administered Tribal Areas (FATA) directly across the disputed Durand Line.

A couple of weeks after I arrived, on July 2, I took my first trip to Pakistan as commander of ISAF. Flying over the border, I was reminded of the historically rooted and obstinate political forces that influenced events on the ground of the war I commanded. The desolate, craggy ridges and pine valleys we flew over on our way to Islamabad, Pakistan's capital, had at one time been coveted by Britain as strategic ground when it believed Afghanistan was indispensible to securing the crown jewel of the British Empire, India. Occasionally harassed by Afghan tribesmen but more seriously threatened by Russian and French designs, India was best protected by an Afghan buffer state kept friendly, weak, and quarantined from other foreign powers. After significant military expeditions into Afghanistan, which included disastrous defeat, heroism, treachery, and privation, Britain settled on a policy of limited engagement, instead trying to influence Afghan leaders through incentive "stipends" for friendly behavior and threats of punishing military retribution for misconduct. The approach wasn't particularly elegant, and while it worked well enough for the British, it also stunted Afghanistan's ability to mature as a state.

On November 12, 1893, Henry Mortimer Durand, the foreign secretary for British India, concluded an agreement with representatives of Afghan ruler Amir Abdur Rahman Khan for the demarcation of a 1,640-mile line establishing a de facto boundary between British India and Afghanistan. The now-famous Durand Line split both the Pashtun and Baloch ethnic groups, with parts of "Pashtunistan" and Balochistan straddling each side. On the day I flew over the line, Afghanistan still refused to admit its legitimacy as an international border with Pakistan.

The purpose of my trip to Islamabad was to meet with our ambassador there, Anne Patterson, and then to hold my first meeting with General Ashfaq Kayani, Pakistan's chief of the army. I'd known Ambassador Patterson from my TF 714 command and found her to be a deeply impressive veteran diplomat.

I'd met Ashfaq Kayani once, back in 2006, when I met Secretary Rumsfeld in Rawalpindi for a late-night meeting with President Musharraf. At the time, Kayani was serving as the director of Pakistan's Inter-Services Intelligence (ISI).

Kayani's biography told the story of the United States' fraught relationship with Pakistan over the prior two decades. When a major, he had won a spot at the U.S. Army's Command and General Staff College in Fort Leavenworth, Kansas. During the 1987–88 academic year, he earned a masters in military arts and sciences and wrote a thesis entitled "Strengths and Weaknesses of the Afghanistan Resistance Movement: A Study of the Capabilities of the Afghan Resistance Problem, Created by the Soviet Invasion of 1979." He was writing, then, about a movement still idealized by many Americans as anticommunist freedom fighters—*Rambo III* hit theaters that May, during Kayani's second semester, and had Stallone's character on a mission to resupply the mujahideen with Stinger missiles. Kayani was an exchange student from an ally helping us fight our Soviet enemy. In a short time, that all changed.

In 1989, the Soviets withdrew from Afghanistan, and with their exit America's strategic interest in the region disappeared. No longer needing Pakistan to help us arm the rebels and frustrated with its persistent nuclear ambitions, the United States refused to vouch that Pakistan was not seeking to gain nuclear weapons. (Earlier, the American government had given Pakistan a pass when the United States needed its assistance in our proxy war.) Thus, in 1990, the Pressler Amendment, passed five years earlier, kicked into effect, immediately cutting off all military aid to Pakistan. It also stopped the United States from bringing Pakistan's military officers to learn and drill with our own—a move that left them feeling spurned. Kayani was one of the last Pakistani officers to be brought to Kansas.

Now, two decades later, with Pervez Musharraf no longer president, General Kayani, in his new role as head of the army, wielded tremendous power. From the Joint Staff, I'd watched Chairman Mullen make a significant effort to build rapport with him. The backdrop of recent events in the region made for a sensitive situation. Clear evidence that the November 2008 Mumbai attacks, conducted by Pakistani terrorists of Lashkar-e-Taiba, were orchestrated from inside Pakistan caused Americans deep frustration. And ongoing accusations that Pakistan's military and intelligence services supported the Afghan Taliban complicated Mullen's and my efforts. Pakistanis were quick to respond with concerns over American violations of their sovereignty, primarily through drone strikes, an ever-perceived U.S. tilt toward India, and a lack of appreciation for the significant Pakistani sacrifices in the war on terror.

Strictly speaking, although my mandate as the NATO commander was limited to inside Afghanistan, it was clear to me that Pakistan would have a role in any lasting solution. At a minimum, ISAF needed access to Pakistani lines of communication for the flow of logistics to our forces. Optimally, for our counterinsurgency campaign inside Afghanistan, the Afghan Taliban could not enjoy support and sanctuaries across the border in Pakistan.

Ideally, our joint ISAF and Pakistani efforts would convince Afghan Taliban leaders that their sanctuaries in Pakistan were no longer secure, and thus their insurgency could not succeed. Effective Pakistani Army operations in the FATA, along with increased levels of coordination with ISAF forces, were necessary in order to produce this kind of rethink inside Mullah Omar's organization. But the FATA was a region where the Pakistani military had traditionally struggled.

The oft-discussed deficit of trust that existed between the United States and Pakistan could only be reduced over time, and personal relationships would be essential to that process. By building as much trust as possible between General Kayani and me, confidence would cascade to some extent down through our subordinates. I believed slow but steady progress was possible. It might not work, but there was no rational alternative.

The next day, July 3, a Pakistani army Mi-17 helicopter went down in the Orakzai Agency of the FATA, killing at least twenty-six Pakistani soldiers. It was a reminder of continuing Pakistani sacrifices in the fight—by early 2010 some two thousand Pakistani soldiers had died fighting in the border regions. I called General Kayani late that evening to express my condolences and followed with a handwritten letter. I knew what it meant to lose soldiers and wanted him to know I shared his sense of loss.

Over the coming months I would spend significant time with Kayani and grow to like and respect him. His perspectives and priorities were, of course, those of a Pakistani army officer, but I found our discussions on the war and our respective strategies to be helpful. Much of our time together was spent alone, simply drinking tea and talking. The talk was substantive but never combative. I never responded well to people who were pushy or arrogant with me, and I came to believe most other people felt the same.

We were still at work on the assessment when, on July 20, I reviewed its initial conclusions with two high-profile Afghans, Minister of the Interior Hanif Atmar, and Minister of Defense Rahim Wardak. Wardak hosted us for a small dinner in his office at the Ministry of Defense. The two men were, on the surface, nearly polar opposites. Atmar, then forty-one years old, was a slender Pashtun who normally wore traditional Afghan clothing beneath a Western sport coat. During the Soviet war, he had served in the Soviet-backed Democratic Republic of Afghanistan's KHAD security service. Badly wounded in fighting around Jalalabad in 1988, he had since walked with a cane. (Former mujahideen who now worked alongside Atmar boasted, half-jokingly, "We gave him that limp.") Courtly in demeanor but passionate and ambitious, Atmar tended to articulate his thoughts in numbered lists. "I have four points on this . . ." he would begin, a habit we learned to tease him about. Atmar had served as both the minister of rural rehabilitation and development and minister of education but now oversaw the Interior Ministry, which controlled the fraught Afghan police.

Twenty-three years his senior, General-turned-Minister Wardak was invariably clean-shaven and dressed in three-piece suits. As a mujaheed, he had fought against the Soviet-backed government in which Atmar served. Although also a Pashtun, his military heritage superseded any ethnic concerns. And though he was more reserved, he was deeply passionate about building the Afghan military.

My relationship with both men had only started in June, but I rapidly came to appreciate the challenges they faced in trying to build functional institutions like the army and police, while dependent upon the largess of western donations and constantly buffeted by the forces that tormented their nation.

In the discussion, I sought their views and their support. I summarized my two primary conclusions about the war. First, the insurgency had grown stronger than at any time since 2001. Second, the weakness of the Afghan government and nationwide corruption had given people what we described as a crisis of confidence. I told them we proposed to change ISAF's strategy to focus on protecting the people, not pursuing insurgents. Further, we aimed to fix ISAF's internal command-and-control structure to achieve unity of command. And finally, we sought to change the ISAF relationship with Afghan National Security Forces by increasing the size of those forces and, for the first time, truly partnering with them. I confided that convincing progress was essential in the next twelve months if we were to retain political support within the Coalition.

Both men expressed gratitude for being included in the process. They agreed that the situation was serious and endorsed the proposed strategy, particularly the value of focusing on protection of ordinary Afghans. Then these two very different men—once battlefield opponents—voiced a single message.

"ISAF is temporary," each stressed. "This must transition to an Afghan-led effort. Our army, police, and other parts of government must be up to the task." Both also asked for international pressure to curtail Iranian and Pakistani interference in Afghanistan.

At the conclusion of our dinner, however, conversation turned to the looming event of the summer. Minister Atmar drove the point home with quiet, haunting power.

"If the elections fail," he said in his characteristically soft voice, "I would recommend that the international community not waste any more blood or treasure here."

With the August 20 presidential election fast approaching, blood and treasure were the uneasy topic of an important meeting that summer. On August 2, Dave Rodriguez, my command team, and I flew to Belgium to meet with Secretary Gates, Chairman Mullen, Under Secretary Michele Flournoy, and a few others. In a small conference room alongside the runway at a military air base we reviewed the initial points of the yet-to-be-submitted strategic assessment and discussed any potential force recommendations.

By then, we'd begun drafting the assessment. Chris Kolenda produced the initial draft containing the core ideas and conclusions. Jeff Eggers would ultimately become the primary "pen" for the final version, and he and I spent countless hours poring over every word. During the day, he and I exchanged drafts by e-mail—I often did my best writing and editing on helicopter rides—and when I returned to headquarters, we would meet well into the night in my office. Jeff was a good partner in this—a critical thinker about the war, and our prospects, he helped prod and challenge me.

The document we submitted was some sixty pages long, including a frank assessment of the war, and some thirty pages of appendices laying out a number of specific recommendations for remedy. Without making any requests, the assessment acknowledged that "continued under-resourcing will likely cause failure." But this was "not the crux" of the problem and "focusing on force or resource requirements misses the point entirely." Rather, "the key to take away from this assessment," I wrote, "is the urgent need for a significant change to our strategy and the way that we think and operate." Crucially, this would mean internalizing that "protecting the people means shielding them from *all* threats." Those threats were not just from insurgent and collateral violence. They were also from the corruption and predation of the Afghans' own government.

In addition to the structural changes to ISAF that I'd explained to Wardak and Atmar, the assessment set a full agenda for that fall. We would institutionalize a reintegration program to make it an avenue for insurgents off the battlefield. And, noting there were "more insurgents per square foot in corrections facilities than anywhere else in Afghanistan," we'd continue our effort under way to revamp our own prisons while cleaning up Afghan-run centers, which were often under de facto insurgent control.

As directed, we kept the basic assessment separate from any recommendations for resources, namely additional troops. Those would be submitted in another document after the assessment. I agreed with that approach, especially because by the end of July it was clear to me that if provided together, any force recommendation would be what policy makers focused on.

Parallel to, and informed by, the work of the strategic assessment team, we'd had a team of planners working on a campaign plan, the key points of which we briefed that day. In the simplest sense, a campaign plan was nothing more than an outline of how a mission would be accomplished. Taking clearly defined objectives, a commander and staff would analyze and select the best course of action to accomplish them, including identifying the required resources, like forces and time. For complex missions, plans could run hundreds of pages and could include countless maps and matrices. Our goal was to identify, refine, and then coordinate the most effective and efficient way to succeed.

Although soldiers, we looked at Afghanistan like a case of electioneering: in our modified "ink spot" approach, we identified 80 of Afghanistan's 364 key districts that we felt we, and then the Afghans, must control in order to ensure the Afghan state's stability and survival. Some of these districts were safe; others we would have to reclaim from the insurgency and transfer to Afghan hands. To a large degree, the pattern made by the eighty key districts would have been unsurprising to students of Afghanistan. It largely overlaid the Ring Road, a highway still under construction that circled Afghanistan, and hewed close to key urban and agricultural areas. Choosing these districts was not merely a matter of numbers; we also weighed the country's historically or culturally influenced sense of important locations. This meant some on-the-surface unimportant rural districts held special psychological or political significance to Afghans, and their fall, we feared, would do disproportionate damage to Afghan confidence.

To allow us to concentrate our limited ISAF and Afghan forces in the most important areas, the following month we began repositioning a number of units out of remote desert or mountain outposts, pulling them closer to the more populous geographic hubs. But what appeared a logical move was also politically sensitive and deeply emotional.

In July 2009, at the passionate request of Nuristan's governor and Minister Atmar, I had approved ISAF forces to reinforce Barg-e Matal, a district capital under Taliban attack in remote eastern Nuristan. I'd been on a patrol to the primitive mountain village with Navy SEALs back in December 2003 and remembered the faces of children who'd gathered to investigate the strangers. But I also remembered the hills that dominated the small garrison and knew long-term defense would be resource-intensive.

With my concurrence, Major General Scaparrotti refined planning to reposition his limited forces to areas where we could better protect large population centers. That process was ongoing when, on the morning of October 3, 2009, Combat Outpost Keating, to the south of Barge-e Matal, was attacked and partially overrun with the loss of eight American soldiers killed and twenty-two wounded. The attack, which highlighted the vulnerability of small bases in difficult terrain, produced calls for rapid withdrawal from exposed positions. As a soldier I understood. But there were other factors to consider as well.

In the early years of the war we had occupied areas that we subsequently abandoned. Afghans who had enthusiastically supported our initial arrival were left vulnerable upon our departure; their hope for the future and our credibility were left shattered as either insurgents or despised warlords moved in. In areas where we reappeared in 2006 and 2007, we encountered cautiously distant attitudes. Departing again would complete their disillusionment. Additionally, even the appearance of ceding territory once under government control was a troubling proposition for Afghan leaders. Traditional military calculations had to be balanced with the psychological effects of every decision. Counterinsurgency in Afghanistan was more complex than moving military symbols on a map.

The Soviets had opted for a version of the "ink spot" strategy during the late stages of their war, as had the Najibullah government that the Soviets left behind. While the Soviets' failure tended to make their actions a cautionary tale rather than a road map for us, aspects of Soviet "pacification" efforts had been successful in engaging the populace. But the "sovietization" efforts they'd enacted within the areas they controlled had offended many conservative Afghans. This offense, and the Soviets' aggressive use of fires in the areas they had ceded control of, undermined their strategy. It was a reminder that we could get the strategy partly, or even mostly, right—and still fail.

Our planners worked hard to determine what was needed to secure the key eighty districts. When we began the process, which I asked Dave Rodriguez to oversee, both he and I had believed no additional forces would be required. We thought, or at least hoped, that the ISAF forces already approved and the projected growth of the Afghan army and police, would be sufficient. But through extensive research, including computer simulations using historical counterinsurgency models, the planners presented evidence indicating otherwise.

Their convincing analysis argued that at least forty thousand troops would be required to establish enough security in enough areas to achieve progress that was credible to Afghans and fast enough to arrest and then reverse the deteriorating situation around the country.

Rod and I struggled with this conclusion. We knew it would be politically contentious, and we challenged the planners repeatedly. But by the end of July, I was convinced that to accomplish the mission we'd been given within the time frame we thought we had, we'd need additional U.S. and NATO forces. Without them, we were unable to halt the insurgency's momentum and buy time until the still-nascent Afghan forces were both big and effective enough to stave off the insurgency and allow the Afghan state to survive. The only other option, as I saw it, was to alter the mission and objectives.

Although we'd finished the guts of the assessment well before the sixty-day deadline of August 30, Secretary Gates directed me to hold the document until after the August 20 Afghan election. He would ask for it then. Given the likely impact of the assessment, the secretary no doubt wanted to ensure that we provided it to the appropriate policy makers before it received wider distribution and scrutiny.

After the long meeting, I sensed Secretary Gates reluctantly accepted the analysis, but recognized the challenge of convincing some in D.C. Its reception would inevitably be affected by factors beyond my view there, but I resolved to try to steer clear of politics. That wasn't always easy. An August visit by a delegation led by Senators John McCain, Joseph Lieberman, and Lindsey Graham had included a pointed exchange in which I declined to outline the recommendations I would provide to President Obama regarding U.S. force levels in Afghanistan. I knew the friction wasn't personal. It reflected the passion that the intersection of policy and politics engenders. But I wanted no part of it.

I left Belgium that afternoon knowing our prescription would be a tough sell. Its reception would hinge, in large part, on how the Afghan presidential elections went.

The elections were already controversial when I arrived in June. After intense wrangling, the date had been pushed from April. There were accusations that President Karzai was unfairly maneuvering to disadvantage potential opponents. Additionally, foreign involvement, including some foreign diplomats' energetic search for opposition candidates, had produced an atmosphere of skepticism and distrust among many Afghans.

For outsiders, the world of Afghan politics was a baffling recipe of ethnicities and personalities seasoned with corruption and intrigue. Even a small taste could produce painful heartburn. Afghans were used to it. The mix of economic, tribal, historical, and personal relationships that produced the colorful swirl of their political scene could frustrate and even enrage them. But they seemed to understand it. The worst amassed power and wealth with callous arrogance. The best cut deals, paid bribes, and even for the best of motives, played by rules they hoped to someday change. The Uzbek commander Abdul Rashid Dostum became the poster child of shifting Afghan loyalties when he turned to, and then against, the Taliban in 1996. But he reflected a long tradition. Often called intractable, Afghan culture was rooted in practicality and compromise.

The election stakes were high. Afghans would select their chief executive for the next five years, a time when the immediate future of that nation and the outcome of NATO's and America's effort in the country would likely be decided. For a weary international audience, and an increasingly worried Afghan electorate, the conduct of the election would be an important metric—and, hopefully, a milestone in the maturation of the fledgling democracy. For ISAF and our Afghan security-sector partners, success in securing a complex election conducted across the country could spur needed improvements and build confidence.

By August, thirty-two candidates were running for president. Karzai, after having been appointed to the office in 2002 and elected by Afghans to a five-year term in 2004, was the clear favorite. But the choices he made that summer for running mates—Marshal Mohammad Fahim, a northern Tajik, and a Hazara, Karim Khalili—worried some onlookers, who hoped for a new crop of leadership to supplant the existing power brokers whose roots were in the country's civil war. Karzai's main rival was another northerner, Dr. Abdullah Abdullah, a confidant of the late Ahmad Shah Massoud and Karzai's foreign minister until 2006. The candidates included a number of other prominent Afghans—including Dr. Ashraf Ghani, a well-respected Pashtun economist and onetime minister of finance, and Ali Jalali, the former interior minister and a journalist by trade. Throughout the summer, Karzai polled at roughly 45 percent of the vote, but Afghanistan's constitution required that a runoff be held if no candidate won at least 50 percent.

From a security standpoint, I'd been tracking the upcoming elections for almost a year. Dave McKiernan's troop request, which had been a focus of ours in the Pentagon, had identified the need to increase security for the elections, particularly in the turbulent and largely Pashtun south. Now, although preparation for the elections had been under way for some months, there was much left to do. Soon after my arrival, detailed planning for Afghan-led security, backed up by Coalition support, moved into high gear. A credible election would require, at a minimum, making secure polling stations accessible to the vast majority of Afghans, even in physically remote or Taliban-controlled areas. It meant the Afghans, led by the government's electoral body, the Independent Election Commission (IEC), needed to identify voting locations, hire staff to run them, and physically deliver and retrieve ballot materials, all the while protecting not only the polling sites but also protecting potential voters.

Incidentally, the planning and coordination process served to force the ISAF-Afghan partnership Rod and I wanted to materialize. In a series of marathon meetings and video teleconferences with our Afghan partners, we hammered out point after point. Afghan leaders I had barely known

before, like Wardak, Atmar, and chief of the army General Bismullah Mohammedi, first became operational partners, then friends.

Among the Afghan leaders with whom we worked most closely, a young
Tajik named Amrullah Saleh stood out. I'd first met Saleh on September 9,
2004, when he took me to the Panshir Valley for a memorial service at the
old headquarters of Ahmad Shah Massoud, the legendary mujahideen
leader. At that spot three years earlier, Massoud had been assassinated by
Al Qaeda operatives posing as cameramen. As we watched the memorial,
surrounded by a hillside of bearded, serious-looking men, Massoud's former fighters, Saleh, still only thirty-three that day, explained how he'd served
Massoud as a deputy. His crisp, fluent English, intimidating intellect, and
fervor against the Taliban made an immediate impression. Since then, he
had risen to be the director of Afghanistan's National Directorate of Security (NDS), and he remained in that role when I arrived in 2009.

I realized that for many in ISAF, true partnering was new and uncomfortable, but that couldn't dissuade us from it. Just about the time we got
everyone comfortable, we would have lost.

That same day, with elections nearing, I spoke to the Afghan National
Security Force Partnering Working Group. "Looking for a decisive battle is
our instinct. We're in it now," I said. "Elections are about what is in people's minds, and that is what will ultimately determine success."

The enemy was surely thinking the same. On the morning of Saturday,
August 15, five days before the election, the headquarters staff sat assembled in the tiered rows of our operations center for our morning update.
Suddenly, a loud explosion shook the small ISAF compound. A voice on the
sound system immediately directed the briefing to end and all personnel to
depart the operations center. Mike Hall leaned over to me. "And where are
we going to go, to the bunkers? What are we going to accomplish there?"
he asked. "I suggest we let the people responsible for securing the compound do their jobs, and we stay here and do ours."

It was sage advice that I transmitted as an order. The evacuation of the
command center stopped abruptly, people settled back into their seats, a
few with obvious nervousness, and the briefing continued. We weren't noncombatants disconnected from the fight; we were going to command it.
Within minutes, it was reported that a car bomb had detonated just outside
our main gate. The explosion had burst the cinderblocks lining the street,
spraying chunks of cement into a large group of Afghans queued up outside
our gate. The tall concrete slabs lining our compound had withstood the
blast, which sent shock waves reverberating back across the street toward
the unshielded Afghan buildings on the other side, blowing out the glass
windows. Those first on the scene came to find the bomber's sedan, charred
but coursing thick orange flames out of its windows and up from its car-
riage. The blast waves had shot up through the tree limbs overhanging the
usually quiet street, sending leaves fluttering down over the tops of the

pavement and parked cars. Half obscured beneath the green spread of leaves lay the motionless bodies of Afghans. The blast killed seven people, and wounded ninety-one others. It was never entirely clear whether ISAF was the bomber's primary target. But it was a jolt to everyone in the command, and a reminder of the stakes.

Election preparations continued. Challenge after challenge surfaced, from transporting the more than ninety-five thousand ballot boxes, which moved on trucks, helicopters, and even on the backs of some three thousand donkeys, to finding ways to put enough security in embattled areas to allow voting. The election was a significant undertaking for the Afghan government, and the IEC recruited a temporary staff of more than 120,000 for the day of the vote. (Although 40 percent of them were women, there were not enough to staff the women-only voting stations.) The IEC planned to open 27,000 polling stations, for which the U.N. procured 58,000 plastic chairs, 116,000 voting screens, and 180,000 tunics for poll workers. The Afghans were remarkably transparent in admitting that they were making accommodations with insurgents in selected areas in order to facilitate the election. But I sensed there was a genuine effort to secure the polls as well as possible. With the Afghans' limited capacity and the Taliban trumpeting their intent to violently disrupt the vote, the outcome would be imperfect at best. Yet from a security standpoint, a clear failure by the Taliban to derail the process would be a win. However, for the elections to have real credibility, they would have to be judged sufficiently fair. That judgment would be an imprecise, but critical, metric.

The political process moved roughly in parallel, although over an even rockier road. It left IEC director Dr. Azizullah Lodin, a quiet, courtly man, constantly buffeted by demands and accusations of impending problems.

As election day unfolded, in ISAF we were initially pleased with the result. Although the number of Taliban attacks was extremely high, the election was not effectively disrupted. The government opened roughly 90 percent of the polling sites that it had planned to, and on the day of the election, violence or threats inactivated just 12 percent of those originally opened to voters. While hard numbers were scarce, between 35 percent and 39 percent of voters turned out. Fewer people voted than we had hoped for or anticipated—particularly in Helmand and Kandahar.

In most provinces the Afghan army and police had performed admirably. They were out in more areas simultaneously than most of my commanders had ever seen, and the Afghans had taken impressive responsibility for security.

Our guarded satisfaction didn't survive long. Almost immediately there were accusations of fraud, ballot stuffing, and other improprieties. Opposition candidates complained, as did many election monitors. Unquestionably, many of the complaints were valid, but I couldn't judge whether these were typical warts of the democratic process or indicators of a "stolen election."

President Karzai, the incumbent and clear Pashtun candidate in a country that was 42 percent Pashtun, hardly needed fraud to be reelected. But he had sought a convincing mandate. I had no doubt that some of his supporters had, with or without his direction, taken it upon themselves to ensure success by any means they considered necessary.

The entire process had been flawed, and recriminations abounded. U.N. special representative Kai Eide's public break with his deputy, Peter Galbraith, and President Karzai's rage at Ambassadors Richard Holbrooke and Karl Eikenberry increased the toxicity in the atmosphere. Most worrisome, the international community's disgust with apparent fraud led many to call into question the feasibility of our effort in Afghanistan. Although the outcome of the election and the health of the government mattered greatly to our mission, my position as military commander allowed, indeed required, that I stay out of the particular postelection political fray.

O n an early morning at the end of August, I took my regular run around the compound. The tiny enclave made for monotonous laps through alleys and behind buildings and still came up well short of a mile. It wasn't fun running, like an interesting city could be. But it was an opportunity to take stock of what we'd done and where I thought we were.

The aftermath of the elections was becoming a mess. Although the vote count was still ongoing, I could sense a looming political crisis. But there were also reasons for optimism. ISAF was becoming a different organization. We hadn't changed the culture entirely, but we were transforming to a more focused team. When the ISAF Joint Command became active late in September, I expected ISAF would be able to mold itself more effectively toward the strategic role that was needed.

Across Afghanistan, ISAF's operational focus on protecting the people wasn't complete. But there were improvements. The U.S. Marines and Brits in Helmand were producing change, not through miracles that suddenly appeared, but through muddy, often bloody fights under the eyes of skeptical locals, followed by patient engagement. It was two steps forward, very carefully taken to avoid IEDs, and one step backward. But it was real progress. On battlefield visits I'd hear my own words on counterinsurgency echoed back to me by young leaders, often unaware of their origin. With more time, and Rod's leadership, I was confident that sustainable improvement was possible.

We had submitted the strategic assessment on August 30, and I was comfortable with the analysis and recommendations. Although the war was not easy to describe clearly in a document, I felt we had captured the essence of the challenges and risks we faced. More daunting was assessing whether the mission was achievable and what it would take to reach an acceptable outcome. I understood the tendency of military leaders to be optimistic, often dangerously so. But both our analysis and my intuition told me our effort could succeed. My responsibility was to provide my best military judgment, and I had done that. Not once in the months and years that followed did I feel we got it wrong. We now waited to see how Washington would receive the assessment.

In an interview earlier that month with PBS's *Frontline,* the reporter had noted that there was "a lot of talk in Washington that in twelve months we'll have an assessment of how we're doing in Afghanistan." Having surveyed our organization and having started to move it in the right direction, I believed I knew what we needed to accomplish. I also knew, realistically, what we could accomplish.

"I would not expect to be able to sit with you twelve months from now," I answered, "and tell you that we are at victory or near victory or even close to victory. What I would say is, I would hope to be able to convince you we have an organization that is now focused and moving in the right direction with the right culture," so that "you could then believe that this is . . . the kind of effort that could be successful."

The ISAF team, while imperfect, was coming together. And while at best our mission in Afghanistan would be extraordinarily difficult, I felt that it could be done.

CHAPTER 19

Decide

September–December 2009

O n a sunny Friday, September 4, 2009, Ambassador Karl
Eikenberry and I walked across the newly constructed bridge
with local Afghan officials, everyone in apparent good humor. In Kunar Province, bisected by the shallow but fast-moving Kunar
River, bridges are a big deal. This one seemed to represent tangible progress, and we hoped it would stimulate local economic growth. But in counterinsurgency, setbacks lie in wait.

I saw Charlie Flynn walking briskly toward me, cell phone in hand. I
knew from his drawn face something was up. His brother Mike had just
called from ISAF headquarters to inform us that a Coalition air strike in
Kunduz Province, two hundred miles to the northwest, had reportedly
killed a large number of Afghan civilians. As many as a hundred were dead,
he said. Details were limited, but initial reports indicated that U.S.-piloted
F-15 aircraft, responding to a German request, had bombed two fuel trucks
that insurgents had hijacked. The insurgents reportedly planned to use the
tankers as massive vehicle bombs against the Coalition base in Kunduz. But
while still a significant distance from the compound, the trucks had become
stuck on a sandbar as they crossed a small river. When the aircraft struck
the trucks, local civilians had gathered around them to obtain free fuel.

Using Charlie's cell phone while standing on the bridge, I immediately
called the palace and asked to speak to President Karzai. He listened quietly as I explained what I knew of the incident. I said that we would investigate immediately but offered no theories or excuses as to why it happened.

I didn't know enough yet and that was not the way I'd decided to deal with such incidents. I continued: "Mr. President, I want to apologize for the incident. As I promised you when I arrived, I am working to prevent this kind of loss. I'll redouble that effort. I also want to express my sympathy to you, and all Afghans, for the tragic loss."

President Karzai's response was immediate and disarming. He thanked me for the report and for my apology. I sensed he had expected me to communicate something like this in a more guarded fashion, or indirectly.

We flew back to Kabul that evening, and the next day, sensing the seriousness of the situation and a slower reaction than was needed, flew to Kunduz. Arriving by helicopter, we moved first to RC-North's headquarters, and then drove to the site of the strike—a stretch of river four miles from the airport.

From our vehicles, the acting RC-North commander, a small group of Afghan and ISAF leaders, and I walked a twisted dirt track that stopped at the edge of the river, where I paused. Partway across the water, in the center of a long sandbar, sat two blackened fuel tankers. Assorted burned debris surrounded the stranded vehicles in a large, uneven pattern. Across the river, half visible through the trees and bushes, small groups of Afghans milled about, including, we believed, local Taliban. They were likely the same band that had hijacked the trucks whose burned shells we were about to inspect. Patiently pacing or crouching, they watched us.

I stepped down into the cold, muddy water, balanced myself for a moment, and proceeded as the group followed behind and we waded the shallow river to reach the sandbar. As we neared the site, the air hung with a strong, acrid odor of gasoline and burned rubber. Everything was charred. The heat of the fire had melted tires and stripped the trucks of everything but the metal—the frames, tanks, and seat springs in the cabs. Milk containers, brought by Afghans to store the gas, lay on the sand, as did what looked like human hair. There were no bodies. After the flames had died down, the dead had been collected by locals from nearby villages, from which the victims had apparently come when the Taliban invited them to come get free fuel. Few Afghans summoned by the Taliban in the middle of the night would have dared say no. It was clear that, when struck, the trucks had been firmly mired in the mud and could not have presented the immediate security threat the commander had felt they did when ordering the strike.

From the incident site, we visited injured civilians in a very rudimentary local hospital. One young man of about sixteen was badly burned, a bitter reminder of the paratroopers I'd watched suffer back in 1994 at Fort Bragg. The staff and families were stoic and not confrontational. They were doing their best to keep the sheets clean and sterile. It was an atmosphere of quiet tragedy.

Before going to the site of the strike, we'd met in a conference room at RC-North with a group of some fifteen local leaders gathered to provide their thoughts about the situation. Interestingly, they were strongly supportive of the air strike, and the group expressed satisfaction that direct action had finally been taken against the Taliban threat in their area. Kabir Sekander, one of my cultural advisers, was there to translate when one of the elders spoke. Even with a skilled translator like Kabir, communication was always challenging, but today their message was clear.

"We need these kinds of operations to tell the opposition that 'we mean business,' that 'the people are fed up with you,' " the elder said. "The people are hostages in the hand of this opposition; the people do not want to participate; they're forced to participate in these kind of activities. But the people want to live in peace and harmony, so we have to have some of these kinds of operations like we did last night. We have to do these things, so people can live in harmony."

Their views were unusual for the aftermath of such a grisly civilian casualty incident. Usually, we heard outrage. But I wasn't surprised, as I suspected the leaders whom the regional command had invited to meet with us were not broadly representative of all the people in the area. Moreover, I knew they were caught in a particularly tough position: For years, the north, around Kunduz, had remained quiet. But insurgents had been steadily gaining power in the area. Many there wanted NATO to target the Taliban more aggressively. I believed the elders had shrewdly calculated that anything less than effusive support would reduce our willingness to conduct operations against the feared Taliban.

The elders complained that the media was focusing on the air strike—an event that I knew had been a tragic mistake with potentially far-reaching consequences in Kunduz and in Kabul—not the insurgents' use of suicide bombings.

"Tashakur," I thanked them, and turned to Kabir. "Also, please convey that I agree with him that the actions of insurgents on things like suicide bombs are terrible and in no way compare to how we operate." I continued: "And what I want to do is to partner with the Afghan people to protect the Afghan people, so I am here today to ensure that we are operating in a way that is truly protecting the Afghan people from all threats."

That evening, as we headed back to Kabul, I decided to do two things. I directed a general officer to lead an investigation of the incident. I wanted to take quick action; we had a moral responsibility to do so. Also, on the advice of my cultural advisers—Kabir and Abdullah Amini—I recorded a statement of sympathy and issued an apology to the Afghan people for broadcast on local television. Dedicated Afghan Americans who had joined ISAF in 2006, Kabir and Abdullah had worked for the previous two ISAF commanders. I was soon glad I took their advice, and came to rely on their ability to parse interactions I had with Afghans for revealing cues I overlooked. Despite some western concerns and criticism over potentially accepting culpability for the incident before an investigation was complete, the television statement was the right move. Afghans typically knew the reality of incidents like this before we did and thought our sluggishness in acknowledging their loss was disrespectful.

"To the great people of Afghanistan, *salam alaikum*," I said in a recorded statement, which was soon dubbed in Dari and Pashto and distributed on Afghan television. "Friday morning, the International Security Assistance Force launched an attack against what we believed to be a Taliban target in Kunduz, in northern Afghanistan. . . . I take this possible loss of life or injury to innocent Afghans very seriously. . . . I have ordered a complete investigation into the reasons and results of this attack, which I will share with the Afghan people."

If our submission of the strategic assessment on August 30 seemed to end the first phase of my tour at ISAF, the Kunduz civilian-casualty incident seemed to begin the second. The air strike was a clear mistake, and a setback. But I recognized that the tragic event was salutary: After the call with President Karzai, I felt as though our relationship had just taken a step, albeit a small one, from being polite and correct toward something closer to genuine trust. If so, such a development cut against the grain of larger forces in the backdrop. Relations between the United States and President Hamid Karzai were rapidly deteriorating, and had been for the past two weeks since the presidential elections. The postelection controversy of widespread fraud by the Karzai campaign and pressure for a runoff election between Karzai and his strongest rival, Dr. Abdullah Abdullah, were producing bad feelings all around.

From a Western perspective, signs of outright fraud, including stuffed ballot boxes and other irregularities, were damning. Combined with increasingly detailed accounts of widespread corruption, they undermined arguments that Karzai's government was a credible partner. Such determinations were crucial for the United States. The key period of the policy-review and the decision-making process had begun ten days after Afghans cast their votes, when I submitted my strategic assessment. That document, soon accompanied by the associated recommendation that additional forces be deployed, provided a point of reference and debate for the strategy sessions the Obama administration convened over the next three months. From the seats inside the White House Situation Room, as the Afghan elections looked bad, so too did a long-term, large-scale engagement in the country.

Afghan views varied, but President Karzai frequently raised with me his frustration at what he interpreted as Western efforts to find and support other candidates to supplant him. Although I felt much of his frustration stemmed from misinterpretation and misunderstanding, watching events as they unfolded, I could appreciate how he arrived at his perspective. Combined with long-held dissatisfaction over how international forces and agencies operated inside his country, President Karzai strained against what he felt was improper meddling. I reminded myself that my view of what had happened in the elections, even if accurate, must be informed by an appreciation of how Afghans viewed it. This proved to be critical on most issues.

As President Obama began a necessarily rigorous and deliberative review of our strategy, and the election controversy grew more heated, the war meanwhile continued apace. Against that backdrop, we worked to lay a foundation for the way ahead, using the strategic assessment to clarify the challenges and the necessary changes.

"We can win this war," I told the command on September 14, as part of the normal morning update that included personnel at ISAF headquarters and other locations by teleconference. "But we can only win one war. We need to stop fighting multiple wars."

Three months into my command, we still waged an uncoordinated campaign. In some areas of Afghanistan, ISAF soldiers conducting autonomous operations and those advising Afghan forces worked for different commanders and reported up separate chains. So too did Special Forces building local capacity, and special operating forces conducting precision raids against the Taliban. And within those different elements I saw varying interpretations of our mission, strategy, relationship with Afghan security forces, and use of firepower. Our disjointed military effort was complicated further by similar misalignment on the civilian side. It was a recipe for failure.

Secretary Gates's decision to create IJC was a significant step toward redressing this. A strong operational headquarters, empowered with robust communications and intelligence assets, helped foster long-needed synergy. Further, Rod and I pushed relentlessly to achieve "unity of command," the simple military concept that a single person should be in charge of every significant mission.

Viewed broadly, achieving unity of command was vital to our counterinsurgency, which had to be effective in both its civilian and military components. But achieving such unity of command across the more than forty nations of ISAF's Coalition and the wider international community sometimes felt impossible. I remain convinced that a single leader, most appropriately a talented civilian willing to spend at least several years in the job, with authority to direct and coordinate all military, governance, and development efforts, would have been the best step toward unifying our war effort. But that fall, no such person existed.

Although I'd outlined my position to Dave Petraeus and Admiral Mullen that I needed control over all U.S. forces in Afghanistan, I faced resistance from some organizations. This was a historically contentious issue, and I didn't obtain formal operational control over Marine and special operations forces until Secretary Gates directed it, months after I'd assumed command.

On September 18, a couple of weeks after Kunduz, I arrived into Lisbon for a two-day conference of the NATO Military Committee, typically the chiefs of defense of the NATO member nations.

At Chairman Mullen's request I'd flown in to provide an update on Afghanistan. Ever mindful of the time Annie and I had been apart, Mullen had flown her over with him.

Seeing Annie at that time was important to me. About a month after my departure for Afghanistan, in response to intelligence reports indicating a potential threat, Annie had been placed under protective security. I'd long accepted the reality that my role in TF 714 could put me at risk, but it was unnerving to have Annie identified as a potential target. I understood both the rationale behind the protection and the impact it would have on Annie. In addition to the pressure of uncertain danger, Annie's life for almost the next full year involved a security detail who controlled her movements. Trips to the store became orchestrated procedures, and her morning runs through Washington, D.C., required that detail members run or bike close by. Predictably, she maintained her sense of humor, became close to the professionals who spent so much time with her, and tried to ensure that her situation was as little a concern for me as possible.

On September 19, the first morning of the conference, Chairman Mullen and I met for breakfast. Over coffee he gave me a D.C. update. It was a bombshell.

"The strategic assessment was leaked. Bob Woodward is reporting he has it, and the *Washington Post* is going to print a version of it," he stated flatly. "I'm not happy about it, but it's out there."

I wasn't shocked, as things in D.C. leaked often. But having it leak so quickly after reaching Washington was frustrating. I'd expected the analysis to receive wide scrutiny, and I was comfortable with what we'd written, but the leak meant that the media and public would form their judgments at the same time as the policy makers. That would create pressures for each of the players and wouldn't help the subsequent decision-making process. That morning I didn't anticipate insinuations that I, or my staff, had been the source of the leak, which we were not.

Nor did I fully appreciate that morning that many observers and some policy makers felt the leaking had begun six weeks earlier, when the civilian advisers who had participated in our strategic assessment returned to the United States and began to say more forces were needed. They weren't speaking for me, nor in concert, but it often appeared that way when they carried a byline that listed them as an adviser to me. Upon seeing this, members of my team contacted them and sought to put an end to any such announcements. But it was a shortcoming on our part to assume, and not to take preemptive steps to ensure, that they would respect the confidential way in which my team sought to guard the assessment's conclusions. The trickle of opinions from these civilian advisers came on top of other prominent public statements made in D.C. by members of the military. As a result, some in the White House felt as though the military had limited the president's options before he had a chance to weigh our professional advice. This was never my intent, nor that of my staff.

Five days later, in Germany, I again met with Chairman Mullen to review and submit by hand, through Central Command, the resource requirements for the strategic assessment. After the previous week's leak experience, the documents to be submitted were tightly controlled, and we inserted markings unique to each copy to make it easier to narrow down the source of any leak. In a long session with Mullen, Petraeus, and Admiral Jim Stavridis, the Supreme Allied Commander–Europe, my staff and I briefed in detail our analysis and conclusions for how to implement the recommendations of the strategic assessment.

Since we had briefed Chairman Mullen and Secretary Gates on our initial thoughts in early August, continued analysis had reinforced our conclusions. Counterinsurgency doctrine argued for 20 security force members, military or police, for every 1,000 residents in an area. Afghanistan, with a population crudely estimated to be about 24 million people, would require 480,000 soldiers and police. That rough math had to be adjusted for the severity of insurgency in each geographic location, and we graded the security of all 364 districts to determine the necessary force ratio in each. Our assessment found the Afghans needed at least 400,000 security force personnel—240,000 from the army and 160,000 from the police—to have a reasonable ability to combat the threat. We explained that if we were willing to accept moderately or significantly more risk, the targets could be lowered to 328,000 and 235,000, respectively. Although we did detailed modeling and analysis, I understood that counterinsurgency doctrine on security force levels was as much art as science.

At the time, the army was roughly 92,000 strong, approved to grow to 134,000, while the police were 84,000 strong. This was too small for a country of Afghanistan's size and terrain to fight an ongoing insurgency. So, as we worked to grow the army by 150,000 (or 100,000 past its previous target) and the police by 80,000, we recommended deploying an additional 40,000 Coalition forces, no doubt mostly American, to provide a "bridge" capability of sufficient security forces until the Afghan army and police could assume a larger role.

We also shared what we believed the impact of smaller and larger force numbers would be, but recommended 40,000 forces were necessary to implement our strategy within the essential time frame and with what we assessed as "acceptable risk."

I received advice to recommend a higher number to give myself "negotiating room" to the lower, true requirement, but I decided against it. This was no time for games; I had to provide accurate, honest inputs. I viewed the troop calculation not as a request, but as providing what is termed "best military advice" to the commander in chief on what I felt was necessary to accomplish his articulated mission with an acceptable amount of risk. I remain comfortable we followed the right approach, but not "asking high" likely made me appear unwilling to compromise in later stages of the decision-making process.

"I want to defend Afghanistan," the frightened young soldier said in Dari. The skinny, dark eyed young man from northern Afghanistan wore a baggy green fatigue uniform, nylon "web" gear holding his basic combat equipment, and a curiously shaped steel helmet of indeterminate age. In his hands he held a worn AK-47 rifle his leaders had told me was now inaccurate due to overuse. The soldier was young and uncertain, but seemed sincere in his desire to serve.

That fall afternoon in 2009, I was on a bare dirt maneuver area on the Afghan National Army's training center, on the north side of Kabul. With staccato gunfire on a nearby range as an appropriate soundtrack to the moment, I was heartened by the young soldier's commitment to the fledgling Afghan National Army. But after a lifetime of training soldiers, I could see how far we had to go.

I had left the August meeting in Belgium with Mullen and Gates confident that all the participants understood and accepted our analysis that Afghan forces needed to expand sizeably. But in Afghanistan, like everywhere else in the world, building an army and police force takes time, money, leadership, and patience. Afghanistan's long, proud military tradition had endured a three-decade-long hiatus when the country went without a functioning national army. That hiatus had depleted both its stores of equipment and reservoirs of human talent.

In combat, the performance of Afghan National Army units had shown promise, but the dominance of former Northern Alliance leaders, corruption, and uneven leadership continued to hobble their development. Initiatives like the Afghan Military Academy—Afghanistan's West Point—helped. But leaders needed time and political will to create a self-sustaining institution.

The police were far behind, almost depressingly so. They had received little international attention since 9/11, and despite Minister Hanif Atmar's energetic efforts, they lacked training and leadership and suffered from chronic corruption and drug use. By nature, police are far harder to build than armies. Their decentralized employment disperses them in small elements that are vulnerable to improper pressure and corruption. It also makes small-unit leadership critical, something that in Afghanistan was weak. Further, in the press to field police around the country, the Ministry of the Interior adopted a recruit-deploy-train model, instead of the more logical recruit-train-deploy one, guaranteeing that most police in service lacked even a basic level of training.

As a result, the police struggled for legitimacy with the people. In a number of locations, predatory police were the single greatest factor undermining support for the Afghan government. Still, against the cacophony of withering criticism they regularly received, I'd point out that the Afghan National Police were dying in far greater numbers fighting the insurgency than any other force.

Finding fault with both the army and police was easy, but that wouldn't get the job done. So we pushed to expand the existing organization responsible for their training and development into a vastly more capable international effort called NATO Training Mission–Afghanistan (NTM-A). At the same time, we sought increased force levels for both the army and the police.

There were a number of reasons to doubt this goal. We knew that rapid expansion of Afghan security forces risked producing units that lacked the training, discipline, and needed professionalism. And we projected that for a decade or more, Afghanistan could not afford forces of this size without donor funding. But we knew that fielding Afghan forces cost a fraction of what it did to deploy Coalition forces, and that the final stages of the war would be fought not by Americans, but by Afghans.

Leadership would be critical. But development of leaders was a long-term prospect. So Rod and I intended to leverage partnership with ISAF forces to help mitigate the risks of fielding Afghan units that lacked a seasoned leadership cadre. The only way to build not just more security forces but better policemen and soldiers was to put into motion the "radically improved partnership at every level" I had called for in the assessment. Afghans and NATO soldiers would train, eat, bunk, plan, patrol, fight, celebrate, and mourn together. We knew this course of action, however, carried its own risks. It'd be impossible to keep out all attempts by the insurgents to infiltrate the forces, or prevent soldiers turning sides. And we anticipated there would be cultural friction. Most difficult to stomach were tragic cases when uniformed Afghans killed NATO service members. Still we judged true partnering was the only viable option in the time frame we believed we had for the mission.

Piercing stares, animated conversation, and pointing followed my every move. Even separated by chain-link fencing and carefully placed sheets of Plexiglas, the prisoners were menacing. I was visiting the detention facility at Bagram air base, still housed in the same old buildings I'd visited in 2002. As I walked among the series of small chain-link group "cells" occupied by eight to ten detainees each, I was struck by the seething rage coming from what looked like cages. The Plexiglas was there to prevent food and other things from being flung at the guards, who, for the conditions, remained impressively professional. Construction was already under way for a new facility. But it couldn't come quickly enough.

Sensitive to both the importance and risks of detention operations, I was anxious to create a detention operation like I'd seen developed in Iraq in 2007–2008. I remembered sitting in a meeting in Baghdad in early 2007 when a Marine Reserve major general named Doug Stone had arrived to take command of detention operations. I'd known Doug from his tour in Islamabad back in 2003–2004 and frankly doubted he would be up to the task.

I was dead wrong. He began by creating a short but frightening video illustrating the depth of the problems we had in the theater detention system in Iraq. To haunting background music, his video showed escapes, frequent violence, even buildings being burned down by prisoners. It also revealed the systematic indoctrination of countless Iraqis who'd arrived into the system with little ideological fervor, but were soon exposed to the extremism then plaguing our detention system in Iraq. He argued that inside our detention facilities, we were losing to the insurgency. Then, in a systematic campaign, Doug and his team changed the environment inside the prisons. What had been a dramatic vulnerability for the Coalition became an effective component of its counterinsurgency campaign.

Now, in 2009, with Dave Petraeus's support, Doug came out to Kabul to lay the groundwork for the creation of a new organization we named Joint Task Force 435. It would redesign our detention operations in Afghanistan with the objective of transitioning them to Afghan control as quickly as possible, we hoped by January 1, 2011. When Doug became unavailable for long-term assignment to Afghanistan, I sought Vice Admiral Bob Harward. Bob was a relentlessly energetic SEAL who'd been one of my assistant commanding generals in TF 714 for my last two years in command. I tasked him with implementing Doug's design. A Dari speaker, Bob brought an ability to drive change and build key relationships with Afghan counterparts.

Bob completed the new detention facility, managing every aspect of its operating plan. It was superb, allowing us to provide better living conditions, conduct effective interrogations, and prepare detainees for integration back into Afghan society. To eliminate Afghans' recurring concerns over the typically opaque way the United States detained their countrymen, we hosted a series of visits and tours by officials, media, and Afghan opinion makers. From the beginning, there was a robust Afghan government presence in the facility, and I directed Bob to place a high priority on the transition to Afghan control as quickly as possible.

More important than reforming how we handled the detention of insurgents, we sought to reestablish the "rule of law" in Afghanistan. Traditional tribal systems—called *shuras* or *jirgas*—and the more official police and judicial functions provided by the districts, provinces, and national government were in disarray. Courts, which should have provided essential government services for common problems like land disputes, were plagued by corruption, inefficiency, or a complete lack of capacity. The Taliban had skillfully exploited this vacuum, and further highlighted the government's failings by providing basic legal arbitration.

Joint Task Force 435's operations quickly became far wider than U.S.-run detention operations and, in concert with the U.S. embassy, included an effort to transform the Afghan government's ability to build up the rule of law. We brought to Afghanistan Mark Martins, an army brigadier general I'd known at Fort Bragg and in Iraq, and now asked him to spearhead urgent change. Mark had been first in his West Point class and a Rhodes Scholar, but his energy was just as critical as his intellect in the task ahead.

At the beginning of October, I got a serious wake-up call. I was in London for engagements conducted to explain and strengthen support for ISAF's efforts, which had expanded significantly with our campaign to secure the Helmand River valley. The rising violence and risks within Afghanistan prompted political challenges to the leadership of contributing nations, such as Germany and Italy, which had joined ISAF with the expectation of nonviolent peacekeeping operations. Over my year in command, I recieved a number of requests for me to provide such direct ISAF commander observations and insights, and I wasn't able to fulfill most of them in person. But given the ongoing Helmand operations and the British role in them, I judged this invitation to be particularly important. After consulting with Secretary Gates, I agreed to speak in London.

I was awakened in the early-morning hours of October 2 by Admiral Mullen relaying concerns over remarks I'd made the previous day at London's International Institute for Strategic Studies. A reporter had asked whether I felt a more limited counterterrorism—CT-only—strategy was viable for Afghanistan. I'd answered that, in my estimation, a more holistic effort than a counterterrorism capture-and-kill campaign was required to leave Afghanistan stable. Although Vice President Biden was not mentioned in the question, and I was not thinking of him in my answer, my response was reported as a rebuttal of other policy options for Afghanistan and as criticism of the vice president's views.

It wasn't intended as such, but I could have said it better. I was a commander focused on explaining the mission I understood I'd been given and the strategy currently being prosecuted. Pending alteration through the current review, that strategy was a counterinsurgency campaign to win what Obama had, a few days before the Afghan elections, declared was "not a war of choice" but "a war of necessity." The London venue allowed me explain to a British audience the soundness of that strategy—under which, on that day, British troops were fighting and dying in Helmand. Still, I should have better understood that the president's review process, begun in September, was not just evaluating my strategy and force request to accomplish counterinsurgency mission but was reevaluating the mission itself.

Redefining ISAF's—and America's—mission in Afghanistan became a central issue. In June, I'd directed our team to conduct the strategic assessment based upon our understanding of the mission as outlined by President Obama in speeches prior to that time. Although the importance of Al

Qaeda was never in doubt, we had interpreted that our mission included helping the nation of Afghanistan develop the ability to defend its sovereignty. This necessarily included building capacity across the government and providing the opportunity for economic development.

After Iraq, "nation building" was an unpopular term. But our assessment had concluded that Afghanistan's inherent weakness in governance was at the core of the problem. Security had to come first, or else the government could not function. But absent legitimate governance, real progress was impossible. We didn't think the country's government needed all the attributes and trappings of Western democracy, but Afghans needed to believe it was responsible and legitimate enough to offer a credible alternative to Taliban or local warlord control.

In the weeks ahead, policy makers reviewed a variety of alternative approaches. One envisioned maintaining control of a limited number of secure areas in Afghanistan and prosecuting a counterterrorist strategy of pinpoint kinetic strikes and raids against insurgents. It had the potential advantage of requiring fewer forces and avoiding the daunting challenge of pacifying areas long under insurgent influence or outright control. A counterterrorist approach shared some attributes with Britain's late-nineteenth-century "butcher and bolt" tactics in India's Northwest Frontier, now Pakistan, where potential adversaries were kept weakened and "in line" by periodic raids that demonstrated Britain's power.

My background in counterterrorism made the approach tempting, but I reluctantly concluded it wouldn't work. Watching efforts like Doug P.'s and Sean MacFarland's fight in Ramadi, I'd left Iraq with the conviction that strikes could damage insurgent forces, but I felt that a counterterrorism strategy would ultimately cede control of an area, and of its population, to the enemy. If our mission included an Afghanistan capable of defending its people and sovereignty, it would require more.

The day after the London speech, I flew to Copenhagen for a previously scheduled Air Force One meeting with President Obama, who was in the region to receive the Nobel Peace Prize. I took Annie with me, and in both our initial greeting with spouses and our one-on-one meeting, the president was focused but friendly and supportive. I don't remember either of us raising anything about the speech.

Still, in retrospect, I never felt entirely the same after the leak of the strategic assessment and then the unexpected storm raised by the London talk. I recognized, perhaps too slowly, the extent to which politics, personalities, and other factors would complicate a course that, under the best of circumstances, would be remarkably difficult to navigate.

Not long before I spoke in London, I'd sat with David Martin of *60 Minutes* in front of a camera in ISAF's Kabul compound. "Can you imagine ever saying to the president of the United States, 'Sir, we just can't do it'?" he asked.

"Yes, I can," I said. "And if I felt that way, the day I feel that way, the day I'm sure I feel that way, I'll tell him that."

His question got to a fundamental paradox military leaders face in communicating about the effort they are leading. The public deserves candor about the situation and prospects for success; politicians demand it. Anything less is deemed incompetence or equivocation. But once a decision has been made to conduct an operation, a commander has to believe it can be accomplished and has to communicate that confidence in countless ways to the soldiers he leads. Failure to do so can undermine the determination of the force and can risk a fear of failure becoming self-fulfilling.

The paradox was real. As I watched from the Pentagon during the year leading up to my assignment to Afghanistan, I thought I understood the political sensitivities that existed around America's and NATO's role in Afghanistan. I had assumed command believing we needed to reverse both the reality and perception of a deteriorating situation, and through the assessment had concluded that only with significant changes, energetically implemented, could we succeed. After three months of command that included extensive travel around Afghanistan and daily interaction with Afghans from Kabul to rural villages, I also believed the mission was worthy of the risks and sacrifices it would entail. But in the coming months I found myself in a balancing act between trying to aggressively accomplish the mission I believed I'd been given, and not corrupting a valid policy-review process that quickly came to question whether the mission itself was the correct one.

Like many soldiers of my generation, my ideal for how a military leader should advise and answer to civilian, democratic authority had been drawn from Samuel Huntington's seminal treatise, *The Soldier and the State*. He argued a military commander should endeavor to operate as independently of political or even policy pressures as possible. And yet I found, as much as I wanted my role to be that described by Huntington, the demands of the job made this difficult. The process of formulating, negotiating, articulating, and then prosecuting even a largely military campaign involved politics at multiple levels that were impossible to ignore.

My position as director of the Joint Staff had offered a window into civil-military interaction that was at once disconcerting and instructive. Inevitably, as the Obama administration decided whether to increase our forces in Afghanistan, some drew comparisons between Afghanistan and Vietnam. As a student of history, I was sensitive to the Vietnam analogy. That summer, I reread Stanley Karnow's *Vietnam: A History*, which portrayed the challenges of that war. During a memorable night in Kabul, Richard Holbrooke and I spoke on the phone with Karnow. But the lessons to be drawn were anything but incontrovertible. Civilians looking back on Vietnam had cause for wariness when reading of the military's propensity for unrealistic assessments of the probability of success, exemplified by Westmoreland's famous "light at the end of the tunnel" phrase.

I also thought of Daniel Ellsberg's book *Secrets: A Memoir of Vietnam and the Pentagon Papers*, which I'd listened to on audiobook while in Iraq commanding TF 714. Ellsberg's story, intensely controversial in my youth, now offered me more nuanced lessons. His outrage stemmed from his conclusion that many of the failures in Vietnam owed not to flawed analysis but to politically driven decisions to ignore the difficult conclusions the analysis offered. The Pentagon Papers, which he famously leaked, convinced him that decision makers had not been misled into disaster by ignorance or bad advice. Rather, faced with two politically toxic but militarily sound options—withdrawal or full escalation—they chose to pursue other policies for political reasons, even though analysis told them these policies were likely to fail. It was a chilling thought.

At one point, a story arose that I was considering resigning if not provided the forty thousand troops I'd recommended. That was simply not true. As a professional soldier I was committed to implementing to the best of my ability any policy selected by civilian leadership.

The following week, on October 8, a version of the "What is our mission?" question surfaced during one of the early National Security Council–sponsored video teleconferences, organized to review America's policy. Beamed into the White House Situation Room from our headquarters in Kabul, I began the briefing by explaining the mission as I understood it: "Defeat the Taliban. Secure the Population." It prompted a participant on the other screen to ask why I interpreted our mission as requiring the destruction or eradication of the Taliban. I said I wasn't. The word we'd used was "defeat," which in military doctrine was defined as rendering an enemy incapable of accomplishing its mission. As Sun Tzu had advised, if that could be accomplished cheaply, with little actual fighting, so much the better. I was then asked why we'd defined our mission as defeat, and not some lesser objective, like "degrade."

"Because that's the mission we provided them in a tasking document," I remember Lieutenant General Doug Lute interjecting into the discussion. "They are using what we told them."

Recognizing the disconnect, I walked into the next VTC with a slide that outlined the sources from which we'd derived the mission we'd used for our assessment, including the president's public speeches and the marching orders that flowed from the administration's March strategy review. We also showed the origins of NATO's mission statement for ISAF. It seemed to surprise some of the participants in the session.

Not the president, however. "Stan is just doing what we've asked him to do," he explained. But it was clear to me that the mission itself was now on the table for review and adjustment.

Redefining the mission was an important, maybe the most important, task in front of policy makers. I'd repeatedly advised my staff not to be wedded to our first interpretation of the mission. We would have to provide our best military advice on the course of action and resources necessary to accomplish whatever directives we were given. Our strategic assessment provided a partial foundation for the process, but had not considered significantly different missions.

While the review debated whether to defeat or degrade the Taliban, I never thought we'd crush the Taliban in a conventional military sense; I calculated we didn't need to. I hoped to defeat it by making it irrelevant: We'd do so through limiting its ability to influence the lives and welfare of the Afghans, and reducing the grievances that pushed recruits to its ranks. But we also needed to craft realistic avenues and opportunities for insurgents to reconcile with the government in safety. Five months earlier, almost immediately after being alerted I would deploy to Afghanistan, I had decided I wanted to create an organization to orchestrate that process. To lead it, only one man came to mind: Soon-to-retire Lieutenant General Sir Graeme Lamb, the Scottish maverick who had so quietly done so much in Iraq to produce much needed spurts of momentum in our favor during a crucial time.

In a gross adaptation of Churchill's famous tribute to the heroes of the Battle of Britain, I'm confident never has so much been extracted from someone for so little. Instead of offering an impressive dinner for a man who is a closet gourmet, I had taken Graeme to a cheap Mexican restaurant near the Pentagon before I'd deployed. Over burritos and beer I asked him to put all his plans for retirement life on hold, come to Afghanistan for an undetermined length of time, and do a job I couldn't precisely define. I had no idea what the mechanics of his employment would be, or what he'd be paid. He had no time to consult his wife, Mel, or his daughters, who'd waited years for Graeme to settle.

"Of course, Stan," he answered with his characteristic laugh, "but I can't believe I'm selling myself for a pathetic Mexican dinner, yeah."

Graeme arrived in Kabul in August and soon began organizing his team and establishing connections with relevant Afghan leaders. The Force Reintegration Cell, or F-RIC as it was named, became ISAF's arm to help provide both organization and energy to what was an almost nonexistent Afghan effort to reintegrate smaller bands of Taliban insurgents into society and to set the conditions for potential large-scale, top-level reconciliation between the Afghan government and insurgent leaders.

Years of halfhearted, mostly failed efforts to reintegrate former Taliban into society had produced deep skepticism. Insurgents doubted they would be adequately protected while loyal Afghans were unreceptive to the idea that former enemies might receive land, money, or political stature while they struggled.

Because feelings on the issue were so passionate, Afghan domestic politics were entrenched. Efforts to organize and implement reintegration and reconciliation programs moved at a frustratingly deliberate pace. The international community, anxious for an acceptable accommodation, struggled to maintain a consistent position on the issue. Into this environment I inserted Graeme Lamb, with confidence he would get people talking and, I hoped, acting.

"You can't roll up your sleeves while you're wringing your hands," Graeme would aptly remark.

The increasing friction between the United States and Afghanistan was painfully evident a few weeks later, on October 20, in a press conference from the presidential palace. At the podium President Karzai appeared flanked by U.S. and Afghan flags, Senator John Kerry, Ambassador Karl Eikenberry, and U.N. special representative Kai Eide. A month before, the Afghan government's electoral body had announced Karzai had won 55 percent of the vote, compared to Abdullah's 28 percent, initially making it appear Karzai had avoided a runoff and gained a significant mandate beyond his Pashtun base. But the independent U.N.-backed monitor, the Electoral Complaints Commission (ECC), announced widespread fraud. The day before, the ECC had announced revised numbers, which put Karzai at less than 50 percent. Now he reluctantly agreed to accept a runoff election. In Afghan society, where a leader's personal stature and presence mattered, the press conference may have reinforced the image of Karzai as a puppet of the West—a portrayal that I knew cut him to his core. Less than two weeks later, the runoff was canceled when Dr. Abdullah withdrew over concerns the second round of voting would be no less susceptible to fraud than the first.

Although blame for getting to that point could fairly be spread far and wide, the scar tissue, particularly the indignation that Karzai felt, was deep and permanent. The mistrust on both sides became a critical issue, further hindering the partnership between NATO and Afghans and eroding confidence in the viability of the mission.

Despite the controversy, and perhaps more so because of it, I increasingly made my relationship with Karzai a priority and sought to base it on genuine respect. I was aware of his flaws, and the allegations against his brothers. I had seen him exhibit both impressive and poor leadership in my first three months. But I increasingly understood the unique challenges of the physical and political environment in which he had to work to make the partnership to which NATO, America, and Afghanistan had committed as effective as possible.

My close relationship with Dave Rodriguez remained important to me on both a personal and a professional level. Whenever I could, often at the end of trips to locations across the country, I'd land at Kabul's airport and walk the two hundred meters to Rod's headquarters to see him for a few minutes before I moved across the city to ISAF's compound. We'd developed the strategy together and were now partners in implementing it. Sitting in his small office, we would often compare notes and talk candidly about the war. Seeing the poster-size photo Rod kept of his son, Andrew, whom I'd known from birth, in his West Point football uniform, I'd remember all Rod was missing.

Late one evening after flying back from Kandahar at the beginning of November, two months into the president's review process, I went to Rod's office and became aware of a set of cables U.S. Ambassador Karl Eikenberry had recently sent. In them, he raised a number of questions and concerns on the troop increase and the Afghans' ability to take responsibility for their country in a reasonable time frame. I would later learn that he had written these at the request of Secretary of State Hillary Clinton in order to provide her with a candid and personal assessment of the campaign. While I may not have agreed with Karl on all matters, I always valued his analysis and judgment, particularly given his years of government service in Afghanistan as a soldier and then as a statesman.

In the cables Karl voiced a number of reservations about the counterinsurgency approach and the impact of more troops, including the American public's patience for a relatively long and expensive campaign. He expressed concerns that the U.S. civilian effort was underresourced: A recent request for increased funding by the embassy, he reminded Secretary Clinton, had been rejected. He also noted that NATO and the U.N.'s wider civilian effort remained uncoordinated and thus undermined—an unsettling reality when the civilian component needed to be an equal pillar in a joint counterinsurgency strategy.

But Karl's strongest criticisms were of the Afghan government. He worried the Afghan army and police were unlikely to be able to establish and maintain security, and the Afghan government lacked the institutions and manpower to establish governance in areas we cleared. Combined with his reservations about President Karzai's personal commitment and effectiveness, it was a powerful warning from a soldier-diplomat with extensive Afghan experience.

Karl's cable reminded me of Bob Komer's well-known 1972 Rand study raising the alarm about U.S. performance in Vietnam, a document I'd read and reread for the instructive way it captured the pitfalls counterinsurgency efforts too easily fall into.

There was little of Karl's analysis that I disagreed with. But based on my understanding of the mission the president had given us, I concluded that we had few options, and none of them were easy or enticing. Complete withdrawal would reopen Afghanistan to Al Qaeda and enable the Taliban's resurgence. And at the status quo, the situation had been steadily deteriorating. So, as we'd outlined in our strategic assessment, I believed that if we were going to pursue the objectives that comprised our current mission, we had to simultaneously do more, and also do it better.

While our objective had to be the most rapid transition possible to Afghan defense of their own sovereignty, by the fall of 2009, for a variety of oft-cataloged reasons, Afghanistan was not yet ready to assume responsibility. As expensive as it would be, particularly in the lives of our service members, I had concluded that in order to provide both the Afghan government and its security forces an opportunity to grow the necessary capabilities, we would need additional U.S. and Coalition forces to enhance security and to accelerate training of the army and police. These Afghan units would need to be mentored by U.S. and international forces in the field, as they jointly fought back the enemy. Doing so, in time, would bring the insurgency down to a size that the Afghan security forces, with continued improvement, could then manage. Rather than increasing the Afghan army and police's dependence, more American troops, seriously focused on integrating the Afghans would set conditions, as President Obama later put it, so that "more Afghans can get into the fight."

Karl proposed President Obama take more time before making a decision on a strategy or troop levels, and instead extend the review process and bring in further viewpoints. In the meantime, Karl suggested, the president might incrementally add smaller amounts of troops to mentor and fight, adding more forces only as the Afghan government's performance improved. I shared the desire to see the Afghan government make significant improvements before putting more Americans in harm's way. But I felt that incrementally adding troops would parallel our experience in Vietnam and, to a degree, in Iraq. In those wars, we had underestimated, then lagged the insurgency. By periodically adding more troops but not enough to finish off the insurgency, we'd made it stronger: The combat made the enemy a wiser foe, and their ability to survive made them appear more credible and fearsome to the population.

Unfortunately, within days of his sending the cables, the broad outlines of Karl's conclusions were leaked to the *New York Times*, which paraphrased many of his concerns. Like the leak of our strategic assessment, it was disruptive to have such classified documents shared with the press, particularly at that sensitive period of the campaign. Then, and again when the *Times* released the cables in their entirety in January, my immediate concern was the impact they would have on the Afghans, particularly President Karzai. As is typical in confidential correspondence, the language was frank. Karl took the position that Karzai was "not an adequate strategic partner." Karzai and his administration soon read that phrasing themselves. I did not share Karl's viewpoint, knowing that a relationship with any one person, even the president, in a campaign as complex as the one in Afghanistan would not make or break the entire effort. Instead, the partnership that we had with Afghanistan collectively—its government, its security forces and, most important, its people—would drive our success or failure.

Two weeks later, on November 23, President Obama convened the last of his full National Security Council sessions on the direction forward in Afghanistan. The president opened the floor, and Vice President Biden spoke first. Secretary Clinton followed. Throughout the fall, she'd been a strong voice during the deliberations. Now she quickly made clear that she supported sending forty thousand additional troops to pursue our strategy. As it had been refined, that strategy involved protecting select geographic centers; continuing to target Al Qaeda; and growing and improving the Afghan army and police to be able to secure the state against a weakened insurgency. Even on the wide angle of the VTC screen and through our headquarters speakers in Kabul, her strong tenor was unmistakable. Secretary Gates spoke immediately after her, and echoed her sentiment. So did Ambassador Holbrooke when it came time for him to weigh in.

Six days later, on November 29, President Obama conducted a VTC with just Karl and me. From our seats in the Kabul embassy's secure conference room, the president appeared alone, and the feeling was strangely intimate. His tone was friendly but serious as he explained his decision to approve the deployment of thirty thousand additional U.S. troops, beginning in December, and to press our Coalition partners to provide the additional ten thousand I'd requested. He also stated his intent to begin withdrawing those surge forces in July 2011. The president then directly asked Karl and me if we could live with the decision as outlined, and we each said yes.

Among other things, the president seemed to be eliciting my reaction to an announced withdrawal date. Earlier, Secretary Gates had asked what I thought about the idea. I cited concerns that it would give the Taliban a sense that if they survived until that date, they could prevail, and that it might decrease confidence in the strategic partnership we were trying to build on so many levels with the Afghans. But I also knew it would provide a clear impetus for Afghans to speed up efforts to assume full responsibility for their future.

I recognized there were political realities outside my view, and I judged that the combination of our ability to expand secured areas over the next eighteen months, and to increase Afghan security force capacity during that period, could allow us to reduce the force size with acceptable risk. If I'd felt like the decision to set a withdrawal date would have been fatal to the success of our mission, I'd have said so.

On December 1, the day before President Obama was to announce his decision publicly, I flew to Chaklala Airfield, the military part of Islamabad's primary airport. Security was tighter than ever. Seven weeks earlier, on October 10, six terrorists had conducted a daring assault of the base, killing six Pakistani soldiers, including a brigadier general I'd known and a lieutenant colonel. It was the equivalent of an attack on the Pentagon to kill senior Defense Department officials and highlighted the serious nature of the threat the Pakistanis were facing.

The Taliban had, since their expulsion in 2001, used Pakistan's undergoverned border areas as sanctuary from which to recruit, lead, and organize the fight in Afghanistan, often with Pakistani support. But their focus had always been primarily across the border, where they sought to reclaim

Afghanistan, or parts of it. Parallel with their rise, however, was that of a Taliban movement focused not only on Afghanistan but also internally, on Pakistan. In December 2007, smaller, independent Pakistani militant groups that had existed in the border region organized themselves into a connected movement. They took the name Tehrik-i-Taliban Pakistan, or TTP, but established themselves outside the formal command and domain of the Afghan Taliban's leaders, such as Mullah Omar.

Instead, at the helm was Baitullah Mehsud, an uneducated thirty-four-year-old who controlled large swaths of South Waziristan. He brought his five-thousand-strong force under the TTP structure and sat atop a leadership council that drew from the agencies and districts along Pakistan's border. At its inception, the group included a patchwork of various militant groups, some old, some new, with anti-Islamabad, anti-American, and anti-Indian leanings. Concretely, however, they aimed to expel ISAF forces from Afghanistan and, importantly, to contest Pakistani military incursions into the border areas.

At the time, I felt the growing threat from the TTP had the potential to cause a shift in Pakistan's strategic calculus, aligning it more closely with NATO's objectives for Afghanistan. The TTP was becoming increasingly effective and lethal. The previous twelve months had been the deadliest year yet for suicide bombings in Pakistan. A Taliban-controlled Afghanistan, once envisioned by Pakistan as a desirable northern neighbor, would more likely become a sanctuary for the TTP, bent on opposing Islamabad. I knew we would not get Pakistan to cooperate fully, which would have involved aggressive operations to root out all Afghan Taliban. We would seek as much cooperation as possible, but I felt we could succeed in Afghanistan even without Pakistan's full partnership.

That day, General Ashfaq Kayani and I discussed President Obama's upcoming speech. We also surveyed the current state of both ISAF and the Pakistani army's ongoing campaigns against insurgents. Kayani was characteristically candid and clearly proud when describing Pakistani operations. I found his insights valuable. He expressed overall support for the ISAF strategy I outlined in this and earlier meetings. But he was openly skeptical that we would succeed. He stated quietly, in his low, sometimes inaudible voice, that while we had the correct approach, he felt we lacked the time to accomplish all that was necessary before support for our effort would fade. He particularly doubted our ability to create effective Afghan security forces to which we could later transfer control. I respected his perspective but felt our chances were better than he believed.

Like my relationship with President Karzai, I sought to build genuine trust with General Kayani. I was aware of the policy and cultural differences between us, but believed that different views, even strong disagreement on hugely substantive issues, would only be exacerbated by personal animosity or disrespect, particularly when expressed publicly or through the press. Despite frustrations I might have had with the Pakistanis, or they with me, I'd found it essential to offer small gestures, engage in honest conversations, and persistently commit to real relationships.

Early the next morning, December 2, in Kabul, I decided, instead of running or lifting weights, to use an hour on an elliptical trainer for exercise so that I could watch President Obama's speech announcing his decision on Afghanistan. He was speaking at eight o'clock in the evening of December 1 in the United States. In front of the president's podium was a sea of gray wool. Young cadets in their slate dress uniforms filled the auditorium's tiered seats. In a moment, the memory of the particular itch and stiffness of the wool brought into focus my thirty-four-year career that had begun on the plain, so near to where the president was speaking. I remembered how our full dress uniforms had all been accidentally shrunk in the academy's washing machines the night before graduation, and how big Ken Liepold's frame had looked inside his tight gray tunic. Earlier that fall, I had phoned Kenny from Kabul. Stricken by throat cancer, he could not talk much, but expressed his support. Even at a distance, his company meant as much as it had when we shared a small dorm room at West Point decades earlier.

On the screen above the elliptical, the camera periodically panned to the faces of the cadets. The youngest would have been ten years old when September 11 struck. Now, as the president spoke, the decision he outlined would likely send some of them to a war that had until then been far away. For those of us already close to it, his speech was an important development for ISAF and a milestone for our long war in Afghanistan.

"We will pursue the following objectives within Afghanistan. We must deny Al Qaeda a safe haven," he said. "We must reverse the Taliban's momentum and deny it the ability to overthrow the government. And we must strengthen the capacity of Afghanistan's security forces and government so that they can take lead responsibility for Afghanistan's future."

To provide the means to accomplish this, Obama announced he would send thirty thousand additional U.S. forces and said he expected our Coalition partners to provide their proportion as well. As a means of demonstrating limits to the mission, he also announced that the increase in forces was for the next eighteen months only and stated his intention to begin withdrawing U.S. forces in July 2011. The surge forces would be one part of a three-part strategy that included a surge in U.S. civilian personnel to help with governance, development, and other efforts, and the pursuit of a new, more effective partnership with Pakistan.

As with most presidential decisions in wartime, there was something for everyone to like and something for everyone to hate. Those who opposed the war decried the escalation, while those who supported it found the stated plan to withdraw counterproductive.

Because I had been through the gestation of his decision, its public birth was anticlimactic. For me, and the command I led, it was simply guidance to execute.

L ater that morning, I drove out the small ISAF gate that had been the site of the lethal car bomb attack in August, and down familiar Bibi Marhru Road to the palace to meet with President Karzai. I went to brief him, as well as ministers Wardak and Atmar, and others from his national security team on the implications of his American counterpart's speech. I'd briefed Karzai earlier in the fall on what I had recommended to President Obama and he offered his concurrence. But, as always, I sensed ambivalence toward any actions that he feared were likely to increase the violence.

I then began a journey to disseminate President Obama's intent across my command. We drove from the palace to a helipad at the Ministry of Defense and flew by UH-60 helicopter to Bagram Airfield to meet with Lieutenant General Mike Scaparrotti and the other leadership of RC-East. We spent the remainder of a long day flying first to RC-North in Mazar-e-Sharif, then to RC-West in Herat, and finally to Kandahar to meet with RC-South. In each location I met face-to-face with ISAF leaders to talk to them about President Obama's decision and what it meant. Earlier in my career, I'd found that reaching or making a decision was sometimes less critical than communicating it effectively.

On Thursday, December 3, we continued. After briefing a meeting of Afghan ministers at ISAF headquarters, I went to the parliament to meet with selected representatives of the people. I explained our strategy and how the additional forces would be employed. I sensed general support. Not surprisingly, despite the exigencies of the situation in their country, some were more concerned with political maneuvering than with addressing the looming issues that threatened the survival of their government.

After parliment, we went to the airport and Brussels for a NATO foreign-ministerial conference scheduled for the following day. That venue provided an opportunity to explain the U.S. decision, and included a strong endorsement of the course of action by Secretary General Anders Fogh Rasmussen. At the conclusion, we reboarded the aircraft and continued on to D.C., where Karl Eikenberry and I would testify before Congress on December 8 and 10.

That next week was a whirlwind. Saturday and Sunday were spent intensively preparing for our upcoming congressional testimony and included two full dress-rehearsal "murder boards," exquisitely humbling experiences where several old "Washington hands" grilled Karl and me with seemingly sadistic pleasure. But as always, the preparation paid off and our testimony went smoothly.

There was time to visit the wounded at Walter Reed Army Medical Center, which was, as always, a difficult but uplifting experience. We gave a series of media interviews, attended a meeting of Army four-star generals, and took a couple of days off before redeploying.

As we often did, Annie and I drove to Gettysburg for the night. En route, we stopped at a used bookstore. Old books, carefully selected and inscribed to people I worked with, were my favorite gift to give. We arrived in town in the late afternoon and Shawn Lowery and I ran the battlefield to clear our heads after the week's work. First making our way south from town into the heart of the battlefield, we turned north near Pennsylvania's monument on Cemetery Ridge and ran the line where federal forces who had been rushed to the frontmost line had stood firm on the critical third day.

It was cold and the day was nearly done. After months of politics, the diplomacy of coalition warfare, and the scrutiny of the media, seeing the stone markers and the cannons in the frigid, fading light brought things into focus. The president's decision was no longer a policy issue for pundit analysis. It was an order sending more Americans to war.

I wasn't tortured by doubts that the president's decision to deploy additional troops was the wrong one. Although our path to that point could be endlessly debated, by December 2009 reversing the rapid deterioration of Afghanistan demanded decisive action. The thirty thousand Americans soon to deploy were the first step of that reversal. The president's speech did not signal success in Afghanistan, nor was it even a promise that we were on a road to it. It simply gave us the tools. It gave us an opportunity. I strongly believed we could succeed, and committed myself completely. As I ran that evening alongside the grass of the battlefield, gray and dry in the wintry early evening, I knew that despite all I'd done, all I'd learned, and all of myself that I was prepared to devote, in war, nothing was certain.

More important, I knew that regardless of victory or defeat, the costs would rise. Soldiers just then being alerted for deployment would die or be grievously wounded. Even in the best of outcomes, fighting would keep our field hospitals busy. Afghan families, long tossed about by the war, would suffer, as would families far away who would never see the country where their loved one died. On most evenings ahead, I would sit quietly at my place in our operations center and write letters to the next of kin. These were sincere but pitifully inadequate efforts to ease their devastating pain. We would use our forces judiciously, but they would go in harm's way. And I was responsible.

| CHAPTER 20 |

▼

Execute

January–June 2010

On the evening of Sunday, February 12, 2010, we gathered in the living room of Palace Number 2. The loftily named but modest two-story building lay on Kabul's palace grounds but outside the historic walled-in compound where the kings and other rulers of Afghanistan had traditionally lived. It was now President Karzai's residence, where he, his physician wife, and their young son, Mirwais, lived. The house was comfortable though hardly palatial. The living room where we waited for President Karzai had the feel of a prosperous but not wealthy American home, circa 1964.

Gathered with me were Afghanistan's security-sector leadership, including Minister of Defense Rahim Wardak; Minister of the Interior Hanif Atmar; Director Amrullah Saleh of the NDS, Afghanistan's intelligence service; and General Bismullah Mohammedi, or "BK," as he was known, Afghanistan's army chief. I found it a comfortable group. In the seven months since I'd arrived, military operations, the elections, and efforts to grow Afghanistan's security forces had brought us into almost daily interaction.

The president was expected down shortly, and we chatted in subdued voices. We'd never met in the president's home before, and I felt slightly guilty having first requested, and then demanded, the evening meeting. The president kept his family life private, and I knew that invading his home that night was an imposition. I also knew he was sick in bed with a cold, but I felt my purpose was important enough to warrant it.

Earlier in the day I had pushed this meeting to secure his final approval for the launch of Operation Moshtarak, the next major step in the campaign we'd begun in June 2009 to reassert Afghan government control over the Helmand River valley. Operation Moshtarak (Dari for "together") was also an advancement in the integration of ISAF and Afghan forces in operations. As we waited, talking through details of the operation, Coalition and Afghan forces were marshaled with vehicles and helicopters some 360 miles southwest, in Helmand. They were poised to begin with a dramatic encircling maneuver.

The operation that awaited them was to be a complex and tedious counterinsurgency. It required they seal off, then clear Marjah, a locale about the size of Washington, D.C., that included gridded urban areas, interlinked bazaars, and agricultural fields, all crisscrossed by a series of irrigation canals designed by American engineers in the 1950s and 1960s. Then the difficult work of local governance and development programs had to begin. The population had to see the benefit of supporting the Taliban's expulsion.

The campaign in Helmand had really begun with the British assault on Babaji the previous June. But the added attention Afghanistan had received from Washington and Europe since then had increased anew with President Obama's December 1 announcement of additional forces. The leadership in Coalition capitals expected these forces be quickly employed, and there was an appetite for an operation with rapid, observable impact.

Before I had arrived at the palace, I'd spoken with General Rod. If we didn't relay a go to the field commanders by 9 P.M., we couldn't start the operation that night. And the weather the next day, he'd said, was not good. We'd have to delay twenty-four hours. We'd lose tactical surprise and Taliban defensive preparations would continue. More IEDs would be buried. The soldiers and Marines who were gathering then in the dark, double-checking equipment, steeling themselves, would be told to marinate another day.

It was now after 7 P.M.

A few days earlier, I'd traveled to the city of Lashkar Gah, Helmand's provincial capital, and met with elders from Marjah who had come from their district to discuss the impending operation with us.

"We support the operation to liberate our district, but only if it can be done following three important conditions," a bearded elder in a turban said in a clearly rehearsed statement.

"First, the operation must be conducted in a manner that avoids killing civilians or destroying our homes.

"Second," he continued, "when it is completed, the corrupt police that have preyed upon us cannot be allowed to return.

"Finally, if you come, you must stay. If you don't, the Taliban will return and we," he said, gesturing to his colleagues in the room, "will all be killed."

This was classic counterinsurgency. From frightened, vulnerable strangers, I was asking for a leap of faith.

"I understand," I said, turning my head slowly to make eye contact with

each of the men. "Your conditions represent our intentions for this operation." And they did. We had crafted Moshtarak to drive out the enemy and
simultaneously reassure Afghans across the country that we intended to
focus on their protection.

As we met, I was judging the elders' sincerity and legitimacy in representing the desires their district's people. As the international community
had learned through painful missteps over the previous eight years, it could
be difficult to identify real leaders in war-jumbled Afghanistan. Wealth,
clothing, or fluency in English were false indicators. And dealing with men
mistrusted or hated by the population was not only ineffective; it made us
appear either complicit or clueless.

The elders were conducting their own assessment—whether this time
would be different. Whether for the first time since the high expectations of
2001 our efforts would both succeed and provide permanent change. They
recognized our power and probably our sincerity. But they also knew that
for us and the nations we represented, our time in Afghanistan was finite. I
suspected they harbored doubts.

With my statement, the meeting ended with head nods, two-handed
handshakes, and right hands touching hearts. We were ready to go.

A t Palace Number 2, a few minutes after we were all present, President
Karzai appeared. He was friendly and gracious as usual, but fatigue
and the effects of his cold streaked his face. He asked how I was, thanked
me for coming, and then asked me directly the purpose and importance of
the meeting I'd requested.

I reminded him about the January 21 briefing Major General Nick
Carter, the British RC-South commander, and his Afghan counterpart,
Brigadier General Sher Mohammad Zazai, had given him in the National
Security Conference Room in the palace. At that time, with all Karzai's
ministers, Rod, Mark Sedwill, and me in attendance, Nick and Zazai had
explained Moshtarak in detail. Mark Sedwill has recently moved from being Great Britain's capable ambassador to Afghanistan to be my civilian
counterpart as NATO's senior civilian representative in Kabul. After the
brief, President Karzai had asked some pertinent questions and issued appropriate guidance. My objective had been to bring him increasingly into
an active role as commander-in-chief, and immersing him in the tactical
plan felt like a good step forward.

Now, three weeks later, I looked at him directly. "Mr. President, the
forces are in position and ready to launch the operation tonight, but I won't
do so without your approval."

It was a critical moment. President Karzai glanced briefly at his key leaders and then turned back to me.

"General McChrystal, you'll have to forgive me. I've never been asked to
approve this kind of operation before."

His statement spoke volumes. On one level, I think he questioned the genuineness of my request, fearing it was a charade to put a fig leaf, or "Afghan face," on what was still an entirely Coalition-controlled operation. That would push him yet further into the puppet-ruler role he feared for himself and for his nation.

But on another level, I think President Karzai knew me well enough by that evening to decide I was sincere. And if so, this operation and his decision represented a paradigm shift, or at least the start of one. He'd never been allowed or encouraged to assume this role, and we'd have to be patient while he and his team grew into it. The decision would affect some one hundred thousand Afghans who made their home in and around Marjah.

Since he'd assumed the presidency in the fall of 2001, Coalition forces had rarely invited any substantive planning or execution by Afghan forces when conducting military operations in Afghanistan. While never asked to be a real commander-in-chief, Karzai, brought his own hesitations, as well. He had an instinctive aversion to violence—not squeamishness, but something he came to intellectually. Even during the heady days of October 2001, when he crossed into Afghanistan on a motorbike to raise an anti-Taliban tribal rebellion, he had delegated military matters to his compatriot Jan Mohammad Khan, and instead concentrated on inspiring political and tribal support. Over the past eight years Karzai had come to view it as the Coalition's war against foreign terrorists, which we fought on his land, among his people. As leader of the country, he was reluctant to classify the Taliban as a largely Afghan insurgency against his government. This was an attitude that needed to change. We both knew that approving Moshtarak, an operation in which Coalition forces were still the strongest component, was not going to transform his role and attitude about the war overnight. But it was an important start.

The moment carried implications for the conduct of the war beyond the operation set to begin that night. Asking President Karzai to assume a genuine role as commander-in-chief meant that we would necessarily surrender some of the independence ISAF had enjoyed—at the cost of developing a capable Afghan partner. We couldn't ask Karzai to assume responsibility and then constrain his authority. And he clearly held different views from ours on many aspects of how the war should be fought. But I knew that ISAF could never win the war; the Afghans must do that. And they couldn't win it until they owned it. That ownership started at the top.

As the launch deadline grew nearer, President Karzai asked his ministers some pointed questions, then gave his approval. Whatever doubts he had weren't obvious in the firm tone in which he directed Moshtarak to begin. The president never asked me if I would have gone forward with the operation if he had not sanctioned it. I would not have done so.

The operation President Karzai set in motion had been eight months in the works. The previous summer, Dutch Major General Mart de Kruif, then the RC-South commander, first discussed with me the concept of retaking Marjah as an essential step in expanding our initial security zones in Helmand. Securing Marjah, we all recognized, would require a special effort because of the stronghold the Taliban and drug traffickers had maintained since it fell in September 2008. Doing so, however, would consolidate hard-won improvements in the rest of the province, and remove a staging perch from which the Taliban could dispatch assassins and suicide car bombs into Lashkar Gah, to frighten the population and attrit its political elite and governing class. The operation would also continue to show our desire and ability to reestablish Afghan government sovereignty over the most Taliban-controlled areas.

The effort to retake Marjah may have appeared to begin on that night. In reality it had been ongoing for weeks with a series of "shaping" actions designed to force out, or isolate, the Taliban in the district; refine our intelligence picture; and increase the confidence of the population in their decision to support us.

A key component of our strategy, as it had been in several locations in Afghanistan, was to use our ISAF special operations forces, and also an expanded TF 714 force, in intelligence-driven raids against identified Taliban leadership. From my experience in Iraq, I'd come to believe that for counterinsurgency to work in Afghanistan, an aggressive but carefully orchestrated campaign of precision strike operations was essential to degrading insurgents' strength and undermining their confidence.

Soon after arriving in June 2009, I reviewed the existing TF 714 force structure—distributed in the east and south of Afghanistan—and confirmed we needed more capacity. But because TF 714 assets, particularly helicopters and surveillance aircraft, were limited, increasing capability in Afghanistan was a zero-sum game. Any additional TF 714 forces for Afghanistan would have to come from Iraq.

The issue was made easier that summer in a VTC with Ray Odierno, then commanding in Iraq; Bill McRaven, commander of TF 714; and Dave Petraeus, who commanded CENTCOM, the command in charge of both Iraq and Afghanistan. Dave stated unequivocally that for CENTCOM, Afghanistan had become the main effort. This meant that the campaign enjoyed priority for the distribution of limited resources, including TF 714 forces. Armed with his decision, I requested he quickly shift as much of TF 714's intelligence capacity and as many of its strike teams as possible to Afghanistan.

This was not a move I took lightly. My classmate and friend Ray Odierno was employing Bill McRaven's forces with a deft touch to maintain progress. Removing TF 714's forces would increase his risk. Because I had invested so much of myself in the mission in Iraq, I was loath to endanger the outcome there. But if we were going to turn things around in Afghanistan, we'd need to maintain pressure on the insurgents while we executed the slow process of counterinsurgency.

As it played out, Ray was gracious in losing combat power in a way that I suspect only a seasoned commander and old friend could be. In his position I would have desperately wanted to maintain as many of Bill's specialized forces as possible, but Ray said he knew we needed them more. This from the formidable center of our Naval War College basketball team, who I knew could be hard to move if he wanted to be.

Like Ray, Bill McRaven understood our priorities and began to reposition forces to Afghanistan. Over the next twelve months, beginning that fall, his footprint multiplied, with bases spread over most of Afghanistan. As important, Bill and his primary command team moved to Bagram, just as I had done in reverse five years earlier. TF 714's pace of operations grew proportionally, as did its impact on the enemy.

In addition to using strike teams to unbalance insurgents in and around Marjah, we conducted information operations to communicate what was coming. We dropped leaflets and in more nuanced ways that used other media to sow discord within the enemy, channel tribal sentiment in our favor, and build popular support for the wisdom and safety of pledging allegiance to the Afghan government. The Taliban responded with a trump card: In their night letters, they promised the coming American offensive would reinstall Abdul Rahman Jan and his predatory police. The honor of Helmandis required they resist this man, who had robbed them and raped their boys.

There was much discussion about the risks involved in so clearly "telegraphing" our forthcoming punch. No doubt the enemy was able to prepare his defense. But we had to communicate that this operation would be different. ISAF had conducted limited-duration actions into the area before. In March and again in May 2009, Coalition forces had entered Marjah in force, only to withdraw. These incursions, although tactically successful in temporarily disrupting the insurgents and drug traffickers, actually made us look weak rather than strong. The population saw that our arrival did not herald a permanent presence—we lacked the strength to stay—and showed that the Taliban would be free to resume its control. This time, I wanted to let the population, and the Taliban, accept the idea that we would stay.

Major General Nick Carter planned and would lead the operation. Nick's concept was to rapidly project overwhelming power, while limiting the actual employment of fires, in order to reduce damage to the area and civilian casualties. That was a tricky business. Air strikes and massed artillery fires, followed by a methodical sweep by armored vehicles, would most protect troops as they advanced. But such actions would leave devastation in their wake. Instead, Nick's Afghan, British, U.S., and other Coalition forces would maneuver rapidly, much of the force by helicopter, into positions to "unhinge" any deliberate Taliban defense. They would then begin the process of clearing and securing the district. The use of fires would be tightly controlled.

A key aspect of the plan was to rapidly institute as many Afghan government services as possible in order to build legitimacy with the populace.

Rod, Nick, and their teams spent months working with Helmand provincial governor Mohammad Gulab Mangal and Afghan government ministers to create a cadre of technocrats to deploy to the area. A superficial description we'd mistakenly coined "government in a box" distracted from the serious effort to bring Afghan governance into what had been enemy territory.

Establishing credible local governance in rural Afghanistan involved a number of challenges. This was especially the case in Marjah. In truth, there were rarely real power vacuums in Afghanistan—in every area, someone or some group was in charge. Therefore installing a new local administration necessarily took power, influence, and access to wealth away from either traditional or nontraditional leaders.

Identifying these power brokers often took months. Other districts in Helmand were somewhat homogenous—Nawah-ye Barakzai was the valley of the Pashtun tribe Barakzai—but more than sixty tribes were represented in Marjah, making it one of the province's most diverse districts. As Marjah became a central processing site for opium, many of the elites depended on money from the drug trade, funds they feared would dry up if the government eradicated the crop. Many therefore opposed the change, some aggressively.

Finding competent, honest civil servants to work in troubled areas was difficult. The educated talent whom we needed to govern on the local level often had more lucrative and far safer opportunities in Kabul or other large cities. Meanwhile, in places like Helmand, locally available candidates too often lacked the education, were involved in corruption, or were caught up in tribal rivalries to function effectively.

Before dawn on February 13, just hours after President Karzai had given his approval, rotor blades on more than sixty helicopters stirred the night sky. American Marine MH-53s, CH-46s, and AH-1 gunships, Army UH-60 Black Hawks, CH-47 Chinooks, and AH-64 Apaches, joined by Canadian and British helicopters, ferried Afghan, British, American, French, and Canadian forces onto carefully chosen locations around Marjah. As one part of this air assault, two mixed companies of U.S. Marines and their Afghan army counterparts landed in helicopters in Marjah itself. The idea was to suddenly present insurgents with threats from multiple directions, thwarting any Taliban effort to conduct a deliberate, phased defense. Two days earlier, on February 11, soldiers on foot and in vehicles had occupied a series of positions, including key canal crossings that controlled access into and out of the area. Neither day featured traditional prep fires; no artillery or aircraft hammered targets ahead of advancing infantry.

In the short term, it would have been vastly simpler if there had been such fires. But the rubble that the soldiers would have walked through would have been the remnants of the bodies, homes, and livelihoods of the very people we sought to protect. Instead, young soldiers and Marines, from Ottawa, Phoenix, Marseilles, and Mazar-e-Sharif, moved carefully through packed-dirt streets and rutted fields sowed with crippling IEDs and scoured by Taliban snipers.

Many civilians had fled the district, some to relatives in neighboring villages, some to refugee camps we'd established outside the zone where we expected fighting. Most were stoic but frightened by the current combat and, even more, by the uncertainty it brought. Taliban rule, financed largely with drug cultivation, was not popular. But the residents hated it less than the other rulers in their recent memory, namely Abdul Rahman Jan and his sadistic police. Early rumors of his impending return piqued local anxieties.

The first day, February 13, went well. By nightfall, Afghan soldiers and U.S. Marines had settled into the center of Marjah. Initial Taliban resistance was less organized than feared. But, as anticipated, this was just the beginning of the clearing phase. On Sunday, Valentine's Day in America, two Marine companies in Marjah continued to clear the town, whose roads were thickly laid with IEDs and whose buildings were booby-trapped. The fighting evolved into a series of small but intense and complex engagements, and the painstaking removal of the enemy's carefully hidden, homemade mines made it slow, dangerous work. Likening it to Fallujah, experienced Marines found these Taliban fighters far more tactically proficient than other Taliban they had encountered.

During the fighting that Saturday, a U.S. rocket launcher called HIMARS targeted a compound, killing twelve Afghan civilians. Initial reports indicated the normally accurate system had impacted three hundred meters short of its intended target. But further investigation pointed to likely engagement of a Taliban-controlled compound that Coalition forces later discovered was also occupied by civilians. To protect the credibility of our commitment to Afghans to conduct operations with their protection foremost, we temporarily suspended use of HIMARS pending investigation. I also directed my staff to issue a statement apologizing for the incident.

To some, issuing an apology to Afghans—for whom our soldiers were risking their own lives, often displaying extraordinary "courageous restraint" in the process—symbolized the inherent contradictions in much of the Afghanistan war. Afghans' resentment of mission-critical actions often mystified soldiers and those who sent them to combat. Such an attitude can strike the military as ungrateful. I recognized and respected those feelings and frustrations, but I also knew improving Afghan perceptions was critical to victory.

The coming days saw continued fighting, interspersed with signs of success. On Wednesday, February 17, while Governor Mangal was briefly in town, Afghan soldiers hoisted a red, black, and green Afghan flag on top of a bamboo pole in one of the city's bazaars. As they raised the flag, forces continued clearing other parts of the district.

A week later, on Thursday, February 25, Governor Mangal and Brigadier General Zazai, commanding the Afghan 205th Corps, hoisted the Afghan flag in the center of Marjah. At the new government center, a proper flagpole replaced the bamboo staff from a few days earlier, and almost seven hundred Marjah residents watched the flag rise. The town's new administrator, Abdul Zahir Aryan, who had been sleeping in the town that week, was in attendance.

Nick Carter, walking without helmet or body armor, told a nearby reporter that "the point at which you have enough security to do something symbolic like this is the point at which the hard work of delivering governance starts." His counterpart, General Zazai, addressed the obvious concerns of the people who had come out for the ceremony. "We promise we won't abandon you," he said.

E ven before my arrival in June 2009, I believed an important component of President Karzai's role as head of state and commander-in-chief of Afghan military forces would be his willingness and his ability to travel around the country providing visible leadership, particularly to troubled areas. Since the increase in violence, he'd left the Kabul palace less and less, except for rumored late-night rides in the passenger seat of a beat-up sedan to see the city that was changing outside his view. I felt he needed to break free of the often-cloistered environment of the palace, where he developed his perspectives based on secondhand, often biased, information, and the routine pummeling he took from the media often inflamed his frustrations. Inside the palace walls, he was also susceptible to the manipulation of members of his inner circle, who stoked his emotions to their benefit through whispers and innuendo. While retaining a balanced perspective was a common challenge for many national leaders, the situation in Afghanistan multiplied both the difficulty and importance of such balance. Further, the population needed to see and hear Karzai. Too often they were informed by rumors and propaganda, rather than direct communication with their leaders. I judged that he needed regularly to visit locations ranging from the battlefields of Helmand to northern provinces like Kunduz.

Such trips were easier proposed than done. Afghanistan's insecurity made adequate protection an extensive effort. Additionally, each trip's location and timing had domestic political ramifications that required Karzai's input. My staff dedicated a large amount of its time to scheduling, coordinating, and executing these trips. We planned them to align with prominent events over upcoming months—central military operations as well as international conferences and decisions. We also sought to visit lower-profile areas and to continue to strengthen his connections beyond the Pashtun south, where his family and tribe were prominent.

The logistics mattered, not least because the Taliban were anxious to kill him. A poorly executed trip risked undermining President Karzai's stature, and could reduce his willingness for future travel. To reach most locations in Afghanistan required a series of vehicle, airplane, helicopter, and ultimately foot movements, each phase of which had to be resourced and integrated into what we hoped would feel like a seamless string of coordinated actions. Each stage involved more than moving just the president. An entourage of selected ministers, aides, and presidential security people always accompanied him.

Although Afghanistan was in the process of fielding a small air force, to include presidential aircraft, the yet-nascent fleet meant that we normally had to use ISAF planes. We had nothing equivalent to Air Force One to fly the president in, so initially he buckled in shoulder-to-shoulder with fifty or sixty Afghan government and ISAF personnel in the noisy cargo bay of a U.S. Air Force C-130. The roar of the aircraft's engines made conversation impossible, and Karzai would maintain as much dignity as possible as we droned toward our destination.

One of the passengers on many of these flights was then-Major Khoshal Sadat, or Kosh, who had joined our team that January. Since taking command, I had been anxious to bring a young Afghan officer onto my staff as an aide-de-camp. Too often, we discussed Afghanistan without a single Afghan in the room. After a few months, a British special forces officer recommended Kosh to us. He came from a military line, like so many of the Americans in his country: Kosh's grandfather had been a senior noncommissioned officer in the king's guards, and his father had been a pilot in the Afghan Air Force. But when his father died in an accident in 1988, Kosh's mother had to raise him and his siblings during the long decade of war that followed. It was a childhood few of us could imagine, one hitched to the weathervane fate of Kabul. As a boy during the civil war anarchy, he caught a ricochet in his arm. As a teenager, he went to get bread but soon wandered over to a crowd, and saw what they saw: the bloodied body of Najibullah, hanging from a candy-cane striped traffic beam. As a young man under the Taliban's dystopian regime, he evaded an unknown fate by escaping out of the back of a pickup after the Taliban had arrested him for carrying cassette tapes. Through it all, his mother insisted that he get an education and learn English. He did well in both, and after joining the military in 2003, he soon won a spot at Britain's Royal Military Academy at Sandhurst. He now came to us after several years of combat as a squadron commander of an elite all-Afghan commando unit trained and mentored by the British SAS.

Kosh was the first and only Afghan to work full-time in the ISAF headquarters building. It was a necessary cultural change, but was not as easy as it should have been. Although he was an important symbol of a new level of partnership and trust, inside the headquarters Kosh often received suspicious looks or requests for identification papers. I watched him closely, impressed that he intuitively understood the importance of his role and handled the friction with impressive maturity. In his shoes, I would have been less good-humored.

After a few such trips on the C-130s with everyone including the president strapped in, we requested and received a "pod," a small capsulelike room that sat five or six people and could be loaded inside a C-130. Although President Karzai had never complained about riding on normal nylon seats in the cargo bay, the pod was quiet enough that we could have substantive conversations while traveling to and from our various destinations. On several occasions, two Afghan government ministers, my NATO civilian counterpart Mark Sedwill, President Karzai, and I were able to frame key issues during uninterrupted flights in a way that hectic palace schedules often prevented.

Despite his often one-dimensional depiction in the media, outside the palace President Karzai was gifted at retail politics. Once on the ground in the various locales we visited, his ability to communicate with local leaders, his "presence," and his natural empathy with his countrymen seemed to resonate in a way that surprised many westerners. In such environments, I was struck anew by his courage and self-discipline.

On one trip north over the Hindu Kush to Kunduz, a rocket attack forced us to forgo our planned return to Kabul by C-130 aircraft. Instead we flew in German MH-53 helicopters ninety-nine miles west to Mazar-e-Sharif. En route, a haboob engulfed the MH-53s in a soupy fog of suspended dust. Sitting next to Karzai, I began to envision the impact on our mission of losing Afghanistan's president in the crash of an ISAF chopper and was irritated at my failure to have asked hard questions about the weather before adopting this plan. I smiled to myself when I remembered that if the aircraft went down, at least I wouldn't have to be the one to explain to President Obama how I'd lost his counterpart. President Karzai likely sensed my frustration but maintained his calm poise and never once, then or later, mentioned anything about it.

The more travel we did, the more I believed that the visits had value. The trips deeply affected President Karzai, as they would any leader exposed to what we called "ground truth." Firsthand contact with the people and the realities of insecure and corruption-racked areas produced thoughtful conversations on our return flights to Kabul.

Such presidential reflection was evident three weeks after Moshtarak began, when on, March 7, I sat quietly, legs crossed, on the floor of Marjah's main mosque. Though the troops I commanded had become the dominant feature of Marjah's landscape for the past three weeks, here I was a guest, a listener. The humble mosque just outside the bazaar was a low box of clay, with rough timber ceiling supports and cracked beige plaster walls inside. Mark Sedwill was next to me. Amrullah Saleh and Minister Wardak sat a few feet away, quietly watching as well. From our position at the front of the room, we saw the crowd that now filled the rug-covered floor. Some two hundred local elders sat cross-legged and still. Quarters were tight, and everyone sat touching. The men a few feet in front of me had significant beards, and sun-darkened faces. Past them I could see the tops of swirled fabric, a sea of thick turbans. As the initial commotion quieted, all gazes were directed to our left. There, President Karzai stood at a small wood podium, topped with a clump of microphones angled toward him.

"I'm here to listen to you, to hear your problems," the president said. This was his first visit to Marjah.

The words came to me, delayed a few seconds, through my translator's voice in an earpiece. The elders sat remarkably still. No uncomfortable shifting or side conversations. On occasion, their work-worn fingers rubbed weathered chins, or silently fingered white beards. With flat faces, they listened with attentive respect. This was the first time in memory such a senior figure from the distant Kabul government had visited their district. Karzai was welcome here, as was I. But this was not scripted theater, and the small space soon got loud when it was the crowd's turn to address him.

The questions were blunt. A man, clearly a father, complained that military units had turned the schools into bases. Another said that the Americans had detained innocent farmers. At one point, an old man, in thick layers of robes, rose, but then turned away from Karzai and squared himself with a man who was off to the side. The old man quivered and shouted, cracking his arm like a whip in front of him as he pointed and denounced the man as a drug trafficker. The seated men nodded and cheered their approval, clapping vigorously, while Karzai raised his hands out to bring quiet again.

Only then did I see them. I hadn't originally. But to the side was Sher Mohammad Akhundzada, along with his hated former police chief Abdul Rahman Jan. These were dangerous men to accuse openly.

And yet the elders did so, sometimes obliquely, sometimes directly, as in the case of the pharmacist appointed by the town to speak for them.

"Their hands have been stained with the blood of innocents and they have killed hundreds of people," he said, pleading with Karzai. "Even now they are being imposed on the people." The message in Marjah was clear: *We do not like the Taliban, but Adbul Rahman Jan and his police gangs are intolerable. They steal from us and rape our children.*

Almost five years earlier, at the request of the British, Karzai had sacked Sher Mohammed Akhundzada as governor of Helmand. Karzai did so reluctantly, and sometimes seemed to regret the firing. Every year since, the province had seen greater Taliban presence, more violence, and more western troops. It wasn't hard to imagine how from his seat in Kabul, the president could conclude that removing Akhundzada had lost him Helmand, and set off a cycle of violence. But from our perspective, with Akhundzada and his men, Karzai could have order, but it would be corrupt and criminal— and thus impermanent. If Helmand landed back under the Akhundzada empire and Marjah came under the thumb of Abdul Rahman Jan, the Taliban hardly had to work to regain the people's favor. As in 2006, and

1994 before that, the pendulum of power would swing back to the Taliban just as soon as the predations became too much for the people to bear. But if the government could unmoor itself from warlords and drug lords, and install something better, it would shift initiative to itself and the Coalition.

The people of Marjah had good reason to be afraid. Abdul Rahman Jan had already organized a thirty-five-man local Marjah *shura* to gain a toehold. He was actively campaigning against the newly installed governor of the district, Haji Abdul Zahir, defaming the Coalition effort, and politicking in Helmand and Kabul to get Marjah back in his hands.

Inside the mosque, President Karzai reacted carefully, his political instincts guiding him. He listened attentively to everyone. He answered complaints he thought unjustified, and he accepted legitimate criticism. The crowd continued to express their grievances to Karzai, but they were not against him. He was quick and conversational with his responses. He got them laughing at one point, and when he asked if they supported Abdul Zahir, the new district chief, the whole crowd erupted in cheers. After one litany that blamed Karzai for letting Akhundzada's men run roughshod over the area in the first place, the president turned to one of the men whom an elder had singled out.

"Shame on you," Karzai said simply and loudly to much applause. From the floor, it appeared to be a first step away from Rahman.

After more than two hours of tense back-and-forth, and some deft politicking, Karzai appeared to win much of the crowd.

"Are you with me?" he asked. "Do I have your support?" The president raised his own hand toward the crowd.

"We are with you," came from the crowd. "We will support you," some said, as many of them raised their hands back at their president.

When the meeting concluded, everyone filed out of the small mosque into the grassless courtyard outside. I sat and slid on my boots, the soles heavy with mud, as Karzai addressed the press outside, this time in English. "We exchanged views. I heard them, they heard me. They had some very legitimate complaints. Very legitimate. They feel as if they were abandoned, which in many cases *is* true."

He walked off, the crowd pressed close around him. He clasped the hand and shoulders of greeters. As I lost site of Karzai into the huddle of people that glided away, out of the corner of my eye I saw a man approach. The first thing I noticed when I turned were the shoes, stepping gingerly through the mud. Beneath the skirt of his *salwar kameez* were black patent leather shoes with long, slender toes that to me seemed absurdly out of place. I looked up at his face. His wide smile parted his ruddy, almost maroon cheeks and black, wooly beard. With outstretched hand, Sher Mohammad Akhundzada introduced himself to me.

I was surprised that he had approached me, although I probably shouldn't have been. Even the appearance of a genial relationship between he and the ISAF commander could send a powerful, potentially frightening message to the throng of locals streaming out of the mosque—the kind of message that could undermine the change we were promising.

"It is good to see you," I told him with a smile, and quickly turned to catch up with Karzai.

I walked with the president through the nearby bazaar. While we were in a small shop, with curious residents surrounding us, Taliban rocket fire impacted some distance away. It was far enough off to have been little immediate danger. But it signaled the Taliban's awareness of Karzai's visit and their intent to target him. With the crump of the rocket, President Karzai looked at me inquisitively. When I shrugged, he smiled back and continued his conversation as if oblivious to any hazard.

I caught up with Kosh, and asked him what he thought. He's good, Kosh said, impressed. Karzai was thickening his Kandahari accent, giving his folksy greetings a twang I couldn't hear.

Meetings like these put tremendous pressure on Helmand's Taliban, who since the town's anticlimactic clearing had regrouped and were intimidating the liberated people. Their threats were making it difficult to convince the scared citizens to use the local government being slowly erected. Much of the menacing came from local insurgents, whom Marjah's people knew were playing the long game. But other more grisly attempts to terrify came from the Mullah Dadullah Front. This large, roving *mahaz* still bore the imprint—fanaticism and cruel tactics—of Dadullah, a man we'd killed two years earlier. Around this time, unsettling news of beheadings arose in the district. It appeared Quetta's newly appointed military chief Qayyum Zakir—who had stolen across the border from Pakistan for a midnight pep talk to Marjah's Taliban before Moshtarak—had dispatched the Dadullah Front to contest our front-page effort to reclaim and rebuild Marjah.

That evening, we marshaled the president and the polyglot collection of travelers in a muddy field to board helicopters back to Kandahar. But the desert skies turned dark, and a steady rainstorm moved in. Worried about getting the entire party stuck in Marjah, I stood outside with our team coordinating aircraft as President Karzai waited inside the small Marine base, rain plunking on the roofing. After a time, the first MH-53 descended into the tight landing zone and we boarded. President Karzai and I sat near the front of the aircraft, next to open windows through which machine guns protruded for protection. As we flew through the now-black night sky, the downpour and wind battered President Karzai and me mercilessly and I shivered from the chill. Directly across from me, Karzai sat motionless. His only move was to reach into his pocket and produce a dry handkerchief that he didn't use to wipe his face—but instead reached across the aisle and handed to me.

As I'd anticipated, because of its timing after President Obama's December speech, the fight for Marjah, never in doubt militarily, became a litmus test for the validity of our strategy in Afghanistan. On display was our ability to conduct effective counterinsurgency in Afghanistan. It also tested the performance of Afghan soldiers, and the Afghan government's commitment and ability to bring legitimate governance to a skeptical population. Finally, the action offered the chance to examine whether it was possibile and appropriate to sharply limit the use of our overwhelming advantage in lethal fires. That judgment would have accompanied the operation regardless of where we'd conducted it.

The natural eagerness in Washington and Brussels to see tangible results following the announcement of more troops created expectations difficult to satisfy with the often glacial speed of counterinsurgency. The drumbeat ahead of the operation, and the dramatic kickoff on February 13, made matters worse. I should have worked harder to tamp down unrealistic expectations of how quickly and dramatically we'd see progress.

That spring there was talk of my returning to Washington, D.C., later that year, as Dave Petraeus had in September 2007 to show progress in Iraq. I remembered his convincing presentation to Congress wherein he showed graphs with steep downward lines and dramatic metrics. Afghanistan, I thought, would never yield anything that clean, or clear. Only over time—a span of months, then years—would we cumulatively be able to produce convincing change.

Indeed, as the first operations of 2010 began, we asked what psychic effect among Afghans we could produce through material gains. Would Afghanistan *feel* the addition of troops and the benefits of security they brought? Would such turns in feeling be large enough, and happen fast enough?

Inevitably, some came to label the decision to increase forces in Afghanistan a surge, and drew comparisons with events in Iraq during 2007 and 2008. The situation we faced in Afghanistan, however, was much different. In Iraq, violence reverberated and was animated along sectarian lines. The 2006 bombing of the Golden Mosque in Samarra set off sectarian purges hundreds of miles away. Our strategy in Iraq reflected that reality, and that of the insurgents: The U.S. campaign began by focusing on sixteen key cities, then narrowed to twelve, then to nine, until we eventually came to realize that the war's center of gravity was one city, Baghdad. Whoever controlled the capital controlled the country, and American planners designed the surge to lock down Baghdad.

More rural and significantly less developed than Iraq, Afghanistan could absorb the effects of violence, and the swings of power between the diffuse insurgency and the NATO-backed government, more than could a country of highly connected urban centers. Unlike infusing the majority of surge troops into Baghdad, in Afghanistan we would spread our troops across the eighty districts whose control we judged could be decisive. We hoped gains made in the coming year would bring about the critical mass of confidence that we thought necessary to keep Afghans from perceiving the cause lost. If they felt the effort was a failure, they would act accordingly by siding with the Taliban, or arming themselves for the civil war that they thought would follow America's departure.

In Iraq, perceptions had a very real ability to be self-fulfilling. Matt Sherman was a State Department official who joined my strategic advisory team that January after a yearlong tour advising a U.S. brigade in Logar and Wardak provinces. Matt noted that when he was in Iraq during the winter of 2006, he'd seen that as the American debate over whether to surge grew louder, it seemed to affect Baghdad's security prospects: Muqtada al-Sadr fled to Iran, sectarian designs on Sadr City quieted, and political calculations among Iraqi leaders altered. We hoped something similar might nudge Afghanistan, though we knew we could not rely on it.

Though no single center of gravity existed in Afghanistan, if the south had a nerve center, it was Kandahar. And the citizens there reflected all the very human contradictions of a people long under the duress of war's whim. Thirty years of it had made them both more stoic and more conspiratorial. They wanted better security, yet many had made a perhaps necessary peace with their plight that made them skittish about any operations there.

This anxiety we would now have to confront: Kandahar was next.

In truth, the fight to secure Kandahar had begun in Helmand. Our effort to expand contiguous areas of security between them was meant to stitch together key districts of what was known as Greater Kandahar, and before that Zabulistan—a subregion formed by the provinces of Helmand, Kandahar, Zabul, and Oruzgan whose economies, tribes, and politics were interlinked. The key node was Kandahar City itself, which sat at the juncture of immemorial trade routes between Kabul in the east, Herat and Persia in the west, and India to the south. The modern Afghan Ring Road that circles the nation, connecting Kabul, Kandahar, Herat, Mazar-e-Sharif, and Kunduz, added to the city's economic importance, as did its proximity to the agricultural breadbaskets along the Helmand and Arghandab rivers and the import lanes from Pakistan.

The city had been the site of many of Afghanistan's most historical pivots. Alexander the Great reputedly laid out the city in the fourth century BCE, and it bore his mark—it's said Kandahar is a corruption of "Iskander," the locals' name for him. It was also where the modern Afghan state was born, thirty years before the United States. In 1747, a nine-day-long council of elders elected Ahmad Shah Durrani their leader, and he went on to congeal Afghanistan into the Duranni empire. His Durrani tribe produced each of Afghanistan's rulers for the next two hundred and forty years, until the coup in 1978. The city hosted a massive Soviet garrison during the mujahideen war of the 1980s, and was later the seat of the Taliban government. The Afghan government's ability to secure the nation's second-largest city—Pashtun, Afghanistan's most important center, and President Karzai's family home—was an important measure of its capacity to assert sovereignty.

Long before Operation Moshtarak launched forces into Marjah, Rod had identified the importance of securing Kandahar to convince its residents and the wider population of Afghanistan that the city was neither a Taliban-controlled enclave nor perpetually threatened with strangulation by insurgent forces. In the spring of 2010, although Kandahar bustled with daily activity, security had deteriorated in the previous four years. The city was not under siege, but mortars and attacks had harassed the August 2009 elections. And the insurgents waged a meticulous assassination campaign against key leaders that sent a clear message to the population that if they didn't call the shots, neither did the government.

While, unlike Marjah, Kandahar did not need to be recaptured from the Taliban, its sheer scale defined the challenge. The city's population had swelled in recent years to over five hundred thousand, and the area grew dramatically when we considered the need to secure the environs around the city. Much like the belts that Al Qaeda had sought to dominate and use as staging grounds to funnel violence into Baghdad from 2005 to 2007, the districts that encircled Kandahar were the traditional keys to controlling the city. Since 2006 and 2007, the Panjwai, Zhari, Daman, Shah Wali Kot, and Arghandab districts had been grinding battlegrounds. ISAF forces, led by a Canadian task force, had been struggling for several years to gain firm control over these critical approaches to Kandahar. But after a series of stiff fights, the districts remained unstable and contested in the face of growing insurgent strength. The fate of Kandahar City rested largely on our ability to secure these avenues, particularly the Arghandab River valley.

At the end of February 2010 I received an e-mail from a staff sergeant serving in the valley. He led a squad in an infantry battalion task force in the Zhari district, west of Kandahar. I'd made several trips to the districts around Kandahar, particularly Arghandab, where one of our Stryker units, an organization built around wheeled armored vehicles, had suffered significant casualties. But any note like his struck a chord inside me.

I don't believe you fully understand the situation we face in this district, and I think you should come down and see it up close, Staff Sergeant Israel Arroyo wrote. Senior commanders don't get many notes directly from squad leaders, particularly notes like that. I told Charlie Flynn to arrange for us to go down the following day.

We flew by C-130 cargo aircraft to Kandahar airfield and transloaded to UH-60 helicopters for the flight to their battalion's main base before driving the final miles in Strykers to a sandbagged outpost on a small rise that overlooked an expanse of farm fields. There I met Arroyo's platoon. After a short brief we went on a combat patrol. Departing from the outpost, we moved on foot for several hours, sweeping the area until we reached a small Afghan village, then returned. As we moved, I listened to the young leader's thoughts and got to know members of his squad, in particular one of his team leaders, Mike Ingram—a corporal responsible for four soldiers. It was difficult ground to soldier in, and always had been. Southern Afghanistan had been the site of the only known mutiny of Arab troops during their global conquest thirteen hundred years earlier. Now both the physical and human terrain seemed to resist the platoon's best efforts. The Afghans were distant in their demeanor, but that wasn't uncommon. It was the cultivated fields that were striking. I felt as though I were walking through the grooves of corduroy: Instead of using wooden trellises to support fruit vines, the local farmers used packed mud. In long lines, they built walls six feet tall, four to five feet apart at the tapered tops, and narrower at the ground where the supporting base was wider. For soldiers, it was like operating in a maze, each corridor of sun-caked mud perfectly designed to channel them into waiting IEDs or well-placed ambush positions. It was still too early in the year for the vines to have fully bloomed, but by late spring the corridors would become like tunnels under a canopy of foliage, any movement inside largely hidden from the air.

The corduroy terrain of Zhari was almost a metaphor for these infantrymen's war. The could see eighteen inches to their left and right, and rarely more then fifty feet to their front or rear. Above, only a slice of sky. Fighting was bloody, and unsatisfying. Rarely was there a hill to take, or a stalwart enemy to take it from. Any progress I could see from a wider view of Afghanistan was impossible to discern from their mud-walled world. War has often been that way. Like leaders before me, I was asking soldiers to believe in something their ground-level perspective denied them. I was asking them to believe in a strategy impossible to guarantee, and in progress that was hard to see, much less prove. They were asked to risk themselves to bring improvements that might take years to arise. Although war is a product and instrument of national policy, that reality feels distant and theoretical to the soldier leaning exhausted against a mud wall. As a commander, I was asking them to believe in me. Whether they did was often hard to judge.

Later that evening I got two more e mails, one from Arroyo, and another from Corporal Ingram, the team leader. Both thanked me for patrolling with them that day. I responded, thanking both for all they were doing. I was grateful to Sergeant Arroyo for having the courage to send his initial note to ensure a fellow leader understood the situation on the ground.

A month later I got another e-mail from Staff Sergeant Arroyo informing me that Mike Ingram had been killed not far from where we'd patrolled. I remembered the young corporal's quick smile and agile movements through the muddy terrain, and his mature insights on the local population. I traveled back to the outpost in Zhari. I felt like I needed to see and listen to the platoon again. I knew it would be a difficult visit—they would be smarting from a big loss. With us would be a reporter from *Rolling Stone* who was periodically interacting with our team, to give him an appreciation for the difficulty of the task they faced.

We met on a hot afternoon, gathering inside the fortified walls of their small compound. The body armor was off. Some quietly sipped water as I

spoke, then invited questions. As on so many visits, there were a few standard questions before the queries became blunt and frank. As I expected,
they were frustrated. Some were openly bitter over their loss and the seem-
ing impossibility of their mission. *Why are we here, Sir? What's the point?*
I listened and we talked. I couldn't solve the platoon's problems that day, or
curtail their mission. The district had to be secured. For many, I lacked the
eloquence to assuage their concerns and could only explain the strategy
they were a part of. I tried to show them I understood, and cared.

As we flew back that night I compared in my mind leading these soldiers
in this counterinsurgency campaign with my experience in TF 714. There
were many similarities. America's military in 2010 was stunningly professional and the past decade of combat had produced a seasoned force. But
there were also differences. In TF 714, most notably in Iraq, although our
special operators had fought almost every night, we largely chose the time
and place of the fight. When our helicopters landed, our operators normally
had the benefit of surprise, the cover of night, and intimate knowledge of
whom they would find on their objective. Over time, even as friends were
given over to Arlington, we could both see and feel the impact we were having on Zarqawi's organization. The bulk of fighting in Afghanistan in 2010
yielded no such mental analgesic. Progress couldn't be measured by direct
attrition of a terrorist network. Combat often erupted unexpectedly: A
boom and a plume of dust or the crack of bullets from the distance, yelling,
rushing to maneuver, return fire, then silence. Then the same thing the next
day. And the day after that, until the geysers of dust claimed a friend, or the
bullets clipped a mentor. And then back out yet again.

The Kandahar Convention Center was a world apart from the sun-
cracked mud trenches of Zhari only a few miles away. But it was here
within the whitewashed plaster walls and the low ceiling of its basement
meeting room that much of our ability to secure Kandahar rested. In an
expansion of the pattern we'd set with Moshtarak, we sought to prepare
the ground for securing Kandahar by fully engaging President Karzai and
leveraging his influence with Kandahari leaders to solidify their support.
Now, on April 4, 2010, some fifteen hundred of them filled the room. I felt
out of place in my light green combat uniform in a sea of traditional Afghan clothing: Blacks, grays, dark maroon, and, at one point, a flash of
azure as three burkas shuffled through and settled to the ground in a curtsy.
I compared it to my small February meeting with Marjah elders; Hamkari,
as the effort to secure Kandahar was called, was a whole new, and vastly
different, ball game.

In Marjah, uncontested Taliban control required shaping operations,
followed by a dramatic initial seizure, before the lengthy process of erecting
a local government could truly begin. Kandahar would need shaping, and
this *shura* was part of that. But operations would involve little drama. In-

stead, we planned deliberately to increase security-force density and effectiveness in the city, and to clear then hold the strategic environs.

The distinction between our concept for Kandahar and more traditional military operations was critical. Much as the residents of Marjah had expressed their fear we would destroy their district to liberate it, Kandaharis trembled at the thought of full-force battles. The term "operation" brought anxious looks, and triggered memories of a nasty time in their history. In 1986, the Soviets began the decimation of Kandahar, and nightly the sky would erupt with tracers and flares and fires from aerial assaults and blanket bombing runs. By 1987, they reduced much of the city to ash and rubble, and when they moved inside, they conducted urban patrols with punishing tanks. "Operations" there devastated the city's population, which dispersed from two hundred thousand down to about twenty-five thousand in less than two years. Through that lens, most Kandaharis I met viewed the Taliban threat as significant but not overwhelming. When asked about it they nodded, "Yes, security must be improved," but then went on to highlight issues of governance and corruption as equally important. The meeting here was meant to soothe their fears, and gauge their sentiment.

One corner of the basement had a platform about twelve inches high that had been furnished with flowers and lined by several large wooden chairs. Beneath a large photograph of President Karzai, Mark Sedwill and I were in two of the chairs. We sat self-consciously, fearful of looking like feudal lords above the sea of Kandaharis. A podium rested on the edge of the platform closest to the assembled audience. The crowd was like earlier *shuras* I'd attended, but larger. Rows of impressive looking elders sat cross-legged on carpets laid for the occasion, and I could see them craning their bodies to see around the television cameras interspersed throughout the hall. Despite the hall's size, the overflow gave the gathering an unexpected feeling of intimacy.

When Karzai walked in, people stood and applauded. Had "Happy Days Are Here Again" erupted from a waiting band it would have felt like an old-fashioned campaign rally. Someone in the audience threw flowers, and the president took his seat on the stage. As he did, Dr. Tooryalai Wesa, the governor of Kandahar, rose to welcome everyone. Wesa was a soft-spoken man who had grown up in Kandahar. An accomplished academic who helped found Kandahar University in 1991, serving as its first president, Wesa had returned to Afghanistan after fourteen years abroad, most recently living in British Columbia, Canada. Governor since 2008, he and Nick Carter had done extensive work to "shape the environment" in the preceding weeks.

Wesa was representative of a group of highly educated, honest, and patriotic Afghans I'd met who accepted leadership positions in the years after 2001. Talented but often outclassed in the bare-knuckle power struggles of places like Kandahar, most found themselves unable to wrest real control from local personalities. In Wesa's case, that personality was a quiet man with an almost obsequious manner. Ironically, as Wesa spoke that day I could watch his nemesis moving around at the very back of the crowd—far from any position of overt prestige or influence. Yet Ahmed Wali Karzai— the president's forty-nine-year-old brother, leader of the Popalzai tribe and chairman of the Kandahar Provincial Council—was the essential power broker for Kandahar.

After Wesa's remarks, President Karzai moved to the podium, and asked the camera crews to move. He wanted a better view of the people, he said, though I suspect he really wanted them to have an unobstructed view of him. He was glad to be face-to-face with them, Karzai said, including his sisters, and began his remarks. I sat and listened, with simultaneous translation of his words coming into the earpieces Mark and I wore.

The *shura* came after a difficult week between Karzai and the United States. Still sensitive from his belief that the international community had unfairly accused and then undermined him during the lengthy election process and its contentious aftermath, Karzai had made recent remarks that brought new controversy. He'd reportedly told a group of Afghans that if pushed too far by the United States, he would join the Taliban. His words became public a mere month before a planned visit for him to the United States, and the White House indicated his remarks put that trip in jeopardy.

I knew that in the claustrophobic palace, bad advisers could goad President Karzai during moments of fatigue and sadness, leading him to say things he did not really feel. But I was bothered by his comments. They were dispiriting to my soldiers fighting to sustain his government. I questioned whether I was too respectful of him and his position, whether I'd gone native. Shouldn't I take a harder line? But in the hall-of-mirrors politics of Kabul, I looked to his actions, not his words. Western observers, and many Afghans, had a menu of items they wanted Karzai to address. For most, corruption was at the top. That was clearly important for our campaign. But as I looked at the rest of my menu for the past ten months, there was room for satisfaction. President Karzai wanted night raids to stop, and yet we'd quadrupled the number of precision strike teams and raids, even taking the president for his first-ever visit to TF 714's in-country headquarters. Through an evening of detailed briefs, he saw the precision that marked each operation, and the direct involvement of Afghan officers that ensured effective collaboration. And although I knew he was deeply skeptical of our logic for bringing more foreign forces to his country, he'd agreed to support my recommendation to add forty thousand. He visited multiple locations like Marjah, and moved closer, albeit haltingly, to his role as commander-in-chief of a nation at war. It was maddeningly incomplete, but he'd made some tough concessions for a partnership that was badly stressed by missteps on both sides. One reason he did so, I felt, was the relationship we'd built.

That April morning in Kandahar, President Karzai insisted I be inside the *shura* room. He sat me close to him, and at one point told the crowd of his close partnership with Mark Sedwill and me. It was an interesting move on his part. On the surface our presence provided a clear signal of NATO and U.S. support, and could also indicate ISAF endorsed anything he said. For me, there were clear risks in that, particularly after the previous week. But there were risks for him as well. Mark and I were visible symbols of Karzai's continued dependence on foreign support, and of Afghanistan's still incomplete sovereignty. Regardless of what he said, I represented much of what frustrated ordinary Afghans about their situation. In the end, I thought he put us on the stage less out of shrewd calculation than intuition. At his core, Hamid Karzai was a man of strong emotions and loyalties. Rubbed raw, sometimes to cynicism, by long years of politics, he was slow to trust but committed to relationships.

After greeting the crowd, Karzai began a wide-ranging speech. He said the tribes needed to secure the peace, and he castigated them for not sending sons to serve in the National Army. He talked of a peace *jirga* as a solution. As he spoke, dressed in black, with a black turban, Karzai's face appeared more dour than usual, almost combative. The crowd appeared cool. Eventually, he broached the topic of Hamkari.

"These days the foreigners speak of an operation in Kandahar," he said. "I know you are worried. Are you worried?"

Shouts came back: Yes!

"Well, if you are worried, then there won't be an operation, if you are not happy."

Some observers judged the exchange that day indicated Hamkari lacked the support it needed. I had no such reservation. It was how the question had been asked, how the game was played. Karzai had asked the question he knew would elicit genuine concerns—which he wanted us to hear. I was confident that both Karzai and the Kandahari leaders welcomed better security in and around the city. But like Marjah's elders, they had articulated their conditions. Karzai was placing a marker that we couldn't ignore. For a leader who'd felt helpless to check eight years of escalating foreign military operations inside Afghanistan, it was a good move. He knew Hamkari had to happen, as did I. But he was forcing us to listen in ways we'd done too rarely in the past.

On Saturday, April 10, 2010, a twenty-year-old Tupolev Tu-154 aircraft flown by pilots of the Polish Air Force crashed in a thick fog in western Russia, ironically en route to the Katyn Forest, site of a World War II massacre of Polish military officers by the Soviets. The Polish president, Lech Kaczynski, was among the eighty-eight souls lost in the accident.

Poland was stunned. In addition to the president, a significant contingent of Poland's most influential leaders were killed, sadly including my friend Franciszek "Franc" Gagor, the chief of the general staff of the Polish Army. Franc and his wife had befriended Annie and me back at the Lisbon

Conference in September 2009, and his special warmth and friendship made him a valued comrade. We'd worked through a variety of operational issues associated with the Polish brigade that operated in Ghazni Province, and I'd promised Franc I would visit Warsaw so I could explain in person to the Polish political leadership the ISAF strategy and war in Afghanistan.

When the accident occurred, I was less than a week from fulfilling my promise to Franc with a stop in Warsaw on a trip to Europe that also included Paris, Berlin, and Prague. In each location, the objective was the same: To meet requests like Franc's from leaders in the four countries and, as the commander of ISAF, provide insights and address questions firsthand. Each nation was an important member of the ISAF Coalition. After the accident I canceled our visit to Warsaw but felt the remainder of the trip needed to go as planned.

On April 14, 2010, we flew to Europe, conducting a short visit to NATO headquarters in Brussels and then continuing to Paris, the first stop of the original four. We had an itinerary of office calls, ceremonies, a dinner, and a talk at the Staff College, all of which began as coordinated.

The same day, seismic activity in Iceland produced an ash cloud that closed most of Europe's airspace for the next five days. Unable to keep our original schedule, I modified the plan, ultimately canceling our stop in Prague and reaching Berlin by a lengthy bus ride. Our schedule there was similar to that in Paris, and highlighted by laying a wreath with Defense Minister Guttenberg at a memorial service for German soldiers recently killed under my command in Kunduz, Afghanistan. They had been Germany's first loss in direct combat since World War II, and I very much wanted to demonstrate my respect for their sacrifice.

In response to official invitations from each nation, I arranged for Annie to join me in Europe, and she participated in all the events that often helped build relationships. We enjoyed the chance to be together, particularly on Friday, April 16, when I took Annie for dinner at a small French restaurant to celebrate our thirty-third wedding anniversary. Mike and Lori Flynn joined us.

Inside a small, bunkered post on a bluff in Surobi District overlooking the Kabul River, they had assembled an honor guard for me to review, each legionnaire selected for his English-language skill. It was April 30, 2010, Camerone Day, a sacred date for the French Foreign Legionnaires assembled in front of me. It commemorated the 1863 stand of sixty-five of their forebears under the legendary Captain Jean Danjou against a force of twelve hundred Mexican cavalry. Captain Danjou, a Crimean War hero with a wooden left hand, led his men in a determined but ultimately fatal defense, reportedly declaring, "We have munitions, we will fight."

For a boy who'd grown up on stories of legionnaires, it was easy to feel the thick spirit that filled this small outpost, home to the parachute battalion that had this corner of the fight. I had come to thank them for their service and their courage. Talking to young soldiers, some already seasoned warriors, who had purposely selected a life of expeditionary service, I thought of their predecessors in Indochina and Algeria. I looked over at two of my aides, one a German officer, another an Afghan. How different wars could be, I thought, but the soldiers seemed the same.

Two weeks later, on May 12, 2010, President Karzai arrived to the United States for four days to meet with President Obama and other U.S. leaders. At President Karzai's request, Karl Eikenberry and I made the trip as well. It closely followed a visit by General Kayani and other Pakistani leaders to Washington, D.C., a few weeks earlier, and was meant to strengthen our partnership with President Karzai and his government. Both relationships, with Afghanistan and with Pakistan, needed improvement.

By May 2010, the wounds created by the August 2009 Afghan elections had healed somewhat, although scars remained. President Karzai's support of operations Moshtarak and Hamkari, though more lukewarm than enthusiastic, had made us feel more aligned than we had in the fall. President Obama had briefly visited Afghanistan on March 28, in an effort to tighten the relationship between the nations and leaders. Even so, underlying tensions remained.

The most poignant moments of the stay involved visits President Karzai made to Walter Reed Army Medical Center to visit wounded soldiers and to Arlington National Cemetery to recognize the fallen. At Walter Reed, Karzai was visibly moved by the courage of badly wounded American soldiers. When several amputees said they'd been wounded in Arghandab, he seemed sobered by the ferocity of the fighting they described. In Arlington Cemetery we walked among the markers of the recently fallen and when I came upon headstones of soldiers I knew, I described the men to Karzai.

On May 26, I met with the latest group of "Afghan hands" to arrive for duty in Afghanistan. The program, conceived by Scott Miller in my office in the Pentagon over a year earlier, had graduated its second round of officers and dispatched them to theater. Although I was frustrated with what appeared to be half-hearted service support for the program—they sent a number of nonvolunteers and noncompetitive officers—it still represented a step forward, and I spoke during an orientation course we conducted before sending this contingent forward to specific duty positions around the country.

After almost a year in command, I was more convinced than ever that a cadre of language-trained professionals, steeped in the culture and assigned for multiple tours to establish genuine relationships, would be the single most powerful asset we could field. This most recent group—which included my former TF 714 aide-de-camp, then-Major Donny Purdy, now fluent in Dari—could begin to provide a more educated, nuanced capability to complement our already overwhelming conventional military power.

As I navigated the first month of my second year in Afghanistan, I recognized that we were a different team than the one I'd joined the previous June. Rod's IJC had matured into a headquarters capable of executing a nuanced counterinsurgency campaign across a collection of very different regional commands. Leavened by the arrival of additional combat-experienced U.S. forces, these commands were approaching the 2010 fighting season with resolve. It would be brutally violent, we knew. Already, in stark rejection of Mullah Omar's *layha* from the previous year, it appeared insurgents had turned toward targeting civilians in order to defeat our attempt to protect them. Since January, the enemy had wounded and killed more Afghan civilians than it had during the first six months of 2009, using more IEDs, suicide bombs, and a ramped-up assassination campaign. While the insurgents killed and wounded more civilians, ISAF and Afghan security forces were responsible for fewer civilian casualties than we had been during the first half of 2009. But we were still killing far too many Afghans, particularly at checkpoints, and needed to better shield them.

I wasn't satisfied with where we were; that's not my nature. But I was fiercely proud of the effort so many people had put forward to get us this far. We thought if we didn't blink, we would come out in a better position than we had been in the previous year.

On Monday, June 21, we gathered again at Kandahar's convention center. Afghan and ISAF military and civilian leaders convened in a large room outfitted with tables facing a briefing screen. As we mingled before the session began, familiar faces engaged in animated conversation: Karl Eikenberry, Mark Sedwill, Abdul Rahim Wardak, Dave Rodriguez, Sher Mohammad Karimi, and Richard Holbrooke—who'd flown in from the United States for the session—and a host of key planners and staff.

Eight days earlier, Karzai had held a second *shura* in the same location. Smaller than the April *shura*, it brought together only a few hundred elders. As before, Karzai brought Mark and me. There, as I'd anticipated, after some discussion the elders had voiced their support for the operation. We now collected to rehearse the specifics of Hamkari. Under Rod's patient guidance, we drilled into almost every aspect of the complex plan. More interesting than the operation, to my eye, was the interaction between Afghans, Americans, Brits, and Australians. Relationships, now scuffed and dented by regular use, had the power of familiarity among comrades that was so vital, yet took so long to develop. If Hamkari succeeded, it would owe less to any brilliance of concept than to the sinew of trust.

That night, at about 10:30 P.M. I went to my room above the operations center and read, as usual, for about twenty minutes before drifting off to sleep. My PT clothes were arranged to work out early before the day's activities began full bore. About 2:00 A.M. Charlie Flynn woke me.

"Sir, we have a problem," Charlie said in the darkness of my room. "The *Rolling Stone* article is out, and it's really bad."

How in the world could that story have been a problem? I thought, stunned. But I replied simply, "Thanks, Charlie. I'll be right down."

I put on my PT clothes and went quickly downstairs to where Charlie and Rear Admiral Greg Smith, our director of strategic communications, waited and handed me a printed copy. The article was the work of a reporter writing for *Rolling Stone* magazine who had interacted with my command team several times over the previous few months, including during parts of our April trip to Europe. This story, one of a number we'd done over the year in Afghanistan, was designed to provide transparency into how my command team operated. But, beginning with the provocative title "The Runaway General," the article described a hard-driving general, a struggling U.S. policy, and attributed a number of unacceptable comments to my command team.

I was surprised by the tone and direction of the article. I thought back to the night of Annie's and my thirty-third wedding anniversary in Paris. At the end of the evening Annie had said she was glad the reporter had been present to see what she had seen: the command team, including American, British, Afghan, and French officers, all together. Annie felt the brotherhood among the soldiers, each a veteran of multiple combat tours over the past decade, was evident and was something the reporter needed to see and understand. I had agreed with her. The printed story cast it in a very different light.

For a number of minutes I felt as though I'd likely awaken from what seemed like a surreal dream, but the situation was real. Regardless of how I judged the story for fairness or accuracy, responsibility was mine. And its ultimate effect was immediately clear to me.

After an hour or so of meeting with key staff and making several phone calls, including one to Annie, I went outside to run. When faced with something frustrating, frightening, or confusing, I've found it is often the best thing I can do. Well before normal physical training time, I ran alone in the darkness around the inside of ISAF's small compound. It was a good opportunity to think, and I needed to. For thirty-four years I'd served knowing many fates were possible. But I'd never anticipated the one before me now.

That evening, as the controversy swelled, I was directed to fly back to D.C. for meetings the following morning with the secretary of defense and the president. The flight provided hours for reflection, free from the cacophony of opinions I knew were filling the media. A number of e-mails came in. One in particular struck me. A member of Staff Sergeant Arroyo's platoon who'd been present at the meeting described in the *Rolling Stone* article expressed frustration with the account, and his support.

From the moment I'd seen the article, I'd known there were different options on how to act, and react, to the storm I knew I would face. But I knew only one decision was right for the moment and for the mission. I didn't try to figure out what others might do; no hero's or mentor's example came to mind. I called no one for advice.

It was light when we landed at Andrews Air Force Base and we drove to my quarters to shower and put on dress green uniforms before going to the Pentagon to meet with Admiral Mullen and then Secretary Gates. Two hours later I left the White House after a short, professional meeting with President Obama and drove to Fort McNair to tell Annie that the president had accepted my resignation.

Entering our quarters, I met Annie, who had been waiting. I told her that our life in the Army was over.

"Good," she said, clear-eyed and strong. "We've always been happy, and we'll always be happy."

Looking into her blue eyes, I knew she was right—and why.

Epilogue

He went like one that hath been stunn'd,
And is of sense forlorn:
A sadder and a wiser man
He rose the morrow morn.

> —SAMUEL TAYLOR COLERIDGE,
> "The Rime of the Ancient Mariner"

In the late afternoon of July 23, 2010, Secretary of Defense Bob Gates came to our quarters on Fort McNair, and we sat briefly in the living room before walking across the street to McNair's parade field. We had moved into the large brick quarters in the summer of 2008 after leaving TF 714. For the first year I'd run each morning alongside the field as I headed out the wrought-iron gates of the post, along the Potomac River, and across Memorial Bridge to the Pentagon. On weekends I'd cross the field to McNair's gym, often passing soldiers practicing drill.

Today the field was uncharacteristically crowded with a formation of 3rd Infantry "Old Guard" soldiers and a setup of chairs and bleachers on either side of the brick reviewing stand. In and around the seating were a sea of family and friends who'd gathered. My father, the now-old soldier, was too weak to travel, but my four brothers and a group of classmates from West Point, one of whom had flown from his farm in North Dakota, were on hand. Importantly, some of the men and women with whom I'd shared the fight of the last decade were there. I wanted to thank them. The occasion was simultaneously happy and sad, a beginning and an end. I'd been to countless retirement ceremonies in thirty-four years, but never my own.

We walked out the door and to our designated seats. Although we'd set the ceremony for early evening, it was still blazing hot. I'd asked an old friend, Major General Karl Horst, commander of the Military District of Washington, if the Old Guard could do the ceremony in army combat uniforms, ACUs, instead of the normal dress blues. Although it was uncommon, he'd readily agreed. I wanted the last uniform I'd ever wear to be the one I believed most reflected the soldier I'd been. And in the heat, I hoped it was more comfortable for the troops that stood on the field.

As I stood on the field, I thought about the future. In a few days Annie and I would clear our quarters and make what I assumed would be our last of so many moves. Everything else was unclear.

I had no idea that a few days later I'd get a note from Jim Levinsohn, the director of Yale University's Jackson Institute of Global Affairs, and in September begin an extraordinary experience teaching young people.

Life would go on. In April 2011, the Department of Defense inspector general's office would release a summary of its review into the allegations outlined in the *Rolling Stone* article. The investigations could not substantiate any violations of Defense Department standards and found that "not all of the events occurred as portrayed in the article." These conclusions came out quietly, almost a year after the tornado of controversy the article created, but they were important to me. Maybe more important, also that month, I would accept First Lady Michelle Obama's request to serve my country again, this time on the board of advisers for Joining Forces, a White House initiative for service members and their families.

That evening on the field, as they were supposed to, every part of the ceremony went smoothly. The precision of the soldiers on the field, the sequence of speeches and awards, and even the emotional appearance of old friends, projected a sense of orchestrated perfection. It was life, as we might have once hoped it would be. No friction, no mistakes, and no casualties.

But my life hadn't been like that. Instead it had been a series of unplanned detours, unanticipated challenges, and unexpected opportunities. Along the way, more by luck than design, I'd been a part of some events, organizations, and efforts that will loom large in history, and many more that will not. I saw selfless commitment, petty politics, unspeakable cruelty, and quiet courage in places and quantities that I'd never have imagined. But what I will remember most are the leaders.

I remember events through the personalities who shaped or responded to them. The examples they set, the decisions they made, and sometimes the price they paid are the lens through which I view the sliver of history I shared. The leaders I studied inspired me. The leaders whom I knew, those who touched me directly, share a special place in my mind, and often in my heart.

As a child I'd been fascinated with heroes, first fixating on their talent, bravery, and commitment. I read again and again of the new American John Paul Jones on the deck of the *Bonhomme Richard* declaring he had "not yet begun to fight," and of the Scot Robert Bruce regaining lost hope by watching a spider spinning a web fail six times without giving up. I'd listened to my father's letters from Vietnam and seen occasional photographs of his lean frame in green jungle fatigues and combat gear. It was a romantic, sometimes two-dimensional model of leadership, embodied in heroism, wrapped in service, most often in uniform.

Over the years, through age, experience, and example, my model of a leader matured. My mother was raised in the south and deeply admired Dr. Martin Luther King, Jr.'s, stubborn leadership of the civil rights movement. She made me understand how someone breaking the law and disrupting an orderly way of life could represent leadership, while those in uniform holding water cannons might not. She taught me that leadership is not command. Some of the greatest leaders commanded nothing but respect. And I learned of, and sometimes saw, commanders who never tried to lead.

So, after a lifetime, what had I learned about leadership? Probably not enough. But I saw enough for me to believe it was the single biggest reason organizations succeeded or failed. It dwarfed numbers, technology, ideology, and historical forces in determining the outcome of events. I used to tell junior leaders that the nine otherwise identical parachute infantry battalions of the 82nd Airborne Division ranged widely in effectiveness, the disparity almost entirely a function of leadership.

"Switch just two people—the battalion commander and command sergeant major—from the best battalion with those of the worst, and within ninety days the relative effectiveness of the battalions will have switched as well," I'd say. I still believe I was correct.

Yet leadership is difficult to measure and often difficult even to adequately describe. I lack the academic bona fides to provide a scholarly analysis of leadership and human behavior. So I'll simply relate what, after a lifetime of being led and learning to lead, I've concluded.

Leadership is the art of influencing others. It differs from giving a simple order or managing in that it shapes the longer-term attitudes and behavior of individuals and groups. George Washington's tattered army persisted to ultimate victory. Those troops displayed the kind of effort that can never be ordered—only evoked. Effective leaders stir an intangible but very real desire inside people. That drive can be reflected in extraordinary courage, selfless sacrifice, and commitment.

Leadership is neither good nor evil. We like to equate leaders with values we admire, but the two can be separate and distinct. Self-serving or evil intent motivated some of the most effective leaders I saw, like Abu Musab al-Zarqawi. In the end, leadership is a skill that can be used like any other, but with far greater effect.

Leaders take us where we'd otherwise not go. Although Englishmen rushing into the breach behind Henry V is a familiar image, leaders whose personal example or patient persuasion causes dramatic changes in otherwise inertia-bound organizations or societies are far more significant. The teacher who awakens and encourages in students a sense of possibility and responsibility is, to me, the ultimate leader.

Success is rarely the work of a single leader; leaders work best in partnership with other leaders. In Iraq in 2004, I received specific direction to track Zarqawi and bring him to justice. But it was the collaboration of leaders below me, inside TF 714, that built the teams, relentlessly hunted, and ultimately destroyed his lethal network.

Leaders can call to the best in us. I thought often of the inspiring flag signal Horatio Nelson sent on the eve of Trafalgar. "England expects every man will do his duty." The flags above the *Victory* didn't ask or demand obedience in the upcoming fight; they expressed Nelson's unshakable admiration for and faith in the sailors and patriots he knew them to be. And I remembered the effect Major General Bill Garrison's faith had on me when I was a major.

Leaders are empathetic. The best leaders I've seen have an uncanny ability to understand, empathize, and communicate with those they lead. They need not agree or share the same background or status in society as their followers, but they understand their hopes, fears, and passions. Great leaders intuitively sense, or simply ask, how people feel and what resonates with them. At their worst, demigods like Adolf Hitler manipulate the passions of frustrated populations into misguided forces. But empathy can be remarkably positive when a Nelson Mandela reshapes and redirects the energy of a movement away from violence and into constructive nation-building.

Leaders are not necessarily popular. For soldiers, the choice between popularity and effectiveness is ultimately no choice at all. Soldiers want to win; their survival depends upon it. They will accept, and even take pride in, the quirks and shortcomings of a leader if they believe he or she can produce success.

On the evening of May 7, 1864, Ulysses Grant's Army of the Potomac cheered when, after bitter fighting in the Wilderness, they turned south into more fighting, instead of north to refit in safety. They were not celebrating the fights to come but instead their belief that in Grant, they finally had a leader willing to do what it took to finish the war.

The best leaders are genuine. I found soldiers would tolerate my being less of a leader than I hoped to be, but they would not forgive me being less than I claimed to be. Simple honesty matters.

Leaders can be found at any rank and at any age. I often found myself led by soldiers many levels junior to me, and I was the better for it. Deferring to the expertise and skills of the leader best suited to any given situation requires enough self-confidence to subjugate one's ego, but it signals a strong respect for the people with whom one serves.

Personal gifts like intellect or charisma help. But neither are required nor enough to be a leader.

Physical appearance, poise, and outward self-confidence can be confused with leadership—for a time. I saw many new lieutenants arrive to battalions and fail to live up to the expectations their handsome, broad-shouldered look generated. Conversely, I saw others overcome the initial doubts created by small stature or a squeaky voice. It took time and enough interaction with followers, but performance usually became more important than the advantages of innate traits.

Later in my career, I encountered some figures who had learned to leverage superficial gifts so effectively that they appeared to be better leaders than they were. It took me some time and interaction—often under the pressure of difficult situations—before I could determine whether they possessed those bedrock skills and qualities that infantry platoons would seek to find and assess in young sergeants and lieutenants. Modern media exacerbate the challenge of sorting reality from orchestrated perception.

Leaders walk a fine line between self-confidence and humility. Soldiers want leaders who are sure of their ability to lead the team to success but humble enough to recognize their limitations. I learned that it was better to admit ignorance or fear than to display false knowledge or bravado. And candidly admitting doubts or difficulties is key to building confidence in your honesty. But expressing doubts and confidence is a delicate balance. When things look their worst, followers look to the leader for reassurance that they can and will succeed.

People are born; leaders are made. I was born the son of a leader with a clear path to a profession of leadership. But whatever leadership I later possessed, I learned from others. I grew up in a household of overt values, many of which hardened in me only as I matured. Although history fascinated me, and mentors surrounded me, the overall direction and key decisions of my life and career were rarely impacted by specific advice, or even a particularly relevant example I'd read or seen. I rarely wondered *What would Nelson, Buford, Grant, or my father have done?* But as I grew, I was increasingly aware of the guideposts and guardrails that leaders had set for me, often through their examples. The question became *What kind of leader have I decided to be?* Over time, decisions came easily against that standard, even when the consequences were grave.

Leaders are people, and people constantly change. Even well into my career I was still figuring out what kind of leader I wanted to be. For many years I found myself bouncing between competing models of a hard bitten taskmaster and a nurturing father figure—sometimes alternating within a relatively short time span. That could be tough on the people I led, and a bit unfair. They looked for and deserved steady, consistent leadership. When I failed to provide that, I gave conflicting messages that produced uncertainty and reduced the effectiveness of the team we were trying to create. As I got older, the swings between leadership styles were less pronounced and frequent as I learned the value of consistency. But even at the end I still wasn't the leader I believed I should be.

All leaders are human. They get tired, angry, and jealous and carry the same range of emotions and frailties common to mankind. Most leaders periodically display them. The leaders I most admired were totally human but constantly strove to be the best humans they could be.

Leaders make mistakes, and they are often costly. The first reflex is normally to deny the failure to themselves; the second is to hide it from others, because most leaders covet a reputation for infallibility. But it's a fool's dream and is inherently dishonest.

There are few secrets to leadership. It is mostly just hard work. More than anything else it requires self-discipline. Colorful, charismatic characters often fascinate people, even soldiers. But over time, effectiveness is what counts. Those who lead most successfully do so while looking out for their followers' welfare.

Self-discipline manifests itself in countless ways. In a leader I see it as doing those things that should be done, even when they are unpleasant, inconvenient, or dangerous; and refraining from those that shouldn't, even when they are pleasant, easy, or safe. The same discipline that causes a young lieutenant to check his soldier's feet for blisters or trench foot, will also carry him across a bullet-swept street to support a squad under pressure.

In the end, leadership is a choice. Rank, authority, and even responsibility can be inherited or assigned, whether or not an individual desires or deserves them. Even the mantle of leadership occasionally falls to people who haven't sought it. But actually leading is different. A leader decides to accept responsibility for others in a way that assumes stewardship of their hopes, their dreams, and sometimes their very lives. It can be a crushing burden, but I found it an indescribable honor.

When the ceremony ended Annie and I stayed on the field to greet friends, many of whom had traveled to share the ceremony with us. In one respect it was a difficult day at the end of a difficult month. But in the broader view of life, it was a magical evening at the end of an incredible journey we had shared. We walked back over to the quarters we would move out of a few days later, and found friends in the yard and in almost every room. At one point I saw Mike Hall, Charlie Flynn, Shawn Lowery, and Casey Welch standing in the fading summer light. I thought of my father, of my first day at West Point, and of our cold Christmas Eve flight over Afghanistan seven months before. The final words of my last speech in uniform, spoken just an hour before were repeated in my mind:

"If I had it to do over again, I'd do some things in my career differently, but not many. I believed in people, and I still believe in them. I trusted and I still trust. I cared and I still care. I wouldn't have had it any other way. . . . To the young leaders of today and tomorrow, it's a great life. Thank you."

Acknowledgments

The people who made this book possible fall into two groups. The first are those who made the life I've enjoyed all that it has been. Beginning with my parents, that group includes a cast of family, friends, teachers, coaches, comrades, friends, and countless figures who shaped me and the age I experienced. To them, I hope the life I led, imperfect as it has been, reflected my admiration and gratitude.

To the officers, commissioned and noncommissioned, who taught me the profession of arms I owe more than I can adequately describe. Possibly more important than the commanders were the experienced noncommissioned officers, who epitomized the professionalism the U.S. military regained in the decades following Vietnam.

As an American, I owe special thanks to a collection of people, military and civilian, who answered the call time and again. The decade following September 11, 2001, confronted a small military with years of relentless combat, often waged by the same selfless professionals. Alongside our civilian and allied partners, this generation served, often at great cost.

Much of the first group is also part of the second: those who directly contributed to the creation of this book. The common denominator has been selfless and generous donations of time and wisdom to a novice author. Where the book soars toward real literature, you have been the reason. Where the wings fall off and Icarus plummets, I am to blame. In every case I am in your debt. A number of the soldiers, civilians, and diplomats who shared their insights and recollections are still out there—keeping the bridge.

Their continued service, and in some cases their safety, requires that they go unnamed here. I have thus chosen not to list anyone by name, though I hope all who participated see how their generosity of time and energy has left a positive mark on the book—and know, thus, how indebted I am.

This book would not have been possible without the fine reporting of a number of true professionals. I've relied on their articles, books, and stories to augment my own memory and in some cases to build out descriptions of events. I did not always agree with them, nor they with me, but their ability to consistently produce clear-eyed and humane stories from the midst of political turmoil and war is testament to their courage and integrity. My research assistants and I found ourselves returning to the work of a number of journalists who've become household names to those who've sought to understand the past decade of war; they populate the endnotes.

Mark O'Donald and David Alvarado were not just skilled photographers, but were welcome travel companions on our many shared trips around Afghanistan. I appreciate their generous permission, and that of Joshua Treadwell, to use their fine work in this book.

To help craft the book into something coherent, I relied on the sage wisdom of colleagues and friends, including Jim Levinsohn and Jeff Siegel. John Gaddis, Mike O'Hanlon, Michele Malvesti, and others read repeated drafts and provided invaluable counsel. As he did in Afghanistan, Matt Sherman shared his frank advice and good humor. Dan Darling leavened the book through his always-impressive feedback.

The team at Penguin, led by Adrian Zackheim, were trusted partners throughout the process. Their encouragement to write the kind of book I wanted was key—and appreciated.

Building the book required the dedication and skill of a team of professionals. I'd become friends with Ben Skinner while we were both at the Council on Foreign Relations years ago, and Ben provided me the initial encouragement to attempt the project. His constant partnership and candid but loyal sagacity were essential. Martin Beiser brought his skills as an editor and storyteller. Alexandra Everett put in long, tedious hours transcribing interview after interview. Eric Robinson and Spencer Bradley contributed rich research, as did Phil Kaplan who, from the start of the project to its end, was relentless and meticulous in his work.

But it was Sam Ayres, a young Yale graduate whom Ben Skinner introduced me to in the fall of 2010, who made my story come alive. Building on his extraordinary gifts as a writer, Sam immersed himself in the history, personalities, politics, and emotions of the entire sweep of my life. Becoming expert in even the most arcane aspects of special operations and counterinsurgency, Sam became my constant partner, confidant, and counselor for almost two years as we attempted to reconstruct and make sense of a lifetime of experiences. I've never known a better young man.

I want to thank my family. Through ups and downs I enjoyed the love and support of a family who guided and encouraged. Without them neither this book nor my life would have been even a shadow of what it is. And thanks to my son, Sam, who was an integral part of all that made our lives so special. I could have been a better father, but not a prouder one.

Finally, and most important, I want to thank my wife, Annie. From the day we met in 1973, she has been a gift to my life. Almost nothing I did, nor who I was, would have happened without her. She was the patient partner as this book consumed our first years of long-awaited retirement, knowing I believe that it is as much her story as mine.

Notes

CHAPTER 2: JOURNEY TO THE PLAIN

10   **1,378 new cadets:** Exactly 1,378 new members arrived on July 3, 1972 (U.S. Military Academy, "1973 Annual Report of the Superintendent," 4).

10   **before the summer was over:** During New Cadet ("Beast") Barracks, 180 cadets were separated ("for all reasons"), which was roughly 13 percent of the class (ibid., 38).

11   **when all rooms went dark:** U.S. Military Academy, "West Point 1973–1974 Catalog," 132.

11   **"The subjects which were dearest":** Winston Churchill, *My Early Life, 1874–1904* (Touchstone, 1996), 15.

12   **the Rutgers football game:** U.S. Military Academy, "West Point 1972–1973 Catalog," 142.

12   **"surrounded by attacking Indians":** Rick Atkinson, *The Long Gray Line* (Holt, 2009), 396.

12   **"prima donnas and spoiled brats":** Ibid.

14   **dramatically upset Air Force:** Gordon S. White, Jr., "Long Run Decides: Hines Races 49 Yards for Cadet Score with 5:53 Remaining," *New York Times,* November 5, 1972.

15   **rooms were to be kept:** During the 1976 honor code hearings, Lieutenant General Sidney Berry explained, "Now, regulations require cadets to keep their rifles cleaned and without rust. If a cadet has a dirty rifle bore and rust on the trigger housing guard, he has violated regulations and will get a minor number of demerits but we do not believe that that is indicative of a lack of integrity" (House Armed Services Committee, *Hearings on the United States Military Academy Honor Code* [U.S Goverment Printing Office, 1977], 24).

15   **usually in a formal fistfight:** A report completed as part of the congressional investigation states that such an issue of honor "was then settled in some sort of duel, the most popular type in the Corps being fisticuffs," (House Armed Services Committee, *Hearings on the United States Military Academy Honor Code*, 152).

15   **scope of the code narrowed:** The report indicates that this emphasis on cadet honesty was the only "tenent [sic] which had been consistently in existence since the early 1800's [sic]" (ibid.).

15 **"Don't let the bastards grind you down":** Atkinson, *Long Gray Line*, 319. While the charges against Koster were ultimately dropped, he was censured and demoted and left the Army in disgrace.

16 **an electrical engineering exam:** By April 4, 1976, 117 cadets had been implicated (ibid., 398), but by graduation *Time* magazine was reporting it might be a larger scandal: "There is talk . . . that hundreds of others may be in deep trouble" ("What Price Honor?" *Time*, June 7, 1976). Atkinson notes that one West Point lawyer and graduate of the academy, Arthur Lincoln, suspected as many as 600 cadets were "involved"; eventually, 149 cadets left the academy because of the scandal (*Long Gray Line*, 405 and 416). In August 1976, Secretary of the Army Martin Hoffmann granted amnesty, and 93 of these cadets were allowed to rejoin the academy after a "year of reflection" (ibid., 414–15).

16 **commandant almost always expelled:** "Report of Superintendent's Special Study Group on Honor at West Point," House Armed Services Committee, *Hearings on the United States Military Academy Honor Code*, 154.

17 **near the Cambodian border:** United Press International, "Viet Cong Regiment Is Cut to Ribbons," *Williamson Daily News*, June 30, 1966.

18 **fewer than seventy thousand:** Gideon Rose, *How Wars End: Why We Always Fight the Last Battle* (Simon & Schuster, 2010), 181–82.

18 **only three years earlier:** Ibid., 171.

19 **broke apart in mid-December:** Kissinger writes that talks "finally exploded" on December 13, 1972. Henry Kissinger, *Ending the Vietnam War: A History of America's Involvement in and Extrication from the Vietnam War* (Simon & Schuster, 2003), 407.

19 **an intense bombing campaign:** The bombings took place from December 18 to 29. It is worth noting that Kissinger quotes the *Economist* when writing in his book that the civilian death toll in Hanoi from the Christmas bombings was "smaller than the number of civilians killed by the North Vietnamese in their artillery bombardment of An Loc in April" (ibid., 415).

19 **quit their academy posts:** James Kitfield, *Prodigal Soldiers* (Simon & Schuster, 1995), 142. Kitfield writes that thirty young officers quit their posts in one eighteen-month period around 1973.

21 **"The last two years wore":** Ulysses S. Grant, *Personal Memoirs* (Penguin, 1999), 19.

22 **834 other members of my class:** "The Class of 1976 graduated 835 cadets on 2 June" (United States Military Academy, "1976 Report of the Superintendent," p. 2), while others graduated later in the summer, bringing the total for the class of 1976 to 855 members (United States Military Academy, "2008 Register of Graduates and Former Cadets," Biographies 3–459).

CHAPTER 3: THE ARMY IN WHICH I SHOULD LIKE TO FIGHT

23 **historical and fresh political animosities:** Bernard K. Gordon, "The Third Indochina Conflict," *Foreign Affairs*, (Fall 1986), 66–68.

24 **"There was no fighting":** "Transcript of President Carter's Statement on the Hostage Situation," *New York Times*, April 26, 1980. Carter delivered the address at 7:00 A.M. from the Oval Office on Apirl 25, 1980. Hours earlier, at 1:00 A.M., the White House had released a short statement about the operation. Mark Bowden, *Guests of the Ayatollah: The First Battle in America's War with Militant Islam* (Grove, 2006), 468.

24 **seized sixty-six Americans:** Of the sixty-six hostages they initially seized, the Iranians held fifty-two captive for the next fourteen months. "The

Hostages and the Casualties," Jimmy Carter Library and Museum website, July 5, 2005.

24 **Many Iranians believed:** Ray Takeyh, *Guardians of the Revolution: Iran and the World in the Age of the Ayatollahs* (Oxford University Press, 2009), 39.

25 **the hostages' release:** Bernard Gwertzman, "Reagan Takes Oath as 40th President; Promises an 'Era of National Renewal'—Minutes Later, 52 U.S. Hostages in Iran Fly to Freedom After 444-Day Ordeal," *New York Times*, January 21, 1981.

27 **first out of their planes' doors:** James M. Gavin, *On to Berlin: Battles of an Airborne Commander, 1943–1946* (Viking, 1978), 105.

27 **two discs in his back:** Stephen E. Ambrose, *The Victors: Eisenhower and His Boys: The Men of World War II* (Simon & Schuster, 1998), 239.

28 **carried a rifle:** Gavin, *On to Berlin*, 103.

32 **high-profile weapons:** David Halberstam, *The Best and the Brightest* (Ballantine, 1992), 22. Ironically, the staffer who suggested Kennedy "adopt" the Green Berets was Daniel Ellsberg; he later said the excesses of the Green Berets were a final motivation for leaking the Pentagon Papers (United Press International, "Ellsberg: Beret Case Caused Disclosure Move," *Modesto Bee*, July 15, 1971).

32 **"mark of distinction":** Alfred H. Paddock, Jr., *U.S. Army Special Warfare: Its Origins*, rev. ed. (University of Kansas Press, 2002), 156.

32 **"unrest and ethnic conflicts":** John F. Kennedy, "Remarks at West Point to the Graduating Class of the U.S. Military Academy" (West Point, NY, June 6, 1962), The American Presidency Project website.

32 **"enveloped in the sinister":** "Mystery of the Green Berets," *Time*, August 15, 1969.

34 **hostage at two locations:** Charles Cogan, "Desert One and Its Disorders," *Journal of Military History* (January 2003), 208.

34 **more than four million people:** Cogan writes there were four million ("Desert One and Its Disorders," 206), while Bowden estimates "more than 5 million" (*Guests of the Ayatollah*, 435).

35 **outskirts of Tehran:** The site was fifty miles outside Tehran (Cogan, "Desert One and Its Disorders," 210).

35 **forty-four aircraft:** Ibid., 211.

35 **columns of suspended dust:** James L. Holloway, "The Holloway Report," Joint Chiefs of Staff, August 23, 1980, 9.

35 **for hours, obscuring anything:** "He climbed to one thousand feet and was still in the cloud. . . . For three hours they flew like this on instruments" (Bowden, *Guests of the Ayatollah*, 449).

36 **insufficient bandwidth of every type:** "When the on-scene commander happened to be away from his radio to consult with others, his radio operator broadcast that the RH-53 and the C-130 had collided. Unfortunately, the transmission was incomplete and no call sign was given. This resulted in several blind radio calls from support bases in an attempt to find out what had happened and where. These unnecessary transmission blocked out other radio calls" (ibid., 51). Years later, I would still face the need for ever more bandwidth to transmit information and support operations in Iraq and Afghanistan.

36 **pilots later admitted:** Ibid., 50.

36 **fully rehearsed:** Ibid.

36 **security concerns prevented:** "The AWS team . . . did not have direct contact with the helicopter and C-130 aircrews. Weather information was passed through an intelligence officer to the pilots on regular visits to the training sites. . . . Information flow to the mission pilots was filtered as a result of

organizational structure. The traditional relationship between pilots and weather forecasters was severed. This was done to enhance OPSEC" (ibid., 38).

36 **"directed against" the United States:** Holloway, "Holloway Report," 61.

36 **Iranian state television looped footage:** Takeyh, *Guardians of the Revolution*, 44.

36 **press conference in Tehran the next day:** Bowden, *Guests of the Ayatollah*, 479.

CHAPTER 4: RENAISSANCE

39 **produce the real metal ones:** U.S. Army, "Fort Stewart History," Fort Stewart website.

40 **the size of Rhode Island:** U.S Army, "Fort Irwin History," Fort Irwin website.

40 **Patton's 2nd Armored Division:** Anne W. Chapman, *The Origins and Development of the National Training Center, 1976–1984*, Office of the Command Historian, U.S. Army Training and Doctrine Command, 2010, 7.

40 **train as they would fight:** Information on the NTC comes from Chapman, *Origins and Development of the National Training Center*, 8, 17, and 20–22.

48 **major in the commandos:** Lawrence Wright, *The Looming Tower: Al Qaeda and the Road to 9/11* (Alfred A. Knopf, 2006), 204.

49 **rising to two hundred:** Numbers on Afghan Arabs come from Camille Tawil, *Brothers in Arms: The Story of al-Qa'ida and the Arab Jihadists* (Saqi Books, 2010), 16–19.

49 **four thousand strong:** Steve Coll, *Ghost Wars* (Penguin Press, 2004), 201.

49 **behind the wheel of bulldozers:** Mary Anne Weaver, "The Real Bin Laden," *New Yorker*, January 24, 2000, 34.

49 **Beal Brothers boots:** Ibid.

49 **between the two quickly shifting:** Steve Coll, in his biography of the family, notes that at this time, "Osama associated himself with Azzam's radical voice, yet he remained an entirely orthodox Saudi figure, a minor emissary of its establishment." Steve Coll, *The Bin Ladens: An Arabian Family in the American Century* (Penguin Press, 2008), 256.

49 ***al-qaeda al-sulbah***: Thomas Hegghammer, "Abdullah Azzam, the Imam of Jihad," in *Al Qaeda in Its Own Words*, ed. Gilles Kepel and Jean-Pierre Milelli (Belknap Press, 2008), 100.

49 **his homeland of Egypt:** Wright, *Looming Tower*, 150.

49 **through coordinated coups:** Hegghammer, "Imam of Jihad," 100.

49 **"To establish the truth":** Al Qaeda's bylaws can be found on the website of the West Point Combating Terrorism Center. These lines are also quoted in Wright, *Looming Tower*, 162.

49 **September 10, 1988:** "Government's Evidentiary Proffer Supporting the Admissibility of Coconspirator Statements: *U.S. v. Enaam M. Arnaout*," *United States District Court, Northern District of Illinois, Eastern Division*, January 6, 2003, 36–37. This document, which has served as a basis for much of the public understanding of Al Qaeda's founding, is a court document from the 2002–2003 case *U.S. v. Enaam M. Arnaout*. It provides a summary of one of the files recovered in March 2002, when Bosnian authorities raided the Sarajevo offices of the Benevolence International Foundation, an Islamic charity. The file, "*Tareekh Usama*" ("The History of Usama"), contained a firsthand account of Al Qaeda's founding and the events surrounding it. Peter L. Bergen, *The Osama bin Laden I Know* (Free Press, 2006), 75.

49 **"Trusted sources" would vouch:** "Government's Evidentiary Proffer," 36.

49 **separate from the conventional one:** Wright, *Looming Tower*, 162. Bergen notes that "prosaic" concerns over security—as Middle Eastern governments

may have been trying to infiltrate the volunteer ranks—prompted Al Qaeda's creation and that the organization was mostly a separate guesthouse to prevent its being compromised. Peter L. Bergen, *Holy War, Inc.* (Free Press, 2001), 62.

49 **hardened Egyptians:** Wright, *Looming Tower*, 162.

51 **met with the king:** *US News & World Report* staff, *Triumph Without Victory: The Unreported History of the Persian Gulf War* (Random House, 1992), 82; Wright, *Looming Tower*, 178.

51 **one hundred thousand Muslims ready:** Wright, *Looming Tower*, 178–79. Wright notes that bin Laden's offer "was a bizarre and grandiose replication of General Schwarzkopf's briefing."

52 **hundreds of pamphlets:** Central Intelligence Agency, "Usama Bin Ladin: Islamist Extremist Financier" (declassified 1996 memorandum), available on the George Washington University's National Security Archives website.

52 **Yemen:** Abu Musab al Suri, quoted in Tawil, *Brothers in Arms*, 27. For a discussion of bin Laden's early focus on fighting communism, see Wright, *Looming Tower*, 150.

CHAPTER 5: PREPARATION

57 **killed nineteen White Devils:** The crash resulted in 130 casualties, including 24 fatalities. Mary Ellen Condon-Rall, *Disaster on Green Ramp: The Army's Response* (Center of Military History, U.S. Army, 1996), appendix.

61 **parachute drop since World War II:** John R. Ballard, *Upholding Democracy: The United States Military Campaign in Haiti, 1994–1997* (Praeger, 1998), xiii.

61 **"the most violent regime":** Bill Clinton, "In the Words of the President: The Reasons Why the U.S. May Invade Haiti," *New York Times*, September 16, 1994.

62 **sixty-one war planes:** Douglas Jehl, "Haiti's Military Leaders Agree to Resign," *New York Times*, September 19, 1994.

67 **deaths occur on the field:** "Historically, approximately 90% of combat-related deaths occur prior to a casualty reaching a medical treatment facility (MTF)." Russ S. Kotwal et al., "Eliminating Preventable Death on the Battlefield," *Archives of Surgery* (December 2011), 1350.

67 **emergency medical technicians (EMTs):** "100% were trained as first responders, 10% as emergency medical technicians" (Sherry Wren, "Invited Critique," in Kotwal et al., "Eliminating Preventable Death," 1358).

67 **more than eight thousand operations:** The time frame for these raids was October 1, 2001, to March 31, 2010. Kotwal et al., "Eliminating Preventable Death," 1351.

67 **complications from surgery:** "None of the 32 deaths resulted from the 3 major potentially survivable causes of death . . . defined in the literature. One casualty with potentially survivable extremity wounds died of post-surgical complications following evacuation" (ibid., 1352).

67 **rate proved to be lower:** "Although the DOD does not have a process to systematically evaluate potentially survivable deaths, the regiment's 3% rate (1 in 32) is significantly lower than the 24% rate (232 in 982) previously reported for a subset of US fatalities from Operation Enduring Freedom and Operation Iraqi Freedom" (ibid.).

68 **wounded 4,500—mostly Kenyans:** "U.S. Grand Jury Indictment Against Usama Bin Laden: Usama Bin-Laden, Muhammad Atef et al.," (Counts 4 thru 238), *United States District Court, Southern District of New York*, November 6, 1998, 37.

68 **blinded:** Wright, *Looming Tower*, 308.
68 **immediately suspected Osama bin Laden:** Commission members and staff: Thomas H. Kean et al., *The 9/11 Commission Report: The Final Report of the National Commission on Terrorist Attacks upon the United States*, July 22, 2004, 115–16.
68 **lived in Sudan:** Wright, *Looming Tower*, 187.
68 **fax machine from the Hindu Kush:** Notes to Osama bin Laden, "Declaration of Jihad Against the Americans Occupying the Land of the Two Holy Sanctuaries" in *Al Qaeda in Its Own Words*, ed. Gilles Kepel and Jean-Pierre Milelli (Belknap Press, 2008), 274.
68 **primarily a financier:** Central Intelligence Agency, "Usama Bin Ladin: Islamic Extremist Financier" (declassified 1996 memorandum), available on the George Washington University's National Security Archives website.
68 **"these young men love death":** The full text of this fatwa can be found translated as Osama bin Laden, "Declaration of War Against the Americans Occupying the Land of the Two Holy Places," in *Princeton Readings in Islamist Thought: Texts and Context from al-Banna to Bin Laden*, ed by Roxanne L. Euben and Muhammad Qasim Zaman, (Princeton University Press, 2009), 436–59.
69 **volley of cruise missiles:** Commission members, *9/11 Commission Report*, 117.
69 **including nerve gas:** Wright, *Looming Tower*, 320.
69 **produced pharmaceuticals:** Ibid.
69 **deprived thousands of Sudanese of medicine:** Thomas Cushman and Simon Cottee, eds., *Christopher Hitchens and His Critics: Terror, Iraq, and the Left* (New York University Press, 2008), 223.
69 **filed suit against the United States:** Ibid.
69 **sixty-six Tomahawk cruise missiles:** Wright, *Looming Tower*, 320.
69 **thought bin Laden would be:** Ibid., 321.
69 **on the road to Kabul:** Ibid., 321–22.
69 **wounding twice that number:** The various casualty claims were reported in Ibid., 323.
69 **thirty militants were killed:** Commission members, *9/11 Commission Report*, 117.
69 **twenty of its trainees:** Weaver, "Real Bin Laden," 37.
69 **snow-tracked Afghan mountains:** Ibid., 32.
70 **"killed Pakistani intelligence officers":** Ibid., 38.
70 **less inclined to act that way:** Ibid., 37–38.
71 **counts against the accused:** Figures related to the trial are from Benjamin Weiser, "4 Guilty in Terror Bombings of 2 U.S. Embassies in Africa; Jury to Weigh 2 Executions," *New York Times*, May 30, 2001.
71 **former members of Al Qaeda:** Vernon Loeb and Christine Haughney, "Four Guilty in Embassy Bombings," *Seattle Times*, May 30, 2001.
71 **send him to the American courts:** "Taliban Won't Hand Over Osama Bin Laden," PBS: Online, *NewsHour*, May 29, 2001.

CHAPTER 6: THE FIGHT BEGINS

72 **That same morning:** The four hijacked flights that morning departed between 7:59 A.M. and 8:20 A.M.
72 **"Tighten your clothes well":** Muhammad 'Ata al-Sayyid, "Final Instructions," in *Princeton Readings in Islamist Thought: Texts and Context from al-Banna to Bin Laden*, ed. by Roxanne L. Euben and Muhammad Qasim Zaman, (Princeton University Press, 2009), 436–59.

73   "When you board the airplane": Ibid., 469.
73   four hundred miles per hour: "Final Report on the Collapse of World Trade Center Building 7," National Institute of Standards and Technology, November 2008, 15.
73   "for the sake of God": Muhammad 'Ata, "Final Instructions," 471.
74   fifty thousand reserve troops: Jane Perlez, "After the Attacks: The Overview: U.S. Demands Arab Countries 'Choose Sides,' " *New York Times*, September 15, 2001.
74   "with the terrorists": George W. Bush, "Address to a Joint Session of Congress and the American People," The George W. Bush White House website, September 20, 2001.
74   his ambassador to Pakistan: This scene is recounted by the former ambassador, Abdul Salam Zaeef, in his memoir, *My Life with the Taliban* (Columbia University Press, 2010), 149.
74   "resort to anything beyond threats": Ibid.
74   Green Berets into northern Afghanistan: Gary Bernsten, *Jawbreaker: The Attack on Bin Laden and Al-Qaeda* (Crown, 2005), 78.
74   Mullah Omar's compound outside Kandahar: Ibid, 82.
75   blows against the United States: The effectiveness of these attacks—infrequent but more and more spectacular—were inseparable from bin Laden's drumbeat of messaging that played on the increasingly unblinking media environment of the 1990s, including the growing private Arab TV stations. See Omar Saghi, "Introduction," in *Al Qaeda in Its Own Words*, ed. Gilles Kepel and Jean-Pierre Milelli (Belknap Press, 2008), 24–28.
75   "wherever they find them": Osama bin Laden, "World Islamic Front Statement Urging Jihad Against Jews and Crusaders," in *Al Qaeda in Its Own Words*, 55.
78   two army engineer officers: Steve Vogel, *The Pentagon: A History* (Random House, 2008), xxiii–xxv.
78   air-conditioned office space: Ibid., 40. Other details about the concept for the Pentagon come from the same work, especially 137, 155.
78   17.5 miles of corridors: Ibid., xi.
78   thirty-three thousand workers: Ibid., 356.
78   first occupants in April 1942: Ibid., 213.
78   eighteen months from concept: Ibid., 295.
80   after midnight on October 11: "Vote Summary on the Joint Resolution (H.J. Res. 114)," U.S. Senate Roll Call Votes, 107th Cong., 2nd sess., October 11, 2002 available from the Library of Congress THOMAS website. President Bush signed it into law five days later, on October 16, as Public Law 107-243.
82   refused to contribute: Robin Wright and Sonya Yee, "Mobilization of Iraqi Exiles Falls Short," *Los Angeles Times*, March 29, 2003.
82   only seventy-four Iraqis: Ibid.
82   ninety million dollars: Ibid.
82   invited to attend: David Lightman, "Top Secret," *Hartford Courant*, April 2, 2003.
82   ask questions or request information: "The most valuable part," Senator Levin was quoted as saying in the *New York Times*, "is you can ask questions, you can press for information" (Carl Hulse and Eric Schmitt, "Pentagon Strokes Lawmakers Every Morning, and They Seem to Like It," *New York Times*, March 29, 2003).
82   while Levin had not: "Vote Summary on the Joint Resolution (H.J. Res. 114)."
82   mulling plans to attack: The first briefing delivered to the chiefs of staff in "the Tank" (where they convene) occurred on Memorial Day, May 27, 2002.

Micah Zenko writes an account of the briefing in *Between Threats and War* (Stanford University Press, 2010), 97.

83 **lower limit of the No Fly Zone:** Ibid., 98.

83 **in Europe and perhaps beyond:** When this facility was attacked and captured, chairman of the Joint Chiefs of Staff Richard Myers suggested on CNN's *Late Edition with Wolf Blitzer* that the facility was the source of the ricin and terrorist operatives implicated in the 2002 Wood Green ricin plot to attack the London subway. "U.S. Troops Search for Chemical Biological Weapons," *Late Edition with Wolf Blitzer*, CNN, March 31, 2003.

83 **dispatching American bombers:** Zenko, *Between Threats and War*, 98.

83 **inserting a ground force:** Ibid., 100.

83 **attacking the Hussein regime:** Ibid., 106

83 **larger force package than envisioned:** Ibid., 100.

84 **equipment Ansar al-Islam had used:** Ibid., 108–109.

84 **soldiers and their families:** Robert F. Worth, "Extension of Stay in Iraq Takes Toll on Morale of G.I.'s," *New York Times*, July 19, 2003.

84 **more Americans had died:** Sergio Vieira, "U.S. Deaths in Postwar Iraq Equal to Those in Conflict," CNN, August 25, 2003.

CHAPTER 7: THROUGH THE HOURGLASS

92 **drove through a field:** R. Jeffrey Smith, "After 10 Months in Iraq, U.S. Marks 500th Military Death," *Washington Post*, January 18, 2004.

92 **another eight times over:** At the time of writing, 4,486 Americans had died in the Iraq war, according to icasualties.org.

98 **"responsibility and duty and engagements":** T. E. Lawrence, *Seven Pillars of Wisdom* (Vintage, 2008), 41.

100 **four square miles:** William Langewiesche, "Welcome to the Green Zone," *Atlantic*, November 2004.

100 **busts from their perches:** Joel Brinkley, "A Joyful Palace Event: Four Heads Roll in Baghdad, and All of Them Are Hussein's," *New York Times*, December 3, 2003.

102 **rebuilding the stock market:** George Packer's description of the palace is unfortunately quite accurate: "Amid the grotesque faux-baroque furnishings, the palace was a hive of purposeful activity. . . . Most of them seemed to be Republicans, and more than a few were party loyalists who had come to Iraq as political appointees on ninety-day tours. They were astonishingly young. Many had never worked abroad. . . . Some were simply unqualified for their responsibilities. A twenty-five-year-old oversaw the creation of the Baghdad stock market, and another twenty-five-year-old, from the Office of Special Plans, helped write the interim constitution while filling out his law school application." George Packer, *The Assassins' Gate: America in Iraq* (Farrar, Straus and Giroux, 2005), 183–84. See also Yochi J. Dreazen, "How a 24-Year-Old Got a Job Rebuilding Iraq's Stock Market," *Wall Street Journal*, January 28, 2004.

102 **only a fraction of their size:** Eight thousand seven hundred soldiers from the 2nd Infantry Division replaced the 101st in January 2004. Eric Hamilton, "The Fight for Mosul," *Institute for the Study of War*, 7–8.

104 **left my key TF 714 staff behind:** My recollection of this October trip and helicopter flight was confirmed in interviews with team members present.

104 **the administration's official line:** That week President Bush said, "The more progress we make on the ground, the more free the Iraqis become, the more electricity is available, the more jobs are available, the more kids that are going

to school, the more desperate these killers become." "Week of Violence," *NewsHour*, PBS, October 31, 2003.

105 **Sunni stronghold after the invasion:** Eric Hamilton, "The Fight for Mosul," 4.

105 **sandbags, burlap sacks:** These processes were described in interviews with participants.

107 **at 4:30 P.M.:** Langewiesche, "Welcome to the Green Zone."

107 **KAMAZ flatbed truck:** Sameer N. Yacoub, "FBI: Deadly U.N. Headquarters Bomb Made from Materials from Saddam's Old Arsenal," *Associated Press*, August 20, 2003.

107 **"they can rape the land":** "The Insurgency," *Frontline*, PBS, February 21, 2006. Zarqawi later claimed responsibility for the U.N. attack, among others, saying, "God honored us and so we harvested their heads and tore up their bodies in many places."

107 **during East Timor's independence:** Abu Omar al-Kurdi, an Al Qaeda in Iraq operative, said Zarqawi targeted Vieira de Mello specifically as "the person behind the separation of East Timor from Indonesia." Quoted in Samantha Power, *Chasing the Flame: Sergio Vieira de Mello and the Fight to Save the World* (Penguin Press, 2008), 514.

108 **a cap attributed to Secretary Rumsfeld:** Interview with senior military official.

108 **critical step to secure authority:** Interview with participant.

CHAPTER 8: THE ENEMY EMERGES

112 **a framed exhibition case:** Don Van Natta, "Hussein's Gun May Go on Display at Bush Library," *New York Times*, July 5, 2009.

113 **three concentric circles:** This understanding of Al Qaeda's structure appears in Coll, *Ghost Wars*, 474. Coll notes that by the late 1990s, such a description of the terrorist group was "common" at the CIA.

113 **core was a bureaucracy:** Commission members and staff: Thomas H. Kean, et al., "Overview of the Enemy: Staff Statement No. 15," National Commission on Terrorist Attacks upon the United States, June 16, 2004, 2–3 (hereafter, "Overview of the Enemy").

113 **"centralization of decision":** Khalid al Hammadi, "Bin Ladin's Former 'Bodyguard' Interviewed on Al-Qaida Strategies," *Al-Quds al Arabi*, trans. by the Foreign Broadcast Information Service, August 3, 2004. The article quotes Abu Jandal (a former "personal guard" to bin Laden) explaining this operational model in 2004. Since then, this statement has been cited by both Lawrence Wright (*The Looming Tower*, 359) and Peter L. Bergen (*The Osama bin Laden I Know*, 253). The organization, as Steve Coll describes it, "was tightly supervised at the top and very loosely spread at the bottom" (*Ghost Wars*, 474).

113 **top-level Military Affairs Committee:** Al Hammadi, "Bin Ladin's Former 'Bodyguard.'"

113 **staying to clean their tracks:** "Overview of the Enemy," 8.

113 **in Europe, and elsewhere:** Contrary to reports, bin Laden did not personally finance Al Qaeda; estimates of his fortune were chronically inflated, and determining his actual wealth was a persistent difficulty for the intelligence community. Steve Coll, *The Bin Ladens*, 347–48, 488–96.

113 **twenty other groups:** Commission Members, *9/11 Commission Report*, 470, note 80.

113 **bin Laden attempted to bring:** Leah Farrall, "How Al Qaeda Works," *Foreign Affairs* (March/April 2011).

114   **ten thousand and twenty thousand:** *9/11 Commission Report*, 67. This figure is also cited by Thomas Hegghammer ("Global Jihadism After the Iraq War," *Middle East Journal* [Winter 2006], 14) and Wright (*Looming Tower*, 341).

114   **as high as seventy thousand:** Bruce Hoffman, "Leadership Secrets of Osama bin Laden," *Atlantic*, April 2003.

114   **hard, poor lives:** Coll, *Ghost Wars*, 474–75.

114   **science and engineering degrees:** Wright notes the "strong bias" toward these specific academic disciplines (*Looming Tower*, 340–41).

114   **physical training alongside indoctrination:** Behavior we witnessed on the battlefield validated Norwegian terrorism scholar Thomas Hegghammer's assessment: "Here lies the key to understanding the extremism and the internal cohesion of the so-called 'al-Qa'ida network.' The training camps generated an ultra-masculine culture of violence which brutalized the volunteers and broke down their barriers to the use of violence. . . . [T]he harsh camp life built strong personal relationships between them. Last but not least, they fell under the ideological influence of Osama bin Ladin and Ayman al-Zawahiri, who generated a feeling among the recruits of being part of a global vanguard of holy warriors, whose mission was to defend the Islamic world against attacks by the Jewish-Crusader alliance" ("Global Jihadism After the Iraq War," 14).

114   **invited attendees to brainstorm:** "Overview of the Enemy," 9.

114   **an Al Qaeda trademark:** Wright, *Looming Tower*, 211.

114   **prestige of such "martyrdom operations":** "Overview of the Enemy," 10.

114   **graduating to advanced training:** Ibid.

114   **endorsed the same strategy:** Hegghammer writes of the "ideological unity" among men who had passed through the camps ("Global Jihadism After the Iraq War," 14).

114   **across sixty countries:** Coll, *Ghost Wars*, 474.

114   **control over the disparate network:** "The eviction from Afghanistan in 2001 made al Qaeda Central more dependent on franchises to maintain operational reach, while local groups were attracted by the strength of the al Qaeda brand name." Thomas Hegghammer, "The Ideological Hybridization of Jihadi Groups," *Current Trends in Islamist Ideology*, November 18, 2009.

115   **under orders from bin Laden:** Farrall, "How Al Qaeda Works."

117   **"In no class of warfare":** C. E. Caldwell, *Small Wars: Their Principles & Practice*, 3rd ed. (Bison Books, 1996 [1906]), 143.

119   **"We have recently seen":** J. B. L. J. Rousseau, quoted in Alexei Vassiliev, *The History of Saudi Arabia* (Saqi Books, 1998), 97.

120   **conquer the peninsula:** Vassiliev, *History of Saudi Arabia*, 98. The state established by Saud and Wahhab's army briefly united most of Arabia but flamed out ten years later, in 1815, following an Egyptian invasion.

120   **"12,000 Wahhabis suddenly attacked":** J. B. L. J. Rousseau, quoted in ibid., 97.

120   **too passive or too compromising:** On understanding how historical Salafisim and Wahhabism have given rise to the more global and violent modern Salafisim of figures like Zarqawi, I found useful Roel Meijer's introduction to the volume he edited, *Global Salafism: Islam's New Religious Movement* (Columbia University Press, 2009).

120   **largely avoided the sectarian targeting:** The exceptions were the smaller, explicitly anti-Shiite extremist groups that had existed in Pakistan and were allied with Al Qaeda in the years leading up to the Karbala attack. But their impact was minimal compared to Zarqawi's impending program: "Although

Salafi discourse has always been virulently anti-Shi'ite, Arab Islamist militants have never in modern times targeted Shi'ites on the scale we are now witnessing in Iraq" (Hegghammer, "Global Jihadism After the Iraq War," 27).

120 **to bin Laden and Zawahiri:** Details of Hassan Ghul's capture appear in Yuri Kozyrev, "Fields of Jihad," *Time*, February 23, 2004.

121 **"They are an easy quarry":** "Zarqawi Letter," trans. by Coalition Provisional Authority, Department of State website, February 2004.

121 **almost thirty years:** Jeffrey Gettleman, "A Ritual of Self-Punishment, Long Suppressed, Is Shattered by a Mortar Attack," *New York Times*, March 3, 2004.

121 **"display of heathens and idolatry":** Hamid al-Ali, quoted in "Why the Aggravation?" *Economist*, March 6, 2004.

121 **outside a hotel and a shrine:** Details of this scene of the Ashura bombings are drawn especially from Anthony Shadid's vivid reporting of the event in *Night Draws Near: Iraq's People in the Shadow of America's Wars* (Henry Holt and Co., 2006), 422–25. I read *Night Draws Near* the year it came out, and it had a tremendous impact on me. I was in Iraq at the time, and it highlighted the superficiality of our understanding, which was tough to accept in ourselves.

121 **169 dead and hundreds wounded:** Casualty figures are from "Will the Blood-stained Shias Resist the Urge to Hit Back?" *Economist*, March 6, 2004.

121 **protectors of their fellow Shia:** Rajiv Chandrasekaran, "Iraq's Shiites Renew Call for Militias," *Washington Post*, March 4, 2004.

CHAPTER 9: BIG BEN

125 **pick up kitchen equipment:** A lot about the event remains unclear, especially the exact reason the Blackwater convoy entered Fallujah that day. Tom Ricks in *Fiasco* says the contractors (traveling without the flatbed trucks) were "checking out a route that Kellogg Brown & Root's logistics convoy would take the next day" (*Fiasco: The American Military Adventure in Iraq* [Penguin Press, 2006], 331). However, the guards were not under contract with KBR, but rather a firm called ESS. The *Raleigh News & Observer*'s six-part series on the incident and a *Frontline* documentary are most authoritative and suggest the contractors were escorting empty flatbed trucks that were going to get kitchen equipment.

125 **stopped at a checkpoint:** "Interview with Colonel John Toolan," *Frontline*, PBS, April 5, 2005. John Toolan (who was a colonel commanding the 1st Regiment, 1st Marines at that time) reported to *Frontline* that the contractors "ignored" the Marines' warnings and then somehow bypassed the checkpoint.

126 **its driver slumped over:** Details of the scene come from an extended series by the *Raleigh News & Observer* on the ambush: Jay Price et al., "The Bridge: Chapter 6: Fury Boils to the Surface," *Raleigh News & Observer*, July 31, 2004.

126 **"cemetery of the Americans":** John Berman, "Outrage in Fallujah," *Nightly News*, ABC, March 31, 2004.

126 **in front of news cameramen:** The front page of the *Rocky Mountain News* for April 1, 2004, carried an image of a Fallujan holding up a sheet of paper that had this slogan printed on it, underneath a skull-and-crossbones logo.

126 **" 'as if they were lollipops' ":** Quoted in Alissa J. Rubin and Doyle McManus, "Why America Has Waged a Losing Battle on Fallouja," *Los Angeles Times*, October 24, 2004.

126 **seat of the lead vehicle:** Price et al., "The Bridge: Chapter 6."

126   **city of 285,000:** Rubin and McManus, "Why America Has Waged."
126   **boasting 133 of them:** Multi-National Forces–Iraq, "Operation Al Fajr: Roll Up" (briefing), November 28, 2004.
126   **produced chemical weapons:** Jon Lee Anderson, "Letter from Baghdad: Invasions," *New Yorker*, March 24, 2003.
128   **a long, combustible history:** Iraqis with a better historical memory than our own knew this was not the first time the Fallujah area had been scene to a murder that drew the ire of a superpower and altered geopolitics. Much of this story is found in H. V. F. Winstone, *Leachman: "O.C. Desert": The Life of Lieutenant-Colonel Gerard Leachman DSO* (Quartet Books, 1982), 215–20.

In August 1920, eighty-four years before the contractors' SUVs merged onto the asphalt of Highway 10, a British lieutenant colonel named Gerard Leachman and his Iraqi driver motored the same road from Baghdad toward Fallujah, stopping at a police station outside the city. A contemporary of T. E. Lawrence, Leachman was a skilled Arabist who had been deployed to the Middle East during the First World War. Now, with Mesopotamia under British control, Leachman was the political officer responsible for a stretch from Najaf to Ramadi in Anbar, or as the desert district was known then, due to its largest confederation, Dulaim. With what Lawrence described as "a plucked face and neck," Leachman "was full of courage" but had "an abiding contempt for everything native," (T.E. Lawrence to Alec Dixon, *The Letters of T. E. Lawrence*, ed. David Garnett [Jonathan Cape, 1938], 489–91). Years earlier, in the midst of the First World War, Lawrence had sent Leachman away from his desert camp because he treated his Arab servant "so unmercifully."

On the day the thin tires of Leachman's armored Rolls-Royce scratched to a stop in the sandy lot of a police station outside Fallujah, Iraq was upset by revolt. The Shia tribes in the south were rising against British occupation following their exclusion from the 1919 Versailles Peace Conference, which had given the British mandate over the three Ottoman provinces of Mosul, Baghdad, and Basra—thus creating Iraq. Hostility toward the British occupation had blown north, and some of the Sunni sheikhs in the Anbar stretch were considering joining the revolt alongside the southern Shias. Leachman was there to meet with a local tribal leader, Sheikh Dhari. The meeting did not go well: Dhari had just met in secret with "hostile shaikhs," while Leachman was now advocating "wholesale slaughter" against insurrecting tribes. Whether the sheikh or his son fired the shot isn't clear, but Leachman took a bullet in the back and died. News of Leachman's murder uncorked the rebellion, and within two weeks the upper Euphrates was under revolt.

The revolt inaugurated a long and uncomfortable relationship between Iraqis and foreign forces. By the time Britain regained control of the provinces, it had deployed one hundred thousand British and Indian troops and spent tens of millions of pounds sterling. Faced with the rising cost of occupation and a diminishing defense budget, then–War Secretary Winston Churchill suggested that employing the Royal Air Force would offer "a prompt and drastic curtailment of expenditure" in Iraq. (Martin Gilbert, *Winston S. Churchill: Volume IV Companion*, Part Z, Documents July 1919–March 1921 [William Heinemann, 1977], 1078). For the rest of the mandate, the British policed Iraq's vaster tribal areas through aerial surveillance and bombing runs.

British planes returned to Fallujah twice more before the century was over. Following a coup in 1941 in which the Iraqi government in Baghdad sought to align with the Axis powers, British relief forces coming east from Palestine through Syria fought a series of battles against the Iraqis, pushing them down through Anbar toward Baghdad. Fighting bunched up at Fallujah, and the Royal Air Force and the Luftwaffe bombed each other in and around the city, pummeling the area. The British bombed the city again in the 1991 Gulf War, aiming for its bridges across the Euphrates, but an errant bomb reportedly killed scores of civilians. (Ahmed Hashin, *Insurgency and Counterinsurgency in Iraq* [Cornell University Press, 2006], 27).

128 **system of patronage:** Packer, *Assassins' Gate*, 277.

128 **home to many military officers:** Steven Komarow, "Favored by Saddam, Fallujah Seething Since His Fall," *USA Today*, April 1, 2004.

128 **night-vision goggles:** Rubin and McManus, "Why America Has Waged."

128 **another seventy-five injured:** "Violent Response: The U.S. Army in al-Fallujah," Human Rights Watch, June 2003.

128 **compensation even as a gesture:** *Al-Anbar Awakening: U.S. Marines and Counterinsurgency in Iraq, 2004–2009*, vol. I, ed. Chief Warrant Officer-4 Timothy S. McWilliams and Lieutenant Colonel Kurtis P. Wheeler (Marine Corps University Press, 2009), 242.

128 **"the massacre" for years afterward:** Ibid., 242.

128 **proud Fallujans rejected it:** Packer, *Assassins' Gate*, 223. By contrast, after the two large urban battles in Fallujah, the Marines undertook a painstaking process to distribute compensation to the families affected by the violence.

128 **rocket-propelled grenades:** Eric Westervelt and Melissa Block, "U.S. General Unhurt as Insurgents Attack Iraqi Facility," *All Things Considered*, National Public Radio, February 12, 2004.

129 **freed eighty-seven prisoners:** Paul Wiseman, "Beleaguered Police Keep Faces Hidden in Fallujah," *USA Today*, February 15, 2004.

129 **twenty Iraqi policemen:** "Fallujah Mayor Questioned in Police Station Attack," CNN, February 16, 2004.

129 **"lying in wait for him":** "New 'al Qaeda' Warning on Iraq," BBC, April 6, 2004.

129 **Los Angeles Police Department:** Interview with James N. Mattis in *Al-Anbar Awakening, vol. I*, 25.

129 **through a few weeks earlier:** Dexter Filkins, "Up to 16 Die in Gun Battles in Sunni Areas of Iraq," *New York Times*, March 27, 2004.

129 **two more with homemade bombs:** Dexter Filkins, "Marine and 11 Iraqis Die During Fighting in Sunni Triangle," *New York Times*, March 26, 2004.

129 **the cloverleaf to its east:** "Marines of RCT-1 conduct offensive actions at the northeastern sector of the city of Fallujah, succeeded in taking control of the Cloverleaf intersection." Kenneth W. Estes, "U.S. Marine Corps Operations in Iraq, 2003–2006" (occasional paper), United States Marine Corps History Division, 147.

129 **the detainees got away:** Interview with task force member.

130 **police chief in Fallujah:** Interview with James T. Conway in *Al-Anbar Awakening, vol. I*, 49.

130 **within seventy-two hours:** Interview with James N. Mattis, *Al-Anbar Awakening*, 34 and 36.

130 **Mosul, Aleppo, and Amman:** Rashid Khalidi, *Resurrecting Empire: Western Footprints and America's Perilous Path in the Middle East* (Beacon Press, 2005), xii.

131 **even before the attack began:** Carter Malkasian, "Signaling Resolve, Democratization, and the First Battle of Fallujah," *The Journal of Strategic Studies* (June 2006), 438.

131   **newspapers repeated these claims:** "After U.S. artillery hit a mosque that
       the Americans said had been sheltering insurgents, [Al Jazeera reporter
       Ahmed] Mansur reported that a family had been killed in a car parked
       behind the mosque. He also said 25 members of a family were killed when
       their house was hit" (Rubin and McManus, "Why America Has Waged").

131   **did not shoot any artillery:** Interview with James N. Mattis, *Al-Anbar
       Awakening*, 36.

131   **momentary period of sympathy:** Details of Shia-Sunni cooperation during
       Fallujah are drawn from several sources, especially Jon Lee Anderson, "The
       Uprising: Shia and Sunnis Put Aside Their Differences," *The New Yorker*,
       May 3, 2004.

131   **blood donations for Fallujah:** Shadid, *Night Draws Near*, 451–53.

131   **stop the offensive in Fallujah:** For a description of the mounting political
       pressure on the Marines and the United States during the battle, see
       Malkasian, *Signaling Resolve*, 437–41.

131   **Lakhdar Brahimi, threatened to quit:** Paul Bremer III, *My Year in Iraq*
       (Threshold, 2006), 326–27; cited in Malkasian, *Signaling Resolve*, 440.

131   **potentially fatal to a new Iraq:** Interview with senior military official.

131   **Bush ordered the assault stopped:** David Cloud and Greg Jaffe, *The Fourth
       Star* (Three Rivers, 2009), 153.

131   **the Marines' Camp Fallujah:** Ibid.

131   **knowing they would be irate:** Ibid.

132   **one of his top aides:** Patrick Cockburn, *Muqtada al-Sadr and the Battle for
       the Future of Iraq* (Scribner, 2008), 145; Shadid, *Night Draws Near*, 441.

132   **in honor of Muqtada's martyred father:** Cockburn, *Muqtada al-Sadr*, 91.

132   **continue fighting Sadr's militia:** The letter, dated April 8, was reported on
       April 9, though the story ran on April 10. Thom Shanker, "Letter Tells
       Soldiers Their Tour May Extend," *New York Times*, April 10, 2004.

132   **"one thug to replace another":** Ibid.

132   **trucks stopped moving:** "One day in mid-April during the Shia uprising in
       southern Iraq, all 122 Coalition convoys traveling the roads in Iraq were
       attacked. Worse was the fact that for a short period in April, CJTF-7's supply
       lines were shut down, including MSR Tampa—the main supply route from
       Kuwait to Iraq" (Donald P. Wright and Colonel Timothy R. Reese, *The
       United States Army in Operation Iraqi Freedom, May 2003–January 2005*
       (Government Printing Office, June 2008), 506.

134   **more frequently that summer:** Thomas Hegghammer, "The Iraq Hostage
       Crisis: Abductions in Iraq, April–August 2004," Norwegian Defense
       Research Establishment, October 2004.

135   **enemies with pig carcasses:** See Donald Smythe, "Pershing and the
       Disarmament of Moros," *Pacific Historical Review* (August 1962), 244–45
       and relevant footnotes.

135   **the Fallujah Brigade:** According to the Marines' history, "On 25 April, both
       Lieutenant General Conway and Major General Mattis met with former
       Iraqi Army generals to discuss the possible formation of a military unit in
       al-Fallujah. . . . By 28 April the Fallujah Brigade had begun assembling and
       on the 30th, a turnover led to the phased movement of the 1st Marine
       Division out of al-Fallujah." Estes, "U.S. Marine Corps Operations," 37.

136   **ran six times:** Details of the events on April 24 come from interviews with
       task force members, as well as Oren Dorell and Gregg Zoroya, "Battle for
       Fallujah Forged Many Heroes," *USA Today*, November 9, 2006.

136   **alone on the rooftop:** Dorell and Zoroya, "Battle for Fallujah."

136   **acting like his Salafists:** See Michael Ware's report from that summer: "Meet
       the New Jihad," *Time*, June 27, 2004.

139 **AK-47 rifles and munitions:** Additional details of the tracking and intercepting of the trucks come from interviews with task force members.
140 **"get more aggressive here":** My recollection of the dialogue and details of the meeting with John Abizaid was aided by interviews with him, as well as other military members present.
141 **Marines had promised:** Confirmed with senior Marine official.
143 **mistaken the initial explosions:** "Several cars and nearby buildings were damaged by what witnesses described as two missiles, one of which appeared to have left a 20-foot crater." Edmund Sanders, "U.S. Airstrike Kills 18 in Fallouja," *Los Angeles Times,* June 20, 2004.
143 **dolls among the rubble:** Interview with senior military official.
143 **"slogans and vowing revenge":** Sanders, "U.S. Airstrike Kills 18."
144 **and we bombed those:** Interviews with task force members.
144 **guesthouses and restaurants:** In addition to open sources, locations of jihadists within Fallujah that summer come from interviews with military intelligence officials.
144 **Brigade was no real challenge:** Malkasian, *Signaling Resolve,* 448–49.
144 **meetings in the backseat:** Interview with task force member.
144 **leaders to be his deputies:** Hannah Allam, "Fallujah's Real Boss: Omar the Electrician," *Seattle Times,* November 22, 2004. Some, including the author of this article, suggest that Omar Hadid may even have been more powerful than Zarqawi within Fallujah. Hadid, a Fallujan and member of the Mujahideen Shura Council, was technically Zarqawi's deputy in the city. While Zarqawi leveraged Hadid's local appeal, he also aided Hadid by raising his profile from that of an electrician to that of a feared and famous jihadist.
145 **truck that roved through town:** Hamza Hendawi, "Fast Resembling an Islamic Mini-State, Fallujah May Be Glimpse of Iraq Future," Associated Press, May 25, 2004.

CHAPTER 10: ENTREPRENEURS OF BATTLE

146 **At the outstation:** Interviews with task force members.
148 **dropped him to the deck:** Adam Nicolson, *Seize the Fire: Heroism, Duty, and the Battle of Trafalgar* (Harper Collins, 2005), 255.
148 **minutes later he was dead:** Ibid., 254, 274.
148 **"No Captain can do very wrong":** This memorandum was written on October 9, 1805, "a fortnight before the battle" (ibid., 45).
148 **strategy with the French captains:** Ibid.
148 **"It takes a network":** This phrasing first appeared in 2001 in a monograph by John Arquilla, and the idea was one he and others had espoused before then.
150 **"absolutely intoxicating in its intensity":** Richard Williams, quoted in Robert D. Kaplan, "Man Versus Afghanistan," *Atlantic,* April 2010, 61.
152 **between bin Laden and Zarqawi:** The full reporting of Abdul Hadi al-Iraqi's trip to Iraq that summer comes from Sami Yousafzai & Ron Moreau, "Terror Broker," *Newsweek,* April 11, 2005.
152 **unrestrained targeting of Shia Muslims:** Lawrence Wright, "The Master Plan," *New Yorker,* September 11, 2006.
152 **challenge Al Qaeda's leadership:** Leah Farrall, "How Al Qaeda Works," *Foreign Affairs* (March/April 2011).
155 **voluntarily sharing it with others:** This point is made in Lamb and Munsing's article about TF 16 in Iraq: "SOF Task Force personnel were directed to set the example by being first to give more information. They were told to 'share until it hurts.' As one commander explained it, 'If you are sharing information

to the degree where you think, "Holy cow, I am going to go to jail," then you are in the right area of sharing.' The point was to build *trust,* and information-sharing was the icebreaker." Christopher J. Lamb and Evan Munsing, "Secret Weapon: High-Value Target Teams as an Organizational Innovation," *Strategic Perspectives* (March 2011), 46.

155 **"He would create the market":** Nicolson, *Seize the Fire,* 45.

156 **a brigade-size force:** Interview with task force member.

157 **broadband Internet and cell towers:** This point is explored by Peter Bergen in his book *The Longest War* (Free Press, 2011), 162–63.

157 **technically illegal under Saddam:** "Iraq Awards Mobile Phone Licenses," BBC, October 6, 2003.

157 **spread after the American invasion:** The Department of Defense indicated (through graphics) that as of June 1, 2004, there were about 500,000 subscribers; 1.5 million by January 1, 2005; and more than 3.5 million by August 31, 2005 (U.S. Department of Defense, "Measuring Stability and Security in Iraq," October 13, 2005, 16). Further data on cell phone and Internet usage in Iraq can be found on the World Bank's "Data" website, which can generate a variety of metrics on the country. In 2004, it lists 574,000 cellular phone subscriptions and, interestingly, only 300,000 Internet users (1 percent of the population).

159 **had not been convinced:** Interviews with three task force members.

159 **140 Iraqis were wounded:** The details of this event and the casualty toll come from Edmund Sanders, "35 Children Die in Baghdad Bombings," *Los Angeles Times,* October 1, 2004.

160 **barracks for our operators:** Interview with Lieutenant General (retired) John Sattler.

160 **enlisted Prime Minister Allawi:** Ibid.

160 **first week of November:** The operation was originally planned for November 5 but was then changed to November 7. Kenneth Estes, "U.S. Marine Corps Operations in Iraq, 2003–2006" (occasional paper), United States Marine Corps History Division, 55.

160 **real attack from the north:** Interview with Lt. Gen. Sattler.

160 **fortified the terrain:** "Three hundred and six well-constructed defensive positions were identified, many of which were interlaced with improvised explosive devices (IEDs)" (John F. Sattler and Daniel H. Wilson, "The Battle of Fallujah—Part II," *Marine Corps Gazette,* July 2005.)

160 **daisy-chain IEDs:** Interview with Lt. Gen. Sattler.

160 **cut the power:** Estes, "U.S. Marine Corps Operations," 58.

161 **Zarqawi pledged:** The message was posted on October 17, 2004, the third day of Ramadan. Jeffrey Pool, "Zarqawi's Pledge of Allegiance to Al-Qaeda," *Terrorism Monitor,* December 16, 2004.

161 **"our most generous brothers":** Translated by Pool in "Zarqawi's Pledge of Allegiance to Al-Qaeda."

161 **websites a few days later:** Ibid.

165 **next door, in Iraq:** Al Qaeda's leadership had sounded the alarm over the looming Iraq war in 2002, and bin Laden had spoken of Iraq as the "new crusade" since 2003. See, for example, Osama bin Laden, "Quagmires of the Tigris and Euphrates (October 19, 2003)," in *Messages to the World: The Statements of Osama bin Laden,* ed. Bruce Lawrence (Verso, 2005), 207–211.

165 **Muslims to wage jihad there:** In January 2004, bin Laden said, "Before concluding, I urge the Muslim youths to carry out *jihad,* particularly in Palestine and Iraq." Osama bin Laden, "Resist the New Rome (January 4, 2004)" in *Messages to the World,* 231.

166   **"regret it afterwards":** Osama bin Laden, "Depose the Tyrants (December 16, 2004)" in *Messages to the World*, 272.

166   **maintain their good work:** "Osama bin Laden to the Iraqi People" (Special Dispatch no. 837), Middle East Media Research Institute, December 30, 2004.

166   **bin Laden had tied his own fate:** To determine when this shift in focus occurred, Thomas Hegghammer examined Islamist Web forums and estimated the jump in interest occurred between April and September 2004. From that point on, Iraq dominated the concerns of the global jihadist movement. (Thomas Hegghammer, "Global Jihadism After the Iraq War," *Middle East Journal* (Winter 2006), 20–21.

CHAPTER 11: OUT WEST

167   **by the sandwich bar:** Elliott D. Woods, "A Few Unforeseen Things," *Virginia Quarterly Review*, Fall 2008, 6–31.

167   **bowing forward in silence:** "Lion in the Village" (transcript), *Anderson Cooper 360*, CNN, March 1, 2007.

167   **past noon, he ignited:** Ibid.

167   **Saudi medical student:** Friends of the twenty-year-old Saudi medical student reported that insurgents in Iraq had contacted the man's father, informing him that his son, who had withdrawn his tuition money and left his studies in Sudan for the jihad, had martyred himself in Iraq. Associated Press, "Report: Mess-Hall Bomber Was Saudi Student," MSNBC website, January 3, 2005. The *New Republic*, examining the 430 martyr biographies in the jihadist text *The Martyrs of the Land of the Two Rivers*, found a description of al-Ghamidi: "And Ahmad Said Ahmad Al Ghamidi, also of Saudi Arabia, was studying medicine at Khartoum University when he broke off his studies and used his tuition money to go to Iraq." Husain Haqqani and Daniel Kimmage, "Suicidology," *New Republic*, October 3, 2005, 14.

168   **"Caravan of Martyrs":** Thomas Hegghammer, "Saudi Militants in Iraq: Backgrounds and Recruitment Patterns," Norwegian Defense Research Establishment, February 5, 2007, 8.

168   **restoring the caliphate there:** "[T]he recruitment message relies not primarily on complex theological arguments, but on simple, visceral appeals to people's sense of solidarity and altruism." Thomas Hegghammer, "The Rise of Muslim Foreign Fighters: Islam and the Globalization of Jihad," *International Security* (Winter 2010–11), 90.

169   **three dozen agencies:** Interviews with JIATF members.

171   **between 12,000 and 20,000 men:** John F. Burns, "Iraq's Ho Chi Minh Trail," *New York Times*, June 5, 2005.

171   **with that stated intention:** This is based on what became known as the "Sinjar records," which indicated that 56 percent of foreign fighters were recruited to be, or joined with the intention of becoming, suicide bombers, while 42 percent came or were tasked to be fighters. Joseph Felter and Brian Fishman, *Al-Qai'da's Foreign Fighters in Iraq: A First Look at the Sinjar Records* (Combating Terrorism Center at West Point, January 2, 2007), 18. Interviews with a number of task force members indicated that some of the foreign fighters picked up had been recruited to fight but upon arrival to Iraq were assigned martyrdom missions (at times against their desire). But interviews also indicated that there was likely similar cross-assignment, where the more talented recruits who came with a desire to be suicide bombers were diverted to positions that would keep them alive.

171   **see a template emerge:** The path of recruitment and of the "ratline" is based
       upon my memory, as well as interviews with task force members involved in
       both intelligence and operations.

172   **if not thousands, of dollars:** Joseph Felter and Brian Fishman, "Becoming a
       Foreign Fighter: A Second Look at the Sinjar Records," in *Bombers, Bank
       Accounts, and Bleedout: Al Qa'ida's Road in and out of Iraq*, ed. Brian
       Fishman (Combating Terrorism Center at West Point, July 2008), 53.

173   **they had been treated:** Felter and Fishman, *Al-Qai'da's Foreign Fighters*, 25.

173   **how strong their relationships were:** Translated versions of the filled-out
       questionnaires were released as part of the Sinjar records, and an English
       version is available on the Combating Terrorism Center at West Point
       website.

173   **USS *Cole* overslept:** He "slept through the page on his phone that would have
       notified him to set up the camera." Wright, *Looming Tower*, 361.

173   **Christmas Eve that year:** This man survived the attack, and his account can
       be found in the first chapter of Ken Ballen's *Terrorists in Love: The Real
       Lives of Islamic Radicals* (Free Press, 2011), 3–44.

175   **openly doubted our assessment:** My recollection of these meetings is aided by
       interviews with other participants.

175   **more than fifty named insurgent groups:** Mohammed M. Hafez, *Suicide
       Bombers in Iraq: The Strategy and Ideology of Martyrdom* (United States
       Institute for Peace Press, 2007), appendix 1, 243–49. Other reports indicate
       around forty insurgent groups during the summer of 2005.

175   **old Saddam apparatchiks:** "Its [MNF-I JIATF's] mission was abruptly
       changed in November 2004 to the identification of former Ba'athists who
       posed a threat to the occupation, at which point its name changed to JIATF–
       Former Regime Elements." Lamb and Munsing, *Secret Weapon*, 15.

176   **calling democracy heresy:** "Zarqawi and Other Islamists to the Iraqi People:
       Elections and Democracy Are Heresy" (Special Dispatch no. 856), Middle
       East Research Institute, February 1, 2005.

176   **mentored a younger Zarqawi:** Jean-Charles Brisard with Damien Martinez,
       Zarqawi: The New Face of al-Qaeda (Other Press, 2005), 43–44.

177   **other hard-line insurgent groups:** The three groups—Ansar al-Sunnah,
       Islamic Army of Iraq, and the Jihad Warriors Army—said, we "call upon all
       Muslims zealous for their religion not to participate in this act of heresy"
       (Middle East Media Research Institute, "Zarqawi and Other Islamists").

177   **"The martyr's wedding":** Ibid.

177   **overran no election sites:** Kenneth Katzman, "Iraq: Elections, Constitution,
       and Government," Congressional Research Service, February 27, 2007, 2.

177   **freeze them into a minority role:** A number of Sunni parties had boycotted
       the election since December 15, 2004. Max Sicherman, "Iraqi Elections:
       What, How, and Who," Washington Institute for Near East Policy, January
       24, 2005.

177   **2 percent of the population:** Michael Knights and Eamon McCarthy,
       "Provincial Politics in Iraq: Fragmentation or New Awakening?" Washington
       Institute for Near East Policy, April 2008, 6.

177   **secured a mere 17:** Katzman, "Iraq: Elections, Constitution, and Government."

179   **independently of the Coalition's control:** Matt Sherman, interviewed in
       "Gangs of Iraq," *Frontline*, PBS, October 4, 2006.

179   **uniforms on Badr militiamen:** Ken Silverstein, "The Minister of Civil War:
       Bayan Jabr, Paul Bremer, and the Rise of the Iraqi Death Squads," *Harper's*,
       August 2006, 67–73.

179   **more than sixty suicide bombings:** Burns, "Iraq's Ho Chi Minh Trail."

180 **mangers for their sheep:** James Janega, "Too Much Border, Not Enough Patrol," *Chicago Tribune*, April 19, 2005.

183 **"featureless, a muddy brown":** Viscount William Slim, quoted in *The War: 1939–1945*, ed. Desmond Flower and James Reeves (Cassell, 1960), 198.

183 **South Carolina–size:** *Al-Anbar Awakening, vol. I*, 10.

183 **attempted to breach the gate:** Steve Fainaru, "The Grim Reaper, Riding a Firetruck in Iraq," *Washington Post*, April 19, 2005.

183 **Marine lance corporal:** An account of the young Marine's actions can be found in Elliot Blair Smith, "Pa. Native Thwarts Car-Bomb Attack," *USA Today*, April 17, 2005.

184 **flown to Germany:** Dates and information on soldiers Jerak, Diesing, Shea, and Kolath can be found on the U.S. Army Special Operations Command "Memorial Wall" website.

184 **"A lot of emotion attached":** E-mail to Annie, August 28, 2005, 9:22 A.M.

185 **"Governments saw men":** T. E. Lawrence, *Seven Pillars of Wisdom*, 199.

186 **proportion of the car bombings:** Craig S. Smith, "U.S. Contends Campaign Has Cut Suicide Attacks," *New York Times*, August 5, 2005.

186 **10 incidents killed 97 people:** These figures were calculated using data from the NCTC's Worldwide Incidents Tracking System database.

186 **had fought with the insurgency:** Kirk Semple, "U.S. Forces Rely on Local Informants in Ferreting Rebels in West Iraq," *New York Times*, December 10, 2005.

186 **AQI and another tribe:** Ibid.

186 **female body parts commingling:** "Al-Qa'eda in Iraq Alienated by Cucumber Laws and Brutality," *Telegraph*, August 11, 2008.

187 **executed nine members:** Ellen Knickmeyer and Jonathan Finer, "Insurgents Assert Control over Town Near Syrian Border," *Washington Post*, September 6, 2006.

187 **"Islamic Republic of Al Qaim":** Ibid.

187 **"I've been able to do":** E-mail to Annie August 28, 2005, 6:54 P.M. (edited for punctuation).

CHAPTER 12: THE HUNT

188 **head of the conference table:** Details of this meeting and the dialogue are based upon my recollection but aided and confirmed by interviews with two individuals present at the meeting.

188 **excluded these Iraq officials:** Interviews with two senior members of National Security Council staff.

190 **"being done to get him":** A memorandum with the subject "Meeting with POTUS" was sent from Donald Rumsfeld to General Dick Myers and Steve Cambone on May 19, 2005. It is available from the Rumsfeld Papers website.

192 **self-stated main effort:** In audio tapes, bin Laden "characterized the insurgency in Iraq as the central battle in a 'Third World War, which the Crusader-Zionist coalition began against the Islamic nation.' " Christopher M. Blanchard, "Al Qaeda: Statements and Evolving Ideology," *Congressional Research Service*, February 4, 2005, 5.

193 **brothers and seven sisters:** The most definitive list of Zarqawi's nine siblings and their ages can be found in Brisard, *Zarqawi*, 10, note 13. However, it is worth noting that, like many aspects of Zarqawi's early biography, contradictory information exists. For example, one otherwise very accurate *Los Angeles Times* article claims Zarqawi was the "second of five children."

Megan K. Stack, "Zarqawi Took Familiar Route into Terrorism," *Los Angeles Times*, July 2, 2004.

193   cemetery near his apartment: Fouad Hussein, "Al Zarqawi . . . The Second Generation of Al-Qai'da, Part 1," Al-Quds-al' Arabi, trans. by the Federal Broadcast Information Service.

193   dropped out at age seventeen: Stack, "Zarqawi Took Familiar Route."

193   sweeping Zarqa's brown streets: Eli Lake, "Base Jump," *New Republic*, November 28 and December 5, 2005, 19.

193   reputation for his temper: Jeffrey Gettleman, "Zarqawi's Journey: From Dropout to Prisoner to an Insurgent Leader in Iraq," *New York Times*, July 13, 2004.

193   tattoos gave his skin: Stack, "Zarqawi Took Familiar Route."

193   case of attempted rape: Brisard, having reviewed Jordanian records on the matter, is most reliable on this event (Brisard, *Zarqawi*, 13–14).

193   knife in a fight: Ibid., 13.

193   strict Salafist bent: Zarqawi's mother "enrolled him . . . at a mosque in Amman known for its Salafist stance." Hala Jaber, "A Twisted Love," *Sunday Times*, July 31, 2005.

193   worked as a correspondent: Stack, "Zarqawi Took Familiar Route."

193   their heroic exploits: Gettleman, "Zarqawi's Journey."

193   for use against Israel: Brisard, *Zarqawi*, 37.

193   1994: Zarqawi was arrested and sent to Suwaqah in 1994, but his trial did not finish with sentencing until November 1996 (ibid., 43).

193   spent in Jordanian prisons: He was eventually moved to Al-Salt and then Jafar prisons (ibid., 49).

194   using hydrochloric acid: Ibid., 50.

194   keep people in line: "He would attack us with his fists," attested fellow prisoner Yousef Rababa, quoted in Gettleman, "Zarqawi's Journey."

194   homemade weights: "Cellmates remember his barbells, made from pieces of bed frame and olive oil tins filled with rocks" (ibid.). This fact is also cited in Brisard, *Zarqawi*, 49.

194   respect of his followers: Brisard, *Zarqawi*, 48–49.

194   "just by moving his eyes": Gettleman, "Zarqawi's Journey."

194   Released in March 1999: Brisard, *Zarqawi*, 58–59.

194   Jordanian wife in tow: Alissa J. Rubin, "Jordanian's Mother Denies He Has Ties to Terrorism," *Los Angeles Times*, February 8, 2003.

194   in Herat in 2000: Herat, near Iran, might also have produced or deepened Zarqawi's bile toward Shiites; Saif al-Adl, quoted in Fouad Hussein's biography of Zarqawi, indicates that the Shiites in Herat worked with the "opposition" to rout the jihadists once the American invasion began. Hussein, "Al Zarqawi, part 8."

194   married a second wife: "Al-Jazeera TV Investigates Iraqi Militant Al-Zarqawi's Al-Qa'idah Links," *BBC Monitoring International Reports*, July 2, 2004.

194   informal relationship with bin Laden: Reportedly, Al Qaeda's insistence on making war with the United States was a barrier to Zarqawi's pledging his full allegiance to bin Laden when invited to do so in 2000. It is also possible that bin Laden's forbidding Zarqawi from teaching Maqdisi's texts was a nonstarter. Vahid Brown, *Cracks in the Foundation: Leadership Schisms in al-Qa'ida 1989–2006* (Combating Terrorism Center, January 2, 2007), 19–20.

194   a set of broken ribs: Saif al-Adl in Hussein, "Al Zarqawi, part 8."

194   was on Zarqawi's mind: Ibid.

194 **line to Zarqawi himself:** Interviews with task force members implied that by being an Iraq-wide player in the insurgency, Abu Zar was more likely linked to AQI senior leadership.

195 **shrine on the other side:** Robert F. Worth, "950 Die in Stampede on Baghdad Bridge," *New York Times*, September 1, 2005.

195 **Some drowned:** Dan Murphy, "Panic of Terror Sparks Human Tragedy in Iraq," *Christian Science Monitor* (reprinted in *USA Today*), September 1, 2005.

195 **that many were injured:** Casualty figures are from "Iraqis Bury Victims of Baghdad Stampede," *New York Times*, September 1, 2005.

196 **of sectarian paranoia:** A rumor spread that the pilgrims had been poisoned. As Robert Worth noted, "Shiite Muslims believe that Imam Kadhim was poisoned by agents of Harun al-Rashid, the Sunni caliph, in the late eighth century, and history often merges with the present among religious pilgrims here" (Worth, "950 Die in Stampede").

196 **tragically entrenched:** And yet even against Zarqawi's encroaching dark dream for Iraq, a few defiant heroes stood out: A young Sunni man, nineteen years old, heard calls from a local mosque to help people drowning in the nearby Tigris, ran to the river, and ferried out Shia victims until he had exhausted himself, drowning in the water. "Sunni Rescuer Hailed as a Hero," BBC, September 5, 2005.

196 **released from prison in Jordan:** About a year before his release, from within the walls of Qefqefa prison, Maqdisi had posted an open letter to his website addressed to Zarqawi and criticizing his tactics in Iraq, but it went largely unnoticed. Nibras Kazimi, "A Virulent Ideology in Mutation: Zarqawi Upstages Maqdisi," *Current Trends in Islamist Ideology*, September 12, 2005.

196 **its most influential ideologue:** Joas Wagemakers, an expert on Maqdisi, writes that "Maqdisi is one of the most prominent radical Islamic ideologues in the world today" but notes that the description of him as "'the spiritual father of the al-Qa'ida movement' . . . may be an exaggeration." Joas Wagemakers, "Abu Muhammad al-Maqdisi," *CTC Sentinel*, May 15, 2008. Maqdisi famously referred to the West Point Combating Terrorism Center's *Militant Ideology Atlas*, to argue that he was "the most influential living Islamic thinker . . . among jihadi groups." Thomas Hegghammer, "Maqdisi Invokes McCants," *Jihadica* (blog), April 18, 2009.

196 **made Iraq a "crematory":** This translation is from Steven Brooke, "The Preacher and the Jihadi," *Current Trends in Islamist Ideology*, February 16, 2006.

196 **wiped out like another race:** Kazimi, "A Virulent Ideology."

196 **"Six months ago, every day":** Y. Yehoshua, "Dispute in Islamist Circles, Over the Legitimacy of Attacking Muslims, Shi'ites, and Non-combatant Muslims in Jihad Operations in Iraq," Middle East Media Research Institute, September 11, 2005. This was strong stuff coming from Maqdisi, whose excommunication of the Saudi royal family in the early 1990s had been too radical for bin Laden and whose own website was stocked with anti-Shia literature (Kazimi, "A Virulent Ideology").

196 **"liquidate" the Sunnis:** Zarqawi responded in an audiotape posted online, later in the day after Maqdisi's Al Jazeera interview aired (Yehoshua, "Dispute in Islamist Circles"). On July 6, the next day, Maqdisi was put back in prison, leaving behind an Internet statement praising Zarqawi as a "beloved brother and hero" and acknowledging that the "mujahadeen brothers in Iraq have their own interpretations and choices that they choose as they see fit in the battlefield that we are distant from" (ibid.).

196   **days later on July 9:** "Letter from al-Zawahiri to al-Zarqawi," Office of the Director of National Intelligence website, October 11, 2005.

196   **fulsome if perfunctory praise:** "I want to be the first to congratulate you," he begins, "for what God has blessed you with in terms of fighting battle in the heart of the Islamic world, which was formerly the field for major battles in Islam's history, and what is now the place for the greatest battle of Islam in this era" (ibid.).

196   **"the strongest weapon":** Ibid.

197   **"Expel the Americans from Iraq":** Anti-Shiism had been ingrained in the fundamentalism of Al Qaeda, but Al Qaeda had occasionally flirted with cooperating with Shias to strike its far enemies. During the Soviet war, Shiites had fought alongside the Sunni groups and even found quarter in bin Laden's camp. Zawahiri's Egyptian al-Jihad had supported the Iranian revolution, and he reportedly took two million dollars of funds from Iran. But by the late 1990s, Al Qaeda was teaching the thousands of men who passed through its training camps in Afghanistan that the "enemies of Islam" were first, apostate Arab leaders; second, Shiites; third, America; and fourth, Israel. Wright, *Looming Tower*, 340–42.

197   **website on September 14:** Zarqawi released another tape on September 19, 2005, clarifying some of his September 14 tape, including that his group would not target Sadrists "as long as they do not strike us," because Sadr's followers weren't collaborating with the Iraqi government. Anthony H. Cordesman with Emma R. Davies, *Iraq's Insurgency and the Road to Civil Conflict* (Praeger Security International, 2008), 155.

197   **"decided to declare a total war":** "Leader of Al-Qaeda in Iraq Al-Zarqawi Declares 'Total War' on Shi'ites, States That the Sunni Women of Tel'afar Had 'Their Wombs Filled with the Sperm of the Crusaders,'" Middle East Media Research Institute, September 16, 2005.

197   **wounded in that day's blasts:** Casualty figures are from "Iraq Timeline 2005," Council on Foreign Relations, October 13, 2005.

197   **nihilistic revenge on a wide scale:** In his July 2005 interview with Al Jazeera, Maqdisi said, "My plan is not to blow up a bar or a movie theater. My plan is not to kill an officer who tortured me. My plan is to restore the nation to its glories and establish the Islamic state for all Muslims" (Brooke, "The Preacher"). Zarqawi acknowledged these criticisms in his July 5 audiotape: "Some of those [*ulama*] want us to stop our Jihad in Iraq, claiming that the Jihad in Iraq is merely a Jihad which causes harm to the enemy but is not a Jihad that can lead to the establishment of Islamic government, and therefore there will be those who reap the benefit of this Jihad and achieve power at the expense of the blood of the Jihad fighters" (Yehoshua, "Dispute in Islamist Circles").

197   **three hotels in Amman, Jordan:** Michael Slackman and Suha Ma'ayeh, "Attacks at U.S.-based Hotels in Amman Were Minutes Apart," *New York Times*, November 9, 2005.

197   **The deadliest attack:** Hassan Fattah and Michael Slackman, "3 Hotels Bombed in Jordan; At Least 57 Die," *New York Times*, November 10, 2005.

197   **an Iraqi from Anbar:** "Bomber's Wife Arrested in Jordan," BBC, November 13, 2005.

197   **mingling quietly with the partygoers:** "Jordan Says 3 Iraqis Linked to al-Zarqawi Carried Out Amman Bombing," *New York Times*, November 13, 2005.

197   **unable to set hers off:** Fattah and Slackman, "3 Hotels Bombed in Jordan."

197   **on hotel luggage carts:** Ibid.

197 **claimed responsibility for the attack:** "Al Qaeda Explains Amman Bombings," Middle East Media Research Institute, December 8, 2005.

198 **in and around those buildings:** Cordesman, *Iraq's Insurgency*, 94. Cordesman notes elsewhere in his volumes the links that began surfacing between jihadists captured in Europe and Zarqawi, such as the eighteen suspected Ansar al-Islam adherents picked up in Germany and the "Chechen-trained group" in Paris arrested in 2002 (ibid., 161).

198 **throughout Jordan, Iraq, and Syria:** Hussein, "Al Zarqawi, Part 2." The Arabic name for this greater Syria region is "Bilad al-Sham."

198 **forbade Salafists from praying there:** Lake, "Base Jump."

198 **"was an unintended accident":** "Al Qaeda Explains Amman," MEMRI.

200 **"This is our Achilles' heel":** Dana Priest reports that upon touring our screening facility at BIAP, I commented, "This is how we lose." Dana Priest and William M. Arkin, *Top Secret America: The Rise of the New American Security State* (Little, Brown, 2011), 248.

203 **"information was reported":** "TF 6-26 Update," FBI e-mail retrieved from "Documents Released Under FOIA," American Civil Liberties Union website, June 25, 2004.

203 **each time we acted:** The *New York Times* reported that on December 9, 2004, a Pentagon spokesman said four SOF personnel had been given "administrative punishments" for "unauthorized use of [a] Taser." Thom Shanker, "For Abuse of Detainees, Military Disciplines 4 in Special Unit," *New York Times*, December 9, 2004.

204 **help spur civil war:** Stathis Kalyvas makes the case that given how infrequently insurgents control cities (preferring rural areas), the inability for the United States to "pacify" cities (like Samarra or Ramadi) from 2003 to 2005 was an indicator of far too few troops spread too thinly around Iraq. Stathis N. Kalyvas, *The Logic of Violence in Civil War* (Cambridge University Press, 2006), 133.

204 **from or around the sites:** Additional details regarding Named Area of Interest 152 came through interviews with four task force members involved in intelligence.

204 **90 percent Sunni population:** Multi-National Force–Iraq, "Operational Update," February 23, 2006.

204 **before his disappearance:** Robert F. Worth, "Blast at Shiite Shrine Sets Off Sectarian Fury in Iraq," *New York Times*, February 23, 2006.

204 **seven o'clock that morning:** Ibid.

204 **Thousands of men:** Ellen Knickmeyer and K. I. Ibrahim, "Bombing Shatters Mosque in Iraq," *Washington Post*, February 23, 2006.

204 **backs of flatbed trucks:** Worth, "Blast at Shiite Shrine."

204 **torched or strafed with bullets:** Ellen Knickmeyer and Bassam Sebti, "Toll in Iraq's Deadly Surge: 1,300," *Washington Post*, February 28, 2006.

204 **a thousand Iraqis:** Ibid.

205 **bag used to suffocate them:** Ibid.

206 **teams landed at NAI 152:** Additional details, including the exact times and casualties at NAI 152, come from interviews with members of the task force, including a senior intelligence official.

206 **bound for Baghdad's streets:** Interview with task force member involved in intelligence.

207 **knew something was awry:** Significant details regarding the interrogation of these detainees came from extensive interviews with multiple task force members.

208 **eighteen thousand detainees:** Michael O'Hanlon and Ian Livingston, "Iraq Index," Brookings Institution, January 31, 2012, 12.

211   **aliases was Yusif al-Dardiri:** Ellen Knickmeyer and Jonathan Finer, "Maliki Aide Who Discussed Amnesty Leaves Job," *Washington Post*, June 16, 2006.

213   **"en route to that objective":** Quoted in Sean Naylor, "SpecOps Unit Nearly Nabs Zarqawi," *Army Times*, April 28, 2006.

213   **raising al-Masri's profile:** On May 16, 2006, Rumsfeld sent a memo to Hadley, Rice, Negroponte, Pace, Abizaid, Ambassador Zal Khalilzad, and Eric Edelman on this subject: "Have received a proposal from George Casey and John Abizaid recommending that we make some adjustments in the current $25 million reward for Abu Musab al Zarqawi (AMZ). Their goal is to try to marginalize AMZ in the eyes of the Iraqi people by reducing his stature and forcing him to act to regain it, with the thought that this might increase his visibility and vulnerability." He sent a second memo on May 24, 2006, outlining how it would be publicly announced. Both have the subject "Reward for Zarqawi" and are available from the Rumsfeld Papers website.

CHAPTER 13: HIBHIB

218   **auditorium inside the Green Zone:** Dexter Filkins and Richard A. Oppel, Jr., "Iraqis Form Government, with Crucial Posts Vacant," *New York Times*, May 21, 2006.

218   **group of Sunnis storming out:** Ibid.

218   **Nouri al-Maliki:** Details of Maliki's biography are drawn from "Leader Profile: PM Nouri al-Maliki," Islamic Dawa Party website, 2012.

218   **both interior and defense:** Filkins and Oppel, "Iraqis Form Government."

218   **abducting and killing them:** See the description detailing these actions in Dexter Filkins, *The Forever War* (Vintage Books, 2008), 315–18.

218   **a thousand corpses:** Bobby Ghosh, "Why Iraqis Aren't Cheering Their New Government," *Time*, May 20, 2006. Iraq Body Count breaks down Baghdad deaths by month and similarly finds 1,066, 1,315, and 1,090 Baghdad deaths in February, March, and April, respectively. "Iraqi Deaths from Violence 2003–2011," Iraqi Body Count website, January 2, 2012.

219   *The Exorcist:* The movie begins in northern Iraq (Mosul), so it became a joke with Mubassir that Mosul was the source of evil in the world.

219   **below the operational tempo:** A close participant estimated that the squadron hit thirty-two targets in twenty-one days.

219   **eighty thousand Iraqis:** Department of Defense, "Measuring Stability and Security in Iraq," May 26, 2006, 41.

219   **victims of the city's bombs:** Louise Roug, "Baghdad Morgue Reports Record Figures for May," *Los Angeles Times*, June 4, 2006.

223   **that Sunday, June 4:** The best estimate is that the squadron positively identified Abd al-Rahman on Sunday, June 4, though it may have been on June 3. Several interviewees remember strongly that the event occurred over the weekend but cannot recall whether it was on Saturday or Sunday.

224   **The next morning:** The events of June 7 are based upon my recollection as well as multiple interviews with participants at all levels of the task force.

225   **Al Qaeda enjoyed alarming support:** Around this time frame, the *New York Times* accurately labeled the area "one of the most violent in the country." Sabrina Tavernise, "Gunmen in Iraq Execute 20 Bus Passengers," *New York Times*, June 4, 2006.

225   **together in banana crates:** Roug, "Baghdad Morgue Reports Record."

225   **take their final exams:** Tavernise, "Gunmen in Iraq Execute 20."

226 *what we've been waiting for:* We ran kinetic-strike profiles on every building that we would potentially strike. Any time we sent troops to an objective, we ran kinetic-strike approvals so that if things went bad, we already had a head start on the approval process. This was no different. As Rahman stopped at this location, the squadron fires NCO ran the kinetic-strike numbers to the Combined Air and Space Operations Center for a Collateral Damage Estimate.

227 **At 4:55 P.M.:** Multi-National Force–Iraq (Major General William B. Caldwell IV), "Iraq Operational Update" (briefing), June 15, 2006.

230 **had been improperly worded:** When the JTAC had told the pilot he was "cleared to engage," he provided one type of authorization that was incorrect and resulted in the abortive bombing run. He should have authorized the run by telling the pilot he was "cleared hot." "JFIRE Multi-service Tactics Techniques and Procedures for the Joint Application of Firepower," Air Land Sea Application Center, December 2007, 56.

230 **second hit the house:** MNF-I (Caldwell), "Operational Update," June 15, 2006.

231 **out of his nose and ears:** Multi-National Force–Iraq (Major General William B. Caldwell IV), "Iraq Operational Update" (video), June 26, 2006.

231 **air sacs in his lungs:** Zarqawi's autopsy and means of death were discussed in the MNF-I press briefing on June 12, 2006.

231 **Five other bodies:** MNF-I (Caldwell), "Operational Update," June 26, 2006.

231 **Zarqawi gurgled blood:** Multi-National Force–Iraq (Major General William B. Caldwell IV), "Iraq Operational Update" (briefing), June 12, 2006.

231 **Zarqawi was dead:** Time lines emerge from Caldwell's June 12 and June 15 press briefings.

234 **minutes after 3:30 A.M.:** Multi-National Force–Iraq (Major General William B. Caldwell IV), "Iraq Operational Update" (briefing), June 8, 2006.

234 **announcing Zarqawi's death:** John F. Burns, "Leader of Al Qaeda in Iraq Has Been Killed," *New York Times*, June 8, 2006.

234 **"Although the designated leader":** "Statement by U.S. Forces in Iraq," *New York Times*, June 8, 2006.

234 **parliament dropped their vetoes:** "The killing of Mr. Zarqawi brought immediate political results in the form of parliamentary approval, immediately after the news conference, of Mr. Maliki's nominees" (John Burns, "U.S. Strike Hits Insurgent at Safehouse," *New York Times*, June 8, 2006).

235 **relieved to see him go:** Lawrence Wright, author of *The Looming Tower*, wrote in *The New Yorker* following the strike, "Among those quietly celebrating the death of Abu Musab al-Zarqawi last week, no doubt, were Osama bin Laden and Ayman al-Zawahiri, the leaders of Al Qaeda, who have watched their nominal ally wreck the standing of their organization among Muslims around the world" ("The Terrorist," *New Yorker*, June 19, 2006). Some commentators went further. Michael Scheuer, who ran the CIA's Alec Station during the late 1990s, claimed that killing Zarqawi had been a strategic error—that our enemy was making such grand mistakes we should not have interrupted him. I find this untenable.

236 **"fight the apostate infidels simultaneously":** Nibras Kazimi, "Zarqawi's Anti-Shi'a Legacy: Original or Borrowed?" *Current Trends in Islamist Ideology*, August 2, 2006, 53–54.

236 **self-propelling cycle:** The Pentagon's August 2006 report "Measuring Stability and Security in Iraq" gave the following assessment of violence: "Since the last report, the core conflict in Iraq changed into a struggle between Sunni and Shi'a extremists seeking to control key areas in Baghdad, create or protect sectarian enclaves, divert economic resources, and impose

their own respective political and religious agendas. Death squads and terrorists are locked in mutually reinforcing cycles of sectarian strife, with Sunni and Shi'a extremists each portraying themselves as the defenders of their respective sectarian groups. However, the Sunni Arab insurgence remains potent and viable, although its visibility has been overshadowed by the increase in sectarian violence." Department of Defense, "Measuring Stability and Security in Iraq," August 2006, 26.

236 **previously mixed neighborhoods drained:** Between the late February Samarra mosque bombing and August of 2006, 22,977 families, or 137, 862 individuals, had been displaced (ibid.).

236 **3,149 Iraqis died:** Michael O' Hanlon and Ian S. Livingston, "Brookings Iraq Index," Brookings Institution, December 21, 2006, 10.

236 **1,855 Iraqi corpses:** Edward Wong and Damien Cave, "Iraqi Death Toll Rose Above 3,400 in July," *New York Times*, August 15, 2006.

236 **90 percent of them executed:** DOD, "Measuring Stability," 34.

CHAPTER 14: NETWORKED

237 **On June 5, 2006:** Information about Ramadi and my recollection of this event were aided by interviews with members of the task force who served there and were on this operation.

237 **Only one hundred policemen:** These figures, from May 2006, are from page 44 of Neil Smith and Sean MacFarland's paper recounting their campaign for Ramadi ("Anbar Awakens: The Tipping Point," *Military Review* (March–April 2008).

237 **insurgents operated undisturbed:** Ibid., 42.

237 **insurgents focused on the Americans:** Interview with task force member.

237 **rates there were extraordinarily high:** Mark Kukis, "The Most Dangerous Place in Iraq," *Time*, December 11, 2006.

240 **five Marine and army battalions:** Smith and MacFarland, "Anbar Awakens," 43.

241 **third-tier sheikh:** Najim Abed Al-Jabouri and Sterling Jensen, "The Iraqi and AQI Roles in the Sunni Awakening," *Prism* (December 2010), 12.

241 **reimagined as his guests:** Ibid., 15.

241 **officially under way:** Smith and MacFarland, "Anbar Awakens," 48. The same event is recounted in Al-Jabouri and Jensen, "The Iraqi and AQI Roles," 11.

241 **wrote to Nouri al-Maliki:** Khalid Al-Ansary and Ali Adeeb, "Most Tribes in Anbar Agree to Unite Against Insurgents," *New York Times*, September 18, 2006.

242 **Iraqi government payroll:** Al-Jabouri and Jensen, "The Iraqi and AQI Roles," 14–15.

242 **did not like having an American tank:** Sheikh Sattar's attitude toward the tank, and the rotation of Iraqi and American models, was recounted in an interview with Sterling Jensen. It also appears in his article, written with Al-Jabouri (ibid.,13).

242 **now a token of power:** Sheikh Abdul Sattar was assassinated a year later, in September 2007, but not before he had served as a rallying point for the Sunni Awakening in Ramadi. His brother assumed his mantle as a leader of the Awakening.

243 **my old friend Graeme Lamb:** Lamb took the title of Deputy Commanding General/Senior British Military Representative in MNF-I on September 7, 2006.

243 **and declare a national position:** My recollection of the early Awakening was confirmed by interviews with task force members and with Graeme. As the Awakening gathered steam and consolidated, Graeme noted in January 2007

that "a conference of tribal chiefs in Anbar ended with a pledge to support the national government's campaign against Al-Qaeda insurgents." Graeme Lamb, "Dispatches from Baghdad: A Soldier's View on Iraq," Ministry of Defense, January 9, 2007.

243   created the "COIN academy": For details of the COIN Academy General Casey established, see Thomas E. Ricks, "U.S. Counterinsurgency Academy Giving Officers a New Mindset," *Washington Post*, February 21, 2006.

243   cited its teachers' precepts: Lawrence F. Kaplan, "Letting Go," *New Republic*, July 10, 2006.

244   Squeeze Chart: Graeme's description that day would later that fall be visualized in a series of increasingly descriptive diagrams that we called "The Squeeze Chart." While they underwent a number of iterations, the most lasting chart that summarized his concept was a Venn diagram, with three circles laterally spaced. The leftmost circle comprised Sunnis, the rightmost Shia. They did not overlap, but where their edges touched was at the center of the third circle, in the middle. This central circle represented those groups assisting, or not resisting, a legitimate Iraqi government.

244   permeated the rest of the Coalition: This point is made in Mark Urban, *Task Force Black* (Abacus, 2011), 186.

244   terms helped us conceptualize: While Ambassador Khalilzad described groups as "irreconcilables" that summer, General James Mattis gives credit to Graeme for meaningfully introducing these terms—and the attendant logic—into the Coalition's mindset. *Al-Anbar Awakening, vol. I*, 30.

244   "not an independent phenomenon": See book eight, chapter six of Carl von Clausewitz's great work *On War* for his extended treatment of this famous quote. Carl von Clausewitz, *On War*, ed. and trans. Michael Howard and Peter Paret (Princeton University Press, 1984).

245   just shy of the most extreme: If we wanted to excise violence from the system, Graeme's thinking went, we needed to approach the most violent groups that could realistically be approached. Cleaving the most radical irreconcilables away from the rest—by killing and capturing them and by separating them psychologically from the people—was key to breaking their hold on the other potentially reconcilable groups. "They will poison the people on the fence," he said.

246   Iraqis were fleeing every month: Sabrina Tavernise, "Civilian Death Toll Reaches New High in Iraq, U.N. Says," *New York Times*, November 23, 2006.

247   perhaps at its all-time low: On November 29, 2006, the *New York Times* published a memo written on November 8 by National Security Adviser Stephen Hadley. He wrote, "Despite Maliki's reassuring words . . . the reality on the streets of Baghdad suggests Maliki is either ignorant of what is going on, misrepresenting his intentions, or that his capabilities are not yet sufficient to turn his good intentions into action."

247   assaulting the Ministry of Health: Kirk Semple, "Sectarian Attack Is Worst in Baghdad Since Invasion," *New York Times*, November 24, 2006.

247   another 250 wounded: Casualty figures are from Associated Press, "Death Toll in Sadr City Rises to 202 Iraqis," *USA Today*, November 24, 2006.

247   hold that record for long: On August 15, 2007, four car bombs killed 250 and wounded 350. James Glanz, "Death Toll in Iraq Bombings Rises to 250," *New York Times*, August 15, 2007.

247   Ansar al-Sunnah's leadership: Information on the ten captured leaders comes from an MNF-I press release: Multi-National Force–Iraq, "Capture of Terrorist Emirs Gives al-Qaida in Iraq Nowhere to Turn" (press release), December 6, 2006.

248   **mess-hall tent in Mosul:** Ansar al-Sunnah was the biggest and most violent indigenous Iraqi insurgent group that had a pro–bin Laden ideology. Prior to the U.S. invasion, AAS had set up a Taliban-like enclave in the ungoverned parts of Kurdistan, banning music, dancing, and liquor, as reported, for example, by C. J. Chivers, "Kurds Face a Second Enemy: Islamic Fighters on Iraq Flank," *New York Times*, January 13, 2003.

248   **Kurdish leaders had reported:** Interview with task force member aware of intelligence on this matter.

248   **merger between the two groups:** Bill Roggio, "A Zarqawi Letter and a Potential Merger with Ansar al-Sunnah," *Long War Journal*, September 21, 2006.

248   **These were conversations:** Details of these meetings with Abu Wail come from interviews with Graeme Lamb.

248   **"you're a face of occupation":** Interview with Graeme Lamb. Note that this quote from Abu Wail has elsewhere been incorrectly attributed to Abu Azzam (Fairweather, *A War of Choice*, 294). In fact, it came from the Ansar religious emir.

248   **FSEC's first strategic release:** The timing of Abu Wail's release comes from interviews with members of FSEC.

249   **"Annie, another Christmas apart":** E-mail to Annie, December 25, 2006. Edited slightly for punctuation.

249   **new strategy in Iraq:** George W. Bush, *Decision Points* (Crown, 2010), 377.

249   **stretching back to the spring:** Peter D. Feaver, "The Right to Be Right: Civil-Military Relations and the Iraq Surge Decision," *International Security* (Spring 2011), 101.

249   **believed Al Shabab was sheltering:** Daveed Gartenstein-Ross, *Bin Laden's Legacy: Why We're Still Losing the War on Terror* (John Wiley and Sons, 2011), 148.

249   **Abu Taha al-Sudani:** Bill Roggio, "U.S. Gunship Fires on Al Qaeda Leader and Operative in Somalia," *Long War Journal*, January 8, 2007.

252   **"Succeeding in Iraq":** George W. Bush, "President's Address to the Nation," White House, January 10, 2007.

252   **there were four vectors:** Department of Defense, "DOD News Briefing with Secretary Gates and Gen. Pace," February 2, 2007.

252   **explosively formed projectile IEDs:** In 2004 Iranian-backed Special Groups had introduced to Iraqi roads a deadly new device known as an explosively formed projectile, or EFP. For years, "shaped charges" had been used in high-tech weaponry to penetrate armor plating. In the late 1990s, however, insurgents in southern Lebanon had adapted the technology for use in portable roadside bombs against Israeli vehicles. The technology migrated from their source, Iran, to Iraq, and according to Rick Atkinson in the *Washington Post* (October 1, 2007) the first EFP was detonated in May 2004 in Basra. By late 2006, the device was all too common and frighteningly lethal. The large number of EFPs was clear evidence of the extent of direct Iranian involvement in the conflict.

EFPs varied in size; most were about the size of a small oil drum or a five-gallon paint bucket, but they could be even smaller. Insurgents positioned them a few feet above the ground and aimed them to shoot laterally into the roadway. Once triggered, often by hidden infrared sensors, an explosive charge on the back of the drum forced a concave metal cone to be reshaped into a dartlike stream in the direction of the target. The dense molten stream, often the size of a bowling pin and traveling at twice the speed of a bullet, punctured inches of metal plating like water through snow. Inside the vehicle, the molten slug cut through legs and torsos, and its heat often lit the cab and the men inside on fire. Our heaviest armored vehicles were vulnerable and despite extensive countermeasures, in large numbers they were a potential game changer.

253 **In the early evening:** One source claims the attack took place at 6:00 P.M. (Mark Kukis, "An Ambush in Karbala," *Time*, July 26, 2007). Another article times the event at 5:00 P.M., providing further details about the number and line of SUVs and the PJCC. (Department of Defense, "Karbala Attackers Used U.S. Army–Styled Uniforms to Gain Access," Armed Forces Press Service, January 26, 2007).

253 **wore U.S. Army uniforms:** Department of Defense, "Karbala Attackers Used U.S. Army–Styled Uniforms."

253 **roughly a dozen:** Ibid.

253 **weapons through the doors:** Kukis, "An Ambush in Karbala." Details of this event draw on this article.

253 **suspicions about their involvement:** Ibid.

253 **neighboring province of Babil:** Borzou Daragahi, "Military Provides Details of Slain Soldiers' Abduction," *Los Angeles Times*, January 27, 2007.

253 **scrawled his name in the film:** Kukis, "An Ambush in Karbala."

CHAPTER 15: THE LONG WAR

255 **could avoid producing antibodies:** Then-Major Ben Connable used this same terminology describing Abizaid's position in volume 1 of *Al-Anbar Awakening.*

255 **eighty-five of their comrades:** Casualty figures come from Smith and MacFarland, "Anbar Awakens," 52.

256 **could not knowingly target:** Throughout the time Task Force 17 was active, it coordinated its target list with MNF-I and the State Department. Any time it posted a slide with "SCIRI" on it—referring to one of the main political parties that used the Badr Brigade as its violent arm—embassy officials would offer fierce objections.

257 **feverishly triaging the material:** My recollection of this event was aided by interviews with those closely involved.

257 **twenty-two-page document:** My recollection of the contents of this material was confirmed and elaborated upon in interviews with two individuals privy to it.

257 **attack on our outpost in Karbala:** General Petraeus later said in a press conference, "[T]he heads of the Qazali network and some of the key members of that network that have been in detention now for a month or more . . . When we captured these individuals . . . we discovered, for example, a 22-page memorandum on a computer that detailed the planning, preparation, approval process and conduct of the operation that resulted in five of our soldiers being killed in Karbala." Department of Defense, "DOD News Briefing with Gen. Petraeus from the Pentagon," April 26, 2007.

257 **as well as postoperation assessments:** Multi-National Force–Iraq (Brigadier General Kevin Bergner), "Situational Update" (briefing), July 2, 2007.

257 **military IDs taken:** Jack Fairweather, *A War of Choice: The British in Iraq 2003–2009* (Jonathan Cape, 2011), 297.

257 **life inside the camp:** Then–Brigadier General Kevin Bergner described in detail the capture of the Khazalis and the contents of the twenty-two-page document in his MNF-I press briefing, July 2 cited above: "The document that we captured showed the following. It showed that the group that

attacked the Provincial Joint Coordination Center in Karbala had conducted extensive preparation and drills prior to the attack. Quds Force had developed detailed information regarding our soldiers' activities, shift changes and fences, and this information was shared with the attackers."

257 **immediate pressure to release Qais:** Indeed, according to Fairweather, Maliki called Dave Petraeus early that morning to demand the Khazalis' release. Fairweather, *A War of Choice*, 297.

258 **seized an opportunity:** Petraeus later reflected, "We told Maliki now was the time to take action against the Jaish al-Mahdi to demonstrate his authority." Fairweather, *A War of Choice*, 297.

259 **sought to capture in Irbil:** "Interview with Mohammed Jafari," *Frontline*, PBS, August 2, 2007.

260 **sought to convince its leadership:** Details of arguments presented to Ansar leadership were provided by those closely involved.

261 **twenty-three hundred men patrolling:** Richard A. Oppel, Jr., "Mistrust as Iraqi Troops Encounter New U.S. Allies," *New York Times*, July 16, 2007.

261 **Daraji was ambushed:** Edward Wong and Damien Cave, "Attack on Sadr City Mayor Hinders Antimilitia Effort," *New York Times*, March 15, 2007.

261 **leader of its operations in Iraq:** Multi-National Force–Iraq, "Capture of Terrorist Emirs Gives al-Qaida in Iraq Nowhere to Turn" (press release), December 6, 2006.

261 **cleansed many of the neighborhoods:** Some of the best work on this subject was done by Dr. Michael Izady of Columbia University as part of The Gulf/2000 Project. His maps of increasingly homogenous neighborhoods are available on the project's website.

262 **giving Graeme greater latitude:** Interview with Graeme Lamb.

262 **Whitehall had ordered:** Fairweather, *A War of Choice*, 316.

262 **to the airport in September:** Ibid., 318.

263 **wounded each of these months:** Iraq Coalition Casualty Count, "Fatalities by Year and Month," iCasualties website, 2012; Iraq Coalition Casualty Count, "U.S. Wounded Totals," iCasualties website, 2012.

263 **blood on their hands:** This exchange is based on my recollection, as well as interviews with participants. A form of this episode is also told in Fairweather, *A War of Choice*, 292. Note: While this book implies this discussion took place at Maude House, I remember it at the Friday meeting.

263 **never to sugarcoat or obscure:** Interviews with members of FSEC.

263 **time for a decision:** My recollection of these meetings is aided by interviews with two task force members present.

263 **Jihad and Reform Front:** The "JR Front Establishing Statement" was posted to an English-language Islamic Army in Iraq website on September 15, 2007, but was signed and dated May 2, 2007.

263 **to avoid killing innocents:** One of the Front's policies covered this issue: "Mujahedeen operations target the occupiers and their agents, and don't target innocents whom one of Jihad goals is [*sic*] to support them and achieve a good life for them, and use kindness as the way that we treat Muslims." "JR Front Establishing Statement," Islamic Army in Iraq website, September 15, 2007.

263 **led by Abu Wail:** "Jihad and Reform Front," *Jane's Terrorism and Security Monitor*, March 20, 2009.

263 **a faction came with him:** Ibid. See also Evan F. Kohlmann, "State of the Sunni Insurgency in Iraq: August 2007," NEFA Foundation, 15, 18–19.

263   **collaborating with the United States:** "Jihad and Reform Front." *Jane's.*

263   **target the leaders:** Stanford University, "Islamic Army in Iraq," Mapping Militant Organizations, project website, 2012.

263   **clashed with AQI, petered out:** Ibid.

263   **dissension within Ansar's ranks:** "Jihad and Reform Front," *Jane's.*

264   **Dadullah the Lame:** Dadullah may have led one of the earliest meetings that set the still small Taliban resurgence movement into action in 2002. See Antonio Giustozzi, *Koran, Kalashnikov and Laptop: The Neo-Taliban Insurgency in Afghanistan* (Columbia University Press, 2008), 11. In 2003, Mullah Omar dispatched Dadullah to lead recruitment in Baluchistan and Karachi, where he was rumored to be accompanied by Pakistani officials. Elizabeth Rubin, "In the Land of the Taliban," *New York Times Magazine*, October 22, 2006.

264   **anti-Soviet resistance of the 1980s:** According to a Taliban biography, he joined the anti-Soviet resistance in 1983. Alex Strick van Linschoten and Felix Kuehn, *An Enemy We Created: The Myth of the Taliban-Al Qaeda Merger in Afghanistan, 1970–2010* (Hurst and Co., 2012), 275.

264   **quit school to join:** Ibid., 275–76.

264   **stepped on a mine:** Omid Marzban, "Mullah Dadullah: The Military Mastermind of the Taliban Insurgency," Jamestown Foundation, March 21, 2006.

264   **"preceded him to Paradise":** Abu Yahya al-Libi, quoted in "Islamist Website Monitor No. 110," Middle East Media Research Institute, June 8, 2007.

264   **Mullah Omar retired him:** Elizabeth Rubin notes, "His fighters slaughtered hundreds of Hazaras . . . in Bamiyan Province, an act so brutal it was even too much for Mullah Omar, who had him disarmed at the time" ("In the Land of the Taliban").

264   **"I no longer need them":** Kate Clark, "The *Layha:* Calling the Taliban to Account," *Afghanistan Analysts Network*, July 4, 2011, 3, note 7.

264   **United Front in the north:** Linschoten, *An Enemy We Created*, 276.

264   **the atrocities he carried out:** Carlotta Gall, "Northern Alliance Presses for Surrender of Taliban Commander and Troops," *New York Times*, December 4, 2001.

265   **relied increasingly on suicide bombs:** This point is made in Linschoten, *An Enemy We Created*, 279.

265   **bombs on the roads of Iraq:** Sami Yousafzai, "Suicide Offensive," *Newsweek*, April 15, 2007.

265   **there were 141:** Ahmed Rashid, *Descent into Chaos: The U.S. and the Disaster in Pakistan, Afghanistan, and Central Asia* (Penguin, 2009), 366. Other accounts give slightly different numbers, but the magnitude of increase is the same. Linschoten, for example, reports 3 suicide bombs in 2004 and 123 in 2006. Linschoten, *An Enemy We Created*, 279.

265   **distance from Al Qaeda:** This is one of the central arguments made in Linschoten, *An Enemy We Created.*

265   **four dollars a disc:** Matthias Gebauer, "The Star of Afghanistan's Jihad," *Der Spiegel Online*, March 1, 2007.

265   **ridgelines and beheading "spies":** Rubin, "In the Land of the Taliban."

265   **relief when he was disposed of:** This is explained in Clark, "The *Layha*," 4.

265   **eulogies from Al Qaeda:** "I announce to you today the passing of a hero among the heroes of Jihad in this era and a knight among its knights," mourned Ayman al-Zawahiri (Ayman al-Zawahiri, "Elegizing the Commander of the Martrydom-Seekers Mulla Dadullah [May Allah Have Mercy on Him]." World Analysis, May 22, 2007.) Abu Yahya al-Libi also had praise for Dadullah. "Today," he said, "we take leave of one of these noble commanders, Mullah Dadullah, who has joined the ranks of the

martyrs . . . after having spent his life on the battlefronts fighting the infidels." Abu Yahya al-Libi quoted in "Islamist Websites Monitor No. 110," Middle East Media Research Institute, June 8, 2007.

268 **target a Special Groups leader:** Multi-National Force—Iraq, "Coalition Forces Target Special Groups Leader, 49 Criminals Killed" (press release), October 21, 2007.

268 **kidnapping and death squads:** Paul von Zielbauer, "Iraqi Journalist Reported Missing After Driver's Body Found," *New York Times*, October 23, 2007.

268 **an IED as they withdrew:** That the teams were under fire while clearing buildings and were hit by an IED on departure comes from my own recollection as well as interviews. These details are confirmed in Multi-National Force–Iraq, "Coalition Forces Target Special Groups."

268 **killed teenagers and children:** "U.S. Raid of Baghdad's Sadr City Kills 49," *USA Today*, October 21, 2007.

268 **fewer Americans were dying:** The specific metrics I cite are from Iraq Coalition Casualty Count, "Iraq Coalition Casualties: Fatalities by Year and Month," iCasualties website, 2009.

269 **helicopter was flying near Baghdad:** UK Ministry of Defense, "Two UK Military Personnel Killed in Puma Helicopter Crash" (press release), November 21, 2007.

270 **same thing eight weeks earlier:** The previous attempt occurred at roughly 3:30 A.M. on Monday, March 3, 2008. Jeffrey Gettleman and Eric Schmitt, "U.S. Forces Fire Missiles into Somalia at a Kenyan," *New York Times*, March 4, 2008.

271 **shot in the back:** Ben Dowell, "Journalist Shot Dead in Somalia Was in High-Risk Area, Says BBC Safety Head," *Guardian*, November 25, 2008.

271 **split from the Islamic Courts Union:** Daveed Gartenstein-Ross, *Bin Laden's Legacy: Why We're Still Losing the War on Terror* (John Wiley and Sons, 2011), 149–50.

271 **striking beyond its borders:** "After Somalia we will proceed to Djibouti, Kenya, and Ethiopia," Fazul Abdullah Mohammed, a now-dead Al Shabab intelligence chief declared in November 2009. Gartenstein-Ross, *Bin Laden's Legacy*, 150.

CHAPTER 16: THE TICKING CLOCK

280 **vacationing in Europe:** Rodric Braithwaite, *Afgantsy: The Russians in Afghanistan, 1979–89* (Oxford University Press, 2011), 31.

281 **wash away the excesses:** As Afghanistan scholar David Edwards notes, while the violence and eccentricities of the warlords gave them a degree of celebrity, the Taliban adeptly portrayed themselves very differently: "An additional point in the Taliban's favor was the relative invisibility of their leadership. . . . One can only speculate on the motivation behind this strategy, but it seems reasonable to conclude that it might be related to the people's disillusionment with the all-too-visible leaders of the established religious parties who did so much to divide the country. In this sense, the Taliban in their first period seemed to represent something like an anticharismatic movement; the emphasis was . . . the movement itself." David B. Edwards, *Before Taliban: Genealogies of the Afghan Jihad* (University of California Press, 2002), 294.

282 **an insurgency soon gestated:** A description of the Taliban's reinfiltration between 2002 and 2006 can be found in chapter 4 of Giustozzi, *Koran, Kalashnikov, and Laptop*, 97–145.

282 **waged blanket assassination campaigns:** Giustozzi, *Koran, Kalashnikov, and Laptop*, 102.

282 **whom we paid handsomely**: Ahmed Rashid, "How Obama Lost Karzai," *Foreign Policy* (March/April 2011).

282 **swift courts**: Giustozzi, *Koran, Kalashnikov, and Laptop*, 111.

282 **"shadow governors"**: International Security Assistance Force (Major General Michael T. Flynn), "State of the Insurgency: Trends, Intentions and Objectives (Unclassified)," December 22, 2009.

283 **More Americans**: Michael O'Halon and Ian S. Livingston, "Afghanistan Index," Brookings Institution, March 31, 2012, 11.

283 **more Afghan civilians**: "Afghanistan: Annual Report on the Protection of Civilians in Armed Conflict, 2008," United Nations Assistance Mission to Afghanistan, January 2009, 7.

283 **four times as many**: In 2007, insurgents laid 2,700 IEDs. In 2008, that number rose to 4,169. ISAF (Flynn), "State of the Insurgency," 2009.

283 **requested additional forces**: On September 22, the *New York Times* reported: "Last week, Gen. David D. McKiernan, the top American commander in Afghanistan, said he needed as many as 15,000 combat and support troops beyond the 8,000 additional troops that Mr. Bush had recently approved for deployment early next year. The general's announcement came after he sent his request to the Pentagon; it has not yet been acted on." Eric Schmitt and Thom Shanker, "Bush Administration Reviews Its Afghanistan Policy, Exposing Points of Contention," *New York Times*, September 22, 2008.

285 **by 50 percent**: The *New York Times* estimates there were 36,600 troops in Afghanistan that month. Hannah Fairfield et al., "Troop Levels in Afghanistan Since 2001," *New York Times*, October 1, 2009.

285 **"disrupt, dismantle, and defeat"**: "White Paper of the Interagency Policy Group's Report on U.S. Policy toward Afghanistan and Pakistan," White House website, March 2009, 2.

285 **"take the lead"**: Ibid.

287 **"I knew wherever I was"**: William Tecumseh Sherman, *Memoirs of General William T. Sherman* (Library of America, 1990), 428.

289 **"In Afghanistan, despite impressive progress"**: "Hearing to consider the nominations of Admiral James G. Stavridis, USN for reappointment to the grade of Admiral and to be Commander, U.S. European Command and Supreme Allied Commander, Europe; Lieutenant General Douglas M. Fraser, USAF to be General and Commander, U.S. Southern Command; and Lieutenant General Stanley A. McChrystal, USA to be General and Commander, International Security Assistance Forces, Afghanistan," Senate Armed Services Committee, June 2, 2009, 10.

289 **"we must succeed"**: Ibid.

289 **killed the vast majority**: According to the U.N., 2,118 Afghan civilians died from conflict in 2008, up from 1,523 in 2007. Of those killed in 2008, 55 percent were killed by the Taliban or their sympathizers and 39 percent by pro-government elements. "Report on the Protection of Civilians (2008)," UNAMA, January 2009, 14.

289 **the gunfight subsided**: U.S. Central Command, "USCENTCOM Unclassified Executive Summary: U.S. Central Command Investigation into Civilian Casualties in Farah Province, Afghanistan on 4 May 2009," June 18, 2009, 6. CENTCOM estimated the strikes killed seventy-eight Taliban (ibid., 11).

289 **to evacuate two wounded**: Ibid., 7.

289 **8,500 pounds of bombs**: Ibid., 8 (notes 7 and 9), 9 (note 10).

289 **nearly 140 Afghan civilians**: Reuters, "U.S. Strikes Killed 140 Villagers: Afghan Probe," May 16, 2009.

289 **estimated roughly 90**: "Balabolook Incident" (press release), Afghan Independent Human Rights Coalition, May 26, 2009, 2. This report further

stated that no evidence was advanced by the Afghan government for the figure of 140 casualties. The CENTCOM report acknowledged the AIHRC's work: "[T]he [CENTCOM] investigative team notes that the report by the Afghan Independent Human Rights Commission . . . represents a balanced, thorough investigation into the incident, citing as many as 86 civilian casualties" (U.S. Central Command, "USCENTCOM Unclassified Executive Summary," 11.) However, the CENTCOM report's own estimate of civilian casualties from the incident was considerably lower, approximately twenty-six (ibid.) The above Reuters article reported that the Afghan government produced a list of names to substantiate its claim of 140 casualties, but that list's authenticity was questionable, according to the U.S. military (Reuters, "U.S. Strikes Killed 140").

289   **in front of the governor's house:** Patrick Cockburn, "Afghans Riot over Air-Strike Atrocity," *Independent*, May 8, 2009.

289   **"Death to the government":** Ibid.

289   **"Our willingness to operate":** "Hearing" (June 2, 2009), Senate Armed Services Committee, 11.

291   **"The better part of one's life":** Abraham Lincoln, letter to Joseph Gillespie, July 13, 1849, in Abraham Lincoln, *Speeches and Writings 1832–1858* (Literary Classics of the United States, 1989), 239.

291   **eighteen to twenty-four months:** In my Senate confirmation testimony on June 2, I said, "I believe that we need to start making progress within about the next nineteen to twenty-four months to know" how long the campaign would take. "Hearing" (June 2, 2009), Senate Armed Services Committee, 17.

291   **"All you have to do is win":** Notes taken by my aide, who was present in the meeting.

291   **"decided within a year":** Jeff Eggers, "Patience Is Paramount but Time Is of the Essence" (memorandum), June 5, 2009.

CHAPTER 17: UNDERSTAND

295   **"And in one single blinding flash . . . ":** Bernard Fall, *Street Without Joy*, (Stackpole, 1994), 292–94. Fall added, while observing the short, saluting master sergeant, "Something very warm welled up in me. I felt like running over to the little Cambodian who had fought all his life for my country, and apologizing to him for my countrymen here who didn't care about him, and for my countrymen in France who didn't even care about their countrymen fighting in Indochina . . ."

296   **forty-two different nations contributed troops:** These numbers come from International Security Assistance Force, "International Security Assistance Force and Afghan National Army Strength and Laydown," June 15, 2009, ISAF website, 1–2. Within a year, the coalition would grow to have troops from forty-six nations.

296   **57,600 troops:** Hannah Fairfield and Kevin Quealy, "Troop Levels in Afghanistan Since 2001," *New York Times*, October 1, 2009.

296   **nearly fifty years of peace:** Thomas Barfield, in his book *Afghanistan*, argues this to be the case, as he divides Afghanistan's twentieth century into three periods and notes, "Under the rule of the Musahiban brothers and their sons, the second period from 1929 to 1978 gave Afghanistan its longest interval of peace and internal stability." Thomas Barfield, *Afghanistan: A Cultural and Political History* (Princeton University Press, 2010), 169.

298   **Nearly all his predecessors:** Rodric Braithwaite, in his account of the Soviet war in Afghanistan, notes that along with keeping the country glued together, independent, and on the track to modernity, the fourth and final task

for recent Afghan heads of state was to "remain alive": "Between 1842 and 1995 seven of them fell victim at an accelerating pace to family feud, palace coup, mob violence, or outside intervention. Between 1878 and 2001, four more were forced into exile. Others prudently abdicated while the going was good" (*Afgantsy*, 13–14).

299 **five American ambassadors:** These ambassadors were Ryan Crocker, Robert Finn, Zal Khalilzad, Ronald Neumann, and William Wood. In addition, James Dobbins was the special envoy to Afghanistan, the senior civilian and U.S. representative at the Bonn Conference, so it could be said Karzai dealt with six.

299 **eleven other ISAF commanders:** Generals McColl (UK), Zorlu (Turkey), Van Heyst (Germany), Gliemeroth (Germany), Hillier (Canada), Py (France), Erdagi (Turkey), del Vecchio (Italy), Richards (UK), McNeill (USA), and McKiernan (USA) all served as the commander of ISAF.

301 **"General, aren't you going to wear":** Interview with Mike Hall.

306 **"We and the people of Balkh Province":** Atta Noor's speech was reported by Balkh TV, a news station in Mazar-e-Sharif. The newscast was translated by the BBC's International Monitoring Service, the source of this English quote. "NATO Commander Meets Northern Afghan Governor," BBC Monitoring South Asia, June 24, 2009.

308 **modernity itself:** A layer beneath the political power struggles for much of Afghanistan's twentieth century was a contest between cultural conservatism and advocates of Western-influenced social progress. As a people, Afghans were conflicted over the issue. King Amanullah's reform-focused reign, from 1919 to 1929, was a source of pride to many Afghans, but ultimately, concern over the by-products of Amanullah's initiatives led to a conservative backlash that unseated the young king. Popular outcry over a photograph of his young queen in a sleeveless gown while on a visit to Europe is frequently cited to demonstrate the fragility of the march to modernity.

308 **"fighting Taliban":** These classifications, and the Pashtun transliterations, can be found in Martine van Bijlert, "Unruly Commanders and Violent Power Struggles: Taliban Networks in Uruzgan," in *Decoding the New Taliban: Insights from the Afghan Field*, ed. Antonio Giustozzi (Columbia University Press, 2009), 160.

309 **twenty fighters:** While more entrenched networks, like those centered around Haqqani, Mansour, or Dadullah, were thousands strong, young upstart commanders had more modest goals. The latter case is described in an excellent chapter by Tom Coghlan, "The Taliban in Helmand: An Oral History" in *Decoding the New Taliban*, 142–44.

309 **unable to fire the local commanders:** The tenuous relationship between the Taliban's central leadership and local commanders in Uruzgan is detailed in van Bijlert, "Unruly Commanders," 169–70.

309 **Outbreaks of insurgency:** Most Taliban infiltration followed a general pattern: Sensing fertile soil, the Taliban sent a vanguard element that became a menacing presence around town who met with and co-opted local leaders who were not in power but who stood to gain from a change in the status quo. They then targeted powerful leaders, stirred sentiment, and corralled it into a sprouting resistance.

309 **varying degrees of success:** In parts of Uruzgan, for example, the Taliban's judges and political officers often had little ability to defy the fighters. Van Bijlert, "Unruly Commanders," 168.

310 **one of my civilian advisers reported:** Correspondence with Matt Sherman.

310 **"What is it that we don't understand?":** My recollection of this meeting was confirmed in an interview with Charlie Flynn.

310   **shortage of Afghan and ISAF manpower:** This shortage of troops had, in General McKiernan's estimation, made for "a greater reliance on air" power than he would have liked. Robert Burns, "Call for Troops in Afghanistan: Promised Brigade Is Not 'Sufficient,'" *Boston Post*, September 17, 2008.

311   **Lore grew:** Interview with Afghan military officer.

311   **for years:** Amy Waldman, "Afghan Leader Warily Backs U.S. Bombing," *The New York Times*, January 2, 2002.

312   **"I expect leaders at all levels":** Stanley A. McChrystal, "Tactical Directive," July 6, 2009, 1–2. This as well as other directives are available on the "Official Texts" section of the ISAF website.

312   **"This directive does not prevent":** Ibid., 2.

313   **answering e-mails:** Interview with Charlie Flynn.

313   **That summer:** While the text was "published" on May 9, 2009, it did not begin leaking out until July, when Al Jazeera obtained a copy. That August, the Taliban posted Pashto and English versions on the Internet. Quotes come from an English translation posted to the Afghan Analysts Network website: Kate Clark, "The *Layha*: Calling the Taleban to Account: Appendix 1. The Taleban Codes of Conduct in English," Afghan Analysts Network, June 2011.

313   **the *layha*:** The official title of the book is "The Islamic Emirate of Afghanistan Rules for the Mujahideen." In official releases and press statements, the Taliban refer to themselves as the Islamic Emirate of Afghanistan, to portray themselves as a competitor to the Islamic Republic of Afghanistan—the sovereign, recognized government.

313   **"Mujahedin":** Omar quoted in Clark, "Taleban Codes of Conduct," 23.

313   **"fiercely" forbidden:** Ibid., 22.

314   **"A brave son of Islam":** This translation comes from Al Jazeera, "Key Quotes from New Taliban book," Al Jazeera, July 27, 2009. Clark has it translated as, "The Islamic nation's sacrificing heroes shall not be used against minor and valueless targets" ("The Taleban Codes of Conduct," 21).

314   **the entire 1980s:** With some rare exceptions, during the 1980s suicide bombing was largely confined to Lebanon, and viewed as a peculiar aspect of that war's internecine violence.

314   **following the book's release:** Kate Cark, "The Layha: Calling the Taleban to Account," Afghan Analysts Network, June 2011, 23.

314   **polio vaccination programs:** Yaroslav Trofimov, "Risky Ally in War on Polio: the Taliban," *Wall Street Journal*, January 15, 2010.

315   **even in areas like Helmand:** Coghlan notes that most estimates for the population who "actively support" the Taliban are "in the range of 10–20 per cent" (Coghlan, "The Taliban in Helmand," 133).

CHAPTER 18: DESIGN

317   **"First, tell me":** Notes of ISAF military officer present at June 20, 2009, meeting.

318   **largest operators:** International Security Assistance Force, "3 SCOTS Launch Massive Air Assault into Taliban Stronghold" (press release), June 2, 2009.

318   **three thousand British, Afghan, Estonian, and Danish troops:** Jeffrey Dressler, *Securing Helmand: Understanding and Responding to the Enemy* (Institute for the Study of War, September 2009), 34.

318   **Nasim Akhundzada:** Biographical details about Mullah Nasim Akhundzada are drawn from Antonio Giustozzi and Noor Ullah, "'Tribes' and Warlords in Southern Afghanistan, 1980–2005," Crisis States Research Center,

September 2006, 9–15, and Joel Hafvenstein, *Opium Season: A Year on the Afghan Frontier* (The Lyons Press, 2007), 128–32.

319 **platform he built overtop the soil:** Giustozzi and Ullah, " 'Tribes' and Warlords," 9. That Nasim had engaged in this practice was confirmed in correspondence with an intelligence analyst deployed to Helmand, 2009–11.

319 **a fatwa he issued:** Hafvenstein, *Opium Season*, 129.

319 **He was on his way:** Ibid., 130.

319 **durable drug cartel:** Giustozzi and Ullah, " 'Tribes' and Warlords," 12–13.

319 **checkerboard of roadblocks:** Hafvenstein, *Opium Season*, 131.

319 **the Karzais:** Giustozzi and Ullah, " 'Tribes' and Warlords," 12.

319 **Taliban program took hold:** Coghlan, "The Taliban in Helmand," 124–25.

319 **Taliban showed themselves unqualified:** Ibid., 124.

320 **mustered networks of aggrieved:** Ibid., 125

320 **posterboy of insurgents' propaganada:** Ibid., 126

320 **brigade-size task force:** The overall task force contained 3,500 personnel, but only 600 infantrymen. Anthony King, "Understanding the Helmand Campaign," *International Affairs* (March 2010), 314.

320 **married two sisters:** Giustozzi and Ullah, " 'Tribes' and Warlords," 13.

320 **eased the population:** Coghlan, "The Taliban in Helmand," 140.

321 **as a fourth tenet:** This was originally a suggestion of Jeff Eggers in his memo, "Patience Is Paramount but Time Is of the Essence" (memorandum), June 5, 2009.

322 **last four summers:** Stephen Grey, "Cracking On in Helmand," *Prospect* (September 2009), 46–51.

322 **Nawa and Garmsir districts:** Dressler, *Securing Helmand*, 38.

327 **"Soviet Invasion of 1979":** U.S. Army Command and General Staff College, "Abstracts of Master of Military Art and Science (MMAS) Theses and Special Studies, Annual Edition 1987–88," 16–17.

327 **left them feeling spurned:** A 1993 *New York Times* article notes: "For five years, the Reagan and Bush Administrations certified that Islamabad did not possess the cability [sic] to detonate a nuclear bomb, a finding widely considered to be a good will effort toward a country that was helping guerrillas fight Soviet forces in Afghanistan. In 1990, after Soviet soldiers had withdrawn from Afghanistan, the Bush Administration stopped protecting Pakistan from the amendment's sanctions and the aid was cut off." Steven A. Holmes, "Clinton Plans Change in the Law Banning Military Aid to Pakistan," *New York Times*, November 27, 1993.

329 **crisis of confidence:** Stanley A. McChrystal, "Commander's Initial Assessment," International Security Assistance Force, August 30, 2009, section 1, 1.

330 **"continued underresourcing":** Ibid., Section 2, 1.

330 **"focusing on force":** Ibid., Section 1, 1.

330 **"from *all* threats":** Ibid., Section 1, 1-3. Emphasis in original.

331 **"per square foot":** Ibid., Appendix F, 1.

332 **more insurgents:** For more on this, see Steve Coll, "Ink Spots," *New Yorker*, September 28, 2009.

332 **aggressive use of fires:** Chapter 5 of Gilles Dorronsoro's *Revolution Unending* is an informative take on the Soviets' later approach and the Najibullah regime they left in place. Gilles Dorronsoro, *Revolution Unending: Afghanistan, 1979 to the Present* (Columbia University Press, 2005), 173–201.

334 **thirty-two candidates:** Kenneth Katzman, "Afghanistan: Politics, Elections, and Government Performance," Congressional Research Service, March 30, 2012, 22.

335 **burst the cinderblocks:** Interview with U.S. military officer present at the scene.

336 **killed seven people:** Carlotta Gall, "Bomb Kills 7 Near NATO's Afghan Headquarters," *New York Times*, August 15, 2009.

336 **women-only voting stations:** United Nations Development Programme Afghanistan: Enhancing Legal & Electoral Capacity for Tomorrow, "Annual Progress Report–2009," 31.

336 **tunics for poll workers:** Ibid., 29–30.

336 **Taliban attacks was extremely high:** The BBC reported that ISAF said there were 400 attacks, but in 2012 the Congressional Research Service reported that there were roughly 280 ("NATO/ISAF announced that there were about 380 total attacks, about 100 more than in 2009"). Katzman, "Afghanistan: Politics, Elections, and Government," 28.

336 **90 percent of the polling sites:** The IEC website indicated that it opened "95.1% of the planned number" of polling centers, but this turned out to be a slight overestimate. Originally, there were 6,970 polling centers planned, but before election day that number was whittled down to 6,210 due to security concerns. A further 760 polling centers were closed the day of the election, again for security reasons. "Press Release of the Independent Election Commission with Reference to Announcement of Preliminary Results of 2009 Presidential Elections," Independent Election Commission of Afghanistan website, September 16, 2009.

336 **threats inactivated just 12 percent:** Ibid.

336 **39 percent of voters turned out:** Voter turnout was at 38.7 percent according to the IEC (ibid.); it was 35 percent according to the Congressional Research Service (Katzman, "Afghanistan: Politics, Elections, and Government," 24).

338 **"a lot of talk in Washington":** The full transcript of the interview, parts of which aired in the episode "Obama's War" on October 13, 2009, is available on the *Frontline* website.

CHAPTER 19: DECIDE

340 **From our vehicles:** My recollection of these events was confirmed and augmented by interviews with two team members present on this trip.

341 **"We need these kinds of operations":** The dialogue of this scene comes from a publicly available video of the meeting. "Stanley McChrystal in Kunduz After 2009 Air Strike" (video), YouTube, May 22, 2009.

344 **my team contacted them:** Interview with a senior military officer involved in coordinating the civilian advisers.

345 **lowered to 328,000:** These numbers reflect our calculations at that time and come from notes taken by a team member on October 6, 2009.

345 **approved to grow to 134,000:** Numbers for the Afghan National Army come from an annex in my assessment, an unclassified version of which was printed by the *Washington Post*. McChrystal, "Commander's Initial Assessment," Annex G, 1.

345 **84,000 strong:** Ibidi., Annex G, 2.

347 **than any other force:** In 2008, 880 ANP policemen died; 646 died in 2009 and 961 in 2010; 155 American troops died in 2008; 312 in 2009; and 499 in 2010. Ian S. Livingston, Heather L. Messera, and Michael O' Hanlon, *Afghanistan Index*, Brooking's Institution, March 30, 2012, 14, 11.

349 **"a war of necessity":** These comments by the president—"This will not be quick, nor easy. But we must never forget: This is not a war of choice. This is a war of necessity"—were delivered on August 17, 2009, during a veterans convention. "Remarks by the President at the Veterans of Foreign Wars Convention," White House website, August 17, 2009.

358 **districts along Pakistan's border:** Details of the TTP come from a fuller account of their rise by Hassan Abbas, "A Profile of Tehrik-i-Taliban Pakistan," *CTC Sentinel*, January 2008.

358 **border areas:** Abbas, "A Profile of Tehrik-i-Taliban Pakistan."

CHAPTER 20: EXECUTE

365 **instinctive aversion to violence:** President Karzai has noted that his role models are famous pacifists—Gandhi, and his friend and contemporary, a Pashtun leader named Ghaffar Khan. See Elizabeth Rubin, "Karzai in His Labyrinth," *New York Times Magazine*, August 4, 2009.

367 **trump card:** Content of Taliban propaganda comes from an interview with an intelligence analyst deployed to Helmand 2009–11.

368 **more than sixty tribes:** Interview with intelligence analyst deployed to Helmand 2009–11.

369 **slow, dangerous work:** Jeffery Dresser, *Operation Moshtarak: Taking and Holding Marjah*, Institute for the Study of War, March 2, 2010, 4–5.

369 **Taliban they had encountered:** Julius Cavendish, "Afghanistan War: Marjah Battle as Tough as Fallujah, Say U.S. Troops," *Christian Science Monitor*, February 14, 2010.

369 **apologizing for the incident:** Afghanistan International Security Assistance Force, "ISAF Weapon Fails to Hit Intended Target, 12 Civilians Killed" (press release), February 14, 2010.

369 **On Wednesday, February 17:** Details of Governor Mangal's appearance that day can be found in Patrick Baz, "Afghans Raise Flag as U.S. Says Offensive 'Going Well,'" *Sydney Morning Herald*, February 18, 2010.

369 **on top of a bamboo pole:** "Afghan Governor Raises Flag over Marjah Bizaar," *AFP*, February 17, 2010.

370 **staff from a few days earlier:** Ibid.

370 **seven hundred Marjah residents:** Dressler, *Operation Moshtarak*, 6, citing the Associated Press, "Afghan Government Claims Taliban Stronghold," MSNBC website, February 25, 2010.

370 **that week, was in attendance:** They had been there since Tuesday (ibid).

370 **"the point at which you have":** Carter and Zazai are quoted in Michael M. Phillips, "Afghan Flag Marks a Turning Point in Marjah," *Wall Street Journal*, February 26, 2010.

373 **school into bases:** Sangar Rahimi and Richard A. Oppel Jr., "Afghanistan's President Receives a Mixed Reception in a Visit to Newly Won Marjah," *New York Times*, March 7, 2010.

373 **an old man:** Mel Preen, "President Karzai Visits Marjah" (news video), NATO TV, March 8, 2010. Available on the NATO TV website.

373 **"Their hands have been stained":** Mohammed Elyas Daee and Abubakr Siddique, "In Marjah, New Gains Could Offer Escape from Tragic Past," Radio Free Europe Radio Liberty, March 9, 2012.

374 **to gain a toehold:** Ibid.

374 **actively campaigning against:** Paul Wiseman, "Despite U.S. Gains, Afghan City Still Feels Intimidation," *USA Today*, June 11, 2010. The article reports that Abdul Rahman Jan accused the Americans of bringing in an "outsider," since Abdul Zahir was from Musa Qala, not Marjah.

374 **crowd erupted in cheers:** Rahimi and Oppel Jr., "Mixed Reception," *New York Times*, March 7, 2010.

374 **"Shame on you":** Aziz Ahmed Tassal, "Karzai Faces Anger in Marjah," *Asia Times*, March 19, 2010.

374 **"We exchanged views"**: Preen, "Karzai Visits Marjah" (news video).

375 **folksy greetings**: Interview with Afghan military officer present on the trip. The *New York Times* similarly noted that Karzai "appeared to win [the crowd] over on occasion with his crisp and simple language, spoken in the accent of his native Kandahar." Rahimi and Oppel Jr., "Mixed Reception."

375 **large, roving *mahaz***: Before he was killed, Mullah Dadullah went on Al Jazeera and bragged about the connections between his *mahaz*, Al Qaeda in Iraq, and the central leadership of Al Qaeda: "We consider it a friendly and brotherly organization, which shares our ideology and concepts. We have close ties and constant contacts with it . . . may have sent our people to Iraq, and [the Iraqis] may have sent their friends to us. We have continuous contacts with them, whether by phone or by other means" ("Taliban Military Commander Mullah Dadallah: We Are in Contact with Iraqi Mujahideen, Osama bin Laden & Al-Zawahiri," Middle East Media Research Institute, June 2, 2006).

375 **beheadings**: Dion Nissenbaum, "Knocked Out of Power in Afghan Town, Taliban Turn to Intimidation," McClatchy, March 14, 2010. The article reports on decapitations, once a trademark of Zarqawi's in Iraq, and a tactic that was on display in an infamous Taliban propaganda video featuring a twelve-year-old executioner, who according to the caption on the video was trained by Dadullah. Bryan Glyn Williams, "Mullah Omar's Missiles, A Field Report on Suicide Bombers in Afghanistan," Middle East Policy Council, Winter 2008.

375 **pep talk to Marjah's Taliban**: In this way, as Dadullah had, the front's new leader—Qayyum Zakir—was well known for stealing over from Pakistan to personally motivate his troops. Anand Gopal, "Qayyum Zakir: The Afganistan Taliban's Rising Mastermind," *Christian Science Monitor*, April 30, 2010.

376 **sixteen key cities**: Correspondence with Matt Sherman.

379 **the only known mutiny**: Hugh Kennedy, *The Great Arab Conquests: How the Spread of Islam Changed the World We Live In* (Da Capo Press, 2007), 194–95.

381 **decimation of Kandahar**: For a description of the devastation the Soviets wrought, see Robert Kaplan, *Soldiers of God: With Islamic Warriors in Afghanistan and Pakistan* (Vintage, 2001), 187–88.

381 **two hundred thousand**: Ibid., 188.

381 **Karzai walked in**: The sequence of events comes from notes taken by a member of my ISAF strategic advisery group, as do the paraphrased remarks, originally transcribed from the live English translation of Karzai's speech. Quoted remarks are from Golnar Mortevalli, "Karzai Rallies Tribes, Distances Self from West," Reuters, April 4, 2010.

382 **would join the Taliban**: According to a CRS report, an English translation of the exact comments was never produced. Kenneth Katzman, "Afghanistan: Politics, Elections, and Government Performance," Congressional Research Service, March 30, 2012, 11.

382 **put that trip in jeopardy**: In an April 6 press briefing, a reporter asked if the White House was considering canceling Karzai's visit. Robert Gibbs, the White House press secretary answered, "We certainly would evaluate whatever continued or further remarks President Karzai makes as to whether that's constructive to have such a meeting, sure." "Briefing by White House Press Secretary Robert Gibbs," White House website, April 6, 2010. Three days later, Denis McDonough said the trip was still on.

386 **in rejection of Mullah Omar's *layha***: The United Nations calculated that from January through June 2010, the insurgency killed and wounded 2,477 Afghans, a 53 percent increase from the same period in 2009, and 76

percent of all civilian casualties. ISAF and Afghan security forces, meanwhile, caused 30 percent fewer civilian casualties than they had during the first six months of 2009, decreasing their share of the civilian toll to 12 percent. "Mid Year Report 2010 Protection of Civilians in Armed Conflict 2010," United Nations Assistance Mission in Afghanistan, August 2010, i–iv.

386 **assassination campaign:** Details of Taliban activity in early 2010 are from Ibid., 2–3, 6.

386 **responsible for fewer civilian casualties:** Ibid., i.

Index

Photo Credits

Insert page 1: Courtesy of Stanley McChrystal

2 (top): Courtesy of Stanley McChrystal

2 (bottom): Courtesy of Stanley McChrystal

3 (top): U.S. Air Force

3 (bottom left): Courtesy of Stanley McChrystal

3 (bottom right): Courtesy of Stanley McChrystal

4 (left): Courtesy of Stanley McChrystal

4-5: AP Photo/Brennan Linsley

6: Courtesy of Stanley McChrystal

7 (top): U.K. Ministry of Defence / Paul A'Barrow

7 (bottom): Courtesy of Stanley McChrystal

8 (top): Multi-National Force-Iraq (MNF-I)

8 (middle): Multi-National Force-Iraq (MNF-I)

8 (bottom): Courtesy of Stanley McChrystal

9 (top): Courtesy of Stanley McChrystal

9 (bottom): Courtesy of Stanley McChrystal

10 (top): Courtesy of Stanley McChrystal

10 (bottom): AP Photo/Manuel Balce Ceneta

11 (top): ISAF Public Affairs

11 (bottom): U.S. Army Command and General Staff College

12 (top): ISAF Public Affairs / David E. Alvarado

12 (bottom left): U.S. Embassy Kabul

12 (bottom right): ISAF Public Affairs / Chris Haylett

13 (top): U.S. Department of Defense / Mark O'Donald

13 (middle): U.S. Department of Defense / Jerry Morrison

13 (bottom): Courtesy of Stanley McCrystal

14 (top): Courtesy of Stanley McChrystal

14 (bottom left): ISAF Public Affairs / David E. Alvarado

14 (bottom right): U.S. Department of Defense / Mark O'Donald

15 (top): U.S. Army / Brandon Pomrenke

15 (bottom): ISAF Public Affairs / Joshua Treadwell

16 (top): U.S. Department of Defense / D. Myles Cullen

16 (bottom): ISAF Public Affairs / David E. Alvarado